BISMARCK'S FIRST WAR

The Campaign of Schleswig and Jutland 1864

Michael Embree

Helion & Company Ltd

Despite Zanzibar

Helion & Company Limited
26 Willow Road
Solihull
West Midlands
B91 1UE
England
Tel. 0121 705 3393
Fax 0121 711 4075
Email: publishing@helion.co.uk
Website: http://www.helion.co.uk

Originally published by Helion & Company Limited 2006. Reprinted in paperback 2007.

Designed and typeset by Helion & Company Ltd, Solihull, West Midlands
Cover designed by Bookcraft Limited, Stroud, Gloucestershire
Printed by Lightning Source

© Michael Embree 2006

ISBN   978 1 906033 03 3

British Library Cataloguing-in-Publication Data.
A catalogue record for this book is available from the British Library.

Dustjacket illustration: Storming of the Königshügel at Ober Selk, 3rd February 1864, by the Austrian 18th Feldjäger Battalion. Painting by Siegmund l'Allemand (courtesy of the Heeresgeschichtliches Museum, Vienna)

For details of other military history titles published by Helion & Company Limited contact the above address, or visit our website: http://www.helion.co.uk.

We always welcome receiving book proposals from prospective authors, especially those of nineteenth century interest.

Contents

Chapters

Appendices

List of Illustrations

Key to Sources (see bibliography for full citations)

Bredsdorff *Paa Feltfod*

Bremen *Düppel und Alsen*

Bruun *Fra Krigens Tid*

Camphausen *Ein Maler auf dem Kriegsfelde*

Illustrated London News 1864

Illustrierte Kriegs-Berichte aus Schleswig-Holstein 1864

Larsen & Dumreicher *Krigen 1864*

Liljefalck & Lütken *Vor sidste Kamp vor Sønderjylland*

Pflug *Der Deutsch-Dänische Krieg*

Schiøtt *1864*

Stilling *1 Bataillon 1763-1913*

Voss *Illustrierte Geschichte der deutschen Einigungskriege 1864-1866*

List of Maps & Plans

List of Tables

Acknowledgements

I am very lucky to have received tireless help, advice, and criticism from many people, to complete this work. It is with extreme gratitude to them all that I name a few of them here.

Alan Aimone, Michael Aitken, Morten K. Andersen, Søren B. Andersen, Stuart Arnold, Jesper Asmussen, Bruce Bassett-Powell, Andrew Baus, Elisabeth Briefer, Robert Burke, Bent L. Christensen, Keith and Kirsten Crosby, Marcus Dechange, Flemming Deleuran, Michael Gandt, Peter Gundelach, Peter Hammerich, Flemming Hansen, Ian Harvie, Tom Hill, Markus Jasker, Erik L. Jensen, Tom Jerichow, Jan Bøll Jespersen, Lars E. Kristensen, Pete Larsen, Gert Laursen, Michael Lenz, Tim O'Brien, Mogens Pedersen, Stuart Penhall, Sten Boye Poulson, Pete Royea, Mogens Rye, Jan Schlürmann, Chris Seidenfaden, Harald Skala, Dave Spender, Jesper Stenild, Gerd Stolz, Palle "Rebel" Thomsen, Bernhard Voykowitsch, Bruce Weigle, Dirk Wendtorf, and finally, to Sally and Kathryn for putting up with all this!

Foreword

> Only three people have ever really understood the Schleswig-Holstein business
> – the Prince Consort, who is dead – a German professor, who has gone mad –
> and I, who have forgotten all about it.

There are many versions of this famous quip by Lord Palmerston on the vexing issue of Schleswig-Holstein. This particular one is from, *Queen Victoria*, by Lytton Strachey, 1921. It is very probable, likely even, that "Old Pam" himself recycled the statement on more than one occasion.

That the issue was a vexing one is not in doubt, and it was only with the death of King Frederik VII of Denmark in November 1863, that the master opportunist and manipulator of events, Prussia's Minister-President, Otto von Bismarck, was able to turn the matter to his advantage. Bismarck was prepared to cut the Gordian Knot irrespective of the niceties. This was crucial and led directly to the matter's resolution – by force.

Bismarck was given the perfect opportunity to act by the foolish actions of the Danish Government, who in fact initiated the crisis, and he took full advantage of it. It cannot be doubted that he would in any case have precipitated action of some sort, and that international opposition would then have been much more vocal.

All through 1863 matters had gone from bad to worse, though the Danes always actually believed that the Western powers, at least, would actively support them. Indeed, Palmerston had strongly implied as much in the House of Commons. The final straw was to be the death in November 1863, of Frederick VII.

This must be the great, "What if?" of this story. Both before and after the death of Frederick VII added even further complications, the Hall and Monrad ministries in Copenhagen pursued a reckless policy of antagonising the great powers, which alone could have helped them. The Swedish King had previously promised support, but could not back up his promise.

The military campaign itself was a microcosm of war and technology on the cusp of a new age. The methods and machinery of the past and of the future were seen together as they were being seen at exactly the same time thousands of miles to the West in the American Civil War.

It is a story worth telling and one which should be heard. This was the first, and the smallest, of the three conflicts for which Bismarck, one day to be the 'Iron Chancellor', was responsible. Together they would forge the united nation of Germany, under the leadership of Prussia. It started here.

A Note on Place Names

It has been decided, as a rule, to use only one place name for each place of habitation or feature, natural or man made. Constantly having to use two names written for the same place was unacceptable to me. Therefore, it will be seen that, after advice, I have used the existing border to delineate names. South of that border, names in the text are German. North of it, they are in Danish. For those seeking an apology on this subject, I give it here. A decision had to made on how to proceed, and I have chosen this manner. I apologise to all concerned when, as is sometimes the case, English is used. In many cases, too, contemporary spellings of place names are used. A glossary of place and feature names showing some of the alternatives mentioned in the text can be found in Appendix I. Please note that the Frisian language has not been used. Of course, the responsibility for all errors of fact, interpretation, or judgement, is entirely mine. I hope that this book will add a little knowledge to that of the English speaking reader and, perhaps to one or two others as well.

A corporal of the Danish 18th Infantry Regiment (Bruun)

1

The Long Road to War

The dynastic and constitutional issue of 'Schleswig-Holstein' was one of incredible and very long-lived complexity. Though the two Duchies were linked at various times in earlier periods, in 1460 the nobles of Schleswig and Holstein formally granted King Christian I of Denmark the titles of Duke of Schleswig, and Count of Holstein, later the Duke of Schleswig and Holstein. Under this "Capitulation", Schleswig and Holstein were to be forever united in a personal union to the King and his male descendants or rightful heirs. Though the issue would become ever more complicated and involved, it was only with the growth of nationalism in the early 19th Century that the matter came to be, if only briefly, of European importance.

After the Napoleonic Wars, the Danish Crown had four component parts; the Kingdom of Denmark, and the Duchies of Schleswig, Holstein and Lauenburg. The Kingdom of Denmark comprised Jutland and the Danish islands. The linked Duchies of Schleswig-Holstein were subject to the authority of the Duke, who was the King. The small Duchy of Lauenburg, south-east of Holstein, was appended to the Crown in 1815, in partial compensation for the loss of Norway to Sweden.[1] Holstein and Lauenburg were both populated by German speakers, and the Kingdom proper by Danish speakers. The population of Schleswig/Slesvig was mixed with more Danish speakers in the north, and vice versa in the south.

In March 1848, as political unrest swept through Europe, the Danish Crown was forced to accept a liberal constitution within the Kingdom. The Danish ruling nationalist party, the National Liberals, further proposed that the Duchy of Schleswig be tied more closely with the Kingdom, separating it from Holstein. Known as the 'Eider Danes', since the River Eider formed the boundary between Schleswig and Holstein, they were regarded in Holstein as an illegal government. As a result, the authority of the National Liberal Government was not recognised there. War followed between the new government and a break-away provisional government set up in Holstein.

Whether a revolt or a civil war the struggle went on, with several breaks, until 1850. The Holsteiners had some military support from Prussia and other states of the German Confederation, but pressure from the other Great Powers, especially Russia and Great Britain, forced Prussia from the war, and the Holsteiners were defeated. Denmark's victory was tempered by the fact that peace was imposed by the Great Powers. Various accords were agreed during negotiations throughout 1851 and 1852. Prussia and Austria insisted that a universal constitution for all the

---

1   To further confuse the issue, both Holstein and Lauenburg were within the German Confederation, which was set up in 1815 as a loose organisation of German states replacing the defunct Holy Roman Empire. Prussia and Austria constantly struggled for control of the Confederation.

Map 1: Denmark and Schleswig

lands of the Danish Crown be written, with its provisions being agreed by each of the monarchy's component parts.

The Treaty of London, of May 8th 1852 encapsulated the previous agreements of 1851-52. It recognised the integrity of the Danish monarchy as being necessary in the makeup of Europe, and also that the future succession to the throne would be through the line of Prince Christian of Glücksburg. Should the Prince's line become extinct, the Powers would reexamine the question. The Danish King, Frederik VII, was reminded of his obligations as Duke of Schleswig–Holstein. Imposed by the Great Powers and Sweden/Norway, the German Confederation was allowed no part in it. The agreement was practically unworkable, and pleased none of the interested parties. Equally, the Treaty itself actually guaranteed none of these things.[2] It was a treaty, "…made only to be broken.[3]"

Throughout the 1850's and early 1860's, successive Danish governments struggled unsuccessfully to produce a joint constitution for the Crown lands, which had differing constitutional aspirations. Two, which were proposed, were found unacceptable. The first, in 1854, was opposed by the 'Eider Danes', and the other, of 1855, by the Schleswig and Holstein Germans. The latter actually came into force in October 1855, even though it was not in accordance with the agreements of 1852.

The Great Powers paid little attention until after the Crimean War. Austria and Prussia then, however, began to take an active interest in the issues, taking up the grievances of the Duchies against the Copenhagen government. Unable to accept this intervention in the Monarchy's affairs, the Danish Government resigned in April 1857. A new National Liberal ministry was appointed in May, headed by Carl Christian Hall. Hall would remain Council-President, with one short break, for six and a half years.

Although Hall was an able and flexible politician, he was still faced with the inherent impossibility of pleasing all sides. The 'Eider Dane' movement, to which Hall subscribed, was growing in strength and the Germans of the Duchies more obdurate. Negotiations, proposals and counter-proposals came and went without result, the Great Powers themselves frequently altering their stance in relation to one another.

In 1859, the Holstein 'Estates' (Assembly) rejected the Danish government's constitutional proposals. In January of the following year, the Schleswig 'Estates' acted in similar vein. The laying aside of the 1855 Constitution for Holstein and Lauenburg was declared by them as a back-door incorporation of Schleswig into the Kingdom by breaking the historic link between Schleswig and Holstein. The status of Schleswig itself was now again in the international arena.

In March 1860, the Diet (Parliament) of the German Confederation in Frankfurt declared that no laws passed in Copenhagen were valid in Holstein or Lauenburg unless agreed by the Estates there. In July, the imposition of the budget for Holstein was questioned in the Diet, since the measure had not been agreed by the Duchy's Estates. Despite the Danish government's contention that this was not a law, in February 1861 Denmark was given six weeks to comply with the

2   Steefel, Lawrence D., *The Schleswig-Holstein Question*, Harvard University Press, Cambridge 1932, p. 7.
3   Ward & Wilkinson, *Germany 1815-1890*, Cambridge University Press, 1916-18, Volume II, p. 123.

submission of the Budget to the Holstein Estates, or face a 'Federal Execution', or occupation, of Holstein by troops representing the German Confederation.

Russia, Britain, France, and Sweden averted this crisis, and the by now normal round of proposed solutions resumed amongst the diplomats.

Bismarck and Prussia

In Prussia, at the beginning of the 1860's, there was political disarray over the issue of the reform of the army. A major overhaul of the army had been planned by the War Minister, Lieutenant-General von Roon, in answer to a request from the Regent, later King Wilhelm I.[4] It called for a substantial increase in the size of the army, and also the extension of the term of service for conscripts by one year, to a total of three years (four in the Guards and specialist arms), and a shake up of the *Landwehr*, or militia.[5] The scheme was extremely costly. The Liberal parties opposed it, whilst the Conservatives in general supported it.

Two Bills on the subject were placed before the Lower House in early 1860, one for the extension of the length of service, the other for the budget. Consideration of the issues was so protracted that a temporary granting of funds was agreed by the House, and the reorganisation went ahead.

The following year, a second granting of funds was passed by the Lower House, but with only a small majority. The benefit of the doubt extended by the House to the government over the army reforms was fast dissipating.[6]

Elections at the end of 1861 again produced a very great majority of the Centre-Left. Although the House first sat in January 1862, it was unable to come to agreement with the King's Ministers, and was dissolved in March. Further elections took place in April-May, and resulted in a crushing defeat for the Conservatives. Of the 350 seats in the House, they held only ten.[7] When the House met on the budget, it was clear that the King's position might be in danger.

Facing a seemingly impossible constitutional crisis, Wilhelm considered abdication, but was dissuaded by his Foreign Minister, Count Bernstorff and the Crown Prince.[8] With nowhere else to turn, he was persuaded by Lieutenant-General von Roon to call upon the Prussian Ambassador in Paris, Otto von Bismarck, who himself had spent the summer considering where his own future lay.[9]

Bismarck, then 47 years old, was an arch conservative, and a brilliant diplomat without any moral scruples. The second son of a landed noble Pomeranian family, Bismarck had started his career in the diplomatic service, and then entered conservative politics. Appalled by the revolutionary violence of 1848, he had

4   Wilhelm had become Regent for his brother, King Friedrich Wilhelm IV, when the latter suffered a stroke in 1857. After Friedrich Wilhelm's death, Wilhelm became King in January 1861.
5   See the following chapter for further details.
6   Anderson, Eugene N., *The Social and Political Conflict in Prussia 1858-1864,*
7   Ibid, p. 412. Other sources say 11, but Anderson does not regard Deputy Hoffman, representing the district of Oppeln II in Silesia, as a Conservative.
8   Ward & Wilkinson, *Germany 1815-1890*, Volume II, pp. 80-81.
9   On previous occasions, Wilhelm had consistently refused advice to consult Bismarck, whom he admired, but was also worried by.

advised King Friedrich Wilhelm IV to suppress the rioting in Berlin, though his advice was not followed.

Elected to the Prussian Lower House in 1849, in 1851 Bismarck was appointed by the King as the Prussian representative at the German Diet in Frankfurt. Here he remained for eight years, honing his already considerable diplomatic and political skills and becoming increasingly convinced of the necessity of excluding Austria from the affairs of Germany, to Prussia's obvious advantage. Subsequently appointed as Ambassador to St. Petersburg, Bismarck developed a belief in the absolute necessity of good relations between Prussia (later Germany) and Russia. Sent to Paris in the spring of 1862, he was recalled because the King had run out of options, the possibility of revolution staring him in the face. Following a telegram from von Roon, a meeting was arranged between the King and Bismarck, to take place at Babelsberg near Potsdam, on September 22nd.

At the meeting, the deeply depressed King again brought up the subject of abdication. Bismarck appealed to his sense of honour as a soldier and a monarch, and promised, if appointed as Minister-President, to serve the Crown faithfully and unceasingly. Wilhelm was finally convinced, and Bismarck's chance for power had come, though in extremely difficult political circumstances.

The following day, the Prussian Lower House overwhelmingly rejected the Army Budget by 273 votes to 68. The budget was cut by the House, which then passed its own finance bill by 308 votes to 11. That same day, Bismarck was announced as interim Minister-President. His post was confirmed as permanent on October 8th and, at the same time, he was also named Foreign Minister.

Guaranteed the support of the (noble) Upper House in Parliament, the Minister-President's first direct clash with the Lower House was to come over the Army Budget. Facing an insurmountable majority, he simply ignored it. Until the budget issue was finalised, the Government would continue to spend the money, which it had allocated. With taxes continuing to be paid and collected, the members of the House were powerless to do anything about it and could only seethe with impotent rage. The political instability in Prussia continued to appear insoluble.[10]

In the latter part of November 1862, Bismarck ordered the Army to produce a plan to defeat Denmark militarily.[11] Lieutenant-General von Roon, the War Minister, instructed Lieutenant-General von Moltke to submit proposals for action in the case of a conflict with Denmark by early December. A possible campaign had long been foreseen, and Moltke replied on the 6th of that month, with basic information on the objectives, requirements and difficulties of such an operation, together with specifics on the forces necessary for its execution and on the strength of the forces likely to be faced. The letter began:

> In reply to Your Excellency's confidential letter of the 28th ultimo, I have the honour to respectfully answer first of all that the eventuality of a military solu-

---

10 Faced with the parliamentary obstinacy, Bismarck stated in late January that since the Upper and Lower Houses could not agree on the budget, it was within the King's power to enforce it. Friedjung, *Der Kampf um die Vorherrschaft in Deutschland 1859 bis 1866*, Stuttgart & Berlin 1912, Volume I, p.53.

11 Steefel, Lawrence D., *The Schleswig-Holstein Question*, pp. 52-53.

tion to the long standing issue with Denmark has been continually borne in mind by this office.[12]

He very promptly followed this up with a detailed operational plan.[13] In practice these plans were not to be needed for a little over a year.

Compromise Fails

A scheme put forward in the spring of 1861 by Sweden/Norway for a separation of Holstein and Lauenburg from the Crown Lands outside the German Confederation received no serious consideration by the Powers, including Great Britain. Then, extraordinarily, in May Britain itself put forward a similar plan that also fell by the wayside.

During March/April, the Hall Government conducted negotiations with the Holstein Estates, which failed just as had previous attempts. The talks did, however, lift the immediate threat of 'Federal Execution' by the German Diet. The deadline set by Frankfurt expired in March, and when the details of the Estates proceedings were presented to the Diet at the end of April, the matter was referred to a committee where it remained buried.[14]

None of the Powers were looking for trouble at this time. For Great Britain and France especially, much of their attention was elsewhere. On April 12th, the first shots were fired in what was to be the American Civil War. For Britain with possessions in Canada, this was potentially very serious. Britain and France were also suspicious of one another after a recent war scare, which had largely been inspired by the British Prime Minister, Lord Palmerston. Austria was preoccupied with major military reforms after the 1859 defeat in Italy, and its own constitutional affairs, whilst Prussia, as shown, had internal difficulties largely related to her own military reforms. Russia was fully occupied by the latest of the reforms of Tsar Alexander II, that of the emancipation of the Serfs. Her local concerns in the Baltic were of maintaining the *status quo*.

Diplomatic activity, therefore, again became preeminent through the remainder of 1861 and 1862. In May, Hall offered complete independence for Holstein, but Russia and France, fearing Prussian influence over such a state, would not approve this. Likewise, a partitioning of Schleswig, suggested by von Schleinitz the Prussian Foreign Minister was rejected by Denmark.

During the summer, the British Foreign Secretary, Lord Russell, attempted by means of pressing Denmark to accede to some the demands from Frankfurt, to remove the German Diet from the equation, allowing more flexibility to the Powers, Denmark, and Sweden/Norway. This, too, failed.

Further Danish talks took place from October 1861, with the new Prussian Foreign Minister, Count Bernstorff, and also Austrian representatives. These

---

12 Moltke, H. von, *Moltkes Militärische Korrespondenz. Krieg 1864*, Berlin 1892. Letter Nr. 1 to the War Minister, 6th December 1862.

13 Ibid, letter Nr. 2.

14 Another clash over the Holstein budget was averted in August, when a face–saving concession allowed the Diet to suspend further 'Federal Execution' on Holstein.

dragged on for ten months over the issue of the Powers', and Frankfurt's right to discuss the future of Schleswig at all.

In September 1862, Lord Russell, who was accompanying Queen Victoria on a visit to Germany, on the 24th, issued lengthy proposals for settlement of the entire problem. Known as the 'Gotha Dispatch', this document completely supported the 'German' position, recommending independence for Schleswig, and supporting all of the demands of the German Confederation as regards Holstein and Lauenburg. Accepted immediately by all the Powers, particularly Russia, the plan was flatly rejected by Copenhagen.

The March Patent and the Federal Execution

The beginning of 1863 seemed to offer a window of opportunity for the 'Eider Dane' movement. The political crisis in Prussia, soon compounded by events in eastern Europe, diverted attention from Schleswig-Holstein. Britain was perceived as being pro-Danish, especially in relation to the coming wedding (in March) of the Prince of Wales to Princess Alexandra, daughter of Prince Christian of Glücksburg, heir to the Danish throne. On January 21st, the *Landsthing* (Parliament) in Copenhagen voted that a joint constitution for the Kingdom and Schleswig be formulated.[15]

In this atmosphere, with Danish diplomats abroad informing Copenhagen that the time was right for 'Eider Dane' policies to be initiated, and the public within the Kingdom fully in favour, the government chose to act. A Royal Ordinance was promulgated, upon which Hall obtained the King Frederick VII's signature, setting Holstein and Lauenburg on a different legal basis to the other Crown Lands.[16]

The so-called March Patent was announced on March 30th, to take effect from January 1st 1864. As a constitution for Holstein and Lauenburg only, the Act once and for all announced that the search for a joint constitution for the entire monarchy was at an end. Hall's ministry was, to German eyes, preparing for some form of incorporation of Schleswig with the lands of the Kingdom.[17]

The Danish government's perception of the attitude of Great Britain and Sweden certainly encouraged them to issue the constitution. Sweden had been supporting a separation from Holstein for some time; the Swedish Foreign Minister, Ludvig Manderström, put forward a scheme in 1861 for a largely independent Duchy.[18] Negotiations for a defensive alliance between Denmark and Sweden went on throughout the summer of 1863, but as Sweden came to realise

---

15 Ward & Wilkinson, Volume II, p. 131.

16 Halicz, Emanuel, *Russia and Denmark 1856-1864. A Chapter of Russian Policy towards the Scandinavian Countries*, Copenhagen 1990, pp. 221-222.

17 Steefel, Lawrence D, *The Schleswig-Holstein Question*, pp. 55-56.

18 Koht, Halvdan, *Die Stellung Norwegens und Schwedens im Deutsch-Dänischen Konflikt, zumal während der Jahre 1863 und 1864*, Kristiania 1908, pp. 70-72. The plan received short shrift from the Great Powers.

that neither Great Britain nor France would be likely to intervene militarily, its interest in the issue cooled, and nothing came of the negotiations.[19]

Throughout Germany, there was outrage at the news of the March Patent, though few initial demands for immediate action. On April 16th, the issue was laid before the Diet of the German Confederation in Frankfurt, which again referred it to a committee for a report. It was not brought forward until mid June and finally, on July 9th, the Diet gave Denmark a six-month deadline to withdraw the ordinance, or face a 'Federal Execution'.[20]

The day after the Patent was first discussed at Frankfurt, Bismarck, speaking in the Prussian Lower House, declared that should war with Denmark prove necessary, it would be undertaken with or without the agreement of that body.

Although it may appear odd that the German Confederation allowed the matter to drag on in this way, its members were heavily involved in their own internal disputes. The Powers, too, were in disarray. In late January 1863, a serious revolt had broken out in Russian Poland, which would last until the summer of 1864 and this would occupy much of her attention. The other Powers were split over the issue, Prussia supporting Russia, with Britain, France and Austria being more sympathetic to the Poles. Bismarck, who throughout his life mistrusted the Poles, and was always anxious to maintain good relations with Russia, sent General von Alvensleben to St. Petersburg. The general rapidly concluded an agreement (February 8th) with the Russian government on cross-border cooperation against the insurgents.[21] This dangerous divergence amongst the Powers took centre stage for some while and could have led to war.[22] Denmark, in the meanwhile, had also shown sympathy for the insurrection, thus weakening her own hopes for support from Russia, already stretched by the enthusiasm shown by Russia for Russel's 'Gotha' plan.

The November Constitution

The eventual reply to the German Diet from Copenhagen on August 27th refused to withdraw the March Patent. A Congress of Princes, called by Austria to discuss reform of the German Confederation, was sitting at the time and could have been asked to decide on further action. Prussia, though, had declined to attend the Congress, and Count Rechberg, the Austrian Foreign Minister, considered that she should be consulted in such a potentially explosive matter.[23] It was therefore left to the full Diet.

Even before this met, however, Council-President Hall defiantly announced a new Constitution for the Kingdom and Schleswig to the *Rigstinget* (Parliament) on

19 The possibility of a Swedish/Danish alliance was of great concern to Russia. See Halicz, Emanuel, *Russia and Denmark 1856-1864*, p. 252.

20 See Steefel, pp. 56-57, and Ward & Wilkinson, Volume II, pp. 132-133.

21 The officially 'Polish' population of Prussia numbered about two million in 1864, out of a total of some 19,200,000 – Anderson, Eugene E., *The Social and Political Conflict in Prussia 1858-1864*, pp.10 and 426.

22 Ward & Wilkinson, Volume II, pp. 87-89.

23 Ibid, pp. 91-98. This Congress was part of the continuing 'tug of war' between Austria and Prussia over control of the German Confederation.

September 28th, clearly stating that the affairs of the Kingdom and Schleswig would be more closely entwined. Buoyed by the negotiations with Sweden, the Danish Government had also been encouraged by a speech in the House of Commons in London on July 23rd. In it, Lord Palmerston stated that should anyone threaten to interfere with Denmark's rights and independence, that it would not only be Denmark that they would have to deal with. Whilst this may have reflected the opinion of the British press and public opinion, it was certainly not an outright threat to the Federal Diet.[24]

In Frankfurt, the vote for a Federal Execution in Holstein was passed in the Diet on October 1st against Frederick VII in his capacity as Duke of Holstein, requiring him to abide by its previous resolutions. In case of non-compliance, Hanover and Saxony were called upon to provide troops to enter the Duchy along with Civil Commissioners to administer it. Austria and Prussia would provide additional troops to back them up, and further forces if needed.

A military commission of four officers was established at Frankfurt to implement the necessary measures.[25] Its first meeting took place on November 23rd and the commission completed its deliberations by December 1st. The force to carry out the 'Execution' was to be commanded by a Saxon, Lieutenant-General von Hake.[26]

The troops, which were to enter Holstein and Lauenburg, consisted of two brigades, one Saxon, and the other Hanoverian. These were composed of the following:

Royal Saxon Brigade – Major General von Schimpff
  1st, 2nd, 3rd, and 13th Infantry Battalions, 1st and 4th Jäger Battalions, six squadrons drawn from the 1st and 3rd Cavalry Regiments, two foot batteries, one horse battery, and a pioneer detachment with a bridging train.
  4692 infantry, 720 cavalry, 16 guns

Royal Hanoverian Brigade – Lieutenant-General Gebser
  II/1st, II/3rd, II/5th, and II/7th Infantry Regiments, the Guard and 3rd Jäger Battalions, three squadrons of the Crown Prince's Dragoons, three squadrons of the Duke of Cambridge's Dragoons (these latter brigaded with the Saxon cavalry), two foot batteries, and one horse battery.
  4674 infantry, 750 cavalry, 16 guns

Remaining along the frontier to support the advance, if necessary, were two additional brigades. These were the Austrian brigade of Major-General Gondrecourt, and the reinforced 11th Prussian Brigade of Major-General

---

24 Sandiford, Keith A.P., *Great Britain and the Schleswig-Holstein Question 1848-64*, University of Toronto Press 1978, p, 59, where he also emphasises British attempts to moderate Danish aims.

25 These were Lieutenant-General, Baron von Moltke (Prussia), Major-General, Baron Rzikowsky (Austria), Major von Brandenstein (Saxony), and Major-General Schulz (Hanover).

26 Grosser Generalstab, *Der Deutsch-Dänische Krieg 1864*, Berlin 1886-87, Volume I, pp. 26-27 for these details and strengths.

Canstein, together about 10,500 men. Further large Austrian and Prussian forces were held in readiness in case of need.[27]

Whilst Frankfurt deliberated, Council-President Hall, in spite of his country's apparent isolation, continued with a belligerent policy. The third and final reading of the new constitution took place on November 13th, the measure passing with almost 75% of the votes in the *Rigstinget.* It now only remained to obtain the signature of the King. Two days later, however, Frederick VII died suddenly, on his deathbed refusing to sign the constitution, even though he was the architect of many of the proposals.[28] His death precipitated an immediate crisis.

As discussed, the succession to the throne had been agreed by the Powers in the Treaty of 1852, whereby Prince Christian of Glücksburg would become King upon the extinction of the existing male line. Christian, neither an orator nor a self-publicist, was an honourable man, politically a Conservative, far removed from the Eider Dane movement. He and his wife were the only members of his family to remain loyal to Denmark in 1848. He was, nevertheless, still seen as 'German' by many Danes.[29] The accession of 45 year old King Christian IX was announced in Copenhagen on the 16th. The situation was tense, with crowds cheering for the new constitution.

Without significant political support, King Christian was in no position to question the adoption of the Constitution, let alone oppose it. He signed the document on November 18th, to come into effect on January 1st, 1864, and almost immediately sought to form a government whereby it could be repealed. His position, once again, was impossible. On December 21st, the government dissolved the *Rigstinget* despite pleas from Britain and Russia. Christian desperately attempted to form a more moderate Cabinet, but was unable to do so. Hall's resignation was accepted on December 28th, and on New Year's Eve, the previous Minister for Education and Religious Affairs, Ditlev.Gothardt. Monrad, took office as Council-President with a Cabinet of mainly inexperienced ministers.

Monrad, a hard-line 'Eider Dane', fully supported the November Constitution and was prepared for war over it, believing that Denmark would be supported at least by the Western Powers. A former newspaper editor and bishop, he also almost certainly suffered from manic-depressive disorder, a condition causing extreme shifts in mood and energy.[30]

For Bismarck, the situation was a great opportunity. His plans were always flexible. It was clear to him that the two Duchies were ripe for picking by Prussia, although the King and many others were of the opinion that the claims of the

27 See Appendix V. The two Austrian and Prussian brigades mentioned above, together with these other troops would become the Allied intervention force.
28 Sandiford, Keith A.P., *Great Britain and the Schleswig-Holstein Question*, p.67.
29 Lindeberg, Lars, *De Så det Ske*, Copenhagen 1963, p. 7. The King's reserved manner was in sharp contrast to that of his gregarious predecessor.
30 Schioldann-Nielsen, Johan, *The Life of D.G. Monrad 1811-1887. Manic-Depressive Disorder and Political Leadership*, Odense University Press 1988.

Duke of Augustenburg should be accepted.[31] "Bismarck stood alone in his opinion that Prussia must, if possible, take advantage of the King of Denmark's death, by which the question of the succession was reopened, to annex the Duchies."[32] Bismarck was skillfully able to manipulate liberal, but nationalist feeling in all of Germany on the issue.

During November, Prussia and Austria had begun to come together on the Danish issue, largely from fear of isolation by the other Powers.[33] Count Rechberg made overtures to Bismarck, which, after an agreement that Austria not pursue an anti-Prussian agenda in the German Confederation, resulted in a joint policy of upholding the Treaty of London on Schleswig. The two Powers forced a vote through the German 'Diet' by only one vote on December 7th, calling for the Execution in Holstein to be carried out as soon as possible. Discussions on the fate of Schleswig would follow.

Whilst Copenhagen lurched through the political crisis, Von Hake's troops began entering Holstein and Lauenburg on Christmas Eve. Following the strong advice of Britain and Russia, they were unopposed by the Danes, whose troops withdrew before them, abandoning the fortress of Rendsburg and the important Baltic port of Kiel. Both Duchies were fully occupied by the Saxon/Hanoverian troops by the New Year. Of the voluntary Danish withdrawal, Sir John Maurice has fully blamed Great Britain in harsh terms. It had,

> …persuaded the Danes to surrender to Prussian aggression the first line of their defences and the fortress of Rendsburg, expressly on the grounds that, till that was done, she could afford no material assistance, drew back and left the Danish monarchy to be dismembered avowedly by sheer force.[34]

Concern that the 'Diet' might take matters over Schleswig into its own hands prompted Austria and Prussia to propose at the end of December that the German Confederation should also occupy that Duchy, to fulfill the obligations of the Treaty of London. The high handed manner in which the two Powers had behaved in relation to the earlier vote, however, frustrated their hopes of gaining a majority. The two states now formulated their own agreement for joint action. In Frankfurt, the 'Diet' rejected the Austro-Prussian proposals on Schleswig on January 14th. It was then informed that Austria and Prussia were to take bilateral action and occupy Schleswig, against which there were protests from member states.

Two days later, the Prussian and Austrian special ambassadors in Copenhagen sent, on behalf of their respective governments a final ultimatum to the Danish Foreign Minister, von Quaade. It read:

31 Duke Christian had renounced his claims on Schleswig-Holstein in 1852, in exchange for a large sum of money. His sons, however, had not, and there was support both in the Duchies and in Frankfurt for an Augustenburg Duke.

32 Kohl, Horst, *Bismarck's "Reflections and Reminiscences"*, p. 120.

33 Bismarck once stated that in 1849, Prussia had felt what it was like to be one against four. "Two against three is a better ratio", he said. Friedjung, H., *Der Kampf um die Vorherrschaft in Deutschland 1859 bis 1866.*

34 Maurice, J., *The Balance of Military Power in Europe*, Edinburgh & London 1888, p. 11.

The Governments of Austria and Prussia had hoped that the Common Constitution of the 18th of November last year, for Denmark and Schleswig sanctioned by His Majesty King Christian IX, and appointed to take effect from the 1st of January 1864, would have been suspended before that date. This hope has not been fulfilled. The Constitution came into operation on the 1st of January of the present year, and the incorporation of Schleswig was thereby accomplished. The Danish Government has thus unequivocally broken the obligations which it undertook in 1852, as well towards the German Confederation, as especially against the two German Powers, and has thereby created a state of affairs which cannot be regarded as justified by treaties. The above named two Powers owe it to themselves, and to the Federal Diet, in consequence of the part they played in those proceedings, the result of which was also approved by the Federal Diet at their recommendation, not to allow this situation to continue.

They address, therefore, to the Danish Government once more an express summons to withdraw the Constitution of the 18th of November, 1863, which rests upon no legal foundation, and thus, at any rate, to restore the preceding *status quo* as the necessary preliminary to any further negotiations.

Should the Danish Government not comply with this summons, the two above named Powers will find themselves compelled to make use of the means at their disposal for the restoration of the *status quo*, and the security of the Duchy of Schleswig against the illegal union with the Kingdom of Denmark.

The undersigned Ambassadors of the two Powers – whilst not formally accredited, are acting by special appointment of their Governments – are directed to require the withdrawal of the Constitution of the 18th of November last year, and to leave Copenhagen in the case of not receiving information by the 18th inst., that such action has been taken.

The undersigned take the opportunity of expressing & c

Brenner Balan[35]

The formal agreement between Prussia and Austria was signed in Berlin on the 17th.[36] Assisted by Danish inflexibility, the two nations would ostensibly go to war to defend the Treaty of 1852. The ultimatum by the two Powers threw Europe into disarray.

Minister-President Monrad initially asked for more time to consider the ultimatum. When this was refused, he rejected it on the 18th.

That same day, Franz Josef addressed his officers, assembled in Vienna. He told them:

I have assembled you here for a farewell greeting. Keep on good terms with your Prussian brothers-in-arms. I know that you will do your duty as if you were at home, and should it come to blows, will show your courage.

The Danes had thus precipitated a crisis, for which they were unprepared and the consequences of which they completely misjudged. There had been no serious

---

35 Fischer, Friedrich von, *Der Krieg in Schleswig und Jütland im Jahre 1864*, Vienna 1870, p. 39.

36 Article 5 of this Convention would later be the cause of difficulties for the current allies. It provided that a settlement in the Duchies would be achieved by mutual agreement of the two Powers. Ward & Wilkinson, Volume II, p. 235.

appreciation of the determination of the new allies to undertake a winter campaign, and this miscalculation was to cost them dearly.

The elderly Prussian Field Marshal Wrangel assumed command of the Allied Army on January 20th. The next day, that army entered Holstein on its march to the river Eider. To avoid any possible clash with General Hake's troops, arrangements were made to move those Saxon and Hanoverian units quartered along the Army's line of march further to the west. Hake's cavalry, strung along the south bank of the Eider, was to stay in place until relieved by the Austro-Prussians.[37]

Diplomacy, for now, was at an end. It is ironic that the otherwise progressive liberal parties on both sides of the argument were equally blinded by pure nationalism.

37 Moltke, H. von, *Militärische Korrespondenz. Krieg 1864*, Letter Nr. 33, to the War Minister, 20th January 1864.

2

Opposing Forces and Plans

Preparing to fight over the lower portion of the Cimbrian Peninsula were the entire armed forces of the Kingdom of Denmark, and a small portion of those of the Kingdom of Prussia and the Empire of Austria. What follows is a brief examination of those forces.

Denmark

Army

The Army Plan of 1842 called for an army of:

1 battalion of Royal Life Guards Infantry (four companies)

17 battalions of line infantry (four companies each)

5 battalions of light infantry - Jæger Korps (four companies each)

1 squadron, Life Guard Cavalry

2 squadrons, Guard Hussars

6 dragoon regiments (four squadrons each)

2 artillery regiments (twelve batteries, six to be maintained in peacetime)

2 companies, engineers

1 bridging train company

Quartermaster Generals dept.

By the time of the 1848 war, much of this plan had yet to be instituted, and a huge amount of improvisation took place during the war, including the raising of Reserve and 'Reinforcement' battalions. Victory in that conflict led to calls for retrenchment, and many of the hard learned lessons were forgotten in the demands for cuts in expenditure. As a result, the Army remained in the doldrums through the 1850's. A proposal for a new Army Bill in 1857 did not pass the legislature. Similar proposals for expensive works to the main defensive positions of the Danewerke, Dybbøl, and Fredericia, were also the subject of heated debate.

Conscription was introduced under the provisions of the June 1849 Constitution, and was applied not only in the Kingdom proper, but also to the Duchies. This was to have serious consequences for the army. Conscription was theoretically universal, but some exemptions were allowed, and, more importantly, it was possible to pay for substitutes. Service was theoretically four years, followed by four years in the reserve, and eight years 'reinforcement', or supplementary reserve. In practice, many men were sent home after initial training.

As negotiations continued with the Great Powers and the German Confederation in the early 1860's, the Minister of War, General Thestrup, began to push expansion of the Army and the building of fortifications. For the infantry Thestrup proposed to double the number of self-standing battalions to 44. The Life Guards Infantry would remain as one battalion. The Jægerkorps had been abolished in 1860, becoming Infantry Battalions 17 to 22. The artillery, both Field and Fortress, were to be rearmed with rifled guns.

After a disagreement with the Finance Minister, Lieutenant-General Thestrup resigned on August 13th 1863. A notoriously difficult and strong-willed man, Colonel C.C. Lundbye, replaced him. Lundbye brought with him to the Ministry, Major S. Ankjær. After troop manoeuvres at the Danewerke in September, the two men introduced sweeping new measures. Between September and November, three different sets of proposals came and went, including the increase of battalions to six companies. These measures caused a great deal of confusion amongst units that had only just begun to settle down. Finally, at the beginning of December, regiments were reintroduced for the first time since 1842. As previously planned, brigades were to comprise four battalions, each of four companies, but each brigade would now have an additional layer of command, a regiment of two battalions. Otto Vaupell comments on the whole that,

"In requiring 10 new regimental commanders, 22 new battalion commanders, 88 new company commanders, and 40 new adjutant etc. posts, and by taking away a huge number of NCOs from their former units, the entire infantry structure came loose – down to each battalion."[1]

An additional problem was the regiments from Holstein: the 14th, 16th, 17th, and 22nd. The first of these had to be disbanded altogether, and reconstituted with "reinforcement" men, that is, older men from earlier classes who had to be called up to fill the gaps. The 16th and 17th Regiments also had their soldiers from Holstein replaced before the outbreak of hostilities, but the 22nd did not reach a war footing until after this. The last Holstein soldiers did not leave the army until March.

The basic tactical unit of the infantry was the company, which was composed of four officers, ten NCOs, three musicians, 20 Undercorporals, and 180 men (plus four volunteers). Four companies, plus a battalion commander, adjutant, and one musician formed a battalion, and two battalions, a regiment. A regiment's full strength was 38 officers, 80 NCOs, 27 musicians, 160 undercorporals 1,440 men, and 32 volunteers. Note, however, that this strength was rarely, if ever, met.[2] The 1863 regulations stressed fire and movement, and the use of skirmishers, but had only been in force for 9 months when war started. Many senior officers still favoured the bayonet.

The cavalry faced less expansion than the infantry, but had its own share of last minute confusion. The four squadron regiments were ordered at the beginning of December, to add a fifth squadron, made up from the other four, and then, at the end of the month, to create a sixth. They were also required to create a regimental subdivision, or 'half-regiment', capable of operating independently. In spite of a shortage of horses, this was almost fully achieved before war broke out. The Field

1   Vaupell, Otto, *Kampen for Sønderjylland. Krigene 1848-1850 og 1864. 1864*, p. 61. Especially for the infantry, the officer shortage was acute. Experienced NCOs, too, were in short supply.
2   See Appendices IV, XII and XX.

Artillery's main problem was also horses, but since the existing 12 batteries were to be supplemented by only one more, the disruption was not too great.

A cavalry squadron comprised three officers, ten NCOs, 2-3 trumpeters, eight Undercorporals, and 112 men. The six squadron regiment comprised 21 officers, 69 NCOs, 12-15 trumpeters, 48 Undercorporals, and 670 men. Field Artillery Batteries, armed with rifled 4 pounder guns, had a strength of 189 combatants, and 29 non-combatants.

In the matter of weapons, the situation could not be said to be ideal. Like most of Europe, and indeed one of her two opponents, the Danish infantry were equipped with muzzle-loading rifled muskets. Six types, three on the minié system, and three pillar-breech, were issued, in two different calibres. In terms of effectiveness, there was little to choose between the performances of these weapons. For the artillery, matters were more difficult. The field artillery was in the process of receiving the iron M.1863 rifled muzzle-loading guns, sited from 500 yards up to a range of 3,750 yards. The majority of the position guns were, however, still smoothbore, varying from 6 to 84 pound weapons. (Note that in the text Danish smoothbore guns capable of firing shells are referred to as howitzers and others as cannon, purely to highlight this difference.)

The supreme command went to Lieutenant General Christian Julius de Meza, who was appointed on Christmas Day, 1863. The 72 year old was offered command of the army in spite of being somewhat odd. He had had a distinguished career, and was a great hero of the 1848-50 war, despite his undoubtedly strange manner. He would play the piano for hours on end, oblivious to all else.[3] Nonetheless, he was almost certainly the best candidate for the post. Like his future opponent Wrangel in several ways, he was also thought to be lucky, and his luck in the Three Years War at the battles of Fredericia and Isted certainly weighed heavily in his favour for the highest command. Appointed as General de Meza's Chief of Staff, was the very capable Colonel Heinrich Kauffmann of the General Staff.

When the army was mobilised at the end of 1863, many men from German speaking parts of Schleswig did not answer the summons, and the shortfall had to be filled by men from the Kingdom. The partial failure to answer the call-up was further compounded by a problem that would plague the Army throughout the campaign, that of the loyalty of the conscripted soldiers from South Schleswig. Antonio Gallenga, a correspondent for The (London) Times, heard of this firsthand:

> All along the road, by land and water, we met hundreds of old soldiers, chiefly from Schleswig, who obeyed orders lately issued by the Danish Government, calling under arms all the men bound to service up to thirty-five years of age. Most of these men seemed aware that there is a language spoken among the gods and one used among mortals. They conversed in German among themselves, and were ready with their Danish whenever there was a chance of being over-heard by strangers. Some of them were old sailors, familiar with the Western and Southern Ocean; they spoke English almost as well as their native language; they were an intelligent, well-informed set of men. They told me it was not

3 Jensen, N.P., *Den Anden Slesvigske Krig 1864*, p. 84, speaks of "… a certain weirdness …"

without repugnance that they undertook this weary journey, that their hearts were with the Germans, and that it was very hard they should have to bear arms against their own friends and countrymen; that they should have to follow the standards of those very Danes against whom they fought fourteen years ago. They added that they would fain have followed the example of many of their friends who had gone over to Holstein, only that they were not so sure Schleswig might not remain Danish, after all, when they would find themselves banished from their homes during their lifetime. They assured me that Denmark would have little cause to be satisfied with their services and with those of the Schleswigers and Holsteiners, which she held in her ranks against their will; that on the first shot being fired they would all pass over *en masse* to the enemy; that the whole of their Duchy was German to the core, and that even some of those belonging to the Northern Provinces who actually speak nothing but Danish were still devoted to the German cause.

Of course, I did not take these words to the letter, nor did I believe the Danish cause as hopeless as they made it out; what most forcibly struck and amazed me, however, was the boldness and readiness with which they gave utterance to such thoughts before a perfect stranger; for, although I suppose I do not look like a spy or an informer, still, I never told them I shared their feelings in any way, nor gave them any reason to believe they could rely on my discretion. Surely some fire must be smoldering when so much smoke appears; and if only one-tenth of what I everywhere hear is true, Denmark will have no little trouble in guarding against such friends, if ever the day comes in which she is to guide them against her enemies.[4]

On the outbreak of war, the army essentially consisted of one battalion of Life Guards Infantry, 22 infantry regiments (two battalions of four companies each), one squadron, Life Guards cavalry, the Guard Hussar Regiment (six squadrons), five dragoon regiments (six squadrons each), 13 field artillery batteries (eight guns each), six fortress artillery companies, and three companies of engineers.[5]

For better or worse, this was the Army that would fight to keep the Duchy.

Navy

The Danish Navy was in a much better position than the army to fight a war, and, at least in the short term, faced no enemy that could in any real sense challenge it. Like the army, most of its men came from conscription. Its peace time complement was 1881, soon greatly expanded.

Well equipped and trained, within two weeks of the outbreak of war, the fleet had ready for sea one turreted ironclad, two armoured schooners, one screw ship of the line, four screw frigates, three screw corvettes, ten screw schooners, seven screw gunboats, eight paddle-wheelers, and numerous inshore vessels. A further converted ironclad was nearing completion; one more was under construction, and another in the process of being purchased. In the second line was a considerable, if out of date, sailing squadron. Certainly, at the outset, Denmark had nothing to

---

4   A. Gallenga, *The Invasion of Denmark in 1864*, London 1864, Volume I, pp. 105-106.

5   See Appendix IV. It can be seen that not all units were fully formed.

fear from the Prussian Navy, and any potential Austrian threat was a long way away.

Prussia

Prussia's military and naval forces were something of an unknown quantity at the beginning of 1864. All of the other Powers had fought a major campaign within the previous ten years. Not so Prussia, which had not seen large-scale warfare since the end of the Napoleonic Wars. Prussia was a Great Power in military terms, but not as regards its navy. The army was of paramount importance.

Army

The army mobilisation of 1850 had been a spectacular failure, leading to a humiliating climb-down to Austria. Nine years later, at the time of the Franco-Austrian War in Italy, Prussia once again mobilised. Again the result was a complete shambles. Although the initial phase was begun in late April, by mid July the war was over, and the Prussian army was nowhere near a state of being able to fight anyone. Indeed, the very purpose of the mobilisation was unclear, since it had not been decided what was to happen subsequently.

This apparent inefficiency, however, belied the great improvements that had recently been made in the army, but which had yet to be observed from the outside. These improvements were due to several figures, of whom two were of prime importance; Lieutenant -General Helmuth Carl Bernhard von Moltke, appointed Chief of the General Staff in 1858, and Lieutenant General Albrecht Theodor Emil, Count von Roon, appointed War Minister by the King in 1859.

Von Roon was 56 when appointed, and the most junior lieutenant-general in the Army at the time. He had a passionate belief in professionalism, and major plans to completely overhaul the Army. This meant universal conscription from the age of 20, with a basic three year term of service for the average conscript (more in the Guards and specialist branches), followed by four years in the reserve, and then to the *Landwehr*, or militia.

In 1864 the entire army comprised:

9 Guard Infantry Regiments – 4 Foot Guards, 4 Guard Grenadiers, and 1 Guard Fusilier

2 Guard Battalions – Guard Jäger and Guard Schützen

72 Line Regiments – 12 Grenadier Regiments (Nr's 1-12), 52 Line Infantry Regiments (Nr's 13-32 and 41-72), and 8 Fusilier Regiments (Nr's 33-40)

8 Line Jäger Battalions

8 Guard Cavalry Regiments – Garde du Corps, Guard Cuirassier, 2 Guard Dragoons, Guard Hussar, 3 Guard Uhlans

8 Line Cuirassier Regiments

8 Line Dragoon Regiments

12 Line Hussar Regiments

12 Line Uhlan Regiments

1 Guard Artillery Brigade

8 Line Artillery Brigades

The campaign against Denmark was carried out initially by formations from two different Corps, III (Brandenburg) and VII (Westphalia), and the newer regiments of the Guards, but additional units from other Corps areas were also mobilised. Some of these latter units were used with the main army, and others for coast defence at the Prussian Baltic ports. The initial invasion force was one (Combined) corps, and a (Combined) Guard division, with additional troops.[6]

Infantry regiments were composed of three battalions, a brigade, of two regiments, and a division, of two brigades, with supporting elements. The Prussian infantry, during the campaign, were noted by many observers to be young. The reason for this was political. Part of the controversy over von Roon's reforms was an added year to military service. The new terms of enlistment only came into effect in 1859, and by late 1863, not enough men had gone through the new system to mobilise the infantry battalions to 1,002 men, without calling up 24-29 year old *Landwehr* soldiers, many of whom were married and had children. Given the political instability of the country, and that military service was one of the root causes of it, the decision was taken to mobilise only to a figure that could be attained without this step.[7] As a result, infantry battalions in the 1864 campaign were composed of 22 officers, 56 NCOs, 17 musicians, and 729 men. This meant that company and platoon officers had 20% fewer men to control, which proved to be an unforeseen benefit.

Apart from Norway, Prussia was the only state that had adopted breech-loading firearms for its infantry, the M1841 Dreyse *Zündnadelgewehr*, or needle-gun. This rifle would give Prussian infantry an advantage over their opponents, despite its faults, simply because they could fire faster (four rounds a minute, on average). As such, it was a formidable defensive weapon.

The cavalry units in the campaign were, for the most part, attached to their parent division. Cavalry regiments comprised four squadrons, a total of 23 officers, 84 NCOs and 635 men. One regiment, 2nd Westphalian Hussar Regiment, Nr. 8, also fielded its depot squadron in the campaign, and so had five.

For the artillery, the war was largely experimental, and varied in nature. Prussian artillery was organised in brigades, one for each of the Corps in the army. Each brigade had a regiment of field and one of fortress artillery. Each field regiment comprised one horse division of three batteries, and three field divisions of four batteries each. The Fortress artillery regiment had two divisions, each of four companies. In practice, in 1864, batteries were mixed and moved within the structure of the field army, particularly the fortress artillery. The reader's attention is drawn to the relevant appendices and text for details. The partial use of rifled artillery for the first time also meant that the gunners were feeling their way in the matter of doctrine. The new rifled 4 pounder field gun could throw an 8½ pound

---

6   See Appendix V.

7   For those who may consider that Minister-President Bismarck was fully in control at this time, this fact speaks volumes.

shell 4,000 yards with an angle of descent of 17.3 degrees. One 'experimental' battery of these guns was used.

Field Marshal Wrangel's appointment as supreme commander by the King was inevitable given the Austrian insistence upon the commanding general being an officer who had seen active service. In an army that had seen no major conflict since Waterloo, 'Papa' Wrangel was the only realistic choice. Almost 80 years old, he was nevertheless greatly respected by the public, and had the affection of the troops, if not necessarily that of his officers. He was thought to be lucky, a quality which Napoleon himself had considered useful in his generals.

Wrangel had won the *Pour le Mérite* as a young officer in 1807, and was awarded both classes of the Iron Cross for his actions in 1813. He eventually became a Field Marshal in 1856, and had unquestionably seen more of war than probably any living field commander. He was, however, completely out of touch with contemporary military thought. Even had the latter occurred to him, though, he would probably not have thought it important.

Prince Friedrich Carl, the King's nephew, was appointed to the new Allied 1st Combined Corps. He was a stern but compassionate man who was concerned always for the welfare of his men, who returned the affection. The Prince was a first rate organiser and trainer of troops, as he had superbly shown with his III Corps. In the field, however, he could sometimes display a curious hesitancy.[8]

Navy

With the acquisition of Swedish Pomerania in 1815, Prussia gained substantial additional Baltic coastline. Little was done to shape a separate Prussian navy, however, for some time, largely because of the rise of a "German" Navy, under the auspices of the Frankfurt Parliament, and then, the First Schleswig-Holstein War. After the acrimonious demise of the first, and the end of the latter, some progress was made under Prince Adalbert of Prussia, a nephew of King Friedrich Wilhelm III, who had championed the naval cause since the 1830's. Made "Admiral of the Prussian Coasts" in 1853, he worked ceaselessly for naval expansion.[9] Unfortunately, naval funding came into the conflict between parliament and the King from 1859, and continued until the crisis over Schleswig brought war. The Prussian Navy was far from ready.

The fleet had four screw-corvettes, the Royal Yacht, two paddle steamers, six '1st class' steam gunboats and 14 '2nd class', as well as inshore and harbour defence craft, and a squadron of sailing vessels. Of these, the paddle steamer *Preussischer Adler*, and two '1st class' gunboats were in the eastern Mediterranean, and one of the screw-corvettes on her way to the Far East. The rest were stationed variously in the Baltic ports of Swinemünde, Stralsund, and Rügen. Fitting out in Danzig was a screw-corvette, and under construction there were two screw-corvettes and two '1st class' gunboats. During the war, Prussia would also purchase two ironclads and two screw-corvettes, which would not be delivered until after the end of hostilities.

8   There are considerable parallels here with the Union General, George McClellan.
9   Legend has it that King Wilhelm IV would not create Adalbert Admiral of the Fleet, because, 'we do not have a fleet', Sondhaus, Lawrence, *Preparing for Weltpolitik*, Annapolis, 1997.

Naval personnel amounted to one admiral, three captains, 75 other officers, 40 cadets, eight gunnery officers, and 2,146 petty officers, men, and boys.

Austria

One of the Great Powers, the Habsburg Empire had immense resources potentially available for use against Denmark. In practice, of course, a large military mobilisation was never considered to be relevant for the matter in hand and one Army Corps and a naval squadron were actually employed in the war.

Army

In 1864, the major combat units of the Imperial Army comprised:

80 Infantry Regiments

14 Frontier Infantry Regiments

1 Frontier Infantry Battalion (independent)

1 Tiroler Jäger Regiment (6 Battalions)

32 Feldjäger Battalions

12 Cuirassier Regiments

2 Dragoon Regiments

14 Hussar Regiments

13 Uhlan Regiments[10]

12 Field Artillery Regiments

1 Coast Artillery Regiment

4 Fortress Artillery Companies

2 Engineer Regiments

6 Pioneer Battalions

Further details are given only for troops who took part in the "joint action" with Prussia. After the defeat in Italy in 1859 by the Franco-Italians, an immense amount of soul-searching took place in the army. A major reorganisation was formulated and carried out whilst, at the same time, a complete revision of tactical procedures was also developed and put into effect during 1862/63. This implementation of a total reversal of earlier doctrine was a most impressive achievement, but it remained to be seen how the new offensive-minded regulations would fare in the field. Men were theoretically liable for military service from the age of twenty, but a call up was not universal.

---

10 It should be noted that grenadiers no longer existed as a separate entity within infantry regiments, having been abolished in this form under the army reorganisation of 1860. The term "grenadier" was now applied to any soldier in the Line or Grenz infantry who re-enlisted.

One full Army Corps was created and mobilised for the campaign. A "typical" Corps consisted of four infantry brigades, a cavalry regiment, corps artillery reserve, and attached units. The creation of what was to become VI Corps was as follows. The brigade of Major-General Gondrecourt, stationed in Prague, was ordered in early December to join the Federal Executions force for Holstein. The brigade arrived in Hamburg by train on December 21st and was placed at the orders of force commander, the Saxon Lieutenant General von Hake.

A few days after the orders to Gondrecourt, the decision to mobilise a complete Army Corps for the joint action with Prussia was taken. Three other infantry brigades were alerted for this, those of Major-Generals Nostitz and Tomas in Vienna, and of Major-General Dormus in Hungary. The cavalry brigade of Major-General Dobrzhensky, formerly in Bohemia, was added in addition to artillery, engineer, trains, and ancillary units. The whole force, which was to include Brigade Gondrecourt, was designated VI Army Corps.[11]

A Brigade was made up of two infantry regiments, one Jäger battalion, and an artillery "brigade battery" of eight guns.

As, in this case, there was not a full mobilisation each infantry regiment fielded only two battalions in the campaign. The depot battalion remained at home, in that capacity. A battalion comprised six companies. An infantry company was composed of the following combatants: one captain, one oberlieutenant, two lieutenants, 14 NCOs, 16 Gefreite (senior private), 130 men, two drummers, one trumpeter, and two infantry pioneers. Added to the six companies were a battalion staff of one commanding officer, one adjutant, one battalion drummer, one battalion trumpeter, and one Fahnenführer (standard bearer), giving a total combatant strength of 1,019. A Jäger battalion was slightly smaller, with a full strength of 1,050 and a combatant strength of 963.

One hussar and one dragoon regiment, both officially light cavalry, were part of VI Corps. Each had five field squadrons of five officers, 14 NCOs, 1 trumpeter, and 130 men (149 horses) apiece. The regimental combatant strength was 760.

Six batteries of artillery were in the corps, one 4 pounder battery with each brigade, and two 8 pounder batteries, as the Corps Artillery Reserve. All were from 1st Artillery Regiment. Each 4 pounder battery had an establishment of four officers and 160 men, and the 8 pounder batteries, four officers and 193 men. All batteries had eight guns. Only two models of cannon were used during this campaign, both bronze rifled muzzle-loaders. These were the M.1863 rifled 8 pounder (3.83") field gun, and the M.1863 rifled 4 pounder (3.08"). Their maximum ranges with common shell were just under 4,200 yards and 3,750 yards respectively.

Appointed to head VI Corps was 49 year old Ludwig, Baron von Gablenz, who assumed command on January 16th. Born in Saxony, he was initially in the Saxon army, but transferred to the Imperial service in 1835. His early years were under Marshal Radetzky in Italy. Gablenz was a first rate officer, with a sense of duty and honour, neither of which could be compromised. A somewhat nervous man and what today might be termed a 'control freak', he possessed great personal courage and was always at the forefront in battle. His instructions from Vienna included enforcing strict discipline amongst the troops, something for which he was

11 See Appendix V for details.

in any case noted. Gablenz set the highest standards for himself, and expected nothing less from his subordinates.[12] In common with many Austrian officers, he was prepared to take casualties to achieve success.

Navy

The Imperial Navy, based in the Adriatic at Pola, had developed into an appreciable force since its modernisation. This modernisation was begun by the Rear Admiral Hans Birch von Dahlerup who, ironically, was a Dane. Dahlerup's work was continued by the able and enthusiastic Archduke Ferdinand Max, who chose Pola as the main fleet base. He was able to separate naval affairs from the War Ministry by getting a separate Ministry of Marine established in 1863. By 1864 the main fleet comprised one screw Ship of the Line, five ironclad frigates, five screw frigates and two screw corvettes. In reply to requests, a squadron was sent to the North Sea.

12 At the beginning of the campaign, Gablenz sacked the commander of the Liechtenstein Hussars, Colonel Baron Basselli von Süssenberg, for dereliction of duty in the neglect of care of his troops. The unfortunate man was lucky to be retired from the army on grounds of sickness. See, Gründorf von Zebegény, Wilhelm, *Memoiren eines österreichischen Generalstäblers 1832-1866.* Stuttgart 1913, pp. 195-107.

3

The Danewerke

On January 30th, just ten days after taking command, Field Marshal Wrangel sent a wordy ultimatum to Lieutenant-General de Meza, which ended:

...the undersigned has been given orders to occupy the Duchy of Schleswig with the allied troops of Prussia and Austria, unified under his command, and also to take over its provisional administration. In notifying you of this, I ask you to inform me whether you have orders to leave Schleswig and withdraw the Royal Danish troops outside its borders.

I herewith take the opportunity to ensure you of my highest regards.

The next day, this reply was received from Lieutenant-General de Meza:

The undersigned does not accept the right of Prussian and Austrian troops to occupy any part of Danish territory and does not accept the accuracy of the document included in Your Excellency's letter of 30th January. My government has instructed me to oppose your moves and to respond to any acts of violence with armed force.[1]

Hostilities were now inevitable. Upon receipt of this reply from de Meza, Wrangel notified his Corps Commanders. The message ended simply, "In God's name – GO!"

The strength of the forces about to clash across the Eider, were as follows:

Table 1

Allied Army Field Strength February 1st 1864[2]

I Corps (Prussian Combined Corps)

25 Battalions	20,851 infantry
25 Squadrons	3,933 cavalry
96 Guns	3,633 artillery and pioneers
Total	28,417

II Corps (K.K. VI Army Corps)

20 Battalions	19,248 infantry

---

1   von Fischer, p. 80.
2   These figures are extracted from von Fischer, pp. 21-26. Grosser Generalstab, *Der Deutsch-Dänische Krieg 1864*, Volume I, Appendices 10, 11, 12, and 13, reduce the total number by roughly 1500 men. This is still probably a little on the high side. In addition, not all of these troops were immediately available for operations in Schleswig.

10 Squadrons	1,523 cavalry
48 Guns	1,841 artillery, engineers and pioneers
Total	22,612

III Corps (Prussian Combined Guard Division)

12 Battalions	9,972
4 Squadrons	625
14 Guns	290
Total	10,887

Army Totals

57 Battalions	50,071 infantry
39 Squadrons	6,081 cavalry
158 Guns	5,474 artillery, engineers and pioneers
Total	61,626

Table 2

Danish Field Army at the Danewerke[3]

1st Division

12 Battalions

3 Squadrons

16 Guns

2nd Division

12 Battalions

3 Squadrons

16 Guns

3rd Division

12 Battalions

3 Squadrons

16 Guns

---

3 Extracted from Generalstaben, *Statistiske Meddelelser den danske Krigsmagt*, Copenhagen 1867. These figures represent combatants fit for duty in the forward area of South Schleswig.

4th (Cavalry) Division

18 Squadrons

8 Guns (from Feb 2nd)

Infantry Reserve

4 Battalions

Army Artillery

32 Guns

Army Totals

40 Battalions	31,195 Infantry
27 Squadrons	3,153 Cavalry
88 Guns	3,940 Artillery, engineers and other
Total	38,828

Across the Frontier

At approximately 07:00 on Monday February 1st 1864, the first Allied troops crossed the frontier into Schleswig. On the left, II Corps was assembled to the south and east of Rendsburg by 06:30. Brigade Gondrecourt crossed the River Eider via the railway bridge and Brigade Nostitz by the road bridge. Neither was opposed, the Danish Guard Hussar pickets firing a few shots before withdrawing. Brigade Tomas, following behind, used both bridges as did the cavalry brigade and reserve artillery. Brigade Dormus, in the rear, was still marching north from Neumünster.

There was no resistance to the Austrian advance by the Danish outposts of 2nd Division (from the 5th and 7th Infantry Regiments). These, as ordered, withdrew towards the Danewerke, stopping at the village of Oxlev to tear up the railway tracks and, at 12:00, to blow up the rail tunnel. Subsequently they pulled back to the Danewerke itself.

FML Gablenz advanced Brigades Nostitz and Gondrecourt some three miles north to the villages of Ahrenstedt (Nostitz) and Schulendamm (Gondrecourt), with pickets to the west of Witten Lake, a further three miles on.

On their right, I Corps passed over the Eider Canal at four points on a front of some 11 miles. These points were Cluvensiek, (Advance Guard,[4] and most of 13th Division), Königsforde, (one battalion and one squadron), the 'Landwehr' Bridge (Cavalry Division) and Levensau (6th Division, and five batteries of the Reserve Artillery). At the head of the Advance Guard were the four squadrons of the Ziethen Hussars, followed closely by Prince Friedrich Carl and his staff.

---

4   A temporary 'Advance Guard' had been formed for the start of the campaign, from units of other formations. It comprised five infantry battalions (F/IR13, F/IR15, F/IR24, I/IR 60, and 7th Jäger Battalion), six squadrons of hussars (4 and 5/Westphalian Hussars Nr. 8, and the four squadrons of the Ziethen Hussars, Nr. 3), and 18 guns, all under the command of Colonel von Groeben.

The extremely poor weather made the advance hard going for the troops, with heavy snowfalls. Roads were sheets of ice, and especially difficult for horses. The temperature was noted at minus 6.25 degrees Centigrade (20.5 Fahrenheit) during the day.[5]

At Levensau, there was a brief skirmish with a post of the Danish 5/4th Dragoon Regiment. One Danish dragoon was shot and mortally wounded. The main body of the Danish squadron was able to successfully withdraw, but one post was unlucky. After crossing the canal, 3/11th Uhlans, Major von Lüderitz, were detached to their left to move west and make contact with the Prussian Cavalry Division. The squadron surprised a Danish cavalry outpost from the aforementioned unit near the Landwehr Bridge. One undercorporal and five dragoons were captured.

Further west the Danish outpost infantry, from the 18th Regiment, had begun to withdraw before the Prussian advance began. At 06:00, the regiment received a message that the 2nd Division further west was pulling back its forward troops, and that they were to conform to this movement.

Two companies of the Danish regiment's Second Battalion were positioned in the Friedensthal Woods, almost two miles southwest of Eckernförde to cover the other units' withdrawal. At 10:00, two companies of the Prussian I/IR60, Major Karl von Jena, moved into the woods. These units, 2/IR60, Captain von Mach, and 3/IR60, Captain Lesczinski, engaged in a brief firefight with Captain A.C. Volkvartz' company, 4/18th. Volkvartz, however, had no intention of being pinned in an action, and the retreat was continued. Major von Jena had no casualties - Volkvartz lost four men wounded and two missing (the latter taken prisoner).[6]

At 11:30 the 18th Regiment retreated through the fortified position at Kochendorf, held by 3rd Infantry Regiment. Kochendorf itself was held a little longer, but, in accordance with the general instructions for the withdrawal and concentration along the line of the main position, it too was abandoned at 14:00, the troops moving back to Missunde.

Whilst this was going on Lieutenant-Colonel Zimmerman's F/IR13, of the Prussian Advance Guard, had been sent directly towards Eckernförde Bight, and a little after 11:00, just after passing the village of Marienthal, the unit sighted two Danish warships close inshore there. These opened fire on the advancing Prussian columns. A message to this effect was dispatched to the main body, which sent three batteries of artillery hastening to the scene.

The armour-plated schooner *Esbern Snare* (one smoothbore 30 pounder and two rifled 18 pounders) under Lieutenant-Commander Kraft, followed by the screw-corvette *Thor* (twelve smoothbore 30 pounders) under Lieutenant-Commander Hedemann (commanding), had entered the southern part of the fjord on a reconnaissance. Observing enemy troops, at 11:15 both vessels fired upon columns of the Prussian 6th Division, which were moving north towards Eckernförde. In their turn, the ships were fired upon by Prussian artillery.

5   Rüstow, Wilhelm, *Der deutsch-dänische Krieg 1864*, Zürich 1864, p. 190. Rüstow actually says '-5 degrees', since he was using the Reaumur temperature scale, quite common at the time. In this scale, distilled water freezes at zero and boils at 80 degrees. This text gives the Centigrade and Fahrenheit equivalents.

6   Grosser Generalstab, *Der Deutsch-Dänische Krieg 1864*, Volume I, Berlin 1886, p.124, claims 13 Danish casualties.

This was 3rd 6 Pounder Battery/Artillery Brigade Nr. 3 under Captain Minameyer (six guns), which had been hurriedly moved to the shore by the Advance Guard's commander, Colonel Count von Groeben, and deployed at Sandkrug. Shortly afterwards, two additional 6 pounder batteries (2nd and 4th 6 Pounder Batteries, of the Reserve Artillery – 12 guns) were brought in to action east of Goossee. All of these units were equipped with rifled 6 pounders.

The duel between the vessels and the Prussian field artillery continued until about 12:00, when Hedemann pulled his ships out of range of the enemy guns. At one point, Thor had come within 650 yards of the shore. Hedemann had, in any case, been given orders not to engage enemy artillery, and he was lucky to escape lightly. *Esbern Snare* was undamaged. *Thor* had several hits made on her, one putting a hole through her funnel, but no serious damage. The Prussians had one horse killed.[7] *Esbern Snare* withdrew to Sønderborg, and *Thor* to Nyborg.

The town of Eckernförde was given up without a struggle at 14:00, and now all Danish troops in the area were pulled back still further, to the Missunde position, along the Schlei. By late afternoon, I Corps had established a line of forward posts extending from Eckernförde to Windeby Lake, which linked with II Corps to the west.

There had been no casualties amongst the Allies on the first day. Danish losses totaled seven for the 4th Dragoons, and 18th Infantry Regiment lost about 10 or 12 men.[8]

Confident of a favourable reception from the populace, certainly in the southern portion of the Duchy, Marshal Wrangel issued the following Proclamation to the people of Schleswig:

Prussian Headquarters 1st February
Inhabitants of the Duchy of Schleswig – Commissioned by His Majesty the King of Prussia, my most gracious master, to occupy the Duchy with Prussian troops, in conjunction with the forces which His Majesty the Emperor of Austria has been pleased to place under my command for the same purpose, I call upon you to receive these troops with friendship and hospitality.

We come to protect your rights.

These rights are violated by the common Constitution for Denmark and Schleswig sanctioned by his Majesty the King of Denmark upon the 18th of November of last year, by which, in contravention of the agreements entered into in the year 1852, the Duchy has been incorporated into the Kingdom.

---

7 The Danish Navy was most sensitive about ships engaging land artillery. This stemmed from an occurrence during the 1st Schleswig War. On April 4th 1849, in the same area as this, Prussian/Holsteiner shore and field batteries actually blew up the 84-gun ship of the line *Christian VIII* and forced the surrender of the frigate *Gefion*. The Danish navy lost over a thousand men, mostly prisoners. *Gefion* was commissioned into the Prussian Navy, and was still in service in 1864.

8 Generalstaben, *Den danske-tyske Krig 1864*, Volume I, Copenhagen 1890, page 216, gives the total for the day as three wounded (of whom one was captured), and seven unwounded prisoners. However, on the previous page, it states that four men of the regiment were wounded in the fight in Friedensthal woods. As noted, the Prussian claim is higher. Other sources are similarly confusing.

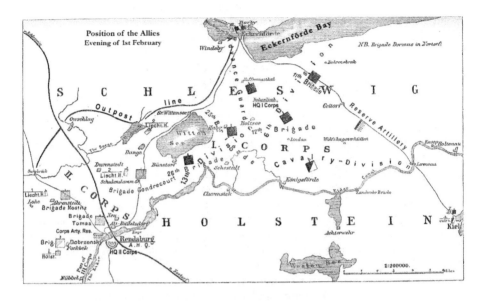

Map 2: Allied Position, evening of 1st February

His Majesty the King of Denmark has been vainly summoned to loose this bond. The Governments of Prussia and Austria have in consequence thereof determined on their part to bring into operation the means at their command practically to abolish the incorporation, and to ensure to the Duchy the rights to which it is entitled by treaty. They will accomplish these objects by occupying the Duchy with their united troops and assuming its temporary administration.

This administration will be undertaken by civil commissioners of the two powers.[9] I call upon you to pay obedience to their orders, and to support them in their efforts for the maintenance of legal and settled conditions. The laws of the country remain valid so far as the security of the troops does not indispensably require momentary and passing exceptions.

I expect of the loyal and reasonable good sense of the inhabitants of the Duchy that they will abstain from all demonstrations, from whatever party they may proceed. You must yourselves be aware that party agitation can only injure your good right, and that I cannot suffer them in your own interest.

Our troops come as friends; as friends you will receive them.

von Wrangel, Field Marshal Commanding

For General de Meza, a further headache was the presence of the King and Council-President Monrad. Christian IX and Monrad arrived in Schleswig on the 1st, intent upon inspecting the army and the defence works. The Council Presi-

9   Here was the sting in the tail. Although it was a perfectly sensible administrative measure to appoint Civil Commissioners, there is no mention here of the Prince of Augustenburg or any authority other than that of the two powers. For those who could or wished to see it, this was the first hint at imposed rule.

dent also wished to see his son Viggo, a second-lieutenant in the 10th Infantry Regiment. There was little de Meza could do other than keep them out of harm's, and his, way as much as possible.

The Action at Missunde, February 2nd

The defence of the Missunde peninsula south of the Schlei, about seven miles east of the town of Schleswig, was entrusted to Major-General C. A. Vogt's 2nd Brigade, elements of which had been involved in the previous day's skirmishes, and also to Captain H.C. Hertel's 6th Fortress Artillery Company. The width of the Schlei here was only some 200 yards but was an important crossing point.

The defences themselves comprised the following (see map in this section. Note that the numbered designations of the defences described here are those used by the Allies):

On the peninsula, redoubts 59 and 60 were at its neck, a little over 100 yards south of the village, on either side of the Eckernförde Road, which crossed the Schlei at Missunde. Their armament consisted of four 12 pounder smoothbore guns and four 24 pound smoothbore howitzers (number 59), and two 12 pounder smoothbore guns and four 24 pound smoothbore howitzers (number 60), commanded by Lieutenants Bache and Klubien respectively. Redoubts 61a and 61b were sited north of the village the former defending the road bridge, whilst 61c was at the north-east tip of the peninsula, covering the temporary 'artillery' bridge, which had been constructed there. Of these, only 61b actually contained any artillery: two 12 pounder smoothbore guns.

Across the Schlei, on the north bank, redoubts 63a, b, c, and d were situated on the heights west of Missunde below the Missunde Ferry house, facing the opposite bank. Numbers 63 e and f were north of this, also facing east. In Number 63a were two 12 pounder smoothbore guns and in 63b, two 24 pound smoothbore howitzers. These were under command of Corporal Würtz.

Vogt had only 8 companies of infantry available in the area of Missunde on the morning of February 2nd. 2/18th Regiment was deployed in Redoubts a and b, half a company in each. 1/18th formed the outpost line, whilst 5/18th and 7/18th were in reserve. Three companies of I/3rd Regiment were north of the Schlei at Brodersby, nearly a mile away, along with the 10th Field Artillery Battery. The 1/3rd was further to the east, on its way from Cappeln. 7/3rd Regiment was defending the northern bridgehead from redoubt f. Captain Hertel's fortress artillery company manned the guns in the defences, and one squadron, 6/4th Dragoons, Ritmester V. Bülow, was also in support.

Marshal Wrangel's orders for February 2nd to Ist Corps were for an advance to the neck of the Schwansen Peninsula, between Eckernförde and Holm. This rendered it necessary to take the fortifications at Kochendorf, which had actually already been vacated by de Meza on the 1st.

Prince Friedrich Carl, unaware of this, issued orders that the Advance Guard move on that position from Moschau, where it was concentrated, at 08:00. They were instructed to move through Windeby Wood and attack and carry the position upon word of the arrival of 13th Division at Osterby. 13th Division's own orders called for them to leave Lehmsiek, also at 08:00, and move via Osterby to occupy the defile at Mölhorst.

The rest of 6th Division was to support 13th Division. 11th Brigade was to assist at Kochendorf if necessary, supported by three squadrons of the Westphalian Hussars (from the Reserve Cavalry). The remainder of the Reserve Cavalry was ordered towards Rendsburg, whilst the Reserve Artillery was to concentrate at 09:00 at the junction of the Sandkrug and Eckernförde roads to Windeby and await developments.

I Corps again moved off in extremely bad weather and poor visibility. Many of the cavalry and artillery were dismounted, leading their horses on the icy roads and by-ways. Progress was unavoidably slow.

No major resistance had been expected at Kochendorf but, soon after 08:00, reports came to the Advance Guard that it was abandoned. This information was soon confirmed. The position had been strongly barricaded, and the bridges at Mölhorst and Holm destroyed. Pioneers rapidly removed the obstacles, and began repairing the bridges. By 09:00, I Corps' objectives for 2nd February were achieved: the line of Eckernförde-Holm was occupied.

Prince Friedrich Carl now decided to advance on the bridgehead at Missunde. He had no way of knowing where the Danes would make a stand, and in any case he would have to force the Schlei at some point. It was even possible that the bridgehead itself might be occupied without resistance. He reasoned that his artillery was stronger than his opponents, and could overpower them. A plan was hurriedly formulated and put into action.

Lieutenant-General von Manstein was given operational command of the Advance Guard and Canstein's 11th Brigade. His instructions were to develop the Missunde position, but not to risk an assault unless it was certain to be successful. The artillery was to be his prime weapon. At the same time, the Reserve Artillery was told to move as quickly as possible to join the action.

The Prussian vanguard F/IR24, 11 and 12/IR15, 2/7th Jäger and 3/Ziethen Hussars, under the command of Major von Krohn, passed the village of Kosel to their right and then began to see obvious signs that the area had been prepared for defence. Paths had been widened and knicks broken through in places. Nearer Missunde, whole knicks had been reduced in height to clear fields of fire. Between Lang See and Missunde, at 10:00, the hussar pickets came under fire from Danish outposts and withdrew. Von Krohn himself pushed forward with 9 and 10/IR24.

At about 10:30, these strong lines of skirmishers forced the Danish outposts up on to the heights of Ornum. 1/18th, Captain F. Baller, fell back into the redoubts. The whole of the F/IR 24 was now engaged. All four companies were on the heights east of the Ornum-Missunde road with the 10/IR24, Captain Baumgarten, on the right nearest to the Schlei, under rifle and occasional artillery fire from the redoubts. Thick fog constantly drifted back and forth across the area, and became thicker and more widespread during the day.[10]

The firing alerted Major-General Vogt, who was shortly joined by Lieutenant-General Gerlach. Vogt took position in Redoubt b, and Gerlach in Redoubt d. The units at Brodersby were summoned to cross the Schlei, and further

10 Anon., "Missunde", *Militärische Blätter*, Volume 12, Nr. 8 Berlin 1864, says, "The weather on 2nd February was so foggy that one had no view of more than 100 paces, and even the approximate position of the redoubts could be recognised only by the flash of the enemy guns firing."

troops alerted. Until the situation was clarified, however, no general call for reinforcements was made. It was not until much later, after the first Prussian artillery eventually became involved, that Gerlach and Vogt finally realised that there was a major enemy force facing them.

Laurence Oliphant, a self styled adventurer, had come directly to Schleswig upon hearing of the death of Frederick VII. A shrewd observer, he was present with the Prussians at Missunde during the whole of the action. His rather pompous account gives a good description of the extremely poor visibility during the fighting here:[11]

> Passing through the village, the inhabitants of which were all excitedly collected to witness from afar the coming engagement, I ascended a hill, on which stood a picturesque church, and from the churchyard, filled with spectators, was just able to distinguish with my glass the indistinct forms of the Danish skirmishers. Unfortunately the mist lay so heavy over the landscape that the fortifications of Missunde itself were not visible, and after leaving the churchyard, we felt very much as though we were groping our way in the dark as we approached the enemy's position. Soon a shot from the Danish batteries enlightened us as to their exact whereabouts, and our artillery was brought up into position, extending itself in a semicircle along the crest of the hill. Fortunately the frost had hardened the surface of the ploughed land across which the guns were to be dragged. The fields were divided by mud banks surmounted by hedges, and pioneers were actively employed cutting gaps through them. These banks afforded very comfortable shelter for amateurs; but the firing was not hot enough to drive one behind them for long. I afterwards understood that no fewer than seventy-four pieces of ordnance were engaged in the bombardment; but I only counted six batteries, and the fire was not kept up with much spirit. In fact, the fog seemed to exercise a depressing influence upon all concerned: our extremities were very cold; but there was not even enough excitement to make one forget one's 'poor feet.' The unhappy Danes did not the least know where the infantry was massed, and could only judge what to fire at by the flashes of our heavy guns. The flashes of theirs alone revealed the position of Missunde, and the consequence was that comparatively little damage was done on either side. The enemy's fire was necessarily feeble, as they had but few guns in position; but the sound of shot and shell was evidently new to the young soldiers who composed the Prussian army, and who paid the tribute of respect to a whistling shell common to novices. Once I perceived, advancing dimly through the fog, the line of Danish skirmishers, and thought that some life was about to be infused into the monotonous artillery combat, which had lasted for about two hours; but they halted two fields distant and retreated in good order, having apparently made themselves acquainted with our position.

11 Oliphant, Laurence, *Episodes in a Life of Adventure*, London 1888. By an amazing coincidence, Oliphant had been the guest at the country estate of the Duke of Augustenburg, when the news came of the death of the old King, thus prompting him to the scene of the turmoil. The Duke's eldest son was thought by many to be the rightful heir to the Duchies. Oliphant left Schleswig a few days after Missunde, having been unable to observe any more fighting and having sorely tried the patience of the Prussian military authorities. Reading of his travels, one feels that he must have been utterly insufferable.

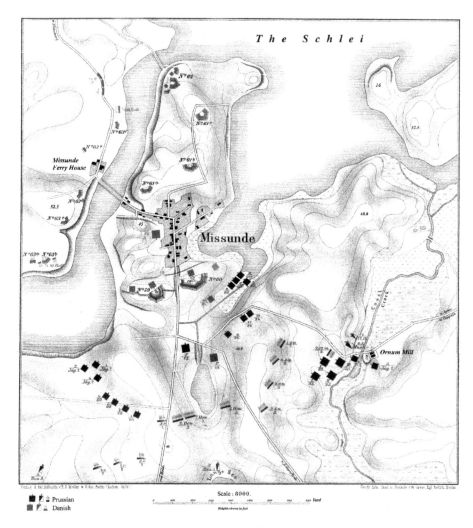

Map 3: Action at Missunde - 2nd February

At 11:30, the rest of the Advance Guard began arriving, and were posted north of the Lang See, to await the Reserve Artillery. Lieutenant-General von Manstein arrived to take command at noon. Artillery Colonel Colomier had, in the meantime, been planning the positions to be occupied by his Reserve Artillery batteries upon their arrival.

At the same time as the Prussian troops were deploying, the other three companies of the I/3rd Infantry Regiment arrived in Missunde from Brodersby. Gerlach and Vogt still had no real idea of the forces opposing them, and were confused by the fact that no enemy artillery had as yet appeared. Consequently, these units were ordered on a reconnaissance to ascertain enemy strength and intentions.

At 12:30, each company advanced, intending to move along the three roads to Ornum, Kosel, and Weseby, respectively. The battalion was followed by a troop of the 6th Dragoons, commanded by Premierlieutenant Meulengracht. The force was instructed to reoccupy the original outpost positions should it discover that there was no major enemy force present.

Little more than 100 yards south of the redoubts, the force came under heavy fire. Engaged in a firefight with the Fusilier Battalions of IR15 and IR24, the 3 Danish companies were quickly pushed back. The centre company, 2/3rd, was thrown back in confusion after the company commander, Captain A. Moltke was slightly, and Premierlieutenant Seyffart mortally, wounded.

The two other companies, 5/3rd under Captain (of the War Reserve) L. Svane, and 6/3rd under Premier Lieutenant (of the War Reserve) Bergmann, covered this retreat with some difficulty, pulling back to the redoubts under heavy fire. To their left, 10/IR24 under Captain von Baumgarten, on the Prussian right flank, seized the moment of confusion and attacked across the ice of the dead arm of the Schlei, pushing forward to occupy an unfinished trench only some 150 yards from Redoubt b. The fire from Baumgarten's men throughout the afternoon would seriously hamper the gunners in this redoubt. An attempt to clear them out of the trench was made by 7/18th, Premierlieutenant H. Ahlmann, but it was repulsed in disarray by heavy rifle fire.

The reconnaissance had established that a large Prussian force was, indeed, south of the position, though how large they had been unable to ascertain. Its intentions were still, briefly, something of a mystery. Prince Friedrich Carl sent a curious message to FML Gablenz at this time, in which he seems to have already changed his mind about the whole enterprise. It read:

> Before Missunde, 2nd February, 1864, 12:30 PM
>   I have encountered no resistance at Kochendorf, Holm, and Mölhorst, other than some barricades and broken bridges, and have taken with the Advance Guard and the 11th Brigade, a position so that a Danish sortie – which, by the way, I do not expect - cannot impede me. The 13th Division, as well as the 12th Brigade, stand along the main road from Eckernförde to Schleswig. I have the Artillery Reserve coming to the front to fire against Redoubts 59 and 60. I will not cross the River Schlei today or tomorrow. My Headquarters today will be at Hemmelmark.[12]

As the Danish infantry pulled back into the redoubts, the first Prussian guns came into action. On the news of the approach of the Reserve Artillery, the two foot batteries (3rd Howitzer Battery – eight guns, and 3rd 6 Pounder Battery – six guns) of the Advance Guard took position either side of the Eckernförde Road and opened fire at a range of about 700 yards. A shell from one of these killed Premierlieutenant Meulengracht, whose dragoon troop had taken up a position near Redoubt b. They were then withdrawn to the north bank.

Gerlach now recognised that a major Prussian force was opposed to him, the great number of guns that had suddenly entered the fight suggesting a very large force indeed. 3rd Brigade was immediately ordered to Missunde, though it would

12 von Fischer, p. 91. This message was not finally delivered to FML Gablenz until 18:00.

be some time before they could arrive. II/3rd Regiment, Captain Krabbe, was ordered to leave one company in position guarding the coast from Brodersby to Ulsnis, and advance the other two companies immediately to Missunde. 10th Field Artillery Battery had arrived at noon, four of its guns being placed on the north bank of the Schlei, in Redoubts g1 and g2 (the other four were deployed opposite the northern bridgehead at Redoubt g6, and never came into action). Later, these would take part in the action against Prussian horse artillery. For the present, there were no other supports to call upon (The two companies of II/3rd would finally arrive in Missunde, along with 1/3rd from Cappeln shortly after 15:00, and were placed in reserve. With their arrival, the Danish force reached its maximum: 2,109 men).[13]

At 13:00 Friedrich Carl's Reserve Artillery began to arrive and enter the fight.[14] The howitzer batteries unlimbered to the west of the Eckernförde road, on the left of the 3rd Howitzer Battery, and the 6-pounder batteries to the east of the road, on its right. The horse batteries were placed further west, initially the 1st and 3rd Batteries, and subsequently by the 4th and 6th.[15] 64 guns, 24 of them rifled 6

Major von Jena, commander of II/IR60, at Missunde (Voss)

13 Generalstaben, *Statistiske Meddelelser angaaende den danske Krigsmagt*, Volume I, p. 136.

14 The artillery had a very difficult time in moving to Missunde, not only because of the weather, but also the sheer volume of traffic and the consequent churning up of the roads, especially through the villages. See von Saenger, "Notizen über die Theilnahme der reitenden Artillerie der Westphälischen Artillerie-Brigade Nr. 7 an dem Gefechte bei Missunde", *Militärische Blätter*, Volume XXI, Berlin 1869, pp. 146-150.

15 Ibid. von Saenger notes the movements and actions of these four batteries, of which he was the commander. He states that the 3rd Horse Artillery Battery finally came as close as less than 450 yards from Redoubt a. The Prussian artillery, however, constantly misjudged ranges on this day because of the weather.

pounders, were now engaged against 24 Danish guns (including those of 10th Field Battery which had reinforced Redoubts g1 and g2) in the redoubts. The 2nd 12 Pounder Battery, attached to Canstein's brigade moved from place to place in an attempt to find a position from which it could take part in the battle, but was unable to do so.[16]

West of the howitzer batteries, I/IR60, Major von Jena, moved forward to cover their left flank towards the Schlei. South of the junction of the Holm-Eckernförde roads, the four companies of F/IR15, Lieutenant-Colonel von François, had also become involved in the firefight with the redoubts. Neither side ever saw more than glimpses of the enemy.

The Prussian horse batteries came under fire from Redoubts g1 and g2 on the north bank. 1st Horse Battery and, when it arrived, the 4th were assigned to suppress this fire, which they were unable to do. Conversely, Captain Hertel requested assistance for Redoubt a, which was seriously harassed by the horse and howitzer batteries.

Colonel Colomier, at 14:00, moved the centre batteries between about 170-200 yards closer to the redoubts. He had perceived that there was a lessening of Danish fire, and wished to press any advantage. This new position, certainly for the howitzer batteries, was somewhat less than 600 yards away.[17] Their positions were peppered with spent rifle bullets as well as artillery fire.

During the cannonade, General Canstein ordered II/IR60, Lieutenant-Colonel Becker-Blumenthal, assembled in company columns at Ornum Mill, forward, both to cover the right flank of the artillery, but also, "… in anticipation of the possible assault to come…".[18] The battalion moved forward into heavy artillery and rifle fire, crossing the frozen dead arm of the Schlei, and coming into line on the right of Baumgarten's 10/IR24, who were still firing into Redoubt b from the unfinished trench that they had occupied. Canstein at the same time pushed the rest of his Brigade across Kosel stream.

On the left, similar forward movement was taking place. By 14:30, both of the remaining battalions of the Advance Guard, F/IR13, Lieutenant-Colonel von Zimmerman, and 7th Jäger Battalion, Major von Beckedorff, were pushed into the line. Three companies of Jäger moved all the way over to the left of the horse artillery, and into line west of von Jena's I/60th. Both battalions moved forward a short way, but halted under heavy fire to await further orders. Clearly, even at this stage, there was still some consideration of a possible assault.

Zimmerman's battalion moved into the gap between von François' F/IR15 and the three companies of F/IR24, Major von Krohn, on the heights above the Ornum Road. The situation at 14:30 can be seen on the map in this section of the book.

It became increasingly clear through the afternoon that a direct assault on the redoubts would be costly, and quite possibly unsuccessful. Friedrich Carl,

---

16 Grosser Generalstab, Volume I, p.145.

17 The distance here is a matter of dispute. Waldersee, Count, *Der Krieg gegen Dänemark im Jahre 1864*, Berlin 1865, states on pages 46-47 that the horse batteries were unable to close further – von Saenger agrees that the batteries did not move, but says that they were already much closer in (see footnote above).

18 Grosser Generalstab, Volume I, p.145.

observing that the fire from the enemy artillery had not diminished under his bombardment, decided to cancel plans for an infantry attack on the works. The fog was becoming even thicker, and darkness would soon follow. At 15:30 he gave orders to break off the action and for a general withdrawal back to the area of Eckernförde, shifting his own headquarters to Hemmelmark, north-east of there.[19] The final rounds were fired by the Prussian artillery at about 16:00. The Danish guns continued to fire as long as any target was vaguely discernable.

The Prussians requested, and were granted, a truce to gather in casualties. During this cease-fire, 150-200 men who had been pinned down behind knicks in front of Redoubt b, only some 500 feet away, used this opportunity to withdraw. They were allowed to do so unmolested by the Danish artillery. After the end of the truce, a five man Prussian picket at Ornum Mill was captured by a patrol of the 4th Dragoons, and that position itself reoccupied (these are not included in the casualty table below).[20]

The Princes' probe was more in the manner of a reconnaissance in force than a major attack, though of course had he perceived the possibility of seizing the bridgehead he would undoubtedly have done so. The idea of doing so must clearly have been in his mind, although, as so often, he was ill at ease with his own intentions for much of the afternoon. Expenditure of ammunition in this gloom-shrouded affair had been heavy, but not prodigious. The Prussian field artillery alone fired 1,256 rounds.[21] The four engaged guns of the Danish 10th Field Artillery Battery, in only intermittent action for perhaps 3 hours, fired a total of 66 rounds.[22]

The losses in the action were surprisingly, perhaps even amazingly, light given the volume of fire that had taken place. This fact once again emphasises the effect of the extremely poor visibility on that winter's day. In Redoubt a, three cannon had been dismounted by enemy fire, and Prussian 'overshoots' had also caused damage and fires in the town. Total casualties were as follows:

Table 3

Prussian Casualties at Missunde, February 2nd 1864

Prussian: 199[23]

19 Waldersee, Count, *Der Krieg gegen Dänemark im Jahre 1864*, Berlin 1865, p.49

20 Liljefalk, Axel, and Lütken, Otto, *Vor Sidste Kamp vor Sønderjylland*, Copenhagen 1904, p. 49.

21 Anon., "Munitionsverbrauch der Preuß Truppen in dem Feldzuge gegen Dänemark", *Militärische Blätter*, Volume 14, Nr's 2 & 3, Berlin 1865. Rüstow, Wilhelm, *Der deutsch-dänische Krieg 1864*, Zürich 1864, p. 194, gives a figure of 4,500 rounds fired by the Prussians.

22 Edsberg, V., *Minder fra 10de Batterie i 1864*, Copenhagen 1889, p. 9. This battery had problems with faulty shell primers that day, using a total of 80 to fire the 66 shells.

23 Grosser Generalstab, Volume I, Appendix 18.

Unit	Killed		Wounded		Prisoners		Missing	
	Officers	Men	Officers	Men	Officers	Men	Officers	Men
Staff	1	—	—	—	—	—	—	—
Fusilier / IR13	—	1	—	21	—	—	—	—
Fusilier / IR15	—	11	4	43	—	—	—	1
Fusilier / IR24	1	4	—	8	—	—	—	—
I / IR60	—	—	1	—	—	—	—	—
II / IR60	—	10	3	25	—	—	—	3
Fusilier / IR60	—	—	—	4	—	—	—	—
FR 35	—	1	—	14	—	—	—	—
Jäger Battalion. Nr. 7	—	—	—	3	—	—	—	1
Hussar Regt. Nr. 8	—	—	—	1	—	—	—	—
Uhlan Regt. Nr. 11	—	—	—	1	—	—	—	—
Artillery Brigade Nr.3	—	—	—	—	—	—	—	—
2nd Howitzer Battery	—	—	—	3	—	—	—	—
3rd Howitzer Battery	1	1	—	7	—	—	—	—
2nd 6lb Battery	—	1	—	—	—	—	—	—
3rd 6lb Battery	—	—	—	2	—	—	—	—
4th 6lb Battery	—	—	—	2	—	—	—	—
2nd 12 lb Battery	—	—	—	3	—	—	—	—
Artillery Brigade Nr. 7	—	—	—	—	—	—	—	—
1st Howitzer Battery	—	—	1	8	—	—	—	—
1st Horse Battery	—	1	—	—	—	—	—	—
3rd Horse Battery	—	—	—	2	—	—	—	—
4th Horse Battery	—	—	—	1	—	—	—	—
6th Horse Battery	—	—	—	1	—	—	—	—
Pioneer Bn Nr.3	—	—	—	1	—	—	—	—
Ambulance	—	—	—	1	—	—	—	—
Totals	3	30	9	152	—	—	—	5

Two Prussian battalion commanders had been wounded, Lieutenant-Colonel von François (F/IR15) and Major von Jena (I/IR60), the former badly.

Table 4

Danish Casualties at Missunde, February 2nd 1864

Danish: 141[24]

Unit	Killed		Wounded		Prisoners		Missing	
	Officers	Men	Officers	Men	Officers	Men	Officers	Men
3rd Infantry Regiment	2	5	2	40	—	4	—	1
18th Infantry Regiment	2	20	—	46	—	3	—	2
4th Dragoon Regiment	1	—	—	—	—	—	—	—
6th Fortress Artillery Company	1	7	1	4	—	—	—	—
Totals	6	32	3	90	—	7	—	3

The Danish rank and file were jubilant at their success, and the country as a whole broke into wild celebration. The matter was hailed and presented as a major victory. Certainly, a little over 2,000 Danish troops had held off a force roughly five times its own size. Any subsequent attack on the position could only expect considerably greater opposition.

In discussions with his staff that evening, Friedrich Carl agreed with them that a different place to effect a crossing of the Schlei must be found. Colonel von Blumenthal, the Prince's Chief of Staff, spoke eloquently on the subject. He had served in this area in the 1849, and knew its topography well. Friedrich Carl relied heavily on his opinion (Blumenthal was equally valued by General von Moltke, with whom he kept up a regular correspondence). Consensus proposed a point further to the north-east, perhaps near Arnis or Cappeln. Already during that evening were being gathered all the boats and pontoons available, as well as a search for further boats in the area of Eckernförde.[25] The Prince reported to Marshal Wrangel his opinion that a crossing at Missunde could not be achieved, and that he would choose a point further east to do so.

In Schleswig town, the artillery fire at Missunde had been clearly audible during the day. General de Meza had considered mounting an attack by his 3rd Division against the Prussian line of communications as soon as he heard initial reports of the fighting there, but there was insufficient time to do so. Instead, a small diversionary move towards Fleckeby was ordered. The force moved from Haddeby at 16:45, but the operation was cancelled upon reports of the Prussian retreat.

24 Generalstaben, Volume I, p.96.
25 Waldersee, p.52.

In Missunde, the commander of 3rd Brigade, Colonel Wørishøffer, riding ahead of his columns, reported to General Gerlach at 19:00, only to be told that his men were no longer needed. His reply to this information is not recorded. The brigade marched to bivouacs in nearby Moldenit, Schaalby, and Winding, west of Missunde.

Further west, the Allied II Corps' orders for the day had been to form along the line of the villages of Hütten, Uscheffel, Klein Breckendorf, and Rohrby. This was accomplished without difficulty. The Corps pickets of Nostitz' Brigade, on the left of this line were pulled out at midday, being relieved by III Corps. The final units of Brigade Gondrecourt also arrived, marching north from Rendsburg where they had been brought from Hamburg by train.

During the course of the morning, Major-General Tomas sent frequent cavalry patrols in the direction of the Schlei. By order of FML Gablenz, one of these, the 3rd Troop, 6/Leichtenstein Hussars, Unterlieutnant Farkas, was strengthened by the addition of an entire squadron, 1/Windischgrätz Dragoons, Major Kutschenbach. Moving north on the road between Gross Breckendorff and Ober Selk, this force encountered a forward post of the 4/1st Danish Infantry Regiment, Captain F. Weyhe, at Hahn Inn. A short skirmish cost the Austrians one wounded hussar, and the Danes 3 prisoners. The cavalry withdrew after Danish supports appeared.

Most of III Corps also arrived in Rendsburg by railway during the day. Two battalions were left to occupy the town (I and Fusilier/3 GGR), and the remaining ten, along with the Brandenburg Cuirassier Regiment and 5th Horse Artillery Battery moved into line to the west of II Corps. Elements of I and Fusilier/4 GGR subsequently relieved the Austrian pickets in their sector at noon, as related above.

Austrian 18th Jäger Battalion in snowstorm at the Danewerke
(*Illustrated London News*)

None of these units had any contact with enemy forces during the day. III Corps was at this point under the operational orders of FML Gablenz.

The Field Marshal himself had his headquarters established in Damendorf, this being midpoint in the triangle of Rendsburg, Ekernförde, and the central area of the Danewerke. The Crown Prince and Prince Albrecht (junior) also established their quarters here. The Marshal busied himself with the orders for the next day.[26]

The Allies had edged to the fringes of the Danewerke in the area south of Schleswig. On the right flank, the rebuff at Missunde was militarily unimportant, and some way around that position had to be found. The main fortifications were a different prospect. Their real strength remained a mystery.[27]

The Defence of the Danewerke

The origins of the Danewerke are disputed, though may date from the 7th Century. It was, for centuries, considered an important military position and was unquestionably established to face invaders from the south. It formed the core defensive position in the initial phase of the campaign.

The main position in 1864 lay from the town of Schleswig west to the marshes of the River Treene, a distance of about 10 miles. West of this, after the marshes, lay the fortress of Friedrichstadt. To the east of Schleswig town is the Schlei, some 26 miles long. At Missunde, as discussed, the Schlei is only 200 yards wide. The distance defended across the whole peninsula was 50 miles. In the east, because the Schlei was a natural obstacle, fortifications had only been constructed at Missunde, although some were planned further east. Near the Baltic coast, therefore, the defences were the weakest in the line.

On the western flank, Friedrichstadt, surrounded by deep water, controlled the point where the rivers Treene and Eider meet, before the latter flows into the North Sea, five miles to the south-west. East of the fortress there were bridgeheads along the Treene four miles away at Schwabstedt and at Hollingstedt, a further eight miles on. All of this area was marshy and could, in season, be deliberately flooded.

The main defensive position lay in the area south and south-west of Schleswig town. Although on the flanks, as shown, there was a degree of natural defence, here it was necessary to construct, as it had been for centuries. From 1852, Danish governments had spent large amounts of money fortifying the area in and around the old ramparts and earth walls, work which continued until the beginning of the campaign. After the decision, in 1861, that the Danewerke would be the primary land defence of the country, efforts were redoubled. Nevertheless, much remained to be done at the commencement of hostilities. Its major weakness was a lack of depth. To the small Danish Army, already overextended in its defence, any enemy breakthrough would be fatal. This was fully understood by General de Meza. This was the line that Field Marshal Wrangel now had to cross.

---

26 Winterfeld, p.85.
27 See Appendix VI for the armament of the whole Danewerke at the beginning of the campaign.

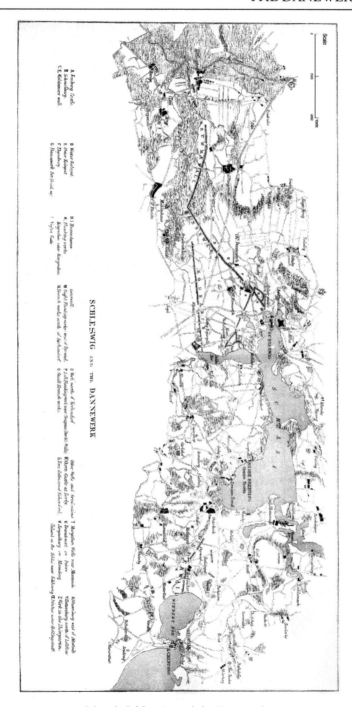

Map 4: Schleswig and the Danewerke

Wrangel's orders for I Corps, on February 3rd, were that it, "…will tomorrow continue its operations against Missunde…"[28] Friedrich Carl had thus been given no orders for the day, since the Danish position there was much stronger on the 3rd than it had been the day before, and the Prince had already informed the Marshal that no further attack would be attempted. Wrangel also directed Friedrich Carl to detach one rifled artillery battery from his Corps, and place it at the disposal of II Corps. This battery (4th 6 Pounder Battery / 3rd Artillery Brigade) was to be at Esperehm by 15:00, and await further instructions. The main body remained in their quarters for the day, with outposts around the Missunde defences, where the Allies thought that the Danes had massed 10,000 men. In fact, Gerlach's entire 1st Division only numbered around 9,000. It was still not fully appreciated on the Allied side how thinly stretched the Danes were.

In Missunde, another attack was expected, and the troops were in their positions by 04:00, work on the defences having been carried on through the night. This concern persisted through most of the day, though no such threat materialised. Significantly, a telegram from the High Command in Schleswig town to 1st Division the previous day had warned that the enemy would attempt to cross the Schlei further to the east of Missunde.

Prince Friedrich Carl meanwhile continued his advance preparations for exactly that – a crossing point further to the east. At midday, three squadrons of Westphalian Hussars (Regiment Nr. 8), quartered individually at the villages of Söby, Holzdorf, and Pommerby, were spread along the south bank of the Schlei, as a *cordon sanitaire*. This stretched from Stubbe, five and a half miles down-stream from Missunde almost to Cappeln, about nine and a half miles further. The 1/8th covered the area around Stubbe and Guggelsby, 2/8th that of Sieseby and Windemark, and 3/8th, the vicinity of Kopperby and Ellenburg. The intention was to completely sever any Danish communication between the Angeln and Schwansen peninsulas, at least across the Schlei itself.

Lieutenant-Colonel Bergmann, I Corps' artillery commander, and Lieutenant-Colonel von Kriegsheim, its senior engineer officer, were together dispatched in a fishing boat to study possible sites for the crossing to take place. These officers considered that it was likely that the north bank might be heavily fortified; though in the poor weather it was difficult to establish this. The water itself had floating ice, and this also caused difficulties in regard to the poor visibility. It was observed that the Danes had carried away, sunk, or destroyed anything that might have been useful in effecting a crossing.

They were able to clearly observe the Danish outposts at regular intervals along the north bank. They discerned from local people that the towns of Arnis and Cappeln were both occupied by Danish infantry, though they were unable to establish their strength (the total infantry available in this area were II/2nd and 1¾ companies of I/2nd, at most, perhaps 1200 men). Their observations established a clear preference for the construction of a pontoon bridge to connect at Arnis, and two provisional points for the use of boats to ferry the infantry. These latter were, first, below the town of Cappeln, in the vicinity of the windmill of Rabelsund, and second, above the same town near the village of Espernis. In these two places, the

28 von Fischer, p. 94.

width of the river was moderate, and most importantly, the riverbanks on both sides were sufficiently low for the use of boats.[29]

Whilst this investigation was taking place, Friedrich Carl went to Army Headquarters to present his views to the Field Marshal. In general terms, Wrangel approved of the enterprise, but he wished to see specific proposals based upon the report of the two colonels on their return. Friedrich Carl returned to his own headquarters at Hemmelmark to await the report, which was duly delivered to him that evening.

In the Danish centre, as at Missunde, the 3rd Division was also assembled and ready for action in their defences by 04:00.[30] The High Command in Schleswig town had decided late the previous evening that there was the very real possibility of a major attack. It was raining heavily, but all the troops were in high spirits after the victory at Missunde. Time dragged, however, and no major enemy move occurred, so, at 11:00, all troops not on outpost duty were allowed to return to their quarters, having spent seven hours standing in the pouring rain. Due to the downpour, they were not allowed to march back to their camps on the main roads, as these were required to be kept in as reasonable condition as possible. They were forced to wallow along muddy tracks, increasing their exhaustion.

During the night, enemy patrols had been reported in the villages of Lottorf and Geltorf, some three and a half miles south-east of the central redoubt line, and about 650 yards south of the Danish vedette line. As a result, a reconnaissance was ordered in this area. At 10:30, Captain Christiani moved off with his battalion II/9th and 2/6th Dragoons, Ritmester H. Castenschiold, to investigate.

Allied plans in the centre called for the Austrian Corps to push its outposts to a line running south-east from the Schlei at the village of Fahrdorf, and through those of Nieder (Lower) Selk, Ober (Upper) Selk, and Jagel. This line was to be established by 16:00, and the Field Marshal ordered that FML Gablenz and Lieutenant-General von der Mülbe meet him in Ober Selk at that hour to receive their orders for February 4th.[31] General von der Mülbe's command was to conform to these movements, crossing the Sorge and extending its forward posts from the junction with II Corps at Jagel as far as Alt (Old) Bennebek, also to be completed by 16:00, giving them a frontage of some 3,000 yards. No major opposition was expected to these moves.

Gablenz made his dispositions as follows. Brigades Tomas and Gondrecourt took the lead. Brigade Tomas, with the second division of the Windischgrätz Dragoons (5th and 6th Squadrons) at the head, was to move on Fahrdorf and Loopstedt. Brigade Gondrecourt was to advance with its main force from Gross Breckendorf directly on Ober Selk. A separate column (from the same brigade) on their left flank would move to Jagel.

---

29 Waldersee, pp. 55-56. These were the same places that the Danish High Command had warned 1st Division of as possible crossing points in the previous day's telegram; Generalstaben, Volume I, p.230.

30 An attack by 3rd Division had certainly been considered. See Bjørk, Kjær, and Norrie, p. 173. Norrie, in his earlier manuscript, "Begivnehederne 1-6 Februar 1864", p. 9, says that an attack was actually ordered, but cancelled during the morning of the 3rd.

31 von Fischer, p. 95.

On Gablenz' right flank, Brigade Tomas had no difficulty in achieving its objectives for the day. On his own left, one company of Tomas' 11th FJB cooperated with Gondrecourt's troops to take Selk Mill. Loopstedt and Fahrdorf were occupied without difficulty, the Danish pickets, 6/20th, Captain J. Riise, falling back to Haddeby across the bridge, and removing the planks as they did so, covered by the fire of two guns of 11th Field Artillery Battery. Subsequently, intermittent fire took place between Tomas' forward posts and the opposing pickets, plus the intended relief company, 5/9th, Captain H. Hansen, (joined later by 1/9th and, in the late afternoon, by 2 guns of 12th Field Artillery Battery, which will be mentioned subsequently) across Selk Lagoon.

Table 5

Austrian Brigade Gondrecourt Order of Battle, January 30th 1864

	Fit for Service	*Fighting Strength*
18th FJB	923	830
Headquarters, IR Martini	38	2
I/Martini	1008	955
II/Martini	887	816
Headquarters, IR Preußen	87	2
I/Preußen	917	858
II/Preußen	934	876
2/1st 4 Pounder Battery	199	199
Total	4993	4538

Brigade Gondrecourt's advance guard, comprising one troop of 2/Liechtenstein Hussars, the 18th FJB, Major Ferdinand Eyssler, and two 4 pounder guns from the Brigade Battery (4/1st Artillery) moved off at about 12:00, the main column following on. This comprised two troops 2/ Liechtenstein Hussars, I/Martini, 4/1 Artillery Battery (minus two guns), II/ Preußen, II/Martini (minus one company), one medical platoon, and finally, the rearguard, one company IR Martini. I/Preußen and the squadron's fourth troop of hussars moved parallel to the main column along the railway, as ordered by Wrangel. This latter force was intended to move north, crossing the railway at Lottorf, and advance directly on Jagel across the moor. The main force was to advance upon Ober Selk.[32]

Behind these units, Brigades Nostitz and Dormus would follow, accompanied by two squadrons of hussars. The first division of the Windischgrätz Dragoons (1st, 2nd, and 4th Squadrons) together with the Corps Artillery Reserve were to remain in Gross Breckendorf and await further orders.

32 These figures are from, "Ordre de Bataille und Dislokation des 6. Armeecorps dem 30 Jänner 1864" KA, AFA, January 1864, Document 149. They are the nearest available.

The Danewerke - The semi-circular rampart of the 'Oldenburg' or 'Saksarmen', near the village of Bustorf, with the 'Königshügel' (King Sigurd's Hill) seen to the south
(*Illustrated London News*)

This area south of Schleswig town and the Little Danewerke was largely small ranges of hills, generally 75 to 100 feet in height, cut through with water courses, with ramparts criss-crossing in all directions, and, in summer, a good deal of marshy ground.[33] Like much of the Duchy, the land in this area was also divided by large and very thick 'knicks'. The massive Kurgraben, a rampart some 6,500 yards long, cut through the middle of the area. It stood from 16 to 20 feet high, and was from 10 to 12 feet wide. The dominating features of this outpost terrain were the 136 foot Königshügel (King Sigurd's Hill), a little over 800 yards north of Ober Selk, some 2,300 yards from Redoubt 10, and the smaller Schwarze Berg, 350 yards further west.

The knicks, used as field boundaries, were almost impenetrable hedges, four to five feet high, and three to four feet thick, and the small entrances to the fields were not in uniform places. They were atop mud banks between the ditches on either side used as watercourses for the fields. Each field was thus virtually its own redoubt. This was very difficult country for cavalry and artillery, and large formations of infantry likewise were very difficult to control in it.

Captain Christiani advanced his force with the majority of his cavalry moving behind his marching infantry. Only a small detachment scouted ahead. This did not make for rapid reconnaissance. He sent a company and a small detachment of dragoons to both Lottorf and Geltorf, whilst he, with the rest of his force remained near Lottorf. Neither detached force discovered any enemy presence, but on the

---

33 There were elaborate plans, with the means at hand to implement them, to flood many of the low–lying areas, which might have been very effective in a summer campaign.

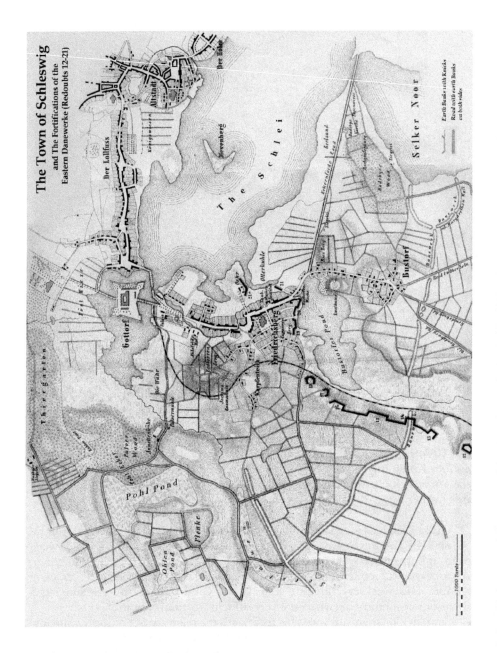

Map 5: Schleswig Town and environs
This map is a contemporary Allied one. The Danish fortifications are numbered with Allied
designations. To correspond with the Danish designations in Appendix VI, from right to
left, Redoubt 21a is Fleche I, and then numbered sequentially as far as Lunette XI.

main Breckendorf Road, Austrian cavalry were reported at 13:00, with infantry behind them. There was a brief exchange of fire between the horsemen, and Christiani pulled back north up the road. He had a report of this sighting sent to Divisional headquarters, but by the time it arrived (14:00), it had been overtaken by events.[34]

Just before noon, three infantry battalions moved out from the Danewerke to relieve the units on outpost duty. I/11th, Major J.M.F.F. Rist (the commanding officer of 11th Regiment), moved to Ober Selk to relieve II/1st, Captain J.C.T. Thalbitzer. II/21st, Major O.C.F. Saabye was to relieve its sister battalion, I/21st, Captain W. Hackke, around Klosterkro, and I/9th, Major J. Nørager to relieve I/20th, Major S.P.L. Schack, on the left. As fate would ordain, the approach of the advancing Austrians coincided with these reliefs. The result would be a confusing series of encounters in two separate actions – one centred around the village of Ober Selk, and the other on that of Jagel.

Brigade Gondrecourt's advance guard encountered Christiani's force along the Breckendorf Road, and reported them quickly falling back. There were considerably more troops behind them. The Danish force in the forward positions at this juncture, comprised seven infantry battalions, two squadrons of dragoons, and six guns, all rifled 4 pounders. They were disposed as follows:

Left Flank
Between Fahrdorf (on the Schlei) and Haddeby; and east of Haddeby Lagoon
5/9th and 6/20th (west of Selk Lagoon) and two guns
Total = two companies and two guns

Central Position
Ober Selk, the southern slopes of the heights, on both sides of the Breckendorf Road
I/11th, II/1st, 1/9th, and 2/20th, plus two guns
Total = ten companies and two guns

Central Position
In reserve on and around the Königshügel and Schwarze Berg
2/9th, 6/9th, 1/20th, 5/20th, and II/9th (Captain Christiani) plus 2/4th and 2/6th Dragoons and two guns
Total = eight companies, two squadrons and two guns

Right Flank

---

34 Curiously, an untimed report reached the Headquarters in Schleswig at 16:00. It read: "The troops in the front line have been pushed back towards Selk and Kongshøj, where the battle is now going on. It appears as if it is a strong reconnaissance, but we are still not certain. Castenschjold." Jensen, N.P. p. 123. Ritmester G. Castenschjold was the commander of the line of outposts that day, and the officer from whom this message came. He made no protest at the assumption of command in the centre by Major Rist. Ritmester H. Casteschiold was the name of the officer in command of the dragoon squadron attached to Captain Christiani's battalion in the initial reconnaissance. Both were in the same regiment.

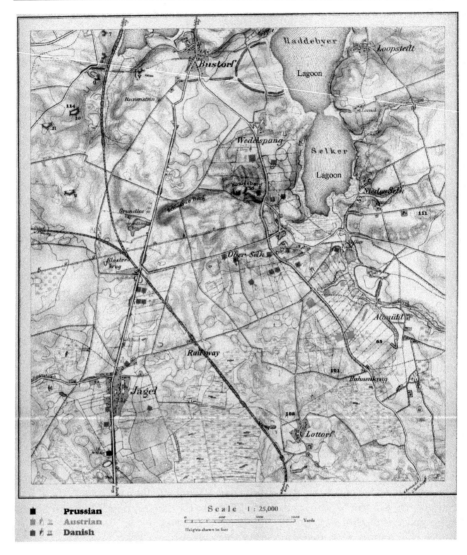

Map 6: Action of Selk/Jagel - 3rd February

In the area around Jagel
1/21st, 2/21st, 5/21st, and 6/21st, in the vicinity of Jagel 3/21st, 4/21st, 7/21st, and 8/21st, around Klosterkro
Total = eight companies and four guns

This made a total of 28 companies, two squadrons, and eight guns: about 6,500 men in all.[35] One relief was successfully achieved before any fighting took place. 8/1st, Premierlieutenant C. Andersen, positioned east of the railway near Klosterkro,

35 Generalstaben, *Statiskiske Meddelelser...* p.136, gives the total as 6447.

was relieved by 7/11th, Premierlieutenant J. Lund, this relief being noted as having been done rapidly and after which Andersen withdrew to the main position.[36]

Upon the reported approach of Gondrecourt's advance guard, and hearing the fire to the south, the aggressive and somewhat hot-headed Major Rist assumed command of the units in the vicinity of Ober Selk.[37] Without regard to chains of command, he rode about the field giving orders to platoons and companies alike, causing a great deal of confusion. In some cases he hurled abuse at units, making the situation more difficult. Perhaps more importantly, he made no attempt to contact the units further to the west around Jagel, and inform them of the situation.

On the Austrian right flank, the right wing of 18th FJB, aided, as discussed, by a company of Brigade Tomas' 11th FJB soon drove 1/9th Regiment from Selk Mill, where it had just relieved 2/20th. The latter company withdrew to a position between the Königshügel and the village of Wedelspang.[38] 1/9th pulled back to occupy the north-east portion of Ober Selk, covering the road. The lone Austrian Jäger company of Tomas' brigade then moved north from Selk Mill towards Loopstedt to rejoin its brigade.

Major Rist was hurriedly deploying his troops along the low hills south of Ober Selk, on a front of some 1600 yards. West of the Breckendorf Road, in the first line were 3/1st, Captain C. Irgens, and 5/1st, Premierlieutenant P. Hammerich. In reserve behind them were 3/11th, Captain Count E. Ahlefeldt-Laurvig. Also in this area, Captain F. Weyhe had assembled his company, 4/1st, which had been on outpost duty. East of the road, 1/11th, Captain M. de Fine Licht formed the first line, with 5/11th, Captain A. Staggemeier in reserve.

The Austrian advance on Ober Selk was slow due to the knicks and broken terrain. Because of the advance on Selk Mill, the two wings of the 18th FJB, Lieutenant-Colonel Tobias Edler von Hohendorf, had become separated, with a considerable gap between them. To close this gap, Gondrecourt pushed I/Martini, Major Franz Oreskovic, between them. The entire line then continued to move forward until engaged in a firefight just short of the village.

The two guns with the advance guard of the brigade in the meanwhile took up a good position on high ground to the east of the road, some 900 yards from the Danish line, from where they were able to effectively support the advance. These guns opened fire at about 13:45 on the Danish troops to the east of the road.

Rist, having no artillery present, immediately dispatched an adjutant, Second-Lieutenant A. Abrahams, to bring forward the two cannon of 11th Field

36 Johansen and Nordentoft, *Hæren ved Danevirke*, p. 201.
37 Liljefalck & Lütken, p. 55, describe Rist as, '…more brave and patriotic than intelligent and calm.'
38 There were two villages called Wedelspang in the vicinity of Schleswig town. The one mentioned in this context is within the Danewerke position (see map), south of Bustorf. The other is north-east of the town of Schleswig, and to which reference will be made in due course.

Artillery Battery which were in reserve on the Königshügel.[39] In the meanwhile, he made bayonet attacks with 1/11th. The reserve company, 5/11th was also heavily engaged. The forward units west of the road withdrew fighting, towards the Schwarze Berg.

Corporal Nielsen's two guns from the Königshügel arrived in Ober Selk just as the Austrian pressure was building against the village. The corporal received no specific orders and unlimbered his guns just as the infantry were retreating. He was able to limber and escape with one piece, but the other was overrun by the first platoon of 2/18th FJB, Cadet Oberjäger Alois Krauss being the first man to reach the gun.[40] Nielsen withdrew his remaining gun to the Königshügel, escorted by 2/4th Dragoons, Ritmester J. Bentzen, which had just appeared. This squadron had been requested from Bustorf by Rist, but had been given no specific instructions. After returning the cannon to the hill, the task-less dragoons returned to Bustorf.

Rist now rode west to 3/11th, still in reserve. He asked what company it was (of his own regiment) and, upon being informed, ordered, "I have heard that people from Jutland can fall, but never give up, so now we go with God!" They made a brave attack, but were pushed back by superior numbers. Count Ahlefeldt-Laurvig then withdrew his company to the west, to link up with 7/11th, still on outpost duty near Klosterkro.

All companies west of Ober Selk were now in retreat. Rist now rode to 5/11th, and ordered Captain Staggemeier to attack, the Captain immediately obeying. This attempt once again met superior numbers from 18th FJB and I/Martini, at one point in a brief close quarter encounter. Staggemeier was pushed back, retreating to the north, and Ober Selk fell to the Austrians at 15:00.[41] Rist gave orders to retreat to the heights north of the village, but these were not in all cases delivered.

Major-General Gondrecourt had now fulfilled his orders in the centre. However, he sensed the possibility of gaining the important heights north of Ober Selk, and therefore there was a slight lull, whilst he reorganised his units for the attack. I/Martini, which had suffered heavy casualties, was placed in reserve. II/Martini, Major Stampfer, II/Preußen, Major Stransky, and 18th FJB would make the assault. Initially, the now complete Brigade Battery of eight rifled 4 pounders, Captain Modricki, was to shell both the Königshügel and Schwarze Berg.

---

39 Ibid, p. 56. Corporal Nielsen, in command of these two guns of 11th Field Artillery Battery, had strict orders not to move forward of his position and, initially bravely refused to follow the command sent by Major Rist. When another officer present urged him to do so, however, he obeyed. See also the official report by Captain Fallesen, *Rapport Fra. 11. Batterie/Fallesen/ Over dets Deltagelse I Træfningerne den 3., 4., og 6. Februar 1864.*

40 Anon, *Die hervorragendsten Waffenthaten der Unteroffiziere und Mannschaft des k.k. 6. Armeekorps aus dem Feldzuge 1864 gegen Dänemark*, Vienna 1864, p.110. Krauss was awarded the Silver Medal for Bravery, 1st Class.

41 Dedenroth, v., *Der Winterfeldzug in Schleswig-Holstein*, Volume 1, Berlin 1864, p.77.

Major Rist, in the meantime, also reorganised his forces. To his right, on the western slopes Königshügel he had 1/20th, Captain H. Daue, with the field piece that had escaped from Ober Selk on their left. Then came 2/9th, Captain C. Knauer, whose left flank rested on the road. East of the road stood 5/20th, Premierlieutenant C. Steinmann, and on the left flank, 6/9th, Captain H. Meincke. Behind the hill, was assembled Captain Christiani's II/9th.

Further to the rear, two companies 1/9th and 2/20th, joined by 5/11th were approximately half way between the heights and Wedelspang.[42] The other units that had taken part in the earlier fighting were either too scattered or disorganised to take any further part. Though Rist could not know it, the final stages of this fighting would be witnessed from Bustorf by King Christian himself. The King had come from Missunde on his way to Headquarters in Schleswig town hearing the sound of cannon for much of the journey. After seeing the loss of the hill he continued on to Headquarters.

At 15:45, Gondrecourt's infantry attack began. He now had a definite advantage, committing two fresh battalions as against Rist's equivalent of one, and artillery supremacy. Though the Königshügel was by no means an ineffectual obstacle, the Imperial troops were confident of success. At the front were Jäger skirmishers.

Cadet Rudolf Pistecky, serving in the 1/18th FJB, was approaching the Königshügel at this time, and describes the scene:

> The combat was fully underway, 18th Jäger Battalion in the very first line, formed as was usual in those days, in *Divisions-massen-linie*, with an advanced skirmish line and supports. Infantry Regiments 30 and 34 of Brigade GM Gondrecourt were in the second line and the reserve.
>
> At this point, our supports had already been used up in the skirmish line, the main columns moved closer, and the battalion stormed ahead from knick to knick.

Having described the nature of the obstacles, Pistecky describes his own luck that afternoon:

> Along such a knick, running headlong at the enemy position, I advanced with part of my platoon, one man behind another, at the double. There, came a sound like a bursting bell and a bright flash of lightning flew past my eyes, and the man in front of me jerked back so suddenly that I almost hit my nose on the mess tin on the back of his pack. He shouted, 'SAKRA!' and with an old Bohemian curse, he threw his bayonet-less rifle to the ground, and continuing to run forward, took up the weapon of a fallen Jäger, making good the damage to his rifle by well aimed shots into the next enemy position.

---

42 Rist also attempted to obtain reinforcements, but was only partly successful. He exchanged words with the commander of I/9th, Major Nørager, calling him a coward. He then ordered the commander of II/1st, Captain J. Thalbitzer, to occupy the Schwarze Berg (He had himself failed to do this, and Christiani's battalion, II/9th, in reserve, seems to have been forgotten by him altogether). Thalbitzer pushed some of his troops up the hill, but before they were able to reach the top the Königshügel had fallen, and they withdrew. See Johansen & Nordentoft, *Hæren ved Danevirke*, pp. 206-207.

IR Martini at the storming of the Königshügel (Pflug)

What had happened? Very simple: an enemy bullet had blown the blade off his bayonet. This made the clear sound and the severed blade made the lightning across my eyes.

Jäger Lukaschek (1st Company, 3rd Platoon) – such is the name of this hero – was awarded the Silver Medal for Bravery, 2nd Class, for his courage in the action.[43]

Initially, the fire of the four defending companies caused many casualties amongst the attacking force. Rist, however, decided upon an attack downhill against his assailants. Once again Christiani's full battalion behind the hill was ignored, and Rist ordered the four companies with him forward. Captain Daue

43 Pistecky, Rudolf, "Selbsthilfe", *Unter Habsburgs Kriegsbanner*, Volume IV Dresden/Vienna/Leipzig 1899. *Divisons-massen-linie* was a tactical formation of columns of two companies (divisions) each with a front of a half-company. A battalion would form three such columns.

(1/20th) flatly refused to participate, but the other three companies went gallantly forward as instructed.

The attacks were met and halted by heavy Austrian fire. Some platoons attempted subsequent charges, but each melted away in the storm of rifle fire. Captain Meinke was killed, as were two of the three Austrian battalion commanders (Stampfer and Stransky). Rist's troops were driven back up the hill, no longer cohesive fighting units, and retreated in disorder to Wedelspang.

With Gondrecourt at the very front, the Austrian battalions gained the top of the Königshügel, where the lone 1/20th awaited them. Corporal Nielsen's single cannon of 11th Battery had also, quite sensibly, been withdrawn. Rist, with his seemingly endless energy, led a brave defence by the company, but in a very short time it was driven from the hill. Rist was seen waving his fist at the oncoming Austrians before wheeling his horse, and following his retreating command. He was shortly to be superseded by a senior officer, Colonel Scharffenberg, 8th Brigade's commander. It was 16:00, only about 15 minutes since the storming of the hill began. Captain Christiani, on his own initiative, withdrew his battalion from its now very vulnerable reserve position.

General Gondrecourt decided to halt and consolidate the captured positions. However, in the heat of the moment, with heavy officer and NCO losses, both infantry battalions, and some elements of the Jäger pushed on. Taking prisoners along the way, the disorganised units captured the settlement of Wedelspang, and in the flush of victory, moved on still further, towards Bustorf. Now, however, they also came under fire from the artillery of the Danewerke itself, and fresh troops manning the defences.[44] The attacks were repulsed, as were several probes by Colonel Scharffenberg towards Wedelspang.[45] As darkness began to fall, and order was restored, the Austrian troops were pulled back from Wedelspang to the Königshügel.

Gondrecourt could be well pleased with the results of his main force's push, certain that Headquarters would be pleased with his having captured the most important outwork along the line. As yet, though, he did not know of the situation of his remaining battalion, I/Preußen, in its move west towards Jagel.

Colonel Benedek, the commanding officer of IR Preußen, accompanied his First Battalion on its march to Jagel, along with a troop of hussars. From 13:00, the column heard the sound of gunfire to their right, becoming more intense as time passed. At 14:30, the hussars at the head of the column developed the first Danish vedettes. They were men of I/21st, which had just relieved its sister battalion in the forward positions.

---

44 Corporal Nielsen's artillery section was also engaged again here. He had replaced his lost gun from the Artillery Park, and gone back into action. He was very justifiably one of those specially commended in the War Ministry report of the action – 'Beretning fra Krigsministeriet om Fægtninger foran Dannevirke (Selk, Kongshøj, Bustrup og Jagel), den 3die Februar 1864'. See also Johansen & Nordentoft, *Hæren ved Danevirke*, p.211-212.
45 Also at this time, the four guns of 11th Field Artillery Battery arrived at Bustorf from Klosterkro (see below). Two of these joined in the closing stages of the action here, whilst the other two were sent to Haddeby to engage the artillery of the Austrian Brigade Tomas.

Upon the approach of the Austrian column, the Danish 21st Regiment was deployed as follows (see map 'Action of Selk/Jagel' above):

At Klosterkro – 3 and 4/21st were just about to be relieved by 7 and 8/21st. The Commanding Officer of II/21st Battalion, Major O. Saabye, was present here. 3/21st, Premierlieutenant E. Voss was just over 100 yards south of the Inn, with 4/21st, Captain C. Zahlmann slightly to the west of them. 7/21st, Captain H. Wedelfeldt, was facing east, half of the company occupying the railway station. 8/21st, Premierlieutenant N. Rovsing stood 550 yards south of the Inn, east of the road. Two rifled 4 pounders of 12th Field Artillery Battery were in a position north-east of the village, also awaiting their relief.

At Jagel – 1 and 2/21st had just been relieved by 5 and 6/21st. All four companies were in or near Jagel. 1/21st, Captain J. Beissenherz, occupied a knick north of the village, to the east of the road. 2/21st, Premierlieutenant H. Larsen, took up position on the eastern edge of the settlement. 5 and 6/21st (Captain E. Recke and Premierlieutenant V. Vaupell, respectively) were south of Jagel, with pickets south of there.

Major Saabye, as the senior officer, and with Captain Hackhe's concurrence, assumed command of the regiment, and sent the following message to the commander in the main position: "From a report by a forward post at Jagel, the enemy has been observed at Lottorf with several companies of infantry and some cavalry. On the left flank there is some firing." Saabye was given little time to react, as Colonel Benedek immediately launched attacks on the village, which consisted of about 20 farmsteads.[46] First division (1 and 2/Preußen), Captain Franz Zimmerman, moved against the east side, whilst the second division (3rd and 4th), Captain Ignaz Gylek came in from the south. The third division (5th and 6th), Captain Alexander Weniger, remained in reserve to the east, in close support of Zimmerman's men.

Both of these speedy assaults drove the defenders back through Jagel. 5/21st attempted a counterattack within the village, but it was unsuccessful, and all four Danish companies were pushed about 400 yards north of it. Having restored order, Major Saabye was considering launching an attack to recapture the place, when the sound of firing came from behind their positions. He moved towards Klosterkro with three companies, leaving Captain Beissenherz' 1/21st facing Jagel.

At Klosterkro, the Danish artillery had fired some rounds against I/Preußen, observed to the south. Once their relief section arrived, they saw that more Austrian infantry were advancing towards Klosterkro from the east. All four guns were immediately limbered, and taken all the way back to Bustorf.[47]

After the fall of the Königshügel, hearing firing to the west, Major-General Nostitz, whose brigade had reached the area south of Ober Selk, sent the third division of his 9th FJB, (5th and 6th Companies) Captain Karl Haradauer, in that direction to investigate. Since the gunfire continued, he followed this up by moving the rest of the battalion in the same direction.[48] Nostitz' foresight would pay dividends.

---

46 Knorr, *Von der Eider bis Düppel,* p. 16.
47 The later use of these guns upon arrival at Bustorf has already been mentioned.
48 Grosser Generalstab, Volume I, p. 161.

North-east of Klosterkrug, at 16:00, Haradauer's two companies encountered 7/11th, the picket company that had come on duty that day, and was still in position, along with the hard used 3/11th, which had retreated here after the fall of Ober Selk. Haradauer swiftly attacked them. After a brief struggle, in which Premierlieutenant Lund (7/11th's commander) was shot dead, he drove both companies west right into the Danewerke, and continued on his way towards Klosterkrug. His battalion commander, Major Schidlach, himself advanced with the second division, Captain Eduard Urschitz, so as to envelop the village from the south, leaving the third division in reserve.

South of Klosterkro, 8/21st found itself under fire from the rear, and immediately retreated to the north-west. 7/21st at the railway station and 3 and 4/21st, both north-west of the Inn were soon under heavy attack by Schidlach, whilst Haradauer moved further west, threatening to cut off their retreat. The open order attacks of the Jäger were especially effective in these encounters. Major Saabye, too late to affect the outcome, and equally concerned about his line of retreat, pulled his companies away to the north-west, and as darkness came, into the main line.

During this action, 1/21st, still north of Jagel, came into a brief firefight with a picket company of the Prussian Guard, which was extending III Corps' outpost line to link with the Austrians near Jagel. For some 20 minutes, a desultory fire was exchanged with skirmishers of 10/4GGR (Queen Augusta), Captain von Notz, who then withdrew to the west. Beissenherz also retreated with his company to the north-west.[49]

A little later than anticipated, II and III Corps had advanced their outposts to the line specified in Marshal Wrangel's orders. Beyond this, of course, a much more important factor was now present. At comparatively small cost, II Corps had, almost by accident, captured the most important outpost terrain opposite the weakest point in the Danewerke defence line.[50]

I/Preußen's commanding officer, Lieutenant-Colonel Friedrich, Count Pötting and Persing, in his report from Jagel of 18:00 that evening, stated that some of his companies were out of ammunition, that his wounded required assistance and that I/Ramming, Major Eliatscheck were present with him to assist with outpost duty.[51] It had been a surprisingly eventful day for all concerned.

Initial reports of losses on both sides were higher than the figures would eventually show. The Austrian attacks proved very costly, especially in officers, although in encounter actions where specific objectives had been identified, there was little choice but to attack. In any case, the whole spirit of the army was offensive minded. Major-General Gondrecourt proved correct in exceeding his orders and chancing an attack on the Königshügel. One good sign for the Imperial

49 Anon., "Die Erstürmung von Jagel am 3. Februar 1864", *Österreichische Militärische Zeitschrift*, Volume I 1864, p. 184.

50 Norrie, J., "Begivenhederne 1-6 Februar 1864", p.11.

51 "Gefechts Relation über das am 3. Februar bei Jagel bestandene Gefecht", KA, AFA, February 1864, Document 66. Lieutenant-Colonel Pötting subsequently became ill, but stayed with the regiment until mid-March, when taken to hospital in Hamburg, where he died. Kreipner, Julius, *Geschichte des K. und K. Infanterie-Regiments Nr. 34...*, p.658.

Army was the excellent cooperation of the artillery in supporting attacks. Major-General Nostitz proved his worth, as did Major Schidlach, whose men did superbly well.

For the Danes, the troops themselves had stood up well in their first test in the open field. Certainly they, like their opponents, were more than ready to undertake infantry attacks. The overall command structure was given no real chance to function in such a fluid and unusual situation, but there appears to have been little high level interest in what was happening immediately in front of the main defence line.

The handling of matters in the centre by Major Rist was the subject of heated discussion, both at the time and later. Much of the criticism levelled at him for the confused and haphazard way that he conducted the defence is perfectly justified, though his courage and determination cannot be faulted. It is possible that he should have pulled back the scattered and disparate units of which he assumed control and avoided action altogether. Very simply it would not have been in his nature to do so and, because of the separate nature of the command structure for the outpost line, none of the other regimental or brigade commanders came forward to see the situation for themselves until it was too late. On the other hand, Colonels Johansen and Nordentoft also pose the interesting question as to what the effect on the morale on both sides might have been had several battalions, obviously and clearly, immediately retreated in front of a small enemy advance guard.[52]

Major Saabye, unluckily caught completely 'flat-footed' at Jagel, took command and did as well as he possibly could under the circumstances. Austrian losses were much heavier in the actions of Ober Selk and the Königshügel than at Jagel. In the latter, Danish casualties were 159, two-thirds of them prisoners or missing, whereas Austrian losses were 43, 41 of them from I/Preußen.[53] Most of the 'missing' on both sides were dead.

The losses on 3rd February were as follows:

Table 6

Allied Casualties at Jagel, Ober Selk and Königshügel
February 3rd 1864

Allied: 432[54]

52 Johansen & Nordentoft, *Hæren ved Danevirke*, p.214-215.
53 Anon, "Die Erstürmung von Jagel am 3 Februar 1864", *Österreichische Militärische Zeitschrift*, Volume I 1864, p. 329.
54 Grosser Generalstab, Volume I, Appendix 19. This does not list the two fatalities of 9th FJB, which are well documented. These totals do not include lightly wounded men who did not leave their units, and whose inclusion would raise the number to 521.

Unit	Killed Officers	Killed Men	Wounded Officers	Wounded Men	Prisoners Officers	Prisoners Men	Missing Officers	Missing Men
Staff	—	—	—	—	—	—	—	—
9th FJB	—	2	—	—	—	—	—	—
18th FJB	5	20	1	54	—	4	—	5
IR Martini Nr.30	6	33	9	146	—	5	—	12
IR Preußen, Nr. 34	3	22	3	79	—	—	—	8
Szluiner Grenz Regiment Nr.4	1[55]	—	—	—	—	—	—	—
IR Coronini Nr. 6	—	3	—	5	—	—	—	—
IR Prinz zu Holstein Nr. 80	—	1	—	4	—	—	—	—
1st Artillery Regiment	—	—	—	1	—	—	—	—
Totals	15	81	13	289	—	9	—	25

Table 7

Danish Casualties at Jagel, Ober Selk and Königshügel
February 3rd 1864

Danish: 419[56]

Unit	Killed Officers	Killed Men	Wounded Officers	Wounded Men	Prisoners Officers	Prisoners Men	Missing Officers	Missing Men
Staff	—	—	—	—	—	—	—	—
1st Infantry Regiment	1	6	2	12	—	29 (4W)	—	11
9th Infantry Regiment	1	11	1	33	—	16 (7W)	—	4
11th Infantry Regiment	2	6	2	21	1W	35 (7W)	—	12
17th Infantry Regiment	—	—	—	—	—	2	—	4
20th Infantry Regiment	—	8	—	16	—	13 (2W)	—	4
21st Infantry Regiment	—	7	—	33	1W	101 (5W)	—	17

55 This officer, Unterlieutenant Elias Badovinac, was attached to IR Martini.
56 Generalstaben, Volume I, Appendix 26, and *Statistiske Meddelelser angaaende den danske Krigsmagt*, pp. 106 & 126. These totals also do not include lightly wounded men, not admitted to hospital.

4th Dragoon Regiment	—	—	—	1	—	1	—	—
6th Dragoon Regiment	—	—	—	1	—	—	—	—
11th Field Artillery Battery	—	—	—	2	—	—	—	—
Noncombatant	—	—	—	—	—	2	—	—
Totals	4	38	3	121	2	199	—	52

W = Wounded

Dawn on the 4th brought a clear, frosty morning. On the Allied right flank, I Corps remained in quarters for the whole day. Prince Friedrich Carl considered the results of the previous day's reconnaissance by the commanders of his artillery and pioneers. It was clear that Arnis, almost 11¾ miles north-east of Missunde, and Cappeln, some two and third miles further on, both on the north bank, should be determined as the points for the crossing of the Schlei. The river at Arnis was just under 250 yards wide, and at Cappeln, a little over 400 yards. In both places, the water was frozen on both banks, though free-flowing in the middle. Colonel von Blumenthal was sent to the Field Marshal's headquarters at Damendorf with a report to this effect and to request permission for the crossing of the river to take place at these points.

Field Marshal Wrangel now agreed to the proposals and ordered that the crossing of I Corps should take place overnight on the 5th/6th, with a small force left to mask the defences of Missunde. Once across the Schlei, the Prince was to move on Schleswig town, directing one brigade towards Flensburg. Should the force at Missunde be threatened from there, an Austrian brigade at Weseby would be made available to support it. Much would depend upon any possible Danish action at Missunde, and the Marshal attached particular importance to the necessity of the force left there to be able to react rapidly to any signs of impending movement. Should the crossing prove impossible, Friedrich Carl was ordered to move his Corps quickly back to Cosel, where plans would be made to integrate it into a major assault on the central Danewerke position.[57]

It was not the Prince's intention after the crossing to move directly upon Flensburg, and the approval of the plan was predicated upon the first move being to take possession of Missunde.

The Allied orders for the centre were to consolidate positions, and await news from the east, where, as related, I Corps hoped to cross the Schlei. There would be no storming of the main line until that news was received. Opposite the Danewerke, the troops were to hold positions taken the previous day and construct defensive works.

North of the Danewerke, King Christian, accompanied by Council-President Monrad, left Schleswig town at 03:30 on the 4th, and travelled to Flensburg. Earlier that morning, Monrad had sought out the Chief of Staff, to discuss the military situation, having heard of discussions of a retreat. Colonel Kauffmann confirmed his understanding of the current instructions in force for the defence of the line, and informed the Council-President that it could not be held for long.

57 Winterfeld, Volume I, pp.92-93.

Monrad stated that it was politically desirable for some defence to be made, and inferred at one point that a loss of 1/3 of the Army may be an acceptable price. Expressing his full confidence in the High Command, Monrad took his leave.[58]

Later that morning an uneasy General de Meza, with his staff, carried out an inspection of the central Danewerke position, his first since the beginning of hostilities (it would also be his last.). It was also the first time that many of the troops had seen him. He found the men generally in good spirits but could see that they were clearly suffering from the freezing weather. Near Bustorf, he witnessed part of an artillery exchange between the batteries in the works in front of the town and Austrian guns now in place on the Königshügel.

Overnight on the 3rd/4th, Austrian engineers of the 11th Company dug an emplacement for three guns, and some works for infantry. Occupying the hill was of Major-General Nostitz' brigade, the engineer company, and the 10th 8 Pounder Battery of the Corps Artillery Reserve. Given the situation, there were too many troops on the Königshügel, and the engineers had not had sufficient time to construct large enough protective works.

At dawn, the guns in Redoubt X (one 84 pound, and two 24 pound howitzers, two 12 pounders, and 2 six pounders) opened a lively fire at the hill. These were soon joined by those in the Bustorf Work Nr. II (one 84 pound howitzer and five 12 pounders), and two rifled 4 pounders of Captain Fallesen's 11th Field Battery. This fire appeared unpleasantly accurate to the Austrians, but actually caused few casualties. A long duel ensued at a range of about 1¼ miles from Work Nr. II, and a little more than 1½ miles from Redoubt X.

The Danewerke - The Bustorf Outwork, known as 'Gibraltar' (Stilling)

58 See Johansen & Nordentoft, *Hæren ved Danevirke*, p. 224, Kauffmann, *Tilbagetoget fra Dannevirke og dets hemmelige historie*, Copenhagen 1865, pp. 24-26 and Schioldann-Nielsen, *The Life of D.G. Monrad 1811-1887*, Odense 1988, pp. 105-106.

Nostitz eventually pulled the artillery off the hill. At noon, FML Gablenz ordered Nostitz to leave one battalion and three guns on the Königshügel (the number for which positions had already been prepared), and withdraw the remainder of his Brigade. There had been no Danish casualties. One man had been killed in the Austrian battery, and three wounded. IR Hessen had two men wounded.

On the Austrian right flank, Brigade Tomas at daybreak took positions on the heights at Fahrdorf, and was soon under fire from three Danish batteries. The guns north of the Schlei at St. Johannis-Kloster (four 84 pound howitzers), those on the island of Möwenberg (four rifled twelve pounders), and also those on the high ground of the Markgrafenberg, south of Haddeby (the eight smoothbore 12 pounders of 12th Field Battery), were all engaged at ranges of between 1,500 and 2,000 yards.

The fire was heavy and accurate, forcing Tomas to pull his troops back out of sight of the guns. At about 11:00, he moved his own artillery battery, 5/1st (eight rifled 4 pounders) together with the 'borrowed' Prussian battery, 4/3rd 6 Pounder (six rifled 6 pounders) and placed them on high ground with a good field of fire south of Fahrdorf. Their fire was initially directed against the St. Johannis Kloster, which was forced to cease firing after its breastworks were demolished.

At 15:00, their attention was turned to the Möwenberg, which, in its turn was also silenced. It remained out of action until the next day. Further exchanges continued across the Haddeby Lagoon but had little effect.

Meanwhile, skirmishes south of Loopsted took place throughout the day between elements of Brigade Tomas and the 9th Infantry Regiment. A great deal of ammunition was used up, but casualties were few, largely due to the good cover provided by knicks in the area, of which both sides availed themselves.[59] One gunner from Tomas' brigade battery, one hussar of 6/Leichtenstein, and an officer and one man from Regiment Coronini were wounded during the day. The Danish 9th Regiment had casualties of one NCO wounded and two men captured (one wounded).[60]

In III Corps sector, a minor skirmish occurred at the village of Klein Rheide, 6½ miles west of Jagel. At 06:30, ½ of 11/4th GGR, Premier-Lieutenant Freiherr zu Putlitz, together with a troop of the 6th Cuirassiers, whilst scouting forward, encountered Danish outposts of 10th Infantry Regiment. After an exchange of fire, the latter fell back on their supports, and there the skirmish ended. One Cuirassier had been wounded. Danish losses were one man killed, and four captured, one of these wounded. A few cannon shots were also fired at Prussian hussars from Redoubt Nr. XIX.[61]

The major alarms and 'scares' of the previous day and firing that morning, had convinced many on the Danish side that a major attack on the Danewerke would take place during the day. For this reason the army was kept under arms and in the forward positions for most of the daylight hours. Not until mid-afternoon was it

---

59 Grosser Generalstab, Volume I, p. 172.

60 Contemporary accounts speak of "a few" or "several" casualties in these various minor encounters. The majority of these were cases of injuries where men did not leave their units.

61 Grosser Generalstab, Volume I, pp. 173-174.

realised that no attack would come, and finally at around 15:00, most of the troops were stood down.

Long before his return to his headquarters, General de Meza knew what must be done. The army was too small to defend the extended position, and was rapidly becoming exhausted bivouacking in the open. He ordered that a Council of War take place that evening at the Prince's Palace in Schleswig.

The meeting began at 18:00, the following officers being present:[62]

Lieutenant-General de Meza, Commanding General

Lieutenant-General Lüttichau, Commander, Army Artillery

Lieutenant-General Hegermann-Lindencrone, Commander, 4th Division

Major-General du Plat, Commander, 2nd Division

Major General Steinmann, Commander, 3rd Division

Major-General Caroc, Commander, Infantry Reserve

Colonel Kaufmann, Chief of Staff to General de Meza

Lieutenant-Colonel Dreyer, Commander, Army Engineers

Major Wegener, Chief of Staff to General Lüttichau

Major Schrøder, Chief of Staff to Lieutenant-Colonel Dreyer

Captain Rosen, Deputy Chief of Staff to General de Meza, and taking the minutes of the meeting.

The 1st Division, on the left flank, was unrepresented as it was considered that they were too great a distance away to attend.

General de Meza took his place at the centre of a large table, with Captain Rosen seated opposite, the other officers around them, and proceeded to address the meeting. He gave a situation report on the defensibility of the position and also of the physical state of the army itself. He also gave his assessment of the enemy's capabilities and intentions. He referred to current muster rolls, and read out loud from the instructions given to him by the War Ministry concerning the defence of the Danewerke line. Then, he dropped the bombshell. Making clear that he thought that it should, he asked his officers if the army should voluntarily withdraw from the Danewerke.

Lieutenant-General Lüttichau was appalled by the idea, and stated that he could not agree to a retreat for the obvious and quite justifiable reason that he would lose a large portion of his position artillery. He was fully convinced that they should stay and fight.

The three divisional commanders present had differing views on what should happen next. Hegermann-Lindencrone, the only other officer present who was equal in rank to de Meza and Lüttichau, took the view that a retreat was necessary, and that the time had come to fall back to the 'Flank' positions of Dybbøl and Fredericia. However, he held the opinion that an attack should first be made to

---

62 See Generalstaben, Volume I, pp. 254-260, Bjørke, Kiær, & Norrie, pp. 188-191 (who give the conference start time as 16:00), and Jensen, N.P., pp. 133-135.

recover the terrain lost the previous day, both as a barrier and to improve the morale of the troops. Colonel Kauffmann pointed out that the logical consequence of fighting taking place at this juncture was that in the case of a retreat, the army would not have the head start necessary to successfully complete it.

General Steinmann also held the opinion that the army must retreat, but also insisted that a sortie be made to recover the glacis in the centre, visualising that a fighting retreat could then take place. He was most worried about the image of the army should it withdraw voluntarily from the fortifications without them having been attacked.[63] Like Hegermann-Lindencrone, he was concerned with the morale of the troops in such a case.

General du Plat spoke in favour of an immediate retreat, and this led to a long discussion, centring on the War Ministry instructions of 22nd January not to hazard the existence of the Army itself. Eventually, a vote was taken on the matter, which resulted in a nine to one majority in favour of an immediate withdrawal. Only Lieutenant-General Lüttichau stubbornly stuck to his original view. Captain Rosen, acting as secretary, did not take part in the voting.

The minutes of the meeting identified seven reasons why a withdrawal from the position should be made:

The integrity of the Danewerke position was based on the obstacles that the Schlei and Eider rivers and the surrounding area posed, and that currently the Schlei was no more than a channel that in frosty weather could be frozen over in two days; that the Reide valley could be frozen over in 12 hours; and furthermore it was no longer possible to break up the ice near the enemy.

Additionally the Danewerke position was based on the most important parts of the position being occupied. However, there was only one hutted camp for 2,000 men and the commanders of the divisions had stated that the season prevented continuous bivouacking.

The defence was based on an army of 40-50,000 men, but that the army at hand did not exceed 35,000 men according to the muster rolls.[64]

The composition of the army and its training by no means met the requirements of a fully trained and well-organised army.

The enemy, who had at least 50,000 men under arms, had occupied the major part of the terrain that should be occupied by Danish outposts to secure their army, and that it was not possible to win back this terrain. The enemy were currently moving their artillery into positions which, within two days, would be able to shell Danish artillery in the redoubts. The length of the Danewerke position made it most unlikely that it could be held in case of an enemy breakthrough.

An orderly retreat of the army after the position had been overrun would have been impossible to carry out, and finally, The War Ministry's instructions for the Commander-in-Chief dated the 22nd of January 1864 demanded as a condition for the resistance in the Danewerke position that the fighting must not compromise the army's survival as an army.

63 Bjørke, Kiær & Norrie, p. 189, mention that the press and public opinion may have been a factor in Steinmann's argument, to which de Meza was supposed to have replied, "We didn't take up a position here in order to put on a show that will meet with the approval of spectators."

64 The figure of 35,000 refers to men fit for duty.

It was declared necessary from a military point of view that the army should be withdrawn from the positions voluntarily for the reasons listed above and that retreat should begin the next day leaving any unnecessary equipment behind, and a protocol was drawn up to this effect.

Once these details were finalised, de Meza proposed that he alone would sign the document. The loyal Colonel Kaufmann, however, would have none of that and insisted that all should sign. In the end, only Lieutenant-General Lüttichau was excused from affixing his signature. Orders for the retreat were to be drawn up the next morning. The meeting finally broke up at about 23:00.[65]

The decision to retreat was unquestionably the correct one. It remained to be seen whether that decision had been taken, even after only four days, too late. The fate of Denmark's irreplaceable army hung in the balance.

65 Jensen, pp. 132-135, Bjørke, Kjær & Norrie, pp. 188-191.

4

Retreat from the Danewerke

The morning of February 5th offered the worst of compromises for the Danish Army. A complicated series of orders had to be written and issued, and all arrangements made, without a large number of persons being made aware of the situation. It was also snowing heavily. This last factor did offer one slight advantage. If it continued, the snowfall would at least help to deaden the noise of an army on the move.

The Danish troops were under arms in the defences by 06:00. From 09:00, for about an hour, there was an intermittent exchange of fire between the Austrian and Prussian artillery batteries at Fahrdorf and those on the island of Möwenberg, which thereafter died away.

At 12:15, Army Headquarters in Schleswig sent copies of the following telegram to King Christian and the Minister of War:

> There are exchanges of fire between the redoubts and the enemy's batteries. There are no skirmishes, but the enemy is occupying more and more of our outpost terrain. On the flanks, all seems calm. The troops are starting to suffer from the freezing weather.

There was, of course, no hint of what was shortly to come. In the meantime, the staff at Headquarters prepared the orders for the retreat to be sent out to all senior commanders marked 'Confidential'.[1] The whole army would retreat from the line that night.

The two wings presented a relatively simple matter. On the right, part of General Wilster's 4th Brigade (2nd Division) had a long march, a little over 30 miles from Friedrichstadt to Flensburg. The plan called for the brigade to withdraw from that fortress and the towns of Schwabstedt and Hollingstedt along the river Treene to the east, at 22:00. They were to move north through Treia, and on to Flensburg.

On the left, the majority of 1st Division was spread along the north bank of the Schlei, and was permitted to assign its own routes of march, averaging a little over 20 miles across the Angeln Peninsula to Flensburg. For 1st Brigade, the divisional commander decided upon Süderbrarup and Cappeln. 2nd Brigade, at Missunde, was to take the route via Wedelspang.[2] 3rd Brigade, already around Wedelspang, also had the direct route north, and was required to march at 20:00, taking up a defensive position upon arrival at the junction of the Schleswig and Missunde Roads, just south of Flensburg.

In the centre, the first troops to depart would be the Reserve Artillery. These were to leave Schleswig at 19:00, followed by the Infantry Reserve an hour later.

---

1   Jensen, p. 140.
2   This is the village of Wedelspang north of the Schlei, north-east of Schleswig town, and not that previously mentioned at the Danewerke.

Their destination was the Sundeved Peninsula, the site of the Dybbøl fortifications, almost 40 miles away.

Most of 2nd Division was to withdraw from the main line and outposts at 22:00, and pull back via Schuby, then joining the Flensburg Road near Idstedt Forest. Their destination was Harrislee, just north-west of Flensburg, a distance of 25 miles. Major-General du Plat was warned, however, that this could be extended to Kværs, 12 miles further north.

3rd Division, like the 2nd, was to withdraw its main body from the fortifications at 22:00, and follow that division north along the main road. It was also to provide the army's rearguard. This latter was composed of troops from 7th and 8th Brigades.

Finally, the last of the fighting troops to be considered, 4th (Cavalry) Division, and the 7th Infantry Regiment of 2nd Division, were to move via Schuby, Friedrichsau, and Eggebek, to Handewitt and Bov (about 25 miles for the infantry), where they would halt and deploy pickets.

The main problems, though, would be the movement of the army's supply trains along the main road, in poor weather, and allowed the least amount of time, as they would in most cases move in front of the fighting formations. The rear echelon officers, officials, and men faced an enormous task. The trains were to move through Flensburg, to positions north of the city at Harrislee and North Smedeby.

The troops, of course, had not been informed that a retreat was to take place, and in many cases, as they assembled, they had thought that they were going to attack. Once they learned the truth, despair and anger set in. There were tears in the eyes of many as the withdrawal began.[3]

Left Flank

On the left flank, General Gerlach, upon receipt of his orders at about noon, issued instructions from his headquarters at Brodersby. 1st Brigade (Lasson), on the far left, began its retreat between 19:00 and 20:00, moving in two columns. The eastern column, consisting of I/2nd Infantry Regiment, two companies of II/2nd, I/22nd, 4/4th Dragoons, and six guns of 13th Field Artillery Battery, marched from the area of Arnis/Cappeln via Sterup to Hardesby, and on to Husby, arriving there at 08:00 the following morning.

The western column, consisting of II/22nd Infantry Regiment, six companies of II/2nd, and two guns of the 13th Field Battery, also marched to Husby, via North Barup, Sörup, and Hardesby, arriving at 06.30. Upon the arrival of the main column, the entire brigade moved on at 09:00, reaching Flensburg at 11:00, after an exhausting weather battered 15 hours.

3rd Brigade (Wørishøffer) was assembled at Wedelspang (see footnote 2, page 82) by 23:00, along with four guns of 1st Field Artillery Battery and moved off. However, at Böklund, less than a mile north, orders were received that because of delays to the main force on the Schleswig-Flensburg Road, one regiment was to remain at Wedelspang until 00:30. 16th Regiment was chosen. An officer in the

3   Bjørke, Kiær, & Norrie, p. 194.

Retreat from the Danewerke - the withdrawal from Friedrichstadt (Liljefalck & Lütken)

17th Regiment, 26 year old Second-Lieutenant Lauritz Borberg, describes the awful conditions that night:

> As we passed Wedelspang, we marched past 16th Regiment, which was lined up in the ditch alongside the road. For a moment we believed that the brigade was to take up a position to oppose the pursuing enemy and offer him battle, but no order came to halt, so with no break we continued marching under the cover of the night's darkness. Due to the blizzard and the dark, we could not see one step on either side. As we left Wedelspang behind us, the men began showing signs of fatigue, though for a time, most kept up. Fear of falling into the hands of the enemy was a mighty inspiration, a much more powerful persuader than any order or threat from our own superiors.
>
> Many men were helped on the march by their stronger comrades, carrying their rifles and giving physical support. Personally, I walked on with an unwell man from Fehmarn on my arm for quite a while, until I gave him up to a supply wagon when he could march no more. The man had a weak chest. These aids did not last long as the road was very icy, and this held up the march. Soon whole groups threw themselves into ditches and could not be made to move, so in the end we gave up trying to get those worn out soldiers moving, and the march continued, broken only by two short breaks of 10 minutes each.[4]

The regiment and the four guns, with a good deal of straggling, reached the assigned road junction south of Flensburg, at 06:30 on February 6th, where they were joined by 16th Regiment two hours later.[5]

2nd Brigade (Vogt) had instructions to break camp at 21:00, and follow 3rd Brigade through Wedelspang. However, after a minor skirmish in the early after-

---

4   Borberg, Lauritz, *I Krig og Kantonnement 1864*, Copenhagen 1938, pp. 46-48.
5   Jensen, pp. 133-134, and Johansen & Nordentoft, *Hæren ved Danevirke 1864*, p.263.

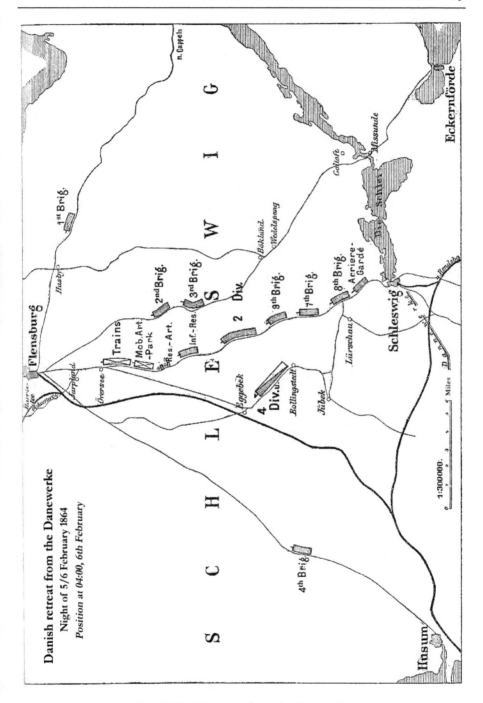

Map 7: Danish retreat from the Danewerke

noon at Missunde, and a further report of an enemy advance around dusk, Major-General Vogt decided that it would be prudent to accelerate the timetable. Troops on the north bank of the Schlei were on the move by 18:30. Unfortunately, in the confusion, no orders were issued to Major Lundbye's I/18th Regiment, at Missunde. On his own initiative, Lundbye had the bridges destroyed, marching with two of his companies at 21:30, and after the destruction was complete, the other two departed at 23:00. The brigade's withdrawal was unhindered by the enemy.

Right Flank

In the west, Major-General Wilster's 4th Brigade moved off from Friedrichstadt, at 22:00 as planned. The brigade moved through Husum, and marched towards Flensburg. It joined the main body of 2nd Division at Harrislee on the evening of the 6th.

Centre

Overnight on the 5th, Headquarters was notified that 1,500 replacements would be sent to Schleswig by rail from Flensburg next morning. The High Command cancelled the troop movement, but requested the freight trains to be sent forward empty. This was done the next morning. However, due to a misunderstanding about the time between Colonel Kaufmann and Major Wegener, the artillery Chief of Staff, no guns were available to be moved. By the time Wegener was able to consider moving some ordnance in the evening, the trains had been sent back to Flensburg, and the bridge across the Treene destroyed.[6]

At noon, Colonel Kaufmann ordered Ritmester W Haffner, commander of the army's wagon trains to begin the move of the Baggage and Provisions Trains north. The first vehicles were soon on the road from the depots, which had been established at Idstedt Inn and Arenholz Lake. Between 350 and 400 wagons were to be moved. This number was not as great as it might have been, since General de Meza had decided that a large portion of the Provisions Train would be deployed to the field units. This would ensure that the troops could be fed before the retreat began, and that they had additional provisions on the march itself. In practice, although necessary for the care of the men, it meant that very many of these wagons would be abandoned.

The artillery and engineer parks, like everyone else, given little time to prepare, also faced a severe shortage of horses. Since the orders stipulated that no vehicles were to be allowed to enter the main road after 19:00, there was little to do but move whatever was possible. Captain Thestrup, commanding the Artillery Park, had 440 wagons, but only 84 horses. A great deal of materiél had to be left behind.

Haffner managed to get his columns under way relatively quickly, in spite of having only a handful of personnel to control and direct the undisciplined and nervous wagon drivers. By mid-afternoon, the last movable vehicles were on the road. The very poor weather meant that progress was necessarily slow, but it continued unhindered, and some 24 hours after they had begun, the army's trains

6   Bjørke, Kiær, & Norrie, pp. 192-193.

rolled into their designated areas at Harrislee and North Smedeby. Ritmester Haffner had, against heavy odds, done a first rate job.

The Reserve Artillery withdrew from Schleswig along the main road on time, and passed the village of Hühnerwasser at around 19:30, as planned. They were followed at 20:00 by the two regiments of the 'Infantry Reserve' some 2½ miles behind. The artillery continued its march to the Sundeved, reaching there the following evening. The main body of 2nd Division (minus 7th Regiment) followed at 22:00, retreating up the main road, and reached Harrislee, where it was reunited with its 4th Brigade the following evening. The Cavalry Division had pulled back to its assigned positions north of Flensburg by 06:00 on the 6th.

General de Meza left Schleswig for Flensburg at 17:00, leaving Colonel Kauffmann in charge at Headquarters. Once the entire operation was under way, Colonel Kauffmann drafted and sent a message to the War Minister. Dispatched at 21:50, the telegram, copied to the King, read:

> After having convened a Council-of War yesterday, the High Command has decided to abandon the Danewerke before the imminent, serious attack is attempted upon the position. The Army marches tonight to Flensburg. The materiél in the Redoubts is being left behind.

Immediately after the message was sent, the telegraph station was closed down and prepared for transportation. No higher authority could now interfere in the immediate course of events. Finally, at 23:00, Army Headquarters left Schleswig town, reaching Flensburg at noon on the 6th.[7]

Most of de Meza's troops had withdrawn from Danewerke untroubled by Allied troops. The last major formation to withdraw was General Steinmann's 3rd Division. Providing the rearguard, its retreat would not prove so simple.

The Prussian Crossing of the Schlei

Whilst the Danish retreat was being organised and carried out, on the eastern flank, Prussian I Corps had been busy with its own logistical problem – crossing to the north bank of the Schlei. The heavy snowfalls were an obstacle to the march downstream, but also cut visibility for the enemy outposts on the opposite bank. From 05:00, the long columns of men and horses began to move north-east. Twelve hours later, I Corps was bivouacked along the Schlei, opposite Arnis and Cappeln. The troops were forbidden to light fires, and had to huddle together for warmth. Prince Friedrich Carl, moving ahead of his troops, established his headquarters in the castle of Carlsburg at 16:00. Left behind to mask Missunde, were F/IR15 and 1/7th Dragoons.

It was planned that Major-General Roeder's 12th Brigade was to be taken, in 30 boats, across to Cappeln, one battalion at a time, whilst the Advance Guard infantry was to cross to Arnis in 45 boats. Both of these operations were scheduled to begin at 04:00 the next morning. Once a perimeter around Arnis had been secured, it was intended that work would begin to construct a bridge to there from the opposite bank, enabling the rest of the Corps to cross. Around 20:00, citizens of Cappeln reported that the Danes had withdrawn from the town. Sergeant Krug,

7   Jensen, p. 149.

Prussian I Corps crossing the Schlei, 6th February
(*Illustrierte Kriegs-Berichte aus Schleswig-Holstein 1864*)

of 7th Pioneer Battalion, volunteered to cross the Schlei to confirm this, which he did. Later, a similar report came from Arnis. Roeder passed this information to the Prince's headquarters at 00:20. The Prince ordered that the crossing be speeded up, if possible.

The transition of Roeder's brigade took a considerable time, and was only completed at 10:00. In the meanwhile, construction of the bridge began at 07:30, after three batteries of artillery were positioned to defend it from Danish warships. Supervised by Major Roetscher, his men of 3rd (Brandenburg) Pioneer Battalion used 49 pontoons to build a bridge almost 800 feet long. In spite of drifting ice, the structure was usable by 10:30[8]. The crossing of the Corps was a lengthy business, not completed until 16:30, the order of march being, Prince Friedrich Carl and his staff, Ziethen Hussars, Advance Guard Infantry, artillery, Reserve Cavalry, 13th Division, Reserve Artillery, 11th Brigade (Canstein).[9]

Although the Reserve Cavalry were then sent to pursue the retreating Danes, the latter had too much of a head start. The weather was awful, with heavy snow storms, the horses finding the icy roads very difficult. By 21:00, the point units of the cavalry had reached the village of Sterup, a little under 9½ miles from Cappeln, about halfway to Flensburg. The exhausted horses and men could do no more. The Advance Guard and Brigade Roeder caught up with them somewhat later. Orders were given that next morning, at 04:00, three squadrons would make a dash for Flensburg.[10]

8   Grosser Generalstab, Volume I, p. 199. Waldersee, p.81, gives the start of the crossing as 09:45.

9   Waldersee, p. 81.

10 Ibid, p. 99.

3rd Division's Retreat

The Danish 3rd Division began its retreat at 22:00 on the 5th, in two echelons. First, 9th Brigade and divisional units began moving north. Major-General Steinmann placed the majority of his cavalry and artillery at the front of 9th Brigade. The second echelon, 7th and 8th Brigades followed, at the start 1¼ miles behind the first. Elements of both of these brigades provided the Army's rearguard (6 and 7/1st Regiment and 3 and 7/20th Regiment), along with 6/5th Dragoons, Ritmester C. Posselt, the whole commanded by Ritmester H. Castenschiold, 6th Dragoons.[11] The last pickets of 8th Brigade, providing the initial cover, withdrew from Bustorf at midnight. The Danewerke had been abandoned without a major battle.[12]

Because of the appalling weather, the condition of the roads, and the inevitable general congestion of the withdrawing columns, most especially the supply trains, 8th Brigade was forced to halt at Tater Inn, only about two miles north-west of Schleswig. It was unable to move on until 03:00, leaving the pickets follow an hour later[13]. Progress towards Flensburg remained painfully slow, although at least they were not as yet facing any form of pursuit. Nevertheless, straggling soon began to occur, particularly amongst the wagon trains, which, of necessity, had been called upon to undertake a major movement in far too short a time to do so efficiently.

The Pursuit

Although the last elements of the rearmost brigade (at this stage, 8th Brigade) had cleared Schleswig town by 01:00 on the 6th, this information did not reach Austrian headquarters until 04:00.[14] FML Gablenz then immediately gave orders for the movement of the whole II Corps, and was himself in the saddle by 04:30. 2nd, 3rd, and 4th Squadrons of the Liechtenstein Hussars were detailed for pursuit of the enemy, although no one could be sure at this point what the apparent enemy withdrawal really entailed.

The entire movement was executed with alacrity and Count Waldersee reports that by 08.15 the last Austrian battalion was at Gottorf Castle on its way into Schleswig town. There was great rejoicing amongst the populace, the tri-coloured Schleswig-Holstein flag appearing everywhere. The troops were welcomed with

---

11 It was standard operating procedure in the Danish army to assign a composite force in such circumstances.

12 This abandonment had been foreseen in the Danish operational planning of 1858, which placed the primary defence on the "Flank" positions of Dybbøl and Fredericia. This policy had been reversed in 1861.

13 *Beretning fra Krigsministeriet [War Ministry Report] om Tilbagetoget fra Dannevirke, for Arrièregardens Vedkommende, og om Kampen ved Sankelmark Sø den 6te Februar 1864*, Copenhagen 1864.

14 See Waldersee, p.87, and Fontane, *Der Schleswig-Holsteinsche Krieg 1864*, p.86, with reference to the lack of, as well as lost and/or misdirected communications that night. Also, von Fischer, p. 121 on the proper use of the telegraph in such circumstances, referring to the American Civil War experience.

brandy. Regiment Coronini was detached to occupy the town itself.[15] Brigade Gondrecourt moved north from Jagel across the Danewerke and over the heights to the west of Schleswig town.

Table 8

Austrian Brigade Nostitz Order of Battle, January 25th 1864

	Officers	*Men*	*Total*
9th FJB	30	1020	1050
4/1st 4 Pounder Battery	5	159	164
I/Belgier (four companies)	26	700	726
II/Belgier	31	1004	1035
I/Hessen	34	1043	1077
II/Hessen	27	1000	1027
Grand Total	153	4926	5079

Behind the hussars, Major-General Nostitz' Brigade was detailed to follow on at as best a pace as they could in the blizzards and extreme cold of a north-east wind. Nostitz moved from Schleswig towards Flensburg at 10:00.[16] The brigade's order of march was: Advance Guard – 9th FJB, Lieutenant-Colonel Schidlach; Main Body – I/Belgier, Lieutenant-Colonel Illeschütz, 4/1st 4 Pounder Battery, Captain Ritschl, II/Belgier, Major Baron von Haugwitz, I/Hessen, Major von

Austrian hussars of 4/Liechtenstein at Hesse Moor during the pursuit, 6th February
(Voss)

15 Waldersee, p.87.

16 The nearest figures for the Brigade are those contained in a "March Plan", dated 25th January, almost two weeks before the battle, in Hamburg. This gives totals only, not fighting strengths, "Marsch Plan KK VI Armeekorps Kommando", KA, AFA, January 1864, Document 113. This also gives the hussar's strength as 43 officers and 851 men.

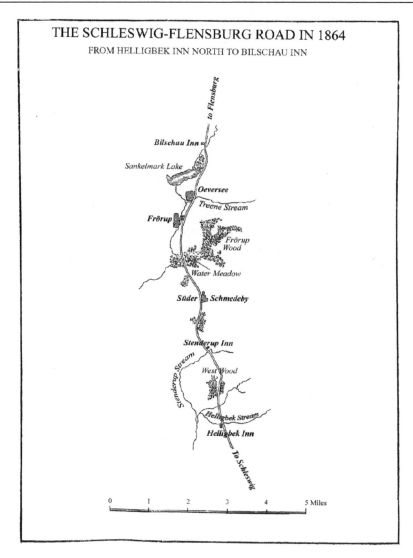

Map 8: The lower Schleswig-Flensburg Road in 1864

Taulow, II/Hessen, Lieutenant-Colonel Count Vetter, and ½ medical platoon. Nostitz' orders were to keep contact with the enemy and push them when and where possible[17]. Gablenz was completing his arrangements for Corps operations, when, at 10:30, Field Marshal Wrangel and the Prussian Crown Prince arrived in Schleswig, with their attendant staffs. After a brief discussion with the Field Marshal, Gablenz de-

---

17 Nostitz, J. K., "Relation über das Gefecht bei Over See am 6 Februar 1864", KA, AFA, February 1864, Document 247.

parted, moving north, taking with him a section (two guns) from Nostitz' brigade artillery.

Two squadrons of hussars had already advanced north through snowstorms along the icy Flensburg Road. 4/Liechtenstein, Rittmeister Johann, Count Attems, in the lead, passed small groups of stragglers and at about 09:00 just north of Hesse Moor, in a confused encounter, captured a supply column which had come from Ober Stolk and appeared completely unaware that a retreat was under way. Mixed in with this column were disparate elements of the retreating force, many of them non-combatants. Some 40 to 50 Danes were made prisoner here, in addition to a large number of vehicles and three 12-pounder cannon.[18]

Attems pushed on to the village of Helligbek, and at 10:00 here encountered the first Danish infantry. These troops were Ritmester Castenschiold's current rearguard, 6/1st, Premierlieutenant L. Beck, and 7/1st, Premierlieutenant Carl Th. Sørensen, of 7th Brigade, who would shortly "leapfrog" with the companies from 8th Brigade, who would relieve them. Beck and Sørensen were further hampered by the fact that a massive wagon jam had occurred at Helligbek, creating chaos and making any movement extremely difficult. Fortunately for them, this also applied to their attackers.

Attems' squadron initially engaged Beck's company at the rear, along the road, and also the confused milling mass from both sides. It was soon obvious to Attems that he was heavily outnumbered, and could make no progress through the crush of vehicles, animals, and men. He pulled back to rally, reorganise, and await support. 4/Liechtenstein was shortly joined by the 5th Squadron, Rittmeister Stolzenberg, ½ of 2nd Squadron (attached to Brigade Gondrecourt, and sent forward on his order), Rittmeister Thurn und Taxis, and a troop of the 6th, the whole now under the personal command of the regiment's commander, Colonel Baselli. Attems' squadron was pulled back into reserve.

The hussars had lost Warrant Officer Strohmeyer killed, and Rittmeister Count Lamberg and Hussar Kiss wounded, along with four horses. Lamberg, who had been grazed by a bullet and fallen from his horse, was rescued by one of his men, Hussar Anda. Anda, under fire, caught the animal, and brought it back to Lamberg, allowing him to remount and escape.[19] The Danes lost one man killed and three wounded.[20]

The retreat continued, Ritmester Castenschiold now handing over the rearguard to 8th Brigade.[21] Baselli's hussars immediately followed up the stragglers, capturing some wagons, including two carrying "Royal Property".[22]

8th Brigade's commander, Colonel Scharffenberg, moved the 20th Regiment to occupy Stenderup Wood, a mile and a quarter north of Helligbek, whilst 9th Regiment barricaded the bridge across the stream at Stenderup Inn. Scharffenberg would now protect the rear until his troops once again moved north, through 7th

18 Generalstaben, Volume I, p. 283, says one 24 and one 84 pound pieces.
19 Smagalski, Ladislaus, *Geschichtliche Skizze aus dem Feldzuge 1864 gegen Dännemark*, Chrudim 1866, p.16. Anda received the Silver Medal for Bravery for this act.
20 It should be noted here that throughout all of the fighting on this day, as on February 3rd, many small arms misfired at various times in the cold and wet.
21 Castenschiold had now decided that the composite rearguard had achieved its purpose, and returned its component units to the operational control of their parent units.
22 Smagalski, p.16. These probably just contained government property.

Brigade. This was to be at the village of Oeversee, seven and a half miles north of Stenderup Inn. His two regiments would 'leapfrog' one another as they withdrew.

20th Regiment retreated slowly to Stenderup Inn, constantly harried by small groups of hussars who darted in to fire their pistols, or to catch an unwary individual. The Danish infantry pulled back across the stream. About this time, FML Gablenz arrived, accompanied by the section of two rifled 4 pounder guns under Oberlieutenant Schmalz, which was quickly sent into action.

The retreat was now considerably more difficult for Scharffenberg's men, with the Austrian artillery moving forward constantly to support the hussars' pinprick lunges. Worse was to come, since four additional guns had been hurried forward by the Austrians.[23] Scharffenberg's Brigade Adjutant, Second-Lieutenant H. Holbøll describes these actions:

> The enemy here used artillery in conjunction with cavalry straight from the rulebook of the art of war. It was well done, and would have pleased the heart of any soldier – if it hadn't been so bad for us.[24]

The cavalry constantly forced the retreating troops to bunch together or form square, so that the artillery could engage them, forcing them to open out their formations once again. The cohesion and discipline of the pursued infantry units was tested to the full. 9th Regiment had a more difficult time of this affair than did the 20th. Holbøll gives an example:

> The Liechtensteiner's sudden attack made the men somewhat nervous. They frightened quite easily, especially when they were marching north and therefore had their backs to the enemy. In one case, as the 9th Regiment's First Battalion was retreating to take up a position, suddenly, for an unknown reason, someone shouted, 'The enemy are there!' The companies to the rear, 1st and 2nd – Premierlieutenant Redsted and Captain Knauer – had just crossed part of the meadow between South Schmedeby and Frörup and were assembled in the road there. Quickly, the company commanders ordered their men to climb up to the high ground on either side of the road, Knauer to the west, where he occupied a barrow, and Redsted to the east, where he took up position behind a hill. Thereby order was restored. Shortly afterwards the Second Battalion of the Regiment retreated through the position.[25]

Some time prior to this, Colonel Scharffenberg had left his brigade and ridden north expecting to find 7th Brigade at the village of Oeversee. Not finding them there, he continued until coming across them deployed on the high ground east of Sankelmark Lake, about ¾ of a mile beyond where he thought they should be. Unfortunately, before departing, he had not informed anyone of his intentions, not even his worried adjutant.

---

23 von Fischer, p.123. Lieutenant-Colonel Weisser, the Corps Artillery commander, on his own initiative sent these guns forward under Captain Ritschl. They were also from Nostitz' Brigade Battery, 4/1st.

24 Holbøll, H., *En Brigade-Adjutants Erindringer fra Krigen 1864*, Copenhagen 1912, p. 92.

25 Ibid, pp. 93-94.

Whilst looking for Scharffenberg, Second-Lieutenant Holbøll encountered Ritmester Posselt's 6/5th Dragoons, along with a troop of 5/5th, halted behind a hill near Frorup, little more than half a mile from Oeversee. Though ostensibly screening the retreat, these troops had been most conspicuous by their absence.

After some argument with Posselt, Holbøll managed to get the dragoons moving south, encountering artillery fire and then the Austrian van, two troops of 3/Liechtenstein (about 30 men were present at this point), Rittmeister Krenosz, at the wood of Süderholz, between Stenderup Inn and South Schmedeby. After a brief clash, the dragoons pulled back, the hussars following up until fired upon by Danish infantry who occupied the village.

Soon after, the retreat continued in much the same way as before, except that Captain Ritschl's four additional guns had arrived and joined the action. In the skirmishing previously and the brief action with the Posselt, Krenosz lost two men killed, four wounded, and two captured, along with 7 dead horses. Posselt's 6/5th Dragoons lost three men wounded and one captured. Posselt then withdrew all the way to Bilschau Inn, north of Oeversee.[26] 8th Brigade continued its withdrawal towards Oeversee, hoping to find their commander on the way.

The Action at Oeversee

At 14:30, General Steinmann halted at what had become the most important point in his defensive plan. Here, in the hilly wooded terrain north of the village of Oeversee and east of Sankelmark Lake, an area that he himself had reconnoitered three years earlier, would stand his rearguard after the passing of 8th Brigade. The difference was that this time the formation would have to stand its ground, giving time for the rest of the Army to withdraw to Flensburg. The enemy pursuit was too large and aggressive to permit further fluid defence.[27] The stand here would require a special kind of doggedness.

This vital and extremely difficult task was assigned to 7th Infantry Brigade, commanded by fifty-six year old Colonel C.F. 'Max' Müller. Müller was a tough, no-nonsense professional who placed his faith in attack. He was a total proponent of the bayonet, and had imbued his subordinates, like Major Rist, with this philosophy. His aggressive nature would not seem to sit well with the task of a rearguard action. His selection, however, was a good one since he could be completely relied upon to keep his nerve under any circumstances.

On the morning of the 6th of February, 7th Brigade comprised 2,752 effectives (1st Regiment – 1,253, 11th Regiment – 1,499).[28] Attached to the

---

26 Smagalski, pp. 20-21. Jørgensen, A., "Eskadronen Posselt Syd for Sankelmark den 6te Februar 1864", *Vort Forsvar*, Nr.503, Copenhagen 1903, quotes a participant in the skirmish, the then Undercorporal Brasch. Brasch places the encounter too far north, but the description of the action puts him here.

27 Steinmann had already been incorrectly informed that 3rd Brigade would take over the rearguard from him immediately south of Flensburg. These already tired troops were, in fact, moving forward to support his left flank.

28 Müller, Colonel M., "Mere i Anledning af Bajonnettens Anvendelse under Fægtninger", *Tidsskrift For Krigsvæsen* 1865, p.22

brigade were the 6/5th Dragoons, which had, as discussed, 'screened' the retreat of 8th Brigade.

The only available artillery to support the brigade were four guns of the 11th Field Battery, Captain Fallesen, which had halted at Bilschau Inn to rest and feed both horses and men. Colonel Müller had ridden to see General Steinmann to request artillery and cavalry support. Steinmann now regretted his decision to put 3rd Division's cavalry and guns at the front of his retreating columns. He dispatched his Chief of Staff, Captain J. C. Blom, with instructions to Fallesen that his guns be placed at Müller's disposal. Fallesen, however, vigorously opposed these orders, so much so that, incredibly, only two of the guns, under Premierlieutenant Grüner, were finally assigned to Müller. Fallesen cannot be criticised for speaking up for his own command, but he certainly should, in the circumstances, have been overruled.[29]

A similar state of affairs occurred with Posselt's dragoon squadron. Though supposed to cover 7th Brigade, they did not actually move forward of Bilschau Inn. A different squadron was requested from Flensburg, but this would take time, especially in the present conditions. Ritmester Posselt's unit did not have a very creditable day on February 6th.

'Max' Müller learned of the approach of Nostitz' brigade after the questioning of a Liechtenstein hussar prisoner captured at Schmedeby, by a Hungarian-speaking officer of 1st Regiment, Premierlieutenant J.A.W. Weiss. Müller was informed that there was one regiment of cavalry involved in the pursuit. In any case itching for a fight, he retorted, "Then they have no more than one brigade. A military power like Austria does not send out a large force without adequate cavalry support. They have a brigade – I also have a brigade. *Parti egal* (we are equal)!"[30]

Müller anchored his right flank on Sankelmark Lake. The lake itself was frozen over, but the ice would not bear the weight of a man. Any move across it was impossible. The 1st Regiment formed the first line in company columns, with skirmishers to their front. I/1st, Captain J. Hansen, was west of the main road – two companies forward, and two in reserve - and II/1st, Captain J. Thalbitzer, to the east – one company forward, two in the second line, and the last further back, in reserve.[31] The westernmost company of all, 2/1st, was the most exposed, deployed too far to the west and with the lake actually behind them.

Immediately in the rear of II/1, east of the main road, Premierlieutenant Grüner sited the two cannon from Fallesen's 11th Battery on the top of a small hill. This was a commanding position, with the guns able to fire over the heads of the infantry. Additionally the horse teams and limbers were able to shelter on the reverse slope, but the guns and their crews were very vulnerable to enemy fire.

29 Johansen, J, and Nordentoft, J., *Haeren ved Danevirke 1864*, p. 293. Fallesen himself does not make any mention of this in his report – Fallesen, M., *Fra 11. Batterie/Fallesen/ Over dets Deeltagelse I Træfningen den 3. 4. og 6. Februar 1864.*

30 Sørensen, Carl Th., *Erindringer fra Første Regiment 1864*, Copenhagen 1891, p. 44. Indeed, Müller had been heard earlier by Sørensen urging General Steinmann to let him attack the Austrians in conjunction with 8th Brigade.

31 The battalion commander, Major Hansen, had been left behind sick, in Schleswig, where he was captured. Captain Hansen was in temporary command.

In a hollow some 200 feet to the rear of 1st Regiment, 11th Regiment was posted where the main road passes through the narrow point between the lake and the high ground to the east. I/11th, Captain W. Stricker, stood west of the road, and II/11th, Captain R. Chabert, to the east. Both units were at this stage formed in battalion columns. Although still extremely cold, it had stopped snowing, affording a good view of the enemy's approach.[32]

Müller had placed his troops in a position to attack whenever possible, not something that General Steinmann had anticipated, but he did not interfere. The General advocated a position further north and east than Müller occupied, although still too large for the force Müller had. The Colonel's frontage was also somewhat longer than he would have preferred, almost 550 yards.[33]

At around 15:30, after 8th Brigade (now reunited with Colonel Scharffenberg) had passed through Müller's positions, Gablenz dispatched an adjutant, Captain Ritter von Gründorf, to undertake a reconnaissance with six and a half troops of Basseli's hussars to discover the enemy's precise whereabouts.[34] The six available guns of Nostitz' brigade battery had already opened their first fire at 7th Brigade from a small hill east of Oeversee Inn. They were joined there soon after, by the remaining two.[35]

Though ostensibly a reconnaissance, it seems clear that the hussars, who may have come into close proximity with the Danish infantry by accident, did attempt to work up some sort of attack. Müller's I/1 Infantry regiment had formed immediately into company squares, and 11th Regiment to their rear, into battalion squares. Most of I/1's skirmishers were well protected behind knicks and a dike close to the main road, which offered almost wall-like cover. In the event, in whatever manner the attack occurred, it was halted by the heavy fire of the skirmishers and, in Gründorf's account, of artillery fire as well. He states that they then withdrew. Müller had announced his intention to stand and fight.[36]

Just after this repulse of the hussars, the adjutant of 1st Regiment, Second-Lieutenant J.C.E.M. Bernth, was injured by a shell fragment, whilst sheltering with Lieutenant-Colonel Beck within the battalion square of Captain Stricker's I/11th. Incredibly, Beck personally accompanied the wounded officer to the field hospital at Bilschau Inn. 1st Regiment was thus left without a commander just as an action was beginning. He was not to return to it until after it was no

32 Johansen, Jens & Nordentoft, Johan, *Hæren ved Danevirke*, p. 294.

33 Ibid, pp. 291-292.

34 The whole of Third Squadron, half of the Second, and half a troop of the Fifth – about 180 men. See, Smagalski, L., *Geschichtliche Skizze aus dem Feldzuge 1864 gegen Dänemark*, pp.26-28. This account has Gablenz calling out, 'Hussars! Attack the guns.'

35 During their shelling by the Austrian guns Second-Lieutenant Bernth recalled that each time a shell came over, the men instinctively ducked, taking no notice of orders from their officers to the contrary. Bernth, J.C.E., "Fra Rendsborg til Sankelmark", *Vort Forsvar*, Nr. 88, Copenhagen 1884.

36 Gründorf von Zebegeny, Wilhelm Ritter, *Memoiren eines österreichischen Generalstäblers*, Stuttgart 1913, pp.206-207. Fallesen's report confirms that Grüner's guns did indeed fire upon the hussars, stating that, "...a squadron placed on the right flank seemed to suffer from our fire." Fallesen, *Fra 11 Batterie...*

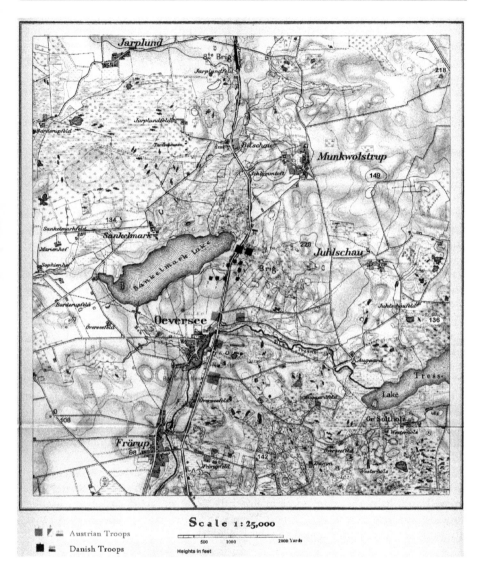

Scale 1:25,000

500   1000   2000 Yards

Heights in feet

Austrian Troops

Danish Troops

Map 9: Action of Oeversee - 6th February

longer a fighting force.[37] At the same time the Austrian artillery battery also got the range of Premierlieutenant Grüner's two cannon, wounding one man. With shells landing near his position, and also in the mistaken belief that the enemy had 14

37 See Johansen & Nordentoft, *Hæren ved Danevirke*, p.296. It is surely impossible to imagine any Prussian or Austrian regimental commander leaving his command on the field of battle in such circumstances. Even more extraordinary is that no mention of it seems to have been made subsequently.

guns present, Grüner limbered up his two pieces, and withdrew to a previously prepared earthwork near Bilschau Inn.[38] Unfortunately, he did this without informing anyone.

Events now occurred in swift succession. An order from Wrangel reached Gablenz at Oeversee Inn at the same time as the head of Nostitz' Brigade, 9th FJB, reached there. Wrangel's order was that II Corps was to take possession of the Oeversee defile, but should not advance beyond the village of Oeversee on that day. Quite apart from it being complete anathema for Gablenz to break off an action, he saw cogent reasons to undertake an immediate assault. Not least was the late hour, leaving him little daylight to force a conclusion. His troops were also extremely tired. Given this situation his view was that an immediate direct attack offered the only possibility for success. 9th FJB, the first available troops, were given the order by Gablenz himself, to take off their packs and attack.

The immediacy of the situation precluded anything other than the committal of units to the attack as they arrived, the inevitable result of which would be heavy casualties. Lieutenant-Colonel Schidlach deployed 4/9th FJB in a firing line straddling the main road, with 1st, 2nd, and 3rd Companies initially in *Zugs kolonne* (platoon width) on the main road behind them. The third division of the battalion, Captain Franz Heller (5 and 6/9th FJB) moved directly north from Oeversee village to the southern tip of Sankelmark Lake following a small lane.[39]

Schidlach launched his assault column directly up the road, where it was met by a withering fire from three companies to the west of the road (1, 2, and 7/1st), and one company east of it (5/1st). The column staggered to a halt, suffering some 30 casualties in the first few moments.[40] It was a critical moment.

A combination of factors prevented a complete repulse here. First, the 3rd division of 9th Jäger were advancing east along the southern shore of Sankelmark Lake, flanking Premierlieutenant Riebau's company, 2/1st, which was already under fire from the 4/9th FJB, deployed in the firing line supporting the attacking column. Secondly, four companies of I/Belgier, Lieutenant-Colonel Illeschütz, had just arrived on the field, and were deployed east of the main road in *Divisions-massen-linie*. Three companies (1, 2, and 5/Belgier)were immediately pushed into the attack, partly flanking I/1st in front of them, and supported by a renewed assault by the main force of 9th FJB along the road. 6/Belgier, for the moment, was held in reserve. Captain Went von Römö, commander of 2/9th FJB had no doubt what had changed the situation:

38 Fallesen, *Fra 11. Batterie...*

39 Nostitz, "K.K. Infanterie Brigade Generalmajor von Nostitz - Relation über das Gefecht bei Over See am 6. Februar 1864"; KA, AFA, February 1864, Document 247. Some sources have asserted that Heller's two companies actually moved westwards around the lake, to attack the Danish right flank/rear. They did not. Time and weather conditions preclude the possibility. Indeed, their absence on such a wild goose chase could very possibly have affected the outcome of the main attack. Bernth describes the Jäger as being, 'in 3 columns.' – *Fra Rendsborg til Sankelmark.* If he saw this himself, the advance must have been slightly earlier, since he was wounded just after the hussars' withdrawal.

40 Schidlach, Major, "Kais. Königl. Feld-Jaeger Battalion No. 9 - Relation über das Gefecht bei Översee am 6. Februar 1864", KA, AFA, February 1864, Document 232.

A gefreiter and three privates of an Austrian infantry regiment, most probably
IR Nr. 27, König der Belgier (Voss)

Our situation was rather awkward; needlessly the calls '*Klumpen*' and 'With-
draw/Retreat', were sounded in quick succession. Then, a brave bugler sounded
'Advance' on his own initiative; others followed his example, and we held
steady, expecting an enemy attack. There, from the left, across the road, we
heard the constant drumming of the 'Storm'. The First Battalion of 'Belgier',
their white standard floating in the wind showing us the Queen of Heaven,
came advancing. Its dead and wounded showed the path it had come. It was a
solemn moment, when salvation prevented our being smashed by enemy forces.

The 'Belgier' battalion crossed the road at the height of our skirmish line.
Its front company immediately clashed with the next Danish mass, which
formed square. Now, a bloody hand-to-hand struggle followed in which the
Jäger quickly joined with the bayonet and the butt. The Danes were over-
thrown. Many scenes of bravery took place during this episode which took far
less time than I can describe it.[41]

Just before the infantry attack Max Müller had ordered 11th Regiment to pull
back to positions in Sankelmark Wood and also to the left, on the heights east of
the road towards Munkwolstrup. This was intended as a preparation to cover 1st
Regiment's withdrawal. Major Rist was none too pleased for his regiment to be

41 Römö, Went von, "1864. Erinnerungen eines österreichisches Kriegsmannes",
Österreichische Militärische Zeitschrift, Volume 39, Nr. 1, Vienna 1898.

Colonel 'Max' Müller at Oeversee (Liljefalck & Lütken)

ordered back. Premierlieutenant Sørensen overheard the following exchange as Rist came to see Müller: Rist, he wrote,

> ...came riding through the hail of shells that by now came from right to left, and asked Max Müller: 'Does the Colonel wish the 11th Regiment to remain in columns, under fire?' Just what the Brigade Commander answered I was unable to hear, but it must have been something like, 'Yes!', as Rist had clearly been dismissed rather brusquely. However, just afterwards, there must have been second thoughts in Max Müller's mind, as Rist had not gone very far when Max called after him, 'Yes, can you get out of there?' after which they (Müller and his staff) departed for the left wing. Shortly afterwards, we saw that the 11th Regiment retreated.[42]

1st Regiment, however, was now under attack all along its line, and in no position to disengage. It was also being shelled by Nostitz' artillery. The renewed Austrian attack met inevitably disjointed resistance from the regiment, which had no commander present, and the officers of which were inevitably heavily influenced by their brigade commander's tactical views, which required attack at every opportunity.

East of the main road, 4/1st, Captain Weyhe, after a brief discussion with his battalion commander (II/1st, Captain Thalbitzer) rushed forward in an attack

42 Sørensen, Carl Th., *Erindringer fra Første Regiment 1864*, p.49.

Oversee, February 6th with the lake to the left and the main road to Flensburg on the right (*Illustrated London News*)

upon Illeschütz' columns, which were already partly overlapped on the right. They were in turn counterattacked by Illeschütz' reserve company, 6/Belgier, Captain Castella. The lead elements of Weyhe's company fought a brief close-quarter action with Castella's men. Captain Weyhe actually crossed swords with Oberlieutenant Count St. Julien, before one of St. Julien's men clubbed him to the ground.[43] Weyhe was taken prisoner, and his men forced back. Lieutenant-Colonel Illeschütz was mortally, and Castella badly, wounded. Captain Entner took command of I/Belgier.

The main Austrian force to the right of the road pushed back 5/1st, already in some confusion, forcing 4/1st on their right to pull back a short way, after which they attempted to halt the enemy advance. 8/1st, which had followed directly behind their attack, was therefore also forced to halt. The remaining company II/1st, 3/1st, Captain C. Irgens, had also attacked Illeschütz' force and been repulsed. Each company, operating without any overall control, was being driven backwards, though continuing individually to fight fiercely, repeatedly firing into their advancing opponents.

West of the road, the resumption of the assault by the Austrian Jäger was initially met by heavy small arms fire. As to the east, however, the ingrained doctrine of the offensive prevailed, and two of the three companies of I/1st Regiment's first line soon counterattacked (1/1st, Premierlieutenant J. Weiss, and 2/1st, Premierlieutenant J. Riebau). Only Sørensen's 7/1st, in the centre, remained

43 Ibid, p. 50. Sørensen witnessed Weyhe's fall from a distance.

in position behind a fence. Captain Hansen, the acting battalion commander, had been killed previously.[44]

Both of these companies were repulsed by Austrian musket fire, then pushed back to their original positions, and subsequently beyond, Sørensen's 7/1st having to conform to their retreat moving into the line. They were still causing many losses amongst their attackers by their steady fire. Nearest to the lake, 2/1st was cut off along with some of Sørensen's men. Attacked from the front, and also now by the third division of 9th FJB, which moved rapidly east against them, along the southern shore of the lake, they had nowhere to go. Trapped against the ice, Riebau being already a casualty, about a half of the company was captured, along with some of Sørenson's men. The survivors, under Lieutenants Hansen and Volkersen, escaped northwards.[45]

1st Regiment was now starting to come apart. On its right, the disorderly retreat of Riebau and Hansen's companies engulfed 6/1st, held in reserve, and it too, began to withdraw. The withdrawal soon turned to panic. II/1st was also becoming more and more disordered as it was driven north through the woods. Max Müller personally tried to rally the regiment, but soon saw that it was hopeless. He then rather pointlessly ordered the retreat to be sounded. Most of the regiment fled the field, though individuals and groups rallied and joined 11th Regiment in their positions to the rear.[46] These positions were already under fire from the Austrian artillery.

During the disintegration of 1st Regiment, Major-General Steinmann had come forward, bringing Lieutenant-Colonel Beck with him. Seeing the fleeing troops, Steinmann had also done his best to rally them, but was unable to achieve much. Around this time, he was wounded in the leg by a rifle bullet. Nevertheless, he remained in the saddle until after the action had ended.

Major Rist's 11th Regiment was, at this point, positioned between Sankelmark Lake, across the main road, and north-eastwards along a track to the village of Munkwolstrup. It was deployed as follows:

I/11th, Captain W. Stricker – Facing south. 1 and 7/11th were posted on the edge of the Sankelmark Woods, between the lake and the main road. Both had lost their company commanders on February 3rd, and were now commanded by Premierlieutenant C. Varberg and Premierlieutenant N. Scheel, respectively.

---

44 The commanding officer of I/1st, Major F. Hansen, was left behind sick in Schleswig, and captured there. Captain J. Hansen had taken command as a result.

45 Volkersen, F., *Rapport fra det 1ste Regiments 2. Kompanie over Fægtningen d. 6 Februar 1864*, 11th February 1864, gives his estimate that the company strength that day was some 140-150, of whom c. 100 became casualties. Riebau, captured in the battle, wrote his report a year later ('Rapport fra 1' Infanterieregiments 2 Compagni over Arriergardefægtningen ved Sankelmark Sø den 6' Februar 1864', 12th February 1865). He gives the company strength as about 130 privates (quite similar to Volkerson's figures), and estimated that about 70 men, including wounded, were captured. He also states that his stand saved 1st and 7th Companies. This may be so, but is unlikely to have been intentional.

46 Johansen & Nordentoft, *Hæren ved Danevirke*, p. 303, state flatly that the retreat of 1st Regiment was a rout, and that only part of it could be rallied.

IR Belgier at Oeversee (*Illustrierte Kriegs-Berichte aus Schleswig-Holstein 1864*)

5/11th, Captain Staggemeier, was east of the road, with 3/11th, Captain Count Ahlefeldt-Laurvig, on the left, both occupying a low ridge.

II/11th, Captain R. Chabert – Facing south-east. 2/11th, Captain E. Stricker, with 6/11th, Premierlieutenant W. Bruun, to their left, occupied a low hill south of the track to Munkwolstrup. 4/11th, Premielieutenant H. Hermannsen, and 8/11th, Premierlieutenant A. Kjærulff, formed a second line, a little under 150 yards behind the first.[47]

East of the lake, the main body of 9th FJB, deployed in open order, pushed into Sankelmark Woods, where they were immediately attacked by 1 and 7/11th. A fierce struggle developed, which was decided by the appearance, once again, of Captain Heller's two companies, moving along the lakeside, and taking the Danes partially in the flank. They fell back slowly, still fighting, but being pushed back and to their left. Both companies were finally scattered, but rallied north of Bilschau. Captain Went was wounded in the fighting in the woods, writing later:

> Squeezed into a small space, we offered the enemy a welcome target. I stood in cover, and squeezed between two crooked trees, my body bent slightly forward to shout to the Jäger, where to direct their fire, when, 'thump', an enemy bullet hit me in the middle of the chest, and went out my right side, slightly injured my arm, and stuck in the tree behind me. By chance, it was of no significance, as I wore two coats, my tunic, and other things. The shot, fired from close range, just tore my clothing.[48]

The attack in the centre stopped the Austrian advance by I/Belgier, and a firefight developed. On the Danish left, II/11th forced I/Belgier back, and threatened to flank the Austrians, but the appearance on the field of II/Belgier,

47 Tusch, E. Jenssen, '11 Battalion I Krigsaarene 1848-50 og 1864', p. 113.
48 Went von Römö, Karl, *Ein Soldatenleben*, p. 97. The modest Went was in hospital for some time.

Major Haugwitz, prevented this. Both Danish battalions (6 companies in the first line) were slowly pushed back. It was about 16:30.

Premierlieutenant Grüner's two guns were also repositioned to aid the retreating infantry. They were ordered to a hill north of the Inn at Bilschau. From here, they fired some rounds in support, but were forced to cease fire in order not to hit their own troops. The guns were then limbered, and, accompanied by Ritmester Posselt's 6/5th Dragoons, were withdrawn to Flensburg.[49]

11th Regiment withdrew towards Bilschau, with those scattered elements of 1st Regiment which had rallied to them. The whole of this force then took up a position just south of Bilschau, and west of Munkwolstrup, from where Max Müller intended to make yet another counterattack against what was now a much larger force than his. Before this could happen, however, Major Rist was heard to shout, "We are flanked on the left! Retreat!"[50]

Rist had seen troop formations near Munkwolstrup. Quickly recovering his nerve, but without informing Müller, he took 4/11th, 6/11th, and half of the 3rd, 5th, and 8th Companies and rushed off in that direction. Müller, arriving just after, was left to defend against the Austrian advance with what was left, and nevertheless took a heavy toll of the attackers. About 17:00, the Austrians captured Bilschau, along with the field hospital there. In the growing gloom of darkness, Müller gathered an *ad-hoc* group of about 300 men, and personally led them in an attack to recover the village, but the assault was beaten off. Some time near the end of the battle, the Colonel of the Belgier, the gallant Duke of Württemberg, had his right foot shattered by a rifle bullet, later having the toes of the foot amputated as a result.

In the meanwhile, Rist had arrived at Munkwolstrup to find that the 'enemy' force on his flank was, in fact, the 17th Infantry Regiment, from 3rd Brigade, sent forward to support Steinmann's left flank. The 17th's commander, Colonel Bernstorff, deployed two of his companies, 3rd and 4th (from II/17th), on the southern outskirts of the village to support Rist, whilst I/17th, Captain F. Lund, was deploying its companies north of it.

With the battalion was Second-Lieutenant Borberg, serving in 7/17th, who witnessed some of the last phases of the action here. He recalled:

> We turned right from the road next to Bilschau Inn towards Munkwolstrup, where we were taking up positions to cover the retreat of 11th Regiment, and to take up the fight if necessary. Now I was going to experience what I had dreamed about, namely how I would feel with bullets flying around me. Lieutenant Nielsen had said that he was convinced that Wolff and I would pass the baptism of fire.[51]

From the south, the second infantry regiment of Brigade Nostitz, IR Hessen, was approaching. I/Hessen, Major Hugo von Taulow, was advancing to the right

49 Fallesen's report, *Fra 11 Batterie…* says that only one round was fired here.
50 Johansen & Nordentoft, *Hæren ved Danevirke*, p. 304. The authors are scathing about this utterance. Vaupell, p. 158, says that Rist had just received a message to this effect from Captain Scheel. Rist was certainly wild and unpredictable, but no coward.
51 Borberg, Lauritz, *I Krig og Kantonnement 1864*, p.53.

of the road towards the position of the Brigade Battery on heights a little south-west of Munkvolstrup. The first division of the battalion was ordered by Taulow to clear out enemy troops on heights to the east. In doing so, 2/Hessen, Captain Mayern, became involved in a firefight with Rist's troops and the forward companies of 17th Regiment. Major Rist was wounded around this time.[52]

Borberg, having just come under fire, was asked by his battalion commander to set an example to the men:

> Lund asked me to remain standing in an opening in the fence, presumably to expose myself to encourage the troops, since I could well have observed the terrain from the front, as I walked up and down behind the centre of the formation. Of course, I obeyed immediately, although I have to admit that it was without inner obedience, as I for certain would have been a victim if we had had any serious fighting, and if darkness had not come shortly after. While we stood there, Lieutenant-Colonel [note – Rist was still a Major at this time] Rist, commander of the 11th Regiment, was carried away badly wounded, in a closed ambulance. An adjutant, I don't know who, came riding by in utter despair at being unable to find a doctor, as the Lieutenant-Colonel [sic.] was lying in there, and could easily bleed to death. Rist's horse was led to the road where my men stood. It had been badly wounded and was bleeding heavily. Shortly afterwards it collapsed and died.
>
> At that moment, Captain Lund went back to the battalion reserves, and made me responsible for the men remaining at their posts until he whistled twice. We should then run as fast as we could over the ridge to the reserves. Shortly after, one platoon after another from 11th Regiment passed, without officers or NCOs, tired and in despair, as they didn't know which way to go. When they were about to mingle with my men, I ordered them further back, where 17th Regiment's reserve was, to gather there. I didn't want them with my men, partly because they belonged to another regiment, but particularly because they might have discouraged them, since the poor fellows were tired by the long fight that they had endured. Luckily, Lieutenant Holstein, of the 11th Regiment, arrived shortly after, and I handed them over to him. He gathered them together, and led them back. Shortly before, units with Captains Ahlefeldt and Stricker had passed.[53]

In the growing darkness, Colonel Bernstorff withdrew his troops to the north, not wishing to become involved in a major action. Almost a hundred of his men would be missing or prisoners by the next day, the fourth highest total for the Army during the retreat, a number only surpassed by three of the regiments most heavily engaged with Gablenz' Corps.[54] Müller also pulled back, rallying and herding as many men as he could. The Austrians ceased their advance at around 18:00, in complete darkness. Regiment Hessen, which had played a negligible part in the fighting, posted pickets for the night north of Bilschau and Munkwolstrup. Perhaps mindful of the orders received from Marshal Wrangel, but certainly aware

---

52 Schütte, Oberst, "Großherzog von Hessen, 14tes Infanteri Regiment - Gefechts Relation am 6ten Februar 1864", KA AFA, February 1864, Document 170.

53 Borberg, pp. 54-55.

54 17th Regiment was partly composed of German-speaking South Schleswigers, some of whom surrendered at the first opportunity.

that his men needed rest, FML Gablenz had no intention of a pursuit into the night, something that would in any case undoubtedly descend into chaos.

The southernmost Danish pickets, drawn from the battered but noble 11th Regiment, were posted some ¾ of a mile north of Bilschau, south of the road junction to Jahrplund. Here, they were joined by 1/4th Dragoons, Ritmester F. Munck. Munck's squadron had earlier been detailed to replace Posselt's in support of Müller's brigade, the latter having actually done nothing of the kind. Later that night, the very tired pickets of 11th Regiment were relieved by men from the 3rd Division's 19th Regiment (9th Brigade).[55]

In the battle, the Austrian infantry had once again proved their courage and discipline. Gablenz had led from the front, and a rifle bullet had hit the hilt of his sabre. His officers had again shown reckless bravery, and many had paid the price. The artillery once more performed extremely well, and their joint pursuit of 8th Brigade together with the hussars had been very skillfully handled.

Austrian losses were very heavy in the persistent attacks during that short afternoon. Given that there was little time or space for much maneouvre, this was inevitable. Total losses for the entire day, hastily calculated immediately afterwards, were frighteningly high, including many men who remained with their units. However, many men were lost, separated from their units, guarding or escorting prisoners, helping the wounded, and doubtless, some malingering.

Initial figures varied from 27 officers and 626 men killed and wounded, up to a total of 710. A staff officer in II Corps, Ladislaus Schnayder, gave what he describes as 'official figures' for the day of 29 officers and 651 men killed and wounded.[56]

Table 9

Austrian Casualties at Oeversee, February 6th 1864 (according to Schnayder)

9th FJB	9 officers and 240 men
IR Belgier	20 officers and 386 men
IR Hessen	5 men
2, 3, 4 / Liechtenstein	18 men
Artillery Battery Nr. 4	2 men

Almost three weeks later, Gablenz issued a detailed supplementary report, showing much lower figures, though grim enough, a total of 434. The lower figures were

55 Tusch, *11 Battalion i Krigsaarene 1848-50 og 1864*, p. 115. Their opposite numbers to the south, IR Hessen, though very lightly engaged that day, had, like their comrades, slept outside for three freezing nights, had had no hot food for 24 hours, and had that day marched almost 20 miles in dreadful weather. They, too, were very tired. Before the last elements of 7th Brigade departed, during a truce for casualty collection, Second-Lieutenant A. Abrahams, was much to his surprise, confronted by Major-General Nostitz, who congratulated him on his troops shooting.

56 Schnayder, Ladislaus, *Oesterreichisch-Preussischer Krieg gegen Dänemark*, Vienna 1865, p. 71.

explained as not including a large number of lightly wounded men, who remained with their units, and other factors as mentioned above. This has been accepted by many, though not all, researchers. It is possible that by this latter date, many of the 'lightly' wounded had already been returned to their units, but this is speculation. As on February 3rd, officer losses were again very high. Those men still shown below as 'missing' were almost certainly dead. These later figures break down as follows:[57]

Table 10

Austrian Casualties at Oeversee, February 6th 1864 (according to Gablenz)

Unit	Killed		Wounded		Prisoners		Missing	
	Officers	Men	Officers	Men	Officers	Men	Officers	Men
Staff	—	—	—	—	—	—	—	—
9th FJB	3	29	6	120	—	1	—	10
IR Belgier	4	29	16	153	—	—	—	31
IR Hessen	—	2	—	3	—	—	—	4
Liechtenstein Hussar Regiment	—	8	—	9	—	2 (1W)	—	—
4/1st 4 Pounder Battery	—	—	—	2	—	—	—	—
Totals	7	70	22	287	—	3	—	45

W = Wounded

Total Danish casualties were higher than the Austrian, but many fewer of them were dead and wounded. This was mainly due to the defensive nature of their mission and the terrain. The large number of unwounded prisoners, however, raised questions about unit cohesion. 11th Regiment appeared to be better disciplined than the 1st, although the 1st Regiment was initially in the forward position, and left isolated by the 11th's first (ordered) withdrawal. It was an argument, initiated on 3rd February, which would continue for years. It was, however, merely part of a larger problem, which there had not been the time or resources to fully address before or during mobilisation. Whilst commending the courage and stamina of the Danish infantry that day, Count Waldersee wrote of this problem: "The root of these defects is the highly unsatisfactory military training of the non-commissioned officer corps and of the numerous reserve officers who make up over half of the officer corps."[58]

57 Supplementary report by FML Gablenz, appended to, "Officieller österreichischen Bericht...."., pp. 313-314 *Österreichische Militärische Zeitschrift*, Volume I, 1864, pp. 313-314, and Anon, *Der Feldzug in Schleswig-Holstein und Jütland 1864*, Vienna 1864, p. 137.
58 Waldersee, pp. 94-95. This is a harsh judgement, but reflects faults of the system, rather than of those within it, and also the very great expansion that the army had undergone in such a short time.

Danish casualty reports were also subject to variation. The War Ministry report gave figures of 18 officers, 944 men and 10 non-combatants. 'Statistiske Meddelelser' later gave a total of 1,068 casualties.[59] Colonel Müller's own account of the losses of his two regiments totaled 796:

Table 11

Danish 7th Infantry Brigade Casualties at Oeversee February 6th 1864

| | Killed | | Wounded or Missing | |
	Officers	*Men*	*Officers*	*Men*
1st Regiment	2	53	8	435
11th Regiment	2	49	5	243[60]

Shown below are the General Staff History figures, totaling 932. Some of the prisoners shown were taken during the night or early next morning. However, prisoners from other units (especially 17th Regiment), probably taken on the 6th, and men missing from those units, are not included. Also note that lightly wounded men not hospitalised are not shown on this table. As with the Austrians, most of the missing men were dead:[61]

Table 12

Danish Casualties at Oeversee, February 6th 1864 (General Staff Figures)

| Unit | Killed | | Wounded | | Prisoners | | Missing | |
	Officers	*Men*	*Officers*	*Men*	*Officers*	*Men*	*Officers*	*Men*
3rd Division Staff	—	—	1[62]	—	—	—	—	—
1st Infantry Regiment	2	22	1	29	8 (2W)	403 (38W)	—	31
9th Infantry Regiment	1	5	1	15	1	84 (9W)	—	3
11th Infantry Regiment	2	14	3	41	—	188 (17W)	—	32
17th Infantry Regiment	—	—	—	2	—	—	—	4
20th Infantry Regiment	—	1	—	3	—	20	—	—

59 *Beretning fra Krigsministeriet [Report from the War Ministry] om Tilbagetoget fra Dannevirke, for Arrieregardens Vedkommende, og om Kampen ved Sankelmark Sø den 6te Februar 1864,* and Generalstaben, *Statistiske Meddelelser angaaende den danske Krigsmagt,* Volume I, p. 136.

60 Müller, M., "Mere i Anledning af Bajonnettens Anvendelse under Fægtninger", *Tidsskrift for Krigsvæsen,* 1865.

61 Generalstaben, Volume I, Appendices 28 & 29.

62 This was Major-General-Steinmann.

5th Dragoon Regiment	—	—		—	3	—	1	—	—
Noncombatants	—	—		—	—	—	12[63]	—	—
Totals	5	41		6	93	9	708	—	70
						(2W)	(64W)		

W = Wounded

'Max' Müller had conducted a brave and determined defence, in accordance with his orders. Attacked by an equally courageous and aggressive opponent, he held his ground as long as possible. It is not possible to state that he saved the army, but he certainly did his absolute utmost to do so. By simply standing to fight, he ensured that in the short time left of the day, the pursuit would be effectively halted. His subordinate regimental commanders behaved in opposite ways. Lieutenant-Colonel Beck's extraordinary behaviour has already been discussed, and his regiment was left leaderless. Major Rist acted in precisely the same way he had at Ober Selk – with little thought but much fast and furious action. That he would always be at the forefront in action, was in no doubt.

Brigade Gondrecourt halted at South Schmedeby for the night, the truncated Brigade Tomas stopping at Gross Solt (IR Coronini having been left to occupy Schleswig town). Brigade Dormus and Major-General Dobrzensky, with the Windischgrätz Dragoons had been ordered (by Wrangel) to cross the Schlei at Missunde. The infantry brigade was duly transported (leaving one company, 5/Khevenhüller in Missunde) but due to congestion and delay, only one squadron of the dragoons was able to cross. Dobrezensky, and the other four therefore moved north in the footsteps of the main body, reaching South Schmedeby in the evening, where they also spent the night.

To the west, III Corps did not move for some time. Gablenz had ordered that news of the general advance be passed on to Lieutenant-General von der Mülbe, by Major-General Gondrecourt. This was, however, not done.[64] For their part, The Prussian Guard outposts did not notice anything untoward. It was not until 09:30, that the advance was started. Orders from Wrangel to advance upon Flensburg were received around this time.

The movement of the Guards was very slow. The advance guard started along the Ox Road north of Jagel at 10:00, the main body an hour later, with the rearguard half an hour after this. The columns crawled along through the snowfalls. By late evening, only the tip of the advance guard had reached Wanderup, about five miles west of Oeversee. The rest bivouacked in the area of Eggbek, Langstedt, and Bollingstedt. The main body did not get beyond Gammellund and Jübeck, an advance, for them, of less than 15 miles. It was a very poor performance.[65]

63 Two officer grade officials of 11th Regiment, and 10 medical staff from the field hospital at Bilschau.
64 See footnote 14, page 89.
65 Grosser Generalstab, pp. 196-197. See also von Fischer, pp. 122 & 130 who attributes some of the problems to friction between Army Headquarters and senior field commanders. During this stately progress, the rail and telegraph lines at

Three out of four of de Meza's divisions had successfully retreated from the Danewerke without major fighting. 3rd Division had been pressed hard, but had at least halted any overnight pursuit. The Allies were, though, less than five miles from Flensburg, and Danish Headquarters, in all of the confusion of the retreat, could not be certain of the actual situation.

Initially, upon hearing the heavy firing to the south, de Meza's headquarters ordered 2nd and 4th Divisions to prepare for action. Once the gunfire ceased, however, and the wounded Major-General Steinmann was able to make a verbal report to the Chief of Staff, these preparations ceased. The wounded Steinmann then finally allowed himself to be evacuated by ship.

Nevertheless, General de Meza was worried by the enemy pursuit, and decided that the retreat must continue immediately. The relevant orders, issued by Colonel Kauffmann, went out at 22:00 that night. The already exhausted army would continue to withdraw, in part to Jutland (primarily 4th Division), but the main body was to pull back to the fortified positions on the Sundeved Peninsula, and the island of Als, just beyond. Some units were evacuated by sea. Army Headquarters quit Flensburg at 03:30 on the 7th.

The three Prussian squadrons detailed the previous evening, marched for Flensburg at 04:00, entering the town at 07:30. Commanded by Rittmeister von Weise, his own 1/Ziethen Hussars, 2/Ziethen, Premier-Lieutenant Thiele, and 1/11th Uhlans, Rittmeister von Rauch, scooped up 22 prisoners, two munitions wagons, eight baggage wagons and several provisions ships in the harbour.[66]

A large amount of ordnance, mostly the position guns, and much materiél was left behind in the Danish retreat.[67] In and behind the centre of the defences, between Redoubts I and XVIII inclusive, and including Schleswig town, were left 104 guns of the following calibres:

31	6 pounders
14	12 pounders
28	18 pounders
15	24 pounders
16	84 pounders

On the island of Möwenberg, the four rifled 12 pounders were found up to their axles in the mud and cracked ice.[68] To the west and east of the main position, a further 50 guns were abandoned, giving a maximum total of 154 guns lost. However, only six 12 pounders, left at Friedrichstadt close to the west coast, were found by the Allies to be usable. All of the rest had been spiked, their sights and carriages

Eggebek were destroyed by units of the Guards, thereby requiring that they immediately needed to be repaired for Allied use.

66 Dedenroth, Volume II, p. 8.

67 Inevitably in such a confused situation, there are numerous different totals for the number of cannon left behind or lost in the retreat. Those stated here are from von Fischer, pp. 120-121, and Liljefalk & Lütken, pp. 108 & 120, unless indicated otherwise. Johansen & Nordentoft, *Hæren ved Danevirke*, p. 262, say 132 guns lost in total. Bjørke, Kiær, & Norrie, p. 193, say 142.

68 These guns are incorrectly referred to as 18 pounders by von Fischer.

damaged, and all the tools and operating equipment smashed. It was not much of a prize, and showed that the retreat had been carefully, though quickly, planned. Great quantities of ammunition and materiél were also, of necessity, left behind

The Danes managed to withdraw 13 guns from the central Danewerke and six more from Missunde. From Friedrichstadt, Süderstapel, and Husum, in the west, it proved possible to withdraw 14 guns (four 84 pounders, two 24 pounders, six 12 pounders, and two 6 pounders). These guns, due to the Herculean efforts of Captain H.P.W. Mønster and his men of 5th Fortress Artillery Company, were taken to Fredericia, finally arriving there on February 11th.[69] This total of 33 guns is all that was saved from the whole of the line.[70]

With some luck, General de Meza had saved the army, but his own future looked bleak. For the present, under a new commander, the bulk of that army was to become acquainted with a different fortified position – Dybbøl.

---

69 Jensen, N. P., p.145.
70 Generalstaben, Volume I, p.278, and Bjørke, Kiær, & Norrie, p. 191. von Fischer puts the number saved at 34.

5

Operations at Dybbøl to February 23rd

De Meza Loses Command

On February 6th, as the army wearily withdrew from the Danewerke, the draft of a proclamation by the King to the Danish Army was published in the Copenhagen newspapers. King Christian and Monrad were in Sønderborg, on Als, when they heard the news of the retreat that morning. The Council-President left for the mainland to confer with the High Command, writing the draft, and sending it to the King for approval. The original, however, was leaked to the press, appearing on the streets of Copenhagen that afternoon. It read:

> Soldiers! – Not alone by valour on the battlefield, but also by enduring with patience, want of rest, cold, and all manner of privations and exertions, the soldier has to prove his fidelity to his King, and his love for his country. There are few amongst you who have not proved in battle against an overwhelming foe that you have not degenerated since Fredericia and Idstedt. You have all had ample opportunity to give brilliant proof of efficiency and endurance, and you have preserved a cheerful courage under long and severe hardship.
>
> Soldiers! – Receive for this the thanks of your King. The Danewerke has been abandoned. The guns which were to have curbed the arrogance of the enemy are in their hands. The country lies open to the enemy. I deeply feel with you that which we have thereby lost. But, my friends, I have but one army for the defence of the country, and your military leaders were of the opinion that I would no longer have had an army if I had not withdrawn you. They therefore came to the determination to retreat.
>
> Soldiers! – I stand alone in the world with my people. Up to the present, no Power has declared that it will support us with action, but I depend upon you and my fleet. You are ready to shed your blood, but we are few against many, and safety must therefore be dearly purchased.
>
> May the Almighty grant that the hour of vengeance may soon strike for all the violence and injustice which has been done to me and my people.
>
> Christian R.[1]

The result of this in the capital was absolute uproar, confirming existing rumours of a retreat. The public was profoundly shocked that the lauded line of fortifications had been abandoned without a battle. Presented to the nation by the press as impregnable, the Danewerke had not even been defended. There was talk that the King and the Council-President were party to the withdrawal.[2] Rioting

---

1 Jensen, pp. 171-172. A slightly altered version was actually presented to the army on the 8th.
2 As discussed, Monrad had actually given mixed signals to the army command, in their conversation at the Danewerke several days previously – See Schilodann-Nielsen, *The Life of D.G. Monrad 1811-1887*, pp. 105-106.

broke out in the city. Upon his return to the city the next day, Monrad had to be smuggled out of the central railway station because of fears for his safety. The departure of the Life Guards Infantry for active service, ordered on the 6th, was postponed.[3]

The Cabinet met the same morning. Immediately after the meeting, Colonel Lundbye, the War Minister, sent a message to Army Headquarters, which read:

> Lieutenant General de Meza and Colonel Kaufmann shall, without delay, report to Copenhagen. Lieutenant-General Lüttichau will temporarily take command, with Major Stjernholm as his Chief of Staff. The High Command will give the necessary orders concerning the absence of Major Stjernholm from the staff of Lieutenant-General Gerlach.

General de Meza received the message at Graasten, on the Sundeved Peninsula, turning over command of the Army to the 69 year old Lüttichau the following morning. He and Colonel Kaufmann then departed for Copenhagen, arriving there on the 9th.[4]

Later that day, Monrad spoke brilliantly in Parliament, removing himself from any responsibility for or prior knowledge of the retreat. He stated that, whilst on his visit to the Danewerke, he had been told that the army would fight there, and he gave his support to the recall of de Meza and Kaufmann by the War Minister.[5]

Lundbye, though he had no authority to recall the Commanding General of the Army, had done precisely that. General de Meza held his command by order of the King, not the King's War Minister, who was also a serving officer. The War Minister did not have the authority of the King to issue this order, and therefore must have had the tacit approval of Bishop Monrad to do so.[6] Lundbye himself was determined to get rid of de Meza. On February17th, the War Ministry ordered a Board of Enquiry set up to examine the circumstances of the withdrawal from the Danewerke.[7]

In Copenhagen, relations between de Meza and Lundbye became more acrimonious each day, de Meza at one point threatening to make their correspondence public. This was the final straw for Lundbye, who insisted that he must now go. The King did not wish de Meza's departure, but Monrad then declared the matter a Cabinet issue. Rather than lose his entire government, Christian capitulated. De Meza's luck had finally and irrevocably run out. By a Royal Order of February 28th, he was formally dismissed. With him went any chance of a flexible defence at Dybbøl.

The Approach to Dybbøl

Unaware of the indignation in the capital, the Army continued its withdrawal, 4th Division and 7th Regiment pulling back into Jutland, and the main body to the

3   Johansen, & Nordentoft, *Hæren ved Danevirke,*p .343.
4   Jensen, N.P., pp. 174-175
5   Schioldann-Nielsen, pp. 106-107.
6   Jensen, N.P., pp. 174-175.
7   Ibid, pp. 176-177. The eventual conclusions exonerated de Meza.

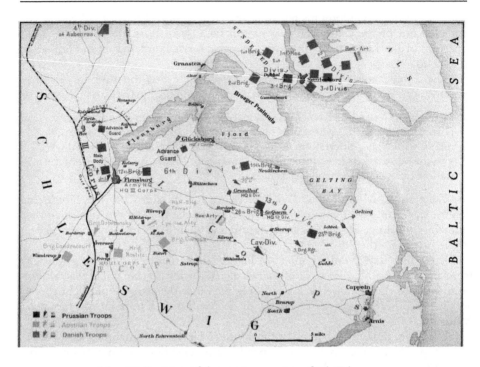

Map 10: Position of the armies, evening of 7th February

Sundeved Peninsula and the island of Als, just beyond. By the evening of the 7th, this latter movement was largely complete. The Allies, meanwhile, remained largely in their positions of the previous night, resting and reorganising, only the Prussian Advance Guard pushing its outposts about 5 miles north of Flensburg.. The surprise retreat by the Danes had caught them unawares, and its success rendered all their previous operational planning irrelevant. A Royal Cabinet Order of February 11th sent Lieutenant-General Moltke to Schleswig, to report to the King on the conduct of future operations.[8]

The defences at Dybbøl, in the Sundeved, at this time were limited to the ten redoubts, numbered I to X from south to north, which contained 84 pieces of ordnance (effective February 7th).[9] Trenches and communications between them, and to the rear, were soon undertaken.

"Dybbøl is abandoned! The Danes have taken ship to Als!" This cry echoed through the streets of Flensburg on the evening of February 9th, and it was doubtless believed by many.[10] That day, the Prussians had begun probing the extent and depth of defence of the Dybbøl position, at this stage not knowing whether or not their enemy would make stand here.

8   Moltke, *Militärische Korrespondenz*, p. 82.
9   See Appendix VII for details.
10 Knorr, *Von Düppel bis zur Waffenruhe*, Hamburg 1864, p. 1.

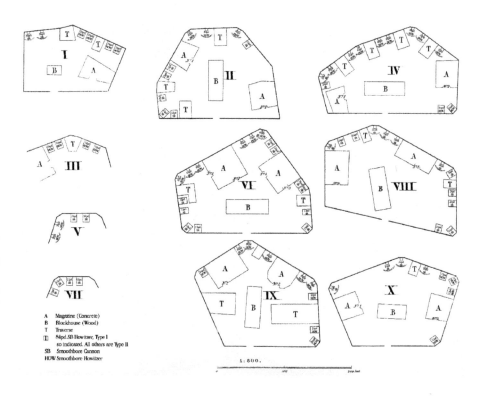

Map 11: The Dybbøl Redoubts, early February

At 06:00 on the 9th February, III Corps' commander, General von der Mülbe, ordered a reconnaisance towards Dybbøl. Consequently, 6 and 7/3rd Foot Guards accompanied by 1/6th Cuirassier Regiment, Rittmeister von Rauch, all commanded by Major von Barby, were sent towards the towns of Graasten and Nybøl. The weather was very poor, with heavy wind-blown snowfalls reducing visibility. On reaching Graasten, the infantry halted and occupied the town and castle. The cuirassiers moved on alone. Immediately west of Nybøl, they surprised and captured a Danish dragoon post of a corporal and three men, who had allowed them to approach in the murk, thinking that they were part of the retreating army. Playing on their luck, one troop of the cuirassiers moved on into the town, where shots were fired at them. They managed to withdraw without loss, bringing six prisoners of the Danish 18th Infantry Regiment with them. The squadron then pulled back to Graasten with their captives.

When the captured dragoon corporal was interrogated, he said that he and his men had been posted in that position since the 7th. Asked about the situation of the Danish Army, he stated that it was moving to Als.[11] Field Marshal Wrangel commanded that a further operation take place the next day.[12] It was the start of almost two weeks of constant aggressive probing.

The following morning, at 09:00, Major von Beeren, commanding officer of I/4GGR (Augusta), ordered his 2/4GGR, Captain von Arnim, to undertake another reconnaissance towards Nybøl. Arnim soon encountered forward posts (one platoon) of the Danish 8/18th Regiment spread out behind knicks. He immediately attacked these, and drove them back into the wooded area called the Bøffelkobbel, where they remained. The Prussians had one NCO wounded, the Danes, one man killed and two wounded.

Shortly after this incident, the force ordered by the Field Marshal was assembled at Graasten, to attempt to gauge the extent of the defensive position and whether it was occupied by the Danes. Comprising Lieutenant-Colonel Liebeherr's I/3rd Foot Guards, two guns from the 3rd Guard 6 Pounder Battery, Captain Reinhardt, and 12 men of the Guard Hussars, the force then moved off. The main body headed towards West Sottrup, five miles to the north-east, intending to continue to Ragebøl village beyond, whilst the 4/3rd Foot Guards moved to Adsbøl and towards Nybøl. The latter soon encountered von Arnim's company, which had just had its skirmish, and went no further.

The main force pushed on towards West Sottrup. Reaching there, the hussars bumped into a Danish patrol of one NCO and nine men of the 5/4th Dragoons. These immediately attacked and drove the hussars back, taking two of them prisoner. The dragoons stopped their pursuit as they approached supporting Prussian infantry near Tørvemosegaard (farm), a mile south of West Sottrup, having one of their own men captured.

The Prussian infantry approached Tørevemosegaard at 12:00, driving in the Danish pickets of 2/2nd Infantry, Captain B.F.J. Thorkelin, and attacking the farm where the rest of his company was, whilst it was also shelled by their two accompanying guns. The Prussians were lucky to have appeared at just the time when Thorkelin's company was in the process of being relieved by 5/5th Regiment, Premierlieutenant Ravn. The two companies were forced to withdraw towards Ragebøl Wood, some 1400 yards to the east, and were driven there in some confusion, Thorkelin himself being wounded.[13] The firing died away around 15:00. Liebeherr's force was back at Graasten by 16:30. Prussian losses totalled 16 – two killed, one officer (Premier-Lieutenant Herwarth) and 11 men wounded, and two men taken prisoner. Danish casualties totalled 38, six men killed, one officer (Captain Thorkelin) and 26 men wounded (two captured) and six

11 Sørensen, Carl Th, *Den anden Slesvigske Krig*, Volume II Copenhagen 1883, p.14. The corporal was wrong – not all of the Army would cross to the island.

12 There was to be little or no pro-active defence by the Danes. Schøller comments that the Prussians, "…had the possibility to take the initiative, whereas we had to await it.", p.28. It is not clear why this had to be the case, and would not have been so with de Meza in command.

13 Rockstroh, K.C., *Fortællinger af 2. Battailons History 1657-1907*, Copenhagen 1907, p. 84.

unwounded prisoners. Of the total, 26 were from Thorkelin's company. Certainly, not all of the Danes had yet withdrawn to Als.[14]

Having established that the enemy was still in the Sundeved, I Corps began its concentration in the area. During the 11th, 6th Division made its headquarters at the castle of Graasten. Elements of 13th Division reached Hønsnap, a little under 7 miles from there.

At Dybbøl, a fixed duty period for the Danish force was established from February 11th. Other than Fortress Artillery, Engineers, and 4th Infantry Regiment, on the Kjær Peninsula (on Als), twelve infantry regiments, six squadrons, and nine field artillery batteries were available for service there. The initial rotation schedule was three days in the position, and six days in camp on Als.[15] The deployment of troops was to be as follows:

In Sundeved - One regiment deployed as outposts from the Vemmingbund in the south, along the south and west sides of the wood known as the Bøffelkobbel, north past the west face of Stenderup Wood and marsh, then north of the village of Ragebøl to Als Sound.

One regiment in support, with one battalion at Dybbøl Church, and the other at (West) Dybbøl village.

One regiment manning the Redoubt Line, with one battalion in the main line, and the other in reserve immediately behind it.

Two squadrons (after 19th February, one) stationed behind the fortifications as pickets, and also for use as orderlies and for patrol duties.

Two guns of a field artillery battery deployed on the Flensburg Road (after February 15th, another two on the Aabenraa Road).

Sønderborg - Two regiments as main reserve.[16]

An important factor in the defence here was to prove the appointment of a commander of the outpost line. Although standard procedure, this was a peculiar arrangement, which took operational control out of the hands of the normal command structure, and would cause innumerable problems, as it had at Selk and Jagel on February 3rd.[17]

On February 15th, Field Marshal Wrangel ordered that I Corps, "...continue its operations against Dybbøl, and will from the 17th expand its quarters to Flensburg, Aabenraa, and west of the main road to Tinglev."[18] It was stressed that the Prince should tie up as many Danish troops as possible, to allow II and III Corps freedom of movement to the west and north.[19]

14 Grosser Generalstab, Volume I, pp. 211-212.

15 See Appendix IX for details of the rotation of infantry units at Dybbøl.

16 Generalstaben, Volume II, p. 119,

17 See Johansen, Jens, *Dybbøl 1864*, pp. 57-60.

18 Grosser Generalstab, Volume I, p. 227.

19 On February 15th, there were 26,223 Danish combatants (effectives) at Dybbøl/Als, out of a total of almost 43,000 – see Appendix VIII. Generalstaben, *Statistiske Medellelser*, Volume I, p. 54, gives the total as 42,885, of whom 26,537 were at

Although there were differing views as to the nature that operations on the Sundeved should take, senior officers at Allied Headquarters were agreed that the Broager Peninsula, on the southern flank of the Dybbøl fortifications, should be occupied. Prussian heavy artillery posted on the Gammelmark heights (some 180 feet) here would pose a grave threat to the Danish position. Friedrich Carl planned to throw a bridge across the Egernsund to Broager at its narrowest point, between Alnor and Egernsund village. A battery of three rifled twelve pounders was constructed at Alnor on the 15/16th, with another battery at Adsbøl. In the early evening of the 16th, two battalions of Canstein's 11th Brigade were ferried across to the Broager. These units, II/IR60, Lieutenant-Colonel Becker, and F/IR60, Major von der Lundt, rapidly occupied Egernsund, established pickets some 650 yards to the east, and scouted almost to Smøl.

The next morning, eight officers, 29 NCOs, and 272 men from 3rd and 7th Pioneer Battalions built a 150 yard pontoon bridge across the Egernsund.[20] Under the direction of Captain Krause, they completed this work in only two hours.

In order to establish any line of circumvallation of the Danish position, it would be necessary for senior artillery and engineer officers to examine the Danish defences from a distance of no more than about a mile. A reconnaissance was planned for the 18th. Colonel Colomier, and Lieutenant-Colonel von Kriegsheim, I Corps' senior artillery and engineer officers respectively were to undertake it, though only from the Broager Peninsula, some distance away.

The Danish High Command had recognised the grave threat posed by an enemy occupation of that peninsula and the commander of naval forces in the western Baltic, (Naval) Captain F. Muxoll, was requested to send the turreted ironclad *Rolf Krake*, (Naval) Captain H. P. Rothe, to destroy the pontoon bridge.

Rolf Krake herself had only been a short time in the area, as described in a letter by the commander of her forward turret, Lieutenant Mariboe:

> Nine days ago (Feb 10) we left the roads at Copenhagen, and sailed, in concert with the *Dagmar*, to Sønderborg. Our crew only came on board the morning of our departure. The men were unpractised, and had rarely been under fire. On the evening of the 17th, we heard that we were next morning to see what was to be done against a bridge, which the enemy had thrown across at Egernsund, shortening the route to Broagerland and the position at Dybbøl. At 7 AM on the 18th we left Sønderborg, and steered for Flensburg Bay (sic).[21]

Entering Flensburg Fjord, the ironclad was heavily shelled by the battery at Holdnæs, but did not answer fire. She steamed to a point 1,400 yards off Egernsund, and anchored. The bridge was not visible from this point, but the vessel's draught of 10' 6" would not allow her any further. At 09:30, she opened fire with her four 68 pounders on the battery of three rifled 12 pounders at Alnor, commanded by Captain Kipping, Magdeburg Artillery Brigade Nr. 4. Two

Dybbøl/Als. Moltke's estimate of Danish strenth at the end of the month was a 'maximum of 34,000'; *Militärische Korrespondenz*, letter Nr. 40 to Colonel Blumenthal, 28th February 1864.

20 Winterfeld, Volume 1, 147.
21 *The Times*, March 9th, 1864

additional guns of the same calibre were hurried from Holnæs to join Kipping. Lieutenant Mariboe takes up the story:

> Here, we anchored, with our broadside towards two fixed batteries, which opened upon us a murderous fire with round shot, conical shell, and shrapnel. A tongue of land prevented our seeing the bridge we had been ordered to destroy. The enemy fired very well. His fixed batteries were masked, and it is therefore impossible to say how much damage we did him; but I sent a couple of shells at a rifled gun that rained conical shot upon us from the heights, and when sheering off bombarded a mill and a house. We returned to Sønderborg after being engaged an hour and a half.[22]

The duel actually lasted until around 10:45, without the *Rolf Krake* doing any serious damage to the artillery positions. She was forced to withdraw, being unable to close with and destroy the pontoon bridge. The ironclad had been hit by about 100 rounds. One man was wounded and Lieutenant Mariboe and two men were lightly injured. 264 shells had been fired at her, and she had sent 57 in return.[23] The lieutenant describes the effect of the Prussian fire on the ship:

> The *Rolf Krake* stood the test well. She was hulled 66 times, each shot being of itself sufficient to sink a wooden ship. The towers (turrets) were hit several times; 16 shots went through the funnel, one through the steampipe, two through the foremast, one through the mizzen, and from 60 to 70 through the bulwarks, small boats, sails, and rigging. The deck is torn up in many places, the tackle much cut, the three boats riddled; every vulnerable point was hit, and I should like to have seen any part of the deck where a man could have been sta-

Prussian 12 pounder 'Beach' battery at Alnor, which engaged *Rolf Krake* on February 18th (Voss)

22 Ibid
23 Generalstaben, *Den dansk-tyske Krig 1864*, Copenhagen, 1891 Volume II, pp. 128-129. Jensen, *Den Anden Slesvigske Krig 1864*, 1900, says one officer and one man, p.228.

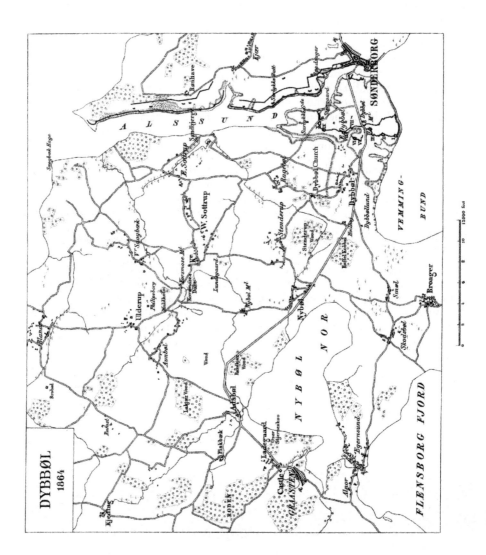

Map 12: The Dybbøl area

tioned without the certainty of death. We calculated that about 5000 lb of iron were expended on us, and you may suppose that we contributed our share. The noise was deafening, produced as much by our fire as the missiles of the enemy, whose shells flew about in all directions. One, which burst directly over the tower in which I was stationed, sent a shower of pieces, which set fire to two mattresses, damaged my frontispiece, grazed my leg, smashed my telescope, and penetrated a coat lying by my side in half a dozen places. I am still deaf of one ear from the din, otherwise not too much hurt. One man in each tower was also slightly wounded, and, curiously enough, each in the left cheek.[24]

Upon the approach of *Rolf Krake*, Prince Friedrich Carl feared that a major Danish sortie against the weak force covering the reconnaissance on the Broager Peninsula might take place at the same time. He ordered Major-General Roeder to move significant elements of his brigade forward through Nybøl to forestall any such movement by launching attacks of his own, with Canstein already pushing troops north from Smøl. Brigade Goeben was to demonstrate on the left.

The Danish outpost line consisted of the 17th Regiment, Colonel A. Bernstorff, just relieving 3rd Regiment, Major H. Mathiesen, which was pulling back to occupy the main line. 17th Regiment was spread from north and east of Ragebøl Wood, west and south around Stenderup Wood and the Bøffelkobbel before swinging back to the Vemmingbund. Behind the outpost line was deployed 16th Regiment, Major C. Wolle, with I/16th at Dybbøl Church, and II/16th immediately west of (West) Dybbøl village.[25]

In the sector of the line east and south of Stenderup Wood, 3/17th Regiment, Captain C.W. Frost, was deployed as outposts. Two platoons were placed in Stenderup Wood, one on the main Sønderborg Road at the farm of Østerskovgaarde, and one south of the road in front of the Bøffelkobbel. Frost's company, at most 200 men, covered a front of about 1¼ miles.[26] 5/17th, Premierlieutenant B. Aarøe, stood between the Bøffelkobbel and the Vemmingbund in two outposts, each of two platoons. Supporting these units, 1/17th, Premierlieutenant E. Troiel, and 2/17th, Captain J. Gandil, were posted at the farm of Hvilhøi, on the main road east of the Bøffelkobbel, and 7/17th, Premierlieutenant J. Nielsen, also east of the Bøffelkobbel on the road from Smøl.

At 09:00, on a clear frosty morning, Roeder advanced I/IR64, Major Hüner von Wostrowsky, along the main road towards the Bøffelkobbel, with II/IR64, Major Kramer, on their left, moving through Stenderup towards Stenderup Wood. It was intended that the battalions would link up east of the Bøffelkobbel, at Hvilhøi. Major Hüner's battalion, was accompanied by two guns of 3rd 12 Pounder/Artillery Brigade Nr. 3, Premier-Lieutenant Müller. Two troops of 4/11th Uhlans accompanied each battalion.

Skilfully exploiting the terrain, moving from knick to knick, the Prussians were able to mask their advance.[27] Major Kramer's battalion was first to make contact, moving in heavy skirmish lines, and rapidly driving the two Danish platoons in Stenderup Wood back to Dybbøl Church.

Further south, near Østerskovgaarde, a barricade blocked the main road. The defending platoon here, commanded by Second-Lieutenant E.C. Hoffmann, opened a lively fire on the approaching Prussians, killing one, wounding five others, and shooting the horse from under IR64's commander, Colonel von Kamienski. Premier-Lieutenant Müller moved his two 12 pounders forward to

---

24   *The Times,* March 9th, 1864.

25   One company of each was assigned work duty in the Redoubt Line.

26   Johansen, J. *Dybbøl 1864*, p. 63. 17th Regiment's strength was 1,628 effectives on February 16th – Anon., *Bidrag til 17 Battalions Historie 1657-1907*, p.50.

27   Bjørk, Kiær, & Norrie, p. 254.

Combat at Nybøl, 18th February
(*Illustrierte Kriegs-Berichte aus Schleswig-Holstein 1864*)

about 325 yards from the barricade, and opened a rapid fire on it. After 18 rounds, the defenders withdrew, leaving one dead and three wounded.[28]

The Prussian infantry both north and south of the main road rapidly stormed into the Bøffelkobbel, capturing the wounded Lieutenant Hoffmann and most of his platoon. The platoon of 3rd Regiment, which Hoffmann had just relieved, also came under heavy fire as it pulled back towards the main line. The shaken and badly outnumbered Danes withdrew to West Dybbøl. The outposts west and south of the Bøffelkobbel had a clear view of the approaching enemy (the pickets of Canstein's brigade), and were able to retreat to the heights of the Avnbjerg with little difficulty. The fighting was over by 10:30.

Considering that no interference with the planned reconnaissance could now take place, Canstein and Roeder withdrew their troops to their original positions, first clearing up the mess in the Bøffelkobbel and Stenderup Wood. They did, however, take the opportunity to extend the Prussian outpost line from Nybøl Lagoon to the Vemmingbund. North of Stenderup, Major-General Goeben's demonstration was largely uneventful, elements of IR15 and IR55 exchanging a few rifle shots with the Danish outposts.

Whilst Friedrich Carl had launched his pre-emptive strike out of concern that a Danish attack might take place, General Lüttichau, who had had no such intention, believed himself to be under attack. He ordered 1st Brigade from Sønderborg, and held 6th Infantry Regiment and 8th Field Artillery Battery in readiness for action. Equally unaware of his enemy's intentions, between 13:00 and 14:00, he ordered General Gerlach to retake Stenderup Wood, which had,

28 Müller, H. von, *Kriegerisches und Friedliches aus den Feldzügen von 1864, 1866, und 1870/71*, Berlin 1909, p. 21.

along with the Bøffelkobbel, been abandoned by the Prussians some time before.[29] Both woods were then once again occupied.

The reconnaissance itself was undertaken from the heights around the village of Dynt on the Broager Peninsula. Although some information could be gleaned, it was of no great use since it was almost 2½ miles from the nearest redoubt.[30]

The losses of the day were extremely one sided, reflecting both the vulnerability of the Danish left flank, the complete surprise achieved and the disparity in numbers at the main point of contact. The total number of Danish troops taking part was 1,819,[31] most of them hardly at all. In the main fighting in the two wooded areas, two battalions of IR64 – perhaps 1200 men, outnumbered their surprised opponents by three to one or more.

Prussian losses totalled two killed and ten wounded. In contrast, Danish casualties were 102. 3rd Infantry Regiment lost one man killed, two wounded (one of them captured), and 22 unwounded prisoners. 17th Regiment lost two NCOs and 12 men killed, two officers (one captured), one NCO, and 33 men wounded (eight captured), and 13 unwounded prisoners. In addition, one NCO and 12 men of the regiment from Schleswig took the opportunity to desert or allowed themselves to be captured. One artilleryman was also wounded.[32]

The following day, Lieutenant-General Lüttichau issued formal orders on the manner in which the redoubts would be defended. These were:

> Each Redoubt, including the rear Bridgehead, will be defended by forces stipulated by the High Command.
>
> Whilst the commander of the artillery detachments in the Redoubts have sole responsibility for the direction of the artillery, the oldest ranking officer in the Redoubt will take overall command in the case of an enemy attack.
>
> At the time of taking command of the individual Redoubt, and in the daily hand-over of command, the new commander must ensure that everything is in order, that the gates can be shut, and the bridge retracted etc. Any issues must be reported, and if of a serious nature, must be reported without delay to the immediate superiors.

That morning, the newly arrived 3rd (Brandenburg) Jäger Battalion, Major von Witzleben, was added to the Prussian force on the Broager Peninsula, bringing it to a total of four battalions, one squadron, and one mobile battery (6 guns). To secure the safety of the pontoon bridge, another new arrival, 1st 6 Pounder/Artillery Brigade Nr. 3 was emplaced west of Egernsund Mill, also on the Broager.[33] The six rifled 12 pounders sited west of the sound near Alnor were moved to two new positions, each of three guns, at Sandager about 2¼ miles to the south.

29 Generalstaben, Volume II, p. 130.
30 Rüstow, pp. 345-346, says, "It is a complete mystery to us what they were supposed to look for and see there."
31 Generalstaben, *Statistiske Meddelelser*, p.136.
32 Generalstaben, Volume II, Appendix 11.
33 Both of these units were part of the recently mobilised 5th Division, Lieutenant-General von Tümpling.

A smaller reconnaissance of the position had also been ordered by Friedrich Carl the same day. Colonels Colomier and Kriegsheim were to examine the Danish left flank covered by Jäger Battalion Nr. 7. The move fizzled out, however, amidst heavy snowfalls. Danish casualties amounted to two wounded from the 17th Regiment. One Prussian Jäger was also wounded.

A further effort to test the defences was made on the 20th, by General Goeben's 26th Brigade. That morning, three Prussian columns moved forward on a wide front towards the Danish centre and right, north of the Sønderborg Road. Farthest north, at 09:30, Lieutenant-Colonel von der Goltz led 5/IR15, and one officer and 27 men each from 6, 7, and 8/IR15, along with a troop of Westphalian Dragoons, from Blans towards East Sottrup and Sandbjerg, on Als Sound. Major von Böcking, leading 1/IR55, 11/IR55, ½ 12/IR55, and a troop of dragoons, left West Sottrup and hour and a quarter later, moving east along the Sottrup-Sønderborg Road towards West Dybbøl and Ragebøl. Finally, Major von Rex, with 10/IR55 and eight dragoons, advanced from near West Sottrup towards Stenderup, covering the right flank of the movement[34].

Once again the attempt was hindered by poor weather, including further snowfalls. The latter, however, permitted Goeben's troops to surprise the Danish outposts. In the swirling snow, three Prussians were wounded, whilst four Danes were killed, and 11 wounded. The conditions once again assured that the reconnaissance itself was a failure.

The weather on February 21st was a considerable improvement. As on the previous day, units of the 26th Brigade probed the Danish right flank, this time much more information being gleaned. A move by 8/IR15, Captain von der Reck, and two platoons of 6/IR15 was successful in occupying Sandbjerg Mill, on Als Sound. There were no losses to either side.

Back at the Danewerke, as recommended by General von Moltke three days earlier, the demolition of the entire works began on the 21st. Initially, 100 Austrian pioneers and 400 civilian labourers worked on the project. Subsequently, some Danish prisoners of war were also put to work on it. Much of the reusable material from the fortifications would soon be used in the operations in the Sundeved Peninsula.[35]

A major, overall reconnaissance was ordered for February 22nd, its prime purpose being the capture and retention of the vulnerable Bøffelkobbel and to reconnoitre, as far as possible, the main defences. A force of 12 battalions, three squadrons, and 26 guns was detailed for the task, about 8,000 men.[36] Friedrich Carl's orders, issued on the evening of the 21st, read:

> Tomorrow, at dawn, a strong reconnaissance force will be thrown out against the Bøffelkobbel and the redoubts at Dybbøl. The Division Manstein will, at 07:00, attack the Bøffelkobbel from Smøl and Stenderup Wood from Stenderup. The division will be reinforced with a rifled battery from the Reserve Artillery.

34 Waldersee, p.128, & Grosser Generalstab, Volume I, p. 227.
35 Report Nr 23, *Die Befreiung Schleswig-Holsteins im Jahre 1864. Nachden Berichten des Königl. Staats-Anzeigers zusammengestellt,* Berlin 1864.
36 Rüstow, pp. 349-350.

At the same time, the Division Wintzingerode will advance Brigade Goeben over Sottrup to Ragebøl, to support Division Manstein's attack. Brigade Goeben will deploy at Sandbjerg. Brigade Schmid will follow as reserve, and will, at 07:00, deploy between Ulderup and Sottrup.

The Advance Guard will concentrate at Feldsted and march to Fiskebæke, at which point they will deploy at 09:00.

Only a few troops of cavalry will follow to serve as patrols and scouts.

The Reserve Artillery will remain in their camps, and the outposts in their positions.

The Commanding General will be at Broager.

This movement was not intended to repeat the error of the 18th, when simply not enough troops were used.

Facing this divisional sized attack, one Danish infantry regiment, the 18th, was thinly spread in the outpost lines, its two battalions covering a distance of some 4½ miles, as with 17th Regiment four days earlier.[37] Six platoons (2/18th, Premierlieutnant F.V Bruun, and one platoon each from 1/18th and 7/18th) formed the forward posts of Major Lundbye's I/18th, two north of the Sønderborg Road, two west of the Bøffelkobbel, and two south of that wood. The remaining 2½ companies were deployed in support, three platoons of 7/18th, Premierlieutenant Ahlmann, at Dybbøllund, and 5/18th Premierlieutenant Lommer with three platoons of 1/18th, Captain Baller, at Hvilhøi.

II/18th, Captain Wehye, was equally stretched on the right flank, though less vulnerable than Lundbye. His forward posts comprised two platoons of 4/18th between the Ravnskøbbel and Ragebøl Wood, two platoons of 8/18th, Premierlieutenant Bentzon, at the Aabenraa Road, and the other two north-west of Ragebøl village. Two platoons of 6/18th continued the line west to link with Lundbye's troops. Supporting these were the other two platoons of 4/18th, Captain Volqvartz at Lillemølle (mill), 3/18th, Premierlieutenant Nielsen, at Ragebøl Inn, and the remaining half of 6/18th, Premierlieutenant Madsen, between Dybbøl Church and Ragebøl.

Behind the 18th, the 22nd Regiment was in support, II/22nd, concentrated west of West Dybbøl village, 3 and 4/22nd near Dybbøl Church, and 1/22nd and 2/22nd south-east of the village of Ragebøl. Four field guns were held in support outside the main line, two just in front of Redoubt X, near the Aabenraa Road, and two in the village of West Dybbøl. Manning the main redoubt line was the 2nd Regiment. One squadron was also immediately available, 5/4th Dragoons, Ritmester Sommer, about 75 men. Including the artillery in the fortifications, these totalled under 3,500 men, though of course, many more could be brought forward to defend the main line if necessary.[38]

From the Broager, Canstein advanced towards the Bøffelkobbel and Hvilhøi with four battalions (FR35, Colonel Elstermann – minus 7/FR35 – and 3rd Jäger Battalion, Major von Witzleben), 2/11th Uhlans, Rittmeister von Kleist, 2nd 12

---

37 Further detailed information was gleaned from two men of the 18th Regiment, both Schleswigers, who deserted to the Prussians the previous evening; Bjørke, Kiær, & Norrie, p. 258.

38 Generalstaben, *Statistiske Meddelelser...*, p.136, gives the number of troops involved as 3,472.

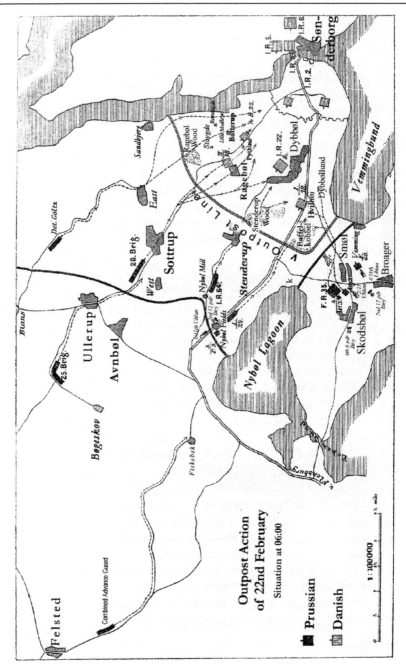

Map 13: Dybbøl - Action of 22nd February

Pounder/Artillery Brigade Nr. 3, and 4/3rd Pioneers. Brigade Roeder, commanded by Colonel Kamienski,[39] advanced I/IR24, Major Grumblow, 1/11th Uhlans, Rittmeister v. Rauch, and Premier-Lieutenant Müller's 3rd 12 Pounder/Artillery Brigade 3, along the main road from Nybøl towards the Bøffelkobbel. The three battalions of IR64 were to move through Stenderup and Stenderup Wood. Further north, Brigade Goeben was to advance four of its five battalions through East and West Sottrup to Ragebøl.[40]

Snow fell overnight, and early morning Danish patrols did not encounter any enemy movements. The Prussian operation began between 06:30 and 07:00, beginning on the Danish left and was screened by fog and further snow showers.[41]

On the Prussian right, complete surprise was achieved, and Major Witzleben's Jäger swept into the Bøffelkobbel from the south, whilst Grumblow's I/IR24 pushed into it from the north-west, and IR64 from Stenderup and Stenderup Wood. There was pandemonium in the wood. Major Witzleben led 2/3rd Jäger, Captain von Erckert, and 3/3rd, Captain von Henning, into the wood's south-east corner. The two west-facing platoons of 1/18th were cut off and forced to surrender, about 80 men being captured.[42] South of the wood, Major Kellermeister von der Lundt's III/FR35, attacked towards Hvilhøi. Hearing heavy firing and realising that his forward posts would be crushed by such a major attack, Major Lundbye despatched a dragoon orderly to inform the outposts to retreat. Unfortunately, the trooper was killed before delivering all of the orders.

9/FR35, Captain von Kirschy, drove in the Danish outpost south of the Bøffelkobbel, driving them north. This move was supported on the left, by Captain Erckert's Jäger company, and 4/3rd Jäger, Captain Paczinsky. Premierlieutenant Bruun, commander of 2/18th, at a farmstead near the north-east corner of the Bøffelkobbel, was fired upon from Hvilhøi. Thinking it to be an accident, he climbed up on a fence and shouted, "Can't you see we're Danish!?", to be almost immediately shot and mortally wounded. As IR64 advanced south from Stenderup, elements of Major von Hartmann's F/IR64 encountered the Danish troops withdrawing from Hvilhøi. These were driven back towards (West) Dybbøl village, some of the men from South Schleswig taking the opportunity to desert.[43] 18th Regiment's southernmost forward posts, nearest the Vemmingbund, were able to withdraw safely, Premierlieutenant Ahlmann retreating with the three platoons of his 7/18th to the commanding heights of the 185 foot Avnbjerg.

At about 07:45, Major von der Lundt decided that, contrary to General Manstein's orders, he would assault the Avnbjerg, since some of his troops had already gone further than intended, in which case the withdrawal to come would

39 Roeder himself was sick.
40 II/IR55 was still in Flensburg.
41 Isenburg, *Brandenburg Füsilier-Regiment Nr. 35 1815-1870*, Berlin 1879, p. 239. The snow became heavier during the morning.
42 Shortly afterwards, two of Paczinsky's men were killed in an accidental exchange of fire with elements of IR64; Kusserow, L., *Geschichte des Brandenburgischen Jäger Bataillons Nr. 3 und des Magdeburgischen Jäger Bataillons Nr. 4 von 1815 bis 1865*, Berlin 1865, pp. 138-139.
43 Bjørke, Kiær, & Norrie, p. 258.

Prussian reconnaissance in force at Dybbøl, 22nd February, viewed from the east. The wood of 'Bøffelkobbel' is seen in the distance to the west (Larsen & Dumreicher)

be subject to flanking fire. Consequently, three of his companies moved forward and took the height at 08:00, under heavy fire from Ahlmann's defending troops.[44]

On the Prussian left, at 07:00, I/IR 55, Major von Bocking, and F/IR55, Major von Rex supported by two guns of 4th 12 Pounder/Artillery Brigade Nr. 7, pushed south-east along the Aabenraa Road towards Ragebøl. Following behind were I/IR15, Major Baron von der Horst, F/IR15, Captain Preuss von Sandberg, four guns of the same battery, and 4/7th Pioneer Battalion. Accompanying the column, escorted by a troop of dragoons, was the divisional commander, Lieutenant-General Wintzingerode. North of this column, Lieutenant-Colonel von der Goltz took three companies of his II/IR15, and two guns of 1st 6 Pounder/Artillery Brigade Nr. 7, from East Sottrup partly through Ragebøl Wood and partly to the left of it.

At the head of the main column marched 3/IR55, Captain von Gerhardt. The company engaged the two Danish platoons on the Aabenraa Road, throwing these back, and then came into action with their supports north of the village. Captain Weyhe, II/18th Regiment's commander, requested the two companies of 22nd Regiment at the Pythuse to support him. Before they could do so, however, Weyhe was driven from Ragebøl, and Goltz' force took Stavegaarde on the right. In the fighting for Ragebøl, four of the five officers of 3/IR15 became casualties.

Under fire from Goltz' two guns, the Danish outposts on the right pulled back to a distance of about 450 yards between Redoubts IX and X. For the first time,

44 Isenburg, pp. 241-242, Grosser Generalstab, Volume I, p. 293.

Troops of 3rd Brandenburg Jäger Battalion, taken at Dybbøl, 22nd February (Bremen)

heavy guns in the Redoubt Line opened fire in support, along with the two field guns along the Aabenraa Road, halting any further Prussian advance in the north.[45]

At around 09:00, Prince Friedrich Carl ordered a general withdrawal to the previous positions, other than the outposts. The troops were back in their camps by noon. Although the thinly stretched Danish forward posts had received a severe handling, heavy snowfalls had also prevented a thorough reconnaissance.[46] Even so, the Danish outpost line had been driven in about a mile and a quarter in the south, and some ¾ of a mile to the north. It now ran approximately north-east from the Avnbjerg to Randsgaard. The whole Redoubt Line had fired fewer than 30 rounds during the entire day in support of the infantry, mostly on the right flank, where its brief intervention had produced an immediate result.[47]

Both sides had learned some interesting lessons. Three days later, an article appeared in a Prussian journal, lauding the performance of the Prussian infantry, most especially their skill in skirmishing and their adeptness at taking cover. This was contrasted with the Austrian inclination to over-expose their troops, resulting in higher casualties.[48]

Casualties in this one-sided affair were in an approximate ratio of ten to one against the Danes. The factor of surprise and weight of numbers explains much of the difference, as do the factors mentioned above, and, to an extent, the more rapid fire of the Prussian breechloading riles.

Table 13

Prussian Casualties during the Reconnaissance Operation around Dybbøl February 22nd 1864

Prussian: 37[49]

---

45 Rüstow, p. 350.
46 Ibid, p. 351.
47 Schøller, F., *Forsvaret af Dybbølstillingen I 1864*, Copenhagen 1867, p. 33.
48 Anon, "Fechtweise der Preußischen und österreichischen Infanterie", *Militärische Blätter*, Volume 12, Nr. 8, Berlin 1864.
49 Grosser Generalstab, Volume I, Appendix 26.

Unit	Killed Officers	Men	Wounded Officers	Men	Prisoners Officers	Men	Missing Officers	Men
11th Brigade	—	—	—	—	—	—	—	—
III/FR35	—	1	—	10	—	—	—	—
Jäger Battalion Nr. 3	—	2	—	1	—	—	—	—
12th Brigade	—	—	—	—	—	—	—	—
IR64	—	—	—	1	—	—	—	—
26th Brigade	—	—	—	—	—	—	—	—
IR15	—	3	4	14	—	—	—	—
IR55	—	—	—	1	—	—	—	—
Totals	—	6	4	27	—	—	—	—

Table 14

Danish Casualties during the Reconnaissance Operation around Dybbøl, February 22nd 1864

Danish: 382[50]

Unit	Killed Officers	Men	Wounded Officers	Men	Prisoners Officers	Men	Missing Officers	Men
1st Brigade Staff	1	—	—	—	—	—	—	—
18th Infantry Regiment	1	23	3	18	2 (1 W)	141 (5 W)	—	85[51]
22nd Infantry Regiment	—	36	3	39	—	24 (5 W)	—	2
4th Dragoon Regiment	—	2	—	1	—	1	—	—
Totals	2	61	6	58	2	166	—	87

W = Wounded

Whilst the defenders had now, after two weeks, been hustled away from the Broager Peninsula and towards the fortifications, it was clear that they had no intention of retreating from Sundeved. How the Prussian High Command would react to this was uncertain to everyone.

---

50 Generalstaben, Volume II, Appendix 13.
51 Most of these were Schleswiger deserters.

Austrian Jäger band playing outside Allied Headquarters in Haderslev
(Illustrated London News)

6

To the Jutland Frontier and Minor Operations

North Slesvig and Jutland, February to Early March

With the retreat from the Danewerke accomplished, Danish forces had withdrawn from the whole of the mainland of the Duchy other than the Sundeved Peninsula. It was not until February 15th, however, that the Prussian 5/4GGR, Captain Dejanicz von Glyszczinski and 8/4GGR, Captain von Studnitz, occupied the abandoned fortress of Friedrichstadt, at the mouth of the River Eider. General von Moltke reported the following day that the fortress was in a good state, and defensible against any Danish attack.[1]

To the north, the Danish 3rd and 4th Divisions had pulled back into Jutland. Upon arrival in the area of Kolding, at the western tip of the fjord of that name, just inside the Kingdom, on February 9th Lieutenant-General Hegermann-Lindencrone requested further instructions. The following day, the Army Commander, now Lieutenant-General Lüttichau, sent him the following message:

> The 4th Division must keep the border of Jutland occupied inasmuch as its strength allows. The commanding general has decided to give control of the 3rd Division to General Hegermann, as long as it operates in conjunction with the 4th Division. The 8th and 9th Brigades, under Colonel Neergaard, are today sailing to Fredericia. Colonel Neergaard has been provided with orders to report to General Hegermann, and, under these orders, to move forward from Fredericia as soon as the troops are ready to march.
>
> In the case of an attack on Fredericia, 3rd Division units are to retire there, and the 4th Division, with 7th regiment, to North Jutland. The Espignol Battery will, when no longer required by the Division, be sent to Fredericia. When possible, the remainder of the 3rd Division will be transported there. For the movement of the depleted trains and 2nd Dragoon Regiment, transport resources are to be sent to Fredericia.[2]

Although these orders were clear, they were optimistic. In fact, due to demands upon overstretched resources and very poor weather, the entire operation was not completed until the 12th. Furthermore, since only a part of 3rd Division

---

1   Moltke, H. von, *Militärische Korrespondenz*, Letter Nr. 36 to the War Ministry, 18th February 1864. In the same letter, he also advised the immediate destruction of the entire Danewerke fortifications.

2   Generalstaben, Volume I, p. 312.

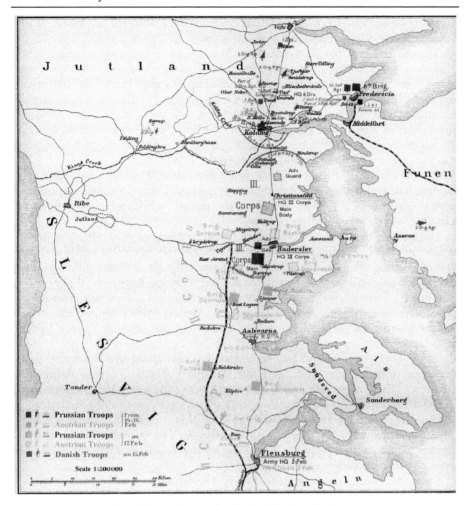

Map 14: Situation, excluding Dybbøl, mid February
Note: Immediately to the lower right of the symbol for Brigade Nostitz, and to the right
of the village of Gjenner, is an unnamed island. This is Barsø. Also, directly under the
letter 'r' in Gondrecourt (Brig. Gondrecourt), is the village of Halk.

was at first sent to Jutland, Hegermann was very weak in infantry, having only 10
battalions (8th Brigade, 9th Brigade, and 7th Regiment).[3]

In the meanwhile, Allied II and III Corps were advancing north. Anticipating
that he could cross the border by the 17th, Field Marshal Wrangel, from Allied
Army Headquarters at Haderslev, reported this to Berlin on the February 14,

3   Ibid, pp. 312-3. The rest of 3rd Division would follow, but by then the situation had
     changed. 7th Brigade arrived in Fredericia on February 20th. The command structure
     in Jutland was further complicated by the fact that Major-General Lunding, the fortress
     commander at Fredericia, considered that his status was equal to that of Hegermann,
     since both reported directly to the War Minister.

requesting permission to do so. Political developments, though, had not kept up with the rapid change in military circumstances.

The Austro-Prussian Convention of January 16th had only agreed a joint occupation of Schleswig, not a violation of the Kingdom of Denmark itself. After the removal of Danish troops from the Danewerke, Emperor Franz Josef had made clear to the Prussian Minister in Vienna that he would not sanction the advance of his troops into Jutland. On February 15th, Count Karolyi the Austrian Ambassador in Berlin had a meeting with Minister-President Bismarck, making clear his government's view that any infringement of the borders of the Kingdom would require a new understanding between the Allies.

On the morning of the 16th, the King telegraphed Wrangel with orders that his operations were to be limited to the territory of the Duchy, although for morale reasons, this was not communicated to the troops.[4] Obviously, some form of incident could only be a matter of time.

Hegermann and Colonel Neergaard had already planned to withdraw in the face of any major Prussian attack. They would certainly not risk a battle over the town of Kolding. The defence of the border was assigned to Colonel Neergaard's own 9th Brigade and three squadrons of the 3rd Dragoon Regiment. By February 17th, the 4th Division was posted in the shallow Alminde Valley, 6½ miles north of the town, with 8th Brigade assembling in Fredericia that evening.

Neergaard's 19th Regiment was now near the hamlet of Gudso, some 7 miles north-east of Kolding, with four guns of the 5th Field Artillery Battery. 3/19th Regiment, Captain J. Darre, was posted as outposts along the Kolding Creek, which ran south of the town, and into the fjord. 3/3rd Dragoon Regiment, Ritmester C. Bruhn, patrolled the area to the west of the town. II/21st Regiment, 1/3 and 2/3rd Dragoons and four Espignols, which were moved to Kolding during the day, that evening were pulled back to Nørre Bjert, two miles to the north-east, with I/21st further north, a little south of Herslev. The outposts were informed that they were to withdraw in the face of any serious attack, or if flanked by enemy troops crossing Kolding Creek to the west.[5]

On the same date, Allied Army Headquarters was established at Christiansfeld, only some 10 miles south of Kolding (Wrangel returned to Haderslev the following day), with the whole of the Prussian Guard Division (III Corps) concentrated in the area, and II Corps to their left and rear. Upon hearing of the continued Allied advance, Hegermann and Neergaard on the evening of the 17th, made the dispositions above-mentioned which were tantamount to abandoning Kolding.[6]

At 08:00, Captain Darre received word, from Ritmester Bruhn, that a Prussian force had appeared at the village of Lejrskov, 4½ miles west of Kolding, and *NORTH* of Kolding Creek.[7] At 09:00, Bruhn reported that he could see Prussian troops to the south. Bruhn requested permission to withdraw northward at around 11:00, and did so shortly afterwards. Darre pulled out of Kolding at

4   Grosser Generalstab, Volume I, p. 231.
5   Vaupell, p. 293.
6   They had clearly decided to do so, Vaupell, p. 292.
7   Ibid, p. 293, and Bjørke, Kjær, & Norrie, p.216. Crucially, these reports were incorrect.

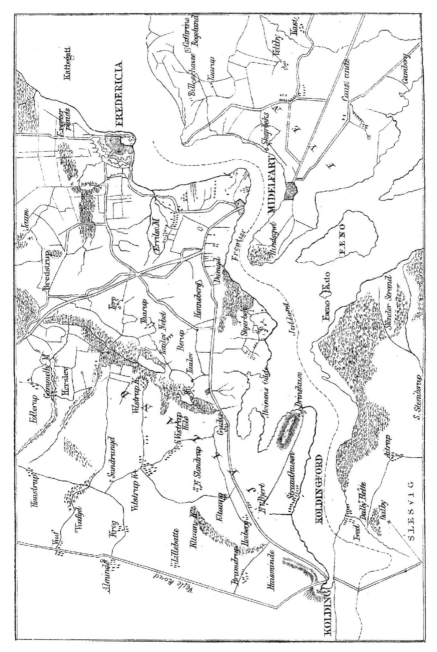

Map 15: General area between Kolding and Fredericia

12:30, moving north-east towards Nørre Bjert, linking up with the outpost company of 21st Regiment, and continued the retreat.

On the morning of 18th, Prussian pickets from 2/4th Foot Guards, had discovered that the village of Vonsild, only two miles south of Kolding, was unoccupied by the Danes. The Advance Guard commander, Colonel Bentheim immediately reported this to the Guard Division commander, General von der Mülbe, who ordered an immediate reconnaissance towards Kolding. By 10:20, this information was in the hands of the Field Marshal Wrangel, in Aabenraa. The Field Marshal was asked if he instructed otherwise.[8] He did not do so.

General Staff Major von Alvensleben was ordered forward with 1 and 3/Guard Hussars. Reaching the town, Alvensleben found it abandoned, sending back word of this. The two squadrons then pushed on north-east along the Fredericia Road. Colonel Bentheim and the rest of the Advance Guard entered the town at 13:00.

The Guard Hussars came up with elements of the 2/3rd Dragoons, Ritmester Scholten, who were also pulling back, and pushed them further in a short skirmish. At about 14:00, however, their advance was halted by the fire of Captain Darre's 3/19th near Nørre Bjert. The hussars withdrew, and rode back to Kolding. Danish losses in this skirmish were two killed and three prisoners (all wounded). Prussian casualties totalled one officer and four men wounded.

A major diplomatic storm erupted over the violation of the frontier of the Kingdom proper. The event took Bismarck himself by surprise, though he rapidly recovered his equilibrium. He subsequently declared the occupation of the town as being necessary in view of the capture by Danish warships of German shipping on the high seas. The outrage was greatest in London, where rumours were also rife as to the despatch of an Austrian naval squadron from the Mediterranean to the North Sea. Although the British public and press called for action on Denmark's behalf, neither the Cabinet nor the Queen would countenance any more hostile act than the recall to home waters of the Channel Squadron.[9]

On February 21st, Lieutenant-General Edwin von Manteuffel was sent from Berlin to Vienna to convince the Austrian Government of the necessity of occupying Jutland, a measure which General von Moltke had recommended five days earlier. The fact that Prussian troops had already occupied a town within the Kingdom without any serious consequences would considerably ease his task. Conversely the complete lack of resistance to a crossing of the border in spite of specific orders to do so was disastrous for the Danes.[10]

After matters calmed somewhat, and no further Prussian advance appeared imminent, a realignment of the Danish defences took place. With the arrival in Jutland of the remaining elements of 3rd Division, the deployment on the mainland (outside the Sundeved) was as follows:

8   Grosser Generalstab, Volume I, p. 235.
9   Steefel, p. 201, & Sandiford, pp. 199-201.
10   Vaupell, p. 295 is scathing about the affair. He says, "We must conclude that the enemy only occupied Kolding because we left the town voluntarily."

Table 15: Danish Forces on the Mainland (Outside the Sundeved), Late February 1864

At Fredericia

Fortress Command, Fredericia	Espignol Battery, 1st, 2nd and 5th Fortress Artillery Companies, 2nd and 4th Engineer Companies

3rd Division

Infantry	8th Brigade, 9th Brigade, 13th Regiment, 14th Regiment
Cavalry	2nd Dragoon Regiment, 1st Half-Regiment-4th Dragoon Regiment
Artillery	3rd, 6th, and 12th Field Artillery Batteries
Total Strength (early March)	Approximately 13,000 effectives.[11]

Elsewhere

4th Division

Infantry	(Attached from 2nd Division) II/7th Regiment, (Attached from 3rd Division) 7th Brigade – deployed from Greis south to Vejle, I/7th Regiment, in detachments west of Vejle
Cavalry	1st Cavalry Brigade, in detachments west and north-west of Vejle, 2nd Cavalry Brigade, in detachments north-east of Vejle
Artillery	½ 5th Field Artillery Battery, with 1st Cavalry Brigade
	½ 5th Field Artillery Battery, with 2nd Cavalry Brigade
Engineers	3rd Engineer Company, at Vejle
Total strength (1st March)	Approximately 6,500 effectives.[12]

Along the 'border' between Schleswig and Jutland, there was almost a *de-facto* truce after the Prussian occupation of Kolding. The Danes were content to remain in position, and without the political will to undertake further operations in the area, there was little for the Allies to do. Both sides still sent out cavalry patrols, but these did not often come into contact.

11 Jensen, p. 216. Approximately 1,000 additional men from some of these units were on the island of Funen.
12 Johansen, J., & Nordentoft, J., *4de Division I Nørrejylland 1864*, Copenhagen 1936, p.88.

Dragoon Niels Kjeldsen (Liljefalck & Lütken)

On February 28th, however, a picket of the Danish 4/6th Dragoons, Ritmester H. Sehested, had a forward post of one corporal and six men at Viuf, on the Kolding-Vejle road some two miles north of Kolding (see map above). This picket was attacked at 10:00 by a detachment of 12 Prussian Guard Hussars under Ensign Count Lüttichau. Lüttichau's detachment was itself the advance guard of a troop of 40 men, commanded by Second-Lieutenant Count Wartensleben, leading a squadron of the regiment north from Kolding. The dragoons made a desperate attempt to reach their main force at Højen Inn, two and a half miles to the north, but were overtaken by the hussars' faster horses.

The corporal and two dragoons were able to escape, but three others (one of them wounded) were taken prisoner. The final man, Trooper Niels Kjendsen, fought single handed against his foes until killed by a pistol shot from the young Count Lüttichau. This incident is celebrated in Danish folklore to this day.

The following day, a much larger skirmish occurred south of the village of Vorbasse, west-south-west of Vejle, ten miles north of Estrup. Having developed Danish patrols in the area on February 26th and 27th, Lieutenant-Colonel von Rantzau, commanding officer of the 8th (Westphalian) Hussars had now also learned from local inhabitants that a Danish dragoon squadron was quartered there.[13]

He devised a scheme to take this unit by surprise on the early morning of the 29th using two of his own squadrons, some 300 men. 2/8th, Premier-Lieutenant von Thaden, was instructed to proceed from Skandrup via Anst and Gjesten to Bække where it would join 4/8th, Rittmeister von Grodzki, which would come via Lejrskov, Ravnholt and Kragelund. From here the united force was to move on Vorbasse.

The Danish squadron based in Vorbasse, 3/5th Dragoons (104 men),[14] Ritmester E.E. Moe, was resting in the vicinity of the town, unaware that any major enemy moves were known of or expected. Normal precautions were in place. Half of the squadron, commanded by Second-Lieutenant W. Sauerbrey was billeted at a farm immediately north of Bække, with a picket to the south. Moe was at Vorbasse with the other half squadron.

13 Grosser Generalstab, Volume I, pp. 323-325, and Vaupell, pp 297-298.
14 Liljefalck & Lütken, p. 187.

The Prussian raid took place as planned, on the morning of the 29th. Leaving three troops of 2/8th Hussars as a reserve at Bække, the remaining five troops of hussars moved on to surprise the dragoon outpost at 11:30, capturing two men. The rest of the Danish outpost galloped back towards the farm to raise the alarm, although the carbine fire had already been heard by the main force.

Sauerbrey's troops at the farm (21 men) were engaged in a horse inspection, and thus completely unready for action, and he himself was some few hundred yards south of there with the remainder. Nevertheless, every man who could mount did so, in all states of dress, and some saddle-less. Somehow this desperate assault repulsed the main Prussian force, which retreated to Baekke, some troopers falling from their horses and being taken prisoner.

From Bække, the hussars' reserve of three troops, assuming the rag-tag half squadron to be the sum total of their enemy, moved forward, only to be attacked by Moe's half squadron which had hurriedly been summoned from Vorbasse. The Prussian hussars were unceremoniously bundled backwards.

The action was over by 12:30 and with the Prussians withdrawing, Moe was not disposed to attempt a pursuit of a force, which he now realised was at least two full squadrons.

Moe's squadron lost one man mortally wounded, five wounded, and two taken prisoner (one wounded) in addition to the loss of five horses. The "Blue Hussars" had one killed, three wounded, and one officer (wounded) and 32 men captured (four wounded), along with the loss of 23 horses. The unfortunate Second-Lieutenant Hällmigt thus became the first Prussian officer to be taken prisoner during the conflict.[15]

The result of this small clash made Field Marshal Wrangel furious, and he had orders issued by his headquarters forbidding any further such incursions into Jutland.[16] The entire strategic situation along the border, however, was soon to change.

General von Manteuffel's mission to Vienna had been a success. The Austrian government was now prepared to allow its troops to take part in a full-blown invasion of Jutland. For the Danes, the consequences of the failure to offer even a token defence of the border on February 18th would not go away.

Minor Operations, March-May

Consistent pressure on the Danish High Command from the War Ministry for offensive action led to some odd adventures. At 15:00 on March 4th, two companies of the Life Guards Infantry embarked in the steamer *Freya*, which then sailed from Copenhagen for Kiel Bay, on the coast of Holstein to conduct a 'raid'. 1/Life Guards, Captain Nægler and 4/Life Guards, Captain Herskind, were to make a descent on the town of Hohwacht, and march inland from there a little over five miles to Lütjenburg and back. There might also be further landings, dependent upon the circumstances. *Freya* rendezvoused with her escort, the steam corvette

---

15 Of him, Field Marshal Wrangel said, "I hope he is dead!" – Rustow, p.373.

16 von Fischer, pp. 170-171. He carefully does NOT mention the size of the enemy force. Contemporary Prussian accounts regularly exaggerated the number of men available to Ritmester Moe. General von Moltke himself mentions the skirmish in one of his letters, calling it, "…most disagreeable…" Moltke, *Korrespondenz*, Letter Nr. 42 to Colonel von Blumenthal, 4th March 1864, p. 95.

Dagmar, Commander G.F.G. Wrisberg, at midday, on the 5th, and the two vessels proceeded towards the north Holstein coast.

They arrived in the area off Hohwacht on March 6th, but no landing there could be effected in the prevailing poor weather. It proved possible to land one platoon of 50 men, some six miles to the east, near the village of Putlos. Even here, however, the men had to wade in water up to their waists. In any case, the decision was taken not to disembark any more men since there were no enemy troops in the area. There were, in fact, no Prussian troops anywhere in the vicinity.

Once the weather had abated, the platoon ashore was re-embarked, and the vessels returned to Hohwacht, to make a further attempt. On the passage, however, they ran into a cold front, with rain and snow. Since the orders for the enterprise allowed only a few days for its execution, the operation was called off, and the troops returned to Zealand.

The Loss of Fehmarn

The island of Fehmarn, though a part of the Duchy of Schleswig, lies just off the north coast of Holstein, its nearest point being less than 2000 yards from the mainland (see main map). On the outbreak of hostilities, it was defended by the screw gunboat *Krieger*, Lieutenant L. Braag (two 30 pounders). Braag's primary duty was the blockade of the port of Heiligenhafen, on the mainlaind west of Fehmarn. During February, a few troops were sent to the island, and in mid-March, the military 'garrison' comprised 111 men. This figure includes a requisition party there to collect 26 horses, and seven non-combatants.[17] The most senior officer present was Gendarmerie Ritmester Benzon. The naval picture was slightly brighter, since *Krieger* had been joined by the gunboats *Marstrand*, Lieutenant MacDougall, and *Buhl*, Lieutenant P.H. Braëhm. Both vessels were similarly armed to *Krieger*.

The Prussian forces in Holstein, in an uncomfortable and sometimes tense joint-occupation of with the original 'Execution' troops from Hanover and Saxony, were mainly of the 5th Division, Lieutenant-General von Tümpling. The eastern coast of Holstein was primarily patrolled by Major-General Schlegell's (Combined) 9th Brigade. Tümpling had learned of the small size of the Danish force on Fehmarn and came up with a plan to take it using one of Schlegell's regiments, IR48, Colonel von Tiedemann, supported by part of the division's artillery.

The troops were concentrated in the area of Heiligenhafen during the 13th and 14th of March. On the night of 14/15th March, this plan was put into action. Tümpling, suddenly getting cold feet about the Danish gunboats, sent a message to von Schlegell that the time was not right for the attack, but by the time it reached him, the movement was already under way.

---

17 Premierlieutenant Tersløw, two NCOs, and 24 men of the Copenhagen Garrison Battalion, 62 men of the 14th Infantry Regiment, one officer (Second-Lieutenant Baggesen), one NCO, and 13 men of the 4th Dragoons. The non-combatants were an officer (Benzon), one NCO, and three men of the Gendarmerie, an official, and a military labourer. Generalstaben, *Statistiske Meddelelser angaaende den danske Krigsmagt*, Volume I, pp. 105, 113, 125 & 129.

II/IR48, Major Zglinicki, was to undertake the crossing from the Ferry House of Heiligenhafen. Two other companies were to be held in reserve there. Overnight, a battery was constructed either side of the Ferry House, under the direction of Lieutenant-Colonel von Scherbening. Each contained three smoothbore 12 pounders, and two 7 pound howitzers, to cover the crossing.

First to cross, at 05:00, was 8/IR48, Captain von Mellenthin. His company had a strength of four officers, 13 NCOs, five musicians, 137 men, and one ambulance soldier.[18] Making good time in the boats, they landed and overwhelmed a shore watch of one Undercorporal and six men, and by 06:30 were at the main town of Burg. Attacking from several directions, Mellenthin's troops, after a few shots from the defender's vedettes, captured all the defenders, mostly still in their quarters.

Following behind the first wave, 5/IR48, Captain Kassner, accompanied by the battalion commander, were slowed in their crossing by a storm, and were still being rowed across at daybreak. The boats were seen by the gunboat *Krieger* at around 07:00. The vessel fired 10 shots intended as the alarm signal for the island's defenders. The Prussian battery at the Heiligenhafen Ferry House opened fire on *Krieger*, whereupon Lieutenant Braag withdrew his vessel.[19]

On Fehmarn, 7/IR48, Premier-Lieutenant von Kamecke, followed the two other companies ashore, but there was then a delay, due to the utter exhaustion of the boats crews. The island was soon fully occupied without further resistance. Prussian casualties were one man killed, and five wounded. One Dane was killed, a Gendarmerie NCO, and all of the remainder captured, one being wounded.[20]

Buhl sailed the following day for Sønderborg to report the loss of the island. The Danish prisoners were shipped to the mainland the same day.

Field Marshal Wrangel initially wished to abandon Fehmarn, but an appeal by General Schlegell and local people changed his mind. Prussian troops remained, and by the end of the month, the island's garrison was one battalion, one battery and one squadron.

Aaroe's *Streikorps*, March/April

(See map above for these operations)

Very much in keeping with the constant urgings from Copenhagen to take the war to the enemy was an idea previously submitted by a serving officer. 36 year old Premierlieutenant Bendt Aarøe, an infantry company commander in the 17th Regiment, had before the war proposed the formation of a mixed arms inter-service force for the purpose of reconnaissance, raiding, interference with enemy communications, supplies, and the like. Aarøe, never lacking in self-confidence, had submitted his plan direct to the War Minister the previous year, to be considered in the event of hostilities. Now, influenced by the small successes of two 'unofficial' units operating largely independently under Hegermann-Lindencrone in Jutland, it was dusted off, and approved by the Army High Command on March 23rd.

18 Mellenthin, X. von, *Jungens holt Fast. Der Überfall auf Fehmarn*, Berlin 1914, p. 88.
19 Lütken, Otto, *Søkrigsbeivenhederne i 1864*, Copenhagen 1896, p. 97.
20 Ibid, p. 34. Prussian figures for prisoners are slightly higher than the Danish garrison, at four officers and 116 men, the difference primarily being that five sailors from the gunboat *Krieger* and three from a transport vessel were sick in Burg that night.

The 'Aarøe *Streifkorps*', commanded by the Premierlieutenant himself, was initially composed of one officer and 24 dragoons seconded from the 4th Dragoon Regiment, and 100 men from the 2nd Infantry Regiment, and at first quartered at Stegsvig, near Nordborg on the northern part of the island of Als. By the end of March, with further additions, including a group of Scandinavian volunteers posted to the unit, its organisation was as follows:

Table 16

Organisation of Aarøe's *Streifkorps*, March 1864

Commander	Premierlieutenant Aarøe
Swedish/Norwegian Infantry Detachment	Premierlieutenant Baron von Raab
	Two sergeants
	Two corporals
	36 undercorporals and men
Danish Infantry Detachment	Second-Lieutenant Bjerager
	Two officers
	Three corporals
	143 undercorporals and men
Cavalry Detachment	Second-Lieutenant Baumann
	Two NCOs
	22 dragoons

In addition, the following vessels were attached to Aarøe's 'Corps':
Steamer *Aurora*
Steam Tug *Marie*
'Iron Troop Transport Vessel Nr. 5'
    The force was also promised full naval co-operation for its operations.[21]
    The force sailed from Als on the evening of March 31st, for the island of Funen, where it was to set up its base at Assens. From here it would have the task of harassing Allied troops on the east coast of the mainland. On April 1st, some 30 men sailed, aboard *Aurora* and *Marie*, with supplies and matériel, to the island of Barsø, at the mouth of Gjenner Bay. Here, they set up a small advanced base for use on operations. The men then returned to Assens.[22]
    With the focus of Allied operations centred on Dybbøl/Als, and secondary considerations concentrated on Fredericia, there were few troops, and no infantry

21 Esmann, N.C., *Det Aarøe'ske Strejfkorps i 1864*, Copenhagen 1884, pp.4-7. Inter-service co-operation was very good in this instance – a rarity in 1864. It should be noted that the 'Corps' was not in any form an elite force. There were few experienced NCOs. The Swedish and Norwegian volunteers could sometimes be wild and undisciplined, and required careful handling.
22 Ibid, p. 7.

available to act as coast watch along the Little Belt.[23] By early April, the only troops in the area were a squadron of dragoons at Aabenraa (1/7th), where lay the main Prussian magazine, and 4/11th Uhlans, Premier-Lieutenant von Bülow. This single squadron was responsible for the entire coastline of some 30 miles between that town and Allied Army Headquarters in Haderslev to the north.

Bülow placed his squadron headquarters in the village of Hoptrup, on the main road between the two towns, where a supply depot was already located. The majority of his troops were spread in small detachments in the hamlets along the coast. With such a large area to cover, he had no choice, and, in any case, there was little concern about offensive moves by the Danes.

Hearing of these dispositions, Aarøe resolved to launch his first raid on the village of Gjenner and the small islet of Kalvø at the westernmost point of Gjenner Bay, north-east of Aabenraa. It was believed that some 30 Prussians were billeted in the area. The move was set for the night of April 4/5th.

The operation went awry at the beginning. The *Marie*, towing 'Iron Troop Vessel Nr. 5', grounded on the mud between Kalvø and the mainland. Some troops went ashore, but the surprise was lost. Shots were exchanged in the mutual chaos. The attackers were fortunate to be able to refloat the vessels and withdraw. The little flotilla steamed back to Assens, arriving at 12:00.[24]

Although there were no concrete achievements from the attempt, news of it created pandemonium at Prussian headquarters. Wild rumours spread as to the size of the force, and it was even supposed that the undertaking was to be in conjunction with a major sortie from Fredericia. Concern for the munitions at Aabenraa was such that next morning 3½ battalions, a squadron, and 8 guns were despatched to the town.[25]

Possibly the very fact that the enemy had made an offensive move at all worried the Allies most, since coastal landings which might interfere with their long and vulnerable lines of communications was always a fear. At least in the Baltic, the Danes could always move troops by sea without interference.

After a reconnaissance of the area, and orders from headquarters, Aarøe's next project was to be a descent upon Aarøsund, on the mainland directly west of Assens, in the lee of the island of Aarø. The operation was scheduled for the night of the 8/9th, and began at 23:30. Commanded by Second-Lieutenant Baumann, three other officers, one senior sergeant, and 40 men were loaded into four barges, and towed by *Marie* to the island. From here, they rowed to the mainland intending to ambush the Prussian coast watch near the Ferry House.

Once again, however, bad luck plagued the expedition. Difficult terrain forced the attackers to alter their route, and approach along the beach. The uhlans were able to escape. The force returned to Assens at 07:45, with nothing to show for their efforts.

Undeterred by previous mishaps, Aarøe immediately planned a return visit to Gjenner Bay. This time, however, his target was the hamlet of Løjt Kirkeby, south of Kalvø island, some three miles south of the landing site. It was known that some

23 Waldersee, p. 258.
24 Esmann, pp. 8-10.
25 von Fischer, p.249. Five platoons of Austrian pioneers, who were in the general area,
    were also sent.

Prussian troops were billetted there. This raid would take place over night on the 10/11th. The force, commanded by Premierlieutenant Baron Raab, would comprise Second-Lieutenants Baumann and Bjerager, Senior Sergeant Andersen, and 53 men (31 Danish and 22 Swedish/Norwegian).

The expedition left Assens at 20:30 on the 9th, *Marie* towing four boats. The force reached the advanced base on Barsø island. *Marie* left the force there, and returned to Assens, with instructions to return on the night of the 11th. The troops stayed on Barsø until 21:00 on the 10th, and then rowed from there to the landing point at 02:00. Disembarking, the troops made their way to Løjt Kirkeby.

The raid was a complete surprise, the houses of the small village quickly cleared, and by 04:00, the force was on its way back to Barsø. Five prisoners were taken in the raid, Premier-Lieutenant Baron von Strombeck, one NCO, one trumpeter, and two men.[26] The *Marie* returned to pick up the raiders at 21:00 on the 11th, and returned in triumph to Assens.

Meanwhile, Headquarters had issued new instructions to Premierlieutenant Aarøe on the 10th, extending his area of operations southwards, and giving him a largely free hand to implement them. There were two especially significant points made in these orders:[27]

Firstly they made clear that,

Any information on enemy deployment, movements, planned operations, the state of his troops, etc, must, as soon as it becomes known to the Corps, be brought to the attention of both Army Headquarters and the nearest military authorities to whom it may have importance.

Secondly:

The High Command authorises operations in the areas of Halk Head, Gjenner, Flensburg, and Eckernforde, and also draws your attention to Broager, which is at present believed to be lightly fortified. At the time these operations commence, the Corps will relocate to Als.

Whilst the descent on Løjt Kirkeby was taking place, Aarøe had been surveying possible landing places, and an operation was planned for the night of 13/14th, which he would command himself. The objective was the capture of an uhlan picket at the village of Halk, about seven miles south-east of Haderslev.

Aarøe's raiding force consisted of Premierlieutenant Raab, Second-Lieutenants Bjerager, Dohlmann, and Baumann, two NCOs and 50 men. *Aurora, Marie* and seven boats were used to transport the troops. The flotilla left Assens at 21:00, on the 13th, landing the troops at Halk Head at 02:00. Aarøe was fortunate enough to encounter an officer and 11 uhlans, who had just returned from patrol. He immediately attacked. The officer and six of his men were able to mount their horses and escape, but the remaining five Prussians were captured, together with their

---

26 Generalstaben, Volume II, p. 290. German language sources insist that the total was six. von Fischer, p. 249, Waldersee, p.260.

27 Generalstaben, Volume II, Appendix 38. It is clear that the High Command was trying to focus Aarøe's attention towards Dybbøl, where direct intervention was now of critical importance. The order to move the base of operations is plain, as is the reference to Broager.

horses, and taken back to the boats. There had been some confusion amongst the Scandinavian volunteers, but the raiding party was soon back under control, and withdrew in good order. The expedition returned to Assens with its captives, and without loss.

After a reconnaissance of Ørosund on the 15th, Aarøe decided upon an undertaking on an altogether different scale. The next raid would involve the entire 'Corps'. It was now known to him of the existence of the Prussian depot at Hoptrup, and this became his next target. The 'Corps' would first capture uhlan pickets at the coastal village of Sønderballe, on the north side of Gjenner Bay. It would then move on to destroy the depot some three miles to the north-west. This ambitious venture was scheduled for the night of 17/18th April. Aarøe also hoped that the move might draw enemy troops north from Dybbøl. He could not know that the final preparations for the Prussian attack on Dybbøl would be made that same night.

The *Streifkorps* sailed from Assens at 23:00 on April 17th. *Aurora*, *Marie*, 'Iron Transport Vessel Nr. 5', and four boats carried the raiders to the landing beach. As the troops rowed ashore, they were greeted with pistol shots from an uhlan patrol. Any hope of surprise was lost.

Equally unknown to Aarøe, a new Prussian brigade had arrived in the theatre of war. 21st Brigade, Major-General Bornstedt, on route to General Münster in Jutland, had been held temporarily in North Slesvig. The dragoons captured two Prussian uhlans, but then encountered Prussian infantry for the first time, a platoon of 5/GR10, commanded by Second-Lieutenant von Montowt, by chance being in Hoptrup that night. Second-Lieutenant Baumann's horse was shot from beneath him. The dragoons withdrew to the main force. Aarøe's troops had a brief skirmish with the Prussian infantry. Once again, confusion occurred before order was restored, and the force withdrew. Aarøe was able to return the force to Assens with the two prisoners, having lost two killed and five wounded of his own.

Dybbøl was lost the same day, and the *Streifkorps* was left without a specific operation to support. No further raids were undertaken before the Armistice in May.[28]

28 Aarøe was promoted to Captain on April 17th, Generalstaben, Volume II, p. 291.

7

The Invasion of Jutland

On March 6th, Field Marshal Wrangel finally received authorisation to invade Jutland. Upon his consequent orders during the 7th, II and III Corps were assembled near the border around Kolding, with instructions to advance the following morning. The initial orders were that II Corps would move directly on the town of Vejle, 15 miles to the north. It was not known that General Hegermann-Lindencrone had been ordered to withdraw his 4th Division to Als, and that one of his three infantry regiments was to begin its move during the day. III Corps was to march against Fredericia, some 12 miles to the north-east, a position that the Danes had no intention of leaving, although there was no question of attacking the fortress itself at this stage.

The Action of Fredericia, 8th March

The main Allied forces began their march at 04:00, General von der Mülbe's Guards in the lead. Mülbe's advance guard, under Colonel von Bentheim, consisted of his complete 3GGR, two squadrons of the Guard Hussars, six guns of the Guard 4 Pounder Battery, 1st 6 Pounder/Artillery brigade Nr. 3, and the bridging train. Behind them, came the main body, the 3rd and 4th Foot Guards, three troops of the Guard Hussars, and the 3rd Guard 6 Pounder Battery, all under the command of Major-General von der Goltz. Finally, came the reserve, under Colonel von Oppell, II/4GGR, one troop of Guard Hussars, 4th 12 Pounder Battery/Artillery Brigade Nr. 3, and the Corps Field Hospital. The whole force marched north on the main road to Vejle, and, upon reaching Alminde, turned right towards Fredericia, with the intention of turning the enemy flank.[1]

A supplementary column, under Major von Beeren, with his own I/4GGR, 1/Guard Hussars, and two 4 pounders of the Guard Battery, left Kolding and moved east along the Fredericia Road at 06:00, with the intention of pinning the defence. Just after crossing the southern tip of the Elbo Valley at 08:00, von Beeren developed pickets of 1/20th Regiment, Captain Daue, and 5/20th, Premierlieutenant Steinmann. These companies withdrew before him, performing intricate movements to appear a larger force.[2] Beeren reported that the Danes had abandoned Gudsø, and were withdrawing along the Snoghøi Road, but that there were still enemy troops north of him. Daue and Steinmann pulled back to Børup, where, at 09:00, they met the battalion commander, Major Schack, and 6/20th, Premierlieutenant Riise. Here, they halted. Beeren also halted just west of Børup, performing his task admirably.

In the meanwhile, further north, Mülbe's advance guard reached Havreballe Pass, at about the same time, encountering 8/20th Regiment, Premierlieutenant Willerup. F/3GGR, Major von Röhl, supported by the artillery pushed the badly

1   Winterfeld, Volume I, p. 220.
2   Vaupell, p. 299.

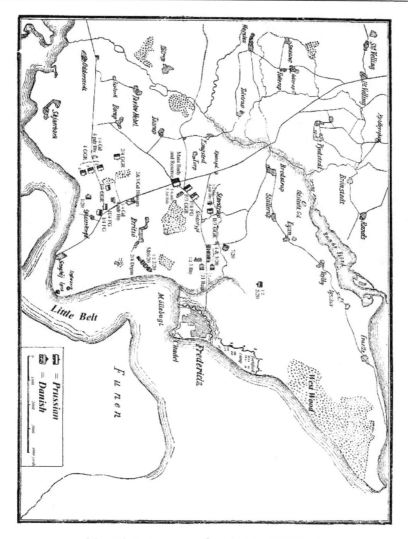

Map 16: Actions west of Fredericia - 8th March

outnumbered Willerup gradually back to Hejse Inn, occupying it at about 10:45. Here, Willerup linked with his support, 3/20th, Premierlieutenant Weien.

Whilst this was happening, Captain Daue, down at Børup, had been listening uneasily to the sounds of battle from the north, to which he drew the attention of the battalion commander, Major Schack. Schack was not greatly concerned at that stage. Daue remonstrated with him:

I turned now to Major Schack, who was still calmly walking backwards and forwards along the main road, and asked him why he had stopped my reserve (from falling back), but he immediately shouted at me that there was no reason to fall back. I then explained my position, and that I was unable to hold it any

Troops of the Danish 20th Regiment engaged with the Prussian Guard west of Fredericia on 8th March (Liljefalck & Lütken)

longer. He then said, 'You must hold it. That's an order.' When I now explained to the Major that he had not been forward and seen the danger of the situation, and insisted that I be allowed to temporarily fall back, perhaps to move forward again later, he finally replied, 'Yes, then you may fall back.' He then added, as if he were displeased with me, 'Perhaps you could pull back through 6th Company.' This, I regarded as an order, but then the Major again burst out, 'There is, in any case, no reason to fall back further.' I asked him if the decision was that I should fall back through 6th Company, and he then finally gave his consent.[3]

First to withdraw, was, in fact, Riise, with 6/20th, followed by Steinmann's 5/20th, leaving Daue to follow. He withdrew to Laadegaard Wood, just west of the Vejle-Snoghøi Road, but halted here at 10:00. In spite of his own concerns, with heavy firing in his right rear, he hesitated before retreating further. It was a fatal mistake.[4]

Major von Beeren had reported that he was still faced by an enemy force, and as a result, Major-General von der Goltz despatched I and II/4th Foot Guards, under Colonel von Korth, south from Hejse Inn, along the Snoghøi Road. By 11:30, Major Schack and his other three companies had withdrawn towards Fredericia, and Daue was surrounded in woods south of the Kolding-Snoghøi Road. The entire company was forced to surrender, having lost two wounded.

Back to the north, Captain Sperling's II/20th had been forced back to Storstrup, where he made a stand, supported by the two guns of 3rd Field Battery.

3   Daue, H., von, "Det 20de Infanteri-Regiments 1ste Compagni under Fægtningen den 8de Marts 1864", *Tidsskrift for Krigsvæsen*, Copenhagen, 1866, p. 239.
4   Vaupell, p. 300.

As the skirmish started here, Major-General Wilster, 3rd Division's commander appeared with his staff, having come forward from Fredericia. A Prussian shell landed amongst them, wounding the General, and mortally wounding Captain Hoffmann, his Chief of Staff. The withdrawal continued to the fortress, the Prussian advance halting along a line between Storstrup and Erritsø. Wary of any possible countermove from Fredericia, General von der Mülbe pulled his troops back to Elbo Valley the next morning.

Casualties in this very one-sided affair were:

Table 17

Prussian Casualties at Fredericia, March 8th 1864

Prussian: Two officers and 18 men

	Killed		Wounded		Prisoners		Missing	
Unit	Officers	Men	Officers	Men	Officers	Men	Officers	Men
3rd Guard Grenadier Regiment (Elisabeth)	—	1	2	13	—	—	—	—
4th Guard Grenadier Regiment (Augusta)	—	1	—	2	—	—	—	—
Guard Hussar Regiment	—	—	—	1	—	—	—	—
Totals	—	2	2	16	—	—	—	—

Table 18

Danish Casualties at Fredericia, March 8th 1864

Danish: Eight officers and 204 men

	Killed		Wounded		Prisoners		Missing	
Unit	Officers	Men	Officers	Men	Officers	Men	Officers	Men
3rd Division Staff	1	—	1	—	—	—	—	—
19th Infantry Regiment	—	—	—	3	—	1W	—	—
20th Infantry Regiment	1	3	1	9	4 (1W)	168 (3W)	—	17
Ambulance and 8th Brigade Magazine	—	—	—	1	—	—	—	2
Totals	2	3	2	13	4 (1W)	169 (4W)	—	19

W = Wounded

The Action of Vejle, 8th March

After the Prussian Guard had left Kolding, between 05:00 and 06:00, II Corps, about 21,000 men, began its march north to Vejle. First to move was Dobrzensky's Cavalry Brigade, followed by Brigade Nostitz, ½ 11th Engineer Company, half of the bridging train, Brigade Gondrecourt, and the Corps Artillery Reserve. This 'right wing' column halted after about 2½ miles, near Bramdrup, to allow the column of FML Neipperg, comprising the rest of the Corps and the Prussian cavalry Brigade of Colonel Fliess, to come level with them, about three miles to the west. Neipperg, however, was seriously delayed in crossing Kolding Creek, due to a sudden rise in the water levels near his crossing point at Eistrup, caused by recent heavy rain. Though he was able to find a ford for the cavalry, not until 11:00 was Neipperg able to get his infantry across.[5] Gablenz' plan for an envelopment of the Danish force at Vejle was thus ruined at the outset, and he was forced to continue with his own column alone, at about 08:00.

Ahead of the main force, General Staff Captain, Count Uexküll, was sent with 6/Windischgrätz Dragoons to scout the area of the advance. At 09:00, the advance patrols of the squadron, as they came out of woods three miles north of Viuf, saw heights to their front, blocking any further view. Uexküll and his aide, escorted by 16 dragoons, moved forward with the intention of gaining an observation from this point, but were surprised at 09:45 by a Danish dragoon outpost of 25 men of 6/6th Dragoons, commanded by Second-Lieutenant Saint Aubain. Uexküll's patrol was quickly bundled back, Oberlieutenant Count Czernin and three of his men wounded and temporarily captured, with Uexküll and a further six men wounded. Saint Aubain had one man wounded. No pursuit was undertaken as he saw the rest of the Austrian squadron to the south. He quickly pulled back to report the presence of enemy cavalry. Initially, the whole of 6/6th Dragoons were then sent forward, as were two platoons of infantry, but once these were fired upon by two guns of Nostitz' Brigade Battery, under Oberlieutenant Schmalz, the force pulled back towards Vejle.

Four volunteers in the Danish 1st Infantry Regiment - from left to right: W. Johansen (Swedish), F. Sorensen , R. E. Ekstrom (Swedish) and O. Boldt (Swedish)
(Liljefalck & Lütken)

5   von Fischer, p. 179.

The position at Vejle consisted of two distinct parts; the forested hills north of the town, and those facing west across Greis Creek. Since these ranges are at right angles to one another, an assault on either enfilades the other. Vejle Creek, from the south, was a considerable obstacle, especially in the then prevailing conditions, but the bridge itself could not be dominated by artillery on the northern heights. The town bridge was the only crossing point, others around the position having been demolished.[6] The slopes rising on both sides of the creek are steep, and the heights to the south, more dominant. Equally, the hills west of Greis Creek dominate those to the east. Hegermann's intention was to defeat any attack upon him, and subsequently retreat to Horsens.[7]

As the Brigades of Nostitz and Gondrecourt marched north, Gablenz ordered frequent halts, both for rest, and to allow straggling elements to catch up. Not until 12:45 were these brigades ready to advance from the woods occupied by the dragoons.[8] An hour later, 7th Brigade's Colonel 'Max' Müller reported to General Hegermann-Lindencrone: "Communications between Fredericia and Vejle are cut off. Intelligence reports suggest that in Blaakær Wood, at least one enemy infantry battalion, 5-6 squadrons, and some guns are stationed. The enemy appears to be bivouacking there for the night."[9]

Without 7th Regiment, General Hegermann-Lindencrone's force at Vejle included only four battalions of infantry, some 3,000 men. His cavalry and artillery added about 2,500 more, with 16 guns. His forces were deployed thus:

1st Cavalry Brigade was stationed west of the town, with most of the 3rd Dragoon Regiment around Bredstrup, 6¼ miles away, one squadron north of this, and 5th Dragoon Regiment further north, with four guns of the 5th Field Artillery Battery. Defending the bridge across Vejle Creek, south of Bredstrup, was 6/1st Regiment, Premierlieutenant (of the War Reserve) Beck. Linking them to the main force at Vejle, 3/1st, Captain Ross, and 4/1st, Captain Povelsen, were positioned at Haraldskjær, almost four miles west of Vejle.

Defending the town, three companies were posted south of the creek. 1/11th, Premierlieutenant Wilhelmi, was placed on the heights facing south, covering each of the three roads to Ribe, Kolding, and Fredericia. 3/11th, Second-Lieutenant Kragh, stood in an entrenched position at the junction of the three roads, with 5/11th, Captain Staggemeier, holding the southern houses of the town, and the bridge, which would be blocked with abbatis on the south, and barricaded on the north side, as soon as friendly units had withdrawn across the creek. One of Staggemeier's platoons was placed north-west of the town at Soph(f)iesminde, covering the road to the west. North of the town, the west facing heights of the valley of Greis Creek were defended by, from north to south, 1/1st, Premierlieutenant Weiss, 2/1st, Captain Stricker, and 7/1st, Premierlieutenant Carl Th. Sørensen. Captain Chabert's II/11th Regiment was posted above the town, all four companies facing south, directly overlooking it. Finally, I/11th Regiment, Captain Count Ahlefeld-Laurvig, was to occupy the east of the position.

6   Tusch, p. 118.
7   Jensen, pp. 252-253.
8   It is also possible that Gablenz had still hoped that Neipperg's column might have been able to make up some time and catch up with him – von Fischer, p.182.
9   Jensen, p. 255.

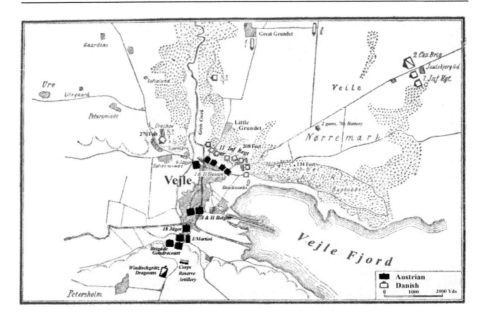

Map 17: Action at Vejle - 8th March

Only 7/11th, retired Captain Bjerregard, was actually there, but the planned deployment was to take place after the three companies south of the Creek abandoned the positions there.

The main position was heavily fortified. 7th Field Artillery Battery, Captain Johansen, had four guns on Little Grundet, sighted across the creek on the heights by the road junction, two guns on the Horsens Road, targeted on the town, and two more in reserve, at the junction of the Horsens and Viborg Roads. About eight miles east of Vejle, was 2nd Cavalry Brigade, with four guns of 5th Field Artillery Battery. Also there was 7th Regiment, which had been on its way to Als, but was halted on the news of the Austrian advance.

At 15:00, the advancing cavalry of Major-General Dobrzensky's cavalry contacted the pickets of 11th Regiment south of Vejle, and the Danish dragoon outposts withdrew through the defences. Soon after, I/Hessen, Major von Taulow, moved forward. Taulow directed 1st division against the heights south of the river. 1/Hessen, Captain Benesch attacked the windmill there, and Captain von Mayern's 2/Hessen, the woods, while Oberlieutenant Schmalz shelled the position with his two guns, placed along the main road. The three defending companies were driven back, and withdrew across the bridge, to take up their positions on the heights north of the town.

With the support of Schmalz's two guns, now on the captured heights, Mayern's company pushed on down the slope into the southern section of the village. With the help of the battalion pioneers, and spite of the heavy fire, they smashed through the obstacles at either end of the bridge, and into the houses of the town, followed by Benesch and his men. A number of defenders were trapped inside buildings in the town before they could escape, and taken prisoner. At about

IR Hessen storming Vejle bridge, 8th March (Pflug)

this time, the other six guns of Nostitz Brigade Battery joined Schmalz, the guns on the hills north and south of Vejle now bombarding one another over the top of the town.[10] Realising the situation, Captain Ahlefeld-Laurvig ordered the evacuation of the town, pulling his troops into the woods to the east.

Ambulance soldier Ludvig Helms, serving in 'Max' Müller's 7th Brigade Ambulance, left his impressions of the action in a letter to an old school friend:

> The affair at Vejle came rather unexpectedly. Before noon, Holmsted and I had driven out on a visit and knew nothing, but as soon as we got back an orderly appeared with a message that we should be ready. We waited and waited. The cavalry positioned itself close by the Juulsbjerg but things stayed calm. In the afternoon the first shells fell on Vejle, wagons came with wounded and we then had to get on with our 'sad business'. It is far from cosy when the cannon thunder outside. One would like to have a little look at the fun, but we had to stay inside, and work on some wounds from shell-fire, which are so terrible that one gets a shiver just thinking about them.[11]

With the cover provided by the guns, Nostitz was able to push his infantry across the creek relatively unhurt by the defenders on the ridges above. Ordered by Gablenz not to attempt a further assault until the infantry of Brigade Gondrecourt could come up, Nostitz posted Benesch's first division (1 and 2/Hessen), and

10   von Fischer, p. 183, Jensen, p. 255. Captain Mayern was awarded the Knight's Cross of the Order of Leopold, for his part in the action.
11   Helms, Ludvig, *Tilbagetoget i Jylland 1864*, compiled by Hege Søgaard, Th. Thrues, Aarhus 1971, pp. 19-20.

Captain von Czako's second (3 and 4/Hessen), to the north end of the village. Captain Achilles Edler von Gröller's third division, with Lieutenant-Colonel, Count Vetter's II/Hessen stood on the eastern edge of town, 9th FJB was sent to the north-west edge, and IR Belgier remained in reserve in the market square. Two of the brigade battery's guns were taken across the bridge, and deployed facing west.

Considering time to be of the essence, Gablenz ordered 9th FJB, Lieutenant-Colonel Schidlach, to outflank the Danish right. This was a difficult undertaking, however, owing to open ground and a canal. Premierlieutenant Carl Th. Sørensen's 7/1st Regiment, was holding this area, as he later wrote:

> In the meantime, the fighting in front of our positions had started; we could hear, but not see it, as our vision to the west was hampered by the steep slopes leading from Lille (Little) Grundet. The fighting intensified and at last we got our little part of it. On the road at Vejle, an Austrian Jäger battalion marched over Stockbro and Gjedebro, on the Varde Road turning towards 7th Company's position west of the creek, a position decided upon for a case like this, some hills, from where the retreat led to a bridge we were building. Then, the Austrians formed a firing line, facing east, flanking 11th Regiment, but the other side of Greis Creek and that part of 7th Company who faced them on that side of the creek. We exchanged some shots with the Austrians, but it was at long range. There was only one place near Vejle, where they tried to cross the creek, but they failed after five or six of them were already in the water. They then kept their distance on the left bank, whilst we, after all our men had crossed to the right bank, were in scattered positions along the bank, behind trees, in thickets, but also, in some places, in close order.[12]

FML Gablenz at Vejle, 8th March (Pflug)

12 Sørensen, Carl Th., *Erindringer fra Første Regiment 1864*, pp. 62-63.

To break this impasse, Gablenz ordered the two 8 pounder batteries of the Corps Reserve Artillery up, and 18th FJB forward in support of Schidlach's battalion. This proved to be the key. The 16 8 pounders, beginning at 16:00, opened a heavy fire on the Danish guns, while 18FJB filed forward through Vejle.

> Whilst Nostitz' troops formed for the attack, Gablenz rode up to them, acclaimed with much cheering. As 18th FJB moved up on Nostitz' left for the flank attack, Gablenz called out to Nostitz' men, 'Today you will be as brave as the valiant 18th!' Referring to 9th FJB, a voice from the ranks of the 18tth shouted, 'Your Excellency, you need two nines to make one 18!' Grinning at the man, Gablenz gave the order for the attack.[13]

At about 17:30, Gablenz ordered a general attack. Hegermann-Lindencrone, who had been considering the situation, also gave orders for a withdrawal around this time. Ludvig Helms recalled the retreat:

> Towards dusk, the firing got alarmingly close, and our Chief Doctor, who is no hero, was of the opinion that it would be best if we left. I was thrown up on to a farmer's wagon to keep a half dead artilleryman alive, in which I succeeded, though with a great deal of trouble. Shells were flying over our heads when we left the Juulsbjerg. We drove to Horsens where I stayed until early the next morning.[14]

Vejle was a spirited little action, in which losses were surprisingly small. Gablenz had a great superiority in numbers over Hegermann, but this could not be exploited until Vejle Creek could be crossed. In the prevailing flood conditions, that could only be achieved at the bridge, the storming of which was a singular feat. Hegermann was also fortunate that these conditions prevented Neipperg's force from carrying out its part of the attack plan. Losses were:

Table 19

Austrian Casualties at Vejle, March 8th 1864

Austrian: Eight officers and 84 men[15]

Unit	Killed		Wounded		Prisoners		Missing	
	Officers	Men	Officers	Men	Officers	Men	Officers	Men
Staff	—	—	—	—	1W	—	—	—
IR Hessen	—	6	2	38	—	—	—	—
IR Belgier	1	5	1	19	—	—	—	—

13 Müller, Alexander, "Sin Stolzer 18er Jäger", *Unter Habsburgs Kriegsbanner*, Volume II, pp. 203-204.
14 Helms, Ludvig, *Tilbagetoget i Jylland 1864*, p. 20.
15 Grosser Generalstab, Volume I, Appendix 36. However, Lieutenant-Colonel Schidlach reports that his 9FJB suffered seven casualties, three of them serious; the latter one would certainly expect to be included. "Relation über das Gefecht bei Veile und die Einnahme der Höhen nördlich dieses Ortes", KA, AFA, March 1864, Document 188.

18 FJB	—	—	2	7	—	—	—	—
Windischgrätz Dragoon Regiment	—	—	1	9	—	—	—	—
Totals	1	11	6	73	1	—	—	—

W = Wounded

Table 20

Danish Casualties at Vejle, March 8th 1864

Danish: Three officers and 176 men[16]

	Killed		Wounded		Prisoners		Missing	
Unit	Officers	Men	Officers	Men	Officers	Men	Officers	Men
1st Infantry Regiment	—	—	—	2	—	3	—	22
11th Infantry Regiment	—	9	2	21	1	111 (3W)	—	5
6th Dragoon Regiment	—	—	—	1	—	—	—	—
7th Field Artillery Battery	—	2	—	—	—	—	—	—
Totals	—	11	2	24	1	114	—	27

W = Wounded

The last shots were fired around 19:00. Hegermann retreated 19 miles to the vicinity of Horsens, the first columns reaching the town at 02:00 on the 9th. Here the division was quartered for what remained of the night. 7th Regiment was billeted in the town, with 11th Regiment, 2nd Cavalry Brigade, and the artillery, to the north across Hansted Creek. Most of 1st Regiment, 1st Cavalry Brigade, and four guns, were spread along the Silkeborg Road to the north-west, with two companies and two squadrons south of the main bodies, something under 10 miles west of the town. These latter troops had retreated directly north from Vejle.[17] Pickets were spread in an arc south of Horsens at a distance of some two miles. The exhausted Austrian troops remained overnight at Vejle. FML Neipperg's weary column did not make it to the town that night.

16 Generalstaben, Volume II, Appendix 4. However, Colonel Schütte's report on the action states that his regiment, IR Hessen, took 319 prisoners – "Über das am 8. März vor Veile stattgehabte Gefecht und die Einnahme von der benannten Stadt", KA, AFA, March 1864, Document 248. Also, the Brigade Chief Doctor for Nostitz' Brigade, Dr. Blohm, in his report states that eight wounded Danes were treated – "Relation über das Gefecht bei Veile", KA, AFA, March 1864, Document 192.

17 Johansen, J., & Nordentoft, J., *4de Division I Nørrejylland*, Copenhagen 1936. pp. 131-133.

4th Division's Retreat to Mors

(see general map – Denmark and the Duchies)

After the fighting the previous day, Gablenz had no intention of a further advance on the 9th. His intention was rest for his men, and for Neipperg's force to catch up. This latter achieved, II Corps stayed in position until the 11th, sending cavalry patrols towards Horsens. A muster of March 10th showed the Corps fighting strength to be 17,147 out of a total of 25,088 men.[18]

Equally, Hegermann had no intention of remaining in Horsens. During the afternoon of the 9th, he began receiving reports of enemy troops along the Horsens-Vejle Road. Fearful of a further attack in overwhelming force, at 21:45 that evening, he ordered a retreat north to Skanderborg. At midday on the 10th, an *ad-hoc* force of 8th Westphalian Hussar Regiment and 22nd FJB, found Horsens abandoned. The town was given a requisition to provide quarters for 10,000 men the following day.[19] Count Neipperg moved to Horsens with Brigades Tomas and Dormus, and the Prussian Cavalry Brigade of Colonel Fliess. That evening, Brigade Gondrecourt and Gablenz' headquarters arrived in the town. Brigade Nostitz was left as a reserve for the Prussian Guard around Fredericia.

Overnight on the 11/12th, the Austrians reconnoitred the position at Skanderborg, a strong one, with lakes on either side, connected by a creek, with only two crossing points. During the night, Hegermann again withdrew, marching north-west towards Silkeborg, 20 miles away. By 08:30 on the 12th, 'Max' Müller's 7th Brigade was already about seven miles from Skanderborg. Gablenz sent Count Neipperg directly on Skanderborg, with five battalions of Brigade Dormus, the Prussian cavalry brigade, and the guns of the Corps Artillery Reserve, as a diversion, whilst he moved to the east to outflank the position with Brigades Gondrecourt and Tomas, and five squadrons of Dobrzensky's brigade. Neipperg, however, at around 13:00, learned that the Danes had retreated once again.

The next day, Neipperg rode north-east to Aarhus with five squadrons, finding no trace of the enemy, the last Danish troops there being the 7th Regiment, which had embarked for Als some days before. At the same time, Gablenz despatched Major-General Gondrecourt with 18FJB and three squadrons of the Liechtenstein Hussars, from Skanderborg north-west towards Silkeborg. Gondrecourt marched the eight miles to the next potential defensive position, also a stream flanked by lakes, but found it empty, with the bridges destroyed. The Danish 4th Division appeared to have vanished.

At this point, Gablenz, seeing no point in a wild goose chase, and mindful of the situation at Fredericia, where the Field Marshal was demanding action, began a concentration of II Corps around Vejle. This took place between the 14th and 16th. On the 16th, orders were received from Wrangel, that two brigades of II Corps and 12 guns of the artillery reserve, were to take part in actions against the fortress.[20]

Meanwhile, after his withdrawal from Skanderborg, Hegermann-Lindencrone had continued to retreat, first to Silkeborg, and then to Skive, a distance of almost 50

---

18 See Appendix X.
19 von Fischer, p. 189.
20 Ibid, p. 194. In fact, all 16 guns were used.

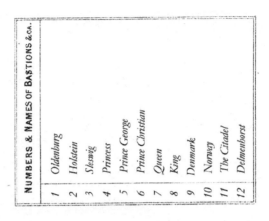

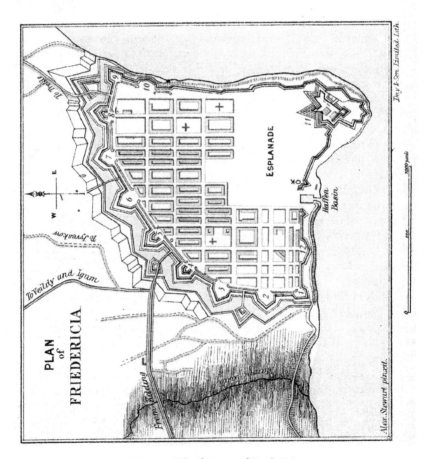

Map 18: The fortress of Fredericia

miles, in poor weather, the troops morale dropping with every step, Hegermann becoming known as 'General Backwards'. The General then decided that the division would only be safe on the island of Mors, in the Limfjord. Three days of storms hindered this, but, finally, on March 17th, the crossing began, and by the following day, the division was quartered on Mors, except for outposts on the mainland. It would remain there for two weeks. Whilst there, the General requested from the High Command that two full divisions be sent to him.[21]

The Bombardment of Fredericia

Unlike either the Danewerke or Dybbøl, Fredericia was a properly constituted fortress, though its fortifications had been rather neglected in recent years, particularly since the change of policy in 1861. Its position was a very strong one, sited on a promontory at the northern end of the 'Little Belt'. The population of the town in 1864 was some 6,500. The fortress formed a triangle, with its base on the northern, or landward, side. The rapid major technological advances in artillery somewhat reduced the effectiveness of the defences, however, particularly so as the fortress had few rifled guns. The fortifications consisted of ten large earthen bastions, linked by curtain walls, reinforced by cavaliers, and ravelins at the entrances. In the south-east corner, separated from the town by an esplanade, stood the citadel. North of the fortress, was a fortified camp, on the site of the former parade ground. Also backing on to the coast, the camp, which fronted to the west, consisted of five redoubts, and flanked the fortress to the north and west. The armament, on March 21st, consisted of 209 pieces of ordnance, six of them unmounted.[22]

On the 14th and 17th of March, Wrangel sent reconnaissance parties forward. In the latter, one man of 4GGR was wounded, Danish casualties amounting to eight. These operations showed that the main defences were complete, but that work was ongoing on the communications lines between the redoubts. Consulted by the Field Marshal about a possible attack on the fortified camp, and a bombardment of the fortress, Lieutenant-Colonel Weisser, the senior Austrian artillery officer, told him that without heavy artillery, a bombardment would achieve little. An attack on the camp, he said, would be pointless, since, even if taken, it could not be held under the guns of the fortress.[23] Wrangel then abandoned the idea of attacking the camp, but the bombardment was to go ahead, "…to cause consternation in the town, if possible set it on fire, and perhaps by this means, force the enemy commander to surrender the position."[24]

During March 19th, battery positions were selected and prepared. That morning, three Allied brigades squeezed the Danish outposts back in preparation. From Trælle and Igeskov, pushed the Combined Guard Grenadier Brigade, the Combined Foot Guard Brigade, from Vejlby, Egun and Stallerup, while Brigade Tomas occupied Sønderbygaard and the woods to the south. Allied casualties totalled 23, and Danish, 15 (see charts below). That afternoon, the guns were placed in their positions. These were:

21 Vaupell, p. 321. Unsurprisingly, the troops were not sent.
22 See Appendix XI.
23 von Fischer, p. 201, & Prybila, Karl Edler von, *Geschichte der Kriege der k. u. k. Wehrmacht von 1848-1898*, Graz, 1899, p.390.
24 von Fischer, p. 201.

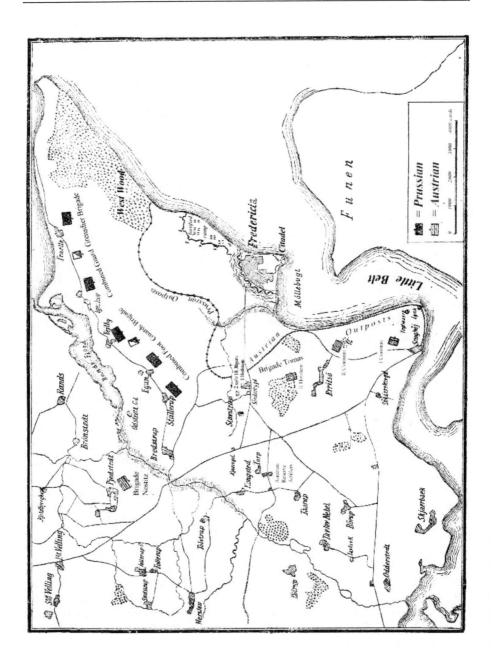

Map 19: Situation at Fredericia, 19th March

Battery I, eight Austrian rifled 8 pounders, east of Erritsø

Battery II, eight Austrian rifled 8 pounders, south-east of Sønderbygaard.

Battery III, twelve Prussian rifled 6 pounders, some 2,500 yards south of Vejlby.

Battery IV, eight Prussian rifled 4 pounders, 1,750 yards north of Battery III

Battery V, six Prussian smoothbore 12 pounders, near the south-west edge of West Wood.

The closest battery to a Danish work was Battery IV, some 1,600 yards away. Battery III opened fire at 05:30, and by 06:00 all were in action, witnessed by Wrangel and the Crown Prince of Prussia. Second-Lieutenant Holbøll, 8th Brigade's adjutant, was in the fortress:

> On the 20th of March, at six in the morning, when Irminger and I had just sat down to drink coffee, we heard a whistling sound in the air, and then an immense bang. 'What was that?!', Irminger asked. 'It was a shell.', I answered, 'It's the start of the bombardment.' One round followed another, and soon the shelling was brisk. We drank our coffee, and then went out to see if fires had started anywhere and that things (sic, furniture etc) were all outside. At the end of Prinsessegade (street), where the Brigade Headquarters was, there was a mill on the Prince Christian Bastion. The enemy had placed one of his batteries along the continuation of the road, and was still aiming at the mill. Thus, the shells were coming straight down the road, exploding, and sending fragments everywhere. It was nice to get past that street.[25]

The shelling continued throughout the day, and was initially briskly answered by the defenders. The Prussian guns concentrated on the fortified camp, and the Austrian, on the town. Lieutenant Holbøll spent the whole day in the fortress, noting the difference in the guns of the two sides:

> We had, when the bombardment started, 188 guns, of which only five were rifled 12 pounders, and 12 rifled 4 pounders. The rest were smoothbores. During the bombardment, a further 21 guns were placed in the batteries, seven of them rifled 12 pounders. When our gunners started to fire the rifled guns, the shells exploded over the heads of our troops, to their great fright, long before they reached the enemy. The shelling, therefore, had to be stopped. It was said that the fuses had been stored for so long, that the wooden tubes where they were to be placed had dried out and cracked. Hence, the fire could spread faster along the crack into the powder, instead of slowly, through the fuse. New fuses were immediately ordered from Copenhagen, but they did not arrive before the night of 21/22nd March. The enemy tried to push back our (out) posts. They did not succeed in the north, but in the west, our posts had to withdraw some distance.[26]

The last comment refers to the series of outpost clashes that occurred throughout the bombardment. It had been Wrangel's intention to cease the bombardment after one day, but FML Gablenz considered that another day would

25 Holbøll, p. 154.
26 Holbøll, p. 161.

indicate whether the defence was suffering unduly, and the order for a further day was given.

The shelling began at dawn on the 21st, ceasing at 13:00. The Field Marshal then sent a Prussian officer into the fortress to offer an exchange of prisoners, but actually to request its surrender. General Lunding agreed to an exchange, but flatly refused any other terms. After this, the shelling was resumed from 15:00 to 19:00. From then, it ceased for good. Lieutenant-Colonel Weisser had been proven correct. If the Field Marshal wanted to hurt Fredericia, a siege train was needed. The fortifications had not suffered very badly, although parts of the town had been hard hit. Casualties in the shelling, and the associated skirmishes were:

Table 21

Allied Casualties at Fredericia, March 19th-21st 1864

Prussian/Austrian: Four officers and 39 men (19th, 20th and 21st March)

	Killed		Wounded		Prisoners		Missing	
Unit	Officers	Men	Officers	Men	Officers	Men	Officers	Men
3rd Foot Guards Regiment	—	—	—	1	—	—	—	—
4th Foot Guards Regiment	—	3	—	3	—	—	—	—
3rd Guard Grenadier Regiment (Elisabeth)	1	3	2	16	—	—	—	—
4th Guard Grenadier Regiment (Augusta)	—	—	—	2	—	—	—	—
IR Holstein	—	1	—	2	—	—	—	—
11 FJB	—	1	1	7	—	—	—	—
Totals	1	8	3	31	—	—	—	—

Table 22

Danish Casualties at Fredericia, March 19th-21st 1864

Danish: Three officers and 84 men (17th – 21st March)

	Killed		Wounded		Prisoners		Missing	
Unit	Officers	Men	Officers	Men	Officers	Men	Officers	Men
3rd Division Staff	—	—	—	1	—	—	—	—
9th Infantry Regiment	—	2	—	8	—	—	—	—
13th Infantry Regiment	—	5	—	9	—	—	—	3
14th Infantry Regiment	—	1	—	2	—	3	—	—
19th Infantry Regiment	—	2	—	7	—	—	—	—

20th Infantry Regiment	—	6	1	16	—	—	—	—
21st Infantry Regiment	1	2	—	8	—	—	—	—
Fredericia Labour Battalion	—	—	1	5	—	—	—	—
3rd Field Artillery Battery	—	1	—	—	—	—	—	—
Fortress Artillery	—	1	—	1	—	—	—	—
4th Engineer Company	—	—	—	1	—	—	—	—
Totals	1	20	2	58	—	3	—	3

To the Fall of Dybbøl

After the bombardment, King Christian and Colonel Lundbye undertook a tour of inspection, arriving in Fredericia on the 25th, and from there went on to the 4th Division on the evening of the 26th. Both Lunding and the War Minister were confused by the Allied movements around Fredericia, and by the purpose of the bombardment itself. Lunding requested and received permission to undertake offensive action, but his Chief of Staff and the brigade commanders were against any large-scale operations. It was therefore agreed that a force of four companies be held in readiness, and that with these, some raids would take place, assisted by accurate and up to date information provided by local people, a permanent advantage for the Danes in Jutland.

With the withdrawal of the majority of the Prussian Guard infantry from Jutland on March 25th, the remaining Prussian troops were reorganised into a 'screen', protecting the rear and lines of communication of II Corps, which remained to blockade Fredericia. It was against a portion of this defensive cordon that the first, and most successful, of General Lundings 'raids' was made. On the evening of March 27th, 100 men of 2/20th Regiment, Captain F. Stockfleth and 100 from 1/19th, Premier-Lieutenant Harboe, accompanied by four Guard Hussars, sailed from the fortress in an iron transport vessel, towed by the screw gunboat *Schrødersee* (two smoothbore 30 pounders), Lieutenant A.E. Christiansen.[27]

The force landed in Sandbjerg Bay, near the village of Julesminde, under 20 miles east of Vejle at 02:30.[28] Leaving 25 men with the boat, the rest of the troops moved off to the west some 10 miles to Hornumkjær. Here, they waited until the evening, before moving on. Their target was the hamlet of Assendrup, some five miles north-east of Vejle, where a detachment of the Prussian Guard Hussars had been earlier billeted.

Reaching Assendrup at 01:30 on the 29th, Stockfleth swiftly overwhelmed the Prussians, a few shots being fired by the hussar sentinels from a barricade. One Dane was wounded, along with two Prussians. 22 more hussars were taken prisoner, along with 23 horses.

Stockfleth was able to withdraw safely with his booty. Lieutenant Chritiansen had steamed, with the transport boat, to the harbour of Rosenvold, on the north

27 Generalstaben, Volume II, pp. 244
28 Inexplicably, Børke, Kjær, & Norrie give the time of landing as 14:00, p.308.

shore of Vejle Fjord, where he embarked the force at 04:00, returning to Fredericia at 09:00.[29] General Lunding was understandably elated at the outcome of the raid.

Whilst this raid was taking place, a sortie was made from the fortress on March 28th in an attempt to capture an Austrian foraging party near Erritsø Mill, north of the village. Four infantry companies were involved, commanded by Major O. Saabye, commander of II/21st Regiment. A planned envelopment went awry, when 6/19th, Captain L. Borring, pushed ahead too quickly and were seen. The Austrian foragers were able to escape, losing one man as a prisoner.[30]

Minor patrol clashes around the fortress took place. Small units demolished gun positions, which had been in the bombardment, on several occasions. A corporal of 21st regiment was taken by a patrol of IR Holstein on March 26th. On April 1st, a patrol from 9th Regiment captured an outpost of one NCO and three men of IR Hessen, at Vejby. From then, Fredericia became quiet until after the fall of Dybbøl. General Lunding lost 8th Brigade, transferred to Dybbøl on April 10th, followed by the Espignol Battery on the 15th.

Ritmester Castenschiold, on March 19th, had taken the 'Østre Streifkorps' south, reporting to General Hegermann later that his patrols had entered towns which were clear of the enemy, among them Skanderborg and Horsens. To the west, the 'Venstre Streifkorps', on March 23rd, had also moved south. On the 30th, Ritmester Sehested, with 4/6th Dragoons, Premierlieutenant Sperling, and two platoons of 2/1st Regiment, Captain Kaas, entered the town of Tørring, ten miles north of Vejle, without having encountered enemy troops. At the same time, 6/6th Dragoons, Premierlieutenant Buchwaldt, and two platoons of the same company, under Second-Lieutenant Christensen, arrived in the village of Kollemorten, some 11 miles north-west of Vejle, where they were informed of Prussian cavalry moving north along the Vejle-Brande Road that morning.

Earlier, Second-Lieutenant Baron von Fürstenberg, and 38 men of 4/8th Hussars were despatched on a reconnaissance from Vejle to the town of Brande, 22 miles to the north-west. To intercept them on the return journey, Premierlieutenant Døcker was sent with 40 dragoons and 20 infantrymen. Døcker chose Hjortsballe Inn, south of Brande, for the confrontation. Leaving the infantry and 13 dragoons in ambush south of the inn, and 12 troopers to flank the hussars, Døcker led the remainder straight up the road. Fürstenberg pulled back to the inn, and his troopers opened fire with their carbines, but as the attack was pressed, the hussars scattered. Ten hussars were taken prisoner, and several others wounded, as were Døcker and two of his troopers.[31] This skirmish caused the by now normal panic at Allied Headquarters, and resulted in large scale patrolling over the next few days. 'Østre Streifkorps' had a further skirmish with advancing Prussian Guard

29 Sørensen, Volume II, pp. 218-221, & Generalstaben, Volume II, pp. 244-245.

30 Michelsen, Poul U., *21. Battalions Historie, 1788-1918*, Copenhagen 1918, pp. 198-199.

31 Johansen & Nordentoft, *4de Division I Nørrejylland 1864*, pp. 180-181, Grosser Generalstab, Volume I, pp. 380-381, and Waldersee, pp. 427-428.

troops near Horsens on April 10th, losing one man killed, one wounded, and one captured.[32]

On Mors, General Hegermann-Lindencrone finally accepted that Allied forces in Jutland were much reduced by the departure of the majority of the Prussian Guards, and that most others were masking Fredericia. On April 3rd, 4th Division began to move back to the mainland. By April 7th, Divisional Headquarters was in Silkeborg. From here, Hegermann considered various ways to attack the Allied forces between Vejle and Fredericia. He now had only two battalions of infantry, 11th Regiment having been ordered, on March 20th, to move to Als, where it arrived on April 1st. As a result, he sent Captain Thomsen, on April 12th, to request four battalions from General Lunding. Lunding, having orders to send a brigade to Als already, sent the officer back with the message that this was not possible. Hegermann then suggested that he take the majority of his cavalry, and attack the Prussian force at Dybbøl in the rear, whilst General Gerlach mounted a frontal assault. This caused Minister-President Monrad to wonder whether Hegermann would also offer to ride to Berlin and take the King of Prussia prisoner.[33] In any case, the officer sent with this offer, once again Captain Thomsen, arrived at Army Headquarters on Als on the evening of April 18th, just after Dybbøl had fallen.

---

32 Generalstaben, Volume II, pp. 257-258. It is also stated here that Prussian losses were three killed and six wounded. Prussian accounts make no mention of casualties.
33 Vaupell, p. 324.

8

The Investment of the Dybbøl Position

Field Marshal Wrangel and Prince Friedrich Carl were both now fully aware that the Danes intended to defend the Dybbøl position. It was obvious to them that heavy artillery on the Broager Peninsula alone would not be enough to subdue the considerable number of guns in the Redoubts, and that the field artillery available to I Corps was not powerful enough.

Replying to an earlier message from the King, Wrangel wrote on February 23rd that a quick assault at Dybbøl might well fail, and expressed his view that a siege was the proper course to follow. He believed that a frontal attack should be undertaken, and emphasised that obtaining the necessary artillery and matériél, as well as the poor weather would mean that such an operation would be lengthy. He did not believe that it would be possible to occupy the island of Als, and that the way ahead was for the capture of the Sundeved as well as an occupation of Jutland. Wrangel attached supporting comments from his senior artillery officer, Colonel Graberg.[1]

Any major attack upon Dybbøl therefore required a siege-train, which would take time to assemble. In addition, General von Moltke considered that an invasion of Jutland was the correct way to proceed, rather than an attack on Dybbøl, which would not, he believed, drive Denmark from the war. Nevertheless, the political situation was fluid following the incident at Kolding, and any action in Jutland depended upon Austrian participation (see Chapter 5). Moltke therefore recommended that if Jutland could not be invaded, heavy artillery should be sent to Sundeved.[2]

In the meantime, I Corps' senior Artillery Officer, Colonel Colomier, was studying the nature of the defences from an observation post established at Gammelmark. From his observations, and such information as had been gleaned from the various recent operations he developed an attack plan, proposing an attack on the southern wing of the fortifications; a plan requiring far more heavy artillery than the army presently possessed in the field.

In Berlin, War Minister von Roon, on the 26th of February agreed to release additional heavy guns, although he did not have the authority to call up the men to use them. On March 1st, Friedrich Carl despatched Colonel Colomier to Berlin with his plan to obtain its approval by the King.

Colomier calculated that 96 guns would be required to implement his attack plan - 12 rifled 24 pounders, 12 rifled 12 pounders, 24 rifled 6 pounders, 12 'short' 12 pounders, 16 7 pound howitzers, and 16 25 pound mortars. From prisoners and deserters, he believed that the defence possessed 106 guns, many of them large calibre.

1   Grosser Generalstab, Volume I, Appendices 27 & 27a.
2   Moltke, *Korrespondenz*, letter Nr. 38, to the King, 22nd February 1864, and letter Nr. 39, to the War Minister, 28th February 1864.

His plan proposed an attack on the (Prussian) right wing in the area of Redoubts I to III. This was the optimum point for an attack for several reasons. Firstly, the terrain in this sector was the most favourable for an assault, the Redoubts south of the Flensburg Road commanding the ground to their front much less than those to the north of it. Secondly, the heavy artillery batteries to be placed on the heights at Gammelmark, across the Vemmingbund would dominate the whole of the fortifications on the position's southern flank.[3] Conversely Danish heavy guns emplaced along the Als Sound could fire upon the flank of any attack made in the north. In the event of a breakthrough in the south, it was possible that the Danish troops in the fortifications north of the main road could be cut off and captured. Finally, the Vemmingbund itself would protect the Prussian right flank, although the possibility of intervention by the Danish fleet might well be expected. Should this happen, the heavy batteries at Gammelmark would also be a powerful factor.[4]

Following the fiasco on February 22nd, General Lüttichau concluded that stronger defences were required at Dybbøl. In future, one brigade would be on outpost duty, another would man the Redoubt Line, and a third would be in reserve in Sønderborg. The outposts were divided into a left and a right wing, each manned by a regiment. The Redoubt Line was similarly divided, between Redoubts VI and VIII (VII being to the rear between the two). Each wing again held a regiment, with one battalion in the fortifications and one in reserve.

Each brigade spent six days in the position - two in Sønderborg, followed by two in the outpost line, and then two in the main line. After this, the brigade would spend six days on Als. The divisional commander whose troops were in the position was the immediate commander, and the commander of the outpost line reported to him. Nothing was done about the inherent weakness of this arrangement in the command chain.

In order to solve the problem of rotating units in and out of duty on the northern part of Als, on February 25th a permanent self-standing unit was created for that area, named 'The Mels Detachment'. Commanded by Captain Wildenradt, the force comprised 550 infantry – divided into three companies – and 20 dragoons.[5]

Prince Friedrich Carl was also busy with administrative tasks in late February. The separate Advance Guard was wound up on the 24th, its units returning to their parent formations. Manstein's 6th Division had its Headquarters at Graasten, with 11th Brigade (Canstein) on the Broager and at Alnor, and 12th Brigade (Roeder) north of Graasten. Wintzingerode's 13th Division had its Headquarters at Bøgeskov, its infantry north and east of 6th Division, with 25th Brigade (Schmid) forward, and 26th Brigade (Goeben) in reserve. The Cavalry Division and the Reserve Artillery were both positioned south-west of Graasten. In

---

3   De Bas, p. 142, describes this as a "fatal flaw" in the defence line. It is difficult to reconcile this with Schøller, p. 43, that, "Although the fire from Broagerland was troublesome, it would not have a considerable impact on the defensive possibilities." De Bas' view is more cogent.
4   Grosser Generalstab, Volume I, pp. 303-304, and Brackenbury et al, p. 33.
5   Schøller, p.36.

the case of a Danish attack, the defence would be along the line Sottrup and Nybøl Mill, rather than Ullerup-Sottrup-Ballegaard as previously.[6]

With both sides thus preoccupied, the last days of February and the beginning of March were relatively quiet at Dybbøl. On the morning of February 23rd, the armoured schooner *Esbern Snare*, Lieutenant-Commander Kraft, was fired upon by Prussian field artillery off Ballegaard on the Als Fjord. The next day, there were minor clashes of patrols, resulting in four Danish and two Prussian casualties. Between the 23rd and the 28th of February, Danish casualties totalled one officer wounded, five men killed, ten wounded, and 66 prisoners, the great majority of whom had deserted.

The problem of desertion of troops from Schleswig was becoming serious. As discussed, many Schleswigers had avoided the call-up, but many had not.[7] At Dybbøl the problem was particularly bad in the 10th and 12th Regiments. From early March, the troops of these units were given the choice of remaining in the ranks, or of being transferred to new labour units. Some 500 men chose the latter option, their places being taken by recruits. Further, 12th Regiment, perceived as the major problem, was transferred to the northern part of Als on March 6th. 4th Regiment moved from there to Dybbøl, and 7th Regiment was ordered transferred from Jutland. Although these were decisive moves, there were troops from South Schleswig throughout the Army, and the problem would persist until the end of the war.[8]

On March 1st, whilst I Corps changed its defensive arrangements against any Danish attack at Dybbøl, Lieutenant-General Gerlach took command of the Danish Army. His temporary predecessor, Lieutenant-General Lüttichau was assigned as Chief of Artillery, a desk job, and left for Copenhagen.

Gerlach made several command changes. Major-General Vogt took command of 1st Division, and Colonel Vahl of the Army Artillery. Colonel H. Kauffmann, formerly the Army Chief of Staff, was given command of 2nd Brigade. Major (soon, Lieutenant-Colonel) Stiernholm stayed on as the Chief of Staff. The largely administrative post of Commandant of Als was abolished as superfluous, Army Headquarters being on the island.

Colonel Colomier's plan of attack at Dybbøl was duly approved by King Wilhelm, and on March 6th, he was appointed to direct the artillery attack, with Lieutenant-Colonel Kriegsheim, I Corps' Senior ('First') Engineer Officer controlling engineering aspects of the operation. It remained for them both to obtain sufficient resources to make the plan a reality.

The firm hold of the Prussians on the Broager Peninsula, and their fortification of the Smøl isthmus to protect it, made it highly likely that they would establish positions for heavy artillery on the Gammelmark heights. Since any such batteries would enfilade the entire defensive position at Sundeved, this possibility could no longer be ignored. On March 8th, General Gerlach ordered the

6   Grosser Generalstab, Volume I, p.302.

7   See Chapter II.

8   Schøller, pp. 20 & 39-40, and Generalstaben, Volume II, pp 111 & 150-151. A Labour Battalion was also formed at Fredericia from 13th Regiment, another heavily Schleswig unit, and Schleswig recruits still in training. Holstein troops still in the ranks were discharged during March.

construction of a second line of defences on the left, south of the Flensburg Road. This would comprise a defensive line, initially stretching from Redoubt IV to the Vemmingbund, and withdrawn at such an angle that it would not be possible to enfilade from the Broager Peninsula.[9]

Work began on the new 'Recessed (or Withdrawn) Line' on March 11th, to take place around the clock. However, the following day, it was seen that construction of earthworks was already taking place at Gammelmark, on the Broager. Once these batteries were established, their fire prevented any work during the day. Nevertheless, construction was continued at night, and the entire line was finished to a relatively low specification by the end of the month.

The line began on the cliffs near the beach of the Vemmingbund, some 700 yards behind Redoubt I, to which it was connected by a communication trench. It consisted of four open works, A, B, C, and D, connected by trenches. The line was not intended to withstand a major assault, being more of a rallying point for the defenders of the main line, should it prove necessary, and also as a trip-wire for the bridgehead defences. It ran north-west close to Redoubt IV. A further line ran north from here to join the main line at Redoubt VII.

Lunette B was constructed about 500 yards north of A, six hundred yards east of Redoubt II. The line then ran almost to Redoubt IV. In the middle of this stretch lay work C. It then ran north to Redoubt VII. Work D was constructed immediately south of the main road, on the site of a trigonometric station. This work was about 300 yards east of Redoubt V.[10]

Minor Prussian patrolling took place on the first three days of the month, and again on the 5th and 9th. The next few days were wet, and extremely muddy, precluding much activity. On March 13th, however, a larger Prussian operation was planned. Major-General Goeben organised a surprise raid on the outposts on the Danish right flank. Before dawn, at 04:30, elements of II/IR15, Lieutenant-Colonel von der Goltz, and F/IR55, Major von Rex, started to move forward. Goltz was east of Ragebøl Wood with Rex on his right. Their advance was masked by a heavy snow storm.

At 05:00, 85 men of 8/IR15, Captain v. der Recke, encountered and attacked a patrol from 16th Regiment near Randsgaard, capturing 12 prisoners. Simultaneously, 7/IR15, Captain Krieg, also surprised an advance post of the same regiment, driving it back and capturing a further 14 men. The Danish forward posts were driven south as far as Batterup.

Further west at Ragebøl Inn, two platoons of 5/16th Regiment under the command of Second-Lieutenant Fischer were attacked by 12/IR55, Captain Bacmeister, a firefight developing on either side of a knick. Fischer sent Sergeant Kok with his reserves, to the left, where Kok was able to flank the Prussians, forcing their withdrawal. One Prussian NCO was mortally wounded in this encounter.[11] 11/IR55, Captain von Flotow, also took a few prisoners, before both Prussian battalions withdrew. They were back in their original positions by 06:00, an hour

9   Schøller, pp. 40-41. It is perhaps surprising that the artilleryman, Lieutenant-General Lüttichau, did not institute such work earlier.
10 Ibid, pp. 41-42.
11 As his men carried him back, a copy of the battalion's orders fell from his pocket, and was found by the Danes; Vaupell, p. 204.

and a half after the operation began. Their loss was one man killed, the Danes had lost two NCOs and 29 men, all captured.

A further Prussian reconnaissance was ordered for the following day, and also that 12th Brigade should occupy the villages of Nybøl and Stenderup, pushing its outpost lines beyond them, in order to protect the growing depots being established. 11th Brigade was also to advance its outposts, whilst 13th Division was to remain in place.

On General Roeder's right, IR64 accomplished its assignment with minimal opposition, the regiment's two Musketier battalions setting out forward posts from Hvilhøi northwards, the main force of I/IR64 taking positions in the farms around the Bøffelkobbel, and II/IR64 around Nybøl. Two companies of F/IR64 occupied Nybøl fields and the water mill.[12] Later, a minor skirmish took place with a patrol of the newly arrived Danish outpost regiment, the 2nd, near Hvilhøi, one Danish officer being wounded, one man killed, and three wounded.[13]

Further north, at 06:00, IR24's Colonel von Hacke pushed towards Dybbøl Church with six companies, whilst his remaining two, 6/IR24, Captain von Görschen, and 7/IR24, Premier-Lieutenant von Görschen, moved on Ragebøl village. Defending Dybbøl Church and its fortified churchyard was a half company of 1/18th Regiment, commanded by Second-Lieutenant C. Hansen, supported by Second-Lieutenant Voldby's platoon from 2/18th, stationed south of the church.

2/IR24, Captain Ballhorn, advanced on the right, to maintain contact with IR64, while 1/IR24, Captain Radowitz, faced the church, the other companies left in reserve. A prolonged firefight took place, in which Ballhorn was wounded. Chr. Bredsdorff was one of the defenders that morning, and left this lively description of the fighting there:

> Our company was assigned the excellent fortified Dybbøl churchyard as our line of defence. I had asked permission to participate in a stealthy patrol and was granted it, and so, just as dawn was breaking, Jungerson, together with a Schleswiger and I started towards Stenderup town, the outskirts of which we reached without having seen or heard anything of the enemy.
>
> Hardly had we returned and reported our findings before a lively rifle fire started from our vedette line, and within 10 minutes we were all – a half-company of 80 men – heavily engaged with the enemy from behind the churchyard dyke. The enemy attacked the centre of our position (First and Second Companies, 18th regiment) and the right flank (3rd Regiment), whereas we heard nothing from the left wing (the other companies of the 18th Regiment). The enemy seemed especially enraged about the church tower; I counted no less than four bullets go through the window in the porch, in which we had sat down and happily chatted while having lunch the previous day. Another 12-14 rounds had gone through the sound hole [sic., openings in the bell tower], where some of our best marksmen were placed. We didn't hesitate to respond to the fire, and did so merrily, until 'Mikkel' gradually began to sneak off again.[14]

12 Grosser Generalstab, p. 400.
13 Sørensen, Carl th., *Den Anden Slesvigske Krig*, Volume II, p. 146.
14 'Mikkel' is an old nickname for a fox, applied to the Prussians.

Two Prussian prisoners at Dybbol, 14th March (Bredsdorff)

Only a few of the enemy had come so far ahead that they could not retreat, and they were now bravely lying firing from behind a hedgerow. However, that position was soon overrun by a patrol of 7-8 men from 2nd Company, who crept up on them, and stormed the 'cuckoos' with a 'Hurrah' and blazing rifles. The patrol returned with two Prussians.[15] It was only a small victory, but it caused great joy, especially to Lieutenant Voldby, who had been involved in taking the prisoners. "Yes, if we could just advance a couple of times, having some luck with us, then you would see a new spirit come over us all."[16]

Firing continued until about 07:30. By this time Hacke has placed his outposts as instructed, could see that no progress was being made, and pulled his main column back. Bredsdorff was present at the close of the action:

Soon after, when only a few shots were fired, Lieutenant Hansen went out with 19 men in order to set out our vedettes again. In a sunken lane we came across the complete equipment of a Prussian, who possibly had been shot and then carried away by his comrades. I 'salvaged' a spiked helmet, which I hung on my sword; it caused quite a sensation wherever I went, but since all 'salvage' was forbidden I was forced to hand it over to the outpost commander. Still, I had looked forward to showing it off when I got home.

During this walk, we were fired upon from close range, particularly from a gateway in a dyke, and we had to spread out in a line along the dyke. Lieutenant Hansen, though, was sure that the fire came from a burned out house about 200 yards away. We fixed our bayonets and advanced towards the house – the final

15 'Cuckoo' was another nickname for the Prussians. Corporal Nielsen, who led this patrol, was awarded the Silver Cross of the Order of Dannebrog – Vaupell, Otto, "Paa Forpost", *Vort Forsvar*, Nr. 43, August 1882.

16 Bredsdorff, Chr., *Paa Feltfod*, Danmark, Copenhagen 1911, p. 208.

part of the way with 'charged bayonets' and a cheer of "Hurrah!" – with Lieuten-ant Hansen at the front, his sword drawn. The enemy, though, had gone, and we had to be content with the satisfaction of having driven them away – a feeling which you can be sure was much more stimulating than the constant retreating.[17]

The smaller Prussian column attacked and drove back 1½ platoons of 3rd Regiment south of Ragebøl, but was then halted and held by 6/3rd Regiment, Premierlieutenant Duus, who was wounded in the skirmish. The Prussians withdrew shortly afterwards.

Roeder's 12th Brigade had achieved its set objectives, but the attempt to go further was unsuccessful. Canstein's 11th Brigade pushed its own outposts to the line of Steenbæk-Bøffelkobbel as instructed. Prussian losses totalled 20, IR24 having one officer and two men killed, one officer and twelve men wounded, and two men captured. IR64 had two men wounded. Danish casualties amounted to two officers and 18 men for the day.

Although possession of the Broager Peninsula had been secured after the fight-ing of February 18th, and the desirability of placing heavy guns on the Gammelmark heights on its northern shore recognised shortly afterwards, it was not until March 10th that any construction was begun. That day work began on Batteries 2 and 3, which were completed and armed on the 13th. Battery 1 was constructed and armed on the night of the 14/15th. These batteries comprised:

Table 23

Prussian Batteries on the Gammelmark Heights, Dybbøl, mid-March 1864

Battery[18]	Armament	Target & Approximate Range
Battery Nr. 1	Four rifled 24 pounders	Redoubts I-IV & Sønderborg 2,600 – 5,000 yards
Battery Nr. 2	Four rifled 24 pounders	Redoubts I-IV & trenches 2500 – 3,500 yards
Battery Nr. 3	Six rifled 6 pounders	Redoubts II, III, & V 2,500 – 3,500 yards

It had previously been ordered that, in the event of Prussian batteries being es-tablished on the Broager, two of the south-facing smoothbore 12 pounder guns in Redoubt II should be replaced by two rifled 12 pounder guns. This was done on the 13th, and that afternoon these fired at the enemy construction works across the Bund. The fire continued the next night and day, a few individual ranging shots being fired in return, but the exchanges had little effect because of storms and poor visibility.

The weather on the morning of the 15th was also stormy, and it was not until 11:00 that the bombardment began. Then, all three batteries at Gammelmark,

17 Ibid, pp. 208-209.
18 These batteries were manned by 8th Fortress Company/Artillery Brigade Nr.7, (Batteries 1 and 2) and 3rd 6 Pounder Battery/Artillery Brigade Nr. 7 (Battery 3).

Prussian 6 pounder battery at Dybbøl (Liljefalck & Lütken)

reinforced by two additional 6 pounder batteries (2nd /Artillery Brigade Nr. 3, and 1st /Artillery Brigade Nr. 7) - a total of 26 guns - opened a regular, heavy fire on Dybbøl. The main targets were Redoubts I, II, and IV, between and 2,200 and 3,000 yards away, across the Vemmingbund. Fire was returned from Redoubt II, one shell landing not far from Prince Karl of Prussia, who was watching the bombardment near Battery Nr. 2.[19]

The shelling continued until 14:00, 463 rounds being fired, 98 of them 24 pounder. 13 projectiles fell in the town of Sønderborg. During the bombardment, the blockhouse in Redoubt II was struck by a shell, killing Second-Lieutenant Voldby, who had performed so brilliantly the day before, and wounding three men from 18th Regiment. In skirmishing on the Danish left flank, Captain Krag, company commander of 4/17th Regiment was badly wounded, and one man of IR24 killed.

On the 16th, shelling began at 10:00, continuing for five hours, answered for a time from the redoubts. A shell hit the blockhouse of Redoubt I, killing two officers, Premierlieutenant E. Bruhn and Second-Lieutenant F. Gløerfehldt, and ten men, and wounding one officer and 39 men (six mortally), all from 17th Regiment.[20] Additional losses in the bombardment were seven killed and three wounded from the artillery, and one man killed from both 2nd and 22nd Regiments. After the two incidents involving the blockhouses, these, formerly very popular with the infantry, were avoided like the plague.

19 In honour of his father's 'close shave', Prince Friedrich Carl ordered that Premier-Lieutenant Mogilowski's battery in future be known as the 'Feldzeugmeister' Battery, since Prince Karl, was 'Master of Ordnance' of the Prussian artillery.
20 Generalstaben, Volume II, p. 164. Schøller, p. 43, gives figures of two officers and 12 men killed, and one officer and 21 men wounded.

General Goeben's 26th Brigade, now in the line facing the Danish right flank, sent small probing patrols forward during the day, and at 22:00, launched a major raid towards Lillemølle and Stavegaarde, with six companies of IR15. They swiftly pushed back the advanced posts in both places, but went no further when faced with their supports. IR15 had three men wounded. The Danish 3rd Regiment has losses of one officer killed, two men wounded, and two more captured.

The Actions of Ragebøl and Dybbøl, 17th March

When the Prussians had finally pulled back to their camps at about 04:00, they left a small detachment for a short time in Ragebøl Wood. General Gerlach was informed at 04:45 that the advanced posts on the right had been reoccupied, but that enemy troops still occupied Ragebøl Wood.[21] Most probably stung by the stream of criticisms that had been coming from the War Ministry as to his lack of action, he decided to clear the Prussians from there.

He gave orders that 2nd Division, before it had completed the relief of 1st Division in the line that day, should drive the enemy from Ragebøl Wood. The task fell to Colonel O. Bülow, commander of 6th Brigade. Bülow would, however, only command one of his own regiments, the 5th. Also under his command for this operation was 4th Regiment, from Wilster's recently revived 4th Brigade (which had not existed while 7th Regiment was in Jutland, and was reactivated on the 16th). It was an unpromising start.

Word soon arrived at Headquarters that the enemy was no longer in the wood, and Gerlach altered the orders to, "Reconnoitre on the right flank without bringing on any engagement of note with the enemy". This ambiguous instruction would bedevil the action to come.[22]

For the Prussians to undertake siege operations, heavy artillery batteries needed to be placed in front of the Danish fortifications to complement those already established at Gammelmark. This required the Danish outposts to be pushed back. Consequently, Friedrich Carl sent orders to Major-General Roeder to take the village of Dybbøl, giving him the choice to do so either that morning or the following day. Roeder had no time to consider these options, however, since at 10:00, to his left, Bülow's advance towards Ragebøl Wood began.[23]

In the bright, clear light of the morning, I/5th Regiment, Major J. Myhre, moved towards the wood, with three companies in the front line, pushing the Prussian outposts from I/IR15 (of Goeben's brigade) before them. Finding the wood itself unoccupied, they moved through it, and deployed some 400 yards to the north-west. II/5th, Captain A. Rothe, moved to their right, passing north of the wood, and coming level with Myhre, halted two of its companies on either side of the road to East Sottrup village.

Further south, 4th Regiment, moving in column, advanced through Ragebøl village, and reached a point immediately north of Ragebøl Inn before halting there at 10:30. Both regiments had moved through the positions of 3rd Regiment, deployed as outposts, which was to be relieved that day.

---

21 Ibid, Volume II, p.165.
22 See Johansen, J. *Dybbøl 1864*, pp. 130-132.
23 Rüstow, p. 429.

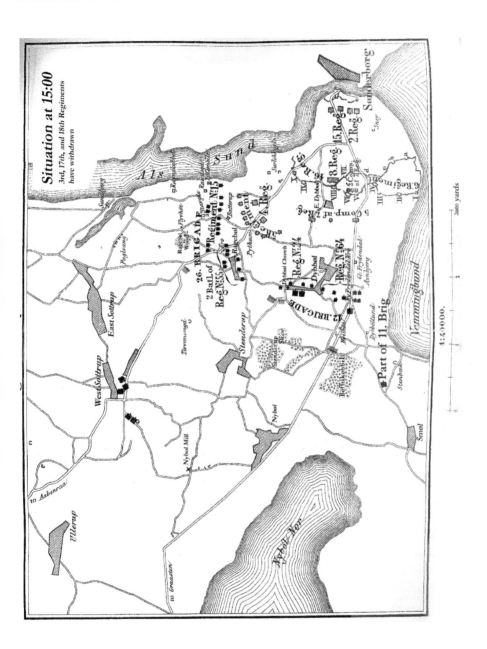

Map 20: Actions of Ragebøl/Dybbøl - 17th March

Goeben, misinterpreting the move, reacted swiftly to the unexpected Danish advance. He despatched a message to Roeder informing him of the situation, and, believing himself subject to a major attack, requested support. He then, at about 11:30, moved I/IR15, Major Baron v. d. Horst and I/IR55, Major Böcking, forward against Ragebøl village. F/IR55, Major von Rex, moved forward to a position along the Aabenraa Road between West Sottrup and Ragebøl Wood.[24]

Goeben's artillery battery (4th 12 Pounder/Artillery Brigade Nr. 7) had difficulty in manoeuvring on the soft ground. Two of its guns moved into position on a rise south of the road, and began to shell Ragebøl village, some 1,000 yards to the south.

The appearance of Goeben's infantry from East and West Sottrup, as well as Fuglsang, appears to have coincided with Bülow's decision that his mission was completed, bearing in mind Gerlach's instructions not to become involved in a serious action. 4th Regiment, seeing the advancing Prussians, had left two companies I/4th north of the inn, with the other two in reserve. II/4th deployed two companies west of Ragebøl village, with two in reserve in the settlement.

The then Premierlieutenant F.F. Hansen, company commander of 4/3rd Regiment, was in the forward posts at this time:

> I moved up in front of Ragebøl to observe the course of events and saw that a beacon had been lit in West Sottrup, and that a unit was advancing in another place. I reported this to the division's Chief of Staff, Major Schau, who then informed General du Plat, who I heard say, 'Will you order a slow retreat?'.
>
> This manoeuvre is very popular in the training areas, and consists of one unit moving some way back, and taking up a defensive position, after which another unit moves back through this and further back, then taking up a defensive position, and so on alternately. On the training grounds, where there are no defence positions, this is done so that one unit takes up a position a few hundred yards behind the other. However, in battle, with long ranges, this sort of manoeuvre is a waste of time and actually disadvantageous, and it is ridiculous to see positions captured in open fields where there are no defensive positions. However, since the troops are almost never trained outside these training areas, they and their young officers rarely understand the manoeuvre's purpose and execute it in the manner which they are used to.
>
> Here, where three regiments were placed in line behind one another, this manner of retreat might, in a critical moment, have the consequence of mixing the units up, and one unit retreating could pull men from another unit with it.[25]

Bülow gave the signal to Major Myhre's 5th Regiment, passed by trumpet, for a "Slow Retreat". The regiment pulled back, under increasing fire from the advancing Prussians. All units, following their original orders, were still wherever possible setting fire to any structures in front of them.

Meanwhile, Prussian I/IR55, Major Böcking, and on their left and I/IR15, Major Horst, moving very swiftly in firing lines pushed in the Danish outposts and stormed into Ragebøl village and Inn. 6/4th Regiment, Premierlieutenant Bodin, and 8/4th, Premierlieutenant Winsløw were ejected from the village, and the badly

24 Grosser Generalstab, Volume II, p. 406.
25 Hansen, F.F., *En Compagniecommandeurs Erindringer fra Krigen 1864*, Copenhagen 1911, p. 47.

wounded Captain P. Bauditz, 4th Regiment's acting commander, captured. Some 40 other men, about half of them wounded, were also taken prisoner.[26] It was now about noon, as 3/IR15, Captain Hoffmüller, and 4/IR15, Captain von der Schulenburg, also joined by 11/IR15, Captain von Flotow, then attacked Stavegaarde to the west. They took the village from the Danes after a sharp action with I/5th Regiment, Captain J. Hammer, during which they came under heavy flanking fire from two of Hammer's companies, 2/5th, Captain Haffner, and 6/5th, Premierlieutenant W. Claussen. Hammer's battalion was already, in any case, falling back as ordered.[27]

By now, the units of 4th Regiment, also given the order, "Slow Retreat", were becoming increasingly mixed up with those of the 3rd Regiment. Confusion was beginning to appear at all levels of the command structure.

By 13:00, Goeben's 26th Brigade had stabilised its front along the line from the Als Sound, through Stavegaarde to Ragebøl village with 5 battalions and the six 12 pounders of his battery. Colonel Bülow, deployed his 5th Regiment at the Pythuse[28] (II/5th) and south of Batterup (I/5th), and ordered the relief of 3rd Regiment in the outposts. 4th Regiment was held in reserve just outside the line of the fortifications, and the two field guns, which had not been used, were sent into the main position. All the while, occasional fire was exchanged.

After several contradictory orders, which had become the hallmark of the day's action, and the approach of enemy troops, Hansen describes his 4/3rd Regiment's last few minutes just east of Ragebøl village, waiting to be relieved. Half of his company was in a skirmish line, and half in reserve, with Hansen standing between the two:

> It did not take long before the enemy swarmed forward at the Inn, and was received with heavy rifle fire, upon which, he stopped. In front, the company was well under cover, as the day before I had the hedges repaired. However, on the flanks, I had no cover. From Ragebøl, a double post (two men) had advanced to a trench that had been constructed as an observation post to observe from Pythuse to Ragebøl. It was situated approximately 400 Alen (800 feet) from my position, and as I stood right between the line (of skirmishers) and the (company) reserve, I posed an excellent target for them. They must have missed five or six shots at me, but oddly enough, they began conferring with one another, and ceased to fire. I was also fired on, by a double post along the road, but they were further away. Besides, the enemy did not advance over the hills of the Ragebøl position. What I feared most was that the enemy from Stavegaarde would make an unobserved advance behind Batterup and Pythuse. Since I was not willing to sacrifice more than was necessary of the company, I ordered the reserve to retreat when the regiment had passed a forward post, placed on the road in the hollow in front of the fortifications. When the reserve had gained a

26 Waldersee, 166. He mistakenly refers to Bauditz as commanding 5th Regiment. 4th Regiment's commander, Major E. du Plat, was sick. Both of the battalion commanders that day were also captains, as were those of 5th Regiment. The army was woefully short of officers. Bauditz, who died of his wounds, was promoted to major.

27 Johansen, *Dybbøl 1864*, p. 136.

28 'Pythuse' is an untranslatable term meaning a number of buildings or structures sited in a dip or hollow.

good start, I suddenly let the whole (skirmish) line run down the hill, and along the road. I thus escaped from this dangerous post without casualties. In my report the next day, I wrote that I had left the position because I saw no sign of the relief coming. When I arrived at the fortifications, the regiment was formed up behind them.[29]

Further south, Major General Roeder had decided that the most effective way for 12th Brigade to support his colleague was to follow the orders given him by Friedrich Carl, and take Dybbøl village immediately.[30] Accordingly, all of Colonel Count von Hacke's IR/24 and I/IR64, Major Hüner von Wostrowsky, were moved forward to the Bøffelkobbel, with the intention of attacking Dybbøl Church, some 1,100 yards south of Ragebol village, and (West) Dybbøl village itself. The advance was supported initially by two guns, and subsequently all eight, of 2nd Howitzer/3rd Artillery Brigade.

Roeder's guns deployed north-west of the Stenderup-Dybbøl Road, about 850 yards from the church, and began to shell the churchyard. At 13:00, F/IR24, Major von Krohn, advanced north of the road, following its two sister battalions to northern part of the village, II/IR24, led by von Hacke, in the van. Major Hüner's I/IR64, along with 9/IR64, Captain von Unruhe, and 10/IR64, Premier-Lieutenant Ewald, attacked towards the western side of Dybbøl, whilst II/IR64, Major Kramer, assaulted the key heights of the Avnbjerg, south of the village. The two remaining Fusilier companies, 11 and 12/IR64, took no part in the action.

Facing them, newly arrived at Dybbøl that morning, was the 7th Regiment, Lieutenant-Colonel L. Muus. The 7th had been transferred from Jutland, and posted to 6th Brigade.[31] It landed on Als on March 13th, and had never been in action before. As there was no apparent enemy movement in the area, it was ordered at 10:30 that 7th Regiment could immediately relieve the 18th in the forward positions. The hand-over was virtually completed between 12:00 and 13:00, shortly before Roeder's attack began. 7th Regiment's deployment was:[32]

II/7th, Major G. Behmann

8/7th, Premierlieutenant S. Munck

Two platoons at Dybbøl Church

Two platoons in the south-west outskirts of Dybbøl village

4/7th, CO sick, for him, Retired Captain E Jacobsen

Two platoons on the Avnbjerg

Two platoons south of the Avnbjerg to the Vemmingbund

---

29 Hansen, pp. 49-50.
30 Definitive orders from the Prince's headquarters were received shortly afterwards. Two guns of Roeder's 2nd Howitzer/Artillery Brigade Nr. 3 had fired in support of Goeben's Brigade during the fighting at Ragebøl, Grosser Generalstab, Volume II, p. 408.
31 2nd Division's infantry was now organised as follows:
    4th Brigade – 4th and 6th Regiments
    5th Brigade – 10th and 12th Regiments
32 Generalstaben, Volume II, p. 172.

3/7th, Second-Lieutenant C. Baggesen

Support – South-east of Dybbøl Church

6/7th, CO sick, for him, Premierlieutenant (of the War Reserve) C. Gersdorff

Support – East of the Avnbjerg

I/7th, CO posted away,

For him, Captain G. Maes 2/7th, Premierlieutenant (of the War Reserve) C. Zoffmann, and 5/7th, Captain G. Meyer

Reserve – At the crossroads north of Dybbøl village and the north-east part of the village.

1/7th, Premierlieutenant F. Nielsen, and 7/7th, Premierlieutenant C. Sørensen

Reserve – Tvinge Farm and the south-east part of the village.

South of the Sønderborg Road, the rapid and unexpected attack of Major Kramer's II/IR64 literally swept the company from the 185 foot high Avnbjerg as well as the supporting 6/7th, and driving away Sørensen's 7/7th, which came forward to assist. The three companies dissolved in panic and fled to the main line. It proved impossible to rally them for some time, but they were eventually reassembled in the afternoon. One of the most important heights in the whole of the Sundeved had fallen into Prussian hands virtually unopposed. Cramer immediately placed his own outposts on the hill.

The rest of 7th Regiment, five companies of untried men, on a front of some 1,300 yards, without direct artillery support, and already flanked on the left, now faced an equally unforeseen assault by 18 companies. Dybbøl village was stormed from the west and south, and taken after a brief struggle.

At Dybbøl churchyard, Premierlieutenant Munck and his men of 8/7th, under flanking fire from Ragebøl village to the north, fought against great odds.

Fighting at Dybbol Church, 17th March (Liljefalck & Lütken)

Munck's men withdrew fighting towards the Redoubt Line. At this point, artillery fire from the fortifications, mainly Redoubts VI and VIII was directed at the advancing IR24, which had reached East Dybbøl. Roeder quickly withdrew the troops to the western parts of (West) Dybbøl to join those elements of IR64 already there. By 14:30, both the Avnbjerg and West Dybbøl were in Prussian hands, and fighting had died down. At Ragebøl, Major-General Goeben made what could have proved a disastrous error, and began to send troops back to their quarters, believing that the fighting was over.

As the Prussians made their advance towards East Dybbøl, General du Plat expected an attack on the main position. He ordered forward the two regiments of the Infantry Reserve, the 8th from its position at the Barracks Line to the ravine between Redoubts VI and VII, and the 15th to the support position behind the main line. The Army Commander, General Gerlach had also warned troops for the possibility of action, and had halted 1st Division's withdrawal to Als.

The morning reconnaissance had gone badly, but not disastrously wrong. Now, however, General Gerlach, seeing the Prussian retirement from East Dybbøl under fire from the Redoubts, most uncharacteristically ordered du Plat's 2nd Division to retake the outpost terrain that had been lost. He did not provide du Plat with any of the additional troops, which he had earlier warned for possible action, and he now allowed 1st Division back to the rest area on Als. In fairness to Gerlach, it seems that du Plat himself was also confident that, with 8th Regiment's assistance, he could regain the lost terrain around Dybbøl without any major clash.[33]

Prince Friedrich Carl himself came forward to the Broager at 14:30. Noting the favourable situation, he ordered General von Manstein to push forward part of Major-General Canstein's 11th Brigade to take the high ground around the farm of Old Frydendal, immediately south of the main road, whilst Roeder maintained his hold on (West) Dybbøl. Canstein accordingly despatched Lieutenant-Colonel Becker-Blumenthal (commander II/60th) with four companies, 6/IR60, Captain Krähe, 8/IR60, Captain Michelmann, 7/FR35, Captain von Schütz and 8/FR35, Captain Lindow, to do so.

Unexpectedly for Friedrich Carl, at 15:00 du Plat's 'counterattack' began. On the Danish left, the main body (five companies) of 7th Regiment, supported to their right rear by II/8th Regiment, Captain G. Møller, accompanied by the 8th's regimental commander, Colonel Hveberg, moved west from the fortifications through East Dybbøl. The three remaining companies of 7th Regiment, now rallied, also joined the advance, moving forward later than the main body. 7th Regiment's Colonel Muus advanced on the lower part of the town, switching II/8th to cover his left flank in the direction of the Avnbjerg. I/8th, Captain J. Grønland, remained for now between Redoubts VI and VII.

7th Regiment was able to enter the eastern part of Dybbøl without resistance, but soon came under heavy fire from elements of both I and II/IR 64, which were at that time being redeployed in their own outpost positions around the town.[34] Two of Captain Møller's companies, 3/8th, Premierlieutenant N. Jensen, and

33 Vaupell, pp. 212-213, and Grosser Generalstab, Volume II, pp. 409 - 410.
34 Gentz, *Geschichte des 8. Brandenburgischen Infanterie-Regiments Nr. 64*, Berlin 1878, pp. 54-55. The first companies to make contact with the advancing 7th

4/8th, Captain Baron H. Rosenkrantz, were also sucked into the fighting along with Colonel Hveberg. To the left, 7/8th, Premierlieutenant F. Pio, stood on heights near Old Frydendal farm, about 450 yards south of the Flensburg Road, with 6/8th, Premierlieutenant (of the War Reserve) F. Lyneborg in reserve.

The stubborn resistance of IR64 in the village stopped the Danish advance, allowing time for the other companies of both battalions, and also the two Fusilier companies (9 and 10/IR64) present, to come to their assistance. Superior numbers soon began pushing Hveberg and Møller's troops back.

At 16:30, Lieutenant-Colonel Blumethal's four companies appeared on the Avnbjerg, driving Premierlieutenant Pio's 7/8th back. Behind Blumethal came five more companies from 11th Brigade, under the commander of IR60, Lieutenant-Colonel von Hartmann, who had obtained General Manstein's permission also to move forward.[35] Leaving 12/IR60, Captain Schulenburg-Wolfsburg, to reinforce Blumethal, von Hartmann moved north across the main road with the remainder, coming under fire from the Redoubts as they did so, and attacked the south-east corner of Dybbøl. At almost the same time, the three 'late' companies of the Danish 7th Regiment joined the fray from the east.

The fighting was very confused through the town and the houses and farms around it. 8th Regiment's Colonel Hveberg was killed, and Major Hüner, CO of II/IR64, wounded. Weight of numbers pressed the Danes inexorably back. General du Plat's Chief of Staff, Major Schau, who had ridden forward into the fighting, now rode to the position of Captain Grønland's I/8th Regiment, still posted in the ravine between Redoubts V and VI, and ordered the battalion forward.

As Grønland's men made their way to the front in march column, two companies forward, and two behind, 7th Regiment and II/8th were being steadily driven back. Moving past East Dybbøl, I/8th moved through the retreating units of 7th Regiment, and their own II/8th. Ordered to attack the vastly superior force facing him, Grønland complied, but the volume of fire directed at his battalion was too much. Launching 8/8th, Premierlieutenant P. Bern, in a covering attack, Grønland withdrew his other three companies. Bern's company, advancing in column along a road, was soon halted and repelled by rifle fire from behind every knick.

At about 17:00, General Gerlach himself rode to the centre, just south of the Aabenraa Road, just as Captain Grønland's battalion was being pushed back. He personally ordered the three companies of Captain Wedege's II/4th Regiment, posted there (and acting as reserves for 5th Regiment in the renewed fighting around Ragebøl), to attack towards Dybbøl Church, in Grønland's support.

Wedege immediately complied, putting Premierlieutenants Bodin's 6/4th and Winsløw's 8/4th in the first line, with Captain Bügel's 4/4th in the rear. All three companies were deployed in company columns with skirmishers in front.

Regiment, were the 2/IR64, Captain Count von Maltzahn, 7/IR64, Captain von Bock and 8/IR64, Premier-Lieutenant von Gerhardt. Gerhardt was mortally wounded in the fighting.

35 Grosser Generalstab, Volume II, p. 412. These companies were 1/3 Jäger, Premier-Lieutenant v. Szwikowski, 2/3 Jäger, Captain von Erckert, 4/3 Jäger, Captain von Paczinsky, 9/IR60, Captain Maurer, and Schulenburg-Wolfsburg's 12/IR60.

The battalion made a courageous effort, advancing through a torrent of rifle fire. From behind a knick on the Danish right 12/IR24, Captain von Sellin, came a particularly effective fire. There was a short firefight, but Wedege's men were pushed back, Premierlieutenant Winsløw being killed, and Wedege himself wounded and taken prisoner. The two forward companies retreated into the fortifications, with Bügel's company covering the retreat.[36] At this point, in the darkness, fighting around Dybbøl ended at about 19:00.

In the meantime on the Danish right, planned or otherwise, the other arm of General du Plat's 'counterattack' had been taking place.[37] After the withdrawal of 3rd Regiment to Als, the artillery in the Redoubts had, somewhat ineffectively, shelled the Prussian left. Major General Goeben, as mentioned, believing the day's fighting over, had started to send his units to their quarters during the middle of the afternoon, to eat and gather their packs and equipment. He had, in fact, already sent two battalions (I/IR15 and F/IR55) back when the Danish advance began at about 16:00, and was forced to hurriedly recall them.

Captain Rothe's II/5th advanced from the Pythuse on Ragebøl, whilst Captain Hammer's I/5th, on their right, moved on Stavegaarde and Randsgaarde with three companies, the remaining 2/5th, Captain Haffner, advancing along the beach. The attack was to be supported by II/4th Regiment. Neither battalion, however, had any direct mobile artillery support, although the batteries across Als Sound would provide powerful indirect support.

In a reversal of the morning's proceedings, von Goeben now received a plea for assistance from Roeder upon the renewal of the attack on Dybbøl, followed by the enemy advance in his own sector. Goeben was in a difficult position. Until he could recall his own troops and/or obtain support from 25th Brigade, still in the area of Sottrup and Landsgaard,[38] he had three battalions and one artillery battery to defend a line from Ragebøl village to the Als Sound, a distance of some 2000 yards. He was also flanked on his left, by the heavy Danish artillery emplaced across the sound.

Defending Ragebøl village were 1/IR55, Captain von Arnim, 4/IR55, Captain von Bosse, and ½ of 2/IR55, Captain Kaweczinski. At Ragebøl Inn, was posted 3/IR55, Premier-Lieutenant Rothenbücher, and the remaining half of 2/IR55 was deployed in defence of 4th 12 Pounder/Artillery Brigade Nr.7, still in its original position north of the village.

---

36 This attack came under fire from elements of six companies of IR 24. Four of these were positioned around Dybbøl Church, 1/IR24, Captain von Radowitz, 3/IR24, Captain von Lettow, 8/IR24, Premier-Lieutenant Marquardt, and 11/IR24, Captain Freiherr Meerscheidt-Hüllesen. The remaining two, in the northern part of the village, were 2/IR24, Premier-Lieutenant von Brodowski, and 12/IR24, Captain von Sellin – Grosser Generalstab, Volume II, p. 416, Voights-König & Becker, Volume II, pp. 87-90, Johansen, *Dybbøl 1864*, pp. 146-147.

37 Johansen, *Dybbøl 1864* states that it is unknown who gave the order for this, p.148. Grosser Generalstab, Volume II, p. 415, states that it was Colonel Bülow.

38 Lieutenant-General Winzingerode, commander of 13th Infantry Division, would not allow his other brigade (Schmid) to move up. Not until after the fighting had ended, did two battalions, I/IR13 and F/IR53 come forward; Grosser Generalstab, Volume II, p. 415 & 417.

The attack on Ragebøl village by II/5th was successful, and pushed the 2½ Prussian companies towards the Inn. They pulled back, and took up positions behind fences and small knicks south of the woods. Their fire from here, together with that of von Arnim's men, who had been pushed back from Ragebøl lnn, and supported by the shellfire of the artillery battery finally brought the Danish advance to a halt a little under 450 yards east of the Inn.[39] A firefight ensued. One of the four companies of Captain Wedege's II/4th Regiment, acting as 5th Regiment's reserves, was brought up, but also could make no ground. There were no further supports to call upon.[40]

On the Danish far right, Captain Hammer's I/5th, supported by the heavy fire of the Surlykk Battery, across the Sound, stormed forward, and took Batterup, Stavegaarde and Randsgaarde, advancing in fine style. It appears that this attack may also have been supported by Premierlieutenant Sarauw's 3/4th, which must, in that case, have been moved to the right immediately after their attack near Ragebøl village.[41] Taking part in the advance here was Private L. Rasmussen, serving in 5/5th. He later wrote:

> I got a place at the front of the storm column. It was lead so well, that we surprised the Prussians and threw them out in such a hurry that they couldn't take their fallen comrades with them. We crossed a large grassy field, where a Prussian had fallen. He had caught a bullet, which had passed through his head and out near the mouth. Our clever platoon leader took his rifle, which lay beside him, and quickly became confident with the mechanism of the needle gun. He asked me to help remove the leather equipment of the casualty so that he could get the cartridges. I was the closest and immediately began. When I tried to lift his upper body, the Prussian made a small movement with one of his arms, as if to say, 'Let me lie!", but it didn't take long before our platoon leader had the cartridges, and we were quickly back in our places amidst a shower of bullets. Our platoon leader was sending the Prussians shot after shot with their own ammunition. There was a great difference between the rate of fire between the Prussian gun and ours.[42]

Observing that Ragebøl Wood was again occupied by enemy troops, Hammer then pushed two companies, 1/5th, Premierlieutenant Stonor, and 6/5th, Premierlieutenant Claussen, towards it from the south-east, but they were unable to make any headway.

39 Mørch, F. *En Dansk Militærafdeling Gjennem 325 Aar* (History of the 5th Battalion), p. 172.
40 This was Premierlieutenant P. Sarauw's 3/4th. It will be recalled that the other three companies of this battalion were moved by General Gerlach personally, and used in the attack against Prussian 12th Brigade a little to the south. I/4th was not ordered take part in the advance.
41 Generalstaben, Volume II, page 179 say that 5th Regiment reports give one company of the 4th Regiment in support here, but cannot confirm this. Johansen, *Dybbøl 1864*, p. 149, also gives the advance as supported by a company of that regiment; Sørensen, Carl Th., *Den Anden Slesvigske Krig*, Volume II, p.158 states that it was 3/4th.
42 Rasmussen, L., *Minder fra Krigen 1864*, Odense 1907, pp. 17-18.

At 16:45, Colonel Bülow sent the following message to Major General du Plat: "The enemy has been driven from Lille Mølle, Randsgaard, Batterup, and Stavegaarde, which are currently occupied by us. The town and Inn of Ragebøl are under enemy artillery fire."

The Colonel's optimism was short lived, however. At 17.00, Goeben's 'missing' units returned to the field. 11/IR55 Captain von Flotow, and 12/IR55, Captain Bacmeister, attacked the north and north-west of Ragebøl village, whilst Hoffmüller's 3/IR15, attacked Ragebøl Inn, supported by Schulenburg's 4/IR15. Captain Rothes II/5th was forced back from Ragebøl village and Inn, and pulled back to the Pythuse, still under fire from Goeben's artillery battery.

Rothe's retreat uncovered the left flank of Hammer's I/5th, still fighting between Ragebøl Wood and the Sound. Hammer was forced to pull back from his gains, but the artillery on Als prevented Goeben's left flank from occupying Lille Mølle, Randsgaard, Batterup, or Stavegaarde. Desultory fire was maintained on the right until, as at Dybbøl, darkness fell at around 19:00, and Bülow pulled all of his troops, apart from the outposts, back into the fortifications.

The result of the day's fighting left the defenders tightly encircled within their defences from the Vemmingbund to Als Sound. The London Conference would, at some point become a reality. The Prussians, with the notable exception of General von Moltke, were now largely convinced of the need to reduce the position, and, over the previous six weeks, the public had been prepared of the necessity for a siege.[43]

The action on the 17th had involved roughly 6000 Prussian infantry, and a total of 8293 Danes.[44] Many of the latter however, were lightly engaged and the figure includes troops of all arms. Neither side had planned an action on any scale; both were surprised that matters escalated in the way that they did.

Prussian casualties were not heavy, considering the number of men engaged, and the length of time involved, although the proportion of officers was very high, almost 12%. In general the troops had behaved well, and no major tactical problems were apparent. It was fortunate indeed that Major-General Goeben's decision in mid-afternoon that the fighting was over, did not have more serious consequences. Losses were as follows:

Table 24

Prussian Casualties at Ragebøl and Dybbøl, March 17th 1864

43 Rüstow, p. 433 & Generalstaben, *Statistiske Meddelelser...*
44 Ibid, p. 433.

Prussian: 138[45]

Unit	Killed		Wounded		Prisoners		Missing	
	Officers	Men	Officers	Men	Officers	Men	Officers	Men
IR Nr. 15	—	2	4	16	—	—	—	—
IR Nr. 24	—	—	—	7	—	—	—	—
IR Nr. 55	2	8	4	21	—	—	—	—
IR Nr. 60	—	4	1	7	—	—	—	—
IR Nr. 64	1	13	4	35	—	—	—	—
Jäger Bn. Nr.3	—	3	—	6	—	—	—	—
Total	3	30	13	92	—	—	—	—

The most senior officer casualty was Lieutenant-Colonel von Hartmann, commanding officer of IR60, who had a painful leg wound.

The muddled nature of the direction of the battle meant that Danish losses were considerably higher than the Prussian, well over four times as many. The troops had shown courage and discipline, and those elements of 7th Regiment which panicked in the morning, in action for the first time, later pulled themselves together[46]. At higher levels, decision making had been abysmal, and the results could have been far worse. Officer casualties were not excessive. Losses were:

Table 25

Danish Casualties at Ragebøl and Dybbøl, March 17th 1864

Danish: 677[47]

Unit	Killed		Wounded		Prisoners[48]		Missing	
	Officers	Men	Officers	Men	Officers	Men	Officers	Men
2nd Infantry Regiment	—	—	—	1	—	—	—	—
3rd Infantry Regiment	—	1	—	5	—	2	—	—
4th Infantry Regiment	4	21	1	46	1W	54 (12W)	—	13
5th Infantry Regiment	1	39	2	68	—	19 (4W)	—	—
7th Infantry Regiment	—	28	—	42	—	128 (10W)	—	6

45 Grosser Generalstab, Volume II, Appendix 44.
46 As chance would decree, this was 7th Regiment's only engagement of the war.
47 Generalstaben, Volume II, Appendix 22.
48 Liljefalk & Lütken, p. 263, say, "The great number of unwounded prisoners aroused, at the time, a feeling close to shame, both in the Army and amongst the people."

8th Infantry Regiment	1	24	1	46	—	82 (9W)	—	12
15th Infantry Regiment	—	—	—	—	—	1	—	—
18th Infantry Regiment	—	1	—	2	—	13	—	—
22nd Infantry Regiment	—	—	—	1	—	—	—	—
Field Artillery	—	2	—	—	—	—	—	—
Fortress Artillery	—	1	—	—	—	—	—	—
2nd Division Ambulance	—	3	—	2	—	3	—	—
Totals	6	120	4	213	1	302	—	31

W = Wounded

von Fischer commented acidly on du Plat's operation; "Such arrangements can never lead to a favourable result. They can lead only to useless bloodshed, to defeat and the demoralisation of the troops, and in all circumstances these dispositions must be regarded as irresponsibly poor."[49]

Whatever the views of his army, any confidence that Gerlach himself may have had in his troops' ability to fight in the open utterly vanished after March 17th. His plans, always defensive, became almost a case of housekeeping. In the days following the chaotic mess of the 17th, he took more steps to confirm the static nature of the defence.

The loss of so much territory and the consequent squeezing of the position necessitated a reorganisation in the defence. The outposts now occupied trenches and rifle pits between 200 and 250 yards outside the lines. These were occupied during the day by the assigned troops, and at night were the assembly points for the vedettes that were posted about a 300 yards further out.

Due to the constricted nature of the defences, it was necessary to be able to deploy forces quickly in support of the outposts in case of attack. The positions were therefore, by an order of March 22nd, manned in the following way:

First Line: The position was still divided into two wings, the right running north from Redoubt VII to Als Sound, and the left running south from Redoubt VII to The Vemmingbund. At night, each of the regiments in the front line posted a full company as outposts in front of the fortifications, and during the day, ½ a company. This gave four companies at night, and two during the day, covering the whole line.

The First Reserve units comprised two brigades, one stationed at the barracks line, along the main road between the Redoubts and the Bridgehead, and the other quartered in Sønderborg. The Second Reserve was composed of two brigades, which would bivouac in the area of Sønderborg.

The duty rota for all of these units was that two brigades manned the fortifications for six days, then became the First Reserve for six days, followed by bivouac on Als for three nights.

One Field Artillery Battery was deployed in the position for duty periods of 24 hours. The batteries so deployed were the 2nd, 8th, 10th, and 11th. A battery's

49 von Fischer, p. 228.

four sections were posted thus – one either side of the Flensburg Road, west of Dybbøl Mill, one between Redoubts VIII and IX, and the fourth on the extreme right, covering the Aabenraa Road.

The cavalry were to muster one officer and 30 men daily, as messengers[50].

General Gerlach continued to have more obstacles placed in front of the Redoubt Line, to the point where only eight narrow passages were allowed for the outposts to move in and out.[51] Any major sortie from the Redoubt line was now all but impossible. It became quite clear during the latter part of March that he was not going to undertake offensive movements of any kind at Dybbøl. This proved to be a great gift to an enemy still largely unsure of his own intentions.

In the days immediately following the actions of March 17th, the Prussian heavy batteries were restricted in their fire, due to a temporary lack of ammunition because of the heavy use that day. Each battery was restricted to firing 40-60 rounds during the day, and 3-4 at night.[52] Positions for new batteries were also identified by reconnaissance parties. 40 officers and 300 men of the infantry were transferred to the Artillery Park at Adsbøl.

Two new Prussian artillery positions were constructed, one at Gammelmark on the night of the 18/19th, and the second on the following night south of Hvilhøi. Both were armed by the 20th. These were:

Table 26

Prussian Batteries established at Dybbøl, March 18th-20th 1864

Battery	Armament	Target & Approximate Range

King Christian IX inspecting repairs in Redoubt II at Dybbol, 22 March
(Liljefalck & Lütken)

---

50 *Beretning fra Krigsministeriet [Report from the War Ministry] om Fægtningen den 28de Marts 1864.*
51 Johansen, Jens, *Dybbøl 1864*, p.156.
52 Ibid, p. 424.

| Battery Nr. 4 | Two rifled 12 pounders | Redoubts II-V[53] (2,600 – 3,500 yards) |
| Battery Nr. 5 | Four rifled 12 pounders | Redoubt I & ships (2,800 yards) |

The following day, Battery 5, in an area where other work was taking place, attracted so much fire from the Redoubts that it was dismantled on the 21st, and not rearmed until March 29th. By the 21st, with the arrival of 1/ Guard Fortress Artillery Company, there were at Dybbøl five Fortress Artillery Companies, with a total of 16 24 pounders, 24 12 pounders, and 16 25 pound mortars.

On the 22nd, King Christian arrived in Dybbøl for an inspection of the position, accompanied by the War Minister, Colonel Lundbye. At 19:30 that evening, he visited the fortifications, going first to Redoubt IV and then to Redoubt II, to see for himself the effects of the daily bombardments and the nightly repair work, speaking to both officers and men. The King left for Fredericia the next day.

On the night of the 25/26th, Battery Nr. 3 had its six rifled 6 pounders removed. They were replaced by four rifled 12 pounders, manned by the 8th Fortress Company/Artillery Brigade Nr. 7. Its target priorities remained the same.

Between the 18th and the 26th of March inclusive, about 1,650 rounds were fired by the Broager batteries, primarily on the southern fortifications, mainly Redoubts II and IV. Return fire, primarily from Redoubt II, amounted to something over 500 rounds. Some additional defensive fire was directed at Prussian working parties from various Redoubts. Damage to the defences was considerable, and although effective repair work was swiftly carried out, the need to continually raise and extend as well as mount new traverses, meant that fewer guns could be mounted. Damage to ordnance in the line was also heavy, although several rifled guns were placed in a number of positions.[54]

On the 27th, Batteries 1 and 3 directed their fire exclusively at Redoubt II, the 'Feldzeugmeister' Battery (2) fired upon Redoubt VI, and Battery 4 swept the area behind the Redoubt Line. 345 rounds were fired, answered by 100 shots from the rifled 12 pounders and 54 from the rifled 4 pounder. Redoubt II was badly pounded, and one cannon damaged. Amazingly, only one Danish military labourer was wounded during the day.

---

53 Grosser Generalstab, Volume II, p.424, also points out that this new battery would have the ability to shell the barracks line, the existence of which the Prussians had recently discovered.

54 Ibid, pp. 424-427, and Generalstaben, Volume II, pp.262-270. See Appendix XIII for details of the armament of the Dybbøl Redoubts on April 2nd.

Map 21: The Island of Als

The Ballegaard Project

Although Major-General Goeben had advocated a landing on Als almost from the beginning of operations there, it was not attempted when it may have been the least difficult. Once it had become clear that Dybbøl was to be held by the Danes, the idea became more attractive to some officers. The simple capture of Fehmarn in mid-March, under the noses of Danish warships, reinforced this view.[55] General von Moltke was always of the opinion that a landing on Als was preferable to any operations at Dybbøl, whereas Field Marshal Wrangel was not. Prince Friedrich Carl fell in the middle of these views. The natural result was that both 'projects' went ahead in tandem. Friedrich Carl deputed his Chief of Staff, Colonel Blumenthal, to plan the operation.

For a landing on Als, there were three possible crossing points, The Flensburg Fjord, Als Sound, and Als Fjord. The first was soon discounted, as the necessity of

55 See Chapter 6.

assistance from the Prussian Navy was vital, and that service was, in the Baltic, essentially immobilised by the Danish Fleet.[56] The second possibility offered the shortest distance of water to cross, and also the best protection from Danish warships by artillery emplaced on the shore. This was rejected because of its proximity to Sønderborg, where the Danish reserves on the island were stationed. By default, therefore, Blumenthal chose the route across the Als Fjord, specifically a crossing from Ballegaard, on the mainland, to Hardeshøi, on the northern part of the island, a distance of just under 2,300 yards.[57]

The forces allocated to the attempt would be the brigades of Generals Canstein, Goeben, Raven, and Roeder, two Jäger battalions, six batteries, and two squadrons. 50 guns would be emplaced around Ballegaard to cover the crossing. The plan was presented to the King in a letter from the Prince on March 10th. Wilhelm was initially most concerned with the danger of such an endeavour, and insisted that the fleet must be involved. Not until the end of the month was Friedrich Carl to learn that he had a 'free-hand' in the operation.[58]

In the meanwhile, boats were being gathered for the crossing. Blumenthal had, as early as February 28th, actually instructed Engineer Captain Schütze, and a sea Captain, Bartelsen, who knew local waters well, to make the transport arrangements. Gathered for the attempt were 42 Prussian iron and 22 wooden pontoons, 4 half pontoons, 36 Austrian half-pontoons, 8 captured Danish pontoons, and 27 local fishing, or 'keel' boats. These could all be lashed together in various combinations to carry different loads. The pioneers and infantry provided the rowers for the boats, and frequent drills took place in Nybøl Lagoon. The Danes were only too well aware of the entire operation.[59]

There was still confusion as to the relative importance of a landing on Als in relation to the operations against Sundeved. Neither plan could be effectively pursued whilst competing for the limited resources available. General Moltke thought that any proposed landing could only be conducted with the co-operation of the Navy, and the start of the siege had awaited this. Neither plan was therefore actually being moved forward to a major extent.

Friedrich Carl considered that there were insufficient troops available for the Ballegaard operation, and also to defend the Sundeved in case of a Danish attack whilst it was undertaken. Therefore, after a telegram from Berlin, Marshal Wrangel, on the 25th, ordered the Guard Division to send nine of its battalions and 20 guns immediately to Sundeved. General von der Mülbe carried out this order by forced-march, the troops reaching quarters around Aabenraa on the evening of the 27th, and marching to Sundeved the next day.[60]

In spite of his own general misgivings about the Dybbøl operation, General von Moltke at this stage held the opinion that the two undertakings should

56 See Chapter 12.

57 Grosser Generalstab, Volume II, pp. 387-389 & 443 and von Fischer, pp. 232-235.

58 Moltke, *Militärische Korrespondenz*, letter from the King to Prince Friedrich Carl, with letter Nr. 46 to the King, 15th March 1864, and letter Nr. 31, to Colonel Blumenthal, 31st March 1864.

59 Grosser Generalstab, Volume II, p. 441, and Liljefalk & Lütken, p. 289.

60 The Guards left three battalions and six guns in Jutland in the division of Major-General Count Münster. See Appendix XVIII.

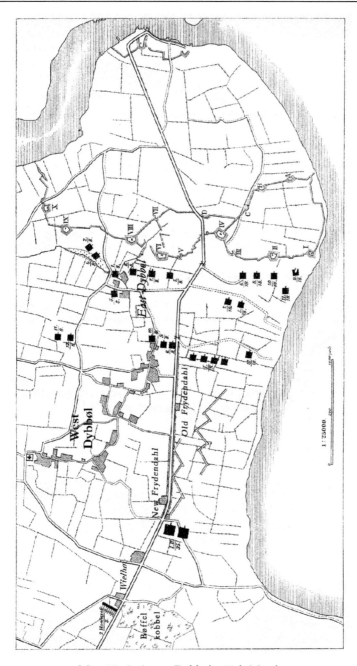

Map 22: Action at Dybbøl - 28th March

continue, complementing one another.[61] In practice the opening of a siege at Dybbøl had been delayed to await the arrival of the fleet. That situation was now reversed, and the opening of the siege was intended to facilitate a landing on the island. The War Ministry telegraphed Army Headquarters asking whether it was intended to await the crossing to Als before the opening of siege works, whilst also making it clear that this was not desirable. Preparations were quickly put in hand to begin a siege.

Edward Dicey wrote from Sønderborg on the 27th of March:

> The sense of their own weakness operates very powerfully upon the Danes. They know only too well that, if Germany hold firm in her purpose, and the Western Powers continue firm to their want of purpose, the ultimate issue of the contest is beyond a doubt. Denmark knows that her only real chance of escape from her foes lies in some Continental complication, or some foreign aid.

Ironically, that night the Danes were to be given a morale boost, from which they would draw the wrong conclusion. Dicey himself would witness some of what occurred.

Before the initial siege works could be constructed it was considered that the Danish pickets should again be pushed further towards the line of fortifications. Covering rifle pits were to be dug from 3-400 yards from the Redoubts on the Prussian right. The newly arrived 10th 'Combined' Infantry Brigade, commanded by 56 year old Major-General von Raven, was chosen for this. It was brought forward from Flensburg on March 19th, arriving at Dybbol on the 22nd, relieving the outposts of Roeder's Brigade at Stenderup and West Dybbol that day. With the addition of three battalions of the 13th Division, released from occupation duty in Schleswig and Holstein, there were now 32 Prussian battalions at Dybbol, outnumbering the Danes' 26 for the first time![62]

Raven's brigade was a temporary formation, as was common with the Prussian Army in this campaign. For administrative and logistical reasons, GR8, the Leib Grenadier Regiment, from 9th Brigade replaced IR52, thus creating the 'Combined' 10th Brigade of GR8 and IR18, leaving the 'Combined' 9th Brigade of Major-General Schlegell, IR48 and IR52 on occupation duties in southern Schleswig and Holstein. Both brigades would revert to their permanent order of battle, within Lieutenant-General Tümpling's 5th Division, at the end of April. Formed on March 19th, the 10th 'Combined' Brigade came immediately under the orders of I Corps.[63]

The Covering Attack of 28th March

Lieutenant General Manstein issued orders to Major-General Raven on the evening of March 27th for his first operation. In the early hours of the next morning, his men were to launch a surprise assault on the Danish outpost line both north

61 Moltke, *Militärische Korrespondenz*, letter number 52 to Colonel von Blumenthal 21st March 1864.
62 On the 28th, the nine battalions of the Guards would arrive from Jutland, bringing the final total to 41 infantry battalions.
63 Grosser Generalstab, Volume II, pp. 393-394.

and south of the Flensburg Road. They were to push it back some 400 paces, and there dig rifle pits for the new Prussian outpost line, giving space for the construction of the siege works to begin. Since the Danes must have no warning, there was to be no preliminary artillery fire.

Raven deployed the GR8 north, and IR18 south of the Flensburg Road, each with 2 battalions forward, and one in reserve, the latter being F/GR8, Major Gaudi and I/IR18, Lieutenant-Colonel von Wietersheim. 100 spades and shovels were issued to each regiment to help dig the new rifle pits. In the event it was far too few. Behind Raven's troops, in the Bøffelkobbel, stood the general reserve, FR35 of Canstein's 11th Brigade and 2 Howitzer Battery/Brandenburg Artillery Brigade Nr. 3. A detachment of pioneers also stood by at New Frydendahl, to assist with the digging of trenches.

At 03:00, a few shots, rapidly followed by the rattle of heavy rifle fire, punctuated by 'wild yells', broke the stillness.[64] In the pitch-black the Danish outposts heard the attacking troops before they saw them. North of the main road, the attackers from I/GR8, Lieutenant-Colonel v. Greiffenberg, and II/GR8, Major Michelmann,[65] were met by a volley, and there was some initial close quarter fighting as the Prussians tumbled into the rifle pits. The Danish outposts hurriedly pulled back into the defences, Second-Lieutenant Dickmeis of 2nd Regiment being killed, and a number of men captured.[66] South of the road, II/IR18, Major Meden, and F/IR18, Lieutenant-Colonel von Boswell, met no resistance, the Danish outposts falling back into the main line. All along the Redoubt Line, a heavy fire of artillery and small arms was directed at the attackers.

By 04:00, IR18's skirmishers were little over 100 yards from the Redoubts. Behind them, (from north to south) 6/IR18, Captain Kessel, 8/IR18, Premier-Lieutenant Raumer, 10/IR18, Captain Count Finkenstein, and 9/IR18, Captain Schultze, had dug-in in front of the position. 7/IR18, Captain Schor, 5/IR18, Captain Schkopp, and 11/IR18, Premier-Lieutenant von Gersdorff also dug-in in a second line behind this. All were within 350 yards of the fortifications and under heavy fire. Apart from the far right, few of the units were able to dig deep enough to be adequately under cover.

In the north, individual detachments of GR8 had pursued the retreating Danish pickets right up to the wire and obstacles of Redoubt VI. Further north 2/GR8, Captain Pohlmann, and 4/GR8, Premier-Lieutenant Wilucki (senior), advanced to East Dybbøl between Redoubts VIII and IX, before halting under heavy fire, and starting to dig in.

Premierlieutenant G. C. F. Tranberg, commanding 4/2nd Regiment, was in Redoubt VI during the attack. His account makes it clear that in at least some places, the Prussian attack had taken on a momentum of its own:

---

64 These 'wild yells' were unfamiliar to the Danish troops, used to hearing the Prussian, 'Hurrah!' The Leib Grenadier Regiment had a unique battle cry, dating from the Napoleonic Wars – 'Heurich!'

65 Seven companies. 6/GR8, Captain von der Hagen, did not advance, and remained posted in reserve near the Flensburg Road south of F/GR8, Major von Gaudi. See map.

66 Liljefalck & Lütken, pp. 290-291.

The attack on Dybbøl, 28th March (Liljefalck & Lütken)

At this moment, the Adjutant, Lieutenant Hindenburg, reported to me, since the battalion commander had been wounded. He appeared at the right time, and I gave him command of two platoons. Except for a small reserve, the whole company was positioned along the parapets. The night's silence had vanished and now it was the rattle of muskets, the zipping of balls and the hurrahs of the enemy. In the Redoubt I found one artillery Aspirant and 4-6 men, and immediately ordered him to fire his gun for the roar to frighten the attackers and the muzzle flame show us how far they had come. The Aspirant refused but as I told him that I was commanding in the Redoubt and that I took responsibility, he obeyed and the thunder of the cannon sounded into the night. Our infantry's fire now opened gaps in the enemy's ranks. Suddenly their 'Hurrah!' vanished, and we could hear their officers beg, swear and shout, 'Forward, men! We will soon be in the Redoubt!' All was in vain, however, and they withdrew to our trenches previously taken by them.[67]

The existing Prussian outpost line, manned by 13th Division, had attempted to maintain contact with the attacking force of GR8, sending first one, and then two more, platoons to maintain communication. Earlier, I/FR35 and II/FR35 had been moved forward to New Frydendal, in case they were requested to assist, but no such request came.

Around 05:00, General von Manstein, having had reports of the positions occupied by the two attacking regiments, decided that the action was effectively over, and about 06:00 returned to Graasten. The supporting howitzer battery also returned to its quarters.[68]

67 Tranberg, G., "2den Paaskedag den 28 Marts 1864", *Danebrog*, Volume 2, Copenhagen 1881-82, p. 755. Tranberg's men were probably engaged with 5/GR8, Premierlieutenant Vogel von Falckenstein.

68 Grosser Generalstab, Volume II, pp. 431-432.

The situation of the two regiments was, however, far from secure. When the initial attack began, Major-General Vogt, the position commander that night, had thought that a major assault was under way. He ordered 5th Brigade (Harbou) forward from the Bridgehead, and 4th Brigade (Faaborg) and the Life Guards Infantry from Sønderborg. The 2nd (Kauffmann) and 3rd (Wørishøffer) Brigades on Als were also put on the move towards Sønderborg. General Gerlach himself came forward and took command, deputing the left wing to General du Plat, and the right to Vogt.

The already heavy fire grew in volume. As day broke, the Prussian batteries at Gammelmark also opened fire, particularly against Redoubt II, in an effort to lessen the Danish shelling, but were unable to do so. Raven's men, and their supporting pioneers, had dug in as best they could, but the lack of effective tools, as well as the loss of control in some units, particularly the Leib Grenadiers, had hampered the work which they had been supposed to carry out. They were under constant fire, that from Redoubts III, VI, and VIII being particularly heavy.[69]

North of East Dybbøl, the firsts units to pull back from the galling fire were the isolated 2 and 4/GR8. These had already pushed too far, and could achieve little on their own. Captain Pohlmann and Premier-Lieutenant Wilucki withdrew to seek cover to the rear.

Infantry counterattacks from the Redoubt Line also began. North of the road, ½ of 8/10th Regiment, Premierlieutenant H.E. Petersen, pushed forward from the fortifications against the Prussian left flank, supported by two platoons from 1/10th led by Second-Lieutenant Goldschacht, and a Swedish officer, Premierlieutenant Bjørck.[70] They advanced against the left of 8/GR8, Captain Cohen van Baren, which, after the retreat of the two companies north of them, was now the left wing of the Prussian force. After several attacks, in one of which Petersen was killed, the attempts were halted.

After holding off these moves, Cohen van Baren began to pull his own company back, but soon found himself again under attack from the units of 10th Regiment facing him. They had been reinforced by four additional platoons (one each from 1, 2, and 7/10th Regiment, and one from 3/6th) under Second-Lieutenant Benzon and Premierlieutenant Hammelef.

8/GR8 withdrew through East Dybbøl, now in flames, and was joined west of the village by 3/GR8, Captain von Unruh, which had been ordered there by the battalion commander, Lieutenant-Colonel von Greiffenberg. Captain Rheinbaben's 1/GR8 continued the fight in the village. Greiffenberg was badly

---

69 *Beretning far Krigsministeriet [Report from the War Ministry] om Fægtningen den 28de Marts 1864.*

70 The number of foreign volunteers in the Danish service from other Nordic countries was not huge, although the number of officers and officials was significant within the total. These were:

Swedish – 529, of whom 80 were officers, one, an officer-aspirant, and 12 officials

Norwegian – 105, of whom 7 were officers, and ten officials

Finnish – 7, of whom 4 were officers

Icelanders – 3 volunteers.

Johansen, *Dybbøl 1864*, p. 102. See Appendices IV, XII and XX for comparison of figures for foreign officers in the Danish Army at different stages in the campaign.

wounded a short time later. Rheinbaben then pulled his company back, pushed all the time by their pursuers. In taking the remains of the village from the Prussians, Premierlieutenant Hammelef was wounded along with Senior Sergeant Pagh. 10th Regiment had the highest casualty figure on the defender's side that morning, a total of 88.

5 and 7/GR8, Premier-Lieutenants Vogel von Falckenstein and von Eckardstein, were still in their forward positions, but their exposed left flank was now under attack. A further push by 7/15th Regiment, Premierlieutenant Neergaard, along with 2nd Regiment's outposts (½ a company each of 5 and 7/2nd) under Premierlieutenant Secher was launched from the main line, south of Redoubt VI, at Falckenstein's 5/GR8. Secher was killed, and this attack stalled.

Word of Secher's death was sent into the fortifications, and Major Gedde, commander of I/2nd Regiment, somewhat peremptorily ordered Second-Lieutenant C. F. Holst out to take his place. Holst did so, got the troops moving again, and kept the momentum going. The Prussians withdrew from their positions, and all the forward companies of the Leib Grenadier Regiment retreated behind the Fusilier Battalion, still in reserve. Fighting north of the Flensburg Road effectively ended at this point. 4/IR13, Captain von Stockhausen, had deployed forward in the area of Ragebøl during the fighting, suffering four casualties, but as no assistance was called for, and GR8 was observed to withdraw, these troops were stood down to resume normal duties.

South of the main road, the Poles of IR18 were slightly better off than their comrades, since they were able to use the ravines in the area as shelter. Nevertheless, only on its right, near the Vemmingbund, had the regiment managed to dig in reasonably well, and enemy fire was still very heavy. To add to their problems, they now faced the intervention of the ironclad *Rolf Krake*, which steamed past the Broager batteries at 05:00, taking several hits from their fire without serious damage.[71]

Edward Dicey, asleep in Sonderborg, had been woken at about 03:30 by the heavy fire, decided that the tempo of the battle was unusual, and quickly dressed. In the early morning darkness, he observed hurried movements of troops. As day began to break he took position near a Danish artillery battery at Sonderborg. From here in the daylight at around 06.30, he witnessed the *Rolf Krake* under fire from the batteries across the Vemmingbund;

> Then I heard a cry raised by soldiers standing near me that the *Rolf Krake* was going into action. Slowly an unwieldy barge-like hull disappeared behind the headland of Dybbol Hill. We could hear the loud crash of her heavy guns, and then the batteries of the Vemmingbund opened fire, not, indeed, at the forts of Dybbol, beneath whose walls the Prussian columns were massed together, but at the gallant ironclad. There was a long pause – so at least it seemed to us, waiting there – and then at length the *Rolf Krake* appeared from behind the headland, steaming furiously beneath the range of the Prussian batteries which lines the southern bluffs of the Vemmingbund bay. Slowly she moved on, amidst a very hailstorm of shells from the cliffs above her. They splashed on every side of her, like giant porpoises playing around her keel. As the shots touched the wa-

71 *Beretning fra Krigsministeriet [War Ministry Report] om Faegtningen den 28de Marts 1864*, Copenhagen 1864.

Rolf Krake in action on 28th March (*Illustrated London News*)

ter, fountains of spray and foam leapt into the air, sometimes enveloping the vessel in a watery mist. We could see the rifle-balls fall into the water like handfuls of pebbles, and still her open deck remained crowded with the crew. Nothing touched her while she remained in sight, and, passing the batteries one by one, she steamed out into the open, till at last the farewell shots the Prussians sent after her fell so far astern that she was allowed to pursue her way in peace.[72]

This rather romantic description belies the extreme importance to Danish morale that the ironclad represented. She had already performed her duty that morning, before Dicey saw her. After passing the Broager batteries, she steamed to a position on the right flank of IR18's forward companies, and opened fire on them with her four 68 pounders from less than 150 yards offshore.[73] These heavy guns at close range had a devastating effect on the morale of the regiment's young soldiers. They had never been under fire before that morning, and certainly the ship's heavy guns were an unexpected additional horror.

The position of Colonel von Kettler's two forward battalions was precarious. Under fire from heavy artillery to their front and right flank, both battalions were also subject to increasing infantry attacks. There was no choice other than to withdraw. The Fusiliers pulled back first, with II/IR18 conforming. *Rolf Krake* had steamed away from the beach into the middle of the Bund, and continued to fire upon all three battalions. Von Kettler pulled the whole regiment behind the Avnbjerg. A further slight advance was attempted after the departure of the ironclad, but by 09:00, IR18 was assembled once again behind the Avnbjerg.[74]

72 Dicey, Edward, *The Schleswig-Holstein War*, Volume II, London 1864, pp. 49-50.
73 Anon, "Das Gefecht vom 28 März 1864", *Militärische Blätter*, Volume 14, Number 6, Berlin 1865.
74 As a turreted vessel, *Rolf Krake's* rate of fire was slow for a shore bombardment role. Had the Danes had a battery ironclad in her place on this occasion, Prussian losses

When the battalions withdrew, isolated detachments were left behind, some of which could not escape through the shelling. As units of 22nd Infantry Regiment advanced from the fortifications, they came across some of these men. Second-Lieutenant Wørmer went forward with a corporal and seven men, encountering 16 Prussians, who surrendered to him. Escorting these to the rear, Wørmer sent Regimental Clerk Klint with three men to see if there were any more stragglers in front of the position. Klint returned with an unwounded officer, Second-Lieutenant Rasper, and seven men.[75] Almost all of the prisoners were from F/IR18.

Firing finally died down around 09:00. The net result of the operation was failure, and only some of 6th Division's outposts had been pushed forward something over 150 yards. The Danish outposts returned to most of their original forward positions, finding that the trenches had been reversed, and had to be reconfigured once again. During the morning, the Prussians requested, and were granted, a truce for the purpose of casualty collection. It lasted from 11:00 until 12:45, although there was some fire from the Broager batteries during the cease-fire, which killed two men.[76]

Dicey's observation was of the skilful withdrawal of the vessel, her skipper, (Naval) Captain H.P. Rothe, steering close in to the southern shore of the Vemmingbund, underneath any possible angle of fire from the Gammelmark batteries, and thus to safely regain open water. The success of the ship's employment on this occasion did not go unnoticed by the Prussian gunners.[77]

Though clearly not an assault upon the main position itself, the defenders appear to have seen it as such. John Skinner, of *The Daily News* later wrote:

> On Easter Monday, we were more cheerful and elated than at any other time during the siege. Overestimating the extent of the battle, as we did, and thinking that a serious assault had been repulsed, it appeared for a moment as though the Danes might be able to hold out until the Conference should bring an Armistice.[78]

This assumption, however misplaced, was nevertheless an excellent fillip for the morale of the Danish troops, and for that reason alone, most beneficial. The Danish countermoves were conducted with spirit, but piecemeal and poorly co-ordinated. A rare opportunity to give the encircling foe a real bloody nose was wasted.

must have been much higher. However, *Dannebrog*, the only other ironclad in service at that point, drew too much water to enter the area.

75 Liljefalk & Lütken, pp. 203-294. Rasper surrendered his sword to Klint. It now hangs in the Dybbøl Center. Wørmer was awarded the Gold Cross of the Order of Dannebrog, and Klint the Silver.

76 *Beretning fra Krigsministeriet [Report from the War Ministry] om Fægtningen dem 28de Marts 1864.*

77 A first step was taken in the next few days. On direct orders from General von Moltke, fishing nets were stretched across the Vemmingbund to hamper *Rolf Krake*, under the supervision of Premier-Lieutenant Saß-Jaworski, of FR 35, Grosser Generalstab, Volume II, p. 433.

78 Skinner, J.E.H., *The Tale of Danish Heroism*, London 1865, p. 150.

The attempt to push the defending outpost line back had failed. One third of the attacking troops were not used. No direct artillery support was made available, and the forward companies, once they had achieved (or exceeded) their objectives, were left to continue as best they could. Overconfidence had certainly played a part in the serious underestimation of any possible enemy response.[79] General von Manstein prematurely decided that the battle was over, just as General Goeben had 11 days before. This time the price was a repulse. The Danish troops behaved well, 2nd and 10th Regiments being particularly commended by General Gerlach.

As on several occasions in this campaign, the casualties suffered by both sides were light considering the volume of fire, and this is especially true of the Prussians here, in makeshift positions and subjected to heavy artillery fire at close range. Colonel Johansen comments that the Prussians, "...got away cheaply...", from this attack. It is difficult to disagree.[80]

Total losses were:

Table 27

Prussian Casualties during the covering attack at Dybbøl, March 28th 1864

Prussian: 188[81]

	Killed		Wounded		Prisoners		Missing	
Unit	Officers	Men	Officers	Men	Officers	Men	Officers	Men
Leib Grenadier Regiment Nr. 8	1	12	2	69	3W	2W	—	—
IR Nr. 18	—	11	5	51	1	27	—	—
IR Nr. 13	—	1	—	3	—	—	—	—
Totals	1	24	7	123	4	29	—	—

Table 28

Danish Casualties during the covering Attack at Dybbøl, March 28th 1864

Danish: 218[82]

	Killed		Wounded		Prisoners		Missing	
Unit	Officers	Men	Officers	Men	Officers	Men	Officers	Men
2nd Infantry Regiment	2	22	1	11	—	21 (2W)	—	14
3rd Infantry Regiment	—	—	—	1	—	—	—	—
4th Infantry Regiment	—	—	—	1	—	—	—	—
6th Infantry Regiment	1	6	1	9	—	—	—	—

79 Grosser Generalstab, Volume II, p. 436.
80 Johansen, Jens, *Dybbøl 1864*, p. 163.
81 Grosser Generalstab, Volume II, Appendix 47.
82 Generalstaben, Volume II, Appendix 33. Of the missing, 18 are likely to have deserted.

8th Infantry Regiment	—	1	—	—	—	—	—	—
10th Infantry Regiment	2	20	1	56	—	6 (1W)	—	3
15th Infantry Regiment	—	—	—	6	—	—	—	—
22nd Infantry Regiment	—	—	—	2	—	14	—	—
Field Artillery	—	2	—	4	—	—	—	—
Fortress Artillery	—	—	—	5	—	1	—	—
2nd Division Ambulance	—	—	—	—	—	—	—	5
Totals	5	51	—	95	—	42	—	22

W = Wounded

The Leib Grenadier Regiment's history comments that more was achieved on the left than on the right, but this is inaccurate and unfair to IR18.[83] During the 29th, Brigade Raven was pulled back into quarters in Graasten, Egernsund, and Ringenæs. For the first time, the newly arrived Guards came into the line, manning outposts from the Vemmingbund, north through Dybbøl, to the Pythuse.

Surprisingly, the failure overnight to gain the required 'elbow room' for the construction of the planned siege works did not cause any delay to the original timetable. The work scheduled would still take place on the night of March 29/30th.

On the 28th, Friedrich Carl received a long message from the War Ministry, a part of which, referring to the possible landing on Als, stated:

> His Majesty has commissioned me to urge Your Royal Highness, with the utmost respect, to inform him by coded or secret message at which point the appearance of the fleet would be most desirable. Accordingly, the fleet will then attempt to get through. Your Royal Highness will be kept informed of its departure, and as far as possible of any obstacles which hinder it. Only if it is clear that the great undertaking being considered cannot be supported in this manner should serious thought be given to carrying it out without the participation of the Navy.[84]

The matter of naval co-operation with the proposed landing remained as fuzzy as ever. On March 27th, Moltke wrote to Colonel Blumenthal that, "I do not know at the moment whether our fleet has come out (or whether they will notify me of this)."[85] In fact, the fleet would never arrive. In the meanwhile, however, a new phase in the operations on the Sundeved was about to start. A formal siege was, at long last, to begin.

83 Horn, Captain A, von, Lichtenstein, Major, *Geschichte des Leib Grenadier Regiments...*, Volume II, p. 25.
84 Grosser Generalstab, Volume II, pp. 427-428.
85 Moltke, *Militärische Korrespondenz*, letter Nr. 56, to Colonel Blumenthal, March 27th 1864.

9

The Siege of Dybbøl

Finally, 51 days after the initial approach to the Sundeved Peninsula, the Prussians started work on the first siege Parallel[1] (see map at the end of the chapter). Unsurprisingly designated the First Parallel, it was opened on the night of the 29/30th March, south of the Flensburg Road at an average distance of roughly 1,000 yards from Redoubts I to IV, and had a length of about 750 yards.[2] Communication trenches from the rear were also constructed. Major-General Canstein's 11th Infantry Brigade was assigned to start the work, along with two pioneer companies (2/3rd and 2/7th Pioneers), all under the command of Lieutenant-Colonel von Kriegsheim. Major Roetscher, commanding officer of Brandenburg Pioneer Battalion Nr. 3, had operational control over the work. The commander of I/IR60, Major von Jena, vividly describes in a family letter what happened:

> The opening of the First Parallel on March 30th was very interesting, and as, with God's help, it went well, so I am happy to have been there. At 6 o'clock (note: 18:00, 29th March) on this side of the Bøffelkobbel, were 1,500 of our men and the same number from the 35th Regiment,[3] who received their tools and were counted and detailed. At half-past eight, when it had become dark, everyone went, without an order, on a signal - they were so attentive - to where our foremost vedettes were, who themselves then crept even further forward. An engineer officer had laid a wide white rope from the Vemmingbund to the main road. The column was led to about the middle of the rope, and then marched off left and right. Two paces from one-another, everyone stuck their spade into the ground. The engineer officer checked whether the distance was correct. A pioneer was allocated to every 12 infantrymen to guide and watch over their work. Now every man laid his rifle behind him and the work began. We had told the men that the Danish forward posts would certainly hear and inform the entrenchments and then we expected shellfire. Thus everyone should try to dig himself in as quickly as possible. This then happened with such an enthusiasm, calm, and order that appeared to be impossible with so many people. Behind

1   Rüstow, p. 445.
2   Fritsch-Lang, A., "L'artillerie rayée prussienne à l'attaque de Düppel, après les auters allemands", *Le Spectateur Militaire*, Volume 50, Paris 1865, is dismissive of the great distance from the Danish works that the parallel was opened, and compares it unfavourably with the French siege of Puebla, Mexico in 1863. This ignores the fact that the operation on the previous night to gain more space to dig the parallel closer to the redoubts had failed to do so. This is also part quoted in, "Notes on the attack of the Duppel Entrenchments", translated by Captain Percy Smith, in *Papers on subjects connected with the Duties of the Corps of Royal Engineers*, Volume 14, Woolwich 1865.
3   Grosser Generalstab, Volume II, p. 439, gives the total number of men involved as 2,737; five battalions of 11th Brigade and the two pioneer companies.

our regiment, the 35th Regiment worked on the approaches. We did not need to worry about people working with exceptional effort, and so I crept forward to the vedette line, and listened. The wind was most advantageous to us, and the night also dark enough. A hundred paces from the workers, I heard almost nothing more from them. On the other hand, I heard music and shouting from the entrenchments. However I still believed that we must be heard and that a flash from the entrenchments would announce a shot, or first they would fire flares, in which case the order was for everyone to keep completely still on the ground and not to move. This did not, however, happen, and after half an hour every man was well under cover, despite the heaviest loam and clay ground. We officers played the worst role, because we could not dig ourselves in. We marched up and down and we were not allowed to smoke, nor could we speak, which, on the eve of battle, was a very sore point for us. When, after two or three hours, everyone was dug in so deeply that rifle and shellfire could no longer be an embarrassment, the work became calmer. We were now so far advanced that every man had dug out 4 feet deep and 4 feet wide by the time we withdrew before daybreak. It was most unfortunate that water entered at many points. To-day, during the day, the Danes were very surprised and constantly looked over with binoculars, and also tried to shoot, but our people, who are now expanding the thing in daylight, are covered. However, tell 'H' that the entrenchments are not the same as 13 years ago. The reason that we can do nothing on our left flank is the formidable batteries on Als, which can shoot as far as Ragebøl and far out. It is easier on the right flank. But the day before yesterday, the *Rolf Krake* brought our 18th Regiment back from Vemmingbund with its shell fire in their rear. In a word, the strongest fortress is easier to take than this position, and unfortunately no-one knew what the Dybbøl Redoubts were. You are surprised that we haven't taken the entrenchments yet, that we haven't even found the small path that was discovered 13 years ago. People are surprised that we don't find cover in the bushes (which have all been cut down), or that we don't advance on the left where, on Als, there are 10 entrenchments and 60 cannon, or along the Vemming shore where the first entrenchment clears the coast, and the *Rolf Krake* appears to our rear despite our batteries. Everyone has an opinion, and no-one is familiar with the situation.[4]

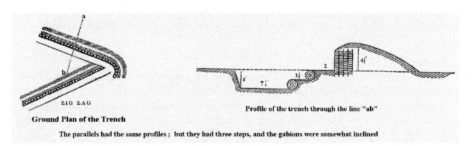

Map 23: Profile of Prussian siege works

4   Von Jena, *Erinnerungen an einen Heimgegangen*, Berlin 1864. Letter Nr. 35, pp. 88-91. The reference to '…13 years ago…' actually refers to the fighting at Dybbøl 15 years before, during the Holstein Revolt.

The work included zig-zag communications trenches to the rear, which were dug at the same time. By 03:30 on the 30th, the parallel had been excavated to a height of 4' 6", a width of just over four feet, and a depth of over three feet. It was discovered at this time that the problem of water seepage into the works would be a problem. During day, as mentioned by Major von Jena, 4/7th Pioneers worked on improving the works, and also on drainage ditches and run-offs, but these difficulties would persist throughout the siege.

That night, the 30/31st, 2,000 men of the Guard Grenadier Brigade worked on widening the parallel to 8½ feet, completing the trenches and approaches, and also started the construction of traverses to protect the position from flanking fire from ships in the Vemmingbund. This work was all completed on the following night (31st March/1st April), by 500 men of I/FR35, Lieutenant-Colonel von Tippelskirch.

I Corps and its supporting Guards units were deployed during the siege, for practical purposes, in three parts. The right flank was to be occupied by the 6th Division, the centre both north and south of the Sønderborg Road, by the Guards and Brigade Raven, and the left flank, to Als Sound, by the 13th Division. In practice, to 6th Division also fell most of the digging and outpost work.

Eight new batteries were established during the same night that the Parallel was widened – 30/31st March – the first of the frontal attack batteries, and the first constructed in nearly two weeks. Seven of these were placed immediately behind the Parallel (Numbers 6-12). The eighth (Number 13) was emplaced on the heights between Dybbøl and Ragebøl. This added another 40 guns, commanded by Major Dietrich, Brandenburg Artillery Brigade, to those already deployed against the fortifications. These batteries, armed overnight 1/2nd April, were:

Table 29

Prussian Batteries established at Dybbøl on the night of March 30th/31st 1864

Battery	Armament	Target & Approximate Range
Battery Nr. 6	Four 7 pound howitzers	Redoubts I & II 1,160 – 1,310 yards
Battery Nr. 7	Four 7 pound howitzers	Redoubts II, II, & IV 1,170 – 1,345 yards
Battery Nr. 8	Six smoothbore 12 pounders	Redoubts II & III 1,165 – 1,200 yards
Battery Nr. 9	Six smoothbore 12 pounders	Redoubts IV & V 1,140 – 1,325 yards
Battery Nr.10	Four 7 pound howitzers	Redoubts V & VI 1,165 – 1,202 yards
Battery Nr.11	Six smoothbore 12 pounders	Redoubts VI & VIII 1,445 – 1,700 yards

Battery Nr.12	Four 7 pound howitzers	Redoubts V & VI
		1,250 – 1,310 yards
Battery Nr.13	Six rifled 6 pounders	Redoubts VI –VIII[5]
		1,200 – 1,700 yards

April 1st

It had been intended that all the batteries would commence the first major bombardment of the Dybbøl fortifications on the 1st of April, but the weather was very stormy. This also impeded the installation of some of the guns. It was therefore decided that the heavy shelling would instead commence on the 2nd.[6]

During the day, Lieutenant-General Gerlach issued new orders detailing how the Redoubts would be occupied and defended by their garrisons. These read as follows:

Instructions of April 1st for duty in the redoubts at Dybbøl
In addition to the personnel serving the guns in the redoubts, the following detachments of infantry will be on duty.

Nr. 1	½ Company
Nr. 2	¾ Company
Nr. 3	¼ Company
Nr. 4	¾ Company
Nr. 5	30 Men
Nr. 6	¾ Company
Nr. 7	¼ Company
Nr. 8	¾ Company
Nr. 9	1 Company
Nr.10	1 Company

The commanding officer in all redoubts is in overall charge of all infantry and artillery detachments in the redoubts.

In case of attack, the oldest serving officer in each redoubt will be in overall command of all troops. Still, however, the commanding officers of the artillery and infantry troops will be individually responsible for the use of the artillery and the deployment of the infantry.

The commanding officer of the artillery detachment is responsible for maintaining order within the redoubt, and the infantry detachment must follow his orders.

It is his responsibility to ensure that the redoubt can be defended and that the bridges can be drawn in, and the entry ports closed. Any damage must be reported to the Duty Officer and must be repaired as soon as possible.

During daylight hours, at least half of the gun crews must be with the guns. One konstabel (gunner) for every one or two guns must at all times watch for enemy movements and also the terrain in order to observe enemy works. The rest of the detachment will then find cover in the terrain behind the redoubt within 300 *alen* (600 feet).

---

5   Grosser Generalstab, Volume II, p.440. Note that Battery Nr. 13 was emplaced NORTH of the Sønderborg Road, east of Dybbøl Church. See Appendix XIII for details of the Danish artillery in place in the redoubts about this time.
6   Ibid, p.442.

If shots are being fired from the redoubt, the artillery detachment must move into the redoubt immediately.

During daylight hours, the infantry detachment must seek cover within 400 *alen* (800 feet) of the redoubt. They must, however, have two to four observation posts in the redoubt in order to observe enemy movements, and when anything is observed, report it immediately to the infantry commander who will, in turn, report to the artillery commander.

Should the enemy appear to attack, the detachment must move into the redoubt as soon as possible and the entry ports must be closed. The infantry commander must immediately take out troops to ensure the closing of the entry port.

During the night the whole garrison must remain inside the redoubt, the bridge must be drawn in and the entry ports closed. The guns will be loaded and sighted in the manner so ordered for the individual redoubt.

The watch at the guns must have tubes and lanyards at hand for their guns.

If work is done in the redoubts during the night, the bridge is not to be drawn in whilst the work is being done.

If a special labour detail is being used and there is a risk of overcrowding, then part of the infantry detachment must be withdrawn and seek cover close behind the redoubt.

If shots are being fired from the outposts, the labour detail will move out and the infantry detachment, which had sought temporary cover outside, will move in, the bridge drawn in and the entry port closed.

The artillery detachment must perform all work related to the artillery, and aid the labour detail in whatever work is to be done on the earthworks and whatever work is assigned by their commander for the purposes of ensuring cover for the troops.

The infantry detachment must supply whatever troops the artillery commander may require.

The Instructions, "The manning and the defence of the closed redoubts at Dybbøl", of February 19th this year, remain in force where they are unchanged or unmodified by the above-stated conditions. However, blockhouses must not be used to stay in or for defence.[7]

April 2nd

On Als, the following ordnance in fixed batteries was in place, from south to north:

Mill Battery	four 84 pound howitzers, type I
Church Battery	six smoothbore 36 pounder cannon
Baadsager Battery	four 24 pounder smoothbore cannon
Flank Battery	six 84 pound howitzers, type I

7 Generalstaben, Volume II, Appendix 17, except that an omission in the text leaves out reference to the infantry garrison of Redoubt VII. This is merely a printing error. The detail for Redoubt VII is taken from De Bas, *L'Armee Danoise en 1864*, p. 277. These orders formalised instructions that the majority of the redoubts' garrisons were actually ordered to spend most of the daylight hours some distance outside the works. This was very sensible in terms of seeking shelter from artillery bombardment, but also potentially highly dangerous in the case of a swift and unexpected infantry assault.

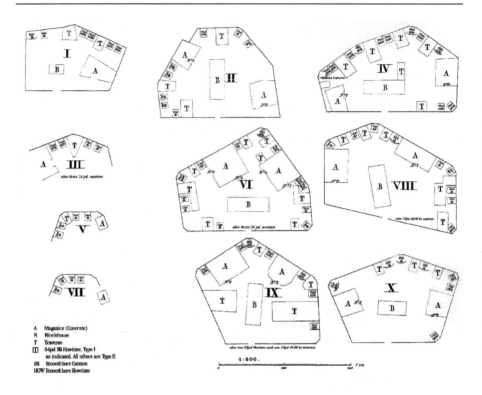

Map 24: The Dybbøl Redoubts, 2nd April

Surlykk Battery	two 84 pound howitzers, type II
	four rifled 12 pounder 'metal' cannon
Kjærvig Battery	two 24 pound howitzers
	two 12 pounder smoothbore cannon
South Rønhave Battery	two 24 pound howitzers
	two 12 pounder smoothbore cannon
'Skov' Battery	two 24 pound howitzers
	two rifled 4 pounder iron cannon
	two 24 pound howitzers
Battery at Arnkilsøre	two 24 pound howitzers
	two rifled 4 pounder cannon

After a request by the Danes, a three-hour truce was arranged to begin at 11:00, for the purpose of a final casualty collection for bodies still lying in front of the redoubts from March 28th.[8] When this truce expired at 14:00, all 52 (so assigned) Prussian guns, including those at Broager, opened fire on the redoubts and

---

8   von Fischer, p. 244. Schøller, p. 66, says two hours, beginning at 12:00.

Sønderborg in the heaviest bombardment seen here up until that time.[9] It grew in intensity, and was particularly heavy between the hours of 17:00 and 19:00, as darkness came.

The intensification of the bombardment was palpable to the defenders. The correspondent with the Danish army from *The* (London) *Times*, Antonio Gallenga, clearly under stress, graphically described the situation from Sønderborg. It should be noted that some of his timings are, understandably, somewhat in error:

> This, April 2nd, is the first day in which we have seen such serious work as may betoken the beginning of the end. We are still all stunned with the din of real war, and it is not without great difficulty that I collect my thoughts and compose my mind so as to give a tolerably distinct and intelligible narrative of passing events.
>
> I set out for a pleasure ride on horseback with a friend a few minutes after three o'clock in the afternoon. The morning had been rainy; but a strong north-westerly wind had driven the clouds from the heavens, and the weather was sharply cold though bright. Our horses were not exactly frisky but fidgety, exhibiting that kind of perverse freakishness, which sometimes, with them, arises from a vague instinct of alarm. The usual slack and unmeaning cannonade had gone on the whole morning; but we had learnt to despise it, and had not even turned out to inquire what its purpose or its results might be. The artillery, however, on Dybbøl Hill soon quickened its fire to a pitch not only unprecedented during the previous phases of this war, but hardly to be matched by anything we had read or heard of in any war. The cannonade was appalling. It was the battle of the angels and demons as imagined by Milton. We flattered ourselves for a moment that all this brisk discharge proceeded from the Danish Bastions. We knew that Prussian Batteries had lately been descried on the Avnbjerg, on several points about Dybbøl village, and on other positions along the line, and fancied that the Danes, bent on the destruction of the enemy's works, wished to show the sluggish Germans with what activity and to what purpose cannon should be handled. The noise became so awful, that after a short hour's ride, we hastened home, and leaving our horses, made our way on foot to the Windmill Battery by the south-eastern shore; then again shifted our place of observation, and went to the top of a hill, in the centre of the windmills which crown Sønderborg on the north, where an arbor in the corner of the garden commands the most extensive view of the Dybbøl heights across the Sound. From the vantage ground we thus successively occupied, we had it in our power to see the flash of every gun, and to follow the path of every shell. The Danes, it soon became apparent, had not taken the initiative in the action; it was the Prussians, who, after all that mere farce of a cannonade, opened their fire with a will, and went to work as if they really meant mischief. Possibly, they had hitherto merely kept up their play at cannon balls to give themselves time to complete their works in front of the Danish lines; possibly, also, their government had, at last, given up all hopes or fears of a Conference, and had telegraphed to their commanders that the time for shilly-shallying was past, and that it be-

9   Grosser Generalstab, Volume II, p.443. On 2nd April, Batteries 1 and 2 each had two 24 pounders operational, and Batteries 3 and 4, each two 12 pounders. Battery Nr. 5 also took part in the bombardment.

hoved them to show that forbearance did not on their part arise from weakness. They had hitherto limited their activity to the throwing of a few hundred shells daily from their batteries at Broagerland. Once only they had tried the range of a few field pieces from the top of Avnbjerg; but today they unmasked their batteries both from that summit and from Dybbøl village, and their 24-pounders thundered all along the line from extreme left to extreme right. The fire was so well maintained that it was difficult for a spectator to follow the reports as they crowded upon one another, and often two or more at one time. Some of us counted as many as twenty-five shots a minute, and an Englishman assured us that 2,500 shells had flown through the air in the lapse of an hour.[10] All this furious attack was mainly directed against the Dybbøl bastions, where the Danes showed the best countenance, and for a long time gave the enemy as good as he sent. The batteries from Broagerland, however, besides aiding in the work immediately before them, found leisure to bestow some of their attention upon Sønderborg, and about 100 of their shells were aimed at the castle, at the *tête de pont* (Bridgehead), and at as many of the lower buildings of the town as were more immediately within their reach.[11] I have not, as yet, been able to ascertain what amount of damage all this shower of projectiles may have done to the Danish line. Some of the officers who have just returned from outposts assure those who are willing to believe them that the mischief is but trifling, and that the bastions are none the worse for the tremendous noise which has been for more than six hours incessantly kept up against them. The evidence of our own eyes, however, would rather induce us to make some abatement to these flattering assertions. The fire of the Prussians was returned by the Danes with less spirit as the day declined, and it is difficult to share the assurance entertained at head-quarters here, that the Prussians, after all the havoc of the day, will be as far from having it in their power to venture on an assault to-morrow as they were in their previous attempts of the 17th and 28th of last month. That none of the batteries on this side have been silenced, we have been able to ascertain. The drawbridge at No. 6 has been burnt, however, and at No. 10 a musketry fire has been heard, a circumstance which might induce a belief that the Prussians have shown themselves at an inconvenient proximity."[12]

10 This was a ridiculous, though understandable, exaggeration. Colonel Neumann gives as the total number of rounds fired by the front attack field artillery batteries, from 2nd April until the establishment of additional batteries on the 7th, as:

12 pounder smoothbore guns	6,005 common shell	28 shrapnel
7 pound howitzers	5,018 common shell	10 shrapnel
6 pounder rifled	1,068 common shell	116 shrapnel
Total	12,091 common shell	154 shrapnel
Grand Total: 12,245		

11 Ibid, pp. 14-15. 40 specially made incendiary shells were used on the town, and had the desired effect.

12 Gallenga, pp.77-81. This article was also found to be of interest to General von Moltke. See *Militärische Korrespondenz*, letter Nr. 59 to Colonel von Blumenthal, April 6th 1864.

The first rounds landed in the town of Sønderborg at 16:30, hitting the castle. One shell landed in the midst of a company of the 16th Regiment in a street, causing 28 casualties. The southern part of the town was set on fire, causing many inhabitants to flee. Surprisingly little damage was caused to the defences by the shelling of April 2nd, and only one 24 pound howitzer was dismounted in Redoubt IV, and a gun carriage smashed in Redoubt III. The Barracks Line to the rear of Dybbøl Mill, however, was set on fire. In spite of the lack of major damage, it was obvious that the redoubts themselves were very large and visible targets.[13] Total military losses for the day were 26 dead and 42 wounded.[14]

Around 17:00, as the bombardment of Sundeved was reaching its height, columns of Prussian heavy artillery and wagons began moving along the roads from Nybøl towards Ballegaard. Many guns had been removed from their batteries to take part in this exercise. The operation that Lieutenant-General von Moltke hoped would end the war was under way.

The excellent weather on April 2nd was a promising start to the Als operation after the 24 hour delay. Almost the whole of I Corps, some 20,000 men were involved in the crossing attempt. Left masking the Redoubts were Brigade Schmid and the nine Guards battalions, under the command of General Wintzingerode. The brigades of Goeben, Canstein, Roeder, and Raven, Jäger Battalions Nr. 3 and 7, one squadron each of hussars and uhlans, plus six artillery batteries moved north towards Ballegaard, on Als Sound, a little over 5½ miles north-east of Graasten.

The major portion of the artillery had left the siege park in Nybøl Fields, starting at 15:00 and moving via Avnbøl and Ulderup to Ballegaard. This first column carried the tools and materials to build the artillery batteries. Upon its arrival at about 19:00, the construction work began. The second column, leaving Nybøl at 18:00, comprised the guns and ammunition.

Around 22:00, storms began to come in from the north-west, bringing snow and rain. This made the work of constructing the batteries a nightmare in the clay soil, and instead of being ready for use by 02:00, some were not ready until 08:30, in spite of strenuous efforts.

13 Schøller, p. 67.
14 Generalstaben, Volume II, pp. 314-316, and Liljefalck & Lütken, pp.297-98. See Appendix XIV for details of Danish casualties at Dybbøl, April 2nd to 17th.

April 3rd

Between 01:00 and 02:00, the boat and pontoon column, 86 vehicles, began to arrive, and around 02:30, Goeben's 26th Brigade, due to cross first, was assembling on the beach. Goeben, though, was uneasy about the weather, which was becoming worse. The swell was reported to have been four feet.[15] The engineer officers expressed doubts, and the naval liaison officer, Commander Henk, flatly stated that a crossing was impossible.[16]

Since Prince Friedrich Carl was ill with a high fever, and so not present at Ballegaard, it fell to Colonel von Blumenthal to communicate the cancellation of the entire operation to Headquarters. The troops were returned to their quarters, although held in readiness for some time in case of a change in the situation. The pontoon and boat column was withdrawn to an assembly area at Blans. With the exception of Henk's sound advice, the Prussian Navy had contributed nothing to the attempt. The Danish fleet had equally played little part in the matter. A storm had defeated 20,000 men.

In the Sundeved, the heavy bombardment of the previous day, which had slackened over night, was resumed from early morning, in support of both the Ballegaard and siege operations. This fire was met with a lively response. In the evening, the shelling of Sønderborg ceased, but Prussian fire on the main position continued through the night.

The redoubt line suffered considerably from this pounding, but many repairs were effected overnight. The palisade of Redoubt III was partly destroyed and the bridges of Redoubt IV and Redoubt V damaged, in addition to the palisade of redoubt VI.

Losses to the shelling during the day amounted to two men killed, and 39 wounded.

April 4th

An order from headquarters empowered Colonel Colomier authority to use any and all artillery within the zone of operations in support of the siege. In addition to this, a Colonel Hurrelbrink from the War Ministry, who had been at Friedrich Carl's headquarters for eight days, announced that a further eight rifled 24 pounders and 16 rifled 12 pounders had been released by the Ministry for service. It was hoped that these would be arriving in less than a week, on either the 9th or 10th.[17] In the meantime, shelling of the defences continued with the guns already present.

This bombardment was again answered by a lively fire from the fortifications on the 4th, and also the following day, although the considerable ranges of over

15 Brackenbury et al, p.35.
16 Grosser Generalstab, Volume II, pp. 444-445. Had the crossing proved possible, in the short term there was only the Mels Detachment of three companies present in the north of the island to oppose it, which could later be reinforced by the 12th Regiment and one field artillery battery. Liljefalk and Lütken, p. 303, considering this, state, "No great force, and we were probably lucky that it didn't happen."
17 Waldersee, p. 257.

1,200 yards meant that most of the smoothbore ordnance in the Redoubts could have little precision effect. The 10th Field Artillery Battery, emplaced between the main road and Redoubt V, was particularly active in its return fire, and took subsequent heavy punishment as a result.[18]

During the day, an 84 pound howitzer was dismounted, and the mountings/gun platform on two others damaged, in Redoubt IV. In Redoubt VIII, a rifled 12 pounder and a smoothbore 24 pounder were put out of action.

For the defenders, a long period of passive suffering had started, as the bombardments became daily heavier. It was worst for the infantry, who had to remain in their posts in the face of concentrated artillery fire. This was made more difficult by the fact that the High Command made no attempt at offensive movements to disrupt the pace of the siege; attempts which would have also helped the morale of the troops.[19]

Losses to the shelling during the day amounted to five men killed, and 26 wounded.

April 5th

Although not held as the universal opinion, Friedrich Carl himself had already become convinced that a landing upon Als as an independent operation would not necessarily gain complete success, and that the siege should be pushed forward. There was now no alternative to a direct attack on the Dybbøl position.

With Lieutenant-Colonel von Kriegsheim sick, the 'First' (Senior) Engineer Officer of the entire Allied Army, Colonel Mertens, took over direction of the engineering aspect of operations. Colonels Colomier and Mertens now formulated an operational plan for the attack. The salient points were:

That night, the outposts were to be pushed forward south of the main road, to gain space for additional siege works.

On the night of 6/7th April, the 'front attack' batteries presently armed with smoothbore 12 pounder guns or 7 pound howitzers should, as far as possible, be rearmed with rifled 6 or 12 pounder guns. The Gammelmark batteries should be reinforced with 12 heavy rifled guns, and a new 'beach' battery – Nr. 15 – constructed, to be armed with four rifled 24 pounder guns.

Fire was to be opened from all batteries on April 7th.

On the night of 7/8th April, a new parallel (later changed to a half Parallel) was to be dug, at a distance from about 275 to 375 yards forward of the 1st Parallel; some 700 to 800 yards from the Redoubts. This would enable mortar batteries to be used to good effect, and give a shorter distance for an assault force.

A continuation of the bombardment on April 8th.

On the night of April 8/9th, the construction of positions for mortar batteries, and the equipping of artillery positions in the new parallel.

A continuation of the bombardment on April 9th.

18 Generalstaben, Volume II. p. 318.
19 Schøller, p. 71.

On the night of April 9/10th, the arming of the mortar batteries would take place.

All batteries to open fire on 10th April. It was hoped that three days of bombardment by all guns would be enough to allow an assault to go ahead from this parallel, on April 13th.[20]

The shelling of the previous days was continued from both the Gammelmark and front attack batteries, although it did not begin until 14:30 and was comparatively ineffective. Breastworks, traverses and palisades all took a pounding. A 36 pounder smoothbore in Redoubt I was dismounted, as was a 24 pounder smoothbore in Redoubt V, and an 84 pound howitzer damaged in Redoubt X.

The new plan was put immediately into effect. The Guards Division received orders to advance the outpost line that night to some 450 to 550 yards from the line of the Redoubts. At 22:00, II/4th Foot Guards, Major von Conta, assembled in the 1st Parallel, along with a platoon of 53 men from 3/7th Pioneer Battalion. I/4th Foot Guards were posted as a reserve.

The Danish outposts south of the Flensburg Road that night were, on the right, 5/5th Regiment, Premierlieutenant F. Ravn (covering Redoubts III to VI), and south of them, 1/10th, Captain E. Hansen (south to the Vemmingbund). Shortly after 22:00, the sentinels of Ravn's company were attacked and driven from their rifle pits after a brief struggle, uncovering the right of Hansen's pickets. Several men from each company were cut off and captured.

The Prussians then halted and occupied the rifle pits, their pioneers effectively working to reverse and link them, in spite of the heavy frost that night.[21] On their left, however, some men had gone further than planned, advancing close to Redoubt V before being pulled back. For much of the night, small arms fire was exchanged.

General du Plat, commanding at Dybbøl that night, hearing of the move and worried that it might be the beginning of a major assault, at 22:45 warned 4th Brigade at the Barracks Line, and 5th Brigade in the Bridgehead, for possible action. Further messages to this effect were dispatched to 3rd Brigade on Als, 10th and 11th Field Artillery Batteries, and to *Rolf Krake*.

Losses to the bombardment during the day were one officer and four men killed, and one officer and 10 men wounded.[22]

April 6th

Although firing between the outposts continued into the morning, no further attack from the Prussians came, and at 03:00, Companies Hansen and Ravn made a cautious move back towards the lost rifle pits. This tentative move was halted by heavy rifle fire. Ravn and one of his officers were killed, and the move fizzled out. Fire continued into daylight, and at about 05:00, Hansen, too, was mortally wounded, and his bugler killed. The combat spluttered out altogether at about 06:00. Half an hour earlier, the units assembled by General du Plat, to oppose any

---

20 Grosser Generalstab, Volume II, pp. 472-473.
21 Winterfeld, Volume II, pp. 24-25.
22 Generalstaben, Volume II, p. 319.

attack on the fortifications, had been stood down. The Prussians remained in the rifle pits they had taken.

Losses in these overnight skirmishes were:

Prussian

4th Foot Guards	Three men killed, and 18 wounded
7th Pioneer Battalion	Two men wounded
Total	23[23]

Danish

	Three officers and 12 men killed, nine men wounded, 13 men taken prisoner, and nine men deserted
Total	46[24]

Large amounts of building materials, much of it taken from the demolished Danewerke, and munitions were now being regularly brought into the Sundeved by the besiegers.

Rear view of the Dybbøl Position from the Church Battery on Als
(*Illustrated London News*)

23 See Appendix XV for details of Prussian losses at Dybbøl from April 5th until the morning of the 18th.
24 Generalstaben, Volume II, p. 321. A breakdown is problematic here. Mørch, *En Dansk Militærafdeling Gennem 325 Aar* (5th Regiment history), gives 5th Regiment's losses as two officers, one corporal, and two men dead, and ten men wounded, p.177. Since this is one more wounded than the total for both regiments given above, there is clearly an error. 10th Regiment was only engaged in this one outpost action at Dybbøl during April, and so its total loss in prisoners and deserters in that time, nine of each, clearly relates to this skirmish – see Appendix XIV. Other figures are similarly confusing. Schøller, p. 74, gives the total Danish losses on 6th April as 14 killed (three officers), 32 wounded, and 23 prisoners.

Exchanges of artillery fire on this day did not begin until 13:00, and continued for the rest of the day, without a great deal of damage on either side. A few shots were fired by the defenders from their 24 pound mortars in Redoubt III. 50 *Voldriffler* were brought to the front, and distributed along the line. These weapons, too heavy for a man to carry, were, in effect, heavy sniper rifles.

During the day, 2,058 shells fell. Casualties amongst the defenders amounted to seven men killed and 16 wounded.

April 7th

Two new batteries were built and armed overnight on the 6/7th. Battery Nr. 14 was established north of Battery Nr. 13, on the high ground between (West) Dybbøl and Ragebøl. Battery Nr. 15 was constructed on the extreme west of the Vemmingbund, commanding its entire length. The lesson taught by *Rolf Krake* on March 28th had been learned. Details of these batteries were:

Table 30

Prussian Batteries established at Dybbøl on the night of April 6th/7th 1864

Battery	Armament	Target & Approximate Range
Battery Nr. 14	Four rifled six pounders	Redoubts III & IV and the area in between 1,180 – 1,355 yards
Battery Nr. 15	Four rifled 24 pounders	Redoubts I, II, and ships 3,060 – 3,150 yards

At the same time Battery Nr. 9 was completely rearmed with two rifled 6 pounders and four rifled 12 pounders. Battery Nr. 11 had two of its smoothbore 12 pounders removed, leaving four. With the construction and arming of the new batteries, as well as the return of guns that had been moved to support the abortive "Ballegaard Project" to their former positions (with the exception of Battery Nr. 3, which had had two of its rifled 12 pounders removed), the besiegers had the following ordnance in place:

Rifled 24 pounders	12
Rifled 12 pounders	20
Rifled 6 pounders	16
Smoothbore 12 pounders	6
Smoothbore howitzers	12

At 09:00, in accordance with the siege plan, all Prussian batteries opened fire upon the Redoubt Line, and continued uninterrupted until about 18:30. Fire was returned by the defenders for a time, particularly from Redoubt IV, the artillery officer commanding this redoubt, Second-Lieutenant Petersen, being wounded. The defending batteries gradually fell silent.

The damage caused by this shelling was considerable, and 12 guns rendered inoperable. During the day, 3,463 shells fell. Casualties amounted to 9 men killed, and one officer and 32 men wounded.

The construction of the Half Parallel and its associated communications, enabled by the pushing back of the Danish outposts two nights previously, took place overnight. The three battalions of IR60, some 1500 men, were once again used for the work, together with eight officers and 190 men of Pioneer Battalion Nr. 7, the whole once more under the command of Major Roetscher.

Work commenced at 22:30. The front attack batteries, which maintained a desultory fire overnight, were directed to increase their fire only in the case of enemy attempts to disrupt the building of the Half Parallel. Since no such attempts were made, work proceeded well along its entire 765 yard length.[25]

April 8th

By 03:00, in spite of the frost,[26] the digging had reached an average depth of just over one yard, and a bottom width of three and a half feet. At this hour, the troops currently working were relieved by I/3GGR, II/3GGR, along with seven officers and 190 men of Pioneer Battalion Nr. 7. These men continued the expansion of the parallel and trenches, and the construction of two new siege batteries, one at either end of the Half Parallel, which would become Batteries Nr. 17 and 18.

A heavy fire from the Redoubts was opened on the Half Parallel at daybreak, particularly from Redoubts IV and VI, causing casualties of four killed and seven wounded within a short time.[27] The siege batteries immediately replied to this fire, and the shelling continued until about noon, when the redoubts on the Danish left were silenced. In the meanwhile, at 07:00, another relief had taken place in the Half Parallel, I and II/4th Foot Guards taking over the work and completing it during the day. On the Danish right flank, Redoubt IX continued a spirited fire through most of the afternoon, but it too was eventually silenced.

A further sign of the increased tempo of events was the arrival of Lieutenant-General Gustav von Hindersin and his staff at Graasten. The 59 year old von Hindersin had been sent from Berlin to assume command of the artillery and engineer operations for the remainder of the siege, once he had acquainted himself with the circumstances of the operations.[28] Count Waldersee observes that from this point, after the opening of the Half Parallel, the siege truly began, its previous direction being only a demonstration.[29] Conversely, General Gerlach sent

25 Grosser Generalstab, Volume II, p. 480.

26 -3 degrees Reaumur; that is 25.25 Fahrenheit, or –3.75 C, Rüstow, p. 459.

27 Grosser Generalstab, Volume II, p. 480. Waldersee, Volume II, p. 31, gives the loss as one NCO and two men killed, three men badly wounded, and one officer (Second-Lieutenant von Trotha), one NCO and four men lightly wounded. All of these were from 3/GGR.

28 Ibid, Volume II, p. 483. This appointment was made by a Royal Cabinet-Order of April 6th. General von Hindersin, an artillery specialist, and foremost champion of rifled cannon, was largely responsible for their adoption by the Prussian service. Later, as 'Second' (Deputy), and then 'First' Inspector-General of Artillery, he would completely overhaul the entire Arm, and see it universally equipped with rifled guns. His staff comprised his Adjutant, Captain von Scheliha, Captains Peters and von den Burg of the artillery, and Captain Meydamm of the engineers.

29 Waldersee, p. 258.

a gloomy message to the War Minister in Copenhagen. He did not think that the position at Dybbøl was long tenable, and considered that a withdrawal from it should take place. Further instructions were requested.

In this second day of intensive bombardment, considerable damage had been done to the parapets and embrasures of the redoubts. In Redoubt I, a 36 pounder gun had been dismounted. In Redoubt II, a rifled 12 pounder was dismounted, and the gun carriage of another smashed. Another gun wheel was also smashed, along with a gun platform. In Redoubt IV the gun carriage of an 84 pound howitzer was destroyed. A rifled 12 pounder 'metal' gun was rendered inoperable in Redoubt V, and in Redoubt VI, the gun carriage of a rifled 12 pounder destroyed. Two gun carriages in Redoubt VIII had been wrecked. Redoubt IX, which had put up such a gallant fight, was badly hit. One 84 pound howitzer there was destroyed, and the gun carriage of another rendered unusable. A third's gun platform was damaged, leaving the gun tilted.

As a result of the heavy pounding, an assault on the position was widely expected overnight or early the next morning. Orders were given to be especially alert that night, and that all ordnance was to remain loaded.[30] As the situation clearly required some action, Gerlach secured the cooperation of (Naval) Captain Muxoll for the assistance of *Rolf Krake* in a bombardment the following morning against the flank of the Prussian works, in conjunction with the army artilllery. This operation was agreed to begin at 05:00. During the night, however, a message from (Naval) Captain Rothe, the vessel's commander, reporting that this was impossible, due to the presence of fishing nets placed by the Prussians in the Vemmingbund, which could easily hamper, and possibly foul the ship, halting her altogether. The operation was called off.[31]

Redoubt VI at Dybbøl under fire (Liljefalck & Lütken)

---

30   Generalstaben, Volume II, p. 329.
31   Schøller, pp. 77-78. Much had been expected of *Rolf Krake* on this occasion, in view of her great success on March 29th.

During the day, 3,694 shells fell. Casualties amounted to 16 men killed, and one officer and 67 men wounded. It had been King Christian IX's 46th birthday.

Beginning at 20:30 that evening, four Prussian mortar batteries were constructed behind the Half Parallel, and designated Nr.'s 18-21. They were not, as yet, armed. This work was carried out under the direction of Major Hendewerk of the Fortress Artillery, who had been specially sent from Berlin. The 900 men assigned for the work also armed and provisioned Batteries Nr. 16 on the (Prussian) right, and Nr. 17, on the left of the Half Parallel. The details of the batteries were:

Table 31

Prussian Batteries established at Dybbol on the night of April 8th 1864

Battery	Armament	Target & Approximate Range
Battery Nr 16	Two smoothbore 12 pounders	Sorties and labour details Variable ranges
Battery Nr. 17	Four smoothbore 12 pounders	Sorties and labour details Variable ranges

April 9th

A telegram from General Gerlach to General Lunding at Fredericia requesting reinforcements elicited a reply that he could spare four battalions and one battery for a very limited period. That evening, 8th Brigade was ordered from Fredericia to Als.[32]

Daybreak brought fog, and it remained murky throughout the day, making both target observation and fall of shot difficult to assess. The bombardment was therefore only fitfully maintained, and was concentrated mainly on Redoubts II, V, and VI.

In addition to other damage, the parapet was destroyed in front of the middle two guns in Redoubt I, and the gun mounting for a 24 pounder smoothbore damaged. In IV, two 12/24 pounder gun carriages were wrecked, in V, parapets and palisades damaged, whilst in VI, the blockhouse and traverses suffered badly, and the material piled against the magazine as protection had partly collapsed.

General Gerlach had a fall from his horse during the day, and probably should have been taken to hospital. Under the prevailing circumstances, he would not consider this, although for the rest of the operations at Dybbøl the 66 year old would remain unwell. Upon hearing of the injury, the War Minister opted for General Steinmann, who had been recovering from the wound he suffered at Oeversee in February, as a replacement should Gerlach be unable to continue in command.[33]

During the day, 1,372 shells fell. Casualties amounted to three men killed and six wounded.

---

32 Liljefalk & Lütken, p.366. Lunding had wanted the troops sent for a specific limited period. He was actually only given the assurance that they would be returned to him in the event of an attack upon Fredericia.

33 Johansen, *Dybbøl 1864*, p. 205.

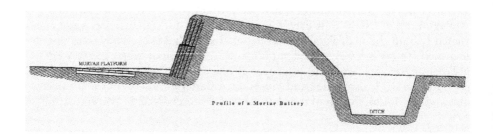

Map 25: Profile of Prussian mortar position

Overnight, Prussian Battery Nr. 3, at Gammelmark, was disarmed and permanently abandoned. On the other hand, the four mortar battery positions constructed behind the Half Parallel on the previous night, were armed and provisioned. These were:

Table 32

Prussian Batteries established at Dybbøl on April 9th 1864

Battery	Armament	Target & Approximate Range
Battery Nr. 18	Four 25 pound mortars	Redoubt III 875 yards
Battery Nr. 19	Four 25 pound mortars	Redoubt IV 1,080 yards
Battery Nr. 20	Four 25 pound mortars	Redoubt V 875 yards
Battery Nr. 21	Four 25 pound mortars	Redoubt VI 850 yards

April 10th

The fire of the Prussian batteries was delayed that morning by thick fog, but was finally opened at 10:30, from both the front attack batteries and the Broager. Redoubts III, IV, V, and VI took a hard pounding from the newly emplaced mortar batteries.

Dybbøl Mill, always a prominent landmark and excellent observation point, was specifically targeted for the first time. Although incidentally damaged previously, now it was on the target list. Around 14:00, after some minor hits, a shell struck the mill. The tower was hit and the upper portion collapsed, causing a great wave of cheering all along the Prussian lines. The hit was 'credited' to the rifled 12 pounders of Battery Nr. 5, Premier-Lieutenant Millies, who had been personally ordered to fire at the mill by Lieutenant-Colonel von Bergmann. The battery hit it from a distance of almost 3400 yards.[34]

Firing against the fortifications died down at around 19:00, though some shelling continued through the night. Damage to the fortifications had been considerable, especially to parapets and traverses, but materiél losses were surprisingly light. Much repair work was done overnight, and the 15th Regiment, posted in the redoubt line, was particularly heavily involved in the work from 20:00 to midnight, not something that the infantry normally relished.[35]

During the day, 4,753 shells fell. Casualties amounted to 12 men killed, and 18 wounded.[36]

On the evening of the 10th, under the supervision of Lieutenant-Colonel von Mertens, the construction of the Second Parallel was begun, some 275 yards forward of the Half Parallel, and having a length of about 600 yards. Initially covered by III/FR35, Major von der Lund, in the outpost line, four officers and 106 men of the 4/3rd Pioneers, and 16 officers and 510 men of II/IR24, Lieutenant-Colonel Kessler, started the work at 19:00, continuing until 06:00 the next morning.

Captain Isenburg, then a Second-Lieutenant, describes the scene:

In the night of the 10th to the 11th of April we went to construct the Second Parallel, 500 paces from the entrenchments. Two battalions of the 24th were given this work, which was to be carried out by means of a 'flying sap'. The 35th Regiment was to provide cover but eventually only the 1st and 3rd battalions under the regiment's commander took up the forward positions, whilst the Fusilier battalion of the 24th Regiment stood ready, half in the first parallel and the other half behind the Avnbjerg. At 6 in the evening the advance through the trenches took place to the forward most (half) parallel. At 8 in the evening the 3rd battalion moved into the outer forward posts. By means of the four companies it covered, in the up to now normal manner, the area from Vemmingbund where the 9th company stood, to the main road where the 12th company took position. At 9 o'clock they were all in place. The sentries had dug themselves in together with their replacements and only a few paces behind, the picket. The supports stood partly in the Half Parallel, and partly in the communication trenches which they had already pushed forward. The 1st battalion was in reserve in the Half Parallel.

Soon after 9, the 3rd battalion received the order to move the sentries, pickets and supports 20-30 paces forward to cover the building of the Second Parallel, but without alarming the enemy so that he would not disrupt the construction.

Between 10 and 11 in the evening this took place. Quietly the posts approached the enemy rifle pits. The lower layers of the air were filled with thick fog, so that it was not possible to see more than 10–15 paces, although the moon shone down brightly from above. Thus the sentries approached very close

34 Pulkowski, *Kurzgefasste Geschichte des Fußartillerie-Regiments General-Feldzeugmeister (Brandenburgischen) Nr. 3*, Berlin 1914, p. 40. Prince Carl of Prussia also gave a personal reward of 20 *Thalers* to the gunner concerned. Winterfeld, Volume II, p. 36.
35 Schøller, p. 84.
36 Generalstaben, Volume II, p. 343. Schøller gives four killed and 26 wounded.

to the enemy. Neither here nor there was there any shooting. Where it was not necessary to move any further forward, the Danes were left in their rifle pits. However here and there the command, 'Danes, back!' was given and was also obeyed until the Danes finally came to a stop at an earth mound and shook their heads vigorously. The sentries and pickets now provided themselves with the necessary protection with earth mounds. They were to withdraw to the Second Parallel as soon as this provided cover. The night passed fairly quietly. Only our guns, and also now our mortars and howitzers sent their shells uninterrupted into the entrenchments. The bombs left their dark red trails over the heads of the detachments at the front, fizzed, rushed, howled and hummed the night's music. Our interest in these fireworks was reduced only by the unpleasant stay in the trenches. These could not be kept dry, despite numerous drainage channels. The running back and forth produced a type of morass, which could only be made able to walk on with the help of brush and straw. The men had therefore already made straw seats in the camps, which they took with them to be able to sit down now and again. They spent the night on these makeshift seats.[37]

April 11th

During the night, Lieutenant-Colonel von der Osten, commander of II/4GGR, ordered three companies (7/4GGR, Captain von Koeppen, 8/4GGR, Captain von Studnitz, and 10/4GGR, Captain von Notz) forward on a reconnaissance to the north of the main road, in the vicinity of Redoubts V and VI. Taking place between 02:00 and 03:00, this move captured nine men of 3/5th Regiment, Captain W. Klüwer, on outpost duty, but also set off a major alarm amongst the defence.[38] Danish 4th Brigade and the 2nd and 8th Field Artillery Batteries were called to 'Alarm' positions, and kept under arms until 0630, when it was decided that no major attack was to follow. During its move forward, 4th Brigade suffered several losses from Prussian artillery fire, clearly demonstrating that any movement of bodies of troops behind the main lines was now a hazardous undertaking.[39]

South of the Flensburg road, at around 04:00, the two outposts, 3/22nd Regiment, Premierlieutenant Behrens, and a platoon from 2nd Regiment, under Second-Lieutenant Stickmann, made a tentative move towards the new parallel. They came into a protracted exchange of fire with the forward posts, mainly of 9/FR35, Captain von Kirschy, and 10/FR35, Captain Barres, joined by 10/IR24, Captain Baumgarten. Danish casualties numbered two officers and about 20 men. Prussian losses were 2 officers wounded, one man killed, and one man wounded.

During the morning, an act of fraternisation took place between opposing outposts as the bombardment raged overhead. With daylight, the two sides saw that they were only some 60 paces from one another. 18th Regiment's Chr. Bredsdorff heard of the incident from his friend, a participant, and discussed it with his comrades:

---

37 Isenburg, p. 271-272.
38 Grosser Generalstab, Volume II, p. 487, states five prisoners. Generalstaben, Volume II, p. 344 says nine, and Mørch, p. 176, gives 10.
39 Schøller, p. 81.

Trading in the forward posts at Dybbøl (Bredsdorff)

Our Senior-Sergeant stated that, 'Even if it would have cost my life, I wouldn't have been able to stop myself from opening fire on that scum!', and I am certain that he would have done so.

But, on this day, both parties had a jovial time. Just as Chr. Leth was sitting in a dugout eating with his men, a Prussian appeared in front of them, trying with hand movements to show that he intended no harm. He wanted very much to obtain one of our excellent water bottles, because the Prussian ones were poorly made out of tin, and so they traded him one. Then the Prussian officers approached our outposts and treated them with *Knackwurst*, tobacco, and cigars.[40]

Still following the operational plan of the 5th, heavy Prussian shelling of all the defensive works continued on the 11th, particularly against Redoubt VI, and, around 16:00, also at Redoubt IV. The batteries on the Broager alone fired 1,026 rounds. In reply, the Surlykk Battery on Als was active, firing 76 rounds during the day, mainly at West Dybbøl village, and Battery Nr. 13, which replied from about 13:00.

The damage in the fortifications was by now such that, south of the main road, almost all the works' parapets, traverses, and palisades were largely destroyed. In Redoubt III, the front wall of the magazine was cracked; in Redoubt IV, a fire – which had been put out – had damaged the blockhouse. In Redoubt VI, one magazine door was damaged, and there were cracks in the concrete around the other. Ordnance hit comprised one smoothbore 12 pounder in Redoubt II destroyed, along with two 24 pound howitzers in Redoubt IV, and a 12 pound howitzer emplaced south-east of Redoubt V. A gun platform in Redoubt II was also wrecked.

40 Bredsdorff, Chr., *Paa Feltfod*, p. 262. Such incidents had taken place throughout the campaign, but became rare at Dybbøl as the siege neared its end.

A telegram from the War Ministry arrived at General Gerlach's headquarters, in reply to his report of the 8th. He was told to continue to hold the position, and await any further orders. By contrast, on the evening of the 11th, Friedrich Carl consulted his General Staff officers, and also General von Hindersin and Colonel Mertens as to how to proceed, since the Second Parallel had now been completed. He had, the previous day, informed his divisions to designate 32 companies to form the storm columns for the final attack, and these had already begun to practice attacking dummy positions constructed in the area near the Engineer Depot at Smøl. Three pioneer companies had also begun daily training, under I Corps' Deputy ('Second') Engineer Officer, Captain Treumann, in the removal or destruction of any and all types of obstacles that the attack might face.

The meeting was to discuss whether the assault should take place from the Second Parallel, or whether another should be constructed closer to the redoubts. The siege of Sebastopol still hung heavily over the conduct of siege operations in Europe almost ten years after the event. It was perceived by the Prussians that any assault must succeed in overrunning the redoubts on the first attempt. Any repulse was potentially disastrous. It was, therefore, vital to have the jump-off point for the storming parties as near as possible to the fortifications. This would have two major advantages. Firstly, the assault troops would not have such a great distance to cover that they would be exhausted in simply reaching the objective, and secondly, the defenders would have much less time to react. A daylight attack might be considered risky, but the besiegers were aware that the majority of the defenders would not be in their defensive positions (owing to General Gerlach's order of 1st April), and that a great degree of surprise could well be achieved. Conversely, the continued approach of the siege works might make the enemy more alert.

General von Hindersin and Colonel Blumenthal both offered the opinion that the attack should not be made from the Second Parallel. They considered that the distance to be covered by the troops – an average of almost 500 yards, and in the case of Redoubt IV, 600 – was too great. Furthermore, they pointed out that pushing forward to an additional parallel would take the last high ground in front of the enemy works, and thus give a valley-like hollow behind the assault troops, affording additional cover for the advance.

The opposing view was that the enemy, on past experience, had shown little energy in previous encounters, and that the Danish artillery was effectively silenced. A key issue for Friedrich Carl was the international situation. It was a political imperative for Prussia to gain a clear and obvious military success before the Conference in London began. This had already been postponed once, and a complete removal of any Danish presence from mainland Schleswig before any possible armistice, was considered vital to Prussian interests.

The Prince decided that an assault should be made from the existing line, and ordered that it take place on the morning of the 14th. The time was fixed for 10:00, and it was to be preceded by a heavy bombardment. The time of the storming was caused by the fact that it was thought that the Danes would not expect an attack during the day, as all previous offensive moves had been made either in the evening or the early morning. Also, the heavy shelling itself was felt to be beneficial to surprise.[41]

41 See Grosser Generalstab, Volume II, pp. 489-90, and von Fischer, p. 253.

During the day, 3,886 shells fell. Danish casualties for the day, including the skirmishes related above, amounted to one officer and 30 men killed, three officers and 40 men wounded, and 10 men taken prisoner.[42]

Prussian fire continued to be heavy during the night, seriously hampering the efforts of the defenders to repair the damage and construct new positions. Nevertheless, mortar positions were established between Redoubts II and III, and work started on gun emplacements between Redoubts VI and VIII, and to the right of Redoubt X. Some positions were restored, and the second (withdrawn) line cut through the main road.

Overnight, the construction of the batteries intended to shell the Danish right flank and the batteries on Als to the north of Sønderborg, took place. The work details were provided by F/IR13, Major von Borries. They would be numbered Batteries 23, 24, 25, 26, and 27.[43]

April 12th

On Als, a battery of four rifled 12 pounders was established in a hollow near the Baadsager Battery, substantially strengthening the north of the Dybbøl defences.

A heavy fire was opened by the siege batteries at 05:00, and maintained throughout the day. The "Feldzeugmeister Battery" alone fired some 500 rounds. The main weight of the shelling was concentrated on the left and centre of the redoubt line.[44]

Redoubt IV had a serious fire. Its palisade, especially near the entrance, was badly damaged, as were the blockhouse, traverses and embrasures. The bridge was in a poor state. A beam in the magazine of Redoubt V was cracked, and the work itself in generally poor condition. Redoubt VI was similarly badly battered. A gun platform for a 24 pound howitzer was destroyed In Redoubt II, and the gun carriage of another destroyed in Redoubt IV, where also another howitzer of the same calibre was damaged. In Redoubt VI, a 24 pounder cannon was dismounted, a 12 pounder lost a wheel, and the gun carriage of an 84 pound howitzer destroyed.

During the evening of the 12th, a Lieutenant-Colonel von Strubberg from Berlin, arrived at Friedrich Carl's headquarters. The Colonel, one of the King's Personal Adjutants, brought a message written by Wilhelm. In it, he approved the Prince's plans for the attack, but offered two concerns for Friedrich Carl's consideration. The first was precisely that which had been discussed the previous night. Was the distance from the Second Parallel to the objectives too great? The King also wondered if the storm columns themselves were strong enough. He quoted the experience of such enterprises in the Duke of Wellington's Spanish campaign during the Napoleonic Wars.[45] Finally, His Majesty offered the view that a delay of a few days would make no difference politically.

---

42 Schøller, p. 82.
43 Grosser Generalstab, p. 482. Colonel Colomier had proposed the establishment of these batteries on April 8th.
44 Waldersee, p. 278.
45 Rehtwisch, p. 150. Wilhelm had actually discussed these matters with the Duke in the past. The conversation(s) clearly had an effect on him.

In accordance with the King's clear wishes, Friedrich Carl postponed the attack, and plans were immediately drawn up for the construction of what would be the Third Parallel. The number of infantry companies designated for the storm columns was raised from 32 to 46, and the practice assaults correspondingly altered.[46]

The arming and provisioning of Batteries 22-27 took place overnight. In addition, two new batteries were constructed and equipped, numbers 28 and 29. The details of all of these were as follows:

Table 33

Prussian Batteries established at Dybbøl on April 12th 1864

Battery	Location	Armament	Target & Approximate Range
Battery Nr. 22	North of Battery 13	Four rifled 6 pounders	Redoubts VII & IX 1500 - 2020 yards
Battery Nr. 23	West of Stavegaarde	Four rifled 24 pounders	Redoubts IX & X, Sønderborg, the Bridgehead 1,660 – 1,880 yards
Battery Nr. 24	West of Stavegaarde	Four rifled 12 pounders	Redoubts IX & X, Sønderborg, the Bridgehead 1,660 – 1,880 yards
Battery Nr. 25	Beach, west of Ragebøl	Four rifled 12 pounders	Batteries on Als & ships in Als Sound Variable Ranges
Battery Nr 26	Beach, west of Ragebøl	Four rifled 12 pounders	Batteries on Als & ships in Als Sound Variable Ranges
Battery Nr. 27	Beach Snogbæk	Four rifled 24 pounders	Batteries on Als & ships in Als Sound Variable ranges
Battery Nr. 28	Beach, Half Parallel	Two rifled 24 pounders & two rifled 12 pounders	Redoubts I & II, and ships 875 – 1,050 yards
Battery Nr. 29	Beach, Snogbæk	Four rifled 6 pounders	Batteries on Als and ships Variable ranges

The effect of the day's pounding was considerable. Both defences and equipment suffered significant damage, and the problem was compounded by the continuance of the bombardment overnight, which seriously hindered repair work.

---

46 Grosser Generalstab, Volume II, pp. 495-496. The troops training for the assault were excused other duties.

Nevertheless, the repair parties did their best, and in addition to carrying out as much repair work as possible, they completed six gun embrasures in front of Dybbøl Mill, and a gun platform between Redoubts VIII and IX. A number of har-rows were also laid out in front of Redoubt V.

During the day, 4,811 shells fell. Casualties amounted to two officers and 27 men killed and one officer and 71 men wounded.

April 13th

The shelling by all of the Prussian artillery began again in earnest at daybreak, con-tinuing without let up until dusk, and much heavier than previously. The most in-tense fire was concentrated on Redoubts I to VI.

By the end of the day, the damage was considerable. Redoubts I and II were serviceable, but parapets and traverses had been badly battered, the bridge in I, destroyed, and that of II, badly hit. All of the guns in Redoubt I had been dismounted, and in II, one 12 pounder gun. Redoubt III suffered severe punishment to parapets, traverses, palisades and embrasures. Three of its guns were workable. Redoubt IV had been similarly pounded, but had six operational guns. Redoubt V had two serviceable guns (another was made operational during the feverish repair work that went on throughout the defences overnight). In Redoubt VI, the door to one of the magazines was left leaning outwards after a shell landed immediately in front of it. The gun-mountings of two rifled 12 pounders had been destroyed, and another gun shot through the muzzle. The work was left with only three fully, and two partially operational guns on its frontal faces.[47]

Eight field guns were added to the defences, emplaced as follows:

To the right of Redoubt X	Two rifled 4 pounders of the 8th Battery
Between Redoubts VIII & IX	Two rifled 4 pounders of the 11th Battery
North of Flensburg Road	Two rifled 4 pounders of the 2nd Battery
South of Flensburg Road	Two smoothbore 24 pound howitzers of the 10th Battery[48]

In general, morale amongst the defenders was beginning to suffer under the constant bombardment, especially in the rear echelon formations. Indeed, during the day, a labour detail initially refused to march to Dybbøl. General du Plat re-ported to Headquarters that there was a growing morale problem. Certainly, the troops were all tired. They were also frustrated by the terrifying, yet monotonous heavy shelling, and what was perceived as the glaringly obvious lack of either the will, or the means, to hit back. Many men realised that their own officers did not consider that the position could be held. There was no crisis of morale, but any dis-ciplinary incidents did certainly require diplomatic handling.

A further problem was the increasing number of men who were sick in hospital. In March, the percentage of men sick had remained around 8% of the total force. During the siege, in the first days of April, this figure had risen to 12%.

---

47 Ibid, pp. 84-85 & Generalstaben, Volume II, pp. 348-351.
48 Ibid, p. 86.

The troops were tiring fast. This total would reach a peak of 17.6% two days later on April 15th; a staggering one in six of the total number of men![49]

There was a much needed boost to the morale of the defenders therefore, with the arrival on Als during the day, of the 8th Infantry Brigade, on "temporary loan" from General Lunding in Fredericia. Colonel Scharffenberg's brigade was assigned to Major-General Steinmann's 1st Division. Apart from being simply additional troops, the brigade was welcome for two additional reasons. First, their presence permitted an alteration in the infantry rotation duty roster. Henceforth, a brigade would spend three days in the Dybbøl position, followed by three days on Als, rather than six days in the position, and three days on Als. From a headquarters standpoint, it was also useful to have four battalions of fresh, fit troops, whose morale had not been sorely tested by the days of endless shelling.

For the construction of the new Prussian siege parallel to be possible, once again the Danish advanced posts needed to be driven back, this time up to the glacis of the main fortifications themselves along the front of the siege-works. This would also have the advantage of securing the last important high ground in front of the redoubts, south of the main road. The operation would take place that evening. The troops called upon were from the Leib Grenadier Regiment (GR8) and IR60 (7th Brandenburg), the two regiments on outpost duty. Two of the latter's companies, 3 and 12/IR60 were guarding the batteries at Broager. I/IR60, Major Karl von Jena was chosen for the attack, and therefore had to borrow a company, 11/IR60, from the Fusilier Battalion.

Lieutenant-Colonel von Hartmann, commanding officer of IR60, came to speak to his troops before the operation. He was still suffering from the wound he suffered on 17th March, and leaned heavily on a stick. He told his men,

> Soldiers of the 60th, you have a good name in the Army and at home, especially in the capital. Now, tonight you will once again have the opportunity to honour your regiment and reputation. We will push the enemy pickets back and capture them. We will face a Copenhagen regiment, so I want to see who are the strongest – Copenhageners or Berliners.[50]

Major von Jena's four companies were deployed in the Second Parallel, in company columns, together with 2 and 3/Brandenburg Pioneers. II/IR60, Lieutenant-Colonel von Blumenthal, was in support behind the Parallel. Further back, in the Half Parallel, stood F/GR8, Major von Gaudi, and finally, in the First Parallel, 9/IR60, Captain Maurer, and 10/IR60, Captain von Wins. The attack was scheduled for 21:30. The signal for the attack was to be the playing of a fife on the left flank.[51] To increase the likelihood of surprise, the troops were forbidden to open fire in the initial phase of the assault. At the appointed time, von Jena moved off. His frontal assault by 1/IR60, Captain von Albrecht, and 2/IR60, Captain von Mach, was held back slightly, to allow 4/IR60, Captain Rödiger on the right and 11/IR60, Captain von Schlieben, on the left, to move around both flanks.

49 Johansen, Jens, *Dybbøl 1864*, p. 220.
50 Bunge, C., *Aus meinem Kriegstagebuch.*, Rathenow 1865, p. 67. Unfortunately for the rhetoric, it was not the case that the Prussians were facing a Copenhagen regiment. One wonders if von Hartmann knew this!
51 Waldersee, p. 283.

In the outpost lines in front of the redoubts, the picket line consisted of rifle pits which held up to half a dozen men. These rifle pits were not far in front of the defensive obstacles of the main line, and could not really any longer be considered as forward posts. Manning these positions was 6/5th Infantry Regiment, Premierlieutenant W. Claussen, awaiting relief by 2/6th, Premierlieutenant J. Grønlund, whom Claussen's men could hear behind them, immediately before the surprise attack hit them.

Claussen's company was entirely overwhelmed by the swift attack. Within minutes, around a hundred men were being handed back towards the Prussian lines.[52] The survivors were pushed back into the relieving 2/6th, and a confused firefight developed. The Brandenburg Pioneers began digging in the new Prussian outpost line, reversing and connecting the Danish rifle pits.

The relieving Danish regiments, 4th and 6th, had reached the redoubts by now, and were firing into the darkness, joined by the guns of the redoubts. This fire was hampered by the presence of their own outpost companies (in addition to the survivors of Claussen's) outside the works. Major von Jena was severely wounded by grapeshot whilst inspecting the newly dug-in outpost line (He died in the field hospital at Nybøl on the 16th). At about 11:30, the two defending Danish outpost companies were pulled back into the fortifications, leaving only a few vedettes outside.

Prost, Danske! (Camphausen)

---

52 Anon., "Der Feldzug in Schleswig", part eight, *Militärische Blätter*, Volume 13, Number 34, comments, "As usual, the Danish outposts were enveloped by this tactic before they were able to offer any serious resistance, and 102 men were taken prisoner." Schøller says, p.87, that the Prussians, "...broke out of the gorges between the Vemmingbund and the road, and without firing a shot, jumped into our trenches." Note that this figure for prisoners relates to the entire operation, and not just Claussen's company.

Heavy fire was kept up through much of the night, causing losses amongst von Ketteler's II/IR60, when they later relieved von Jena's battalion in the new outpost line, the commander of 5/IR60, Captain Redern being among the wounded. I/IR60 withdrew shortly afterwards. The most forward posts of both sides here observed a *de-facto* 'truce' for the rest of the night.[53]

The commander of the Danish outpost line, Ritmester H. Castenschiold, upon hearing of this attack, immediately ordered that the lost positions be retaken at 04:00 the next morning. He recognised that, should the enemy be allowed to keep the newly won ground, the defenders would be effectively penned in the redoubts.[54]

During the day, 7,320 shells fell. Casualties amounted to two officers (including the commander of 10th Regiment, Major Rohweder) and 29 men killed, and 84 men wounded. In sharp contrast, Prussian casualties for the day, excluding the outpost action discussed, were under ten. Urgent repair works on the redoubts and matériel took place overnight.

April 14th

At 04:00, as ordered, Grønland's 2/6th and 8/4th, Premierlieutenant T. Thorson, moved out of the fortifications through the narrow gaps in the wire to attempt to retake the lost positions. Grønlund's men, particularly, met heavy rifle fire. Second-Lieutenant A. Hansen was killed, and the attempt was a failure. The troops were withdrawn, and henceforth only a few sentinels were left outside the works between the Vemmingbund and the main road. Possibly, a larger force could have been used in the counter-attack, but given the severely restricted space and the limited access through the defensive obstacles, more men would have been difficult to deploy, and an easier target.

Casualties in this affair, from the initial Prussian attack to the end of the failed attempt to retake the rifle pits, were:

Prussian – Total - 42
IR60 – Two officers (Major K. von Jena, and Second-Lieutenant von Seydlitz) and four men killed, and one officer (Captain von Redern) and 32 men wounded.[55]
Brandenburg Pioneer Battalion Nr. 3 – Two men killed, and one wounded.
Danish – Total - 118[56]

---

53   Waldersee, p. 284.
54   Castenschiold himself finished his spell commanding outpost line on the morning of the 14th, being relieved by Captain G.F. Schøller. See Sørensen, *Den Anden Slesvigske Krig*, Volume II, p.243.
55   Major von Jena was a rare man, highly regarded by both sides. He had, for many years, been in the Austrian service, serving in Italy under Marshal Radetzky. After the Austrian defeat in 1859, he returned, much decorated, to the Prussian army. He was, therefore, a rarity in that army – a regimental officer who had seen active service. His memorial service, prior to the body being sent home, was a major occasion, even though the siege was at a critical period.
56   No breakdown by unit is available solely for this action, and most of the doubt must lie with attempting to count the losses separately from those caused by the shelling, added to the fact that it took place overnight – i.e., on two different days. Generalstaben,

From this point on, it was realised by the defenders that an all-out assault could be expected any day. Each morning, therefore, the troops were required to rest on their arms from 03:00 until dawn, further increasing their weariness.

The artillery bombardment was resumed from early morning. There was little return fire from the main line during the day, what there was being mainly from the right flank. The Danish batteries on Als, however, carried on a lively fire, the Surlykke Battery being particularly active. A total of 409 rounds were fired by the defenders. At around 08:00, a battery of eight rifled 4 pounder field guns, emplaced south of Rønhave, targeted Prussian batteries Nr. 25 and 26 with a heavy and accurate fire in their left rear flank.[57] Within a short time, both batteries were silenced, with two guns put out of action, two men killed and another wounded (all from 3rd Fortress Company/Rhineland Artillery Brigade Nr. 8). Though again operational within a short time, the batteries were silenced by fire from this battery several times.

The cumulative damage continued to take its toll on the Danish fortifications, though damage to ordnance was limited to three 84 pound howitzers in Redoubt X and one dismounted 4 pounder field gun, emplaced between Redoubts I and II. Orders were issued that day that in redoubts where the bridges were destroyed or beyond repair, attempts to get new cannon into them should cease. In those where the guns were inoperable, the redoubts were to be prepared for destruction if necessary. Some preparatory work was undertaken that night, along with a great repair and replacement effort.[58]

Gerlach dispatched a situation report to Copenhagen, once again recommending a withdrawal from the Sundeved. After an exchange of telegrams between the War Minister and Gerlach's Chief of Staff, Lieutenant-Colonel Stiernholm, the Minister, Colonel Lundby, declined to allow a retreat. The London Conference was too close for the Danish Government to voluntarily withdraw from its last foothold on the mainland of the contested Duchy.[59]

To help gain time, Gerlach once more thought of the Navy. Although the old Ship-of-the-Line *Frederik VI*, (Naval) Captain H. Ipsen, was already in the waters off Als, her value in action was extremely limited since she could not face shore batteries. On the 13th, however, the battery ironclad *Dannebrog*, (Naval) Captain F. Paludan, had also arrived to assist in the defence, anchoring in the northern part of Als Sound. Although well suited for use against shore batteries, she drew too much water to be used in the Vemmingbund. Her status in regard

Volume II, p. 354 gives – One officer and four men killed, 11 men wounded, 98 men captured, and two men missing. Jensen, p. 359 - gives the same total, but counting the prisoners as 100 men (no missing). Combining Schøller's total casualties for the two days (pp.88 & 91), and subtracting the separately listed bombardment losses, gives a figure of 118 casualties in these encounters, which equates with those given, but with a figure of 102 prisoners, that also given by *Militärische Blätter* (see footnote 24, page 213). One feels that this is as close as we will get.

57 Generalstaben, Volume II, p. 362 and Schøller, p. 90. This move came as a surprise to General von Hindersin; see Grosser Generalstab, Volume II, pp. 501-502.

58 Liljefalk and Lütken, p. 372, & Schøller, pp. 89-90.

59 Generalstaben, Volume II, pp. 359-361.

The Third Siege Parallel (Liljefalck & Lütken)

to (Naval) Captain Muxoll's Squadron was also somewhat ambivalent, as she was only intended to stay in the area for a few days. Muxoll was unsure as to the extent of his authority for her deployment.

In an effort to galvanise the naval authorities into action, Gerlach held a meeting with Captain Muxoll to press for the use of *Rolf Krake* on the following day to undertake the operation which had been proposed almost a week before. Once again, it was agreed that she would make a run into the Vemmingbund on the 15th, to shell the Prussian batteries.[60]

During the morning, two saps were dug, by troops of the Leib Grenadier Regiment, out from the Second Parallel to the site for the building of the Third Parallel, some 185 yards to the east. This was achieved with little enemy interference, and the zig-zag approaches built up to the height of the planned new work. The troops then withdrew, leaving the unfilled gabions in place for the building of the parallel that night. Additionally, the Second Parallel itself was widened to allow for the assembly of the reserves for the storm columns.

At 21:00, work began on the parallel itself, the work details provided by IR24, supervised by pioneer detachments. Although it was a clear moonlit night, the construction work was not delayed by the defenders. By 02:00 the next morning, the 650 yard long parallel was largely complete.[61] Work was continued during the following day, subsequently reaching a bottom width of just over seven yards and a depth of nearly four and a half feet. The bottom width of the approaches to the parallel were also later widened to 3½ yards, and steps inserted in the face of the parallel in six places, as jump off points for the storm columns. These were each almost 22 yards wide.

60 Schøller, p. 91.
61 Using the gabions already left in place, this construction so close to the main defensive position clearly showed that the besiegers had little fear of the Danish artillery.

During the day, 4,708 shells fell. Casualties amounted to 27 men killed, and two officers and 63 men wounded.

Overnight, a Prussian officer from IR15, Premier-Lieutenant Weissich, rowed across the northern section of the Sound to Als, and collected valuable information on possible landing areas there. He repeated the feat in a different place the following night.[62]

April 15th

Fire against the fortifications had been continued through the night, mainly answered by the defending batteries on Als. From daybreak, the normal heavy bombardment resumed, and continued all day, the already battered village of Ragebøl being destroyed by a fire as a consequence.[63] On the main line, Redoubt V fired a total of five rounds of shot, and 11 grapeshot in return.

On the Prussian left, the Danish field artillery south of Rønhave once more targeted Batteries 25 and 26 across the Sound. This time however, the latter were ready, and the eight rifled guns of the Guard 4 Pounder Battery, Captain von Ribbentrop, had overnight been emplaced north of them, in anticipation of just such a move. The Danish guns were rapidly silenced. During the afternoon, they opened fire again, and the duel between the opposing batteries continued until dark.

The operation agreed for the employment of *Rolf Krake* once again failed to occur. An officer sent by (Naval) Captain Rothe was sent to Headquarters to inform them that his ship was unable to undertake task for the same reasons as on April 9th. Given the desperate situation in which the Army found itself, Gerlach found it necessary to ask the naval authorities whether, in the event of a surprise attack, the ship could be used to break the bridges linking the Sundeved to Sønderborg should the need arise. The reply was that this was not possible. It was promised, however, that the fleet would do its best to contribute to the defence of Als.[64]

A detachment of Austrian Pioneers, four officers and 160 men, under the command of Captain von Kegeln, arrived at the Engineer Depot at Smøl. Within a short time, these troops were working on the Third Parallel.

On the 15th, Friedrich Carl at last issued to his senior generals the detailed Instruction for the final assault on the fortifications. It stated:

Instruction for the Storm of the Dybbøl Redoubts
    The assault will be carried out simultaneously against works 1 to 6, using 6 columns. Each column will be assigned the number of the work, which it is to attack. Columns of greater strength will be deployed against works 2 and 4, to which communications trenches are connected.
    Columns Numbers 1, 3, 5, and 6 will each consist of six infantry companies, Number 2 of ten infantry companies, and Number 4 of twelve infantry

62 Grosser Generalstab, Volume II, p. 499.
63 Winterfeld, Volume II, p. 48.
64 Schøller, pp. 91-92. There would be much bitter correspondence in military and naval journals generated on the subject. Feelings would run still higher after later operations involving Als itself.

companies. To each of Columns Numbers 2, 4, and 6, a full pioneer company will be assigned, and to each of Columns 1, 3, and 5, half a pioneer company. All companies will be formed in section-front, dressed in caps, without pack, with greatcoats *en bandouliere*.

At the head of each column will march an infantry company assigned as skirmishers. Immediately behind will follow the work detail, with slung rifles. This will comprise, firstly, the pioneers, who will carry with them spades, entrenching tools, axes, crowbars etc., and also 30-pound sacks of powder; secondly, an infantry company to carry ladders, planks, hay sacks, and other equipment. The men in the work detail will keep a sufficient distance from one another to allow other equipment to be transported easily.

At a distance of 100 paces will follow the actual assault column, which, in the case of Columns 1, 3, 5, and 6, will consist of two infantry companies, and in the case of Columns 2 and 4, of four infantry companies. 150 paces behind them will follow the reserve for each column, of the same strength. The latter will include, for each column, one officer, four NCOs and twenty men of the artillery, to operate any guns captured in the trenches. The gunners in each column are to be provided with five pitch torches.

Behind the reserve of Column 5 will follow one artillery officer and half a pioneer company, equipped with spades, axes, entrenching tools, crowbars, and handspikes, whose task will be to clear away the barricades located in the roadway between Redoubts 4 and 5, and make the roadway passable.

Accordingly, the six assault columns will be constituted as follows:

Nrs. 1, 3, 5, and 6, each with 6 infantry companies	24 infantry companies and 2½ pioneer companies
Nr. 2, with 10 infantry companies	10 infantry companies and 1 pioneer company
Nr. 4, with 12 infantry companies	12 infantry companies and 1 pioneer company
To clear the road barricade	½ pioneer company
Total	46 infantry companies and 5 pioneer companies

The infantry will be composed as follows:

Column 1, The Guards	6 companies
Column 2, Brigade Canstein	10 companies
Column 3, Brigade Raven	6 companies
Column 4, Brigade Goeben	4 companies
Brigade Schmid	8 companies
Column 5, Brigade Roeder	6 companies
Column 6, The Guards	6 companies
Total	46 companies

The main reserve will consist of two infantry brigades and four field artillery batteries.[65]

The assault columns will be formed up at the appointed time at the Bøffelkobbel, and from there will be led by their engineer officers to the Second Parallel, which they must reach before dawn, and where the work companies will pick up the equipment which has been deposited there. In addition, each man in the column will there pick up an empty sand bag. From there, the columns will advance to the most forward parallel (note: the Third Parallel), where they will be mustered and formed up. The column reserves, which cannot be accommodated at this point, will remain behind in the Second Parallel, and will move forward from there when the heads of the columns in the most forward parallel begin the assault. Each man in the assault column will half fill the empty sand bag, which he has brought with him, with earth from the inside of the breastwork, and the work details will stand by their equipment so as to be able to pick it up immediately.

In the assault, Brigades Canstein and Raven will form the main reserves, and when the assault begins, will occupy the parallels and the village of Dybbøl. The four field artillery batteries, which have been assigned, will, before dawn, form up near to the Avnbjerg, and the main road.

Before the assault order is given, all of the attack batteries will have maintained a vigorous, uninterrupted six hours fire upon the works to be stormed. The six assault columns will simultaneously debouch from the forward most parallel, with Columns 5 and 6 turning across the road to attack Redoubts 5 an 6, and the half company of pioneers following behind Column 5 going to work on the road barricade. After the leading (note: the *Schützen*, or skirmisher) companies have left the most forward parallel, they will deploy into firing lines, which will advance as quickly as possible. Each company will keep its attention directed on the target Redoubt against which it has been assigned, and will move only against that Redoubt, without regard to maintaining any contact with the column moving forward beside them. In this movement too, the officers of the pioneer companies will act as the leaders.

Should the skirmishers encounter any natural or man-made obstacles, which they cannot cross, these obstacles will be removed by the work details which have been specially instructed and trained for the task.

Once they reach the Redoubts, the skirmishers will surround the works on all accessible sides, and will fire at any enemy occupants they can see. After the work details have cleared the way for them, the assault columns will enter the trenches, spread out through them, and climb the breastworks as soon as the obstacles – palisades etc. – have been cleared away. Once they have mounted the breastworks, the skirmishers will be gathered, and their fire directed against the narrow access way, in order to cut off the retreat of the enemy manning the position.

---

65 Brigades Canstein and Raven. The artillery batteries, commanded by Lieutenant-Colonel Bergmann, were: From the Guards, Four Pounder Battery, Captain Ribbentrop. From Artillery Brigade Nr. 3, 3rd 6 Pounder Battery, Captain Minameyer, 2nd Howitzer Battery, Captain Storp, and 3rd 12 Pounder Battery, Premier-Lieutenant Müller II – Müller, *Kriegerisches und Friedliches aus den Feldzügen von 1864, 1866, und 1870/71*, p. 54.

As soon as the enemy garrison has been driven out, any blockhouses within the Redoubts which have not yet been destroyed, will be blown up by the pioneers using their gunpowder. In addition, the hay sacks which the troops have brought with them, will be stuffed into the embrasures, and set fire to with the pitch torches, in order to set the blockhouses on fire and to drive out the enemy within.

From each of assault columns 2 and 4, each comprising 4 infantry companies, one company, each followed by one company from the reserve, will advance to the right, and one to the left, against the communications trenches attached to Redoubts 2 and 4.

The assault columns must avoid any engagement with enemy troops, which may be advancing between the Redoubts, and must seek to make their way with all possible speed to the Redoubt which they have been designated to attack. Any engagement against advancing enemy troops must be carried out by the main reserve, which will advance for this purpose, on the orders of the most senior commander.

After the assault columns have advanced, the main reserve brigade, on the right wing, will move up to the most forward parallel. Similarly, the four field artillery batteries will continue to move along the main road. Whether the advance should be continued after one or more of the Redoubts have been taken, will be a matter for the most senior commander to assess.

In any event, the troops who have broken into the works should not abandon them, but must hold out there to the last man.

During the assault, the Gammelmark batteries will continue firing upon the advancing enemy columns, and on the enemy trenches to the rear.

Headquarters, Graasten, 15th April 1864

(signed) Friedrich Carl, Prince of Prussia

The planning for the attack was almost complete, and its momentum now unstoppable.

In the late afternoon, largely as a result of insensitive handling, a potentially explosive brief mutiny took place in the Danish 3rd Brigade, then supposed to be resting on Als. The Brigade had been rotated from the frontline in the late afternoon of the 13th, for a normal four-day furlough (see Appendix IX for details of the movements of Danish regiments in and out of Dybbøl during its defence), arriving in their rest area on Als late in the evening. The Brigade commander, Colonel Wørishøffer, was told the next morning that his brigade's rest period had been cut and that it would be moving back into the main position the next day. He informed the men of this, and having done so, relayed to the High Command his view that low morale due to this decision threatened to spread amongst the men. Disappointment and anger had already been expressed in the ranks.

On the morning of the 15th, however, Wørishoffer was pleased to be able to report that the troops had marched off quite readily to their staging areas, in some fields east of Sønderborg. On the way there, though, they had met some of the troops of 8th Brigade, who had relieved them two days earlier, moving in the opposite direction. The latter were on their way to the rest area. The reaction of the men of 3rd Brigade can well be imagined. Waiting in the staging area, their mood became progressively worse.

As soon as he joined the waiting brigade, Colonel Wørishoffer realised that he could have a serious problem. There were murmurings amongst the men. The 3rd Brigade was primarily made up of older men, whereas those of the 8th were generally younger, and also new to the Dybbøl front. Comments such as, "The young soldiers are to be spared, but we; we are to be butchered." were heard. This was compounded by a nearby group of off-duty labour troops and artillerymen, all shouting encouragement to the discontented infantry that their protests were justified.

At 17:00, Wørishøffer issued the order to march. Not a man moved. The Colonel waited for a few minutes. Then, accompanied by his Brigade Adjutant, Premierlieutenant Colding, and his Orderly Officer, Premierlieutenant Heyn, he rode to the acting commander of 17th Regiment, Captain F.W. Lund, (The regiment's commander, Colonel Bernstorff, was temporarily commanding Second Brigade in the main line) and told him to get his men moving. Lund replied, "They won't go". There followed a series of visits to different companies by Wørishøffer and the officers of his staff, in addition to the pleading and cajoling of the regimental and company officers. Eventually, after much effort, the individual companies were started west, and, finally, all passed over the Bridgehead and on to the lines.

Within a very short time, news of these events had, of course, spread everywhere in the defence lines amongst the Danish troops. Reactions were mixed, ranging from shame, through mild amusement, and in some cases, anger at the troops of 3rd Brigade. Nowhere, at least amongst the rank and file, was there any sympathy for the (albeit temporary) disobedience that had taken place.

General du Plat and his Chief of Staff arrived near the end of this affair, which had clearly caused quite a scare. It was the only major occurrence of its kind during the campaign, and was primarily caused by a series of unfortunate coincidences. Nonetheless, the matter could very easily have escalated much further, and at the very least, it was clumsy to allow tired men whose rest had been cut short to meet the particular troops that they were replacing, moving towards a rest area under such circumstances.[66]

In expectation of the impending attack, General Moltke wrote from Berlin to Colonel Blumenthal, "God grant you the victory and that it not be an expensive one, because the material objective to be won is actually worth nothing."[67]

In Redoubt I, all the guns had been dismounted (for the second time), and one in Redoubt IV. The front sight of a 24 pounder in Redoubt III was blown off, and the gun carriage for a rifled 12 pounder damaged. In redoubt IX, a 24/84 pounder gun carriage, and in X, an already damaged 24 pounder smoothbore was shot to pieces.

Across the sound, the Surlykk Battery was badly damaged by return fire, after bombarding Batterup, setting fire to two farms. The Flank Battery, was also heavily shelled, having four cannon dismounted. The fire was so heavy that shell fragments were found in the magazine. As a result, all the ammunition was removed and stored behind a hedgerow near the Baadsager Battery. In Redoubt

---

66 See Liljefalck & Lütken, p. 367-69, and Wørishøffer, General, "3die Brigade Den 15die April 1864", *Vort Forsvar*, Nr. 64, 3rd June 1883.

67 Moltke, H., *Korrespondenz*, Letter Nr. 64, to Colonel Blumenthal, April 15th 1864.

III, the sap coming forward from the Second Parallel had raised fears that the Prussians might attempt plant a mine beneath the work. As a result work on a mine gallery was started to counter the possibility.[68]

During the day, 4,034 shells fell. Casualties amounted to one officer and 17 men killed, and one officer and 39 men wounded.

April 16th

During the course of the morning, Major-General du Plat unsuccessfully tried to persuade the still unwell Gerlach to report sick, and hand over his command to him, as the senior divisional commander. Du Plat had made it clear to Gerlach that should this hand over take place, he would retreat from Dybbøl on the following evening, regardless of instructions from Copenhagen. Gerlach, however, did not feel able to ignore the instructions of the Government nor to relinquish command and allow it to occur by default. He declined the offer.[69]

The bombardment continued at a steady, though reduced, pace throughout the day. Several damaged guns were removed from the fortifications. Once again, the only significant defensive fire came from the batteries on Als, together with some support from the redoubts on the right wing.

In the new emplacements near Dybbøl Mill, were placed two 6 pounder smoothbores, and two 12 pound howitzers. Ammunition totaling 40 rounds per gun was also allocated[70].

By now, the only positions west of the Redoubts still held by the defenders were along a small ridge north of the main road running from Redoubt V past Redoubt VI. From here, it was possible to observe along the length of part of the Third Parallel. Major-General Raven, whose brigade was on outpost duty, was ordered to capture this final obstacle to the main attack.

4/GR8, Premier-Lieutenant Wilucki I, was detailed for the task, to which were attached two officers and 55 men of the 2/7th Pioneers to connect and reverse the trenches. In support were the remaining three companies of the battalion, and F/GR8, Major Gaudi. The assault took place at 21:00.

The company defending the ridge, 3/17th Regiment, Captain C. Gorm[71], was swiftly overrun by the surprise assault, and pushed back off the heights, some 50 men being taken prisoner. The assault troops rapidly dug in. An attempt to retake the position, made by 8/18th Regiment, Premierlieutenant Benzon, failed with a loss of three killed, three wounded, and five taken prisoner. Redoubt VI began shelling the ridge shortly after. Fire from the left flank of the redoubts was continued through the night. The loss of this high ground also caused the Danes to

---

68 Schøller, pp. 93-94.

69 Hansen, F.F., *En Compagniecommandeurs Erindringer Fra Krigen 1864*, p. 68. Gerlach had not recovered from the fall with his horse on the 9th.

70 Generalstaben, Volume II, pp. 370-371.

71 It was certainly this company, although Jensen, p. 362, says that it was Captain Gandil's 2/17th. These troops had been involved in the incident the day before when their Brigade had initially refused to move back to the front lines. It is possible that their morale had not yet altogether recovered.

pull their remaining pickets out of the ruins of East Dybbøl. Prussian losses during the day and overnight on the 16/17th totaled 36.[72]

Redoubt II was largely open in the rear as a result of the ceaseless pounding, and IV badly hit. In Redoubt V, there were large gaps in the palisades. Damage to ordnance in the position on this day was not heavy, partially because so many guns had already been silenced. A rifled 4 pounder was dismounted in Redoubt IV, where also, the gun platform of the left most 84 pound howitzer was destroyed. One 24 pound howitzer was dismounted in the Baadsager Battery.

Incident at the Baadsager Battery on Als (Liljefalck & Lütken)

During the day, 3,032 shells fell. Casualties amounted to one officer and 30 men killed, and one officer and 56 men wounded.[73] A heavy fire was maintained overnight by the besiegers, the most heavy and persistent overnight shelling experienced by the defenders, and amounting to a cross-fire from the front, Broager, and Batterup.[74]

April 17th

On what would prove to be the siege's final full day, the Prussian batteries once again opened a steady fire, somewhat heavier than the previous day. The Front Attack batteries fired with particularly good effect.[75] The shelling was especially brisk during the afternoon and evening. The defenders also replied with gusto. Particularly effective were 150 rounds fired by a "hidden" battery of three rifled 12 pounders emplaced in a small hollow near the Baadsager battery on Als.

---

72 See Appendix XV.
73 Jensen, p. 361. Schøller, p. 98, gives the day's total as one officer and 21 men killed, one officer and 65 men wounded, and 58 men prisoners.
74 Schøller, p. 97.
75 Waldersee, p. 292.

In the mainline, the blockhouse in Redoubt II was hit, and its eastern side set on fire. Temporarily stacked within the blockhouse were a number of unexploded Prussian shells. These exploded as the flames reached them, throwing much of the structure into the air, and showering the garrison and troops in the vicinity with debris. Realising that the magazine itself was threatened, the Redoubt Commander, 27 year old Second-Lieutenant J. Ancker, Bornholm Militia Artillery, immediately ordered his men out of the work, but they refused to leave him there.

Ancker therefore organised volunteers to move sandbags to create a barrier between the fire and the magazine, ably aided by Engineer Premierlieutenant O. Larssen. Singing as they did so, the men erected a wall of sandbags, and the fire itself also died down. Subsequently, the majority of the usable materiél was removed and sent to Sønderborg. The lieutenant and his men remained in the battered redoubt that they had saved from destruction.[76]

Lieutenant-General Gerlach wrote a long report to the War Ministry, with an impassioned plea to be allowed to withdraw from Dybbøl. In places verging on the insubordinate, the dispatch concluded:

> According to the Ministry's coded dispatch of the 14th inst., the Government maintains its earlier view about the importance of holding the position, even if this might result in comparatively heavy losses.
>
> I can only see in this an order not to leave the position unless the troops are being thrown back in a fierce attack. I shall, of course, comply with the wishes of the Government, as it alone is responsible for the orders given to me, and I have not omitted to report on the actual situation. However, I consider it my duty to again point out the weakness of our position. I must emphasise the weakened condition of the redoubts in regard to the stationary obstacles and their effectiveness. I have to stress the numerical weakness of the units - 4 Regiments move into position tonight with 4,200 men - and the low morale amongst the troops. This feeling is caused by the considerable danger that they are exposed to, especially being forced into complete passivity whilst at Sundeved. Above all, I must point out that whether we have two or three bridges, we have in the highest degree failed to secure our retreat.
>
> The confidence in the strength of the Dybbøl position has been broken. The time when we have completely exhausted ourselves might therefore come very quickly and unexpectedly. I shall then necessarily have to expose the best part of the Danish Army to a sad and dishonourable destruction, or to decide, in spite of my best intentions, to act against the orders of the Government. Only when the Government leaves it entirely to me and I can thereby enjoy the necessary confidence, will it be possible for me, in time, to decide not to continue the defence of the position to the bitter end. Only thereby will it be possible for me, in time, to secure an honourable retreat to Als.[77]

---

76 Vaupell, O., "Johan Ancker og Skansen Nr. II's Forsvar", part II, *Danebrog*, Volume II, 1881-82, pp. 616-617.

77 Generalstaben, Volume II, p. 377. Whatever the morale of the troops, General Gerlach's own mental state, combined with his being unwell, had clearly slipped into complete fatalism. This could hardly be thought of as inspiring any kind of confidence in either the army or the authorities.

In a completely different spirit, this was also the day that Prince Friedrich Carl made the final details of the operation known outside his own staff and senior generals – it was now quite clear that the siege had certainly gone as far as it could. The concerns expressed by the King in his message had been satisfied. The Danish artillery in the position had been virtually silenced, and was largely inactive during the day. The whole area, between the redoubts and the bridgehead, was commanded by the Prussian heavy artillery, making any major enemy movement there difficult. The Third Parallel had taken the departure point for the assault troops to under 450 yards from all of the redoubts, and there were now no enemy-held advanced works in front of the main line to be attacked.

The attack would take place the following morning. All senior commanders involved in the operation, as well as the commanders of the storm columns assembled in the Boffelkøbbel at 12:00. The Prince began: "Tomorrow, Gentlemen, you will have the honour to take the redoubts. His Majesty, the King, has requested me to inform him of the hour of the attack, and allows me to tell you that he will be with us in spirit, and will pray for us."[78]

He then verbally gave the necessary orders for the assault to take place at 10.00 the next morning, 18th April, preceded by a colossal bombardment by the artillery. He also gave a detailed 'Disposition' for the attack, copies of which were given to those present by Lieutenant-General von Manstein.[79] It read:

At 01:30 on the morning of 18 April, the companies of the first three columns which have been designated within the orders to carry out the assault, and at 02:00 the other three columns, will assemble at the eastern edge of the Bøffelkobbel, and, on the orders of the general of the day, will advance from there, via the depot, to the Third Parallel, where they will lie down and remain lying until the assault begins.

Brigade Canstein will march under cover via Skodsbøl to the Avnbjerg in order to arrive there at 10:00, to serve as reserve for the assault columns.[80]

Brigade Raven will be in position at Nybøl at 10:00 and from there will march along the road to the Avnbjerg.

Brigade Schmid will, at 10:00, reinforce its forward line of outposts and form up in the area of Ragebøl.

Brigade Goeben will, at 10:00, be in position under cover in the Sottrup woods, where the boats and pontoons will also arrive.

The Guards Division will concentrate at Sottrup at 10:00, and the squadron of uhlans from Baurup will be assigned to them.

At daybreak, all batteries will begin much heavier fire, initially on the Redoubts, and then particularly on the enemy communications and artillery emplacements located there.

78 Rehtwisch, Theodor, *Schleswig-Holstein Stammverwandt. Bilder aus dem Kriege von 1864*, p. 157.
79 Waldersee, p. 294.
80 This was subsequently altered, and Brigade Canstein was instead ordered to take its position behind the storm columns, in the Half Parallel, and follow up from there to the Third Parallel.

At precisely 10:00, the six assault columns will break out of the Third Parallel in the manner specified in their orders.[81] Brigade Canstein will advance to the Third Parallel. Brigade Raven will advance along the road to the high ground at the Second Parallel. The Guards Division will advance from Sottrup to Dybbøl Church through Stenderup. The designated field batteries under the command of Lieutenant-Colonel von Bergmann, will be positioned before daybreak at the Avnbjerg, and at 10:00 will be ready to move forward from there. Of the horse batteries, at 10:00, three will be at Sottrup and two at Nybøl at my own disposition.

With the exception of the squadron remaining in Broager for coast watch duty,[82] the hussar regiment will at 10:00 be positioned behind the Bøffelkobbel.

From the beginning of the attack, the assault columns will be placed under the command of Lieutenant-General von Manstein. All reports will be made to the Avnbjerg, where I shall take up my own position.

Headquarters, Gråsten, 17th April 1864
Commanding General
Friedrich Carl, Prince of Prussia

The scene was now set. All of the arrangements were in place, and planning was at an end. Although the troops themselves were not officially informed until the next morning about the assault, it was widely suspected, and numerous rumours to that effect certainly circulated during the evening.[83]

Major-General Goeben's 26th Brigade, consisting of 16 companies, some 3000 men, was to attempt the crossing of the Als Sound, at his discretion, either as a feint, or if he considered it possible that the opposite bank might be undefended.

After the serious scouting exploits of the previous few nights, a more "freelance" raid on Als took place on the 17th. At 16:00, Captain von Hoffmüller and Premier-Lieutenant Hasselt, with two NCOs and 14 men, all from IR15, embarked in two boats, and rowed across the northern Als Sound. Once across, they found the Arnkilsøre Battery, spiking two guns, a 6 pounder and a 24 pounder. They also attempted to blow up some ammunition, but were prevented from doing this by the rapid approach of the Danish coast watch. The little party were able to return to their boats, and return safely across the sound, bringing with them some of the gun tools as trophies.[84]

---

81 See the 'Instruction' for the storm above, issued on April 15th. It was vital to the operation that each storm column acted independently. In this way, a repulse to one would have no direct impact upon the progress of any other.

82 4th Squadron.

83 Bunge, C, *Aus meinem Kriegstagebuche*, p.76.

84 von Winterfeld, Volume II, pp. 50-51. News of this 'raid' was immediately sent to Berlin, and that very evening, the King himself sent a telegram to Headquarters at Graasten congratulating the two officers, and awarding them both the Order of the Red Eagle. Premier-Lieutenant Weissich went unrewarded for his valuable work previously.

With the arming of Batteries 30, 31, 32, and 33, and the overnight construction of an unnumbered one at East Dybbøl,[85] the artillery massed to pound the Danish positions in support of the attack on the following day was as follows.[86]

Table 34

Prussian Batteries involved in the bombardment of the Dybbøl fortifications, April 18th 1864

Battery	*Location*	*Armament*	*Target & Approximate Range*
Battery Nr. 1	Gammelmark	Four rifled 24 pounders	Redoubts I-IV, trenches, & ships 2,625 – 3,500 yards
Battery Nr. 2	Gammelmark	Four rifled 24 pounders	Redoubts I-IV, trenches, & ships 2,500 – 3,500 yards
Battery Nr. 4	Gammelmark	Four rifled 12 pounders	Redoubts I-IV, trenches, & ships 2,500 – 3,500 yards
Battery Nr. 5	"Beach"	Two rifled 12 pounders	Ships Range variable
Battery Nr. 9	South of the Sønderborg Road	Four rifled 12 and two rifled 6 pounders	Redoubts IV & V 1,135 – 1,325 yards
Battery Nr. 10	South of the Sønderborg Road	Four rifled 12 pounders	Redoubts V &VI 1,165 – 1,295 yards
Battery Nr. 11	South of the Sønderborg Road	Four rifled 12 pounders	Redoubts VI, VIII, & IX 1,445 – 1,800 yards
Battery Nr. 13	East of Dybbøl Church	Six rifled 6 pounders	Redoubts VII &VIII 1,200 – 1,900 yards
Battery Nr. 14	South of the Sonderborg Road	Four rifled 6 pounders	Redoubts III &IV and the area in between 1,180 – 1,355 yards
Battery Nr. 15	"Beach"	Two rifled 24 pounders	Ships Range variable
Battery Nr. 16	Right of the Half Parallel	Two smoothbore 12 pounders	Redoubt I and the area to Redoubt II 750 yards

85 Battery Number 30 and this unnumbered one were both actually equipped in the early morning of the 18th.
86 Grosser Generalstab, Volume 2, Appendix 50.

Battery Nr. 18	Behind the Half Parallel	Four 25 pound mortars	Redoubts II, III, and the area around them 875 yards
Battery Nr. 19	Behind the Half Parallel	Four 25 pound mortars	Trenches and area around Redoubts III & IV 1,080 yards
Battery Nr. 20	Behind the Half Parallel	Four 25 pound mortars	Redoubt IV & the area to Redoubt V 875 yards
Battery Nr. 21	Behind the Half Parallel	Four 25 pound mortars	Redoubts VI, VII & the area around V and VI 850 yards
Battery Nr. 22	Between Dybbøl and Ragebøl	Four rifled 6 pounders	Redoubt IX & troops observed Between Redoubts IX & X 1,530 – 2,010 yards
Battery Nr. 23	West of Stavegaarde	One rifled 12 and three rifled 24 pounders	Redoubts IX, X, the surrounding area and Als 1,660 – 1,840 yards
Battery Nr. 24	West of Stavegaarde	Four rifled 12 pounders	Redoubts IX, X, the surrounding area and Als 1,400 – 1,445 yards
Battery Nr. 25	East of Stavegaarde	Four rifled 12 pounders	Batteries on Als, especially the "Flank" Battery north of Sønderborg Variable ranges
Battery Nr. 26	East of Stavegaarde	Four rifled 12 pounders	Batteries on Als, especially the "Flank" Battery north of Sønderborg Variable ranges
Battery Nr. 27	Snogbæk	Four rifled 24 pounders	Als and ships in Als Sound Variable ranges
Battery Nr. 28	Right Flank of the Half Parallel, close to the Vemmingbund	Two rifled 24 & 2 rifled 12 pounders	Redoubts I & II, communication trenches & ships in the Vemmingbund 875 – 1,050 yards

Battery Nr. 29	Snogbæk	Four rifled 6 pounders	Als, and ships in Als Sound Variable ranges
Battery Nr. 30	Left flank of the Third Parallel	Four smoothbore 12 pounders	Opportunity fire[87] Variable ranges
Battery Nr. 31	Behind the First Parallel, close to The Vemmingbund	Two rifled 24 pounders	Redoubts I & II, communication trenches, & ships in the Vemmingbund Variable ranges
Battery Nr. 32	Left flank of the Second Parallel	Four 7 pound howitzers	Redoubt IV, communication trenches, & positions from Redoubts IV to V[88] 525 yards
Battery Nr. 33	Left flank of the Second Parallel	Four 7 pound howitzers	Redoubts V, VI, & VII[89] 650 yards
(Unnumbered)	South of East Dybbøl	Six smoothbore 12 pounders	Redoubts VII &VIII[90] 350 yards

The final blow was about to be struck, yet although the Danish army commander now expected it daily, he could not be certain when. Refused permission once more to withdraw, Gerlach could only wait for the inevitable attack without any confidence at all in his own situation. For all his many faults as overall commander, a post he had not wanted, one can only feel sympathy for him.

Damage to the fortifications was considerable after more than two weeks of heavy shelling. The defensive works to be assaulted had taken a severe pounding, whereas the line to the north of the Sønderborg Road, though battered, was largely intact[91].

On this, the final day of the siege, 4,222 shells fell. Casualties amounted to 24 men killed, and two officers and 55 men wounded. Of all the long bombardment at Sundeved, that steadfast friend of Denmark, John Edward Henry Skinner wrote,

87 This battery was armed overnight on the 17/18th with the guns from the former Battery 17. They did not, in fact, fire at all from the new position.

88 This battery was armed overnight on the 17/18th with the guns from the former Battery 6, disarmed and abandoned the previous night.

89 As above, but armed with the guns from the former Battery 7, disarmed and abandoned the previous night.

90 As above, but armed with the guns from the former Battery 8, disarmed and abandoned the previous night.

91 See the following chapter for the condition of the defences on the morning of the attack.

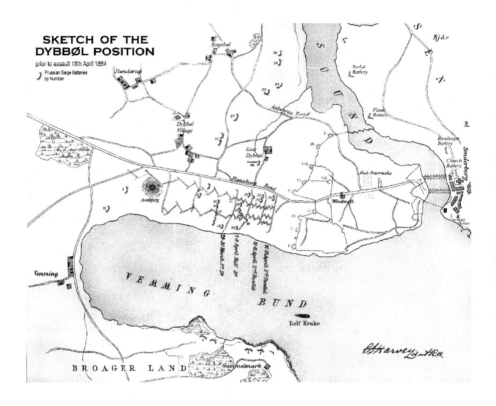

Map 26: Sketch of Dybbøl, morning of 18th April

It may be questioned whether any troops, save the Confederates at Charleston and Vicksburg, have been under such a fire as was poured upon Dybbøl Hill. Old-fashioned campaigners, who thought twelve-pounder guns heavy artillery, and fought every summer in the Low Countries, would find nineteenth century warfare simply astounding.[92]

92 Skinner, J.E.H., p. 184.

10

The Storm of the Dybbøl Position

Orders were issued for all Prussian troop movements to be carried out as quietly as possible during the night of the 17th/18th. The storm columns were formed up on the eastern edge of the Bøffelkobbel, Columns One, Two, and Three, by 01:30, and Four, Five, and Six, by 02:00 on April 18th, as specified in the 'Disposition'. They were then marched to the Third Parallel. Long before dawn, some 10,000 men were mustered here.

Although fire against the lines of fortifications continued overnight, it was not intense and had not prepared the defenders for what was to come. The whole of the Prussian artillery began its pre-assault bombardment at 04:00.[1] It would last six hours. The clocks of all batteries had been synchronised, and were again checked at 09:00 to ensure that the main bombardment would cease precisely at 10:00.[2] The total number of projectiles fired at the Danish positions on the front of the assault – the area between Redoubts I and VI inclusive (Batteries 9, 10, 11, 14, 16, 18, 19, 20, 21, 28, 31, 32, and 33) - from the night of the 17th to the end of the attack has been calculated as:[3]

Table 35

Prussian Artillery projectiles fired during the bombardment of the Dybbol fortifications, April 17/18th 1864

Common shell, rifled 24 pounder	150
Common shell, rifled 12 pounder	1400
Common shell, rifled 6 pounder	719
Shrapnel shell, rifled 6 pounder	46
Shell, 25 pound mortar	1700
Common shell, 7 pound howitzer	640
Common shell, 12 pounder smoothbore	30
Shrapnel shell, 12 pounder smoothbore	30
Total projectiles	4715

The 102 engaged Prussian guns fired some 7,900 rounds in all at the works themselves and the island of Als up to the beginning of the assault. Batteries 5 and

---

1   See previous chapter for details of the Prussian siege batteries on the day of the attack.
2   "Der Feldzug in Schleswig", *Militärische Blätter*, Nr. 37, 1864.
3   Neumann, R., *Über den Angriff auf die Düppler Schanzen in Der Zeit von 15. März bis zum 18. April 1864*, pp. 35-38.

Map 27: Dybbøl , 18th April - Danish positions and subsequent counter-attacks

15 (both 'Front Attack' batteries) were tasked to engage enemy ships, should these enter their field of fire and neither fired a shot on the 18th.[4]

Prior to this massive morning bombardment, the condition of the main Dybbøl defence line and its operational armament was (all guns smoothbore unless otherwise indicated):[5]

Redoubt I   Many repairs to earthworks and palisades
                             had been effected. The bridge was in full
                             working order. One 12 pound howitzer was
                             functional.

4   Grosser Generalstab, Volume II, pp. 523-524.
5   Taken primarily from Generalstaben, Volume II, pp. 380-384, Johansen, *Dybbøl 1864*, pp. 219-222, and Schøller, p. 109.

Redoubt II	The blockhouse had been struck and had caught fire the previous day. As noted, the magazine had been saved by the quick action of Second-Lieutenant Ancker, and its entrance reestablished. The bridge had been destroyed, but a temporary movable one had been constructed. It was possible to defend the position, but one gap still existed to be blocked. The armament comprised one 84 pound howitzer (type II), one 12 pounder gun (capable of firing a few rounds), and one rifled 4 pounder field gun of the 13th Field Battery.
Redoubt III	The work was functional, though there were some gaps in the palisades. The armament comprised one 12 pounder gun, capable of firing one shot.[6] There were also three 24 pound mortars.
Redoubt IV	The interior had been badly damaged, and the earth works partially repaired. The trench palisades were unsatisfactory at the top. The bridge could not be pulled in, and, consequently had been prepared for destruction. The armament was three 84 pound howitzers (type II) and one piece of undetermined calibre, capable of firing one shot.[7]
Redoubt V	The top palisades had been destroyed and the gate could not be closed, but it was considered in a reasonable state for defence. The armament probably comprised one 24 pounder cannon, two 24 pound howitzers (one capable of only a few shots), and one 12 pound howitzer.[8]
Redoubt VI	In a reasonable state. As with Redoubt IV, it was not possible to move the bridge. This was rigged to be blown up if necessary. The armament was made up of two 84 pound

6   Schøller, p.109. Generalstaben, Volume II, p.382, states that this gun was of undetermined calibre.

7   Schøller, p.109, says a rifled 4 pounder. Generalstaben, Volume II, p.382, opts for the 24 pound howitzer.

8   Schøller, p. 109 & *Beretning far Krigsministeriet [Report from the War Ministry] om Kampen den 18de April 1864*, followed by de Bas, p. 229. This is the redoubt's full complement. However, Generalstaben, Volume II, p. 382, followed by Jensen, p. 372, and Bjørke, Kiær, and Norrie, p. 343 all state that only one piece, of undetermined calibre, was operational.

howitzers one capable of firing only one shot (type II), three 12 pounder guns, one rifled 4 pounder field gun, and three 24 pound mortars.

Redoubt VII	Also in a reasonable state. The armament comprised four 12 pounder guns.
Redoubt VIII	Again this was in a reasonable state. The armament comprised four 24 pounder guns, one rifled 12 pounder cannon (damaged), one rifled 4 pounder field gun, and two 12 pound howitzers.
Redoubt IX	In a reasonable state. The armament comprised one 84 pound howitzer (type II), one rifled 12 pounder cannon, two 24 pound howitzers and two 84 pound mortars.
Redoubt X	Also in a reasonable state. The armament comprised two 24 pounder guns and three 12 pound howitzers.

In the trenches between the redoubts the following guns were deployed:

Between Redoubts I and II	Two 24 pound howitzers, of the 13th Battery
Between Redoubts II and III	Two 24 pound howitzers of the 13th Battery
Between Redoubts III and IV	Two 24 pound howitzers of the 13th Battery
Between Redoubts IV and V	Two 24 pound howitzers of the 10th Battery
North of the Flensburg road	Two rifled 4 pounder field guns of the 2nd Battery
South-east of Redoubt V	One 12 and one 24 pound howitzers
Between Redoubts VIII and IX	Two rifled 4 pounder field guns of the 8th Battery and two 24 pound howitzers of the 13th Battery, in two separate emplacements
East of Redoubt X	Two rifled 4 pounders of the 11th Battery

The artillery in the Withdrawn (Second or Recessed) Line was placed as follows:

In Lunette A	Three 24 pound howitzers
In Lunette B	Three 24 pound howitzers
In position C	Two 24 pound howitzers
In fleche forward of Dybbol Mill (D)	Two 6 pounder guns and two 12 pound howitzers
Between Redoubts II and III	Three 24 pound mortars

In the North Bridgehead were emplaced two 84 pound howitzers (type II) and two 12 pounder guns.

Manning the Dybbøl defences that morning were:[9]

Left Flank trenches and Redoubts Numbers I to VI

1st Brigade	2nd Infantry Regiment	1,159 Undercorporals and Men
	22nd Infantry Regiment	1,004 Undercorporals and Men

Right Flank trenches and Redoubts Numbers VII to X (to the Als Sound)

3rd Brigade	16th Infantry Regiment	1,097 Undercorporals and Men
	17th Infantry Regiment	949 Undercorporals and Men

Barracks Line

8th Brigade	9th Infantry Regiment	1,590 Undercorporals and Men
	20th Infantry Regiment	1,384 Undercorporals and Men

Bridgehead

2nd Brigade	3rd Infantry Regiment	1,280 Undercorporals and Men
	18th Infantry Regiment	1,320 Undercorporals and Men
Total		9,733 Undercorporals and Men

The total number of effectives of all arms present was:

Table 36

Danish effectives at Dybbøl, April 18th 1864

Officers	308
NCOs	626
Musicians	200
Men	13006
Military Labour	381
Total	14521[10]

---

9   Generalstaben, Volume II, pp. 384-385. These unit strengths are valid for the evening of the 17th. Note again that the position itself had originally been designed against artillery rather than infantry attack, Schøller, p. 102.

10 Generalstaben, *Statistiske Meddelelser angaaende den danske Krigsmagt*, Volume 1, Copenhagen 1867, p. 137 gives these figures for 18th April. Taking the figures on page 36 for cavalry undercorporals and men, and page 42 for the artillery (both for 15th April), the total number given here appears quite reasonable for the day of the attack.

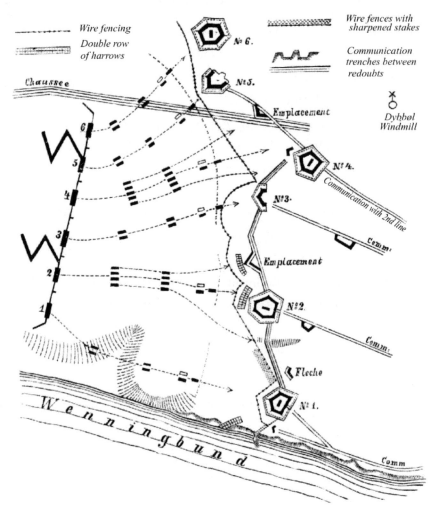

Map 28: Assault of the Prussian Storm Columns - 18th April

The Danish artillery, however, had long since been overpowered, and its influence was minimal. The effective defence of the fortifications was firmly in the hands of the infantry on this day.

In accordance with established procedure, the troops in the main position plus the units in reserve in Sønderborg had been kept in a state of readiness overnight on the 17th/18th, in anticipation of a morning assault that would come at or near dawn. Once again, an exhausting night was spent waiting, snatching any available sleep. The reserve formations were paraded at 03:00, ready to move as soon as the order was given. Not until 06:00, at the height of the shelling, were they stood down.

To 19 year old Peter Frederik Rist, an Officer Aspirant with the 9th Infantry Regiment, in reserve at the Barracks Line, the bombardment was terrifying. He wrote later, "It sounded like the screaming spirits of Hell had been set loose".[11] Significantly however, there was no particular feeling of anxiety in the Danish Command after the early hours of the morning passed. As it was assumed that any attack would take place in the early morning, and since none had occurred, the 'normal' routine of a day of siege automatically fell into place.

At dawn, the commander of the outpost line, Captain Schøller, reported to headquarters: "The day's position has been taken up as ordered. The enemy's works towards the left of Redoubt VI have advanced somewhat during the night. He has established trenches about 220 Alen (about 150 yards) from the Redoubt."[12]

The Deputy Chief of Staff, Major Rosen, made an early morning inspection of the main position, and returned to the Bridgehead at 08:30. Reporting to General du Plat, he expressed his opinion that there would be no assault that day.[13]

Around 09:00 the 'Great and the Good' began to assemble on the Avnbjerg, known to the Prussians as the "Spitzberg", to observe the proceedings. From here, Prince Friedrich Carl, Field Marshal Wrangel, the Crown Prince of Prussia, and their respective staffs along with a host of others, followed the course of the battle.[14] A telegraph line, which had been extended to the hill, kept them in touch with the progress of the attack.

Carl Bunge, serving in 1/IR60, was in the main body of Major-General Canstein's 11th Brigade, in reserve immediately behind the storm columns in the Third Parallel. He noted in his diary:

The selected companies from all the regiments taking parting the siege were formed into six assault columns, corresponding to the six redoubts to be stormed. A detachment of pioneers and artillerymen was attached to each column. The column from our brigade was designated to assault Redoubt II, the strongest and best maintained redoubt of the Danish left flank.

Early on the morning of 18 April, the assault columns marched out and assembled in the Bøffelkobbel, where they removed their helmets and packs, and moved into the last parallel beneath the heavy fire of all the batteries. We followed them at 05:30, removed our helmets and packs as well in the Bøffelkobbel, where we put on our caps, slung our rolled overcoat over one shoulder and waited for further orders. Towards 08:00 the brigade commander appeared and informed us that we would make our assault today, and that we would be part of the 1st reserve on the right flank. As such, we would follow the assault column on foot and support it as required, most likely against the second line of redoubts.

The noise of the batteries, which had orders to shell the enemy position with ever increasing fire from 200 (sic) guns, grew louder and more fearsome by

11   Rist, P.F., *En Rekrut fra Fire og Treds*, Copenhagen 1920, p. 136. Rist went on to become a famous author.
12   Generalstaben, Volume II, p. 379.
13   Bjørke, Kiær, and Norrie, p.344, quote Rosen saying, "Well, it doesn't look like he will come forth today."
14   Grosser Generalstab, Volume II, p. 524.

the minute. We assembled and marched in long lines through the trenches to the 3rd Parallel, in order to take up a preparatory position directly next to the assault column, which was waiting on the steps. It was now nearly impossible to stand the thunder of the guns, and the artillery rounds screamed and whistled through the air over our heads; the ground shook and one had the feeling that the sky would fall. One could not hear the shouts of the person right next to you. In serious, but high spirits, we waited in this hellish noise, each thinking about the next few hours, and anxiously looking at his watch to see how far the hand was from the fateful number 10, since at this hour the artillery fire was supposed to cease and the assault begin. Many thought quietly back on life at home and many others solemnly entrusted their last wishes to their loyal comrade-in-arms. So, there we stood full of expectation and longing, a desire burning in each of us to earn through great effort the reward for the boring and strenuous siege, to have a meaningful part of a great effort and to help earn new laurels for our precious colours. Each of us knew that the thoughts and wishes of our beloved King and Commander in Chief were with us, that his blessings and those of our beloved country accompanied us. How could such feelings, along with memories of the glory of our fathers, of the heroic deeds of the army not but inspire in the heart of every soldier the most loyal and passionate desire to fulfill one's duty and spur him on to greatest possible effort. It was now just a few minutes before ten. The shells, as if driven by a storm, screamed from roaring guns in the direction of the redoubts and a terrible noise, an awful crashing sound filled the air. The Redoubts lay quiet and peaceful as graves - they did not answer our fire at all, but rather patiently bore everything that was going on around them.[15]

At 10:00 the shelling of the main line abruptly ceased, and a mass of men erupted from the Third Parallel. The second-line, the Bridgehead, and Als remained under fire from the Gammelmark batteries. To the accompaniment of martial music from the regimental bands of the 10th (Combined) and 11th Brigades playing in the Second Parallel, the Storm Columns moved quickly towards their objectives.[16] First out of the trench were the *Schützen* companies, providing the covering fire for the main body. Carl Bunge watched them go:

At the stroke of ten the hellish fire suddenly ceased, not a single shot more was fired and an eerie silence fell over the battlefield. We saw the front rows of the assault column hurry over the breastworks, disappear on the enemy side and impatiently push forward in order to get to the jumping off stairs as quickly as possible and be able to follow their brave comrades. The signal to charge was raised, the drums beat and the bugles called to battle and after a few minutes heavy rifle fire crackled from the Redoubts against the assaulting troops.[17]

15 Bunge, C., *Aus meinem Kriegstagebuche. Erinnerungen an Schleswig-Holstein 1864*, Rathenow, n.d. (1865), pp. 76-77.

16 Horn, A., & Lichtenstein, Major, *Geschichte des Leib-Grenadier Regiments Friedrich Wilhelm III...*, Volume II, Berlin 1908, p. 42. These played under the directorship of Gottfried Piefke, Director of Music of the Leib Grenadiers. The bands of four regiments (8th, 18th, 35th, and 60th) would total over 160 musicians.

17 Bunge, C. *Aus meinem Kriegstagebuche*, pp. 77-78.

Storm Column Number One	Major von Conta, 4th Foot Guards
Objective	Redoubt Nr. I
Distance	300 yards (However, the actual route taken so as to flank the work on the seaward side, and avoid flanking fire from Redoubt Nr. II, was 610 yards approximate.)
Schützen Company	4/3rd Foot Guards, Captain v. Reinhardt
Work Column	½ 2/3rd Pioneer Battalion, Premier-Lieutenant Fritze
	5/4th Foot Guards, Captain von Wolfradt
Storm Companies	4/4th Foot Guards, Captain von Stülpnagel
	5/3rd Foot Guards, Captain von Petery
Reserve Companies	1/3rd Foot Guards, Captain von Seegenberg
	5/3GGR, Captain von Hahnke
Fortress Artillery Detachment, Artillery Brigade Nr. 7	
	Second-Lieutenant Schmölder

Captain von Reinhardt's company swiftly moved on Redoubt I, which remained silent, under some shelling from Redoubt II and rifle fire from the trenches between the two redoubts. Attacked from the beach and the front, Redoubt I fell, with minimal resistance, at 10:06.[18] Reinhardt then moved on to take Lunette A, in the Second Line, also with little resistance. Three officers and almost 300 men of the 22nd Regiment were taken prisoner, and handed over to other units of Column One as they came up.

In Redoubt I, meanwhile, artillery Second-Lieutenant Schmölder rapidly organised the work for defence. The only operational gun was moved into a position facing the Vemmingbund, in anticipation of the appearance of the ironclad *Rolf Krake*.

Storm Column Number Two	Major von Fragstein, FR35
Objective	Redoubt Nr. II, the trenches either side, and emplacement to the north
Distance	330 yards approximate (the route taken, however, was 435 yards approximate)
Schützen Companies	2/IR35, Captain von Spiess
	3/IR60, Captain von Leszczynski
	6/IR60, Captain Krähe
Work Column	4/3rd Pioneer Battalion, Captain Daun
	3/FR35, Captain Struensee
Storm Companies	5/FR35, Captain Bachfeld
	7/FR35, Captain von Schütz

18 Each company in the storm columns was given a black and white marker flag to plant on the parapet of captured objectives.

The storming of Dybbøl
Top - skirmishers; centre - work company; bottom - storm companies (Voss)

Reserve Companies	Major von Kettler, IR60
	11/FR35, Premier-Lieutenant von Treskow
	12/FR35, Captain von Kameke
	9/IR60, Premier-Lieutenant von Kaminietz
	10/IR60, Premier-Lieutenant Caspari
Fortress Artillery Detachment, Artillery Brigade Nr. 7	
	Lieutenant Pohlmann

In Redoubt II, the indefatigable Second-Lieutenant Ancker had been answering the Prussian fire with a few shots from the fortification's 84 pound piece. He had also had the 12 pounder gun moved to cover the entrance, and the rifled 4 pounder, the work's interior. At the first alarm, two platoons of 5/22nd Regiment, under Second-Lieutenant Grünwald (about 70 men), hurried in to the Redoubt.

Column II, 11 companies strong (some 1,800 men), was met by canister from the Redoubt, the two guns emplaced south of it, the two to the north, and heavy rifle fire from the work and the trenches either side. 6/IR60, followed by 9/IR60, attacked the southern gun emplacement, overrunning the two guns, although they had already been spiked. Captain Krähe then moved on towards the Second Line. On the right, 3/IR60, supported by 10/IR60, moved against the second gun position, where the guns were also spiked. The first black and white marker flag to be raised in the assault was upon this artillery emplacement north of Redoubt II, by Captain Leszczynski's 3/IR60.[19]

19 Anon, "Der Feldzug in Schleswig", *Militärische Blätter*, Nr. 37, 1864.

Attacking the Redoubt itself, 2/FR35, in the lead, under the heavy fire, instead swept around the work, moving into the trenches on either side, suffering 26 casualties, and was halted in a firefight with II/22nd Regiment's reserve company, 6/22nd, Second-Lieutenant Krogh. Behind them, 3/FR35 and the pioneers had a very difficult time clearing the palisade in the ditch, which finally had to be done with explosives.[20] The two storm companies now coming up, they combined with the pioneers to force their way into the Redoubt, against fierce resistance from the garrison. The first Prussian who attempted to plant a marker flag on the parapet was shot, and the flag grabbed by Corporal Nellemann. Attempting to stop a second flag being planted, Nellemann was killed. Superior numbers overwhelmed the garrison. The work fell at 10:10, Lieutenant Ancker being captured by Second-Lieutenant Schneider of 7/FR35. Schneider said in his report,

> I jumped down into the redoubt and threw myself at two heavy guns which an officer was just attempting to spike. Unfortunately, I was just too late to prevent this. However, I now took from the officer his sword, and made him prisoner. It was Lieutenant Ancker.[21]

Ancker was captured holding a detonator, and had intended to explode the magazine. It was perhaps the ultimate irony that he had worked so heroically to prevent the magazine from exploding the previous day, and was now prevented from blowing it up.[22]

Either side of the Redoubt, the defenders were equally overwhelmed by troops coming through the trenches from the neighbouring works, which had already fallen. Especially around Redoubt III, the line had been broken, with Prussian troops fanning out in the rear.

Storm Column Number Three	Major Girodz von Gaudi, GR8
Objective	Redoubt Nr. III and adjoining trenches: Distance 315 yards approximate
Schützen Company	9/GR8, Captain von Seydlitz
Work Column	11/IR18, Captain von Hanstein
	½ 2/3rd Pioneer Battalion, Premier-Lieutenant Bertram I
Storm Companies	12/GR8, Premier-Lieutenant Sack
	0/IR18, Captain, Count Finckenstein
Reserve Companies	10/GR8, Captain Milson
	12/IR18, Captain von Freyburg
Fortress Artillery Detachment, Artillery Brigade Nr. 3	Lieutenant Millies

20 During the assault, Pioneer Carl Klinke was killed whilst assisting with the explosives in the ditch. He was later elevated to heroic status, as a model of sacrifice and devotion to duty, an icon even in post-1945 East Germany. See Bader, Werner, *Pionier Klinke. Tat und Legende*, Berlin/Bonn 1992.

21 Isenburg, p. 291.

22 Sørensen, *Den Anden Slesvigske Krig*, Volume II, p. 268.

Second-Lieutenant Ancker and Corporal Rasmus Nelleman defending Redoubt II
(Schiøtt)

Redoubt III was defended by 19 men of 4/22nd Regiment, commanded by Officer Aspirant Smidth, with Corporal Hess in charge of the single cannon in the work. As Column Three moved towards the Redoubt, it came under heavy fire from Redoubt IV on its left, the two guns between it and Redoubt III, and by the infantry in the trenches. 1/GR8 stormed the work, meeting fierce resistance from Smidth's handful of troops. Smidth himself shot the first Prussian attempting to plant a marker flag on the parapet, but the struggle was brief, and the work taken at 10:05. One of von Seydlitz' platoons then continued east following the trenches towards Redoubt IV. Two more platoons crossed the Second Line and occupied Dybbøl Mill, driving back 8/2nd Regiment, Second-Lieutenant (of the War Reserve) Reiter, posted in Reserve behind Redoubt IV. The other companies of the column poured through the gap.

Smidth was badly wounded, spending a year in a Prussian hospital. Alfred, Count Waldersee, was to say much later of the young Aspirant, "It is a testimony to a rare amount of energy and skill to defend a work so successfully and with a tenacity given to only a few men."[23] 46 bodies were later found around Redoubt III.[24]

Storm Column Number Four	Colonel von Buddenbrock, Commander, IR53
Objective	Redoubt Nr. IV and trenches between it and Redoubts III and V: Distance 435 yards approximate
Schützen Companies	1/IR53, Captain Boettge (with Engineer-Lieutenant von Brodowski, one NCO, and 5 pioneers)

---

23 Vaupell, p. 264.
24 Sørenesen, *Den Anden Slesvigske Krig,* Volume II, p. 267.

	3/IR55, Premier-Lieutenant Rothenbücher[25]
	4/IR55, Premier-Lieutenant von Sanitz
Work Column	10/IR53, Premier-Lieutenant Wienand (with
	Engineer-Premier-Lieutenant Köhler)
	2/7th Pioneer Battalion, Premier-Lieutenant
	Schotte
Storm Companies	Lieutenant-Colonel von Doering
	4/IR53, Premier-Lieutenant Senckel
	2/IR53, Captain Wolter
	3/IR53, Captain Schalle
Reserve Companies	Captain von Rosenzweig
	9/IR53, Premier-Lieutenant Benkendorf
	11/IR53, Captain Chytraeus
	12/IR53, Captain Henning
	2/IR55, Premier-Lieutenant Delius
	1/IR55, Captain von Arnim II
Fortress Artillery Detachment, Guard Artillery Brigade	
	Premier-Lieutenant Stoephasius, Artillery
	Brigade Nr. 3.

Hearing the first shots, the gunners in Redoubt IV immediately stood to, and the infantry garrison, two platoons (about 70 men) of 3/2nd Regiment, Premierlieutenant Gjørup, quickly moved inside, to be joined by Captain Lundbye, II/2nd Regiment's commander. About a dozen rounds of case shot were fired at the approaching enemy columns. Lundbye ordered Premierlieutenant Crone, the redoubt's artillery commander, to blow up the bridge, but this failed. The Redoubt then came under heavy attack.

Column Four was delayed in its deployment, by the fact that not all troops could be formed in the Third Parallel, and because it was taking flanking fire from Redoubts II and V. Captain Boettge's 1/IR53, the column's leading company, formed in a dense skirmish line, faced case shot and rifle fire from the Redoubt and the positions either side, suffering the heaviest casualties amongst the columns, including the company commander killed. The pioneers, who overtook 10/IR53, rapidly began removing the palisades of the Redoubt, and then forced their way over the counterscarp, together with the latter company, which had caught up. At the same time, the already mentioned platoon of 9/GR8, from Column Three, also assaulted the Redoubt from the south.

Further south, 2 and 4/IR55 attacked the gun emplacement west of Redoubt IV, linking with Column Three. 1 and 3/IR55 attacked the trenches north of the Redoubt, facing stiff resistance from the remaining two platoons 3/2nd Regiment,

25 Rothenbücher would be wounded in the assault, 3/IR55 thus gaining the dubious distinction of having the highest number of officer casualties of any similar sized Prussian unit in this short campaign, a total of eight; Buddenbrock, "Das 5. Westphälische Infanterie-Regiment Nr. 53, das 1. Bataillon 6. Westphälische Infanterie-Regiments Nr. 55 und die 2. Kompagnie des Westphälischen Pionier Battalions Nr. 7 am 18 April 1864", *Militär-Wochenblatt*, Supplement to Nr. 37, Berlin 1864.

under Swedish Second-Lieutenant Ackerhjelm and Senior-Sergeant Nyegaard, but forcing them back.

Under attack from all sides, Captain Lundbye ordered his reserve company, 8/2nd forward, but Second-Lieutenant Reiter's men had already been driven back by troops of Column Three. Lundbye's position was now hopeless, and he was finally forced to surrender, being killed by a stray bullet shortly afterwards. The Redoubt was captured at 10:13. It is estimated that the defending infantry fired some 15 rounds each.[26]

Musketier Kaspar Honthumb, serving in Captain Boettge's 1/IR53, left a gritty account of the action here:

> I was in a platoon of the company, under the command of Lieutenant Löbbecke. To my right and left I saw our men hitting the ground, and suddenly I felt a concussion and fell to the ground. I can recall this moment, my thoughts and feelings now as clearly as if it had just happened. I knew that I had been hit in my left hip, but I did not know at that moment whether the bullet had penetrated or just grazed me. Once I realized it was just a graze, all I wanted to do was get up and continue forward. My attempt to do so failed - I simply did not have the strength to pick myself up. This was not due to the minor wound but rather primarily to the excitement and previous exertions. You could only describe my situation as very unpleasant; I was exposed on the open ground to the continuing hail of bullets - many dead and wounded lay around me, the cries and moans of whom only increased unpleasantness of my situation. In addition to this, I had to stand idly by as my comrades stormed the redoubt in the rush of victory and as the black and white flag flew proudly in the air atop the redoubt. I was gripped by a certain deep-seated rage, and when I saw the Danes piling out of Redoubt IV in front of me in an effort to defend the works further to the rear, I could not deny myself the (blood-thirsty) satisfaction and laid out all the rounds in front of me and fired them at the Danes. You will certainly shake your peace-loving head at this exquisite evil, but I can assure you that when I think of the many men I killed, I find just as much pleasure in that as I would have in saving the lives of the very same number of men.
>
> After having expended all of my rounds, I attempted once again to pick myself up, and this time I succeeded and reached Redoubt IV without any further difficulty. Lieutenant Spinn gathered the remainder of the 1st Company and, as we (a total of 22 men) were standing in a corner, a piece of shrapnel landed in the middle of the group wounding two men and killing Private Flügel, a courageous and valuable soldier through and through. I had just been speaking with him as he told me with tears in his eyes of the death of his best friend and then, just a few minutes later, he lay dead before me. It was very unpleasant in the Redoubt as the *Rolf Krake* and the Als batteries impotently rained shells and shot down on the redoubts, above which the black and white flags were waving in the fresh sea breeze. This is how we huddled together in the corner and sought cover from the enemy fire!
>
> I have to mention one more incident, which made a grand impression on us all. Lieutenant General von Manstein, who led the entire assault, came into

---

26 Schøller, pp. 112-113. He further states that the resistance lasted for over half-an-hour. Even allowing for errors on both sides, and continued resistance within the redoubt after the marker flag was raised, this appears too long.

Redoubt IV and positioned himself on the highest point, where our colours were flying. He grasped them with his right hand and then with inspiring words raised three cheers for His Majesty. Suddenly, a load of canister shot whistled over our heads and everyone ducked - only the brave General remained standing tall and continued speaking calmly. You can well imagine the great enthusiasm with which his three cheers were now returned and which surely must have carried over to the ears of the furious enemy. It was here, amid the singing of the *Preussenlied* (national anthem), in the hail of bullets, among the blood and bodies, that we celebrated the first victory. We had not been in the redoubt for long before our brave chaplain Müller arrived. "Boys", he called to us, 'I knew all along that you would take the redoubts'. He shook hands with many of the men and gave aid and comfort to the wounded.[27]

Carl Bunge, too, was affected by the spell of victory:

By 10:30 all the first-line redoubts were in our hands, Prussian flags waving from them. Suddenly, we heard the hymn "Now Thank We All Our God" coming from the highest of the redoubts, IV, being played by the musicians of eight regiments ordered there by Prince Friedrich Carl. This mighty choral, at this moment - among the dead and wounded, under heavy fire and amid a raging battle made a powerful impression and very few dry eyes remained. Anyone who experienced this overwhelming moment will forever keep it in grateful memory.[28]

Storm Column Number Five	Major von Krohn, IR24
Objective	Redoubt Nr. V and adjoining trenches: Distance 350 yards approximate
Schützen Company	11/IR64, Captain von Salpius
Work Column	1/IR64, Captain von Lobenthal
	½ 4/7th Pioneer Battalion, Premier-Lieutenant Lommatsch
Storm Companies	11/IR24, Captain Baron von Meerscheidt Hüllessem
	12/IR24, Captain von Sellin
Reserve Companies	12/IR64, Captain Windell
	6/IR24, Captain von Görschen

Fortress Artillery Detachment, Guard Artillery Brigade, Lieutenant Gerwien
½ 3/3rd Pioneer Battalion, Lieutenant
Becker to demolish the Sønderborg-Flensburg Road barricade.

The attacking troops were actually able to reach Redoubt V before the majority of the defenders, although they came under effective canister fire from the emplacements either side of it. Corporal Hansen, the artillery commander, had no time to fire any of the guns in the work, and the embrasures were still blocked when the Redoubt was carried in the first rush, at 10:05. 11 and 12/IR64, and the column's pioneers came over the parapets, and through the open rear.[29] The well-con-

27 Honthumb, Kaspar Alexander, *Mein Tagebuch. Erinnerungen aus Schleswig-Holstein von Caspar, Musketier des 53 Regiments*, Münster 1865, pp. 87-89.
28 Bunge, Carl, *Aus meinem Kriegstagebuche*, p. 79.
29 de Bas p. 234.

structed road barricade took Lieutenant Becker's pioneers half an hour to demolish.[30]

Storm Column Number Six	Major von Beeren, 4GGR
Objective	Redoubt Nr. VI
Distance	360 yards approximate
Schützen Company	11/4GGR, Captain von Behr
Work Column	1/3GGR, Captain von Bançels
	3/7th Pioneer Battalion, Premier-Lieutenant Fedkowicz
Storm Companies	1/4GGR, Captain von Rosenburg
	4/4GGR, Captain von der Hardt
Reserve Companies	3/3GGR, Captain Stwolinski
	5/4GGR, Captain von Gliszczynski

Fortress Artillery Detachment, Artillery Brigade Nr. 4, Lieutenant Hübler

The leading companies of Column Six covered the distance to their objective very rapidly, partly protected on the right by the fact that the Danish guns between Redoubts V and VI concentrated their fire on Column Five, but they did receive some fire from Redoubt VIII on their left. Whilst the *Schützen* company swept around the work on the right and left, Captain Bançels' company scaled the face, using the sharpened stakes on the counterscarp to pull themselves up. Once inside, there was a short close-quarter action, before the Redoubt fell, at 10:04½. When the two storm companies arrived, they were then directed to the left. Observing the first marker flag fluttering on the ramparts of Redoubt VI, the first redoubt to fall, Friedrich Carl turned to the Guard Division's commander and remarked, "General von der Mülbe, I congratulate you."[31] The Prince thereupon sent his aide, Count von Haeseler, forward to appraise the situation. Premier-Lieutenant von Haeseler's report resulted in the commitment of the Guard 4 Pounder Battery and 3rd 6 Pounder/Artillery Brigade Nr. 3, later joined by the same brigade's 2nd 6 Pounder Battery. From a commanding position between Dybbøl Stone and the Dybbøl Mill, these batteries provided invaluable fire support from about 11:00.

Column Six's 1 and 44/GGR, having been redirected from Redoubt VI, attacked the trenches between there and Redoubt VII. The survivors from Redoubt VI and the reserve company, which had come forward, 5/2nd Regiment, Second-Lieutenant Holst, put up a stubborn resistance here, but were enveloped on both flanks, and driven east. Lieutenant-Colonel Dreyer gathered what troops he could, and withdrew fighting to a farm south of Dybbøl Stone, where he was forced to surrender.

The two reserve companies of Column Six, also sent to their left, attacked Redoubt VII, which was occupied by a section of 7/17th Regiment, Sergeant Ditmar, with the rest of the company, under Premierlieutenant J. Nielsen in the trenches to the north. The redoubt was overrun, the first marker flag planted on the parapet at 10:30.[32] An attempt by Nielsen to retake it failed. A further effort by

30 Brackenbury et al, p. 30.
31 Braumüller, p. 44.
32 Waldersee, p. 365.

The assault on Redoubt VI (Voss)

the reserve company, 1/17th, Second-Lieutenant Dameck, led by 17th Regiment's commander, Colonel Bernstorff, also failed, Bernstorff being killed.

At the same time, the ironclad *Rolf Krake*, mentioned by Musketier Honthumb, weighed anchor and steamed into the fray, after unusual troop movements were seen at Dybbøl. Once strange flags were seen flying from Redoubts I-IV, it was obvious that a major attack was under way. Standing in towards Redoubt I, she began to shell the attacking Prussian infantry, when they were visible through her smoke, which the wind was blowing on-shore. The vessel was first engaged by Second-Lieutenant Schmölder and his men in Redoubt I, who had brought the fortification's one working 84 pound piece to bear on her and was, in addition, heavily shelled by the Gammelmark Batteries. (Naval) Captain Rothe fired a total of 82 shell and 13 shot against the attackers. One 24 pounder shell pierced the vessel's deck, killing Lieutenant Jespersen and wounding nine men. Hindered in her movement by fishing nets placed by the Prussians in the Vemmingbund, the ship moved out of range of the enemy artillery, and by 12:00, was south of Sønderborg, finally dropping anchor at 16:00.[33]

From Redoubts I-VI, parties from all the storm columns south of the Flensburg-Sønderborg Road had moved swiftly on to the Withdrawn (Second) Line, so quickly in fact, that it is not certain that any artillery rounds were actually fired from there.[34] In this moment of extreme danger, around 10:30, the only major cohesive force immediately available was 8th Brigade, at the burnt out Barracks Line. The Brigade's standing instructions were, in the event of an alarm, to move forward to the Withdrawn (Second) Line, with three battalions, with the fourth temporarily standing on the Aabenraa Road until the 2nd Brigade moved

33 Lütken, Otto, *Søkrigsbegivenhederne I 1864*, Copenhagen 1896, pp. 156-157, quoting Captain Muxoll's report on the action. Lieutenant Jespersen was the only Danish naval officer killed in action in 1864.

34 Schøller, p.116.

forces from the Bridgehead. 8th Brigade was ordered forward, unaware that the Second Line had already fallen.

8th Brigade's Adjutant, Second-Lieutenant Holbøll, was with Colonel Scharffenberg in the Bridgehead, when the brigade received its orders from one of General du Plat's staff:

> After Major Rosen had ridden away, we should have had our lunch. We were about to go to the table, when an orderly came through the doorway with the news that the enemy had attacked. I wrote the time down immediately; my clock showed 10:30. The Colonel ordered two messengers to run and alert the regiments for the attack, and then ordered Irminger ahead to the camp to speed up the previously ordered advance, and move on to Lunette B in the 'Recessed (Second) Line', where he would meet the Colonel. Irminger hastened away – we never saw him again.
>
> I was ordered to follow the Colonel. As I was, for a moment, standing waiting for him, our cook, Dragoon-Orderly Anders Larsen Sonnerup, who had come from Sønderborg into the position to prepare our lunch, came to me and asked to follow me on foot as a messenger. I rejected his request, guided by the old soldier's belief that someone who voluntarily takes part in a battle in which he has nothing to do, will be shot. However, as he continued pleading to come, and promised to use his head, I presented his request to the Colonel, who bluntly answered that dragoon orderlies should not do service on foot. Nevertheless, as Anders Larsen repeated his request again and again, he was allowed to follow.[35]

By the time Colonel Scharffenberg reached the Barracks Line, most of his brigade was already moving forward. On the march, the lead elements of Lieutenant-Colonel Tersling's 9th Regiment encountered General du Plat, who ordered them back, having heard more of the deteriorating situation in the front line. This caused several minutes of confused delay, until further orders from Colonel Scharffenberg got the troops moving forward again.[36] The brigade began to enter the action just before 11:00. At about the same time, General du Plat ordered the withdrawal of Colonel Wørishoffer's 3rd Brigade, on the right flank.

South of the main road, 20th Regiment, Lieutenant-Colonel Scholten, moved towards the Second Line, with I/20th, Major Schack forward, on the right, and II/20th, Major Sperling, slightly behind and to the left. All companies were in company columns. Elements of 22nd Regiment, which had largely ceased to exist as a unit, joined these attacks. The regiment's right flank company, 2/20th, Captain Stockfleth, advanced under heavy fire past Hørlyk towards Lunette C, pushing back two platoons of IR18. These, reinforced by other scattered elements then held their position in the lunette. Stockfleth was halted behind a hedge, under fire from several directions. On his left, the other three companies of Major Schack's battalion took Jensens Gaard from the *ad-hoc* units of Column Two, which had come that far. II/20th Regiment also drove the forward troops of Column One, which had almost reached Sney, back to the Second Line. Whilst preparing Jensens Gaard for defence, Lieutenant-Colonel Scholten was killed.

35 Holbøll, p. 224.
36 Bjørke, Kiær & Norrie, p. 349.

8th Brigade's Counterattack (Liljefalck & Lütken)

Losses in these attacks were heavy, and also included both of the regiment's battalion commanders

9th Regiment, in the meanwhile, had launched its own bayonet charge. Misunderstanding an order from the Brigade Commander, Premierlieutenant (of the War Reserve) Redsted led his 1/9th in a direct attack on Dybbøl Mill, followed by 2/9th, Captain Knauer. Charging through a hail of rifle fire, the attackers forced two platoons of 9/GR8, which had arrived at the mill from Redoubt IV, to evacuate the building and retreat to a hedge behind it. Just north of the main road, the advance of Captain von Sellin's 12/IR24 was pushed back, as were parts of 7. 11, and 12/FR35, a little south of the road. These assembled at Lunette D. The attack of II/9th, Captain Christiani, on the right, under intense fire from units of Columns Four and Five, were able to advance as far as a track running north-south past Dybbøl Stone. On Christiani's right, I/3rd Regiment, Major Arntz, had also been pushed forward extending north across the Aabenraa Road, to cover the withdrawal of the right flank. The remaining three battalions of 2nd Brigade were held in the Bridgehead.

Colonel Scharffenberg was aware that his brigade had suffered great losses in its determined assault. Particularly in the south, he realised the need for more support. An officer dispatched to Headquarters with this information was wounded before he got there. A counterattack was not long in coming.[37]

Shortly before Scharffenberg's countermove, Major-General Raven, north of the main road, sent two companies from his reserve brigade south to support the storm columns in the area around Redoubts II and III. These troops, 2/GR8 and 11/GR8, finding the Redoubts taken, moved through the line, pushing remnants of 22nd Regiment before them, and, by 12:00, were south of Jensens Gaard.

---

37 8th Brigade's losses in the attack were very heavy. Without it, however, precious little from 1st and 3nd Brigades would have escaped.

264   BISMARCK'S FIRST WAR

Linking with troops of Column One, they continued to advance towards the Bridgehead.

The Prussian Reserve Brigades had moved off behind the storm columns as planned, and now began to enter the battle. In the south, Major-General Canstein's reserve brigade started moving forward at about 10:45. Canstein divided the forces into two columns, eight companies of Lieutenant-Colonel von Hartmann's IR60 on the right. On Hartmann's left, Colonel Baron von Puttkammer had six companies of FR35, and two from the Brandenburg Jäger.

Hartmann sent two companies between Redoubts I and II and six between Redoubts II and III. 1/IR60, with Carl Bunge, was in the former pair:

> We forced our way into the communication trenches between redoubts I and II, captured the three guns there and took several prisoners. We pursued and continued to fire on the Danes retreating to the second line of redoubts in order to be able to reach the works at the same time they did, giving them no opportunity to regroup. Elements of the assault column and we took the line at the first rush, spiked several abandoned guns and continued on in the direction of the Bridgehead. From all sides, small (Danish) detachments rushed into the battle in an attempt to force us back or at least to slow our advance; we took fire from all sides and returned it in every direction. It was total confusion - we hardly knew where we were, nor how we got there![38]

The forward units of Column One, plus Hartmann's eight companies made rapid progress against the badly battered 20th Regiment and the remnants of 22nd Regiment which had rallied to them. Captain Stockfleth's 2/20th, on the right of the line was overwhelmed, and after a hard fight, II/IR60, Lieutenant-Colonel von Blumenthal, retook Jensens Gaard. The 22nd and 20th Regiments were steadily forced back, and by 12:00 I/20th had retreated to Sney, with II/20th south-east of them. Each had *ad-hoc* elements of 22nd Regiment in company.

Canstein personally directed 1 and 4/FR35, after passing through a small thicket, to move on Sney, whilst the rest of Puttkammer's troops attacked between Dybbøl Mill and Hørlyk. By 11:30, I/9th Regiment and the survivors of II/2nd had been thrust back from Dybbøl Mill and were being steadily pressed back towards the Barracks Line. North of the main road, Captain Christiani's II/9th Regiment, flanked on the left by Putkammer's advance, and now facing artillery fire to the front, was also forced to retreat towards the Barracks Line.

About this time, du Plat sent the following message, a model of brevity, by courier to the High Command. No time was given:

"Redoubts taken. Troops in retreat.
du Plat"[39]

While this was happening, Major-General Raven's reserve brigade had moved into position south of the ruins of East Dybbøl, along the line of the 2nd Parallel. Shortly after 11:00, Raven received orders to attack on the (Prussian) left wing Redoubts. Perceiving that there was heavy fighting to the south, he had already detached two companies of GR8 in that direction, as discussed. He then advanced,

---

38 Bunge, pp. 78-79.
39 Generalstaben, Volume II, p. 419.

The fighting at Dybbøl Mill (Pflug)

with IR18 in the lead, followed by the remainder of GR8. Passing between Redoubts IV and V, the brigade then deployed south of Redoubt VIII.

After the loss of Redoubt VII, I/17th Regiment's commander, Captain Lund pulled back, forming a line south facing line east of Redoubt VIII, with his 1 and 7/17th, and a platoon of 5/17th. Manning the Redoubt were the remaining three platoons of 5/17th, Second-Lieutenant Galster. As Redoubt VII was already in Prussian hands, Raven dispatched his lead companies 1/IR18, Captain von Treskow, and 2/IR18, Premier-Lieutenant Gersdorff, to storm Redoubt VIII. After some ten minutes of fighting, the work was captured at 11:30.

Captain Lund, now commanding 17th Regiment, had received the orders to retreat at 11.15, and immediately commenced the difficult operation, along with I/3rd Regiment, Major Arntz. On the Danish far-right, Major Wolle's 16th Regiment received his orders some time around 11:30.[40] In a well managed operation, Wolle extricated the regiment, with the exception of three platoons of 6/16th, Captain H. Andresen, from the front line. The regiment withdrew along the beach to the Bridgehead, losing a few men on the way, including Major Hein, commander of I/16th, captured. Andresen's troops, manning Redoubt IX, were already under attack.

After the capture of Redoubt VIII, General Raven went in to the work. Whilst he was away, Colonel von Kettler, incorrectly believing that an attack by Arntz and Lund was about to take place, sent Lieutenant-Colonel von Wietersheim with 3 and 4/IR18, joined by 7/IR18 to assault the farmstead north of Dybbøl Stone, where they were assembled.[41] Hearing of the fighting, Major-General von Raven hastened to the farmstead, where, at 12:30, his lower right leg was shattered by a shell-splinter. Carried to the field hospital at Nybøl, he said, "Finally, a Prussian

---

40 Generalstaben, Volume II, p. 424. Jensen, p. 399, places it earlier, and Bjørke, Kjær & Norrie say 11:45, p. 353.

41 Anon, "Der Feldzug in Schleswig", *Militärische Blätter*, Nr. 39 1864.

general has been wounded in battle. I am glad that it is I who has shed his blood for his King."[42] The Danish units, already in retreat, were pursued all the way to the bridgehead.

At the same time as he visited Redoubt VIII, Raven had ordered GR8 to assault Redoubt IX. The regiment's commander, Colonel von Berger, personally led 3/GR8 in the attack from the south, against heavy fire. The assault was supported by rifle fire from 4/GR8, and a platoon of 8/IR18. A short close quarter struggle ensued, in which Andresen was wounded, and the work taken. Shortly thereafter, at 12:00, Redoubt X was occupied by II/IR13, Major Dürre, of Major-General Schmid's reserve brigade, capturing some unlucky men of 2/16th Regiment, who had been its garrison and left too late. Schmid's outposts had been skirmishing with 16th Regiment's outposts during the morning, appearing to threaten an attack from that quarter. The whole Redoubt Line was now in Prussian hands.

By 12:00, the retreating Danish forces were roughly along a line from just east of Steen Farm in the north, along the Aabenraa Road to the Barracks Line, through Sney, and south-east to the Vemmingbund. While supervising the retreat, at about this time, General du Plat, his Chief of Staff, Major Schau, and the Army Deputy Chief of Staff, Major Rosen, were all hit by enemy fire, near the junction of the Flensburg and Aabenraa Roads. Du Plat and Rosen were killed, and Schau mortally wounded.

As the badly battered 1st, 3rd, and 8th Brigades retreated into the Bridgehead, they were sent across the bridges to Als. General Steinmann had taken command after du Plat was killed. At one point, near 12:00, the Life Guards Infantry were marched across from Sønderborg. In a superb example of quiet courage and discipline, they crossed under artillery fire, only for the decision to be taken that they were no longer required, whereupon they were marched back again, losing 12 killed and 15 wounded altogether. No other infantry were sent into the position since the High Command recognised that it would be a futile waste to do so.

As the Prussian infantry closed in on the Bridgehead, they came under increasing fire from the heavy artillery batteries on Als, especially effective being those north of Sønderborg. The Prussian field artillery present, now 34 guns, 20 of them rifled, attempted to counter this. These were supported, from 12:15, by four rifled 12 pounders which were laboriously brought forward from Battery Nr.10 and emplaced in Redoubt IV. The advance on the Bridgehead slowed, but continued.

Friedrich Carl, still watching the course of events from his observation post on the Avnbjerg, at 12:30 sent orders to Manstein, now directing operations from Redoubt IV, that the Bridgehead should be attacked, "…only if the circumstances were favourable…". Ironically, some 15 minutes later, Gerlach ordered a general withdrawal to Als.[43]

---

42 Zimmer-Vorhaus, Otto, *Offizier Stammliste des Infanterie-Regiments von Lützow (1 Rhenisches) Nr. 25 1813-1913*, p. 440. On April 21st, the King visited him, made him his General Adjutant and presented him the Order *Pour le Mérite*, with the words, 'Here, my dear General, is the order which I myself prize the most.' Raven died of his wounds in the field hospital on April 24th.

43 Grosser Generalstab, Volume II, pp. 562-563.

By 13:30, the point elements of FR35 were less than 200 yards from the North Bridgehead, which then contained three battalions of 2nd Brigade. Half an hour later after the northern pontoon bridge had been dismantled, and the last troops of 18th Regiment withdrew to Als, Lieutenant-Colonel Dreyer ordered the southern pontoon (Frederik VII) bridge broken. Second-Lieutenant Holbøll later paid tribute to the engineers who did this job:

> The performance of the engineer troops during the breaking of the bridges forced recognition upon them. During the work a lot of artillery and rifle fire from the enemy failed to stop them carrying out their task. Despite a total lack of cover, the engineers stood firm and did their work with calm efficiency. The picture of these dark, firm figures remains fixed in my eyes when thinking of them and unqualified pride in them fills my heart.[44]

At 14:03, an unexpected message arrived on the Avnbjerg, "The Bridgehead is ours."[45] The siege of Dybbøl was over. The French military attaché to Berlin, Colonel Count Clermont-Tonnerre, with the army as an observer, remarked to Friedrich-Carl, "We took one Malakoff; you have taken ten!"[46]

During the morning, General Goeben's 26th Brigade in the north had exchanged fire with the Danish batteries in the Kjær Peninsula on Als, and placed some pontoons in the water as if for a crossing. The demonstration proved unnecessary, however, and firing died away around noon.

The entire first line of works had been carried, the second line taken, a counter-attack rolled back, and the whole Danish position occupied in four hours. It was an impressive, if not flawless, feat. Brackenbury et al, writing some 18 months after the event, were highly critical of the lack of naval support for the Danish defence. This criticism still has resonance today. Given the situation ashore at Dybbøl, and the overwhelming naval superiority of the Danish fleet in the Baltic, surely some greater risk could have been taken to support the army at such a time of obvious emergency.

From Berlin, came a telegram from the King. Addressed to Prince Friedrich Carl, it read:

> Next to the Lord of Hosts, I have to thank my splendid army and your leadership for the glorious victory of this day. Express to the troops my highest acknowledgement and my Royal thanks for their performance.
>
> Wilhelm[47]

---

44 Holbøll, p. 257.

45 Waldersee, p. 404.

46 Hellinghaus, O., *Denkwürdigkeiten aus dem deutsch-dänischen Krieg 1864*, p. 180. The 'Malakow', or 'Malakoff' was the major Russian defensive work at Sebastopol during the Crimean War. Its capture by French troops on September 8th 1855 ensured the fall of the city to French and British forces.

47 'Papa' Wrangel immediately pointed to the words, "the Lord of Hosts" on the telegram, and said, "That means me." Stolz, Gerd, *Anekdoten vom Militär*, Husum 1983, p. 30. A different version is given in Rüstow, p. 535.

Captor and captive (Camphausen)

Premier-Lieutenant Stöphasius and men of Storm Column Nr 2, taken after the event
(Voss)

Casualties in the battle were surprisingly light for the Prussians, emphasising their overwhelming artillery superiority, and also the successful gamble in the timing of the assault. The defender's loss was some four times that of the attackers. Casualties were:

Table 37

Prussian Casualties at Dybbol, April 18th 1864

Prussian: 1,201 – 71 officers, and 1,130 men[48]

	Killed		Wounded		Prisoners		Missing	
Unit	Officers	Men	Officers	Men	Officers	Men	Officers	Men
Guard Division	—	—	—	—	—	—	—	—
Staff	—	—	—	—	—	—	—	—
3rd Foot Guards Regiment	—	8	—	18	—		—	—
4th Foot Guards Regiment	—	22	8	76	—	—	—	—
3rd Guard Grenadier Regiment (Elisabeth)	2	6	1	54	—	—	—	—
4th Guard Grenadier Regiment (Augusta)	2	12	2	57	—	—	—	—
Guard 4 Pounder Battery	—	1	—	1	—	—	—	—
I Corps	—	—	—	—	—	—	—	—
6th Infantry Division Staff	—	—	1	—	—	—	—	—
11th Infantry Brigade	—	—	—	—	—	—	—	—
Fusilier Regiment Nr. 35	4	34	8	118	—	—	—	—
IR Nr. 60 (7th Brandenburg	1	17	2	77	—	—	—	7
12th Infantry Brigade	—	—	—	—	—	—	—	—
IR Nr. 24 (4th Brandenburg)	—	8	4	54	—	—	—	—
IR Nr. 64 (8th Brandenburg)	—	15	4	52	—	—	—	3
(Combined) 10th Infantry Brigade	—	—	—	—	—	—	—	—
Staff	1	—	—	—	—	—	—	—
Leib Grenadier Regiment Nr 8 (1st Brandenburg)	2	18	3	85	—	—	—	10
IR Nr. 18, (1st Posener)	2	37	9	83	—	—	—	—
Brandenburg Artillery Brigade Nr. 3	—	1	—	2	—	—	—	—

48 Grosser Generalstab, Volume II, Appendix 61.

Unit	Killed Officers	Killed Men	Wounded Officers	Wounded Men	Prisoners Officers	Prisoners Men	Missing Officers	Missing Men
Brandenburg Pioneer Battalion Nr.3	—	8	1	17	—	—	—	—
13th Infantry Division	—	—	—	—	—	—	—	—
25th Infantry Brigade	—	—	—	—	—	—	—	—
IR Nr. 13 (1st Westphalian)	1	9	—	30	—	—	—	—
IR Nr. 53 (5th Westphalian)	1	27	6	78	—	—	—	2
26th Infantry Brigade	—	—	—	—	—	—	—	—
IR Nr. 55 (6th Westphalian)	—	10	3	32	—	—	—	—
Westphalian Artillery Brigade Nr. 7	—	—	—	1	—	—	—	—
Westphalian Pioneer Battalion Nr. 3	1	12	2	13	—	—	—	—
I Corps Reserve Artillery	—	—	—	—	—	—	—	—
Brandenburg Artillery Brigade Nr. 3	—	—	—	6	—	—	—	—
Fortress Artillery	—	—	—	—	—	—	—	—
Guard Artillery Brigade	—	—	—	1	—	—	—	2
Totals	17	246	54	855	—	—	—	29

Table 38

Danish Casualties at Dybbol, April 18th 1864

Danish: 4,821[49] - 114 officers and 4,707 men

Unit	Killed Officers	Killed Men	Wounded Officers	Wounded Men	Prisoners Officers	Prisoners Men	Missing Officers	Missing Men
Staff	6	—	—	1	1	—	—	—
Life Guard Infantry	—	12	—	15	—	—	—	—
2nd Infantry Regiment	4	56	3	54	11 (2W)	686 (67W)	—	165
3rd Infantry Regiment	1	13	2	36	3	130 (11W)	—	10
5th Infantry Regiment	—	—	—	6	—	—	—	—

49 Generalstaben, Volume II, Appendix 43. Johansen, *Dybbøl 1864*, p. 295, gives a slightly lower total of 4,800, and considers the 'missing' to be primarily Schleswiger deserters.

9th Infantry Regiment	10	65	1	109	6 (3W)	430 (116W)	—	110
11th Infantry Regiment	—	4	—	6	—	—	—	—
16th Infantry Regiment	1	21	—	39	8 (2W)	201 (13W)	—	12
17th Infantry Regiment	2	24	1	32	7 (2W)	372 (47W)	—	45
18th Infantry Regiment	—	9	—	14	—	—	—	7
20th Infantry Regiment	7	74	7	99	1	344 (91W)	—	136
22nd Infantry Regiment	7	45	5	20	11 (1W)	735 (61W)	—	131
Artillery	—	17	1	26	7 (1W)	343 (12W)	—	24
Engineers	—	—	—	4	—	7	—	6
2nd Div. Ambulance	—	—	—	—	—	2	—	—
Rolf Krake	1	—	—	10	—	—	—	—
Totals	39	340	20	471	55 (11W)	3,250 (418W)	—	646

W = Wounded

Dybbøl had been taken, and Bismarck's political imperative satisfied. There was now no Danish presence on the mainland of Schleswig to be used as a pawn in the upcoming international conference. However, as General Moltke had foreseen, the Danish Army had not been destroyed, and only this would have brought about total victory.

11

Naval Operations
February-May

Baltic

The Prussian fleet began preparations for war in late 1863. One of the first moves, before the winter ice set in, was the transfer of the two screw corvettes at Danzig, *Arcona* and *Nymphe*, to Swinemünde, between Stralsund and Stettin.[1] This move would allow, when the time came, cooperation with the gunboat divisions at Stralsund, which themselves could move along lagoons and inshore waterways between the two ports, something which the Danes could do nothing about. When hostilities commenced, Prussian harbours were still iced-in, the thaw not starting until the middle of the month.[2] Even then, preparations were far from complete in regard to both personnel and machinery, and it was not until mid-March that Admiral Prince Adalbert's navy was ready for operations.

Blockade

In Copenhagen, Council-President Monrad sent the Navy Minister a telegram on February 1st, informing him of the outbreak of hostilities, and authorising him to take commercial vessels of any member of the German Federation, as prizes. All such vessels already in Danish ports were also impounded. He further authorised him to plan and impose blockades. International law on the subject of blockades, in 1864, was far from clear cut. The first major attempt to clarify matters was the Declaration of Paris, in 1856. This agreement outlawed privateering and provided for neutral shipping to be exempt from seizure unless carrying contraband. It also provided protection for neutral goods aboard belligerent vessels. Critically, it decided that for a blockade to be binding, it must be effective, and in practice this meant that a port declared under blockade had to have some physical presence offshore, to stop and examine shipping to and from it. Should it be reported that there was no such presence, then the port was not considered to be under blockade, and a fresh notification would be required for its reimposition, together with a period during which shipping could only be warned. The subject caused endless legal wrangling.

The enforcement of the Danish blockade itself presented a fairly elementary problem insofar as Prussia was considered. Her navy was of little importance and posed no threat to the Danish fleet in the Baltic. In the confined space of that sea, and with Prussia's coastline there boasting only the ports of Stralsund, Swinemünde, Stettin, and Danzig of any consequence, comparatively little difficulty in imposing it

---

1 By order of 23rd October, 1863 – Grosser Generalstab, Volume I, p. 98.
2 Anon, "Die preußische Marine im deutsch-dänische Kriege von 1864", *Unsere Zeit*, 1865, p. 82.

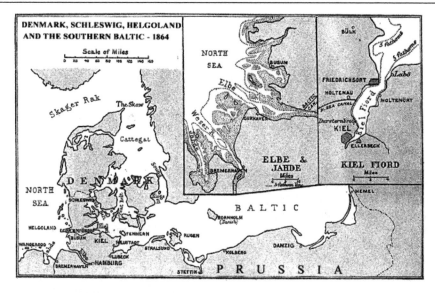

Map 29: The eastern North Sea, and southern Baltic, 1864

was likely.[3] In addition, in the event of a prolonged conflict, it would merely require to be seasonal, since these ports were iced in winter. The blockade itself was to be under the control of Rear-Admiral van Dockum, who had some differences with the government as to the mechanics of its operation. Government policy was to blockade specific ports, whereas the admiral preferred to keep his ships together, in case of Prussian naval incursions.[4] The main incidents of the blockade in the Baltic, other than between naval vessels, were as follows:[5]

The brig *Sara*, coming from Emden, was taken by the watch ship in the Øresund, February 1st, the first prize of war. Next, the Danzig bark *Francisca*, bound for West Hartlepool with a cargo of grain, was taken by the corvette *Heimdal*, in the Roads at Falsterbro (declared a prize). The ship *Alexander*, en route from Colberg to Genoa, with a cargo of spirits, found herself boarded in Copenhagen Roads, February 9th (declared a prize).

One ingenious ruse by the Prussians, on March 23rd, probably had little effect, but has its amusing side. After observations from the light houses at Cape Arkona and Hela (Danzig) confirmed that no Danish warships were visible, three gunboats were ordered to inform neutral shipping that the blockades of the ports of Cammin, Swinemünde, Wolgast, and Greifswald, were no longer in force.

At the beginning of April, the former British frigate *Amphion* was stopped in the Øresund, by corvette *Heimdal* (released). The Dutch Steamer *Rembrandt*, was

---

3 Compare this with more than 3,000 miles of Confederate coastline placed under blockade by the United States at this time.

4 Liljefalk & Lütken, pp. 267-268.

5 Extracted from Larsen, Kay, "Vore Priseskibe 1864", *Tidsskrift for Søvæsen*, Nr. 107, Copenhagen 1936, pp. 174-182, and contemporary newspapers and periodicals.

stopped off Danzig, by armoured schooner *Absalon* as a suspected blockade runner, April 4th (declared a prize).). The ship *Alma*, taken off Jasmund, by the corvette *Thor*, April 14th, was sent to Copenhagen (released). The schooner *Estelle*, of Goole, sailing from Liverpool to Stettin, was taken by the schooner *Fylla*, off Swinemünde, as a blockade-runner, and brought into Copenhagen, May 8th (declared a prize). *Fylla* also took the Dutch schooner *Hermania* off the Oder Banks, on May 1st, for attempting to run the blockade. She was eventually released, and allowed to proceed to Coblenz.

The Action off Jasmund

With military doubts about his fleet's ability to assist in operations, and its apparent impotence against the blockade, it was time for Prince Adalbert to make some show of action. He ordered Captain Jachmann, at Swinemünde, that an attempt to break the blockade must me tried. Jachmann, on the 16th, made a reconnaissance from Swinemünde, with the screw corvettes *Arcona*, Captain Jachmann, and *Nymphe*, Lieutenant-Commander Werner, to establish whether there was only a 'paper-blockade'. Day broke with very poor weather, snow showers and hail, which did not clear until the afternoon. Then, while Captain Kuhn cruised off Greifswalder Bodden (lagoon) with *Loreley*, Lieutenant-Commander Count Monts, 1st Gunboat Division, Lieutenant-Commander Kinderling, and 3rd Gunboat Division, Lieutenant-Commander Arendt, steamed off Swinemünde, Jachmann moved north. Finally, at 15:30, three vessels were seen off Cape Arkona, about 14 miles away. Although Jachmann would have liked to attack them, with at least an hour and a half to steam, by which time darkness would start to fall, it was not practicable. He turned away, and returned to Swinemünde. A blockade was indeed in place, and Jachmann determined to attack the next day.[6]

What Captain Jachmann had seen was Rear-Admiral van Dockum's blockade squadron, which had taken station on the 14th. After Jachmann saw the force, it was joined by a further vessel. The opposing forces on March 17th comprised:

Table 39

Danish naval forces at the action off Jasmund, March 17th 1864

Danish	*Crew*	*Tonnage*	*Speed*
Screw Frigate *Sjælland* (Flag), Captain Grove 30 smoothbore 30 pounders, 8 rifled 18 pounders, 4 smoothbore 12 pounders	423	1,934	10 Knots
Screw Ship of the Line *Skjold*, Captain Wulff 50 smoothbore 30 pounders, 6 smoothbore 18 pounders, 8 rifled 18 pounders	Not known	2,065	8 Knots

6   Anon, "Die Preußische Marine im deutsch-dänischen Kriege von 1864", *Unsere Zeit* 1865, pp. 84-85.

	Crew	Tonnage	Speed
Screw Corvette *Heimdal*, Commander Lund 14 smoothbore 30 pounders, 2 rifled 18 pounders	164	892	9½ Knots
Screw Corvette *Thor*, Commander Hedemann, 10 smoothbore 30 pounders 2 rifled 18 pounders	139	803	9 Knots

Table 40

Prussian naval forces at the action off Jasmund, March 17th 1864

Prussian	Crew	Tonnage	Speed
Screw Corvette *Arcona* (Flag), Captain Jachmann, 6 smoothbore 68 pounders 20 smoothbore 36 pounders	380	2,391	12.4 Knots
Screw Corvette *Nymphe*, Lieutenant-Commander Werner, 10 smoothbore 36 pounders, 6 smoothbore 12 pounders	190	1,202	12 Knots
Paddle Steamer *Loreley*, Lieutenant-Commander Count Monts, 2 smoothbore 12 pounders	65	430	10.5 Knots
'First Class' Gunboat *Comet*, Lieutenant-Commander Kinderling, (I Gunboat Division), 1 rifled 24 pounders, 2 rifled 12 pounders	71	415	9 Knots
'2nd Class' Gunboat *Hay*, Lieutenant Butterlin, 2 rifled 12 pounders	40	279	9 Knots
'2nd Class' Gunboat *Hyäne*, Lieutenant Donner, 2 rifled 12 pounders	40	279	9 Knots
'2nd Class' Gunboat *Pfeil*, Junior Lieutenant Zembsch, 2 rifled 12 pounders	40	279	9 Knots
'2nd Class' Gunboat *Skorpion*, Junior Lieutenant von Rabenau, 2 rifled 12 pounders	40	279	9 Knots
'2nd Class' Gunboat *Wespe*, Junior Lieutenant Heuzner, 2 rifled 12 pounders	40	279	9 Knots

Arcona, followed by *Nymphe*, slipped out of Swinemünde at 07:30 on the 17th, and steamed east. Finding nothing, the ships reversed course, heading towards Rügen. As they approached the island of Greifswalder Oie, at about noon, smoke could be seen to the north. At 13:15 (see map), the corvettes linked up with *Loreley*, and the I Gunboat Division, off Thiessow on the east coast of Rügen. By now, the Danish squadron was visible, and larger than the previous day. *Loreley*

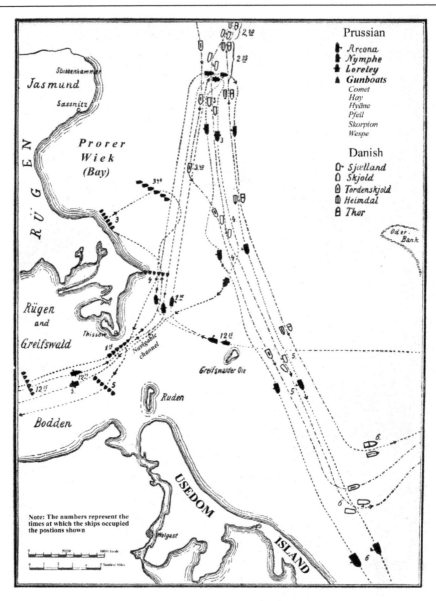

Map 30: Action off Jasmund - 17th March

joined the two corvettes, and moved towards the enemy ships, while the Prussian gunboats turned away, under orders to move inshore north of Thiessow, to cover a withdrawal[7]. The blockading squadron itself, also had eyes to the north, where smoke indicated the expected arrival of another frigate, *Jylland*. As the action be-

7   Ibid, p. 87.

The Action off Jasmünd 17th March (Schiøtt)

gan, the newcomer was identified; not as *Jylland*, but the older screw frigate *Tordenskjold* (38), Captain Meinertz.[8]

Arcona fired the first rounds at *Sjælland* at 14:30, and was answered a few minutes later, at a range of about 1,600 yards, as *Sjælland* turned to starboard and fired a broadside. Jachmann now himself executed a turn to starboard, bringing his port battery into action. He very quickly realised the danger of his situation, and continued his turn until he was heading south. He did not, however, communicate his intent to *Nymphe* and *Loreley*, which for a few minutes steamed east, before they, too, turned south. *Sjælland* switched her fire to *Nymphe* scoring five hits with her first broadside. Her main steam-pipe was hit, the funnel holed, and five men wounded.[9] The ship's speed fell away, but furious work managed to repair the damage.

By 15:00, a full scale chase was underway (see map). Van Dockum made an attempt to exploit a gap between *Arcona* and her consorts, but did not have the speed to do so. The Prussian vessels now pushed their machinery as far as possible, in order to escape the Danish pursuit. *Nymphe* took further hits. As her speed increased, the attempt to cut *Arcona* off failed, and Admiral van Dockum decided to use the frigate's full broadside while she was still within reach.[10] This was unsuccessful in stopping her.

Slightly to the west, *Tordenskjold* made her stately way down the coast of Rügen, coming under fire from the Prussian gunboat division at around 15:40.[11] She was, though, uninterested in them and steamed south firing in passing. The gunboats had their own difficulties. A mechanical breakdown aboard *Hay* meant

8   Dockum, C. van, *Østersøes-Eskadren I 1864*, Copenhagen 1864, p.15. *Tordenskjold* was, at this time, only capable of making 6 knots, and that with difficulty. The 1496 ton vessel's armament comprised 2 smoothbore 60 pounders, 28 smoothbore 30 pounders, 4 rifled 18 pounders, and 4 rifled 12 pounders, and a crew of 400.
9   Anon, "Die preußische Marine im deutsch-dänischen Kriege von 1864", p. 90
10 Lütken, *Søkrigsbegivenhederne i 1864*, p. 124.
11 Anon, "Die preußische Marine im deutsch-dänischen Kriege von 1864", p. 91.

that she had to be taken in tow. The gunboats, unmolested, withdrew towards Stralsund, entering the Greifswalder Bodden at about 17:00.

The main chase went on, both *Nymphe* and *Loreley* suffering under the Danish fire, and *Sjælland* hit several times by the Prussian rifled guns. At 16:00, *Loreley* turned away, towards Stralsund, van Dockum's ships following the corvettes. The last shots were fired at 16:45. The Danish squadron pulled away to the east at about 18:00, a relieved Jachmann steaming on to Swinemünde. That night, *Jylland* (44), Captain Holm, a fast ship, also joined van Dockum's squadron. Jachmann had been very lucky.

Danish casualties amounted to six dead and 16 wounded, all aboard *Sjælland*. Prussian losses were lighter; *Arcona*, three men killed, one officer and two men wounded, *Nymphe*, two men killed, and four wounded, *Loreley*, one man wounded – a total of five men killed, and one officer and seven men wounded. *Nymphe* was the most damaged vessel, taking 19 hull hits, 4 to the superstructure, and 50 to the masts and rigging, with damage to her engineering plant.[12]

The attempt to break the blockade failed as soon as it started. Captain Jachmann immediately saw that he stood no chance in a general engagement, and withdrew. The impossibility of lifting the blockade in the Baltic with the existing Prussian fleet there, had been graphically demonstrated. There had been no battle – only a chase. Equally, any possible support of the army would have to be achieved by evading the Danish fleet, not fighting it. This was emphasised on March 30th, with the assignment to van Dockum, of the newly commissioned broadside ironclad, *Dannebrog*, Captain Paludan. At 2323 tons, armed with 14 smoothbore 60 pounders, and 6 rifled 18 pounders, she had 4½ inches of armour. Though her speed was only 8¾ knots, Prussia had, as yet, nothing with which to touch her.

From Jasmund to the Armistice

After Jasmund, Captain Jachmann was promoted to Rear-Admiral,[13] but both he and Prince Adalbert realised that more was needed than senior officers. On March 19th, *Arcona*, commanded by Commander Hassenstein, and three gunboats undertook a reconnaissance north of Swinemünde, without result. On the 29th, Prince Adalbert had ready a force of 28 ships assembled to support the army in a proposed invasion of the island of Als. Poor weather prevented any such attempt.[14]

Exercises were held on April 6th, in the Greifswald Bodden, with the '1st Class' gunboats manoeuvreing against the '2nd class'. Prinz Adalbert studied the proceedings from the Royal Yacht, *Grille*. They were not a great success, making clear the insufficient training of the crews and problems with machinery.

On April 14th, Prince Adalbert himself undertook a reconnaissance of the blockading vessels off Rügen on board *Grille*. Encountering *Skjold* and *Sjælland* west of Hiddensee, she opened fire on them with her two rifled 12 pounders, whereupon they gave chase. *Grille*, however, the fastest ship in the Prussian fleet at 13 knots, easily outpaced them, and steamed back to Swinemünde, where

12 Grosser Generalstab, Volume II, p. 463.
13 By Royal Cabinet Order of the 18th March 1864.
14 See Chapter 9.

Jachmann's squadron and the 1st Gunboat Division waited to bring her in. Admiral van Dockum's report describes this insignificant affair:

> At 4 o'clock in the afternoon, while *Sjælland* and *Skjold* were busy retrieving the lost anchor, the Prussian gunboat *Grille* arrived from the south, and fired a single shot towards us. *Sjælland* and *Skjold* took up the chase. It turned out to be much faster than we were. We chased it to Swinemünde, from where *Arcona*, *Nymphe*, and a number of gunboats came out. It became dark, however, as we arrived, and they returned to the harbour in Swinemünde.[15]

The same day, Lieutenant-Commander Arendt took his 3rd Gunboat Division east of Rügen, and had a brief skirmish with *Tordenskjold*, and the steamer *Geyser*, Commander Jacobsen (567 tons, two smoothbore 60 pounders, two smoothbore 18 pounders, two rifled 18 pounders, 9 knots). The gunboats fired some 20 rounds without effect, and, as *Geyser* closed the range, they withdrew. The Danish ships did not open fire.[16]

Ten days after this incident, *Grille*, with Prince Adalbert aboard, once more put out of Stralsund, escorted by 2nd Gunboat Division, and engaged *Tordenskjold*. *Grille* kept at a distance whereby the frigate's guns could not reach her. After hits to her rigging, however, *Tordenskjold* bore down on *Grille*, which, with the gunboats, immediately withdrew.

In Danzig, the new Prussian corvette *Vineta*, Commander Köhler, had been bottled up since her commissioning in early March.[17] For some weeks, she had been unable to leave harbour due to low water. On April 30th, however, she was, with considerable effort, gotten over the bar, and confronted the ship of the line *Skjold*, which had recently taken over the blockade duty there, releasing the frigate *Jylland* for duty with a new squadron in the North Sea. Köhler did his best to tempt Captain Wulff in towards the shore batteries, but the latter handled *Skjold* so skilfully that the rifled 24 pounders, even at maximum elevation, could not reach her. Finally, a violent southerly wind caused *Vineta* to break off and return to harbour, as such an occurrence at Danzig heralded a severe drop in water levels.[18]

Admiral Jachmann again left harbour on May 6th, with *Arcona*, *Nymphe*, *Grille*, and the 1st Gunboat Division, when the blockade squadron, now including the ironclad *Dannebrog*, was sighted about nine miles off Swinemünde. Admiral van Dockum maintained his distance, and the Prussian squadron chose not to close it. Six days later, an armistice came into force. During the armistice, Admiral van Dockum was delighted to read, in the Prussian newspapers, that his blockade was considered to have 'hermetically sealed' Prussian ports in the Baltic.[19]

15 Lütken, *Søkrigsbegivenhederne i 1864*, p. 187.
16 These were '1st Class' gunboats *Cyclop*, Junior-Lieutenant Count Pfeil, *Habsicht*, Junior-Lieutenant Baron von Reibnitz, and '2nd Class' vessels *Jäger*, Junior-Lieutenant Pirner, *Salamander*, Junior Lieutenant Baron von Hallerstein, *Sperber*, junior Lieutenant Goeker, and *Wolf*, Junior Lieutenant von Fischer-Treuenfeld. Details for these ships are as for those given for the action of Jasmund.
17 2504 tons, 28 smoothbore 68 pounders, 11.7 knots, 380 crew.
18 "Die preußische Marine im deutsch-dänischen Kriege von 1864", pp. 98-99.
19 Dechange, Marcus, "Die dänische Marine und ihre Operationen im Deutsch-Dänische Krieg, 1864", dissertation, Hamburg 1998.

North Sea Blockade

The blockade of German ports in the North Sea, with a benevolent Royal Navy, was, if anything, a considerably less difficult operation than in the Baltic, barring the intervention of the Austrian fleet. Given that this was based at Pola, in the Adriatic, it was initially considered irrelevant. The frigate *Niels Juel* (42), Captain Gottlieb, had been stationed north of the Kattegat since January, and with the onset of war, extended her activities to The North Sea, Channel, and Western Approaches.

The first merchant ship captured was the Prussian bark *Treue* taken off Lowestoft, with a cargo of oak, by the frigate *Niels Juel* on February 1st(declared a prize). Three days later, the brig *Marie*, with a load of coal, was hauled to, also by *Niels Juel* (declared a prize). On February 6th, the Lübeck brig *Mathilde*, en route home, from Scotland with 180 tons of coal, was boarded in Helsingør Roads by a boat from the frigate *Jylland*. Her crew were imprisoned on prison ships (declared a prize). Next day, the schooner *Friederich Overbech*, Dundee to Germany, with 200 tons of coal, was stopped by the frigate *Jylland* (declared a prize).

In March, the first capture was the Rostock brig *Neptunus*, from Burntisland, bound for Copenhagen with a cargo of coal, boarded by *Jylland* in the Kattegat on the 8th (declared a prize). The Hamburg schooner-brig *Thekla Schmidt*, from Cuxhaven to Cardiff in ballast, was taken by the corvette *Dagmar* shortly after sailing, March 17th (declared a prize).

April began with the Hamburg bark *Eudora*, bound home from Mexico being stopped by the corvette *Dagmar*, off Helgoland, on the 2nd (declared a prize). The Hamburg bark *Betty Louise*, en route from Sunderland to Hamburg, with a cargo of coal, after being stopped by the corvette *Dagmar* was brought into Copenhagen, April 27th (declared a prize). April 13th, the brig *Hertzog von Cambridge* was taken, off Helgoland, also by *Dagmar*, with 327 tons of coal and pottery (declared a prize). The Hamburg schooner-galiot *Victoria*, was taken the same day, by *Heimdal*, off the mouth of the Elbe. Some British faience was released from the cargo (declared a prize). Hamburg Frigate *Albertina*, inbound from South America, with 600 tons of guano, tobacco, and general cargo, was captured by corvette *Heimdal*, April 19th (declared a prize). The *Sophia*, en route from Bremen to Matamoros, was taken, and brought in to Copenhagen on the 23rd (declared a prize).

Austrian Squadron Formed

As early as February 20th, commercial interests had caused the Austrian government to activate naval units for the protection of maritime trade. Initially, these were patrols in the Adriatic and Mediterranean seas, and two vessels (a ship of the line and a corvette) specifically assigned for the Straights of Gibraltar. Subsequently, it was decided to form a powerful squadron specifically for use in the North Sea, comprising the following vessels:

Screw Ship-of-the-Line *Kaiser*

Ironclad frigates *Don Juan* and *Kaiser Max*

Screw frigates *Schwarzenberg* and *Radetzky*

Screw corvette *Erzherzog Friedrich*

Side-wheelers *Elisabeth* and *Lucia*

Gunboats *Seehund* and *Wall*

Command of this force was given to Rear Admiral Bernhard Freiherr von Wüllerstorff-Urbair. It would, however, take time to assemble and ready for sea.

Captain Wilhelm Tegetthoff, in the Levant with the screw frigate *Schwarzenberg* and gunboat *Seehund*, received orders to sail for Lisbon as soon as possible. He left Corfu on March 4th, reaching Lisbon on the 17th, where he found instructions to wait there for other vessels to join him.[20] On the 4th of April, *Radetzky* appeared, and the squadron immediately got under way for Brest. Upon arrival there, Tegetthoff was informed that he was to sail immediately for the North Sea, and not now wait for Wüllerstorff. He was about to enter waters that would prove testing, not least to his diplomatic skills.

Whilst the Austrian fleet was so engaged, three Prussian ships, which had been in the Mediterranean, were ordered to The Texel, in the Netherlands, there to await the arrival of Tegetthoff, and come under his orders. Accordingly, the paddle steamer, *Preussischer Adler*, and '1st Class' gunboats *Basilisk* and *Blitz*, made their way there, arriving on April 15th. While they were there, Commodore Suenson's squadron also paid a visit, but no hostile action was undertaken.

The Austrian squadron proceeded to The Downs, off the south coast of England, to coal, and here discovered the true extent of British hostility. The British public neither wished to see Denmark defeated, nor was pleased to see a new naval force in home waters. Irrespective of the fact that this presence was no threat to Great Britain, it was in many circles perceived as a gross intrusion, and in some, as insolence. On April 27th, *Seehund* appeared in Ramsgate harbour, having been damaged in a storm. With a local pilot on board, she collided with a pier, causing further damage, and a major diplomatic row.[21] Leaving *Seehund* for repairs, Tegetthoff sailed for the Texel, to link up with the three Prussian vessels. The combined squadron then moved on to Cuxhaven, at the mouth of the river Elbe.

The Battle of Helgoland

Officially formed in Copenhagen on March 30th, the North Sea Squadron consisted of the steam frigate *Niels Juel*, and the steam corvettes *Heimdal* and *Dagmar*, the latter already on station. Commanding was 59 year old Commodore Edouard Suenson, his Flag in *Niels Juel*.

On May 6th, the frigate *Jylland* joined Suenson off Christiansand, replacing *Dagmar*, which returned to the Baltic. The squadron then steamed south, towards the island of Helgoland. Tegetthoff left Cuxhaven to look for the enemy on the same day. Both squadrons would, instead, encounter the same British warship. HMS *Aurora*, Captain Sir Leopold McClintock, had been dispatched to Helgoland, by the

---

20 On the way, they took the Danish mercantile brig *Prethe*, and sent her, with a prize crew, to Trieste.

21 Harvie, Ian "HMS Aurora and the Battle of Heligoland (1864)", *Marinehistorisk Tidsskrift*, Copenhagen, Nr. 3 August 2001. This excellent article has a very good account of the incident.

commander of the Channel Squadron, Rear Admiral Dacres, to keep an eye on the belligerent naval forces, and show the flag around Helgoland, a British possession. On the morning of the 7th, Tegetthoff and McClintock sighted one another, both heading north, McClintock to the fore. *Schwarzenberg* closed, and some three hours later overhauled *Aurora*, who then displayed her colours. Noting her as a British warship, Tegetthoff pulled away, his squadron anchoring off the North Frisian island of Sylt.

The following morning, Suenson's squadron appeared from the north-west. McClintock sent an officer to confer with Commodore Suenson, who informed Suenson of the Austrians' last known position. After Suenson had departed, McClintock received further information that Tegetthoff had, in fact, returned to Cuxhaven. He, likewise, returned to Helgoland.[22]

The news that the enemy had been discovered soon spread through the Danish squadron. Lars Andersen, serving in the *Heimdal*, wrote later:

> ...you can believe that there was joy amongst the crew when we saw the frigate Jylland arrive, for then we knew that mail was brought to us. They also brought news; that there were some Austrians at Helgoland whom we were to 'greet', and our answer was: 'Let's go get them.'[23]

Monday, May 9th broke a beautiful, clear day, with a brisk south-easterly wind. Tegetthoff had returned to Cuxhaven to coal the two Prussian gunboats, and was informed by the Austrian Consul, that Danish warships were off Helgoland. He immediately raised steam, and stood out to the north. A little after 10:00, a lookout aboard *Niels Juel* spotted smoke to the south-east. By 13:00, the squadrons had one another in sight, east of Helgoland. At this time, too, Captain McClintock took HMS *Aurora* to a point three miles south of Helgoland's southern tip, in full view of both sides, making clear the international position of the island.

The two squadrons about to face one another comprised:

Table 41

Allied naval forces at the Battle of Helgoland, May 9th 1864

Allied: Captain Wilhelm Tegetthoff	*Crew*	*Tonnage*	*Speed*
Screw Frigate *Schwarzenberg* (Flag), Captain Tegetthoff, 6 smoothbore 60 pounders 28 smoothbore 30 pounders 4 rifled 24 pounders	498	2,614	11 Knots

22 Ibid. McClintock appears to have considered that Tegetthoff had intended to try to enter the Baltic, unseen. Whilst it is quite possible that the Prussian vessels may have wished to attempt this, Tegetthoff was only too aware of the possible political consequences such a step might have, to have made such a move with his own ships. The reason for the move was a reconnaissance of the North Frisian islands for future operations.

23 Christensen, J. Kaare, "Helgoland i Maj 1864", *Krigshistorisk Tidsskrift*, Nr. 3, 1988.

Screw Frigate *Radetzky*, Captain Jeremiasch 4 smoothbore 60 pounders 24 smoothbore 30 pounders 3 rifled 24 pounders	372	2,334	9 Knots
Paddle-Wheeler *Preussischer Adler*, Lieutenant-Commander Klatt 2 smoothbore 68 pounders	110	1,171	10 Knots
'1st Class' Screw Gunboat *Basilisk*, Lieutenant Schau, 1 smoothbore 68 pounders 1 rifled 24 pounders	66	415	9 Knots
'1st Class' Screw Gunboat *Blitz*, Lieutenant MacLean, 1 smoothbore 68 pounders 1 rifled 24 pounders	66	415	9 Knots

Table 42

Danish naval forces at the Battle of Helgoland, May 9th 1864

Danish: Commodore Eduard Suenson	Crew	Tonnage	Speed
Screw Frigate *Niels Juel* (Flag), Captain Gottlieb 30 smoothbore 30 pounders 12 rifled 18 pounders	422	1,934	9.3 Knots
Screw Frigate *Jylland*, Captain Holm 32 smoothbore 30 pounders 8 rifled 18 pounders 8 rifled 12 pounders	437	1,988	12 Knots
Screw Corvette *Heimdal*, Commander Lund 14 smoothbore 30 pounders 2 rifled 18 pounders	164	892	9½ Knots

At 13:30, Tegetthoff signaled to the other vessels, "Our armies have been victorious; we will do the same." Aboard *Niels Juel*, Suenson's message to the crew was equally concise, "Men, there are the Austrians! Now, we will meet them; I trust that you will fight as did our brave comrades at Dybbøl!" Within a few minutes, aboard eight ships, the same order was barked out: "Clear for action!"

At 13:57, *Schwarzenberg* opened fire with her bow pivot-guns on *Niels Juel*, at a distance of 18½ cables (3,750 yards – Map, position 2), and shortly after, her starboard battery. Both sides rapidly closed the range. The two Austrian frigates and the Danish line passed in opposite directions, exchanging fire at about 2,000 yards. One of the first Danish shells exploded on *Schwarzenbergs*' gun-deck, killing or wounding an entire gun crew of the starboard battery.

Tegetthoff now came to starboard, to run south, parallel with Suenson, who was endeavouring to cut off the Prussian gunboats, which had remained west of the Austrian frigates. As *Schwarzenberg* turned, she was fired upon by all three Danish ships, as both frigates initially moved straight towards the Danish line. As they came parallel, however, closing the range to two cables (just over 400 yards), *Niels Juel* fired upon *Schwarzenberg*, and *Jylland* and *Heimdal*, behind her, engaged *Radetzky*. The Prussian vessels remained

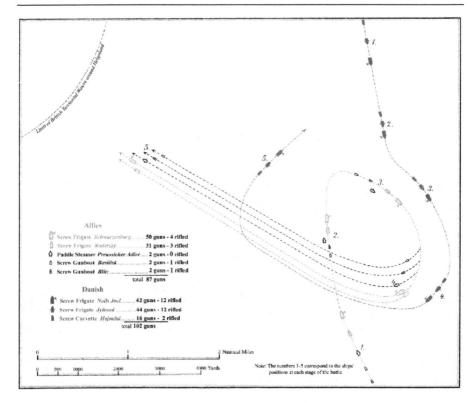

The following is the legend within the map:

Allies

Screw Frigate *Schwarzenburg*	50 guns - 4 rifled
Screw Frigate *Radetzky*	31 guns - 3 rifled
Paddle Steamer *Preussicher Adler*	2 guns - 0 rifled
Screw Gunboat *Basilisk*	2 guns - 1 rifled
Screw Gunboat *Blitz*	2 guns - 1 rifled
	total **87 guns**

Danish

Screw Frigate *Neils Jnel*	42 guns - 12 rifled
Screw Frigate *Jylland*	44 guns - 12 rifled
Screw Corvette *Hejmdal*	16 guns - 2 rifled
	total **102 guns**

Note: The numbers 1-5 correspond to the ships' positions at each stage of the battle

Map 31: Battle of Helgoland - 9th May

in the lee of the two frigates, firing when possible, but with little effect.[24] In this action, an Austrian shell struck *Jylland*, exploding at gun number 9, killing or wounding its whole crew. The crews of the two guns either side recoiled in horror at this, and huddled in a group, staring at their mangled comrades. The battery commander was able to get the men back to their guns, after a sailor named Ludvigsen, from Copenhagen, shouted, 'Here we go again!', and ran back to his gun.[25]

About 15:30, an exploding shell set fire to *Schwarzenberg's* furled foretopsail. She had twice before caught fire during the action, the first from a hull hit, and the second, caused by one which set the sail store ablaze. Casualties had been heavy, but with courage and discipline, both had been extinguished.[26] This one however, was in a very difficult position to fight, especially while the battle raged. Some equipment

24 Lütken, *Nordsø-Eskadren og Kampen ved Helgoland d. 9 Mai 1864*, quoting Commodore Suenson's report, p. 129. A similar, though less bloody, incident involving one gun-crew, took place aboard *Niels Juel* – Anon., "Smaatræk fra Kampen ved Helgoland den 9de Mai 1864", *Danebrog*, Volume II, p. 112.

25 Ibid, p. 103

26 Adami, Rear Admiral Geza Dell, "Die k. u. k. kriegsmarine im Jahre 1864", *Unter Gablenz und Tegetthoff, Vor Vierzig Jahren*, pp. 10-11. Upon the first fire being reported to him, Tegetthoff said, "Well, one will extinguish it."

The battle of Helgoland, 9th May, *Schwarzenberg* turns away, her foretop fire spreading
(Schiøtt)

was manhandled into the main top, and some water pumped, but to no avail. By
16:00, *Schwarzenberg's* entire foretop was ablaze. With her head to the wind, the fire
was spreading rapidly. To carry the flames away from the ship, Tegetthoff was forced
to fall away from the wind, and steam to the north-west, towards Helgoland.
Radetzky was ordered to come to a parallel course, so that both ships could continue
to use their stern pivot guns. In spite of this, Captain Jeremiasch remained on course,
to cover the withdrawal of his consort. A second signal was required before *Radetzky*
obeyed Tegetthoff's order to disengage.[27] (Map 31, position 4).

At this point, Commodore Suenson signaled his ships to turn eight points to
starboard, to pursue, but just as the order was being executed, *Jylland's* tiller rope
and relieving tackle were cut to pieces by a shell, which blew up in the captain's
cabin, to starboard. As the ship would no longer answer the helm, *Jylland*, by far
the fastest of Suenson's ships, was forced to make repairs. It was the effective end of
the action. Unable to follow up without violating British territorial waters,
Suenson, at 16:30, ordered his ships to cease-fire, and pulled away north-east of the
island to await events (Map 31, position 5).

Once in Helgoland's waters, Tegetthoff anchored *Schwarzenberg,* and ordered all
firefighting equipment and crews from the other vessels of his squadron on board her.
Assistance offered by Captain McClintock was, of course, politely refused. The
foremast was finally cut away around 22:00, and after *Schwarzenberg* was made as
ready as possible for sea, the squadron made a run for Cuxhaven, anchoring there at
04:30, on the 10th. The casualties in the ships were landed, and repairs to the ships begun.

Suenson had sailed to the North Frisian island of Föhr, to make arrangements
for his casualties. Here, Lieutenant-Commander Hammer, commander of the

27 Both Tegetthoff and Suenson paid compliment to Jeremiasch, Suenson saying that,
    "*Radetzky* covered the withdrawal honourably, and then followed." – Suenson's
    report, quoted in Lütken, *Nordsø-Eskadren og Kampen ved Helgoland D. 9 Mai,
    1864*, Copenhagen 1884, p. 129. Jeremiasch was himself wounded.

miniscule Danish forces in the North Frisian Islands, handed him a telegram from the Navy Ministry. It contained explicit orders to sail immediately for Christiansand (Norway), and that a cease-fire was to begin soon. Suenson weighed anchor the following morning, and arrived in Christiansand on the 11th, where the wounded were hospitalised, and on the 13th, the dead buried. The squadron returned to a hero's welcome in Copenhagen, on May 15th, when the King himself came aboard *Niels Juel*, and decorated Suenson.

Losses in the battle were:

Austrian

Schwarzenberg – One officer and 31 men killed, four officers and 65 men wounded

Radetzky – One officer and four men killed, one officer and 23 men wounded

Totals – Two officers and 35 men killed, five officers and 88 men wounded

Prussian

None

Danish

Niels Juel – Three men killed, one officer and 21 men wounded

Jylland – 14 men killed and 28 men wounded

Heimdal – Two men wounded

Totals – 17 men killed, one officer and 49 men wounded.

With both commanders honoured by their respective sovereigns, the battle had been conducted with skill and courage on both sides. Suenson made full use of his advantage of 26 rifled guns to 9, and was able to push Tegetthoff into neutral waters after the lucky hit on *Schwarzenberg*. He has often been criticised for not continuing his attack after this, but the presence of a powerful British frigate clearly and rightly urged caution upon him. The strategic situation, however, had changed. With or without an Armistice, additional Austrian naval units were to be in the operational area very soon, and the existence of the North Sea blockade was over. German opinion on the battle was mixed, as Admiral Adami much later wrote:

> Public opinion was in the dark for a long time about the meaning of the Battle of Helgoland. Some considered the outcome as a defeat of the Allied fleet, which was due to the superiority of the enemy. Others were of the opinion that the result was a draw and strongly praised the crews. Only in northern Germany did public opinion, after a few days, conclude that the battle should be considered a glorious success over the enemy navy because the purpose had been served to lift the Danish blockade of the German North Sea ports.[28]

For now, however, the guns were silent. The London Conference had achieved an armistice, which itself had not been easy. Could it now achieve a lasting peace?

28 Adami, p. 11.

12

After Dybbøl: the London Conference and First Armistice

The conclusion of the siege sent waves of interest throughout Europe. In particular, the use of rifled artillery was hailed. The *Journal de L'Armée Belge* published an article, which contained some interesting observations by a Russian artillery officer:

>...one can only conclude that, given the small number of artillery pieces employed, the effect of the Prussian artillery was quite formidable. All the foreign officers present at the siege remarked on this. I believe that it is not without interest to hear the opinion of a Russian officer of artillery, who distinguished himself at the siege of Sebastopol. This officer, having viewed the effects of the Prussian artillery against the redoubts of Dybbøl, had the following to say:
>
>'When one considers the positions of Dybbøl, one sees state-of-the-art defence works constructed by the Danes to produce one of the strongest fortresses of modern times. The Danish officers had the skill to reinforce their positions by the most up to date use of the art of military engineering that we have seen up to now.
>
>One can completely attest to the fact that these defences were infinitely stronger and more difficult to overcome than all the earthworks and defences created around Sebastopol, which halted an Anglo-French army for nearly a year at a cost of 80,000 lives. I am completely convinced that the Prussian Army devoted itself completely to the task of reducing the Dybbøl works with the knowledge that without their diligence in placing the batteries, it could cost the lives of ten times the men it did.
>
>The Danes learned without doubt that the admirable practical instruction by the officers and gunners helped them to serve their weapons as well as any rifleman with his rifle. For them, it was impossible to construct works that could resist for any length of time, projectiles that hit their walls with a precision that matched a revolver on its target. Indeed, these massive redoubts were, for a few weeks, as much abysses, from which resistance became impossible. At the end, these works were completely overrun relatively easily.'[1]

It was not only foreign observers who were impressed. Prince Hohenlohe was to write:

>Our experience with our siege guns were (sic) more instructive. The effect of our rifled siege guns surprised not only the enemy, but also ourselves. At ranges at which the enemy considered themselves absolutely safe from our shell, our 24-pr guns threw their shell beyond the great Wemming Bund, destroying

---

1 A.D.B., Colonel, "Sur le siège de Duppel", *Journal de l'Armée Belge*, Brussels 1864, Nr. 26 pp. 190-191.

blockhouses by their explosion, dismounting the guns on the ramparts which they enfiladed, and causing, on the first day of the bombardment, such annoyance and such a panic, that had we considered such a result as possible, we have held our troops in readiness to take advantage at once of this first terror. We should perhaps have met with less resistance on this first day than we eventually did at the time of the assault. At least the prisoners told us that, on the opening day of the bombardment, the redoubts 1 to 6 were deserted by the whole of their garrisons. We could not see this on account of the heavy snowstorm, which was raging. Later on the defenders became accustomed to our shell, and learnt how to shelter themselves in some degree by throwing up epaulments of earth. When the guns which were captured in the Dybbøl redoubts had been brought back in triumph to Berlin, the state of complete ruin to which they had been reduced by our shell excited general admiration for the effect of our new invention.[2]

The military victory was also a stunning political success. Public opinion was now solidly behind the war, and the army dazzled by triumph. The King arrived at Dybbøl from Berlin on April 21st. A march past was held in his honour.

On the same day, King Christian issued a defiant proclamation to his army, clearly indicating to both sides that, as Moltke had always said would be the case, his Government was not willing to concede. The fall of Dybbøl would not end the conflict.

Brave soldiers! Undaunted and heroic comrades! The army occupying the Dybbøl position has been forced to retreat to Als, after a defence which will be memorable to remotest posterity, not only on account of the inequality of the contest, but also for the heroism with which it was fought.

Heavy, indeed have been the sufferings the development of the contest has entailed upon you; nor will the great and painful losses of the past few days ever be forgotten. But, by God's help neither the sufferings nor the losses will be in vain, for they will bear fruits in the war we are now waging against might and injustice, a war the aim of which is the existence and independence of our beloved country.

I return you the fervent thanks of myself and my people for the perseverance and self-sacrificing heroism you have displayed, and I am convinced that you will still be inspired by the same spirit.

God preserve my brave Danish army! May it receive the reward of its persevering bravery, and may He confer everlasting peace upon our fallen heroes!

Christian R.

---

2   Hohenlohe-Ingelfingen, Prince, *Letters on Artillery*, Roral Artillery Institution, Woolwich 1887, Letter Nr 3.

Jutland to the Armistice

After Dybbøl's fall, considerable Prussian reinforcements were moved north, to re-inforce Allied forces there, and preparations were made to move a siege train to Fredericia. Whilst these reorganisations were taking place, the newly created Division Münster was ordered to clear North Jutland of the enemy as far as the Limfjord.[3] Major-General Münster-Meinhövel's 9 battalions, 12 squadrons, and three batteries, began their move north on April 22nd. During the advance, a re-connaissance patrol of one NCO and six men of 5/8th Hussars, led by Sec-ond-Lieutenant Count Galen, encountered a patrol of five Danish dragoons from 1/6th Regiment, under Corporal Bovense at Torsted. A short, vicious struggle left Galen, his NCO, and one hussar wounded, whilst one dragoon was killed, and two wounded.

Hegermann-Lindencrone could do nothing whatsoever against this force, and withdrew rapidly. Münster was in no rush, his troops entering Hobro on April 29th. By then, Hegermann's troops were across the Limfjord, other than a bridge-head at Aarhus.

Fredericia Abandoned

With the loss of Dybbøl, it was assumed that the next target for the Allies would be Fredericia, as a means to a landing on Funen. As a result, General Steinmann was given command of those troops who were to remain on Als. General Vogt was or-dered to Funen with 3rd Division, and Army Headquarters was also moved there, on April 22nd. The next day, General Gerlach received a telegram from Colonel Lundbye, in which the War Minister expressed his view that Fredericia should be abandoned, and that, with Gerlach's agreement, this should be undertaken as soon as possible. Lunbye's view was that, apart from rifled cannon and relevant ammu-nition, no regard should be paid to any loss of artillery, munitions or stores.[4]

Gerlach was horrified by the suggestion, and sent a telegram back on the 24th, which read:

> After the fall of the position at Dybbøl, Fredericia is our only offensive strongpoint, and should not be evacuated, certainly not before the enemy has clearly shown that he has the intention to attack the stronghold. A detailed statement follows in writing.[5]

Certainly the abandonment of the fortress came as a great shock to friend and foe alike. Without question, it was a much stronger position than Dybbøl, and was in no immediate danger of falling to the enemy.

Gerlach's letter followed later that day. In it, he pointed out that the fortress was in no immediate danger, and that it was tying down considerable Allied forces. He further stated that Fredericia was a more important factor than Als, but that each was tying down enemy forces. The letter closed with the view that no territory

---

3 See Appendix XVIII.
4 Jensen, p. 413.
5 Ibid, p. 414. Given Gerlach's completely passive defence at Dybbøl, this is an amazing statement.

Austrian artillerymen in Fredericia after its abandonment (Voss)

should be voluntarily given up. Lunbye, though, as ever, would not be denied. He wired, at 18:00 on the 25th, that, "My order of the 23rd inst. will be immediately effected. Further official documents may be expected soon. Keep this matter as confidential as possible during the initial discussions."[6]

That afternoon, Lundbye's number two, Major Ankjær, had arrived in Assens (Army Headquarters on Funen), to discuss the general situation of the Army, with Lieutenant-General Gerlach. As an aside, Gerlach asked the Major to raise the matter of Fredericia with Lundbye, on his return to Copenhagen, telling him that it was vital not to vacate the fortress. Ankjær arrived back in Copenhagen after matters had already been settled.[7]

Gerlach sent instructions to General Lunding, in Fredericia, to begin preparations to withdraw from the fortress. Lunding was shocked, and he too, contacted the War Minister, in an attempt to get the orders countermanded. After a flurry of telegrams between the two men during the afternoon of the 26th, Lunding realised that the decision was final, and continued his preparations for a withdrawal.[8] Very likely, the order had been decided upon in a post-18th April fit of depression and panic.

The entire garrison of the fortress was transported across the Little Belt in the next few days. By the 28th, there was only a force of about 1,000 men left in Fredericia, the 'rear-guard' of 3¼ companies of infantry, 200 Fortress Artillery personnel, and a few cavalry and engineers, under the command of Lieutenant-Colonel Nielsen. By 00:45, the next morning, all of these were aboard ship. Austrian

6   Generalstaben, Volume III, pp. 7-8.
7   von Fischer, p. 290. See Appendix XVI, for details of the fortress's armament immediately before the start of the withdrawal.
8   Ibid, pp.9-11. Lunding had already started the 13th Regiment, the Work Battalion, and other units on their way. As ordered, he did his best to disguise the ship movements as transfers to and from the fortress.

patrols entered the city the next morning. 206 guns, and large quantities of ammunition were found in the fortress. The batteries facing the Little Belt were quickly manned. The mainland was effectively cleared of Danish troops. The move certainly confused the Allies. Moltke wrote, to Colonel Blumenthal, "Up to now, nobody knows how to solve the riddle of Fredericia…"

The London Conference

The idea of a conference to discuss the various issues at stake in the Duchies had been in the mind of Lord Russell, since the beginning of the war.[9] Invitations were despatched to the Powers and other concerned parties, at the end of March, to attend talks in London. For some weeks, delays in setting a start date occurred due to protocol, clarification of instructions to delegates, and Danish public opinion. A formal opening of the conference was promulgated for April 12th, but, as previously discussed, was strung out by Bismarck, to enable the Prussians to storm Dybbøl. The new date for the opening was April 20th. The position was stormed on the 18th. This was doubly tragic for the Monrad Government, as they too, had hoped to use Dybbøl as a bargaining chip at the table.

The first full session of the conference took place on April 25th, at No. 11, Downing Street, London. The various representatives were:

Great Britain	Earl Russell (Presiding)
	Lord Clarendon
Russia	Baron Brunnow
Austria	Count Apponyi
	Privy Councillor Biegeleben
France	Prince de Latour d'Auvergne
Prussia	Count Bernstorff
	Privy Coucillor Balan (former Ambassador to Denmark)
Denmark	Baron de Bille
	M. Quaade (Foreign Minister)
	Councillor Krieger
German Confederation	de Beust, Count F. (Saxony)
Sweden	Count Wachtmeister
Acting as Secretary	The Honourable William Stuart
Attending as observers	The Schleswig and Holstein Estates
	Duke of Augustenburg

Although the conference finally started on April 25th, there was no Armistice in force. The acceptance of a cease-fire therefore became its first priority of the British delegation. It was more difficult than they had supposed, however, because of

9   In fact, proposals for a conference to discuss the issues preceded hostilities. Lord Wodehouse and Baron d'Ewers, the Russian Ambassador in Copenhagen, had suggested as much to Monrad, in December, 1863 – Halicz, pp. 320-323.

the vexing issue of the Danish naval blockade. This was the one effective weapon that Denmark had, and was not inclined to allow it to be lifted, especially as, for practical purposes, all three Duchies were occupied. No conclusion could be reached at this session. The suggestion that any cease-fire should allow the Danish fleet to continue the blockade caused outrage in Germany, where newspapers called for it to be lifted. With the appearance of Austrian warships in the Channel, the matter became more acute, but, again, no agreement could be reached on May 4th. Finally, on May 9th, the parties accepted an armistice, to begin on the 12th, and to run for a period of one month, and included a lifting of the blockade.[10]

It was only on May 12th, therefore, that the delegates actually began to discuss the issues for which they had assembled. On this day, Count Bernstorff consigned the 1852 Treaty of London, to history. He stated that the two Allied Powers were ready to consider fresh propositions, it was a relief to many. The board was now cleared, and the delegates agreed to await new ideas from Prussia and Austria, at the next sitting. The treaty thus made 'extinct' finally disappeared without much fuss.[11] Two days later, an attempt by Palmerston to form a united front with France foundered on the mutual distrust that still bedevilled relations between the two countries. Bismarck himself was fully aware of the danger of a joint Franco-British front, and was on his guard against this throughout the conflict.

Five days later, Bernstorff issued a vaguely worded statement, which required, 'the complete political independence and close union of the common institutions of the Duchies'. Whilst all parties wondered as to the meaning of the statement, the French delegate, Prince de Latour d'Auvergne sharply demanded clarification of the proposition. Bernstorff then conceded that it meant the full independence of the Duchies. The Danish representatives protested the package, but indicated that they must await the decision of their government on it. The other mediating powers thereupon reserved their positions until this reaction was known. A further session was planned for May 28th.[12]

Between the two sittings of the Conference, Prussia and Austria were busy formulating a plan, which ended as a compromise. Although both powers could agree that the personal union of the Duchies with the Danish Crown, was a dead letter, their future was a matter of debate. Although Prussian plans were as yet not finalised, there was a growing feeling for annexation. The Austrian position, however, favoured the Prince of Augustenburg, and this Bismarck could not ignore. The Tsar was known to favour another candidate, the Grand Duke of Oldenburg. In accordance with his belief in the art of the possible, Bismarck accepted a move in favour of the Augustenburg Prince, although there would be a get-out clause. As usual, he would back any horse if it were possible to gain any advantage from so doing.

The further Austro-Prussian proposals of May 28th, without giving Prussian recognition of his right to the succession, suggested a resolution for a state of Schleswig-Holstein, ruled by the Prince of Augustenburg. This was pure cynicism,

10 In practice, the action off Helgoland lifted the North Sea blockade the same day.
11 Ward & Wilkinson, p. 172. The agreement of Austria in initiating such a bold step, was hard won.
12 Lecomte, Ferdinand, pp. 230-231 (Danish 1865 edition).

since such a concept would, once again, not be acceptable to Denmark.[13] Russell countered this with the old idea of dividing Schleswig along the line of the Schlei and the Danewerke. The Prussian proposal, as Bismarck had hoped, was rejected. Russell's however, was deemed worthy of further consideration.

With both sides now considering the idea of partition, there seemed to be light at the end of the tunnel. Discussions about where the line of demarcation in a truncated Schleswig would be, went on *ad-nauseum*, though the neutral nations by this time were thinking of the Armistice itself. On June 6th, virtually the whole session was devoted to discussion of an extension of the cease-fire. The Allies wished to prolong it, with an open time frame, to be terminated by either side with notice of one month given. The Danish position, with all of their mainland population occupied, but still sure of the safety of their islands, was against an extension. Under considerable pressure, however, a concession was made. At the next session, on June 9th, agreement was finally reached that, from the 12th, the Armistice was to be extended for a further two weeks.[14]

Throughout these extended negotiations, the Danish position remained unrealistically steady. Whilst the other Powers were able, under severe diplomatic pressure, to obtain Prussian agreement to a border between a line from Flensburg to Tønder, the Danes would accept nothing north of the Schlei.[15] Baron Brunnow, the Russian envoy, did his absolute best to overcome the intransigence, but to no avail. Every idea put forward met the same reply. On June 20th, Brunnow went to see the Danish delegates, with a plea to report the true state of affairs to Copenhagen, and request instructions. This, too, failed.[16] That same day, in Copenhagen, at a crucial meeting of the Rigsraad, Monrad told the King that, should he refuse to compromise, the government would fully support him. Christian was left little option. Only a border at the Schlei was acceptable.[17]

A further meeting of the Conference on June 22nd produced little but harsh words, and, on June 25th, it came to an end, with hostilities due to resume the following day. On the 27th, Palmerston, speaking in the House of Commons, during a speech primarily concerned with economic matters, said, "Whatever wrongs Denmark have sustained – and they are many – she had, in the beginning, been wrong herself."[18] Britain had withdrawn from the issue of the Duchies. Monrad's

---

13 Three days later, Bismarck had a meeting with the Prince, to see if he could, if necessary, do business with him. The Prince, a sincere man, soon realised that he would be in thrall to Prussia. This meeting was the end of his candidature. Bismarck, *Bismarck, The Man and the Statesman*, Volume II, 1899, pp. 31-32.

14 Lecomte, pp. 232-233.

15 Steefel, p. 241. Bismarck had accepted this as early as May 27th.

16 Halicz, Emanuel, *Russia and Denmark, 1856-1864*, p. 460-461.

17 Schioldann-Nielsen, pp. 125-130. Monrad had offered Christian his resignation on the 17th, but the King could find no other possible leader. The King's 'decision' was inevitable.

18 *The Times*, Tuesday, June 28th 1864. Lord Russell, speaking in the House of Lords, also announced that Britain was washing her hands of the matter. The resulting furore produced a Motion of Censure against the Government, which it was lucky to survive.

A corporal and men of the Danish 16th Infantry Regiment, taken during the First Armistice (Larsen & Dumreicher)

complete unreasoning intransigence had caused a renewal of the war. Denmark was now in an utterly hopeless position, without any possible allies.

Military Preparations

During the Armistice, the Danish Army was forced to undergo some reorganisation. At the very top, Lieutenant-Colonel Reich became Minister of War, in place of Colonel Lundbye. Due to the heavy loss of officers, there were a number of transfers. In addition, on June 10th, an order was issued that infantry regimental commanders should also take command of one of their battalions. Prior to this, on May 13th, some older troops were discharged from the army, to be replaced by recruits. The infantry lost all men of the classes of 1853/54/55. In the case of the force on Als, at the end of the Armistice, this meant the loss of about 2,500 experienced men, just over 25% of the infantry strength there.[19] The naval situation in the Baltic remained much the same as before the Armistice. In the North Sea, however, only the 'mosquito' inshore flotilla of Lieutenant-Commander Hammer was in place to defend, as best it could, the North Frisian islands.

Changes in the Allied command structure after the fall of Dybbøl and during the cease-fire were considerable. Field Marshal Wrangel was retired on May 18th, and Prince Friedrich Carl appointed Army Commander. Lieutenant-General von Moltke had already, on May 2nd been appointed the Chief of Staff. The new commander of I Corps was General of Infantry (Lieutenant-General) Herwarth von Bittenfeld, and III Corps, taken over by Wrangel's former Chief of Staff, Lieutenant-General Vogel von Falckenstein. This Corps now comprised the

19 For a detailed order of battle for the army at the end of the Armistice, see Appendix XIX.

Combined Guard Division, Division Münster (10th and 21st Brigades, and Fliess' Cavalry Brigade), and four batteries. The Guards were to come under the command of Lieutenant-General von Plonski. At sea, whilst little could be done in the Baltic, the expected arrival of powerful new Austrian naval units in the North Sea would mean Allied dominance there. The most immediate operation to undertake was by I Corps – the conquest of the island of Als.

This group of five photographs show Prussian officers whose portraits were taken during the Armistice. All photographs by J.B. Bögh of Aarhus, 1864. (From the collection of Duncan Rogers)

13

The Conquest of Als

The island of Als, with an area of some 121 square miles, had a population of some 20,000 in 1864. Very fertile and heavily wooded, it was too large for the force allocated to defend it. The matter of naval co-operation was thus a matter of prime concern to the Danes. All arrangements for the deployment and use of naval forces had to be made by discussion and agreement. At the beginning of May, General Steinmann, now commanding on Als, tried to establish with the commander of the Western Baltic Squadron, (Naval) Captain Muxoll, exactly what he could expect in the way of naval support in the case of an attack. Agreement was reached that naval vessels could operate in Als Sound only to a point on the mainland just above Storskov (Great Wood), opposite the northern part of the Kjær Peninsula. Steinmann also sought assurances that, from the woods of South Wood (Sønderskov), south of Sønderborg, eastwards all around the south, east, and north coast, and back to the point above Great Wood, no enemy landing would be possible by more than 2-300 men. Further, in case of a defeat, he requested that the ships would support the retreat, and rescue the troops. The transport vessels for this purpose, six steamers, four iron transport boats, and four transport lighters (and four sailing vessels on the east coast, added on June 27th) were stationed at Høruphav, east of Sønderborg.[1]

The naval vessels assigned to the defence of Als, were stationed as follows:

Augustenborg Fjord, 'near Arnkils Øre'

	Armoured Battery Ship *Rolf Krake*, (Naval) Captain Rothe.
Sandvig	Gun Sloop Nr. 19, Reserve Lieutenant Marcher.
Hardeshøi Ferry House	Cannon Yawl *Baagø*, Reserve Lieutenant Petersen.
Stegsvig	Steamship Hertha, Lieutenant von der Recke, with the flag of (Naval) Captain Pedersen, Deputy commander, Western Baltic Squadron, Gunboat *Willemoës*, Lieutenant Bærentzen, Gun Sloops Nr. 21 & 22, Reserve Lieutenants Ditzel and Sørensen,
South side of island	Gunboats *Thura*,and *Buhl*, Lieutenants Holm and Skibsted, Gun Sloops 17 and 18, Reserve Lieutenants Christensen and

1   Lütken, *Søkrigsbegivenhederne i 1864*, p. 308.

Clausen, and Cannon Yawl *Kolding*, Reserve
Lieutenant Frantzen.

Kegenæs   Ship of the Line, *Frederik VI*, (Naval)
Captain Ibsen.

As the Armistice came to a close, Steinmann requested confirmation of the
points discussed the previous month, and Muxoll, unaware that his squadron was
to be cut in size, answered in the affirmative. As a result, General Steinmann made
the deployment detailed below.[2] He was potentially faced with a crossing at either
end of Als Sound, and needed a reserve to be able to react in either direction. Aware
that his troops were spread too thin, he had requested another regiment for his
command, to be placed as a reserve below Arnkils Wood, but this was not forth-
coming.[3]

With the resumption of active operations, the troops on the island consisted of
Major-General Steinmann's 1st Division, and the Als Artillery and Engineer Commands (see Appendix XIX). In round figures he had under arms the following:

Infantry	9,600
Cavalry	250
Artillery	1,750
Engineers	350
Total:	11,950[4]

The defending forces were deployed as follows:

In the far north of the island, that is, north of the Augustenborg Fjord, were six
84 pound howitzers and two 24 pound pieces, in temporary positions along the
coast, west of Hardeshøi, manned by a detachment of Fortress Artillery.
Permanent positions for these, in four batteries each of two guns, were under
construction. Steinmann placed 6th Infantry Regiment, Lieutenant-Colonel
Caroc, 2/4th Dragoons, Ritmester J. Bentzen, and four rifled 4 pounders of 1st
Field Artillery Battery, Captain Bruus in this area, under Caroc's command.

Facing Als Sound, the fixed artillery was deployed as follows (June 28th).[5]

On the Kjær Peninsula, north of Kjærvig (cove):

Emplacement Number 1	one rifled 4 pounder – facing south
Emplacement Number 2	two rifled 4 pounders – one facing north
	– one facing south
Emplacement Number 2b	one 12 pounder – facing north

2   Sørensen, *Den Anden Slesvigske Krig*, Volume III, pp. 104-106.
3   Ibid, pp. 107-109. Also, for the area of Arnkils Øre, Steinmann counted on the
     intervention of *Rolf Krake*, which would be stationed in Muxoll's words, 'close to
     Arnkilsøre' – Ravn, Major, "Tabet af Als", *Tidsskrift for Krigsvæsen*, 1865, pp.
     105-106.
4   Ravn, J.T., *Fremstilling af Krigsbegivenhederne paa Als, fra sen 18de April til den 1ste
     Juli 1864*, Copenhagen 1870, pp. 31-32.
5   Ibid, Appendix 7, pp. 197-199.

Forest Wardens House Battery	one 24 pound howitzer and one rifled 4 pounder
Emplacement Number 3	one rifled 4 pounder
Wood Battery	one 24 pound howitzer and one rifled 4 pounder
Emplacement Number 4	one rifled 12 pounder, facing north
North Rønhave Battery	one 24 pound howitzer and one rifled 4 pounder
South Rønhave Battery	one 24 pound howitzer and one rifled 4 pounder
Emplacement Number 5	one rifled 4 pounder, facing north
Emplacement Number 6	two rifled 4 pounders – one facing north, – the other south
Emplacement Number 6b	one 24 pounder smoothbore cannon, facing south
South of Kjærvig (cove):	
Emplacement Number 7	one rifled 12 pounder, facing north
Emplacement Number 7b	one 12 pounder smoothbore cannon, facing south
Emplacement Number 7c	one 24 pound howitzer, facing north
Emplacement Number 8	one rifled 12 pounder, facing north
Emplacement Number 9	one 84 pound howitzer, facing south
Emplacement Number 9b	one 12 pounder smoothbore cannon, facing north
Emplacement Number 10	one 84 pound howitzer and one rifled 12 pounder facing south
Emplacement Number 10b	one 84 pound howitzer, facing north
Emplacement Number 10c	one 12 pounder smoothbore cannon
Møllestedgaard Battery	four rifled 12 pounders
Emplacement Number 10d	one 24 pound howitzer
Emplacement Number 11 (Flank Battery)	one 84 pound howitzer and one rifled 12 pounder facing north
Emplacement Number 12 (Baadsager Battery)	one 84 pound howitzer and one rifled 12 pounder, facing south
Emplacement Number 13	one 24 pound howitzer, facing south
Emplacement Number 13b	one rifled 12 pounder, facing south
Emplacement Number 14	one smoothbore 12 pounder, facing south
Emplacement Number 15	one rifled 12 pounder, facing south
Emplacement Number 16	one rifled 4 pounder, facing north
Emplacement Number 17	one rifled 4 pounder, facing north
Church Battery	one 84 pound howitzer and one rifled 4 pounder, facing north. One 84 pound howitzer and one rifled 4 pounder, facing south. Also six smoothbore 24 pounders, two 84 pound and two 24 pound mortars.

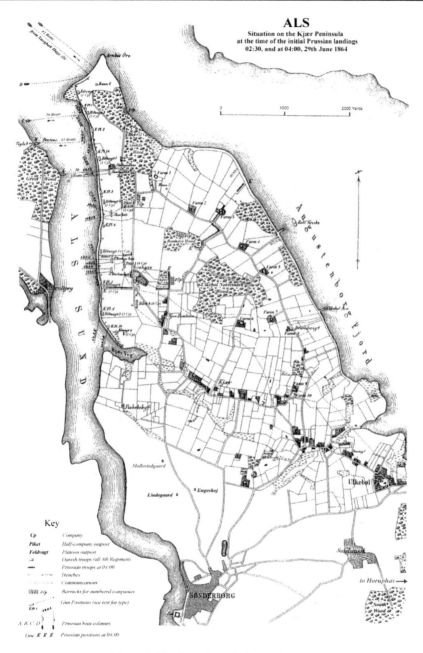

ALS
Situation on the Kjær Peninsula
at the time of the initial Prussian landings
02:30, and at 04:00, 29th June 1864

Map 32: The Invasion of Als - 29th June

| Castle Battery | one 12 pound howitzer and two rifled 4 pounders, facing north |
| Mill Battery | three 84 pound howitzers |

It was in the area facing Als Sound that General Steinmann placed his main force (valid overnight, 28/29th June).

Arnkils Øre to Kjaervig: 4th Regiment, Major Rauch
Arnkils Øre south to Rønhave – I/4th Regiment, Captain Mathiessen
1/4th, Premierlieutenant Linnemann – All four platoons posted as shore watches along the coastline, a distance of some 2,500 yards.
2/4th, Captain Glahn – Two platoons at the-western edge of Arnkils Wood, and the other two at the south-west corner of the Follen Copse.
5/4th, Premierlieutenant Jantzen – In barracks inside Arnkils Wood.
7/4th, Premierlieutenant Westberg – In barracks east of Follen Copse.
Rønhave south to Kjærvig (inlet) – II/4th Regiment, regiment's commander
3/4th, Premierlieutenant Sarauw – All four platoons posted as shore watches as far south as Kjærvig, some 1,800 yards.[6]
4/4th, Captain Bügel – Two platoons north, and two south of Rønhave.
6/4th, Captain Bodin – In barracks in the north section of Rønhave Wood.
8/4th, Premierlieutenant Thrane – In barracks in the south section of Rønhave Wood.

4th Brigade's headquarters was placed at Farm Nr. 5, nearly on the Augustenborg Fjord. This was not only more than two miles from the nearest threatened coast, but out of visual contact. Six 12 pounders smoothbore guns of 9th Field Artillery Battery, Premierlieutenant Bentzon, under Faaborg's command, were stationed near Farms Nr. 9 and 10. The two other guns of this battery were placed west of the Follen Copse.

South of Kjærvig – 6th Brigade, Colonel Bülow, headquarters at the Hvide Hus, east of Sønderborg.
5th Regiment, Major Myhre
Kjærvig south to the Surlykk Battery – II/5th Regiment, Major Rothe.
Surlykk Battery south to the Baadsager Battery – I/5th Regiment, Captain Hammer.
10th Regiment, Major Gedde.
Baadsager Battery south to the Church Battery – II/10th Regiment, Captain Glahn. Two companies in trenches facing the beach, and two in reserve.
Church Battery south to Ladegaard – I/10th Regiment, Captain Vaupell. Two companies in trenches facing the beach, and two in reserve.
Reserve – 3rd Brigade, Colonel Kauffmann, headquarters at Sundsmark. Four rifled 4 pounders of 2nd Field Artillery Battery, Captain Lunn, were at Vollerup Barracks, with two guns at Kjær, and two at Engeshøi. Four guns of 1st Battery were at Sundsmark.
3rd Regiment, Lieutenant-Colonel Mathiesen – Vollerup Barracks
18th Regiment, Major Lundbye,
I/18th, Captain Stricker – Sundsmark Barracks (3½ companies on fatigue duty overnight)
II/18th, Major Weyhe - Ulkebøl

6   Note that this gave the regiment a front of over 2¾ miles.

Major Gerlach, with 3/4th Dragoons, Ritmester Haffner, had headquarters at Augustenborg town.

On the south of the island, connected to the rest of it by a narrow causeway, the fall back position had been designated as the Kegenæs Peninsula, where Major Gulstad, former head of the Slesvig Gendarmerie, had a handful of men. Here, the major had eight 18 pounder cannon from the steam ship of the line, *Frederik VI*, along with their naval gun crews. Finally, at the village of Høruphav, north of this peninsula, were placed two rifled 6 pounders.[7]

At the end of the Armistice, 34 Prussian guns faced Als Fjord from the mainland, and a further 42 fronted Als Sound. The Armistice ceased at midnight on June 25th. Prussian artillery batteries at South Sandbjerg and Batteries 25, 27, and. 29 opened fire at 06:00 on Arnkils Øre and the area around Kjærvig. Their purpose was to unmask the Danish guns there. The Danish artillery did not take the bait, and the firing ceased at 10:00, 73 rounds having been fired. One Danish soldier was wounded.[8]

In complete contrast to the defenders, the Prussians had made attack plans which completely ignored naval support, previous experience having shown this to be unlikely. Although the new I Corps Commander, Lieutenant-General von Bittenfeld, had decided upon a crossing from the original planned site of Ballegaard to North Als, Major-General Manstein insisted that his 6th (Combined) Division could make a successful crossing from Great Wood across the north part of the Sound. Combined with concerns over the time spent crossing in daylight to north Als, this argument won the day. The operation was postponed 24 hours, and would now take place overnight on June 28/29th. The planners calculated that there was sufficient light to begin at 02:00. Boats carrying the first wave of troops could complete the crossing before sunrise at 03:24[9]. For this operation, Manstein's division was to comprise the two most experienced brigades – Major-General Roeder's 12th and Major-General Goeben's 26th. Wintzingerode's follow up division, therefore, comprised Brigades Canstein and Schmid.

Four crossing points were designated, from south to north, Points A, B, C, and D, and from these, troops were to be transported in four separate waves. Point A was situated at the narrowest point of the Sound, embarkation being from the Great Wood, a distance of almost 570 yards. From here, 50 boats, crewed by 325 men, would carry up to 750 troops across. Points B, and B1, were placed either side of the brickworks north of the wood, the crossing here being just under 1,000 yards. From here, 42 boats and pontoons, crewed by 700 men, would carry 6-700 infantry and either 130-40 cavalry or, later, artillery. Point C, also just short of 1,000 yards from Als, was some 500 yards north of B. This was the most unsuitable crossing point, since the boats had to be carried some distance until the water was deep enough to float them. From here, 29 boats, crewed by 218 men, would carry across 400 troops at a time. Finally, Points D, and D1 were located south and north of Snogbæk Hage, a distance from Als of over 2,000 and 1,225 yards

7   Sørensen, *Den Anden Slesvigske Krig*, Volume III, pp. 109-113.
8   Grosser Generalstab, Volume II, pp.644-645 says that the firing lasted for three hours.
9   Ibid, p. 656.

respectively. Only the first wave from here made the longer crossing, subsequent waves being brought from Point D. 42 boats crewed by 440 men, carried 750 troops in each wave here.

The troops were allocated to the crossing points as follows:

First Wave:	A – Regimental Staff & I/IR24
	B – II/IR24
	C – Battalion Staff, 2 & 4/IR64
	D – F/IR64
Second Wave:	A – Regimental Staff, 1 & 3/IR64, and 6 Division Staff
	B – Artillery, Cavalry, and I Corps Staff
	B1 – II/IR64
	C – Battalion Staff, 10 &11/IR15
	D – II/IR15
Third Wave:	A – II/IR55
	B – Artillery, Cavalry and I Corps Staff
	B1 – F/IR55
	C – 9 & 12/IR15
	D – Brandenburg Jäger Battalion Nr. 3
Fourth Wave:	A – Brigades Schmid and Canstein
	B – Artillery, Cavalry, and I Corps Staff
	B1 – Brigades Schmid and Canstein
	C – Brigades Schmid and Canstein
	D – I/IR55

Manstein's orders stated:

After cooking in the evening, the troops are to move to the rendezvous at the Sottrup Wood, so that they are rested there until 01:00, from where an orderly officer will lead them to the crossing points. The crossing to Als will be carried out without packs or helmets; tunics, bread bags, digging and cooking utensils are to be taken, in the latter, food for three days; and 80 cartridges per man, to be protected from damp.

Along the beach from Snogbæk Hage to Sandbjerg, a chain of posts will be established by the hussar regiment. At 01:00, a battalion of Brigade Canstein – the 1st Battalion Regiment Nr. 60 – will be dispersed along the beach, by points B and C, as skirmishers to support the crossing by rapid fire. The best marksmen will be placed in the front of the boats from where they can deal with enemy fire during the crossing. If the crossing succeeds, after taking the trenches and redoubts there, the first wave of Brigade Roeder will press forward to the south edge of the Follen Copse, occupy it, and await the arrival of the second and third waves. Brigade Roeder will then push forward on the left, and Brigade Goeben next to them, on the right, and orders for further action against Rønhave and Kjær will be given.

The Fusilier Battalion of Regiment Nr. 24, with a troop of hussars has the task of observing the beach from Sandbjerg to Egernsund, to protect the beach batteries there, and after 02:00, to direct the enemy's attention to Sønderborg. Using the boats, which will be by the former Redoubt V, they will demonstrate against Als, and cross as soon as a good opportunity presents itself. The hussar regiment has to take over the transport of prisoners to the rear.[10]

The new battery positions to support the crossing were constructed on the night of 27/28th, and armed the following night. Bringing the total number of Prussian guns facing the Sound to 60, the additional batteries were:

Snogbæk Hage	Four rifled 24 pounders
Between Batteries 27 & 29	Two rifled 12 pounders
South-west of Battery 27	Four rifled 12 pounders
North of Great Wood	Four rifled 12 pounders
North of Sandbjerg	Four rifled 24 pounders

The Landings on Als (Camphausen)

The Landings

The first boats went into the water at the most distant Point D 1 at 01:45, June 29th, carrying F/IR64.[11] Within 15 minutes the whole invasion was under way. As Roeder's first wave clambered into their boats, there was some gentle grumbling amongst the men, their officers reminding them that their oath bound them, "…to serve the King on land and sea."[12] Shortly after the departure from D 1, the entire operation was threatened when Prussian hussars on shore watch mistakenly opened fire on the boat column. Though the firing was swiftly stopped, the shots were heard by a patrolling ship's boat from *Rolf Krake*. Although this boat had

10 Gentz, pp. 106-107.
11 Waldersee, p. 490.
12 Rüstow, p. 605.

warning rockets for such a contingency, none were fired, and nothing untoward was reported on the boat's return to the ship at 02:00.[13]

From Point A, the three lines of boats carrying I/IR24, Captain Papstein, were around 100 yards into the Sound before the first shots were fired by Danish vedettes.[14] Thereafter, the fire became heavier, the sharpshooters in the bows of the boats replied, along with I/IR60, posted along the beach south of Snogbæk Hage, and the artillery on both sides joined in.[15] The warning beacons built by the Danes along the Sound were also lit.

The 14 companies of the First Wave, some 2,500 men, began landing at 02:15 (I/IR24, Captain Papstein). Facing them were the widely dispersed immediately available troops of 1 and 2/4th Regiment, about 400 men, and some men working in fatigue parties, one of these from 18th Regiment, unarmed.[16] Though fighting hard, both companies were rapidly overwhelmed, and all of the ground between the shore and Arnkils Wood, taken.

At the first alarm, 5/4th Regiment, in the barracks along the Augustenborg Fjord in Arnkils Wood, assembled and moved north, coming into contact with F/IR64, Major von Unruh. Premierlieutenant Jantzen led his company straight at 9/IR64, Captain von Unruhe, but was halted by rapid rifle fire. 10/IR64, Captain von Großmann, and 11/IR64, Captain Ewald, came forward in support, attacking Jantzen's right flank, driving him eastwards.

7/4th, Premierlieutenant Westberg, also in barracks, but east of Follen Copse, moved north through the copse, taking up a position at the south-west corner of Arnkils Wood, supported by the two guns of 9th Field Battery there. Here, however, they were attacked in front, by I/IR64, Major von Hüner, and in the right flank, by various elements of Unruh's Fusiliers. Westberg was pushed towards Farm Nr. 1, with heavy loss. Both of 9th Battery's guns were captured before they could be removed, one by a mixed bag of F/IR64, led by Second-Lieutenant Klosterstein II after a close quarter struggle, and the other by the skirmisher platoon of I/IR24, Second-Lieutenant Count Yorck von Wartenburg. The Danish troops were driven from Arnkils Wood back to Farm 1. All four companies of Captain Mathiessen's I/4th suffered severely in the fighting, Mathiessen, and two of his company commanders taken prisoner. 4/4th, Captain Bügel, at the first sound of firing, had moved north from Rønhave towards the Wood Battery. It too, was unable to make headway against superior numbers, and Bügel was mortally wounded just after ordering a retreat.

While this fighting continued, Prussian detachments advanced along the beach, rolling up the Danish coastal artillery positions. The batteries north of Kjærvig were only able to fire about 190 rounds before they were abandoned or overrun. Of these, Emplacement Number Two fire approximately 50, the North Rønhave Battery, 47, and Emplacement Number Six, 40 rounds.[17]

13   Ravn, p. 63.
14   Grosser Generalstab, Volume III, p. 662.
15   To the south, the diversionary bombardment of the area around Sønderborg began at 02:30.
16   Ravn, *Tabet af Als*, p. 103.
17   Generalstaben, 211-213.

Danish 4th Regiment's counterattack against the south part of Rønhave wood
(Liljefalck & Lütken)

After I/4th's hammering, 4th Brigade's alarmed commander, Colonel
Faaborg, decided to attempt a counterattack against the southern part of Arnkils
Wood with the survivors of the units to hand, only about 100 men. He personally
led the move, which quickly petered out under heavy fire. Faaborg himself was
lightly wounded. Undeterred, he ordered forward 6 and 8/4th, for another try,
without the knowledge of the regiment's commander, Major Rauch, whose whereabouts was temporarily unknown. Faaborg led Premierlieutenant Thrane's 8/4th,
the first to arrive, forward. At a knick about a hundred yards south of the Follen
Copse, Faaborg's force was attacked by 4/IR64, Captain Count Maltzahn, together with a platoon of 2/IR64. Maltzahn was repulsed, ordering a retreat, and
was killed immediately thereafter. This success was short lived, however, since
3/IR64, Captain Lewinsky, newly landed in the Second Wave, hit Faaborg from
the west, while the previous attackers once again assaulted from the front. Thrane's
company, badly shaken and disordered, was pushed back into the arriving 6/4th,
Captain Bodin, also scattering them. Only a group of about 50 men of the two
companies could be withdrawn in order.[18] Finally, at 03:30, with 4th Regiment
having a remaining effective strength of some 200, Colonel Faaborg requested assistance from Division.[19]

The Intervention of *Rolf Krake*

Rolf Krake's boat rendezvoused with the ship at 02:00, and shortly thereafter came
the sound of firing, followed by the alarm signal for the ship. Between 02:45 and
03:00, the vessel appeared off Arnkils Øre, as the Second Wave was nearing the end

18 Generalstaben, Volume III, pp. 209-210. It was the beginning of a busy morning for
Captain Lewinsky.
19 Ravn, p. 91.

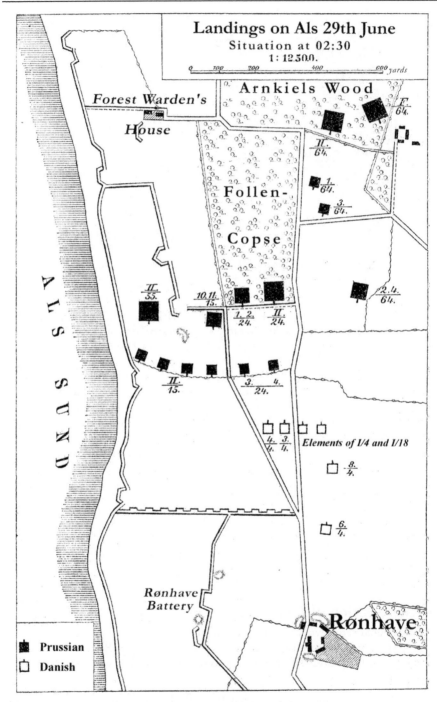

Map 33: Initial Landings on Als

of its crossing of the Sound. She fired upon these, remaining in the area for approximately half an hour, also engaging some of the Third Wave, and the Prussian artillery on the mainland, but made no attempt to close with the small boats. As the sound of battle could be heard fading away to the south, Rothe, in concurrence with his second- in command, concluded that he could be of no further material assistance here. *Rolf Krake* steamed back into the Augustenborg Fjord, in pursuance of her secondary task of supporting the army's flank in a retreat, and assisting in any evacuation.[20]

That *Rolf Krake* could have caused serious disruption and loss to the boat columns by closing with them is not in doubt, although the cost would at the very least have meant severe damage to the ship, with no guarantee of success. That she did not attempt to do so would subsequently cause a furore.[21] After the ship's withdrawal, and with the Danish artillery positions along the Sound falling one after another, there was no further interference with the transfer of men and equipment. This alone, even were there to be a tactical setback, would guarantee the success of the operation.

6th Brigade's Fight

Other than the firing to the north and south, the first that 6th Brigade knew of events was about 04:00, when Major Myhre, commanding 5th Regiment, posted along the shore south of Kjærvig, saw large numbers of Prussians marching south towards Kjær, directly in his regiment's right rear.[22] He pulled back and deployed I/5th, Captain Hammer, around Engelshøj, north of Sønderborg, and ordered II/5th, Captain Rothe, to assemble and move forward. He then reported the enemy presence, as well as his own action, to the Brigade Commander, Colonel Bülow.

About the same time that 6th Brigade received Major Myhre's message, the following order was received from Division:

Morgenstjernes Gaard 29/6   04:00
    The enemy has taken Arnkils Wood. 18th Regiment is marching north. 1st Battalion of the 3rd Regiment is ordered to Morgenstjernes Gaard. According to circumstances, the reserves must be moved to the Right Flank.
    By Order
    Meldahl
    Deputy Chief (of Staff)

20 Timings are crucial to this episode, both in relation to the length of time taken for *Rolf Krake* to reach Arnkils Øre, and how long she remained in position there. Rothe maintained that he was on station longer than the 30-45 minutes in other accounts. See below.
21 After a public outcry, both officers, at their request, were investigated by a special commission, Muxoll, as Squadron Commander focusing upon his responsibility for the defence of Als, and Rothe for his actions that morning. Eventually, Rothe was fully exonerated, but Muxoll was punished with a month under Fortress Arrest (later reduced to 14 days, by the King). See Generalstaben, Volume III, Appendix 21, and Bjørke, Kiær, & Norrie, pp. 438-444. Grosser Generalstab, Volume II, p. 668, which the latter also quote, states that to have caused major disruption to the crossing, the ironclad would have to have arrived earlier.
22 Schiøtt, p. 175.

This order was received at 04:30 and was also explained verbally.[23]

In answer to the summons, I/18th Regiment, Captain Stricker, assembled west of Kjær after a night on fatigue duty, and moved off northwards at 03:45. Some 15 minutes later, with 1/18th, Captain Baller, and 7/18th, Premierlieutenant Ahlmann in the first line, and 2/18th, Captain Baron Adeler, and 5/18th, Second-Lieutenant (of the War Reserve) Schougaard in the second, Stricker encountered Prussian troops in the farms north-west of Kjær. After a mopping up action at Rønhave, three companies of II/IR15, Lieutenant-Colonel von der Goltz, had moved rapidly south along the road towards Kjær, and were in and around several farmsteads east of Kjærvig on the approach of Stricker's battalion.[24] Goltz' troops opened a rapid rifle fire from both front and flank, to which Stricker was unable to make an effective reply, and drove him back from knick to knick, finally into Kjær village. Chr. Bredsdorff, now commissioned, and commanding a platoon in 5/18th Regiment, was involved in this action:

> After we had been in reserve for a while, Captain Baller returned, wounded in his hand, followed by several others. Lieutenant Bokkenheuser and the Senior Sergeant bravely held their ground for some time, but finally had to retreat. 5th Company now took up the fight with them; 1st platoon (Jørgensen) and 2nd platoon (mine) plus Jungersen from 2nd Company, were rushed out in a skirmish line. Our men are firing rapidly, but bit by bit we are forced to retreat from hedgerow to hedgerow, through corn and hedges so dense that it is almost impossible to force a way through them.[25]

While this action bought him some time, Colonel Bülow, correctly anticipating the instructions from Division, had ordered an attack the advancing Prussians by Major Myhre's 5th Regiment, supported by II/10th Regiment, Captain H. Glahn. Major Gedde, 10th's regimental commander, was to concentrate his other battalion, I/10th, Captain Vaupell, in Sønderborg. Immediately available was Captain Hammer's I/5th.

Just after 05:00, Bülow sent the trumpet signal, "5th Regiment, Advance." Captain Hammer moved forward with three companies, from left to right, 1/5th, Premierlieutenant Stonor, 5/5th, Premierlieutenant (of the War Reserve) Snertinge, and 6/5th, Captain Claussen. 2/5th, Premierlieutenant (of the War Reserve) Raabye, remained in reserve. Two platoons of Second Battalion's 3/5th advanced to cover Hammer's right flank. Three and a half companies were attacking almost the entire brigade of Major-General Goeben, which was now supported by four rifled guns of 2nd 6 Pounder/ Artillery Brigade Nr. 3, Captain Lundt, which moved into he north of the village at about 04:30, and deployed across the Rønhave Road.

Hammer was able to advance almost level with the farm of Fiskebækegaard, but then was halted by a murderous crossfire. West of the Rønhave Road, II/IR55 and 9 and 10/IR55, of Major von Rex's Fusilier Battalion, supported by six further

23 Ravn, J.T., *Fremstilling af Krigsbegivenhederne paa Als fra den18de April tilden 1ste Juli 1864*, Copenhagen 1870, p.102.
24 Grosser Generalstab, Volume II, p. 670. The remaining company, 8/IR15, was moving south along the beach.
25 Bredsdorff, pp. 318-319.

companies brought forward by Goeben from behind Kjær engaged the attackers. East of it, II/IR15 (three companies), Lieutenant-Colonel von der Goltz, 9/IR15, 12/IR15, and 2½ companies of the newly arrived Major von Witzleben's 3rd Jäger Battalion, fired into Hammer's right flank. Advancing against this concentration, in Premierlieutenant Snertinge's company was Private Rasmussen, who later wrote:

> We quickly got hold of our rifles and stood ready to march, but a long time went by before orders to advance along the road to Kjær came to the company. We were, however, overwhelmed by the Prussians. We stormed towards them, but the masses of Prussians against our single line forced us to retreat. There were many high fences, and the tall corn made movements difficult.[26]

After this repulse, Colonel Bülow ordered a further effort to retake some lost ground. This time, Hammer's I/5th advance with II/5th, Captain Rothe, on its right. Both battalions were badly hurt. 7/5th, Premierlieutenant Nielsen, and 8/5th, Premierlieutenant Satterup, were able to occupy Møllestedgaard, but unable to hold it for long.[27] Goeben's force was too strong, and able to envelop both flanks. Both battalions were driven east of the Rønhave-Sønderborg Road. Private Rasmussen was one of those taken prisoner:

> The battle rolled backwards and forwards. My comrade in the unit fell close to me, but the Prussians came up so rapidly that I had to abandon him, and soon a great many of our officers and NCOs were wounded and the company torn apart. The Prussians attacked from along the beach and a small group of soldiers, me included, were surrounded at the crossroads and forced to drop our weapons.[28]

During this attack by 5th Regiment, Captain Glahn's II/10th Regiment had been halted at Lindegaard. After the attack was repulsed, Goeben's troops continued to advance. By 05:30, Prussian troops had taken Lindegaard, almost in the rear of the Baadsager Battery on the Sound. Glahn began to deploy his companies to face this advance, some of his troops already jittery. Then Second-Lieutenant Wandler, commanding 4/10th writes,

> The battalion's 4th Company, was in reserve, but already, before the forward companies had become engaged in the fight, they were ordered forward. During the advance Corporal Christensen led the company, but they had not gone far, before he was hit by a ball. He shouted and rolled a couple of times, which caused the advance to stop. The corporal, however, quickly pulled himself together, pulled himself up on his elbow, waved his cap, and shouted: 'Forward Comrades, for old Denmark!'[29]

While this deployment was occurring, at 05:45 Major Gedde received the order for his regiment to retreat. He instructed Glahn to withdraw, followed by

26 Rasmussen, L., *Minder fra Krigen 1864*, p. 21.
27 Schiøtt, p. 176.
28 Rasmussen, pp. 21-22.
29 Wandler, Captain G., "Smaatræk fra Indtagelsen af Als i 1864", *Danebrog*, Volume 3, p. 30-31.

Captain Vaupell's I/10th. Glahn withdrew with three companies to the height of Engeshøi, and then further south to a hill north of Sønderborg. From here, he retreated at 06:30, after coming under renewed fire, 4/10th and 6/10th withdrew south-east towards South Wood, and Premierlieutenant Kühlmann's 3/10th, east. Second-Lieutenant Pætges and 8/10th had become separated from the rest of the battalion, retreating south from Engeshøi, coming under fire from Prussian skirmishers infiltrating along the Als Sound trenches, as so often that morning. They were eventually able to withdraw via South Wood.

Captain Vaupell's I/10th Regiment, was equally beset by confused orders and communications that morning. Vaupell had already, due to a misunderstanding, evacuated Sønderborg, spiking the guns there.[30] He then instituted a countermarch, although this information did not reach 2½ platoons of 2/10th, Premierlieutenant Diechmann and two platoons of 1/10th, Premierlieutenant (of the War Reserve) Huusher. The main force had yet to reach their former positions when, about 05:45, further orders to retreat arrived. Captain Vaupell pushed 5/10th, Captain Lorentzen, and 7/10th, Premierlieutenant (of the War Reserve) Vilstrup to occupy the south-west tip of South Wood. Meanwhile, Diechmann had pulled back to the east of South Wood, and Huusher's troops, believing themselves cut off, signalled to some vessels offshore there, and were picked up and taken to Kegenæs.

After the repulse of 5th Regiment's attacks, Goeben's troops had continued their advance on Sønderborg. The *ad-hoc* units moving down the Sound continued rolling up the coastal batteries one by one. The entry into Sønderborg began at 06:00. From the north, came Major von Böcking, with three companies of his I/IR55, and a platoon of 7/15th, and along the beach from the east and south, Lieutenant-Colonel von der Goltz, with 8/IR55, and 8/IR15, 10/IR15, and 11IR15. Resistance was very light, many defenders giving themselves up. Captain Thesen's 6/10th alone lost some 50 men as prisoners, many of whom remained in buildings within the town until they could surrender.[31] Goeben's troops occupied Sønderborg around 06:30. Colonel Bülow's 6th Brigade was in full retreat.

2nd Brigade's Fight

Whilst these actions were taking place, on the Danish right the decisive action of the morning was fought. Like its sister battalion then to the west, II/18th Regiment was also on the move in response to the calls for help from 4th Brigade. Initially accompanied on foot by 2nd Brigade's commander, Colonel Kauffmann, Major Weyhe moved off from Ulkebøl at about 03:30 with 3/18th, Premierlieutenant Nielsen and 6/18th, Premierlieutenant Madsen, towards Kjær, and then north to the south-west corner of Nørremark Wood. Here they encountered advancing troops of IR64.

30 Lilijefalk & Lütken, p. 537.
31 Ravn, pp, 130-131. He also illustrates the potential pitfalls of relying on after action unit reports, with 3/10th reporting its casualties during the majority of the fighting as 10 NCOs and 68 undercorporals and men, "the greater part dead and wounded". The entire regiment lost less than 50 killed and wounded in the battle.

Major Kramer, after the fighting in the Follen Copse, assembled his battalion at its southwest-edge, and led it south, in company columns, 6 and 7/IR64 in the van followed by 5 and 8. They were followed, in turn, by F/IR64 and 1/IR64. South of Rønhave, Kramer met Major-General Goeben, who ordered him further to the left, as he was in Goeben's zone of operations. In doing so, due to a mix up, two platoons of 6/IR64 became separated from the battalion for the remainder of the battle.

As Kramer moved through the south of Nørremark Wood, he came into a firefight with Weyhe. His own 3½ companies, plus 1/IR64, Captain Lobenthal engaged the two companies to their front, while 3/IR64, Captain Lewinsky, flanked them to the north. The volume of fire from their more numerous enemy drove Weyhe's troops back towards Kjær with considerable loss, particularly to Madsen's 6/18th. Major Weyhe was captured.[32]

The other two companies of II/18th Regiment had moved north along the road east of Nørremark Wood. 4/18th Regiment, Captain Volkvartz, at the front, reached Farm Nr. 4, still held by troops of 4th Regiment. Volkvartz decided to attack Farm Nr. 3, 650 yards further on, occupied by elements of IR64. His attack was repulsed, and he was badly wounded in the chest.

The final company, 8/18th, Premierlieutenant Benzon, was joined on the march by the commander of 4th Brigade, Colonel Faaborg. Faaborg led the company along the same road as Volkvartz, but hearing heavy firing to the south-west and assuming that Major Weyhe needed support, he turned left at Farm 5 and followed the road towards Farm 6, or Tombøll Farm.[33] A request by Benzon to send out skirmishers was denied by the Colonel. Farm 6 had just been occupied by the two platoons of 1/IR64, moved to the east by personal orders from Major-General Roeder. There followed a very strange episode.

As the column, about 04:30, headed by a mounted Colonel Faaborg, approached the farm each side appears to have thought that the other wished to surrender to them. The then Second-Lieutenant Gentz wrote later:

> Curiously, the enemy, who was scarcely 150 paces away, made no attempt to form a battle formation, but marched calmly further with shouldered rifles and on such a wide front that he filled the entire space between the two knicks alongside the road. It was to be suspected that the enemy, who was already cut off, wanted to surrender and this became certain when the Danes waved back at us without doing the slightest hostile thing. Lieutenant Gentz went forward with the platoon, which he had sent to the farm, with the intention of taking the entire unit prisoner extremely happy with the brilliant capture which he had so easily made. When he got closer, it turned out that there had been a complete misunderstanding and that everything would turn out completely different to what one had expected. As it later turned out from the testimony of German-speaking wounded, the Danes had believed that our small unit (the other platoon was hidden by the knick) who they had approached from the rear wanted to surrender. Our waving had been as misunderstood as theirs. The unfortunate result of the false assumptions on both sides soon came to light, for whilst our people, not being able to speak Danish, waited for what had become

32 Ibid, pp. 154-155.
33 Ravn, p. 156.

the conventional surrender movement of lowering the rifles held horizontally, outstretched in both hands, a large red bearded Danish Senior Sergeant grabbed the rifle of Musketier Bernhard of the 1st Company, who as usual was also the first, and tore it away from him despite all his efforts.[34]

At this point all hell broke loose, with firing in all directions, and use of the bayonet. Colonel Faaborg was mortally wounded early on. Second-Lieutenant Stammer's platoon also fired into the column, but the two Prussian platoons were saved by the appearance of Captain Lewinsky's 3/IR64 and elements of 2/IR64. Premierlieutenant Benzon was wounded, and the survivors of 8/18th were withdrawn by Premierlieutenant Graae.

Before this, at around 04:00, Lieutenant-Colonel Mathiesen had also received orders from Colonel Kauffmann to begin moving his 3rd Regiment forward from its 'Alarm' positions towards the advancing Prussians. I/3rd, Captain Schöning, marched via Ulkebøl and Kiær towards Rønhave, and II/3rd, Captain Krabbe, north to the east of Kjær.[35]

Krabbe reached the woods north of Bagmoose at about 04:30, there receiving further instructions from Colonel Kaufmann to attack the flank of the enemy to the west. Unaware of other developments in the area, he advanced, initially with three companies, from north to south, 4/3rd, Premierlieutenant Hansen, 7/3rd, Premierlieutenant Drastrup, and 3/3rd, Captain Fogh, in the first line, and 8/3rd, Premierlieutenant Falkenskjold, behind and to the right. The main body, with two platoons acting as skirmishers, moved westward, while Falkenskjold's company drifted off to the right.

Falkenskjold soon found himself under heavy rifle fire from two platoons of 1/IR64, under Second-Lieutenants Gentz and Stammer, and also 3/IR64, Captain Lewinsky, which had just repulsed 8/18th Regiment, and were now east of Tombøll Farm. Two platoons of 1/3rd Jäger, Captain Szwykowski, also appeared on the right.[36] The rapid fire of this force quickly drove Falkenskjold back, securing the Prussian left flank. In the terrain of wheat and cornfields, with thick hedges, the three Prussian units were actually unaware how close to one another they were.[37]

A few hundred yards to the south, as Krabbe's main force advanced, it came into action with Kramer's II/IR64. Krabbe and his adjutant were both wounded as they attempted to catch up with the advance. Kramer, who by now had pushed south of Farm Number 6 (Tombøll Farm), warned that enemy troops were on his left flank, sent two platoons of 8/IR64, under Second-Lieutenant Möllendorff, in that direction, whilst he, with 5/IR64, and 7/IR64, faced the frontal attack.

34 Gentz, p. 126. Ravn's account, pp. 156-157 says that the column was fired upon as it emerged from the forest, Faaborg was wounded, and that Benzon then ordered his front ranks to open fire.

35 Ravn, J.T., p. 158.

36 The Jäger battalion, having crossed in the third wave, and come under fire from *Rolf Krake*, was marching south, when the battalion commander, Major Witzleben, hearing firing to the east, despatched these troops in that direction – Kusserow, pp. 182-184.

37 Gentz, p. 125.

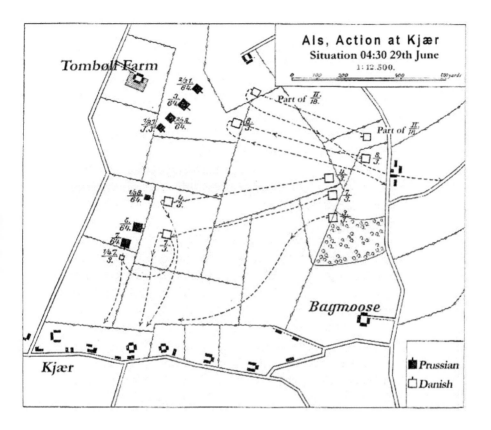

Map 34: Action at Kjær

Without central direction, Krabbe's company commanders, losing sight of one another in the fields, each took different action. Fogh, in the south, hearing heavy fire from the direction of Kjær village, moved there. Hansen, in the north, faced with intense rifle fire, stopped his advance, and then also pulled away to his left, towards Kjær.[38] Drastrup, however, went straight into the attack through the high grain, sending one platoon running towards a hedge flanking the Prussian right.

38 Hansen, in *En Compagnie Commandeurs Erindringer*, page 108, states "With regard to the report of the General Staff, I shall have to point out the following concerning 4th Company. The report states that the company did not engage in the fighting, or only exchanged a few shots. As the company stood isolated, I do not know from where the General Staff can have such information other than from my report. To my mind, it is only written there that a firefight began at a distance of 300 *alen* (200 yards)". Generalstaben, Volume III, p. 228.

The action at Kjær (Pflug)

Seeing this move, Second-Lieutenant Harbou led his platoon of 7/IR64 in a race for the hedge, reaching it 15 to 20 paces before the Danes. The platoon's rapid fire held the flanking movement, long enough for Cramer to reinforce him with two further platoons. Harbou was mortally wounded in the skirmish, but the Danish force was annihilated.[39] In severe close quarter fighting along the main front, Captain Drastrup was also killed. Three of his four platoon commanders became casualties, and the remaining one, Premierlieutenant Lundbye, drew the remnants of the company south towards Kjær.[40]

At this point, advised of the heavy fighting in Kjær village by one of General Manstein's adjutants, Premier-Lieutenant Plötz, Major Kramer gathered his available units and led them, with 7/IR64, Captain Baron von Bock at the head, south into the village to support IR24.

The fight for Kjær village began in earnest at around 05:00, as II/IR24, Lieutenant-Colonel von Kessler, and one company of I/IR24, moved in from the north and west, followed by the rest of Papstein's I/IR24, and Major von Unruh's

39 Gentz, p. 124.
40 Liljefalk & Lütken, pp. 532-533.

F/IR64. South of the Rønhave Road, two platoons of 5/IR24, Captain Münchow, advanced, with, from south to north 7/IR24, Premier-Lieutenant von Görschen, 6/IR24 (minus one platoon), Captain von Görschen, 2/IR24, Premier-Lieutenant von Brodowski, 8/IR24, Premier-Lieutenant Marquardt, and the remaining two platoons of 5/IR24.[41] Facing them was one fresh battalion, I/3rd Regiment, Captain Schöning, two battered companies of its sister battalion, II/3rd, whose commander was wounded, Captain Stricker's I/18th, the hard-used elements of Nielsen's 3rd and Captain Madsen's 6/18th, and Captain Sarauw's remaining troops of 3/4th Regiment.

Especially heavy was the fighting over a farm north of the Rønhave Road, between the two main crossroads in the centre of the village, Christen (or Kristen) Bertelsens Gaard, in the area of the advance by 6 and 7/IR24. The survivors of 7/3rd, some 40-50 men under Premierlieutenant Lundbye, were surrounded and captured by advancing Prussians, who placed them in the farm. Shortly afterwards, Captain Fogh attacked the place, but was repulsed. A second attempt, however, was successful, and Lundbye and his men released.

After another Prussian attack retook the farm, Lieutenant-Colonel Mathiesen ordered 6/3rd, Premierlieutenant Madsen, against it once more. The first effort failed, with both platoon commanders becoming casualties. A second try was also unsuccessful, as was a further one by elements of 1/3rd, and 3/3rd.

Kjær - Fighting at Kristen Bertelsens Gaard (Schiøtt)

41 There is some confusion (in a very confused action) about the precise whereabouts of some units, particularly the four platoons of 8/IR24. Waldersee, p. 509, states that, "8th Company secured the left flank of the 2nd Battalion, and was likewise engaged at Kjær."

318 BISMARCK'S FIRST WAR

North of the village, the Danish right flank was pushed back by elements of 3/IR24, and a platoon of 8/IR24, commanded by Second-Lieutenant Brockhusen. On the Prussian far left, the mixed force of IR64 under Captain Lewinsky continued to push the remaining troops of 4th Regiment, and 4 and 8/18th, south towards Ulkebøl. To the south, 3rd Jäger Battalion moved between the Brigades of Roeder and Goeben, whilst Major Lundbye was attempting to link up with Bülow's 6th Brigade on his left.

As it appeared to Lundbye that the situation south of the Rønhave Road was under control, he pulled back Captain Svane's 5/3rd, leaving only Captain Ahlmann's 7/18th, and Sarauw's 3/4th. It was shortly thereafter that 3½ companies of Major von Witzleben's Jäger came into action, intervening in the fighting of both of General Manstein's brigades. While his battalion was deploying, Witzleben was badly wounded in the chest, and command fell to Captain Paczinsky. He reinforced the existing skirmish line of two platoons of 1/3rd Jäger, and sent Captain Henning's 3/3rd, and Second-Lieutenant von Rheinbaben's platoon of 5/IR24 eastward. This attack partially flanked and cut off part of Captain Ahlmann's company, including the captain himself, driving the remainder back, blocking any possible link between the 3rd and 6th Danish brigades.[42] Paczinsky committed his own 4/3rd, and Captain Erckert's 2/3rd Jäger, to the battle with Bülow's 6th Brigade to his right, as already related.[43]

With mounting casualties, and both flanks in danger, Colonel Kauffmann had little choice. It was not possible to gain any ground, and the Prussians had further troops to commit. Informing General Steinmann, at about 05:30 he ordered the attacks to cease at Kjær, and for 3rd Brigade to withdraw to a position at Ulkebøl Church. At 05:53, Major-General Steinmann sent the following telegram to the High Command: "Following a heavy action on the Kjær Peninsula and heavy casualties, a retreat has been ordered, to rally between Ulkebøl and South Wood. From here, the retreat will continue to Kegenæs."

Retreat and Evacuation

The execution of this order meant that Als was lost.[44] The only possibility of halting, or even delaying, the Prussian advance was on the comparatively narrow Kjær Peninsula, and even this slender hope depended upon no supplementary landings taking place in the area of Sønderborg. With or without the withdrawal from Kjær, Herwarth von Bittenfeld could deploy a fresh division against an already beaten defence. For Steinmann, there was no alternative to a complete withdrawal from the island, and the rescue of as much of his division as possible. He was, once again, dependent upon the Navy.

In truth it is difficult to criticise the Danish company and battalion commanders for committing their units piecemeal as they arrived. Time was

42 Grosser Generalstab, Volume II, p. 680, & Waldersee, p. 513. Waldersee says that Rheinbaben's men were 'probably' of 6/IR24, but they were not. Though many of Ahlmann's men were captured in this move, he managed to escape in disguise, and return to his regiment. – Jensen, p. 493.
43 See Kusserow, pp. 184-188.
44 Generalstaben, Volume III, p. 231.

against them, and as the Prussian force on the island grew stronger, their individual units were also regaining their cohesion. With many of the Danish troops new recruits, there were few evolutions other than a bayonet charge that some units could perform. Despite the confusion of the initial landings, the sheer firepower of the Dreyse's had decimated the first Danish counter-attacks, and continued to do so that morning. Conversely, as at the storming of Dybbøl, many of the attacking Prussian units largely disintegrated in the fighting, although in general they kept moving forward. Had General Steinmann possessed the resources to launch heavy, concentrated counter-attacks, the consequences could have been serious.[45]

With both 3rd and 6th Brigades now in retreat, the question of pursuit remained. Both Goeben's and Roeder's troops were tired and short of ammunition. The advance was to be continued by General Wintzingerode's division. Even so, nearest the Augustenborg Fjord, the indomitable Captain Lewinsky, who did not receive the order to halt, continued to advance to Ulkebøl with his 3/IR 64 and the two platoons of Gentz and Stammer (1/IR64). Here, they linked up with the first troops of the fresh division. A clash occurred with the rearguard of 18th Regiment, which included Second-Lieutenant Bredsdorff:

> We now retreated fighting constantly, although it pulled more and more to our right, where 3rd Regiment was, as far as Ulkebøl Church where the regiments merged. Here a good fire was started in the nose of the enemy, caused by the burning of the barracks at Sundsmark and Vollerup, which forced the enemy to halt for a while although he couldn't have been more than a few hundred paces from us.
>
> Here, a temporary muster was held. We were missing 10 officers; 3rd Regiment likewise. Amongst them, unfortunately was Chr. Leth, and of his company only 12 men remained – it was completely torn apart. Later we heard that the kind Trepka had been killed in action.[46]

At 05:45, before General Wintzingerode's division was fully ashore, the first three complete and united battalions on Als – I/IR13, Major von Borries II/IR53, Lieutenant-Colonel von Moyna, and II/FR35, Major Fragstein, all under the command of Colonel von Witzleben (IR13), were sent south-east towards Ulkebøl.[47] Passing through the main body of IR64, and past Ulkebøl, where von Borries was slightly involved in the skirmish related above, the column continued south, Captain Lewinsky's company going with them.

Due to the confusion caused by its conflicting orders, the Danish 10th Regiment's retreat was cut off by the appearance of Colonel Witzleben's force just east of South Wood, at Høruphav. Trapped between Witzleben and the still advancing brigade of Goeben, the already tenuous cohesion of its scattered elements largely vanished. In a series of encounters in this wooded area, a large number of officers and men of the regiment were captured, including the regiment's commander and one battalion commander, with minimal loss to the Prussians (Witzleben's three battalions suffered a total of 11 casualties on the

45 Showalter, p. 116.
46 Bredsdorff, p. 320.
47 Grosser Generalstab, Volume II, p. 688-699.

29th).[48] The survivors reached the protection of 2nd Brigade's rearguard about 800 yards east of Høruphav.[49] Here pursuit by the very tired Prussians was ended, and Steinmann's troops, joined by Lieutenant-Colonel Caroc's force from North Als (other than II/6th Regiment and the artillery, which were evacuated from there by sea), retreated unmolested to Kegenæs. Firing had ceased by 10:00.

By 13:00, all of Steinmann's troops were at Kegenæs. Plans were agreed with (Naval) Captain Muxoll, that embarkation of the infantry would be managed by the steam gunboats would ship troops from the lighthouse pier to the Ship of the Line *Frederik VI*, and the steamer *Bellona*, which had anchored opposite the pier. The artillery and cavalry were to embark on the transport fleet's vessels, which had steamed down from Høruphav, from the main pier at Østerby.[50]

After the naval commands had been alerted to the emergency, further vessels were allocated to the evacuation. The steamer *Zampa* arrived, and at 17:00, (Naval) Captain Frølich appeared with the steamers *Bleckingen*, *Bergen*, *Glommen*, and *Diana*, along with six iron transport vessels. Also, fortuitously, eight Postal Service vessels were sent to help.[51]

The Danish evacuation of Kegenæs was allowed to continue unhindered over the next two days, because the position was simply too strong to attack. General Herwarth von Bittenfeld himself examined the position as late as July 1st, concluding that he could not proceed with an assault since the causeway had been breached, and the batteries, supplemented by naval support, were too strong.[52]

The Prussians were understandably elated by the success of the operation. Even before the Danes had evacuated the island, Friedrich Carl, by now appointed Army Commander, issued an Army Order:

> Headquarters, Aabenraa, 30th June
> Brave Soldiers of the Allied Army! After my King and Master had tempo-rarily entrusted me with the conduct of the Supreme Command, during the suspension of hostilities, it has pleased His Majesty, a few days ago, to appoint me Commander-in-Chief. My relations with you are no longer temporary but lasting.
> I have opened the second part of this campaign by permitting the valiant Army Corps which I have commanded until now, and with which I have gained nothing but victories, to conquer Als under my own eyes. This expedition is an

48 Generalstaben, Volume III, p. 246, gives 10 officers and c. 220 men. Prussian sources give higher numbers. Grosser Generalstab, Volume II, p. 690, states 13 officers and 329 men. Certainly, 10th Regiment largely fell apart, with many of the German-speaking troops deserting. Nevertheless, the 16 officer casualties that day were also all unwounded prisoners. See casualty totals below.

49 *Beretning fra Krigsministeriet [Report from the War Ministry] angaaende Kampen paa Als den 29de Juni 1864*, p. 11.

50 Ibid.

51 Lütken, *Søkrigsbegivenhederne i 1864*, p. 331. Ironically, some of the ships used in the evacuation had been ready to sail on the morning of the 29th, carrying Colonel 'Max' Müller's 5th Brigade, and supporting units, on an offensive mission to retake the island of Fehmarn, which had been lost in March.

52 Moltke, *Korrespondenz*, Letter Nr. 104, to the King, 3rd July 1864.

instance of the crossing of an arm of the sea unique in the history of war – a storm by water of well defended entrenchments.

May this commencement set a good example for all the troops who may subsequently have the honour to take part in the conflict. May it further serve to gain, for myself personally, that confidence from your leaders and yourselves, without which it is impossible for me to plan brilliant success in war.

Finally, may the unity hitherto existing between the Imperial-Royal and the Prussian troops, to the delight of our respective Masters and the blessings of our countries, to the honour of our armies and the terror of our enemies, remain unimpaired as heretofore.

And, therefore, Three Cheers for the Kaiser and Three Hurrah's for the King!

Friedrich Carl, General of Cavalry[53]

Casualties in the battle for the island had been heavily one-sided, more than eight to one in favour of the attackers. They were as follows;

Table 43

Prussian casualties at the conquest of Als, June 29th 1864

Prussian: 372 – 33 officers and 339 men[54]

Unit	Killed		Wounded		Prisoners		Missing	
	Officers	Men	Officers	Men	Officers	Men	Officers	Men
Headquarters Staff	—	—	1	—	—	—	—	—
I Corps	—	—	—	—	—	—	—	—
6th Division								
11th Infantry Brigade	—	—	—	—	—	—	—	—
Brandenburg Fusilier Regiment Nr. 35	—	1	—	3	—	—	—	—
IR60 (7th Brandenburg)	—	—	—	1	—	—	—	—
12th Infantry Brigade	—	—	—	—	—	—	—	—
IR24 (4th Brandenburg)	—	28	11	64	—	—	—	1
IR Nr. 64 (8th Brandenburg)	3	27	6	82	—	—	—	3
Brandenburg Jäger Battalion Nr. 3	—	4	1	22	—	—	—	—
13th Division	—	—	—	—	—	—	—	—

53 Anon., *Der Befreiung Schleswig Holsteins im Jahre 1864*, Königlich Staats Anzeigers, Berlin 1864, p. 15.
54 Grosser Generalstab, Volume II, Appendix 71.

25th Infantry Brigade	—	—	—	—	—	—	—	—
IR13 (1st Westphalian)	—	1	—	3	—	—	—	—
IR53 (5th Westphalian)	1	—	—	2	—	—	—	—
26th Infantry Brigade	—	—	—	—	—	—	—	—
IR15 (2nd Westphalian)	—	8	5	20	—	—	—	—
IR55 (6th Westphalian)	3	5	2	42	—	—	—	3
Brandenburg Artillery Brigade Nr. 3	—	—	—	2	—	—	—	—
Brandenburg Pioneer Battalion Nr.3	—	2	—	7	—	—	—	—
Pomeranian Pioneer Battalion Nr. 2	—	1	—	7	—	—	—	—
Totals	7	77	26	255	—	—	—	7

Table 44

Danish casualties at the conquest of Als, June 29th 1864

Danish: 3,092 – 73 officers and 3,019 men[55]

	Killed		Wounded		Prisoners		Missing	
Unit	Officers	Men	Officers	Men	Officers	Men	Officers	Men
Staff	1	—	—	—	—	3	—	1
3rd Infantry Regiment	6	40	3	50	1W	174 (38W)	—	42
4th Infantry Regiment	4	25	3	43	12 (2W)	529 (44W)	—	46
5th Infantry Regiment	3	81	2	62	10 (3W)	497 (64W)	—	—
10th Infantry Regiment	—	3	—	5	16	368 (20W)	—	362[56]
18th Infantry Regiment	2	48	3	54	4 (3W)	392 (57W)	—	62
4th Dragoon Regiment	—	—	—	—	—	1	—	
9th Field Artillery Battery	—	1	—	—	—	23 (2W)	—	3

55 Generalstaben, Volume III, Appendix 22, & Jensen, p.499.
56 Almost all of these men were deserters from Schleswig.

Fortress Artillery	—	2	—	2	3 (1W)	75	—	17
1st Engineer Company	—	—	—	—	—	2	—	3
Totals	16	200	11	216	46 (10W)	2,067 (225W)	—	536

W = Wounded

The evacuation continued throughout June 30th, General Steinmann and his staff embarking at 14:30 that day. The final troops withdrew on July 1st. "The last Danish troops had thus left Als, at approximately 15:00."[57] None would set foot there again for almost 60 years. The battle had been a disastrous defeat for the Danes, in many ways worse than Dybbøl, and a hammer blow to the country's morale.

---

57 Ravn, *Fremstilling af Krigsbegivenhederne paa Als...*, p. 181. Generalstaben, Volume III, p. 253, says 15:30.

14

The End of the War
From the Fall of Als to the Second
Armistice

Operations in North Jutland, July 1864

After the capture of Als, the Allied planners were keen to move on to take the island of Funen. However, the Austrian Emperor and his government were against such a move, concerned by the likely hostile reaction of Great Britain to any further action against Danish islands in the Baltic.[1]

Before the end of the Armistice, Bismarck and King Wilhelm met Franz Josef and Count Rechberg, at the Bohemian resort of Carlsbad. Their agreement to a landing on Funen was urged, but the Austrians would not be moved on the subject and would only agree on the occupation of the rest of Jutland, north of the Limfjord. With permission for an attack on Funen at least temporarily withheld, this relatively minor undertaking, along with the capture of the North Frisian Islands off the North Sea coast of Schleswig and Jutland, became the Allied forces' primary concern.

Prince Friedrich Carl conferred with FML Gablenz on the morning of July 1st at Army Headquarters in Haderslev. Details of the move across the Limfjord were agreed. On the right, III Corps was to move north via Randers along the main road, through Hobro, and on to Aalborg. On the left, the two Austrian brigades of Major-Generals Kalik (formerly Dormus) and Piret (formerly Gondrecourt) were to advance with their communications along the line of Holstebro, Skive, and the town of Nykjøbing on the 'inland' island of Mors. Prior to these moves, II Corps was to concentrate in the area between Kolding and Vejle.

To confuse the Danes further, Manstein's Division of I Corps was to make an ostentatious demonstration along the coast between Aabenraa and Kolding, to appear to threaten the north-west coast of Funen. Originally planned for July 14th, these moves were brought forward as conditions appeared more favourable.[2]

On the resumption of hostilities, Danish forces in Jutland were now stationed exclusively north of the Limfjord, except for a 'bridgehead' at Aalborg. They comprised the rather grandly named 'North Jutland Corps', commanded by Lieutenant-General Hegermann-Lindencrone.[3] Though ostensibly a corps, four of its already few infantry battalions had previously been ordered to Funen, leaving the total force composed of only six battalions, 24 squadrons, three field artillery batteries (24 guns), and two engineer companies; a total of some 7,000 men.

1 Steefel, p. 249.
2 von Fischer, pp. 354-355.
3 See Appendix XIX.

Subsequent orders provided for the withdrawal of the remainder of the 'Corps' to Funen at the beginning of July. The only troops to remain briefly in Jutland, to screen this withdrawal, were 1st Infantry Regiment, 2nd Dragoon Regiment, four guns of the 7th Field Artillery Battery, and the 3rd Engineer Company, the whole commanded by Lieutenant-Colonel Beck, commanding officer of 1st Regiment.[4]

On the same day as Friedrich Carl's plans were arranged in Haderslev, three reconnaissance patrols were sent north towards the Limfjord from the Advance Guard of Division Münster of III Corps, at Hobro (10th Brigade, Major-General Kamienski). The westernmost column, commanded by Captain Schor, comprising 11/GR10, 12/GR10, and 3/Brandenburg Cuirassiers was sent north-west towards Løgstør. A central column, 6/GR10, 7/GR10, and ½ 2/Brandenburg Cuirassiers, led by Captain Baron von Dyherrn, moved north along the main road in the direction of Aalborg. The easternmost column, commanded by Major Krug von Nidda, and made up of 1/IR50, 2/IR50, and 5/Westphalian Hussar Regiment Nr. 8, went north-east, over the Lindenborg River (creek).[5]

All three columns advanced without incident, and bivouacked for the night. Major von Krug and Captain Dyherrn made contact through cavalry patrols during the night, from their respective camps at Store Brøndum and Gravlev.

The Skirmishes of Sønder Tranders and Lundby

The various columns were soon spotted, and reported to the Danish headquarters in the town of Nørresundby, on the north bank of the Limfjord, opposite Aalborg. To confirm reports of an enemy force moving along the main road towards Aalborg, Lieutenant-Colonel Beck ordered a reconnaissance by 27 dragoons and a few infantrymen in wagons, commanded by Second-Lieutenant C.W. Christensen, at 02:00 on the morning of July 2nd. Sensing the possibility of surprise, Beck also immediately arranged to attack Major Krug's force.[6]

Christensen's patrol encountered Captain Dyherrn's column near Ellitshøj, less than 10 miles south of Aalborg, exchanging a few scattered shots. Dyherrn, apparently believing that he was facing a superior force, withdrew, pulling back to his previous night's position at Gravlev. Christensen returned to Aalborg.[7]

On the evening of July 2nd, 184 men of 5/1st Regiment, Captain Hammerich, with 16 dragoons were sent south towards the unsuspecting Prussians. Beck led the expedition himself, and several supernumerary officers accompanied him, not wishing to miss the action[8]. A 21 year old volunteer, Holger Petersen, was serving in Hammerich's company at this time. He later wrote to his brother:

4   Generalstaben, Volume III, pp. 169-170 & 269-270.
5   Grosser Generalstab, Volume II, pp. 705-706.
6   Generalstaben, Volume III, pp 271-272.
7   Grosser Generalstab, Volume II, p. 706.
8   At 01:00 the next morning, a reconnaissance patrol of 20 infantrymen and two dragoons, once again commanded by Second-Lieutenant Christensen was also sent south from Aaalborg. Generalstaben, Volume III, p.272.

Map 35: Area south of Aalborg

It was with the best of hope and in the highest of spirits in the world that the company crossed from Nørresundby to Aalborg, and marched south to meet the enemy.

At first, Lieutenant-Colonel Beck gave us a beautiful little speech and encouraged us to go forward in high spirits. On the way, I was given the task of preventing the farmer's dogs from barking, and many a poor farmer had to go out into the cold night dressed in just a night-shirt, to bring his dog in to his own bed. I had to be rude, and had a sense of satisfaction that my 'impossible' mission was fully accomplished.[9]

In the meantime, Major Krug had divided his own force. Having spent the night of July 1st in Store Brøndum, where a cavalry patrol of Dyherrn's column made contact, he pushed on the next morning. Crossing the Lindenborg on July 2nd at the village of that name, he left two platoons of 2/IR50, Captain von Wülknitz, and a corporal and six hussars, to secure his communications, and bivouacked overnight at Gunderup. At 22:00, he received word from Dyherrn that he had encountered a superior enemy force, and withdrawn to his previous day's position, where he would remain until his return to Hobro.[10]

Sending his baggage back to Rosenborg, Krug moved north to Lundby in the early hours of July 3rd convinced that he would encounter an enemy force, having had reports of Danish cavalry there. He then took three troops of hussars, and 20 infantrymen in wagons, commanded by Premier-Lieutenant Klinkowström, and continued northwards. Left behind in Lundby, were Captain von Schlutterbach, with 88 men of his own 1/IR50, 36 men of 2/IR50 under Second-Lieutenant von Wissell II, and two hussars.[11]

Just south of Sønder Tranders, Major Krug encountered Second-Lieutenant Christensen's patrol, which had moved south from Aalborg. Heavily outnumbered, Christensen was able to withdraw to the village, and then to a farm behind it. After a short action, the patrol was forced to surrender. Seven of Christensen's men were wounded. The two dragoons escaped to Aalborg. Krug's casualties totalled two killed, one hussar and one infantryman.[12]

Three miles to the south, Beck's scouts discovered the whereabouts of the main Prussian force at Lundby at 04:00 on the 3rd, by which time his men had marched more than 15 miles. They would cover almost two miles more before coming into contact with their foe. Beck had successfully cut the Prussian force in the village off, and was directly in their rear.

9   Petersen, Holger, *Minder fra 64*, compiled by I. Ravn-Jonsen, Copenhagen 1914, pp. 63-67.

10 "Die Gefechte bei Sönder-Tranders und Lundby am 3. Juli 1864", Supplement to *Militair-Wochenblatt*, October and November 1864, Berlin 1864.

11 Ibid. Krug's entire infantry strength was 216 men in these two weak companies. Of these, 72 had been left at Lindenborg.

12 Ibid. This report states the number of Danish prisoners as 18, of whom three were wounded. The figure shown here is from Stilling, Valdemar, *Danske Livregiment til Fods. 1 Battalion 1763-1913*, p.430.

Beck now sent a dragoon to reconnoitre the enemy position. Unfortunately, this man rode to the top of a hill south of the village, and was seen by the Prussians.[13] Any hope of surprise was gone in an instant.

At the time of the sighting of the Danish cavalry, about 04:30, Schlutterbach himself was on his own reconnaissance north of the settlement. When the news reached him, he immediately returned to Lundby, also sending a message to Major Krug that Danish cavalry had been seen south of Lundby.

By now, Beck and his infantry were on the hill 650 yards south of the village. The colonel ordered an immediate attack. Captain Hammerich asked to be allowed to deploy before moving forward, but was refused permission because speed was of the essence. This decision would prove a costly one. All Hammerich was able to do was open his march column to the width of a half-platoon. He now had a formation which was 10 men wide and 16 ranks deep, exclusive of officers and NCOs.

Schlutterbach now led 76 men in a run for a dyke at the southern edge of the hamlet, whilst his remaining 48 were held as a reserve in the northern part. Reaching the ditch well before the attackers, the Prussians deployed along it, but were not allowed to open fire.[14]

Hammerich's troops had come over 300 yards when Schlutterbach's men reached the dyke. The Danes were tired, and their pace slowed. They were also surprised not to be under fire. At this point, some skirmishers were sent out, as the column moved on. At just over 200 yards, the first volley crashed out. Almost half the attackers fell, either hit, or from sheer shock. The combination of the column moving down hill and the Prussians probably firing high meant that most of the initial casualties were at the rear. The second salvo was delivered a further 50 yards on, and a third about 150 paces from the ditch.[15]

At this point, with the column a complete shambles, the action descended into a chaotic fire-fight, the Prussian reserve also being brought forward. On the Danish right, about 20 men attempted to turn the Prussian left. They were confronted by a half-platoon of 2/IR50, which had just come forward. All of the Danish troops in the attempt became casualties, many of them as they stood up to reload. Some of the attackers may have closed to within 25 yards of the ditch.

Although grazed in the shoulder by a round fired in the first Prussian volley, Hammerich continued to urge his men forward, until there was no further point in doing so. It was whilst he was attempting to rally the company and lead the withdrawal, that he received a wound to his right arm, which brought him down, and caused his capture.[16]

Holger Petersen was one of those to get nearest to the Prussians:

---

13 Grosser Generalstab, Volume II, p. 707.

14 All of the Prussian troops were 'green' and their officers were determined to keep them under strict control.

15 The second and third salvos were not, in fact, ordered volleys. The Prussian infantry were so well drilled, that they individually loaded almost in time with one another. The Danes thought that they were volleys – "Die Gefechte bei Sönder Tranders und Lundby am 3. Juli 1864".

16 Stilling, Valdemar, *Danske Livregiment til Fods. 1 Battalion 1763-1913*, p.426.

Some – I was one of them – charged further forward, but as we were too few to achieve anything, we had to hug the ground very close to the enemy.

I was lying in a low cornfield and fired my rifle a couple of times, but then, I saw the company retreat, and I got up to follow. At that time, the bullets were whistling all over, and as well as I ran, one of the bullets grazed my left thigh and went straight through my right. I got up shortly afterwards and limped away as fast as I could, but I didn't get very far as the loss of blood was too great. Exhausted, I fell down, thinking that it was all over for me.[17]

Seeing absolutely no reason to continue the pointless slaughter, Beck, still on the hill, ordered a retreat. A chaotic and painful withdrawal took place, somewhat eased by the action of the gallant Captain von Schlutterbach, who ordered a ceasefire. Petersen describes how many of his comrades perhaps felt:

It was not really that bad at all, and I will not have my leg amputated. I did not expect the enemy to leave the battlefield as quickly as they did, without bringing all of the dead and wounded. If I had known, I would, of course, have played dead to get to my own (side). Now, there was nothing else to do, other than wait to be picked up by the ambulance.

I was then placed on a farmer's wagon and taken to Hobro. It was a tough trip, as I was utterly exhausted, and hardly fully conscious.[18]

Hammerich's company had been destroyed in less than twenty minutes. He himself had been wounded, and taken prisoner. It was his 35th birthday. The broken remains of Beck's force returned to Aalborg at about 08:00.

The losses in this brief skirmish were dramatically one-sided. Three Prussians were wounded. Danish casualties were, by comparison horrific, Hammerich's command suffering a more than 50% loss. The totals were as follows:

Killed	One officer,[19] one NCO, and 30 men
Wounded	One officer, one NCO, and 24 men
Prisoners	One officer (wounded), two NCOs (one wounded), and 35 men (16 wounded)
Missing	Two men
Total	Three officers, and 95 NCOs and men[20]

---

17 Petersen, Holger, *Minder fra '64*, pp. 63-67. The field is referred to as an oat field in, "Die Gefechte bei Sönder-Tranders und Lundby am 3. Juli 1864".

18 Ibid.

19 This was a Swedish volunteer officer, Premierlieutenant P. Betzholtz. This badly wounded man was seen to stand up and continue to stagger towards the Prussian line, causing Captain Schlutterbach to order his men to cease firing. Betzholtz died in the Prussian field hospital on July 26th. At the church where Betzholtz lay, Schlutterbach wore Betzholtz' sword which he had taken on the field at Lundby. In a noble gesture, he placed the sword and scabbard on the coffin, with the words, "Hereby, I return to you your sword my friend, the sword that you used to your great esteem, but which also led to your misfortune." Møller, M. Friis, & Mentze, Ernst (compiled by), *1864 – et hundredårsminde*, p. 276.

20 Generalstaben, Volume III, Appendix 24. The Prussian troops fired some 750 rounds in this encounter – "Die Gefechte bei Sönder-Tranders und Lundby am 3. Juli

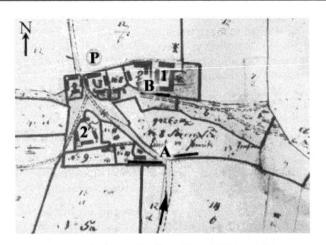

Map 36: Skirmish at Lundby, 3rd July 1864
Map from c.1813
1. Lundbygaard (the main farm in the village)
2. Mellemgaarden (Where the wounded were brought after the skirmish)
Arrow, bottom middle - The Danish attack
A: The main Prussian position
B: Prussian reserve
P: Prussian camp before the skirmish
(with special thanks to Jan Bøll Jespersen)

Major Krug returned to Lundby at 05:30, knowing that his left was uncovered by Dyherrn's retreat, and uncertain of the situation he immediately began a retreat. His force returned to Hobro around 19:30 that evening. Captain Dyherrn's column had returned on the 3rd, after its hasty retreat from Ellitshøj. Captain Schor, commanding the western patrol, had carried out his orders and reconnoitred as far as Løgstør, but encountered no hostile forces. He returned to Hobro on July 5th.

The Allied Crossing of the Limfjord

Although the actions near Aalborg were on a small scale, the fact that the Danes had engaged in any offensive operations south of the Limfjord convinced the Allies that they would meet resistance in crossing it. Initially, therefore, a large number of boats were gathered, and heavy artillery brought forward. Intelligence reports that the main Danish forces were embarking at Frederikshavn, however, clearly showed that no major defence was intended, and the dates of the planned crossings were brought forward.

Lieutenant-Colonel Beck, still commanding the Danish rearguard, aware that his force was very vulnerable, abandoned Aalborg on the 9th, arriving at Frederikshavn at 03:00 on July 10th. During his withdrawal, he received orders for

1864". The skirmish at Lundby was written of endlessly in relation to the use of the breech-loading rifle. It was certainly a graphic example of the defensive value of such weapons, but certainly not the first. The action at Kjær, less than a week before, had also provided a good example – Rothpletz, p. 22.

Lundby ca. 1890, seen from where the Danes attacked

the embarkation of his troops for Funen, and this was immediately carried out, the troops sailing in the provided transports for Nyborg.

On the afternoon of the same day, General von Falckenstein, on a visit to his Corps' Advance Guard at Ellitshøj, ordered an occupation of Aalborg on the 10th. The General had already departed, when, at 18:45 an officer of the 8th (Westphalian) Hussars reported that Aalborg had already been abandoned by the Danes, the last of their troops having pulled out that morning. By 24:00, the town was occupied by forward elements, and the remainder of the Advance Guard moved in on the morning of the 10th, as did the Corps Commander himself. Falckenstein ordered Premier-Lieutenant Boguslawski, with two other officers and 20 men of 12/IR50 across the Limfjord to Nørre Sundby. These reported no enemy presence.[21]

Events now occurred swiftly. No resistance was met anywhere. On the 11th, Prussian pioneers threw a bridge across the Limfjord at Aalborg. To the west, Austrian troops had also moved north, Baron Gablenz himself leaving Kolding on the evening of the 8th, reaching Holstebro late on the 9th. All reports reaching him indicated that Danish troops had been withdrawn. On the 11th, Major Eliatschek, with two officers and 61 men of IR Ramming, crossed the Ørresund on a reconnaissance, finding no enemy forces on the north bank.

Prussian forces occupied Frederikshavn on the 12th, and the Austrians crossed to the island of Mors on the night of the 13/14th. On the 14th, General Vogel von Falckenstein himself, accompanied by Prince Albrecht (senior), with a small escort, travelled to Cape Skagen, the northernmost point of Jutland, and symbolically raised the Austrian and Prussian flags there. During the next few days, the main Allied forces were pulled back from the northern areas with the exception of IR Nr. 50, 8th Westphalian Hussars, and 3rd 6 Pounder/Artillery Brigade Nr. 6, commanded by General von Fliess.[22]

---

21 Grosser Generalstab, Volume II, pp. 716-717.
22 Ibid, pp. 716-722, & von Fischer, 357-361 for exhaustive detail. Less so in Jensen, pp 503-504.

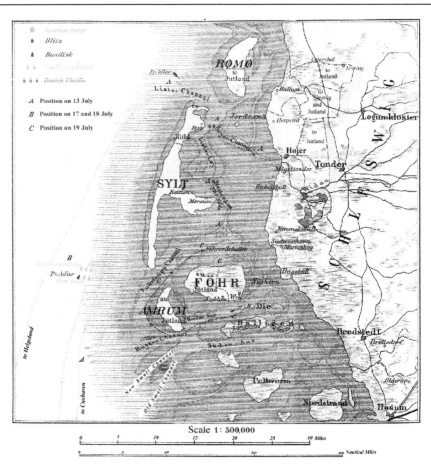

Map 37: North Frisian Islands, July 1864

The Occupation of the North Frisian Islands

With the whole of mainland Jutland occupied by Allied troops, the only areas of disputed territory still in Danish hands were the islands off the mainland's west coast. Matters were put in hand for their capture.

The slender Danish forces in the islands were still under the command of the redoubtable Lieutenant-Commander Otto Hammer. Completely isolated and without any hope of assistance, he was nevertheless determined to do his duty to the utmost, in spite of the hopeless position. It was a Lilliputian force, to be sure, but it had taken him five months of constant badgering of the authorities to get even this. Hammer's command comprised:

A. Paddle steamer *Limfjorden*, Flag, equipped only with two 1 pounders and espignols
B. Cannon-Yawl Division:

Steamship *Augusta*, Lieutenant Holbøll, unarmed other than espignols

Cannon-Yawl *Barsø*, Reserve Lieutenant S. Rasmussen, one 60 pounder smoothbore

Cannon-Yawl *Aarøsund*, Reserve Lieutenant F. Hansen, one 60 pounder smoothbore

Cannon-Yawl *Hørup*, Reserve Lieutenant C. Rasmussen, one 60 pounder smoothbore

Cannon-Yawl *Ekernsund*, Reserve Lieutenant J.Rønnov, one 60 pounder smoothbore

Cannon-Yawl *Ærø*, Reserve-Lieutenant F. König, one 30 pounder smoothbore

Cannon-Yawl *Fænø*, Reserve-Lieutenant N. Rasmussen, one 30 pounder smoothbore

Cannon-Yawl *Middelfart*, Reserve-Lieutenant R. Rasmussen, one 30 pounder smoothbore

Cannon-Yawl *Snoghøi*, Reserve Lieutenant J. Westh, one 30 pounder smoothbore

C. 15 Customs Service cutters, each equipped with two heavy calibre muskets, and crews of three to five men
D. Infantry detachment, composed of two officers and 159 men, commanded by Second-Lieutenant J. Uldall, all now on the northernmost island, Fanø.[23]
E. Six 24 pounder smoothbore cannon, manned by 24 artillerymen, also on Fanø.

The available naval forces of the Allies dwarfed Hammer's command, although fortunately for him, the larger vessels could not operate inshore amongst the inter-tidal sand and mud flats around the islands. Their presence was more concerned with preventing any interference by the Danish fleet.[24] Commanded by 48 year old Rear Admiral Bernhard, Baron Wüllerstorf-Urbair, the combined Allied squadron was formidable.[25] It comprised:

Screw ship of the line   *Kaiser* (Flag), Captain Baron von Böckh, 91 guns

Screw ironclad frigate   *Don Juan d'Austria*, Captain Pokorny, 31 guns

Screw frigate *Schwarzenberg*, Commander Baron Daublebsky von Sterneck, 50 guns

Screw frigate *Radetzky*, Commander Jeremiasch, 31 guns

Screw corvette   *Erherzog Friedrich*, Commander Ritter (Knight) von Wiplinger, 22 guns

Paddle steamer *Kaiserin Elisabeth*, Commander Zaccaria, 6 guns

Gunboat *Seehund*, Commander Kronowetter, 6 guns

Gunboat *Wall*, Lieutenant-Commander Monfroni von Montfort, 6 guns

Despatch Vessel *Preussischer Adler*, Lieutenant-Commander Klatt (Prussian), 2 guns

Gunboat *Basilisk*, Lieutenant Schau (Prussian), 2 guns

23 A subsequent detachment of 55 men was added to Uldall's force just after the resumption of hostilities – Tusch, *11 Battalion i Krigsaarene 1848-50 og 64.*
24 The Danish fleet had no intention of intervening here, and, as will be seen, was solely concerned with protecting the main islands in the Baltic.
25 Technically, Tegetthoff still commanded those vessels which first sailed with him to the North Sea.

Gunboat *Blitz*, Lieutenant Mac Lean (Prussian), 2 guns[26]

The Austrian military forces on Jutland's west coast, and charged with their occupation were commanded by Lieutenant-Colonel Schidlach. His force consisted of 9th FJB, 5/Windischgrätz Dragoons, and two rifled 4 pounders of 4/1st Foot Battery. This force, though not large, was considerably greater than Hammer's. It was positioned as follows (11th July):

Ballum	½ 2/9th FJB
Højer	Battalion Staff and 3, 4, and 5/9th FJB, one troop, dragoons
Møgeltønder	Two troops, dragoons
Tønder	One troop, dragoons
Rickelsbüll	6/9th FJB
Emmelsbüll	1 and ½ 2/9th FJB (with posts at Südvesthörn and Dagebüll)
Marienkog	¼ Foot Battery 4/1st

On the morning of July 11th, the signal, "Steamship in sight", was relayed to Hammer. Investigating the report aboard *Limfjorden*, he discovered the frigates *Schwarzenberg* and *Radetzky*, and was hurriedly forced to turn about when fired upon by them. That same afternoon, *Elisabeth*[27] and the four Allied gunboats sailed north to the Lister channel, and reported the presence of the Allied squadron to Schidlach.

Without arranging for naval support, Schidlach undertook to cross to Sylt and Föhr the next morning. Three separate columns of small boats, many of which had been gathered, were organised to carry troops thus:

A. 5/9th FJB, Captain Kaluschke, from Højer to Morsum, on the island of Sylt, in 24 boats. This was a very considerable 12 nautical miles away.

B. 6/9th FJB, Captain Heller, from Rickelsbüll to Näs-Odde, on the eastern tip of Sylt, in 25 boats, a distance almost six nautical miles.

C. 1/9th FJB and ½ 2/9th, Captain Urschitz, from Südwesthörn to the island of Föhr, in 36 boats, a little over five nautical miles.

The first and third columns set sail on the high tide, at around 05:00 on July 12th, and the second at 06:00. Each column was so arranged that the company commanders were in the centre of their respective groups, communication being passed by horn signals.[28]

26   This force was joined, on July 18th, by another Austrian ironclad, *Kaiser Max*, 31, accompanied by the steamer *Lucia*.

27   Hereafter, *Kaiserin Elisabeth* will be so called.

28   Wiser, Friedrich Ritter von, *Der Besetzung der nordfriesischen Inseln im Juli 1864*, Vienna 1914, p.8.

All of the boat columns found their progress blocked by Danish cannon-yawls guarding the channels. That from Højer was opposed by *Fænø* and *Hørup*, as was the column from Rickelsbüll. Captain Urschitz' boats, from Südwesthörn were faced with *Aarøsund* and *Snøghøi*. Lieutenant Holbøll, in *Augusta*, with *Ærø* and *Eckernsund*, moving out of the harbour of Vyk, on Föhr, also engaged this column.[29] Defenceless against the fire of the Danish vessels, the Austrians withdrew their vessels, the Jäger remaining well disciplined under the shelling.[30] The withdrawal was completed without loss. Lieutenant-Colonel Schidlach had been lucky.

Between 19:00 and 20:00 that evening, Lieutenant Holbøll, in *Augusta*, took the cannon-yawls *Aarøsund*, *Snoghøi*, *Ærø*, and *Eckernsund* across to the mainland at Dagebüll. Here they bombarded and destroyed some of the boats and materiél gathered there, before withdrawing in the face of fire from the two Austrian rifled 4 pounders there.

"It was clear after the first attempt that a crossing to the islands would not succeed so long as the enemy flotilla retained its full freedom of movement within the lagoon."[31] Consequently, by 15:00 that same day, several of Schidlach's officers, including General Staff Captain Wiser, were aboard the gunboat Seehund, to confer with officers of the squadron on plans to repeat the attempt on

Danish gun-yawls destroying enemy boats gathered on the shore at Dagebøl, 12th July
(Liljefalck & Lütken)

---

29 Danish reports mention that a column of boats also came from Dagebüll, but this was
    not the case – Lütken, Otto, *Søkrigsbegivenhederne i 1864*, p.303.
30 Wiser, *der Besetzung der nordfriesischen Inseln im Juli 1864*.
31 von Fischer, p.364.

Syld the next day. By the morning of the 13th, the Prussian gunboat *Blitz* was stationed in the Højer Channel, and *Basilisk* in the Lister Ley, with *Wall* and *Seehund* sealing the Lister Channel.

Under cover of this force, Captain Kaluschke was able to cross from Højer and land the 5th Company and half of the 3rd safely on north Sylt. Captain Heller's 6th Company, one again in small boats, and sailing from Rickelsbüll was once again soon under attack, forcing them to wait until ebb tide, when the Danish yawls were forced into the deeper channels, and the small boats were able to make the crossing.[32] Undefended Sylt was rapidly occupied.

The same day, a message from FML Gablenz was delivered to Lieutenant-Commander Hammer under a flag of truce. Hammer was asked to surrender. He refused this, but subsequently offered to withdraw from the area, if granted safe passage. This offer was not accepted.

Immediately north of Sylt, the island of Rømø was occupied by elements of 2/9th FJB, Captain Went von Römö, on July 13/14th. Went, who had been wounded in the chest at Oeversee in February, had recovered from his wound, and rejoined his company. Crossing to Rømø from Ballum on the mainland, he later described the operation, which was undertaken on his own initiative:

> I knew nothing about the successful undertaking against Sylt, when, on the 13th, I decided to try by means of pressed seamen, to cross over to Rømø that night. Due to the small number of available boats, I could take only 22 Jäger with me. It took great effort to drag the boats to the slipway. Finally, we shoved off. As it was not known whether the enemy occupied the island, it was necessary to steer for its southern tip, which ran out in a long, muddy spit.
>
> Due to the timidity of the seamen, we could take the boats no further. We therefore had to wade the rest of the way. Carefully moving on, at one o'clock in the morning I and my men reached a group of houses near the harbour. Here we met a junior official of the Danish Customs authorities, who, being a native German speaker, immediately gave me the information, which I wanted. The Danish garrison had departed 10 days before.
>
> Early in the morning, I reconnoitred the 7½ mile long by 2 mile wide island, exhorting those persons charged with public positions to comply with the instructions of the Civil Commissioners of the Allied Powers, and I informed the commander of the Austrian warships, anchored in nearby Königshafen, of the occupation of the island which was scheduled to take place by naval personnel on the 15th.
>
> I requisitioned all seagoing vessels we found, and I took the Controller of Danish Customs into custody, since he had once taken a shot from his cutter at my shore watch.
>
> Dunes run through the greater part of the island. Its villages lie on the eastern edge, but lack the affluence found on the mainland. Most of the houses are small and unsightly. Only on the northern part are there some better looking farms and some vegetation. Due to their isolation from the mainland, the inhabitants, mostly seamen, already suffered from a lack of provisions. They knew

32 Anon, *Auszug aus der Geschichte des k.u.k. Feldjäger-Batallions Nr. 9*, p. 139. The advice to do this came from Mercantile Captain Andersen, a Schlesiwger assisting the Allied forces.

nothing of the fall of Als or the political situation in Copenhagen. The women, in their traditional red costume, looked like walking sealing-wax rods.

I was already on Rømø when I received orders from the command on the west coast to try a crossing.[33]

Information regarding a possible Armistice began reaching both Hammer and Schidlach during the next few days. The latter was therefore under considerable pressure to capture Hammer's force. Hammer's own lines of communication were slow and unreliable.

On July 15th, Hammer's flotilla snatched 24 small boats assembled at Hornum, on the south of Sylt. A heavy storm occurred on the night of the 15/16th, but the net was closing on Hammer. By the evening of the 17th, though there was much rumour of an Armistice, Austrian troops were landing on Föhr, supported by *Elisabeth*, *Blitz*, *Seehund*, and *Wall*. Called upon once more to surrender, Hammer refused, and he endeavoured to get his vessels away from the island. He described the scene next morning, with the steamship *Limfjorden* and cannon-yawl *Ekernsund* aground:

> Already, at 05:30 on the morning of July 18th, enemy infantry began to shoot at the flotilla. At 06:00 the enemy squadron was observed in the Wyk Roads. The steam gunboat *Blitz* closed in as far as possible on Näshorn, and together with the other vessels, started a bombardment of the ships, which had been grounded. Due to the long range, these ships sustained no damage. As the first flood approached, *Blitz* was able to get much closer. The infantry fire became more intense, and the danger to the cannon-yawl, the steamer and the crews became so apparent, that I decided to abandon the grounded ships, leaving them with their colours flying. I did not, however, withdraw further than it was possible to deny the enemy the opportunity to capture these ships, and was ready to re-board them should the water level rise enough for them to be moved.
>
> Preparations had been made to blow up *Eckernsund*. When the time came that the steamer could be re-floated, Captain Andresen, 1st Officer Fischer, Chief Engineer Gødecke, Seaman Michelsen, and others went onboard. Under enemy fire, the ship was started up, and was able soon to withdraw from the fire. As the cannon-yawl *Eckernsund* could not be saved, the primed explosives were ignited by a lone NCO of the artillery, Wissmann, who displayed great courage. Having set fire to the boat, he jumped overboard and swam to the nearest vessel.[34]

Hammer was able to move his flotilla to the area between Sylt, Föhr, and the mainland. It was merely matter of time, however, before the force would have no choice but surrender.

Schidlach, in fact, was able to trick Hammer into capitulation. Knowing that an Armistice was to come into effect at 12:00 on the 20th, he despatched an officer to Hammer on the afternoon of the 19th, with a summons to surrender. Unaware of the true position, after a meeting of his officers, he accepted the proposal.

---

33 Went von Römö, Karl, "1864. Erinnerungen eines österreichischen Kriegsmannes", *Österreichische Militärische Zeitschrift*, Volume 39, Number 1, Vienna 1898.
34 Hammer, Otto, *Vesterhavsøernes Forsvar i Aaret 1864*, pp. 89-90.

Austrian Jäger crossing to the island of Föhr (Voss)

Lieutenant-Commander Hammer offered his personal surrender, boarding the Prussian gunboat *Blitz*, Lieutenant Mac Lean, that evening.

Before the surrender, Hammer had burned the cannon-yawls, and military and naval stores. The following were captured:

Limfjorden, Augusta, one Customs cutter, ten Customs patrol vessels, one iron fire ship, two support and three transport ships.

Nine naval officers, and 185 sailors, and two officials and 51 men of the Customs service.[35]

Lieutenant-Commander Hammer had struggled against impossible odds, not only against his enemies, but also against his superiors. If his struggle was doomed, it was also admirable. Otto Vaupell writes of him; "In the writing of Hammer's *Vesterhavsøernes Forsvar i Aaret 1864*, you get a solid sense of his stubbornness and of all the adversities that he brought upon himself due to this stubbornness."

Naval and Military Operations in the Baltic to the Second Armistice

Since the resumption of hostilities, Admiral van Dockum had been able to reimpose his blockade in the Baltic, primarily of Danzig and Rügen, and to continue to bottle up the Prussian fleet with little difficulty. Blockades were declared on June 27th, of the ports of Danzig, Pillau, and Memel, granting neutral shipping 20 days to leave.[36] Two prize ships were taken, both soon after the end of the ceasefire.

First to be taken was *Glen Grant*, which was travelling from Peterhead to Stettin. She was stopped off Greifswalde by the frigate *Sjælland* on June 27th. The vessel and her cargo of 571 barrels of herring, were taken to Copenhagen. The brig

35 von Fischer, p. 369.
36 Grosser Generalstab, Volume II, p. 731.

Lieutenant-Commander Hammer after his capitulation (Pflug)

Die Eiche, en route from Windau to Leith, attempted to pass Helsingør on the night of June 29th, but unfavourable winds forced her to anchor in Humlebæk Bay for the night. The following morning, she was inspected by Customs vessel Nr. 24, and impounded along with her cargo of 2,900 rail ties/sleepers. The vessel was also taken to Copenhagen.[37]

The only challenge to van Dockum came on July 2nd, when the 3rd Gunboat Flotilla Division, (Naval) Lieutenant Arendt, comprising the 2nd Class steam gunboats *Habicht*, *Jäger*, *Salamander*, *Sperber*, and *Wolf*, steamed north from Dornbusch, off north-west Rügen, encountering two Danish blockading vessels after some nine nautical miles. These ships were the screw frigate *Tordenskjold*, (Naval) Captain Meinertz, and the steamer *Hekla*, Lieutenant-Commander Obelitz. Arendt engaged the two ships for about an hour, at an average range of about 3,000 yards. Nothing was achieved in this action, and Arendt withdrew. The Prussian navy still could not seriously worry the Danish fleet.

The existence of a powerful Austrian squadron in the North Sea, however, together with the thunderclap shock of the loss of Als, meant that the situation at sea had fundamentally changed. It was possible, after all, for the Danes to be considered a realistic threat to the major Baltic islands.

On July 10th, Commodore Suenson hoisted his flag in *Dannebrog*. His North-Sea Squadron further comprised the frigate *Niels Juel*, the corvette *Dagmar*,

37 Larsen, Kay, *Vore Priseskibe 1864.*

and the steamers *Slesvig*, *Ejderen*, and *Hermod*. The three steamers patrolled to the north, whilst the other three ships remained in the area between Jutland and Zealand to meet any force coming south. (Naval) Captain Muxoll's squadron in the western Baltic now had the prime responsibility for the defence of Funen.

On land, preparations were also being made to defend Zealand and Funen. Coastal forts were being manned and armed. There could be little optimism, however, as to the real situation in the event of a major attack. The coastal forts of Copenhagen were manned on the 1st of August, over a week after the Armistice, by a total of 907 artillery personnel, of whom 22 were officers.[38] In total there were some 5,000 men available for the city's defence, of very mixed quality.

Called to Copenhagen, General Gerlach resigned as Army Commander on July 5th, and was replaced the same day by General Steinmann. Gerlach was later appointed to command Steinmann's old 1st Division. Steinmann made energetic preparations for the defence of Funen, where the Field Army was now concentrated, and under his leadership, morale in the army rose.

Captain Aarøe's *Streifkorps*, now the strength of a reinforced battalion,[39] continued its limited depredations, much to the annoyance of the Allied high command, but of course could achieve little to alter the course of the war.

The ships of the 'Corps' had already been used in the evacuation of Als. Now operating from their new base at Kallundborg, on the north-west coast of Funen, new orders were issued to the 'Corps' on July 4th, to cover the island of Samsø, raid as and where possible, and to be alert for enemy spies. Operating from their new base at Kallundborg, on the north-west coast of Funen, the troops were anxious for action. Receiving these orders on July 6th, Aarøe resolved that launched a raid that evening to surprise a Prussian coast watch near Grenaa, on the eastern tip of Jutland. The steamer *Jylland* duly sailed with 2nd Company, Premierlieutenant Schulz.

Shortly after midnight three platoons disembarked in poor weather and made their way to the harbour. They surprised and captured seven Prussians, who had taken shelter from the rain in a warehouse along with three horses. Two other members of the shore watch escaped along the beach. By 04:30, the prisoners, one NCO and two men of the Guard Hussars, and four men of the 4th Foot Guards were embarked along with the raiders, and on their way to Kallundborg.

On the morning of the 7th, *Jylland* again steamed west, to transfer some troops from the island of Æbelo to Bøgense, on Funen. At 23:00 that night, she sailed from there for Ashoved on the Jutland coast after a report of an enemy coast watch there.[40] Disembarking at 01:00, Premierlieutenant Essmann, Second-Lieutenant Andersen, three NCOs and 36 men rowed ashore, with a guide.

This force encountered a two-man Austrian patrol along the beach, was able to remain unobserved, and shortly afterwards, discovered eight Austrians from IR Hessen, bivouacked. The camp was rapidly surrounded, and the Austrians called upon to surrender. Instead, they went for their stacked arms. The Danes fired a

---

38 See Appendix XX.
39 See Appendix XX.
40 Generalstaben, Volume III, p.293. These moves were based on intelligence received from the area.

volley and charged, mortally wounding three of the Austrians. One Austrian despite being wounded managed to escape and the remaining four were captured. One of the raiders was slightly injured, with a bayonet wound. The expedition returned to Kallundborg at 11:30 on July 8th.[41] There were no further offensive operations.

The Second Armistice

Whatever the morale of the Armed Forces, that of the Danish political classes and the country as a whole was at rock bottom. The loss of Als had been a profound shock, and there was no more stomach for war.[42] Politically, it was the final blow to the Monrad Ministry. Just before this defeat, the Danish Government had requested British assistance in the resumed struggle. This was refused on July 6th. Any further possible self-delusion on the subject was now impossible.[43] The Government resigned on July 8th, after the King formally requested it. Monrad was shocked, as he believed that he was indispensable.[44] A new Ministry, with Count Bluhme as Council-President, took office on the 11th, proposing an armistice on the following day.

Austrian Jäger on hearing the news of the Armistice
(*Illustrierte Kriegs-Berichte aus Schleswig-Holstein 1864*)

41 Ibid, pp. 292-294, Esmann, pp. 32-41
42 Sandiford, p. 116. Wenck, Captain, "Krigsledelsen I 1864", *Tidsskrift før Søvæsen*, 1914, p.563, says, "However, the morale of the government and people was destroyed by the loss of Als."
43 Sandiford, p. 117, Bjørke, Kjær, & Norrie, p. 464.
44 Schioldan-Nielsen, Johan, p. 132.

Army Headquarters was informed of this the same, day, and Colonel Kauffmann appointed as emissary to the Allied forces. An armistice was agreed to come into force at noon on July 20th. At this time, all acts of war were to cease, including the blockade of German harbours. Hostilities ceased at the agreed time, and, although the possibility of a breakdown of negotiations existed for some time, in fact, the war had ended.

15

Aftermath

Peace negotiations began in Vienna, on July 25th, although Denmark was in no position to negotiate. All of the major demands of the two Allied Powers were agreed to. The Danish delegates managed only to retain three minor enclaves of the territory of Jutland, which lay within Schleswig. It was assuredly a victor's peace. The peace treaty was signed on October 30th, 1864. King Christian's representatives not only had to pay a large financial compensation to Prussia and Austria, but also had to sign away the three Duchies.

For Denmark, the war was an unmitigated disaster, and its effects linger in the national consciousness even today. 40% of the King's subjects in 1863 no longer held that status in 1865. At a stroke, the country had become a nation state, almost without minorities. The Danish speaking majority in north Slesvig would not return to rule from Copenhagen until 1920.

All the participants in the conflict and every country in Europe knew that Denmark could not win a war against one of the Great Powers, let alone two. However, with the practical support of any of the other Great Powers, and even a little flexibility by the Monrad government, she might have avoided catastrophic defeat. To believe blindly in British intervention was simply foolish. That she did not have this support was crucial, and she alone was to blame for the isolation which befell her both in the precipitation of the crisis, and during the London Conference. International political irrelevance was the consequence. She cannot, however, be blamed alone for underestimating Bismarck – everyone did.

As elsewhere in Europe, Danish nationalism was a rampant force in the middle of the 19th Century, and, perhaps inevitably, spawned the Eider Dane movement. Ultimately, however, it could not stand against the huge forces of German nationalism boiling to the south. Those who thought that it could, or simply did not think about it at all, were misguided. The government may have misled the public on the issue of war, but the public wished to be so duped. Little scepticism, and almost no opposition, was voiced against the government's policy on Schleswig. Equally, the romantic vision of Scandinavism proved to be an illusion. In practice, the people of Sweden and Norway were not convinced that the Eider was a vitally important frontier between 'Scandinavia' and 'Germany'.

For Bismarck, the campaign could almost be described as a controlled experiment. After the victory, his prestige in the country grew, and his control of the situation along with it. He felt little respect for the Army, which he regarded as simply another government department which he had turned around. Much later, he would write in his memoirs:

> It is extraordinary that Caprivi (at the time referred to, 1872, a Colonel in the War Ministry) did not remember in that connection how before, and at the time of my taking office in 1862, the army had been attacked, criticised, and curtailed in step-motherly fashion by civilians, and how during my office and

under my guidance it had been raised from its common place garrison existence, and from 1864 to 1871 had passed by way of Düppel, Sadowa, and Sedan, to three triumphal entries into Berlin. I may presume without exaggeration that King William would have abdicated in 1862, that the policy which laid the foundations of the glory of the army would never have come into being, or, at any rate, not in that fashion, if I had not taken over its direction. Would the army have had the opportunity of performing the deeds of heroism and Count Moltke been able to draw his sword if King William I had received other counsels from other persons? Assuredly not, if he had abdicated in 1862 because he could find no one prepared to share and to face the dangers of his position.[1]

Even allowing for the towering ego involved, and the considerable benefit of hindsight, such was the road that the conflict of 1864 had placed him on. An enduring friendship with Russia was the key to success, and he was able to fully benefit from it. That his short-sighted successors squandered this is part of another story.

British policy had proven disastrously wanting throughout the whole of 1863 and the war itself. Only a full rapprochement with France might have altered the situation, and this was never seriously sought. In European matters, her voice would not be taken seriously for almost 15 years.

The one matter not decided by the Treaty of Vienna was what would become of the Duchies themselves. Count Rechberg, the Austrian foreign minister, fell from power three days before the peace treaty was signed. A man who was Bismarck's intellectual, but not political equal, Rechberg was a victim of the growing anti-Prussian faction in the Austrian government. From this point, relations between the two nations began to decline. A power struggle over Germany was inevitable, and the fuse was lit by a disagreement over the future of Schleswig and Holstein. The result would be war just over 18 months later.

Militarily, within the realm of tactics, officers had much to consider from this brief campaign. The breech-loading rifle may not have won the war, but it is absurd to believe that it was thought unimportant or that it went unnoticed. Many thoughtful officers in all armies realised the possibilities of these weapons. Nevertheless, only the Prussian and Danish armies (or perhaps more accurately, treasuries) immediately learned the lesson.

It is quite possible that had further fighting occurred alternative tactical methods might have been tried by the Imperial troops. Heavy loss in attack had been noted by some of those who had undertaken it. On June 23rd 1866, at the start of the Austro-Prussian War, the Duke of Württemberg, promoted to Major-General for his part in the assault at Oeversee (where he had also been wounded) and now a brigade commander, had a chance meeting with officers from his old regiment, the 'Belgier'. Himself a champion of the breech-loading rifle, he said to them, "Gentlemen! Forget everything that I have told you; the bayonet will

---

1   *Bismarck, the Man and the Statesman,* Volume II, New York and London 1899, pp. 166-167.

achieve nothing against the needle gun".[2] Prior to this campaign, nothing was yet 'set in stone'.

Rifled artillery, however, was immediately hailed as a major new force in warfare. Its use here was profoundly felt throughout Europe, and was infinitely more influential than any examples from the American Civil War. The Prussian Army had learned much about siege warfare. Its field artillery, though, had learned little. In the summer of 1866 it would be dominated by the Austrian artillery and, learning from that experience, would go on to become a formidable weapon in yet another war – with a France that would not intervene six years before.

A small conflict in northern Europe thus had incalculable repercussions. How different things might have been, had Council-President Monrad accepted, on either of two occasions, a proposed compromise. After 1864, it was too late.

2   Prybila, Carl, *Geschichte des k.k. Infanterie-Regiments Leopold II. König der Belgier Nr. 27*, Vienna 1882, p.879.

Appendices

Appendices

I

Selective Glossary of Alternative Place/Feature Names

Danish	Place/Feature	Location	German
Amrom	Island	North Frisian Islands	Amrum
Aabenraa/Åbenrå	Town	North of Flensburg	Apenrade
Adsbøl	Village	Sundeved peninsula	Atzbüll
Als	Island	East coast of Schleswig	Alsen
Arnhølt	Village and Lake	West of Schleswig town	Arenholz
Arnæs	Town	North bank of the Schlei	Arnis
Avnbjerg	Height	Sundeved peninsula	Spitzberge
Avnbøl	Village	Sundeved peninsula	Auenbüll
Bilskov	Village	South Schleswig	Bilschau
Bov	Village	North of Flensburg	Bau
Bøgeskov	Village		Beuschau
Broager	Small Peninsula	South of Sundeved peninsula	Broacker
Bustrup	Village	South of Schleswig town	Bustorf
Danevirke	Fortified position	South Schleswig	Danewerke
Dagebøl	Village	West Coast of Schleswig	Dagebüll
Dybbøl	Villages (E&W)/		
Fortified position	Sundeved peninsula	Düppel	
Eckernførde	Town and Bay	North-west of Kiel	Eckernförde
Eggebæk	Village	South of Flensburg	Eggebek
Fartorp	Village	South of Schleswig town	Fahrdorf
Ejder	River/canal	Kiel to Tönning	Eider
Fanø	Island	North Frisian Islands	Fanö

349

Flækkeby	Village	South-west of Missunde	Fleckeby
Flensborg	Town	On Flensburg Bay	Flensburg
Frederiksstad	Fortress	South-west Schleswig	Friedrichstadt
Freydendal	Farmsteads (Old&New)	Sundeved peninsula	Friedenthal
Geltorp	Village	South of Schleswig town	Geltorf
Gettorp	Village	North-west of Kiel	Gettorf
Graasten/Gråsten	Village/Castle	South Schleswig	Gravenstein
Gottorp	Castle	Schleswig town	Gottorf
Haderslev	Town	North Slesvig	Hadersleben
Hanved	Village	West of Flensburg	Handewitt
Harreslev	Village	North of Flensburg	Harrislee
Hellingbæk Kro	Inn/Tavern	North of Schleswig town	Helligbek Krug
Harresby	Village	East of Flensburg	Hardesby
Holsten	Duchy	Holstein	
Hønsnap	Village	North of Flensburg	Hönschnap
Hysby	Village	East of Flensburg	Hüsby
Jaruplund	Village	South of Flensburg	Jarplund
Julskov	Hamlet	East of Oeversee	Julschau
Kappel	Town	North bank of the Schlei	Cappeln
Kjær	Village/Peninsula	On Als island	Kjär
Klosterkro	Hamlet/Rail station	West of Ober Selk	Klosterkrug
Kluvensiek	Village	Along the Eider Canal	Cluvensiek
Kokkendorf	Village/Fortified position	North of the Eider Canal	Kochendorf
Kongshøj	Hill	Central Danewerke	Königshügel
Kurgraven	Early rampart	South of Schleswig town	Kograben/
Kurgraben			

Lyksborg	Town	North-east of Flensburg	Glücksburg
Margethenvolden	Early rampart	South of Schleswig town	Margarethen Wall
Moldened	Village	North of the Schlei	Moldenil
Mysunde	Village	North bank of the Schlei	Missunde
Nybøl	Village	Sundeved peninsula	Nübel
Oversø	Village	South of Flensburg	Översee
Ovreselk	Village	South of Schleswig town	Ober Selk
Øvrestolk	Village	North of Schleswig town	Ober Stolk
Pelvom	Island	North Frisian Islands	Pellworm
Ragebøl	Village	Sundeved peninsula	Rackebüll
Rendsborg	Town	North Holstein	Rendsburg
Rønhave	Village	Kjær Peninsula, Als	Rönhof
Rømø	Island	North Frisian islands	Römö
Saksarmen	Early rampart	South of Schleswig town	Die Oldenburg
Sild	Island	North Frisian Islands	Sylt
Silvested	Village	West of Schleswig town	Silberstedt
Skaleby	Village	North of the Schlei	Schaalby
Skodsbøl	Village	Sundeved peninsula	Schottsbüll
Skovby	Village	North-east of Eckernförde	Schuby
Slesvig	Duchy & Town	Schleswig	
Slien	Fjord	East of Schleswig town	Schlei
Smøl	Village	Broager peninsula	Schmöl
Snogbæk	Villages (E & W)	Mainland opposite N. Als	Schnabek
Sorge	River	South Schleswig	Sorgen
Sottrup	Villages (E&W)	Sundeved peninsula	Satrup

Stavgaarde	Village	Sundeved peninsula	Stabegaard
Sundeved	Peninsula	North-east of Flensburg	Sundewitt
Svansen	Peninsula	South of the Schlei	Schwansen
Sønderborg	Town	South-west Als	Sonderburg
Sønderskov	Wood	South of Oeversee	Süderholz
Sørthoj	Hill	Central Danewerke	Schwarze Berg
Tonder	Town	West of Flensburg	Tondern
Trenen	Creek/stream	South of Flensburg	Treene
Ulkebøl	Village	South Als	Ulkebüll
Ullerup	Village	Sundeved peninsula	Ulderup
Vedelspang ("north")	Village	North of Schleswig town	Wedelspang
Vedelspang ("south")	Village	Danewerke	Wedelspang
Vemmingbund	Bay/Inlet	South of Sundeved	Wenningbund
Vejle	Town	Jutland	Veile
Vindeby	Village	Windeby	

II

Glossary of Terminology, Abbreviations and Symbols in Common Usage in this Book

Abbreviations

Coy.	Company
FJB	FeldjägerBataillons, Jäger battalion (Austrian)
FML	Feldmarschall-Lieutenant – Lieutenant General (Austrian)
F	Fusilier (Prussian)
FR	Fusilier Regiment (Prussian)
GR	Grenadier Regiment (Prussian)
GGR	Guard Grenadier Regiment (Prussian)
How.	Howitzer
IR	Infantry Regiment (Austrian/Prussian)
Nr.	Number
SB	Smoothbore

Symbols

Units are represented by numbers and/or words, placed either side of an oblique stroke. A name or Arabic numeral placed after an oblique gives the name or number of the particular regiment. A battalion of an infantry regiment is shown by a Roman numeral before the oblique. Thus, II/4th represents the Second Battalion of the Danish Fourth Infantry Regiment. II/IR15 represents the Second Battalion of the Prussian Infantry Regiment Number 15. F/IR15 represents the Fusilier Battalion of Prussian Infantry Regiment Number 15. II/Hessen represents the Second Battalion of the Austrian Infantry Regiment Number 14. Austrian regiments are referred to in the text by the name of their owners rather than by their numbers, both because it was common to do so during this period and also to avoid any possible confusion with Prussian units.

A battery, company, or squadron is shown by an Arabic numeral placed before the oblique. Therefore, 1/4th denotes the First Company of the Danish Fourth Infantry regiment, 1/IR15, the First Company of Prussian Infantry Regiment Number 15, and 1/Hessen, the First Company of Austrian Infantry Regiment Number 14. 1/9th FJB represents the First Company of the Austrian 9th Jäger Battalion, whereas 1/3rd Jäger represents the First Company of the Prussian 3rd Jäger Battalion.

Examples for cavalry would be: 1/4th Dragoons, representing, the First Squadron of the Danish Fourth Dragoon Regiment, 2/11th Uhlans, representing

354 BISMARCK'S FIRST WAR

the Second Squadron of Prussian Uhlan Regiment Number 11, and 1/Windischgrätz, representing the First Squadron of Austrian Dragoon Regiment Number 2. As Danish cavalry comprised only dragoons and the Guard Hussar regiment, this identification is greatly simplified.

For artillery, the matter is also simplified. Danish field artillery is referred to by battery numbers only, without reference to higher formations. Austrian artillery represented in the campaign were drawn exclusively from the 1st Regiment. Therefore 4/1st Four Pounder represents the Fourth Battery of First Artillery Regiment. Prussian artillery, at this time organised in brigades, is shown, with some clarified exceptions, in the same way. For example, 2nd Fortress Company/ Artillery Brigade Nr. 4 represents precisely that, whereas 1st 6 Pounder/Artillery Brigade Nr. 7 represents the First Six Pounder Battery of Artillery Brigade Number 7.

Terminology

Aspirant (Danish)	Cadet, either for NCO or Officer
Brigade	Mixed Arms force (Austrian)
Brigade	Single Arm force of more than one regiment (Danish/Prussian). Also the higher organisational entity within the Prussian Artillery.
Corps	Mixed Arms force composed of four brigades (Austrian) or of more than one Division (Prussian), plus other forces
Corps	An ad hoc or mobile force for specific purposes
Division	Mixed Arms force composed of more than one Brigade plus additional units (Danish/Prussian)
division	Austrian tactical sub-unit of two companies (infantry) or two/three squadrons (cavalry)
Gendarmerie	Paramilitary Police
Jäger	Light infantry (Austrian/Prussian)
knicks	Thick hedges with earth banks, commonly found in northern Germany and southern Denmark.
Konstabel (Danish)	Artillery Private who is part of a gun crew. Modern usage would refer to a professional soldier
Oberlieutenant (Austrian)	Lieutenant/First Lieutenant/Lieutenant
Premierlieutenant (Danish)	Lieutenant/First Lieutenant (sometimes hyphenated depending upon period, document etc. This spelling is used for consistency.)
Premier-Lieutenant (Prussian)	Description as above

Ritmester (Danish) Rittmeister(Prussian/Austrian)	Captain (Cavalry)
Uhlan (Prussian)	Lancer
Undercorporal (Danish)	Lance-Corporal/PFC

III

Order of Battle, Royal Danish Army Danewerke Position 1st February 1864

Army Commander	Lieutenant-General Ch. J. de Meza
Chief of Staff	Colonel H.A.T. Kauffmann
Deputy Chief of Staff	Captain L.C. Rosen
Naval Liaison Officer (Naval)	Captain F. Frøhlich
Adjutants	Ritmester H. C. W. F. Deichmann
Captain	C. E. Mehldal
Premierlieutenants	F. F. Jacobi, A.L. le Maire, E.G. Gotschalk, F.W. Count Ahleveldt-Laurvigen, C.H. L. Giese, A. C. N. W.Holstein (of the War Reserve)
Second-Lieutenant	C. A. S. Dalberg
Commander, Artillery	Lieutenant -General M. Lüttichau
Chief of Staff, Artillery	Major J. T. Wegener
Commander, Engineers	Lieutenant-Colonel J.C.F. Dreyer
Chief of Staff, Engineers	Major C.F.N. Schrøder
Commander Train	Ritmester W. Haffner
Orderly Officers	Ritmester C.E. Hansen
Staff Quartermaster	General War Commissary U.C. von Schmidten
Staff Auditor	Senior Auditor N. Tvede
Staff Surgeon	Senior Surgeon J Rørbye
Staff Veterinarian	Staff Veterinarianl C.L. Friis
Army Telegraph & Topography	Lieutenant-Colonel W.H.F. Abrahamson
Head of Administration	Principal of the War Ministry C.J. Westergaard

1st Division

Divisional Commander	Lieutenant-General G.D. Gerlach
Chief of Staff	Major C.F. Stiernholm
Deputy Chief of Staff	Ritmester J.Z. Schroll
Adjutants	Second-Lieutenant L.H. Westphal
	Second-Lieutenant C. Søltoft
Orderly Officer	Second-Lieutenant W.F. Bendz

1st Brigade

Brigade Commander	Colonel G.H. Lasson
Adjutant	Premierlieutenant P.F.W. Hansen
Orderly Officer	Premierlieutenant J.E.C. Rosen

2nd Infantry Regiment - Lieutenant-Colonel C.W.L. Dreyer
    I Battalion (1st, 2nd, 5th, 6th Companies)
    II Battalion (3rd, 4th, 7th, 8th Companies)
22nd Infantry Regiment - Lieutenant-Colonel J.A.F Falkenskjold
    I Battalion (1st, 2nd, 3rd, 4th Companies)
    II Battalion (5th, 6th, 7th, 8th Companies)

2nd Brigade

Commander	Major-General C.A. Vogt
Adjutants	Second-Lieutenant C.F.F.E. Tuxen
	Second-Lieutenant P.E.M. Ramsing
Orderly Officer	Second-Lieutenant J.W.B. Benedictsen

3rd Infantry Regiment - Major H.W. Mathieson
    I Battalion (1st, 2nd, 5th, 6th Companies)
    II Battalion (3rd, 4th, 7th, 8th Companies)
18th Infantry Regiment - Lieutenant-Colonel F.G.H. Hirsch
    I Battalion (1st, 2nd, 5th, 7th Companies)
    II Battalion (3rd, 4th, 6th, 8th Companies)

3rd Brigade

Commander	Colonel J.A.P.F. Wørishøffer
Adjutant	Second-Lieutenant J.G.F. Colding
Orderly Officer	Premierlieutenant (of the War Reserve)
	F.J.L. Hein

16th Infantry Regiment - Major C. Wolle
    I Battalion (1st, 2nd, 5th, 6th Companies)
    II Battalion (3rd, 4th, 7th, 8th Companies)
17th Infantry Regiment - Colonel A. Bernstorff
    I Battalion (1st, 2nd, 5th, 7th Companies)
    II Battalion (3rd, 4th, 6th, 8th Companies)
4th Dragoon Regiment -
    2nd Half Regiment - Major C.A.F. Lillienskjold
    (4th, 5th, 6th Squadrons)

Divisional Troops

Divisional Artillery	Major P.E. Glahn

2nd Field Artillery Battery - Captain O. Lunn
       Eight rifled 4 pounder field guns
          10th Field Artillery Battery - Captain J.C. Johansen
       Eight smoothbore 12 pounder cannon

Divisional Engineers	Major C.T. Jørgensen
	Premierlieutenant O. J. Larssen

5th Engineer Company - Premierlieutenant M.O. Asmussen
    Divisional Magazine with Provisions Column
    Brigade Magazines
    Field Ambulance
    Field Hospital

Wagon Park (Approximately 300 vehicles on 4th February)

2nd Division

Commander	Major-General P.H.C. du Plat
Chief of Staff	Major E.F. Schau
Deputy Chief of Staff	Captain A.J.C.E Madsen
Adjutant	Second-Lieutenant M.S.F. Hedemann
Orderly Officer	Second-Lieutenant H.C.W. Harboe

4th Brigade

Commander	Major-General E.H.C. Wilster
From General Staff	Captain J.A.F. Hoffmann
Adjutants	Second-Lieutenant A. Harttnung
	Second-Lieutenant E.O. Mygind
Orderly Officer	Second-Lieutenant (of the War Reserve)

P.O.R. Olrik

4th Infantry Regiment - Colonel T.C. Faaborg
    I Battalion (1st, 2nd, 5th, 7th Companies)
    II Battalion (3rd, 4th, 6th, 8th Companies)
6th Infantry Regiment - Major G.W. Caroc
    I Battalion (1st, 2nd, 5th, 6th Companies)
    II Battalion (3rd, 4th, 7th, 8th Companies)

5th Brigade

Commander	Colonel J.W.A. Harbou
Adjutant	Premierlieutenant H.C. Baron Haxthausen
Orderly Officer	Second-Lieutenant P.H.W. Lange

7th Infantry Regiment - Lieutenant-Colonel L.H.L. Muus
    I Battalion (1st, 2nd, 5th, 7th Companies)
    II Battalion (3rd, 4th, 6th, 8th Companies)
12th Infantry Regiment – Colonel F.L.A. Hein
    I Battalion (1st, 2nd, 3rd, 4th Companies)
    II Battalion (5th, 6th, 7th, 8th Companies)

6th Brigade

Commander	Colonel O.C.S.A Bülow
Adjutant	Second-Lieutenant C.J.C.F Kranold
Orderly Officer	Second-Lieutenant (of the War Reserve)
	W.L. Dinesen

5th infantry Regiment - Major A.C.J. Myhre
    I Battalion (1st, 2nd, 5th, 6th Companies)
    II Battalion (3rd, 4th, 7th, 8th Companies)
10th Infantry Regiment - Colonel F.C. Lange
    I Battalion (1st, 2nd, 5th, 7th Companies)
    II Battalion (3rd, 4th, 6th, 8th Companies)
Guard Hussar Regiment –

1st Half Regiment Ritmester D.W. Hegermann-Lindencrone
(2nd, 4th, 6th Squadrons)

Divisional Troops

Divisional Artillery   Major W.E. Schøning
      7th Field Artillery Battery - Captain W.P.J. Johansen
          eight rifled 4 pounder field guns
          9th Field Artillery Battery - Major E. Schreiber
          eight smoothbore 12 pounder cannon
Divisional Engineers   Captain N.J. Brummer
                         Premierlieutenant J.H.K. Bangert
1st Engineer Company   Premierlieutenant W. Kolderup-Rosenvinge
Divisional Magazine with Provisions Column
      Brigade Magazines
      Two Field Ambulances
      Two Field Hospitals
      Wagon Park

3rd Division

Commander   Major-General P.F. Steinmann
Chief of Staff   Captain J.C. Blom
Deputy Chief of Staff   Captain C.M.W. Tvermoes
Adjutants   Premierlieutenant W.E.A. Bülow
                    Premierlieutenant F. Grüner
Orderly Officer   Premierlieutenant H.E.E. Nysted

7th Brigade

Commander   Colonel C.F.M. Müller
Adjutant   Second-Lieutenant F.J. Buchwaldt
Orderly Officer   Second-Lieutenant (of the War Reserve)
                    S.F. Fischer
      1st Infantry Regiment - Lieutenant-Colonel H.C.J. Beck
          I Battalion (1st, 2nd, 6th, 7th Companies)
          II Battalion (3rd, 4th, 5th, 8th Companies)
      11th Infantry Regiment - Major J.M.F.F. Rist
          I Battalion (1st, 3rd, 5th, 7th Companies)
          II Battalion (2nd, 4th, 6th, 8th Companies)

8th Brigade

Commander   Colonel P.U. Scharffenberg
Adjutants   Second-Lieutenant H. Holbøll
                    Second-Lieutenant C.J.F. Irminger
      9th Infantry Regiment - Lieutenant-Colonel H.C.G. Tersling
          I Battalion (1st, 2nd, 5th, 6th Companies)
          II Battalion (3rd, 4th, 7th, 8th Companies)
      20th Infantry Regiment - Lieutenant-Colonel J.G. Scholten
          I Battalion (1st, 2nd, 5th, 6th Companies)

II Battalion (3rd, 4th, 7th, 8th Companies)

9th Brigade

Commander	Colonel W. Neergaard
Adjutants	Premierlieutenant (of the War Reserve) J. Petersen
	Second-Lieutenant M.A. Karmark
Orderly Officer	Second-Lieutenant (of the War Reserve) Th. E. Frisch

19th Infantry Regiment - Lieutenant-Colonel L.N. Færch
   I Battalion (5th, 6th, 7th, 8th Companies)
   II Battalion (1st, 2nd, 3rd, 4th Companies)
21st Infantry Regiment - Lieutenant-Colonel G.J.W. Nielsen
   I Battalion (1st, 2nd, 3rd, 4th Companies)
   II Battalion (5th, 6th, 7th 8th Companies)
4th Dragoon Regiment-
   1st Half Regiment - Major A.W. Gerlach
   (1st, 2nd, 3rd Squadrons)

Divisional Troops

Divisional Artillery	Major J.C. Just

   11th Field Artillery Battery - Captain M.E. Fallesen
     Eight rifled 4 pounder field guns
     12th Field Artillery Battery - Major J.D.Z. v.d. Recke
     Eight smoothbore 12 pounder cannon

Divisional Engineers	Captain W.O.W. Lehmann & Captain H. Christensen
2nd Engineer Company	Captain P.F.H. Bruun

Divisional Magazine with Provisions Column
   Brigade Magazines
   Two Field Ambulances
   Three Field Hospitals
   Wagon Park (Approximately 250 vehicles on 4th February)

4th (Cavalry) Division

Commander	Lieutenant C.D. Hegermann-Lindencrone
Chief of Staff	Major F.A. Heramb
Deputy Chief of Staff	Captain C.A.F. Thomsen
Adjutant	Second-Lieutenant T.G. Rohde
Orderly Officers	Second-Lieutenant H.H. Lüttichau
	Second-Lieutenant F.E.W. Paulsen

1st Cavalry Brigade

Commander	Major-General J.J. Honnens
Adjutant	Second-Lieutenant H.B. Dahl
Orderly Officer	Second-Lieutenant A.L. Baadsgaard

   3rd Dragoon Regiment - Major F.L. Brock

(1st, 2nd, 3rd, 4th, 5th, 6th Squadrons)
5th Dragoon Regiment - Lieutenant-Colonel N.S. Brock
(1st, 2nd, 3rd, 4th, 5th, 6th Squadrons)
2nd Cavalry Brigade

Commander	Colonel H.L. Scharffenberg[1]
Adjutant	Second-Lieutenant
	J. F. Hegermann – Lindencrone
Orderly Officer	Second-Lieutenant (of the War Reserve)
	F.S.W. Baron Juel-Brockdorff

6th Dragoon Regiment – Lieutenant-Colonel F.C.A. Bauditz
(1st, 2nd, 3rd, 4th, 5th, 6th Squadrons)

Divisional Troops

Divisional Artillery
5th Field Artillery Battery – Captain C.J.F. Lønborg[2]
Eight 12 pound howitzers
Divisional Magazine with Provisions Column
Brigade Magazines
Field Hospital
Wagon Park (Approximately 200 vehicles)

Army Infantry Reserve[3]

Commander	Major-General F.W.C. Caroc
Chief of Staff	Captain L.E. Fog
Adjutants	Second-Lieutenant G.C.C. Zachariae
	Second-Lieutenant E.A.A. Marcussen
Orderly Officer	Second-Lieutenant C.M. Wildenradt

8th Infantry Regiment – Colonel M.O.B. Hveberg
I Battalion (1st, 2nd, 5th, 8th Companies)
II Battalion (3rd, 4th, 6th, 7th Companies)
15th Infantry regiment – Lieutenant Colonel A.F. Zepelin
I Battalion (1st, 2nd, 5th, 6th Companies)
II Battalion (3rd, 4th, 7th, 8th Companies)
Brigade Magazine
Two Ambulances

Army Artillery[4]

Commander	Lieutenant-General M. Lüttichau
Chief of Staff	Major J.T. Wegener
Deputy Chief of Staff	Major P.C.B. Boeck
Attached from	

1 Colonel Scharffenberg assumed command of the Brigade on 3rd February.
2 Joined the Division on 2nd February.
3 Major-General Caroc assumed command of the Reserve on 3rd February.
4 Also under Lüttichau's command, but not at the Danewerke Position were the following:

General Staff   Major H.A.A. de Jonquières
                                 Captain P.S. Bjerring
                                 Premierlieutenant S.V.W. Pfaff
                                 Premierlieutenant C. Th. Müllertz

Divisional Troops

Reserve Artillery   Lieutenant-Colonel C.U.E. Haxthausen[5]
   1st Field Artillery Battery   Captain N.P.C.T Bruus
      Eight rifled 4 pounder field guns
   6th Field Artillery Battery – Major F. Jürgensen
      eight smoothbore 12 pounder cannon
   8th Field Artillery Battery – Captain F.W.F. Messerschmidt
      eight rifled 4 pounder field guns
   13th Field Artillery Battery – Captain J.W. Salto
      eight 24 pound howitzers (temporarily detached to 1st Division)
Artillery Command, Danewerke Position – Colonel J.Wahl
   1st Fortress Company – Captain O. Moltke
   3rd Fortress Company – Captain T.B. Sick
   5th Fortress Company – Captain H.P.W. Mønster
   6th Fortress Company – Captain H. C. Hertel
Danewerke Position Artillery Park – Captain E.E.S. Thestrup
Fieldpark – Premierlieutenant J.L.C. Pedersen

Engineer Command Field Army[6]

Commander   Lieutenant-Colonel J.C.F. Dreyer
Chief of Staff   Major C.F.N. Schrøder
Attached from   Captain V.A. Thulstrup
General Staff   Premierlieutenant F.L.J. Keyper
                                 Second-Lieutenant S.B.V. Dyhr
   3rd Engineer Company – Captain E.M. Dalgas
   Engineers Park – Captain H.F.F. Jastrau
   Army Trains Command – Ritmester W. Haffner
   Mobile Horse Depot
      Veterinary Horse Depot
      Wagon Park

---

5   Joined on 3rd February by 3rd Field Artillery Battery – Captain A.L. Klein, eight rifled 4 pounder field guns

6   Also under Dreyer's command, but not at the Danewerke Position were the following: On Als, Bridging Company – Captain J.C.G. Hedemann (mustering) and the Reserve Engineer Park. At Fredericia (reporting to the Fortress Commander), 4th Engineer Company – Premierlieutenant C.A. Nielsen.

IV

Danish Army Combatants with Designated Units

Fit for duty - February 1st 1864

| | Officers | | | | NCO's | | | | Musicians | | | | | |
	Line	Reserve & Temporary	Foreign	Total	Line	Reserve	Temporary	Total	Line	Reserve	Total	Undercorporals	Men	Total
1st Infantry Brigade Staff	3	–	–	3	–	–	–	–	–	–	–	–	7	10
2nd Infantry Brigade Staff	3	1	–	4	–	–	–	–	–	–	–	–	3	7
3rd Infantry Brigade Staff	2	1	–	3	–	–	–	–	–	–	–	–	2	5
4th Infantry Brigade Staff	4	1	–	5	–	–	–	–	–	–	–	–	–	5
5th Infantry Brigade Staff	3	–	–	3	–	–	–	–	–	–	–	–	–	3
6th Infantry Brigade Staff	2	1	–	3	–	–	–	–	–	–	–	–	–	3
7th Infantry Brigade Staff	2	1	–	3	–	–	–	–	–	–	–	–	2	5
8th Infantry Brigade Staff	3	–	–	3	–	–	–	–	–	–	–	–	2	5
9th Infantry Brigade Staff	2	2	–	4	–	–	–	–	–	–	–	–	2	6
Life Guards Infantry	15	1	–	16	56	–	–	56	17	–	17	70	637	796
1st Infantry Regiment	17	15	–	32	30	14	21	65	14	11	25	157	1061	1340
2nd Infantry Regiment	20	16	–	36	29	8	35	72	14	10	24	144	1361	1637

3rd Infantry Regiment	16	18	—	34	25	7	36	68	15	11	26	132	1338	1598
4th Infantry Regiment	17	19	—	36	34	12	28	74	15	12	27	146	1303	1586
5th Infantry Regiment	18	14	—	32	31	9	29	69	14	10	24	144	1165	1434
6th Infantry Regiment	18	19	—	37	35	4	33	72	16	10	26	135	1383	1653
7th Infantry Regiment	14	14	—	28	28	26	14	68	17	8	25	136	1352	1609
8th Infantry Regiment	18	14	—	32	28	16	26	70	9	11	20	144	1288	1554
9th Infantry Regiment	19	16	—	35	32	12	31	75	15	8	23	149	1307	1589
10th Infantry Regiment	15	16	—	31	23	8	32	63	16	10	26	139	1170	1429
11th Infantry Regiment	20	14	—	34	30	10	27	67	15	8	23	143	1221	1488
12th Infantry Regiment	17	16	—	33	31	12	25	68	17	8	25	145	1443	1714
13th Infantry Regiment	18	16	—	34	27	7	30	64	16	10	26	146	1243	1513
14th Infantry Regiment	14	15	—	29	24	3	—	27	16	—	16	—	—	72
15th Infantry Regiment	17	14	—	31	26	2	36	64	13	10	23	141	1519	1778
16th Infantry Regiment	17	15	—	32	29	2	32	63	15	10	25	121	1604	1842
17th Infantry Regiment	17	15	—	32	24	4	20	48	14	3	17	123	1446	1666
18th Infantry Regiment	19	17	—	36	29	7	27	63	14	14	28	113	1269	1509
19th Infantry Regiment	15	16	—	31	30	17	22	69	15	11	26	141	1306	1573
20th Infantry Regiment	18	17	—	35	30	8	28	66	14	10	24	135	1294	1554
21st Infantry Regiment	17	18	—	35	29	8	35	72	14	11	25	144	1218	1494
22nd Infantry Regiment	17	18	—	35	26	1	38	65	15	6	21	132	846	1099
Garrison Battalions (note)	4	8	—	12	—	—	—	55	—	—	16	88	1265	1436
1st Cavalry Brigade Staff	3	—	—	3	—	—	—	—	—	—	—	1	6	10

2nd Cavalry Brigade Staff	2	1	–	3	–	–	–	–	–	–	–	–	11	14
3rd Cavalry Brigade Staff	2	1	–	3	–	–	–	–	–	–	–	–	4	7
Life Guards Cavalry	7	–	–	7	13	–	–	13	7	–	7	8	99	134
Guard Hussar 1st Half Regiment	10	1	–	11	20	–	5	25	6	–	6	14	188	244
Guard Hussar 2nd Half Regiment	10	–	–	10	23	–	3	26	5	–	5	21	250	312
2nd Dragoon Regiment	16	4	–	20	38	–	21	59	13	–	13	40	518	650
3rd Dragoon Regiment	15	4	–	19	38	–	15	53	12	–	12	34	480	598
4th Dragoon Regiment/1st Half Regiment	8	–	–	8	18	–	4	22	5	2	7	9	222	268
4th Dragoon Regiment/2nd Half Regiment	8	1	–	9	19	–	2	21	3	1	4	12	194	240
5th Dragoon Regiment	18	1	–	19	38	–	16	54	13	–	13	39	604	731
6th Dragoon Regiment	16	3	–	19	36	3	1	40	12	–	12	42	618	731
Artillery Reserve Staff	2	–	–	2	–	–	–	–	–	–	–	–	1	1	4
1st Division Artillery Command	1	1	–	2	–	–	–	–	–	–	–	–	–	2
2nd Division Artillery Command	2	–	–	2	–	–	–	–	–	–	–	–	1	3
3rd Division Artillery Command	2	–	–	2	–	–	–	–	–	–	–	–	–	2
Artillery Command/Dannevirke	2	–	–	2	–	–	–	–	–	–	–	–	–	2
Artillery Command/Dybbol	1	1	–	2	–	–	–	–	–	–	–	–	–	2
Artillery Command/Fredericia	2	–	–	2	2	–	–	2	–	–	–	–	–	4
1st Battery	2	–	–	2	8	–	1	9	2	–	2	15	136	164

2nd Battery	2	1	–	3	8	–	1	9	2	–	2	19	131	164
3rd Battery	3	–	–	3	9	–	1	10	2	–	2	18	133	166
4th Battery	3	–	–	3	8	–	1	9	2	–	2	22	208	244'
5th Battery	3	–	–	3	9	–	1	10	2	–	2	17	132	164
6th Battery	2	1	–	3	7	–	1	8	2	–	2	21	164	198
7th Battery	2	–	–	2	10	–	1	11	3	–	3	19	145	180
8th Battery	2	–	–	2	10	–	–	10	3	–	3	18	135	168
9th Battery	2	–	–	2	8	5	1	14	3	–	3	22	167	208
10th Battery	2	–	–	2	9	–	1	10	3	–	3	21	172	208
11th Battery	2	–	–	2	7	2	–	9	3	–	3	20	145	179
12th Battery	2	1	–	3	8	2	–	10	2	–	2	21	170	206
13th Battery	2	–	–	2	8	–	–	8	2	–	2	15	165	192
1st Fortress Company	1	6	–	7	4	3	–	7	–	1	1	27	275	317
2nd Fortress Company	1	2	–	3	6	3	–	9	–	–	–	7	164	183
3rd Fortress Company	3	8	–	11	9	11	–	20	–	2	2	29	378	440
4th Fortress Company	1	6	–	7	4	4	–	8	–	–	–	–	125	140
5th Fortress Company	1	5	–	6	5	4	–	9	–	–	–	22	231	268
6th Fortress Company	1	2	–	3	4	4	–	8	–	–	–	13	180	204
Engineer Troops	14	–	–	14	23	22	–	45	1	–	1	31	286	377
Headquarters and Ordnance	13	2	–	15	4	–	7	11	–	–	–	16	154	196
Telegraph & Topography	1	3	–	4	8	–	–	8	–	–	–	2	30	44

Engineer Cmd Field Army	11	–	–	11	3	–	–	3	–	–	–	1	4	19
Army Artillery	6	–	–	6	2	2	–	4	–	–	–	–	–	10
1st Division Staff	6	–	–	6	–	–	–	–	–	–	–	–	–	6
2nd Division Staff	5	–	–	5	2	–	–	2	–	–	–	1	–	8
3rd Division Staff	6	–	–	6	–	–	–	–	26	–	26	–	–	32
4th Division Staff	6	–	–	6	3	–	–	3	–	–	–	–	6	15
Infantry Reserve Staff	5	–	–	5	–	–	–	–	–	–	–	2	10	17
Command on Alsen	2	–	–	2	–	–	–	–	–	–	–	–	–	2
Command at Fredericia	2	1	–	3	–	–	–	–	–	–	–	–	–	3

Source, Generalstaben, *Statistiske Meddelelser angaaende den danske Krigsmagt* Volume I, Copenhagen 1867, pp. 66-67

V

Order of Battle, Combined Allied Army 1st February 1864

Commander	Field Marshal Baron von Wrangel
Chief of Staff	Lieutenant-General Vogel von Falckenstein
Senior Quartermaster	Colonel von Podbielski
General Staff Officers	Lieutenant-Colonel von Schönfeld (Austrian)
	Major von Stiehle
	Captain Count von Hardenberg
	Premier-Lieutenant von Gottberg, Litthauer Uhlan Regiment Nr 12
	Premier-Lieutenant von Roon, 1st Foot Guards Regiment
Attached	Major Geertz, Chief of the General Staff
Topographical Bureau	
Assigned to Headquarters	Lieutenant-Colonel Kraft, Prince Hohenlohe-Ingelfingen
Personal Adjutant to the Field Marshal	Second-Lieutenant Count Kalnein, East Prussian, Cuirassier Regiment Nr 3
Commander, Headquarters	Major von Schack, 2nd Guard Uhlan Regiment
Adjutants	Major von Kleist, 1st Foot Guards Regiment
	Captain von Granach, 4th Rhenish Infantry Regiment Nr. 30
	Rittmeister Count zu Eulenburg, 3rd Guard Uhlan Regiment
	Rittmeister Prince Aremberg (Austrian), Windischgrätz Dragoon Regiment
	Second-Lieutenant von Nostitz, 1st Guard Dragoon Regiment
	Second-Lieutenant Vogel von Falckenstein, 4th Guard Grenadier Regiment
	Second-Lieutenant Baron von Wrangel, 2nd Guard Dragoon Regiment
Artillery Officers	Colonel v Graberg, Commander, Westphalian Artillery Brigade Nr. 7
	Major von der Becke, Pomeranian Artillery Brigade Nr. 2
	Second-Lieutenant Marcus, Artillery Brigade Nr. 7, Adjutant to Colonel Graberg

Engineer Officers	Colonel von Mertens, 6th Fortress Inspectorate
	Premier-Lieutenant Scheibert, 2nd Engineer Inspectorate
	Premier-Lieutenant von Renthe-Fink, 3rd Engineer Inspectorate, Adjutant to Colonel Mertens
Supernumerary	His Royal Highness, Lieutenant-General The Crown Prince of Prussia
Personal Adjutants	Major von Schweinitz, General Staff
	Captain von Lucadou, à la suite 2nd Silesian Grenadier Regiment Nr. 11
Orderly Officer	Prince Karl zu Hohenzollern-Sigmaringen, Premier-Lieutenant à la suite, 2nd Guard Dragoon Regiment
Attached to Staff	His Royal Highness, General of Cavalry Prince Albrecht (Senior) of Prussia
Personal Adjutants	Major von Buddenbrock, à la suite 1st Guard Dragoon Regiment
	Rittmeister von Radecke, à la suite Dragoon Regiment Nr. 1
Temporarily attached	His Royal Highness, the Grand Duke of Mecklenburg-Schwerin
	His Royal Highness, Prince zu Hohenzollern-Sigmaringen, General of Infantry
	His Highness, the Hereditary Prince of Anhalt, Colonel, à la suite 1st Foot Guards Regiment

Royal Prussian Combined Army Corps (I Corps, Combined Army)

Commander	General of Cavalry Prince Friedrich Carl of Prussia
Chief of Staff	Colonel von Blumenthal
Commander, Artillery	Colonel Colomier
Commander, Engineers	Lieutenant-Colonel von Kriegsheim
General Staff Officers	Major G., Count von Waldersee
	Major von Roos
Adjutants	Major von Tilly, Lower Silesian Infantry Regiment Nr. 50
	Major von Bonin, Hohenzollern Fusilier Regiment Nr. 40
	Premier-Lieutenant Count von Haeseler, Ziethen Hussar Regiment, Brandenburg Nr. 3

	Second-Lieutenant von Brösigke, 2nd Brandenburg Uhlan Regiment Nr. 11
Personal Adjutants	Major von Witzendorff, à la suite General Staff
	Second-Lieutenant Baron von Loë, Ziethen Hussar Regiment, Brandenburg Nr. 3
Adjutants to Artillery Commander	Premier-Lieutenant Spangenberg, Brandenburg Artillery Brigade Nr. 3
	Second-Lieutenant Krüger I, Brandenburg Artillery Brigade Nr. 3
Engineer Officers	Captain Treumann, 3rd Engineer Inspectorate
	Premier-Lieutenant Mantey, 3rd Engineer Inspectorate
Attached to Staff	His Royal Highness, Colonel Prince Albrecht (Junior) of Prussia
Personal Adjutants	Major von Massow, à la suite 1st Guard Dragoon Regiment
	Second-Lieutenant von Ploetz, à la suite 1st Guard Dragoon Regiment
Temporary Headquarters Attachment	His Royal Highness, Prince Carl of Prussia
Adjutant	Major von Helden-Tarnowski, Westphalian Artillery Brigade Nr. 7
Personal Adjutants	Lieutenant-Colonel Baron von Puttkamer
	Major von Erhardt
Staff Escort	Second-Lieutenant von Mutius, 2nd Brandenburg Uhlan Regiment Nr. 11

6th Infantry Division

Commander	Lieutenant-General von Manstein
General Staff Officer	Captain von Unger
Adjutant	Premier-Lieutenant von Geissler, Leib-Grenadier Regiment Nr. 8, 1st Brandenburg
	Premier-Lieutenant von Ploetz, 4th Brandenburg Infantry Regiment Nr. 24

11th Infantry Brigade

Commander	Major-General Baron von Canstein
Adjutant	Premier-Lieutenant von Schmiede, 8th Brandenburg Infantry Regiment Nr. 64

Brandenburg Fusilier Regiment Nr. 35 – Colonel Elstermann von Elster
    I Battalion
    II Battalion
    III Battalion

7th Brandenburg Infantry Regiment Nr. 60 – Lieutenant-Colonel von Hartmann
   I Battalion
   II Battalion
   Fusilier Battalion

12th Infantry Brigade

Commander	Major-General von Roeder II
Adjutant	Premier-Lieutenant von Wulffsen, Leib-Grenadier Regiment (1st Brandenburg)Nr. 8

4th Brandenburg Infantry Regiment Nr. 24 – Colonel Count von Hacke
   I Battalion
   II Battalion
   Fusilier Battalion
8th Brandenburg Infantry Regiment Nr. 64 – Colonel von Kamienski
   I Battalion
   II Battalion
   Fusilier Battalion

Divisional Troops

2nd Brandenburg Uhlan Regiment Nr. 11 – Lieutenant-Colonel von Sirthin – four squadrons
   3rd Foot Artillery division, Brandenburg Artillery Brigade Nr. 3 - Lieutenant-Colonel Bergmann
      3rd Howitzer Battery – eight 7 pound howitzers
      3rd 6 Pounder Battery – six rifled 6 pounder cannon
      3rd 12 Pounder Battery – six smoothbore cannon
Brandenburg Pioneer Battalion Nr. 3 – Major Boetscher

13th Infantry Division

Commander	Lieutenant-General von Wintzingerode
General Staff Officer	Captain Baron von Dörnberg
Adjutants	Rittmeister von Kleist, East Prussian Cuirassier Regiment Nr. 3
	Premier-Lieutenant Baronr von Ledebur, 4th Westphalian Infantry Regiment Nr. 17

25th Infantry Brigade

Commander	Major-General von Schmid
Adjutant	Premier-Lieutenant Grach, 6th Westphalian Infantry Regiment Nr. 55

1st Westphalian Infantry Regiment Nr. 13 – Colonel von Witzleben
   I Battalion
   II Battalion
   Fusilier Battalion
5th Westphalian Infantry Regiment Nr. 53 – Colonel Baron von Buddenbrock

I Battalion
II Battalion
Fusilier Battalion

26th Infantry Brigade

Commander	Major-General von Goeben
Adjutant	Premier-Lieutenant Clemen, 5th Westphalian Infantry Regiment Nr. 53

2nd Westphalian Infantry Regiment Nr. 15 – Colonel von Alvensleben
    I Battalion
    II Battalion
    Fusilier Battalion
6th Westphalian Infantry Regiment Nr. 55 – Colonel Stolz
    I Battalion
    II Battalion
    Fusilier Battalion

Divisional Troops

Westphalian Jäger Battalion Nr. 7 – Major von Beckedorff
    Westphalian Dragoon Regiment Nr. 7 – Lieutenant-Colonel von Nibbeck – four squadrons
1st Foot Artillery division, Westphalian Artillery Brigade Nr. 7 – Major Grave
    1st Howitzer Battery – eight 7 pound howitzers
    1st 6 Pounder Battery – six rifled 6 pounder cannon
    1st 12 Pounder Battery – six smoothbore cannon
    4th 12 Pounder Battery – six smoothbore cannon
Westphalian Pioneer Battalion Nr. 7 – Major Count Beissel-Gymnich

Combined Cavalry Division

Commander	Major-General Count zu Münster-Meinhövel
General Staff Officer	Major von Stedink, Magdeburg Dragoon Regiment Nr. 6
Adjutants	Second-Lieutenant von Noville, Westphalian Uhlan Regiment Nr. 5
	Second-Lieutenant von Grimm, Ziethen Hussar Regiment, Brandenburg Nr. 3

6th Cavalry Brigade

Commander	Colonel Flies
Adjutant	Second-Lieutenant von Rudolphi, Brandenburg Uhlan Regiment Nr. 3

Ziethen Hussar Regiment, Brandenburg Nr. 3 – Colonel Count von der Groeben – four squadrons

Brandenburg Cuirassier Regiment Nr. 6 – Colonel, His Royal
Highness, Duke Wilhelm of Mecklenburg-Schwerin – four squadrons
>   1st Horse Artillery Battery, Westphalian Artillery Brigade Nr. 7 – four 12
>   pounder smoothbore cannon

13th Cavalry Brigade

Commander	Major-General von Hobe
Adjutant	Premier-Lieutenant von Bodelschwingh,
	Westphalian Uhlan Regiment Nr. 5

Westphalian Hussar Regiment Nr. 8 – Lieutenant-Colonel von Rantzau –
five squadrons
Westphalian Cuirassier Regiment Nr. 4 – Lieutenant Colonel von Schmidt
– four squadrons
2nd Horse Artillery Battery, Westphalian Artillery Brigade Nr. 7 – four 12
pounder smoothbore cannon

Divisional Troops

Medical Company

Reserve Artillery

Commander	Lieutenant-Colonel von Saenger,
	Commander, Horse Artillery division,
	Westphalian Artillery Brigade Nr. 7

2nd Foot Artillery division, Brandenburg Artillery Brigade Nr. 3 – Major
von Held
>   2nd Howitzer Battery – eight 7 pound howitzers
>   2nd 6 Pounder Battery – eight rifled 6 pounder cannon
>   4th 6 Pounder Battery – eight rifled 6 pounder cannon
>   2nd 12 Pounder Battery – eight smoothbore 12 pounder cannon
Horse Artillery division, Westphalian Artillery Brigade Nr. 7 –
Lieutenant-Colonel von Saenger
>   3rd Horse Artillery Battery – four 6 pounder smoothbore cannon
>   4th Horse Artillery Battery – four 6 pounder smoothbore cannon
>   5th Horse Artillery Battery – four 6 pounder smoothbore cannon
>   6th Horse Artillery Battery – four 6 pounder smoothbore cannon

Ancillary Units

Munitions and Bridging Train – Major Dietrich, Brandenburg Artillery
Brigade Nr. 3
>   Ammunition Trains Nrs. 1, 2, and 3 – Westphalian Artillery Brigade Nr.
>   7
>   Ammunition Trains Nrs. 4, 5, 6, 7, 8, and 9 – Brandenburg Artillery Bri-
>   gade Nr. 3
>> Light Field Bridging Train – Guards
>> Pontoon Trains Nrs. 3 and 7
>> Train Battalion – Major Mechow
>> Provisions Trains Nrs. 1, 2, 3, 4, and 5

Sick Transport Company
Remount Depot
Field Bakery
Field Hospital

K.K. VI Army Corps
(II Corps, Combined Army)

Commander	FML Baron Gablenz
Chief of Staff	Colonel Baron Vlasits
Deputy Chief of Staff	Major Edler von Poppenheim
Quartermaster	
General Staff Officers	Major Baron Dumoulin
	Captain Ritter von Gründorf
	Captain Dimmer
	Captain Edler von Döpfner
Aides	Captain Ochsenheimer, Infantry Regiment Nr. 42
	Oberlieutenant Seracsin, 5th Jäger Battalion
	Oberlieutenant von Ehrlinger
Commander, Artillery	Lieutenant Colonel Weisser
Commander, Engineers	Major Baron Salis-Soglio
Corps Discipline	Rittmeister Ellerich, 2nd Regiment Gendarmerie
Corps Provisions	Captain Purkher, Infantry Regiment Nr. 80

1st Brigade

Commander	Major-General Count Gondrecourt
General Staff Officer	Captain Daublebsky von Sterneck

Infantry Regiment Baron Martini (Regiment Martini), Nr. 30 – Colonel Baron von und zu Lilienberg
    I Battalion
    II Battalion
Infantry Regiment King of Prussia (Regiment Preußen), Nr. 34 – Colonel Benedek
    I Battalion
    II Battalion
18th Jäger Battalion (18FJB) – Lieutenant-Colonel von Tobias
4 Pounder Foot Battery Nr. 2, 1st Artillery Regiment – eight rifled 4 pounders

2nd Brigade

Commander	Major-General Dormus
General Staff Officer	Captain Baron Handel

Infantry Regiment Count Khevenhüller (Regiment Khevenhüller), Nr. 35 – Colonel Camptner
    I Battalion

II Battalion
Infantry Regiment Baron Ramming (Regiment Ramming), Nr. 72 –
Colonel Ritter von Abele
    I Battalion
    II Battalion
22nd Jäger Battalion (22FJB) – Lieutenant-Colonel Ritter von Siller
4 Pounder Foot Battery Nr. 3, 1st Artillery Regiment – eight rifled 4
pounders

3rd Brigade

| Commander | Major-General Nostitz |
| General Staff Officer | Captain Ambrozy |

Infantry Regiment Grand Duke of Hesse (Regiment Hessen), Nr. 14 –
Colonel Freiherr Schütte von Warensberg
    I Battalion
    II Battalion
Infantry Regiment King of the Belgians (Regiment Belgier), Nr. 27 –
Colonel, Wilhelm, Duke of Württemberg
    I Battalion
    II Battalion
9th Jäger Battalion (9FJB) – Major Schidlach (Promoted to
Lieutenant-Colonel, 12th February)
4 Pounder Foot Battery Nr. 4, 1st Artillery Regiment – eight rifled 4
pounders

4th Brigade

| Commander | Major-General Tomas |
| General Staff Officer | Captain Wenzl |

Infantry Regiment Count Coronini (Regiment Coronini), Nr. 6 – Colonel
Fellner von Feldegg
    I Battalion
    II Battalion
Infantry Regiment Prince of Holstein (Regiment Holstein), Nr. 80 –
Colonel Count Auersperg
    I Battalion
    II Battalion
11th Jäger Battalion (11FJB) – Colonel von Schwab
4 Pounder Foot Battery Nr. 5, 1st Artillery Regiment – eight rifled 4
pounders

Cavalry Brigade

| Commander | Major-General Baron Dobrzhensky |
| General Staff Officer | Captain Count Uexkhüll-Syllenbrandt |

Dragoon Regiment FM Fürst Windischgrätz, Nr. 2 – Colonel Count
Bellegarde – 5 squadrons
Hussar Regiment G. d. C. Fürst Liechtenstein, Nr. 9 – Colonel Baron
Baselli von Süssenberg – 5 squadrons

Technical Troops

4th Company, 1st Pioneer Battalion with Bridging Train Squadrons 39 and 40

3rd Company, 1st Pioneer Battalion

11th Engineer Company

Corps Artillery Reserve

Commander   Major Ritter von Neubauer

8 pounder Battery Nr. 9, 1st Artillery Regiment – eight rifled 8 pounder cannon

8 Pounder Battery Nr. 10, 1st Artillery Regiment – eight rifled 8 pounder cannon

1st Medical Company with attached 31st Transport Squadron

Ancillary Units

Commander   Major Arthoffer

Field Magazine, with attached Transport Squadrons 2, 35, and 53

Corps Distribution Depot

Corps Reception Depot

Corps Munitions Park, with attached Transport Squadrons 27 and 28.1st Park Company, 5th Field Repair Company

Munitions Field Depot, with detachment, 1st park company, and 7th Field Repair Company

Field Munitions Depot

Corps Ambulance Nr. 5

Corps Medical Reserve

Field Hospitals Nr's 9, 12, and 16

Field Post Detachment

Field Telegraph Detachment

Gendarmerie (and Courier) Detachment

Escort for Field Munitions Depot - 7th Company, Infantry Regiment Kaiser Alexander, Nr. 2 (Regiment Alexander)

Royal Prussian Combined Guard Division (III Corps, Combined Army)

Commander	Lieutenant-General von der Mülbe
Chief of Staff	Major von Alvensleben
Adjutants	Captain von Notz, 2nd Foot Guards Regiment
	Premier-Lieutenant von Henniges, 1st Guard Grenadier Regiment

Combined Foot Guards Brigade

Commander   Major-General Count von der Goltz

Adjutant	Premier-1 Lieutenant Baron von Ende, Guard Grenadier Regiment

3rd Foot Guards Regiment – Colonel von der Groeben
    I Battalion
    II Battalion
    Fusilier Battalion
4th Foot Guards Regiment – Colonel von Korth
    I Battalion
    II Battalion
    Fusilier Battalion

Combined Guard Grenadier Brigade

Commander	Colonel von Bentheim
Adjutant	Premier-Lieutenant von Wrochem, 2nd Foot Guards Regiment

3rd Guard Grenadier Regiment – Colonel von Winterfeld
    I Battalion
    II Battalion
    Fusilier Battalion
4th Guard Grenadier Regiment – Colonel von Oppell
    I Battalion
    II Battalion
    Fusilier Battalion
Guard Hussar Regiment – Lieutenant-Colonel von Kerssenbroigk – four squadrons
Guard 4 Pounder Battery – eight rifled 4 pounder field guns
3rd Guard 6 Pounder Battery – six smoothbore 6 pounder cannon

VI

Fortifications of the Danewerke Line, Armament planned and those actually in place, February 1st 1864

			Equipped with Stationary Ordnance					
			Armament in Place on the Outbreak of Hostilities					
Works Completed by October 1863	*Completed or Under Construction from late 1863 up to the Commencement of Hostilities*	*Intended Armament*	*84 pd SB How.*	*24 pd SB How.*	*18 pd SB Gun*	*12 pd SB Gun*	*6 pd SB Gun*	*12 pd Rifled Gun*
	A. *Central Position*	4 Cannon	—	—	—	—	—	4
	Battery on Möwenberg (island), south-west of Schleswig town's Altstadt							
	Battery at Holm, east of Schleswig town	4 Cannon	4	—	—	—	—	—
Fleche I	Completed with one powder magazine and infantry position on the left. Moat dug across land spit on which it was sited.	4 Cannon	—	—	2	—	—	—
Battery II	Work completed, with two powder magazines and defensive obstacles	7 Cannon (plus infantry)	—	2	2	—	—	—
Battery III	Work completed with one powder magazine. Position on left flank under construction	2 Cannon	—	—	—	—	—	—
	Battery IV, east of rail line built to cover the rail line and Bustrup Plateau.	4 Cannon	—	—	—	—	—	—
	Battery V, under construction west of rail line, purpose as for Battery IV	4 Cannon	—	—	—	—	—	—
Battery VI	Completed with one powder magazine	4 Cannon	2	—	—	—	—	—
Works between VI & VII for infantry			—	—	—	—	—	—
Battery VII	Completed with two powder magazines, entrance and palisades	8 Cannon	1	2	2	—	2	—
	Link between Work VII and Lunette VIII	4 Cannon	—	—	—	—	—	—

Lunette VIII		8 Cannon	—	—	—	—	—	—
	Link between Lunettes VIII and IX		—	—	—	—	—	—
Lunette IX	Completed with two powder magazines, entrance and palisades	8 Cannon	1	2	2	—	2	—
	Link between Lunette IX and Redoubt X	8 Cannon	—	—	—	—	—	—
Redoubt X	Completed with two powder magazines	11 Cannon (plus infantry)	1	2	2	—	2	—
	Bustrup Outwork. Built as an advanced work to support Battery II, and the gullies leading to it. Built in the hollow of the old escarpment. Constructed with one powder magazine, entrance and palisades.	8 Cannon	1	—	—	5	—	—
Lunette XI	Completed with two powder magazines and defensive obstacles	7 Cannon (plus infantry)	1	2	2	—	2	—
	Danewerke Outwork. Intended as a large outwork able to hold three field artillery batteries		—	—	—	—	—	—
	Also under construction – Links between the Danewerke Outwork, and Redoubt X and Lunette XI, including gun positions.							
Redoubt XII	Completed with two powder magazines and defensive obstacles	11 Cannon (plus infantry)	1	2	2	—	2	—
Lunette XIII	Completed with two powder magazines and defensive obstacles	7 Cannon (plus infantry)	1	2	2	—	2	—
	Under Construction – Links between Works X and XIII, including positions for one battery each between Works X and XI and Works X and XIII, including a battery between X and XI. Works between XII and XIII, and for a Half-battery between Works XI and XII		—	—	—	—	—	—
	Also, a link between Works XIII and XIV across the Ox Road, including gun positions for one battery.							
Redoubt XIV	Constructed with two powder magazines and Defensive obstacles.	11 Cannon (plus infantry)	1	2	2	—	2	—
Redoubt XV	Constructed with two powder magazines and Defensive obstacles.	11 Cannon (plus infantry)	1	2	2	—	2	—
Redoubt XVI	Constructed with two powder magazines and Defensive obstacles.	11 Cannon (plus infantry)	1	2	2	—	2	—

Work	Description	Intended Armament	84 pd SB How.	24 pd SB How	18 pd SB Gun	12 pd SB Gun	6 pd SB Gun	12 pd Rifled Gun
Redoubt XVII	Constructed with two powder magazines and Defensive obstacles.	11 Cannon (plus infantry)	1	2	2	—	2	—
Redoubt XVIII	Constructed with two powder magazines and Defensive obstacles.	11 Cannon (plus infantry)	1	2	2	—	2	—
	Link under construction between Works XVIII and XIX.		—	—	—	—	—	—
Lunette XIX	As for Redoubt XVIII	19 Cannon (plus infantry)	—	—	—	—	4	—
Lunette XX	Completed with one powder magazine	5 Cannon (plus infantry)	—	—	—	—	2	—
Lunette XXI	Completed with one powder magazine	4 Cannon (plus infantry)	—	—	—	—	2	—
Lunette XXII	Completed with one powder magazine	4 Cannon (plus infantry)	—	—	—	—	2	—
Lunette XXIII	Completed with one powder magazine	4 Cannon (plus infantry)	—	—	—	—	2	—
Lunette XXIV	Completed with one powder magazine	4 Cannon (plus infantry)	—	—	—	—	2	—
Fleche XXV		4 Cannon	—	—	—	—	—	—
Fleche XXVI		4 Cannon	—	—	—	—	—	—
Fleche XXVII		4 Cannon	—	—	—	—	—	—
Total guns in the centre			20	24	26	5	36	4

| | Equipped with Stationary Ordnance | | | | | | | |
| | | Armament in Place on the Outbreak of Hostilities | | | | | | |
Works completed by October 1863	Completed or under construction from late 1863 to the commencement of hostilities	Intended Armament	84 pd SB How.	24 pd SB How	18 pd SB Gun	12 pd SB Gun	6 pd SB Gun	12 pd Rifled Gun
B. Left Flank								
MISSUNDE Position								
Lunette a.	Some works carried out, including trenches and palisades	18 Cannon (plus infantry)	—	4	—	4	—	—
Lunette b.				4		2		
Fleche c., Lunettes d.&e.	One powder magazine constructed in d. Armament in d.	14 Cannon (plus infantry)	—	—	—	2	—	—
South Bridgehead, f.	Infantry work with palisades		—	—	—	—	—	—

	Intended Armament	84 pd SB How.	24 pd SB How.	18 pd SB Gun	12 pd SB Gun	6 pd SB Gun	12 pd Rifled Gun
North Bridgehead g – seven works constructed south to north for artillery		—	2	—	2	—	—
g.1 Work with one powder magazine							
g.2 Work with one powder magazine							
Schlei Defences		—	—	—	—	—	—
Palörde, Reesholm. Infantry breastworks and three lunettes	12-15 Cannon (plus infantry)	—	2	—	—	—	—
Batteries on the eastern Schlei, all constructed at the narrows, some occupied by field artillery (2-4 guns) at the following: Goltoft, Hestoft, three near Nis, Arnis, Grödersby, Dothmark, three at Cappeln, Rabelsund, and south of the Schlei at Espenis. Those for the position guns were finished by January 9th, but only at Goltoft and one of those a Nis had a powder magazine.	24-48 Cannon	—	12	—	—	—	—
Total guns on the left flank		—	24	—	10	—	—

			Equipped with stationary ordnance					
			Armament in place on the outbreak of hostilities					
Work completed by October 1863	*Completed or under construction from late 1863 to the commencement of hostilities*	*Intended Armament*	*84 pd SB How.*	*24 pd SB How.*	*18 pd SB Gun*	*12 pd SB Gun*	*6 pd SB Gun*	*12 pd Rifled Gun*
	C. Right Flank							
Lunettes at Süderstapel a.&b.	Both completed with one powder magazine	4 Cannon (plus infantry)	—	4	—	2	—	—
	East of Süderstapel were built two batteries each for two guns. Also one powder magazine.	4 Cannon						
	Breastwork for infantry constructed between Wohlde and Bünge.							

Along the line of retreat from Friedrichstadt and Süderstapel through Schwabstedt:			—	—	—	—	—	—
Redoubt south of Schwabstedt	South of the Treene. A further work for artillery was begun on the north bank.	4 Cannon (plus infantry)	—	—	—	—	—	—
Fleche east of Mildte Koog		4 Cannon (plus infantry)	—	—	—	—	—	—
Fleche east of Drage		2 Cannon (plus infantry)	—	—	—	—	—	—
Fortress of Friedrichstadt Nine works, a., b., f., g., h., i., k., l., m.	Completed with six powder magazines and defensive obstacles.	56 Cannon (plus infantry)	4	—	2	10	—	—
Work south of the Eider	Work in the loop of the river.							
Fleche south of Husum	Completed with one powder magazine	3 Cannon	—	—	—	2	2	—
	Battery completed south of above work							
Total guns on the right flank			4	6	—	14	2	—

VII

Armament of the Dybbøl Redoubts
February 7th 1864

Gun Mounting	36 pd Gun high	24 pd Gun high	low	12 pd Gun low	84 pd How Type I high	84 pd How Type II high	low	24 pd How high	low	12 pd How low	Total
I	2	—	—	—	—	—	—	—	4	—	6
II	—	—	—	6	1	2	—	—	—	—	9
III	—	—	—	2	—	—	—	—	2	—	4
IV	—	—	—	—	1	5	—	3	3	—	12
V	—	—	2	—	—	—	—	2	—	—	4
VI	—	—	5	5	1	5	—	—	—	—	16
VII	—	—	—	4	—	—	—	—	—	—	4
VIII	—	5	5	—	—	—	—	—	—	2	12
IX	—	—	—	—	1	4	—	—	4	—	9
X	—	4	—	—	—	—	—	—	—	4	8
Total	2	9	12	17	4	16	—	5	13	6	84

Note: All ordnance is smoothbore. How = Howitzer

Source: Schøller, p. 14.

VIII

Danish Army Combatants at the Dybbøl Position Fit for Duty 15th February 1864

Units	Officers	Nco's				Musicians			Undercorporals	Men	Total
		Line	Reserve	Temporary	Total	Line	Reserve	Total			
General Staff	19	5	—	3	8	—	—	—	4	49	80
Telegraph & Topography	3	9	—	—	9	—	—	—	2	31	45
Artillery Staff	7	4	—	—	4	—	—	—	—	—	11
Engineer HQ Staff	13	4	—	—	4	—	—	—	1	4	22
1st Division Staff	6	1	—	—	2	—	—	—	—	7	15
2nd Division Staff	6	2	—	—	2	—	—	—	1	—	9
Infantry Reserve Staff	5	—	—	—	—	—	—	—	2	10	17
Total Staff	59	25	—	4	29	—	—	—	10	101	199
Engineer Troops	—	—	—	—	—	—	—	—	—	—	—
1st, 3rd, 5th, 6th (Bridge) & 7th (Park) Companies	8	—	—	—	39	—	—	—	—	336	383
Total Engineers	8	—	—	—	39	—	—	—	—	336	383
Reserve Artillery Staff	3	1	—	—	1	—	—	—	1	1	6
1st Battery	2	8	—	—	8	2	—	2	20	137	169
4th Battery	3	6	2	—	8	2	—	2	22	201	236
11th Battery	2	7	1	—	8	3	—	3	18	148	179
13th Battery	2	8	—	—	8	2	—	2	19	166	197
1st Division Arty Command	2	—	—	—	—	—	—	—	—	—	2
2nd Battery	3	8	—	—	8	2	—	2	18	139	170
10th Battery	2	9	—	—	9	3	—	3	20	175	209
2nd Division Arty Command	2	—	—	—	—	—	—	—	—	—	2
8th Battery	2	9	—	—	9	2	—	2	18	139	170
9th Battery	2	8	5	1	14	3	—	3	20	182	221
Total Field Artillery	25	64	8	1	73	19	—	19	156	1,288	1,561

Arty Command Dybbøl	3	—	—	—	—	—	—	—	—	—	3
3rd, 4th, & 6th Fortress Companies	19	22	20	—	42	—	1	1	52	1,052	1,166
Total Fortress Artillery	22	22	20	—	42	—	1	1	52	1,052	1,166
Artillery Depot	6	22	1	7	30	—	1	—	50	207	293
Total Artillery	53	108	29	8	145	19	1	20	258	2,547	3,023
1st Division Cavalry Staff	2	—	—	—	—	—	—	—	—	—	2
4th Dragoon Regiment, 2nd Half-Regiment	6	20	—	5	25	3	1	4	18	281	334
2nd Division Cavalry Staff	2	—	—	—	—	—	—	—	—	—	2
1st Half-Regiment, Guard Hussars	8	16	—	3	19	5	—	5	14	182	228
Total Cavalry	18	36	—	8	44	8	1	9	32	463	566
1st Infantry Brigade Staff	3	—	—	—	—	—	—	—	1	17	21
2nd Infantry Regiment	34	28	8	29	65	11	10	21	148	1,240	1,508
22nd Infantry Regiment	37	28	1	39	68	13	6	19	162	1,490	1,776
2nd Infantry Brigade Staff	4	1	—	1	—	—	—	—	1	5	11
3rd Infantry Regiment	30	22	8	36	66	14	11	25	125	1,599	1,845
18th Infantry Regiment	32	27	6	28	61	12	14	26	103	1,165	1,387
3rd Infantry Brigade Staff	3	—	—	—	—	—	—	—	1	17	21
16th Infantry Regiment	33	28	8	29	65	11	10	21	148	1,240	1,508
17th Infantry Regiment	33	28	1	39	68	13	6	19	162	—	—
4th Infantry Brigade Staff	4	—	—	—	—	—	—	—	—	—	4
4th Infantry Regiment	31	32	14	28	774	14	12	26	148	1,680	1,959
6th Infantry Regiment											
5th Infantry Brigade Staff	3	—	—	—	—	—	—	—	—	—	3
12th Infantry Regiment	31	31	11	21	63	16	6	22	143	1,452	1,711
6th Infantry Brigade Staff	3	—	—	—	—	—	—	—	—	—	—
5th Infantry Regiment	31	30	9	28	67	14	8	22	166	1,543	1,829
10th Infantry Regiment	31	26	9	31	66	15	10	25	136	1,442	1,700

Infantry Reserve, 8th Infantry Regiment	29	30	16	26	72	8	11	19	143	1,245	1,508
Infantry Reserve, 15th Infantry Regiment	30	24	2	37	63	10	10	20	126	1,400	1,639
Total Infantry	437	362	94	394	850	163	121	284	1,774	18,713	22,058
Total	575	531	123	414	1,107	190	123	313	2,074	22,160	26,229

Schøller, pp.147-148

IX

Rotation of Danish Infantry Units at the Dybbøl Position February-April 1864

Grouping of columns: **Main Position** covers Outposts (Left Flank, Right Flank), Redoubts (Left Flank – Left wing/Right wing; Right Flank – Left wing/Right wing) and Barracks Line. **Reserve** covers Bridgehead and Sønderborg.

Date	Outposts Left Flank	Outposts Right Flank	Redoubts L.F. Left wing	Redoubts L.F. Right wing	Redoubts R.F. Left wing	Redoubts R.F. Right wing	Barracks Line	Bridgehead	Sønderborg	Coast Watch Kjær Peninsula, Als	Coast Watch North Als	In Camp on Als	Remarks
Feb. 7th	2 Brig 3R 18R	1 Brig 2R 22R		3 Brig. 17R		16R			9 Brig 19R 21R; 8 Brig 9R 20R			4 Brig 4R 6R 12R I/13R; 6 Brig 5R 10R; 7th Brig 1R 11R; 5 Brig 8R 15R	
8th	2 Brig 3R 18R	1 Brig 2R 22R		3 Brig 17R		16R			9 Brig 19R 21R; 8 Brig 9R 20R			4 Brig 4R 6R 12R I/13R; 6 Brig 5R 10R; 7 Brig 1R 11R; 5 Brig 8R 15R	
9th	2 Brig 3R 18 R	1 Brig 2R 22R		3 Brig 17R		16R			6 Brig 5R 10 R			4 Brig 4R 6R 12R I/13R; 5 Brig 5R 10R; 7 Brig 1R 11R	
10th	5R outpost 10R support	5R outpost 10R support			12R				3 Brig 16R 17R	4R		1 Brig 2R 22R 6R I/13R; 2 Brig 3R 18R; 5 Brig 8R 15R; 7 Brig 1R 11R	

11th	10R outpost / 12R support	10R outpost / 12R support	5R	3 Brig 16R 17R	4R		1 Brig 2R 22R 6R I/13R	2Brig 3R 18R	5 Brig 8R 15R	7 Brig 1R 11R	8&9 Brig to Fredericia
12th	12R outpost / 5R support	12R outpost / 5R support	10R	3 Brig 16R 17R	4R		1 Brig 2R 22R 12R	2 Brig 3R 18R	5 Brig 8R 15R	7 Brig 1R 11R	I/13R to Funen
13th	6R outpost / 8R support	6R outpost / 8R support	15R	3 Brig 16R 17R	4R		1 Brig 2R 22R 12R	2 Brig 3R 18R	6 Brig 5R 10R	7 Brig 1R 11R	7th Brig to Funen
14th	8R outpost / 15R support	8R outpost / 15R support	6R	3 Brig 16R 17R	4R		1 Brig 2R 22R	2 Brig 3R 18R	6 Brig 5R 10R	12R	As above
15th	15R outpost / 5R support	15R outpost / 5R support	8R	3 Brig 16R 17R	4R		1 Brig 2R 22R	2 Brig 3R 18R	6 Brig 5R 10R	12R	As above
16th	16R outpost / 3R support	16R outpost / 3R support	17R	1 Brig 2R 22R	4R		4 Brig 6R 12R	5 Brig 8R 15R	6 Brig 5R 10R	18R	
17th	3R outpost / 17R support	3R outpost / 17R support	16R	1 Brig 2R 22R	4R		4 Brig 6R 12R	5 Brig 8R 15R	6 Brig 5R 10R	18R	
18th	17R outpost / 16R support	17R outpost / 16R support	3R	1 Brig 2R 22R	4R		4 Brig 6R 12R	5 Brig 8R 15R	6 Brig 5R 10R	18R	
19th	22R outpost / 2R support	22R outpost / 2R support	18R	6 Brig 5R 10R	4R		3 Brig 16R 17R	4 Brig 6R 12R	5 Brig 8R 15R	3R	
20th	2R outpost / 18R support	2R outpost / 18R support	22R	6 Brig 5R 10R	4R	II/16R	3 Brig 16R 17R	4 Brig 6R 12R	5 Brig 8R 15R	3R	
21st	18R outpost / 22R support	18R outpost / 22R support	2R	6 Brig 5R 10R	4R	II/16R	3. Brig 16R 17R	4 Brig 6R 12R	5 Brig 8R 15R	3R	
22nd	6R outpost / 22R support	6R outpost / 22R support	5R	5 Brig 8R 15R	4R	II/16R	1 Brig 2R 22R	2 Brig 3R 18R	3 Brig 16R 17R		
23rd	5 Brig 15R	5 Brig 8R	4 Brig 6R 12R	6 Brig 5R 10R	4R	I/22R	1 Brig 2R 22R	2 Brig 3R 18R	3 Brig 16R 17R		

Date									
24th	6 Brig 10R	6 Brig 5R	5 Brig 15R 8R	4 Brig 6R 12R	4R	I/22R	1 Brig 2R 22R	2 Brig 3R 18R	3 Brig 16R 17R
25th	4 Brig 6R	4 Brig 12R	6 Brig 10R 5R	5 Brig 8R 15R	4R	I/22R	1 Brig 2R 22R	2 Brig 3R 18R	3 Brig 16R 17R
26th	5 Brig 15R	5 Brig 8R	4 Brig 6R 12R	6 Brig 5R 10R	4R	I/22R	1 Brig 2R 22R	2 Brig 3R 18R	3 Brig 16R 17R
27th	6 Brig 10R	6 Brig 5R	5 Brig 15R 8R	4 Brig 6R 12R	4R	I/22R	1 Brig 2R 22R	2 Brig 3R 18R	3 Brig 16R 17R
28th	2 Brig 18R	2 Brig 3R	3 Brig 17R 16R	1 Brig 2R 22R	4R	Det at Mels	4 Brig 6R 12R	5 Brig 8R 15R	6 Brig 5R 10R
29th	1 Brig 2R	1 Brig 22R	2 Brig 18R 3R	3 Brig 16R 17R	4R	Det at Mels	4 Brig 6R 12R	5.Brig 8R 15R	6 Brig 5R 10R
March 1st	3 Brig 17R	3 Brig 16R	1 Brig 2R 22R	2 Brig 3R 18R	4R	Det at Mels	4 Brig 6R 12R	5 Brig 8R 15R	6 Brig 5R 10R
2nd	2 Brig 18R	2 Brig 3R	3 Brig 17R 16R	1 Brig 2R 22R	4R	Det at Mels	4 Brig 6R 12R	5 Brig 8R 15R	6 Brig 5R 10R
3rd	1 Brig 2R	1 Brig 22R	2 Brig 18R 3R	3 Brig 16R 17R	4R	Det at Mels	4 Brig 6R 12R	5 Brig 8R 15R	6 Brig 5R 10R
4th	3 Brig 17R	3 Brig 16R	1 Brig 2R 22R	2 Brig 3R 18R	4R	Det at Mels	4 Brig 6R 12R	5 Brig 8R 15R	6 Brig 5R 10R
5th	6 Brig 10R	6 Brig 5R	4 Brig 6R 12R	5 Brig 5R 15R	4R	Det at Mels	1 Brig 2R 22R	2 Brig 3R 18R	3 Brig 16R 17R
6th	5 Brig 15R	5 Brig 8R	6 Brig 10R 5R	4 Brig 4R 6R	12R	Det at Mels	1 Brig 2R 22R	2 Brig 3R 18R	3 Brig 16R 17R
7th	4 Brig 6R	4 Brig 4R	5 Brig 15R 8R	6 Brig 5R 10R	12R	Det at Mels	1 Brig 2R 22R	2 Brig 3R 18R	3 Brig 16R 17R
8th	6 Brig 10R	6 Brig 5R	4 Brig 6R 4R	5 Brig 8R 15R	12R	Det at Mels	1 Brig 2R 22R	2 Brig 3R 18R	3 Brig 16R 17R

9th	5 Brig 15R	5 Brig 8R	6 Brig 10R 5R			4 Brig 4R 6R	12R	Det at Mels	1 Brig 2R 22R	2 Brig 3R 18R	3 Brig 16R 17R
10th	4 Brig 6R	4 Brig 4R	5 Brig 15R 8R			6 Brig 5R 10R	12R	Det at Mels	1 Brig 2R 22R	2 Brig 3R 18R	3 Brig 16R 17R
11th	1 Brig 2R	1 Brig 22R	2 Brig 18R 3R			3 Brig 16R 17R	12R	Det at Mels	4 Brig 4R 6R	5 Brig 8R 15R	6 Brig 5R 10R
12th	3 Brig 17R	3 Brig 16R	1 Brig 2R 22R			2 Brig 3R 18R	12R	Det at Mels	4 Brig 4R 6R	5 Brig 8R 15R	6 Brig 5R 10R
13th	2 Brig 18R	2 Brig 3R	3 Brig 17R 16R			1 Brig 2R 22R	12R	Det at Mels	4 Brig 4R 6R 7R	5 Brig 8R 15R	6 Brig 5R 10R	7R to Als
14th	1 Brig 2R	1 Brig 22R	2 Brig 18R 3R			3 Brig 16R 17R	12R	Det at Mels	4 Brig 4R 6R 7R	5 Brig 8R 15R	6 Brig 5R 10R
15th	3 Brig 17R	3 Brig 16R	1 Brig 2R 22R			3R 7R	12R	Det at Mels	4 Brig 4R 6R	5 Brig 8R 15R	6 Brig 5R 10R
16th	2 Brig 18R	2 Brig 3R	3 Brig 17R 16R			2R 7R	12R	Det at Mels	4 Brig 4R 6R	5 Brig 8R 15R	6 Brig 5R 10R
17th	1 coy 6R / 1 coy 4R	1 coy 15R / 1 coy 8R	4 Brig 6R 4R	5 Brig 15R 8R	6 Brig 5R 7R	2R 16R	12R	Det at Mels	2 Brig 3R 18R	22R 17R	10R
18th	1 coy 2R / 1 coy 7R	1 coy 10R / 1 coy 5R	10R 2R	6 Brig 7R 5R	5 Brig 8R 15R	4 Brig 4R 6R	12R	Det at Mels	2 Brig 3R 18R	3 Brig 16R 17R	22R
19th	1 coy 6R / 1 coy 4R	1 coy 15R / 1 coy 8R	4 Brig 6R 4R	5 Brig 15R 8R	5R 7R	2R 10R	12R	Det at Mels	2 Brig 3R 18R	3 Brig 16R 17R	22R Guards	Guards to Als
20th	1 coy 17R / 1 coy 16R	1 coy 18R / 1 coy 3R	3 Brig 17R 16R	2 Brig 18R 3R	4 Brig 4R 6R	5 Brig 8R 15R Guards	12R	Det at Mels	1 Brig 2R 22R	6 Brig 5R 10R 7R
21st	1 coy 15R / 1 coy 8R	1 coy 6R / 1 coy 4R	5 Brig 15R 8R	4 Brig 6R 4R	2 Brig 3R 18R	3 Brig 16R 17R Guards	12R	Det at Mels	1 Brig 2R 22R	6 Brig 5R 10R 7R

22nd	1 coy 3R 1 coy 18R	1 coy 17R 1 coy 16R	2 Brig 3R 18R	3 Brig 17R 16R	4 Brig 4R 6R	5 Brig 8R 15R Guards	12R	Det at Mels	1 Brig 2R 22R	6 Brig 5R 10R	
23rd	1 coy 10R 1 coy 5R	1 coy 2R 1 coy 22R	6 Brig 22R 2R	1 Brig 10R 5R	3 Brig 16R 17R	2 Brig 3R 18R Guards	12R	Det at Mels	4 Brig 4R 6R	5 Brig 8R 15R	7R to Funen
24th	1 coy 16R 1 coy 17R	1 coy 18R 1 coy 3R	3 Brig 16R 17R	2 Brig 18R 3R	6Brig 5R 10R	1 Brig 2R 22R Guards	12R	Det at Mels	4 Brig 4R 6R	5 Brig 8R 15R	
25th	1 coy 22R 1 coy 2R	1 coy 10R 1 coy 5R	1 Brig 2R 22R	6 Brig 10R 5R	2 Brig 3R 18R	3 Brig 16R 17R Guards	12R	Det at Mels	4 Brig 4R 6R	5 Brig 8R 15R	
26th	1 coy 4R 1 coy 6R	1 coy 8R 1 coy 15R	4 Brig 4R 6R	5 Brig 8R 15R	6 Brig 5R 10R	1 Brig 2R 22R Guards	12R	Det at Mels	2 Brig 3R 18R	3 Brig 16R 17R	
27th	1 coy 2R 1 coy 22R	1 coy 10R 1 coy 5R	1Brig 22R 2R	6 Brig 10R 5R	5 Brig 8R 15R	4 Brig 4R 6R Guards	12R	Det at Mels	2 Brig 3R 18R	3 Brig 16R 17R	
28th	1 coy 8R 1 coy 15R	1 coy 4R 1 coy 6R	5 Brig 8R 15R	4 Brig 4R 6R	6 Brig 5R 10R	1 Brig 2R 22R Guards	12R	Det at Mels	2 Brig 3R 18R	3 Brig 16R 17R	
29th	1 coy 3R 1 coy 18R	1 coy 16R 1 coy 17R	2 Brig 3R 18R	3 Brig 16R 17R	4 Brig 4R 6R	5 Brig 8R 15R Guards	12R	Det at Mels	1 Brig 2R 22R	6 Brig 5R 10R	
30th	1 coy 6R 1 coy 4R	1 coy 15R 1 coy 8R	4 Brig 6R 4R	5 Brig 15R 8R	3 Brig 16R 17R	2 Brig 3R 18R Guards	12R	Det at Mels	1 Brig 2R 22R	6 Brig 5R 10R	
1st	1 coy 17R 1 coy 16R	1 coy 18R 1 coy 3R	3 Brig 17R 16R	2 Brig 18R 3R	5 Brig 8R 15R	4 Brig 4R 6R Guards	12R	Det at Mels	1 Brig 2R 22R	6 Brig 5R 10R	

April												
1st	1 coy 10R 1 coy 5R	1 coy 2R 1 coy 22R	6 Brig 10R 5R	1 Brig 2R 22R	2 Brig 3R 18R	3 Brig 16R 17R Guards	7 Brig 11R 12R	Det at Mels	4 Brig 4R 6R	5 Brig 8R 15R		11R to Als
2nd	1 coy 3R 1 coy 18R	1 coy 17R 1 coy 16R1	2 Brig 3R 18R	3 Brig 17R 16R	1 Brig 2R 22R	6 Brig 5R 10R Guards	7 Brig 11R	7 Brig 12R Det at Mels	4 Brig 4R 6R	5 Brig 8R 15R		
3rd	1 coy 22R 1 coy 2R	1 coy 10R 1 coy 5R	1 Brig 22R 2R	6 Brig 10R 5R	3 Brig 16R 17R	2 Brig 3R 18R	1 coy Guards / 7 Brig 11R	7 Brig 12R Det at Mels	4 Brig 4R 6R	5 Brig 8R 15R	3 coys Guards	
4th	1 coy 8R 1 coy 15R	1 coy 6R 1 coy 4R	5 Brig 8R 15R	4 Brig 6R 4R	6 Brig 5R 10R	1 Brig 2R 22R	1 coy Guards / 7 Brig 11R	7 Brig 12R Det at Mels	2 Brig 3R 18R	3 Brig 16R 17R	3 coys Guards	
5th	1 coy 5R 1 coy 10R	1 coy 2R 1 coy 22R	6 Brig 5R 10R	1 Brig 2R 22R	4 Brig 4R 6R	5 Brig 8R 15R	1 coy Guards / 7 Brig 11R	7 Brig 12R Det at Mels	2 Brig 3R 18R	3 Brig 16R 17R	3 coys Guards	
6th	1 coy 4R 1 coy 6R	1 coy 15R 1 coy 8R	4 Brig 4R 6R	5 Brig 15R 8R	1 Brig 2R 22R	6 Brig 5R 10R	1 coy Guards / 7 Brig 11R	7 Brig 12R Det at Mels	2 Brig 3R 18R	3 Brig 16R 17R	3 coys Guards	
7th	1 coy 16R 1 coy 17R	1 coy 18 R 1 coy 3R	3 Brig 16R 17R	2 Brig 18R 3R	5 Brig 8R 15R	4 Brig 1 bn 4R 6R	1 coy Guards / 7 Brig 11R	7 Brig 12R Det at Mels	1 Brig 2R 22R	6 Brig 5R 10R	3 coys Guards	1 bn 4R N of Barracks Line
8th	1 coy 15R 1 coy 8R	1 coy 4R 1 coy 6R	5 Brig 15R 8R	4 Brig 4R 6R	2 Brig 3R 18R	3 Brig 16R 1 bn 17R	1 coy Guards / 7 Brig 11R	7 Brig 12R Det at Mels	1 Brig 2R 22R	6 Brig 5R 10R	3 coys Guards	1 bn 17R N of Barracks Line

9th	1 coy 3R 1 coy 18R	1 coy 16R 1 coy 17R	2 Brig 3R 18R	3 Brig 16R 17R	4 Brig 4R 6R	5 Brig 1 bn 8R 15R	1 coy Guards	7 Brig 11R	7 Brig 12R Det at Mels	1 Brig 2R 22R	6 Brig 5R 10R	3 coys Guards	1 bn 8R N of Barracks Line
10th	1 coy 22R 1 coy 2R	1 coy 5R 1 coy 10R	1 Brig 22R 2R	6 Brig 5R 10R	3 Brig 16R 17R	2 Brig 1 bn 3R 18R	1 coy Guards	7 Brig 11R	7 Brig 12R Det at Mels	4 Brig 4R 6R	5 Brig 8R 15R	3 coys Guards	1 bn 3R N of Barracks Line
11th	1 coy 17R 1 coy 16R	1 coy 18R 1 coy 3R	3 Brig 17R 16R	2 Brig 18R 3R	6 Brig 5R 10R	1 Brig 2R 1 bn 22R	1 coy Guard	7 Brig 11R	7 Brig 12R Det at Mels	4 Brig 4R 6R	5 Brig 8R 15R	3 coys Guard	1 bn 22R N of Barracks Line
12th	1 coy 5R 1 coy 10R	1 Coy 2R 1 coy 22R	6 Brig 5R 10R	1 Brig 2R 22R	2 Brig 3R 18R	3 Brig 1 bn 16R 17R	1 coy Guards	7 Brig 11R	7 Brig 12R Det at Mels	4. Brig 4R 6R	5 Brig 8R 15R	3 coys Guards	1 bn 16R N of Barracks Line
13th	1 coy 6R 1 coy 4R	1 coy 8R 1 coy 15R	4 Brig 6R 4R	5 Brig 8R 15R	1 Brig 2R 22R	6 Brig 5R 1 bn 10R	1 coy Guards	7 Brig 11R	7 Brig Det at Mels	2 Brig 3R 18R 3 coys Guards	3 Brig 16R 17R	8 Brig 9R 20R	1 bn 10R N of Barracks Line 8 Brigade to Als
14th	1 coy 5R	1 coy 20R 1 coy 9R	6 Brig 10R 5R	8 Brig 20R 9R	5 Brig 8R 15R	4 Brig 4R 1 bn 6R	1 coy Guards	7 Brig 11R	7 Brig 12R Det at Mels	1 Brig 2R 22R 3 coys Guards	2 Brig 3R 18R	3 Brig 16R 17R	1 bn 6R N of Barracks Line
15th	1 coy 17R	1 coy 4R 1 coy 6R	3 Brig 16R 17R	4 Brig 4R 6R	8 Brig 9R 20R	6 Brig 1 bn 5R 10R	1 coy Guards	7 Brig 11R	7.Brig 12R Det at Mels	1 Brig 2R 22R 3 coys Guards	2 Brig 3R 18R	5 Brig 8R 15R	1 bn 5R N of Barracks Line
16th	nil	1 coy 20R 1 coy 9R	2 Brig 3R 18R	8 Brig 9R 20R	4 Brig 4R 6R	3 Brig 1 bn 17R 16R	1 coy Guards	7 Brig 11R	7 Brig 12R Det at Mels	1 Brig 2R 22R 3 coys Guards	5 Brig 8R 15R	6 Brig 5R 10R	1 bn 17R N of Barracks Line

17th	nil	1 coy 17R	1 Brig	3 Brig	8 Brig	2 Brig	1 coy Guards	7 Brig	7 Brig	4 Brig	5 Brig	6 Brig	1 bn 3R N
		1 coy 16R	22R 2R	17R 16R	9R 20R	1 bn 3R		11R	12R	4R 6R	8R 15R	5R 10R	of Barracks
						18R			Det at	3 coys Guards			line
									Mels				

Schøller, Appendix II. Brig = brigade, R = regiment, bn = battalion, coy = company

Note that the 'Infantry Reserve' was formally designated as 5th Brigade on March 19th. For the sake of clarity, it is so identified here for the whole of the period.

X

Order of Battle and Location
K.K. VI Army Corps (II Corps, Combined Army)
10th March 1864

Unit	Battalions	Companies	Squadrons	Guns	Location	Fit for Service Men	Fit for Service Horses	Combat Strength Men	Combat Strength Horses
Combat Formations									
Headquarters	—	—	—	—	Vejle	166	137	32	—
Brigade Gondrecourt									
Brigade Staff	—	—	—	—	Vejle	12	2	3	—
18 FJB (Jäger Battalion)	1	—	—	—	Lærbek	985	33	880	—
Regiment Nr. 30: Staff	1	—	—	—	Vejle	86	9	2	—
Regiment Nr. 30: 1 Battalion	1	—	—	—	Vejle	710	21	658	—
Regiment Nr. 30: 2 Battalion	—	—	—	—	Vejle	842	21	782	—
Regiment Nr. 34: Staff	—	—	—	—	Vejle	60	7	2	—
Regiment Nr. 34: 1 Battalion	1	—	—	—	Husum, Tønning, Vejle, Tonder	899	20	853	—
Regiment Nr. 34: 2 Battalion	1	—	—	—	Vejle, Lærbek	995	21	951	—
2nd Squadron Liechtenstein	—	—	1	—	Vejle	146	135	—	135
5th Squadron Liechtenstein	—	—	1	—	Vejle	147	141	—	140
Pioneer Detachment	—	—	—	—	Vejle	—	—	—	—
½ Provisions Troop	—	—	—	—	Vejle	—	—	—	—
4 Pounder Foot Battery 2/1	—	—	—	8	Vejle	198	127	—	—
Brigade Totals	5	—	2	8		5,083	507	4,131	275
Brigade Nostitz									
Brigade staff	—	—	—	—	Vejle	11	2	3	—
9 FJB (Jäger Battalion)	1	—	—	—	Vejle	907	30	800	—
Regiment Nr. 14: Staff	—	—	—	—	Vejle	91	7	2	—
Regiment Nr. 14: 1 Battalion	1	—	—	—	Vejle	892	23	836	—
Regiment Nr. 14: 2 Battalion	1	—	—	—	Store Grundet	873	23	835	—
Regiment Nr. 27: Staff	—	—	—	—	Vejle	94	7	2	—
Regiment Nr. 27: 1 Battalion	1	—	—	—	Vejle	1,005	23	956	—

Regiment Nr. 27: 2 Battalion	1	—	—	—	Hornstrup	1,005	23	956	—
Liechtenstein 4th Squadron	—	—	1	—	Vejle	143	138	—	138
½ Provisions Troop	—	—	—	—	Vejle	—	—	—	—
4 pounder Foot Battery 4/1	—	—	—	8	Vejle	146	117	—	—
Brigade Totals	5	—	1	8		5,167	390	4,390	138
Gondrecourt and *Nostitz* Brigade Totals	10	—	3	16		10,316	1,067	8,553	413

Brigade Tomas

Brigade Staff	—	—	—	—	Vinding	12	2	3	—
11 FJB (Jäger Battalion)	1	—	—	—	Vinding	900	30	766	—
Regiment Nr. 6 Staff	—	—	—	—	Schleswig	56	7	2	—
Regiment Nr. 6 1 Battalion	1	—	—	—	Kolding	1,028	23	875	—
Regiment Nr. 6 2 Battalion	1	—	—	—	Schleswig	1,035	23	875	—
Regiment Nr. 80 Staff	—	—	—	—	Skjaarup	56	7	2	—
Regiment Nr. 80 1 Battalion	1	—	—	—	Skjaarup	929	23	897	—
Regiment Nr. 80 2 Battalion	1	—	—	—	Andkjer	933	23	904	—
Liechtenstein 6th Squadron	—	—	1	—	Engom	145	131	—	127
½ Provisions Troop	—	—	—	—	Tvinholdt	—	—	—	—
4 pounder Foot Battery 5/1	—	—	—	8	Vinding	148	95	—	—
Brigade Totals	5	—	1	8		5,242	364	4,324	128

Brigade Dormus

Brigade Staff	—	—	—	—	Engom	11	2	3	—
22 FJB (Jäger Battalion)	1	—	—	—	Engom & Constatinkro	961	30	869	—
Regiment Nr. 35 Staff	—	—	—	—	Louisenkost	98	7	2	—
Regiment Nr. 35 1 Battalion	1	—	—	—	Lysholt	1,002	23	877	—
Regiment Nr. 35 2 Battalion	1	—	—	—	Harborhuss	1,002	23	831	—
Regiment Nr. 72. Staff	—	—	—	—	Juulsberg	95	7	2	—
Regiment Nr. 72 1 Battalion	1	—	—	—	Sonntagaard	1,005	23	843	—
Regiment Nr. 72 2 Battalion	1	—	—	—	Bredballe	1,005	23	843	—
Liechtenstein 3rd Squadron	—	—	1	—	Stenderup	135	12	120	118
4 pounder Foot Battery 6/1	—	—	—	8	Engom	164	117	—	—
1 Provisions Troop	—	—	—	—	Hogholt	—	—	—	—
Brigade Totals	5	—	1	8		5,478	375	4,270	118

Cavalry Brigade

Brigade Staff	—	—	—	—	Petersholm	17	14	—	3
Liechtenstein Staff	—	—	—	—	Vejle	43	34	—	10

Windischgrätz Dragoons Regiment HQ	—	—	—	—	Petersholm	46	40	—	10
Windischgrätz 1st Division Staff	—	—	—	—	West of Vejle	3	2	—	2
Windischgrätz 1st Squadron	—	—	1	—	West of Vejle	152	136	—	134
Windischgrätz 2nd Squadron	—	—	1	—	West of Vejle	152	137	—	135
Windischgrätz 4th Squadron	—	—	1	—	West of Vejle	152	136	—	134
Windischgrätz 2nd Division Staff	—	—	—	—	West of Vejle	3	2	—	2
Windischgrätz 5th Squadron	—	—	1	—	West of Vejle	152	136	—	134
Windischgrätz 6th Squadron	—	—	1	—	West of Vejle	152	136	—	134
Brigade Totals	—	—	5	—		873	779	—	698
Corps Artillery Reserve	—	—	—	—		—	—	—	—
Staff	—	—	—	—	Petersholm	9	6	—	—
8 pounder Battery 9/1	—	—	—	8	Petersholm	188	158	—	—
8 pounder Battery 10/1	—	—	—	8	Petersholm	174	158	—	—
Artillery Reserve Totals	—	—	—	16	Petersholm	371	322	—	—
Combat Formations Totals	20	—	10	48		22,280	2,901	17,147	1,357

Miscellaneous Support Units

Corps Munitions Park

1st Park Company	—	1	—	—	Vejle	115	84	—	—
6th Field Repair Company	—	1	—	—	Vejle	29	—	—	—
Transport Squadron Nr. 27	—	—	—	—	Vejle	89	135	—	—
Transport Squadron Nr. 28	—	—	—	—	Vejle	89	136	—	—
Park Totals	—	2	—	—	Vejle	322	355	—	—
3rd Company, 1st Pioneer Battalion	—	1	—	—	Vejle	190	15	—	—
4th Company, 1st Pioneer Battalion	—	—	—	—	Vejle	205	15	—	—
39th Bridging Train Squadron	—	—	—	—	Vejle	84	128	—	—
40th Bridging Train Squadron	—	—	—	—	Vejle	84	128	—	—
1 Medical Company, with Transport Squadron Nr. 31	—	1	—	—	Vejle	177, 70	112	—	—
½ Pioneer	—	—	—	—	Vejle	6	9	—	—
11th Engineer Company	—	1	—	—	Vejle	154	11	—	—
Corps Munitions Column	—	—	—	—	Vejle	—	—	—	—
Field Magazine	—	—	—	—	Vejle	21	—	—	—
Transport Squadron Nr. 2	—	—	—	—	Vejle	156	228	—	—
Transport Squadron Nr. 35	—	—	—	—	Vejle	156	228	—	—
Transport Squadron Nr. 53	—	—	—	—	Vejle	156	228	—	—

Corps Distribution Depot	—	—	—	—	Vejle	29	—	—	—
Corps Reception Depot	—	—	—	—	Aabenraa	26	—	—	—
Field Supply Magazine	—	—	—	—	Schleswig	16	—	—	—
Field Post Detachment	—	—	—	—	Vejle	7	12	—	—
Field Telegraph Detachment	—	—	—	—	Vejle	27	42	—	—
Corps Ambulance Nr. 5	—	—	—	—	Vejle	43	68	—	—
	—	—	—	—	Vejle	20	36	—	—
	—	—	—	—	Vejle	4	8	—	—
Field Hospital Nr. 9	—	—	—	—	Kolding	136	—	—	—
Field Hospital Nr. 12	—	—	—	—	Schleswig	136	—	—	—
Field Hospital Nr. 16	—	—	—	—	Rendsburg	135	—	—	—
Artillery Field Depot	—	—	—	—	Neumünster	—	—	—	—
7th Field Repair Company	—	1	—	—	Schleswig	30	—	—	—
1st Park Company (part)	—	—	—	—	Schleswig	31	—	—	—
7th Company, IR 2 Alexander	—	1	—	—	Schleswig	160	2	—	—
Totals	—	5	—	—		2,427	1,508	—	—
Corps Totals	—	—	—	—		25,088	4,764	17,147	1,357

Extracted from, Anon, 'Ordre de Bataille und Dislocation des k.k. 6 Armee Corps, 10de März 1864', KA, AFA, March, 1864, Document 195

XI

Armament of the Fortress of Fredericia
21st March 1864

	84 Pd Howitzer Type I	84 Pd Howitzer Type II	24 Pd Howitzer	24 Pd Cannon	12 Pd Rifled Cannon	12 Pd Cannon.	6 Pd Cannon	4 Pd Rifled Cannon	3 Pd Cannon	24 Pd Mortars	84 Pd and 168 Pd Mortars
Delmenhorst Bastion	—	—	—	—	—	—	—	—	—	2	—
Oldenborg Bastion	4	—	—	—	—	—	—	—	—	2	2
Oldenborg Fausse Braie	—	—	—	—	—	—	—	2	—	—	—
Oldenborg Outwork	—	—	—	—	—	2	3	—	—	4	—
Holsten Bastion	—	2	—	1	—	—	—	2	4	—	—
Slesvig Bastion	—	1	—	2	—	—	—	2	4	—	—
Slesvig Ravelin	—	—	—	—	—	—	—	2	—	—	—
Fuglesangsveien (Road)	—	—	—	—	—	—	—	2	—	—	—
Curtain to Princess Bastion	—	—	—	—	—	—	—	—	—	—	2
Princess Bastion	—	1	—	2	—	—	—	—	4	—	—
Kolding Road Outwork	—	—	—	—	—	—	4	—	—	—	—
Prince George Bastion	—	2 (+1)*	—	2(+1)*	(4)*	—	—	—	—	4	—
Curtain to Prince Christian Bastion	—	—	—	—	—	—	—	—	—	—	2
Prince Christian Bastion	—	2	—	2	—	—	—	—	4	—	—
Curtain to Queen Bastion	—	—	—	—	—	—	—	—	—	—	2
Queen Bastion	—	1	—	2	2	—	—	—	4	—	—
Curtain to King Bastion	—	—	—	—	—	—	8	—	—	—	2
King Bastion	—	2	—	1	2	—	2	—	4	—	—
Denmark Bastion	—	1	—	2	—	—	—	—	2	4	—
Norway Bastion Fausse Braie	—	—	—	—	—	—	—	4	—	—	—
Redoubt I	—	2	—	2	1	—	5	—	—	2	—
Redoubt II	—	3	—	3	2	6	5	—	—	2	—
Redoubt III	—	6	1	8	1	—	3	—	—	—	—
Redoubt IV	—	8	1	7	—	—	5	4	—	—	—
Redoubt V	—	—	7	—	—	—	—	—	—	—	—
Totals	4	32	9	35	12	12	37	12	34	12	10

*Ordnance in brackets indicates unmounted guns

Generalstaben, Volume II, Appendix 28

XII

Danish Army Combatants with Designated Units

Fit for duty - April 1st 1864

	Officers				NCO's				Musicians					
	Line	Reserve & Temporary	Foreign	Total	Line	Reserve	Temporary	Total	Line	Reserve	Total	Undercorporals	Men	Total
1st Infantry Brigade Staff	3	—	—	3	—	—	—	—	—	—	—	—	7	10
2nd Infantry Brigade Staff	4	—	—	4	—	—	—	—	—	—	—	—	4	8
3rd Infantry Brigade Staff	2	1	—	3	—	—	—	—	—	—	—	—	5	8
4th Infantry Brigade Staff	2	1	—	3	—	—	—	—	—	—	—	—	4	7
5th Infantry Brigade Staff	5	—	—	5	—	—	—	—	—	—	—	—	4	9
6th Infantry Brigade Staff	2	1	—	3	—	—	—	—	—	—	—	—	4	7
7th Infantry Brigade Staff	2	1	—	3	—	—	—	—	—	—	—	—	2	5
8th Infantry Brigade	3	—	—	3	—	—	—	—	—	—	—	—	3	6
9th Infantry Brigade Staff	2	1	—	3	—	—	—	—	—	—	—	—	3	6
Life Guards Infantry	14	—	—	14	31	—	—	31	44	—	44	77	607	773
1st Infantry Regiment	13	16	—	29	20	11	25	56	11	7	18	123	1447	1673
2nd Infantry Regiment	14	11	—	25	26	7	27	60	12	8	20	132	1254	1491
3rd Infantry Regiment	15	13	4	32	24	6	40	70	15	10	25	127	1380	1634
4th Infantry Regiment	13	11	2	26	25	12	31	68	13	12	25	134	1397	1650
5th Infantry Regiment	14	12	1	27	28	9	20	57	15	7	22	146	1383	1635
6th Infantry Regiment	14	16	—	30	29	2	30	61	14	10	24	137	1378	1630
7th Infantry Regiment	15	13	—	28	31	12	21	64	12	14	26	110	1076	1304
8th Infantry Regiment	12	17	1	30	27	14	28	69	4	4	8	134	1334	1575
9th Infantry Regiment	15	9	—	24	26	7	32	65	14	8	22	137	1514	1762
10th Infantry Regiment	10	14	2	26	19	7	21	47	14	9	23	115	1425	1636
11th Infantry Regiment	15	16	—	31	23	6	27	56	11	8	19	127	1164	1397
12th Infantry Regiment	12	14	—	26	28	8	22	58	17	5	22	126	1315	1547
13th Infantry Regiment	12	12	1	25	28	7	29	64	16	8	24	132	1416	1661
14th Infantry Regiment	15	12	1	28	19	1	58	78	16	9	25	148	1499	1778
15th Infantry Regiment	17	14	1	32	20	1	42	63	14	9	23	137	1326	1581
16th Infantry Regiment	17	14	—	31	22	—	42	64	13	9	22	138	1287	1542

17th Infantry Regiment	14	13	3	30	30	1	33	64	13	3	16	115	1287	1512
18th infantry Regiment	11	12	2	25	27	6	32	65	13	14	27	101	1371	1580
19th Infantry Regiment	15	15	—	30	24	15	27	66	14	11	25	145	1656	1922
20th Infantry Regiment	15	11	2	28	24	6	28	58	12	11	23	126	1354	1589
21st Infantry Regiment	14	16	—	30	29	6	30	65	11	12	23	136	1687	1941
22nd Infantry Regiment	17	12	—	29	21	—	44	65	9	7	16	118	1142	1370
Detachment at Mels	4	7	—	11	6	3	14	23	3	—	3	49	544	630
Garrison Battalions note	5	14	—	19	—	—	—	56	—	—	9	54	651	789
1st Cavalry Brigade Staff	3	—	—	3	—	—	—	—	1	—	1	—	6	11
2nd Cavalry Brigade Staff	2	1	—	3	—	—	—	—	—	—	—	2	8	13
Life Guards Cavalry	6	—	—	6	13	—	—	13	7	—	7	12	99	137
Guard Hussar 1st Half Regiment	7	1	1	9	23	—	4	27	6	—	6	17	283	342
Guard Hussar 2nd Half Regiment	8	—	—	8	23	—	2	25	3	—	3	14	201	251
2nd Dragoon Regiment	12	5	—	17	33	—	22	55	13	—	13	43	478	606
3rd Dragoon Regiment	14	3	—	17	37	—	20	57	12	—	12	41	628	755
4th Dragoon Regiment 1st Half Regiment	9	1	—	10	18	—	12	30	3	5	8	18	321	387
4th Dragoon Regiment/ 2nd Half Regiment	6	1	1	8	19	3	5	27	4	2	6	20	258	319
5th Dragoon Regiment	15	—	—	15	37	—	20	57	12	—	12	52	652	788
6th Dragoon Regiment	15	—	2	17	33	2	16	51	11	—	11	42	603	724
1st Division Art. Command	1	1	—	2	—	—	—	—	—	—	—	—	2	4
2nd Division Art. Command	2	—	—	2	—	—	—	—	—	—	—	—	2	4
4th Division Art. Command	2	—	—	2	—	—	—	—	—	—	—	—	1	3
Artillery Command/Dybbol	3	—	—	3	—	—	—	—	—	—	—	—	—	3
Artillery Command/Fredericia	4	2	—	6	2	—	—	2	—	—	—	—	—	8
1st Battery	2	—	—	2	8	—	1	9	2	—	2	20	133	166
2nd Battery	2	1	—	3	7	—	—	7	2	—	2	19	132	163
3rd Battery note	2	1	—	3	6	1	1	8	1	—	1	20	136	168
4th Battery	2	—	—	2	7	—	1	8	2	—	2	18	164	194
5th Battery	3	—	—	3	8	—	1	9	2	—	2	19	148	181
6th Battery note	2	1	—	3	8	—	1	9	2	—	2	21	177	212
7th Battery	2	—	—	2	7	2	1	10	3	—	3	18	138	171

8th Battery	2	—	—	2	9	—	—	9	3	—	3	20	134	168
9th Battery	2	—	—	2	7	3	1	11	3	—	3	19	187	222
10th Battery	2	—	—	2	7	1	2	10	3	—	3	19	170	204
11th Battery	2	—	—	2	10	1	—	11	3	—	3	18	150	184
12th Battery note	2	—	—	2	9	2	—	11	2	—	2	22	190	227
13th Battery	2	—	—	2	10	—	—	10	1	—	1	30	314	358
Espingol Battery	2	2	—	4	2	7	3	12	1	—	1	3	80	100
1st Fortress Company note	1	5	—	6	5	2	—	7	—	1	1	30	314	358
2nd Fortress Company note	1	6	—	7	6	2	—	8	—	—	—	28	441	484
3rd Fortress Company note	1	6	—	7	7	11	—	18	—	2	2	18	400	445
4th Fortress Company note	1	5	—	6	7	8	—	15	—	—	—	18	535	574
5th Fortress Company note	1	5	1	7	5	4	—	9	—	—	—	27	234	277
6th Fortress Company note	2	4	—	6	10	7	—	17	—	—	—	15	487	525
Engineer Troops	26	3	—	29	37	32	—	69	2	—	2	51	501	652
Headquarters and Ordnance	16	3	1	20	6	—	3	9	27	—	27	9	38	103
Telegraph & Topography	1	2	—	3	9	—	—	9	—	—	—	2	31	45
Engineer Cmd Field Army	11	—	—	11	4	—	—	4	—	—	—	1	4	20
Army Artillery	4	2	—	6	3	—	—	3	—	—	—	1	6	16
1st Division Staff	5	1	—	6	1	—	1	2	—	—	—		7	15
2nd Division Staff	6	—	—	6	3	—	—	3	—	—	—	3	9	21
3rd Division Staff	7	—	—	7	—	—	—	—	23	—	23	7	11	48
4th Division Staff	9	2	—	11	—	—	—	—	1	—	1	1	17	30
Command at Fredericia	4	4	—	8	1	—	—	1	—	—	—	1	19	29

Source, Generalstaben, 'Statiskiske Meddelelser angaaende den danske Krigsmagt', Volume I, Copenhagen 1867, pp. 68-69

XIII

Armament of the Dybbøl Redoubts April 2nd 1864

Redoubts / Gun Mounting	36pd. Smoothbore high	36pd. Smoothbore low	24pd. Smoothbore high	24pd. Smoothbore low	12pd. Smoothbore low	84pd. Howitzer Type I high	84pd. Howitzer Type II high	24pd. Smoothbore low	24pd. Smoothbore high	12pd. Smoothbore low	12pd rifled low	4pd. rifled low	(low)	84pd. Mortar	24pd. Mortar	Total
Redoubt Nr. I	1	1	—	—	—	—	—	—	—	4	—	—	—	—	—	6
Redoubt Nr. II	—	—	—	—	3	—	—	1	—	—	—	3	1	—	—	8
Redoubt Nr. III	—	—	—	—	2	—	—	—	—	2	—	—	—	—	3	7
Redoubt Nr. IV	—	—	—	—	—	1	1	4	1	5	—	—	—	—	—	12
Redoubt Nr. V	—	—	—	2	—	—	—	—	—	2	—	—	—	—	—	4
Redoubt Nr. VI	—	—	—	2	4	1	—	3	—	—	—	2	—	—	3	15
Redoubt Nr. VII	—	—	—	—	4	—	—	—	—	—	—	—	—	—	—	4
Redoubt Nr. VIII	—	—	1	3	—	—	—	—	—	—	2	3	1	—	—	10
Redoubt Nr. IX	—	—	—	—	—	1	1	3	—	3	—	—	—	2	—	10
Redoubt Nr. X	—	—	4	—	—	—	—	—	—	—	3	—	—	—	—	7
Total	1	1	5	7	13	3	2	11	1	16	5	8	2	2	6	83

Schøller, p. 60

XIV

Danish Casualties at Dybbøl from the 2nd to the 17th of April

Unit	Killed			Wounded			Prisoners			Missing		
	Officers	Ncos	Men	Officers	Ncos	Men	Officers	Ncos	Men	Officers	Ncos	Men
Staff	—	—	—	—	—	3	—	—	—	—	—	—
Foot Guards	—	—	—	—	—	4	—	—	—	—	—	—
2nd Regiment	—	2	14	2	1	30	—	—	1	—	—	1
3rd Regiment	—	—	19	—	3	38	—	—	—	—	—	—
4th Regiment	—	1	12	—	1	25	—	—	—	—	—	1
5th Regiment	2	2	29	—	2	62	—	3	88	—	—	1*
6th Regiment	2	1	17	—	3	40	—	1	19	—	—	1
8th Regiment	—	—	4	1	—	12	—	—	—	—	—	—
9th Regiment	—	—	6	1	—	9	—	—	1	—	—	2*
10th Regiment	2	1	25	—	2	64	—	—	9	—	—	9*
11th Regiment	—	1	—	—	—	2	—	—	—	—	—	—
15th Regiment	1	—	10	—	2	15	—	—	—	—	—	—
16th Regiment	1	4	32	2	1	100	—	—	1	—	—	—
17th Regiment	1	2	11	3	2	56	—	1	57	—	2*	3*
18th Regiment	—	—	35	1	2	47	—	—	6	—	—	2*
20th Regiment	—	—	3	—	2	8	—	—	—	—	—	—
22nd Regiment	—	2	11	1	—	19	—	1	—	—	—	—
Artillery	2	1	52	1	4	90	—	—	—	—	—	—
Engineers	1	—	2	1	2	10	—	—	—	—	—	—
Gendarmerie	—	1	—	—	—	—	—	—	—	—	—	—
Work Detail, Als	—	—	2	—	—	5	—	—	—	—	—	—
1st Division Ambulance	—	—	—	—	—	2	—	—	—	—	—	—
2ndDivision Ambulance	—	—	1	—	—	1	—	—	—	—	—	—
Work Detail, Other	—	—	—	—	—	1	—	—	—	—	—	—
Totals	12	18	285	13	27	643	—	6	185	—	2	22

* Those so marked are shown as deserters

Generalstaben, Volume II, Appendix 42

XV

Prussian Casualties at Dybbøl from the 5th to the Morning of the 18th of April

		Killed			Wounded		
Date	Unit	Officers	Men	Horses	Officers	Men	Horses
5th April	4th Foot Guards	—	—	—	—	1	—
5/6th April	4th Foot Guards	—	3	—	—	18	—
6th April	4th Foot Guards	—	1	—	—	3	—
6th April	4th Guard Grenadiers	—	—	—	—	3	—
6th April	Leib Grenadiers Nr 8	—	—	—	—	2	—
6th April	Artillery Brigade Nr 3	—	—	—	—	1	—
6th April	Pioneer Battalion Nr 7	—	1	—	—	2	—
7th April	4th Guard Grenadiers	—	—	—	—	3	—
7/8th April	3rd Guard Grenadiers	—	4	—	—	7	—
7/8th April	FR Nr 35	—	—	—	—	2	—
7/8th April	IR Nr 60	—	—	—	—	2	—
8th April	FR Nr 35	—	—	—	—	3	—
8th April	Artillery Brigade Nr 3	—	—	—	1	—	—
9/10th April	IR Nr 55	—	—	—	1	1	—
10th April	Artillery Brigade Nr 3	—	—	—	—	1	—
11th April	FR Nr 35	—	1	—	2	1	—
11/12th April	4th Guard Grenadiers	—	—	—	—	2	—
11/12th April	IR Nr 13	—	—	—	—	1	—
11/12th April	IR Nr 24	—	1	—	—	2	—
12th April	IR Nr 15	—	—	—	—	2	—
12th April	IR Nr 64	—	1	—	—	1	—
12th April	Guard Artillery Brigade	—	2	—	—	2	—
12th April	Artillery Brigade Nr 3	—	—	—	—	1	—
12th April	Artillery Brigade Nr 8	—	—	—	—	1	—
12/13th April	IR Nr 13	—	—	—	—	3	—
13th April	Pioneer Battalion Nr 3	—	1	—	—	2	—
13th April	Artillery Brigade Nr 3	—	—	1	—	—	1
13/14th April	Leib Grenadiers Nr 8	—	—	—	—	1	—
13/14th April	IR Nr 60	2	4	—	1	32	—

13/14th April	Jäger Battalion Nr 3	—	—	—	—	1	—
14th April	IR Nr 64	—	—	—	—	1	—
14th April	Artillery Brigade Nr 8	—	2	—	—	1	—
15th April	IR Nr 15	—	—	—	—	1	—
15th April	IR Nr 18	—	—	—	—	1	—
15/16th April	IR Nr 53	—	—	—	—	1	—
15/16th April	IR Nr 64	—	1	—	—	4	—
16th April	4th Foot Guards	—	1	—	—	1	—
16th April	IR Nr 55	—	—	—	—	1	—
16/17th April	4th Guard Grenadiers	—	4	—	—	5	—
16/17th April	IR Nr 64	—	—	—	—	4	—
16/17th April	Artillery Brigade Nr 7	—	—	—	—	1	—
16/17th April	Artillery Brigade Nr 4	—	1	—	—	—	—
16/17th April	3rd Guard Grenadiers	—	—	—	—	3	—
16/17th April	IR N · 24	—	5	—	—	10	—
17/18th April	IR Nr 60	—	—	—	—	2	—
Total		2	33	1	4	137	1

Grosser Generalstab, Volume II, Appendix 52

XVI

Armament of the Fortress of Fredericia
29th April 1864 at the Start of the Danish Withdrawal

	84 Pd Howitzer Type I	84 Pd Howitzer Type II	24 Pd Howitzer	24 Pd Cannon	12 Pd Rifled Cannon	12 Pd Cannon.	6 Pd Cannon	4 Pd Rifled Cannon	3 Pd Cannon	24 Pd. Mortars	84 Pd and 168 Pd Mortars
Delmenhorst Bastic n	—	—	—	—	—	—	—	—	2	—	—
Oldenborg Bastion	4/	—	—	—	—	—	—	—	/2	—	2/
Oldenborg Fausse Braie	—	—	—	—	—	—	2	—	—	—	—
Oldenborg Outwork	—	—	—	—	—	2	3	—	—	4	—
Holsten Bastion Salient	—	—	—	1	—	—	—	—	—	—	—
Holsten Right Face/Right Flank	—	1/	—	—	—	—	2/	—	/2	—	—
Holsten Left Face/Left Flank	—	1/	—	—	/2	—	—	—	/2	—	—
Slesvig Bastion Salient	—	1	—	—	—	—	—	—	—	—	—
Slesvig Right Face/Right Flank	—	—	—	1/	—	—	—	—	/2	—	—
Slesvig Left Face/Left Flank	—	—	—	1/	—	—	2/	—	/2	—	—
Slesvig Ravelin	—	—	—	—	—	—	2	—	—	—	—
Work in front of Ravelin	—	—	—	—	—	—	2	—	—	—	—
Curtain to Princess Bastion	—	—	—	—	—	—	—	—	—	—	2
Princess Bastion Salient	—	—	—	—	—	—	—	—	—	—	—
Princess Right Face/Right Flank	—	—	—	—	—	—	2/	—	/2	—	—
Princess Left Face/Left Flank	—	—	—	—	—	—	—	—	/2	—	—
Princess Cavaller	—	1	—	2	—	—	—	—	—	—	—
Ravelin at Princes Gate	—	—	—	—	—	—	3	—	—	—	—
Kolding Redoubt	—	—	—	—	—	6	—	—	—	—	—
Work S. of Redoubt	—	—	—	—	—	2	—	—	—	—	—
Prince George Bastion, Blunted Salient	—	—	—	—	—	—	—	—	—	—	—
Prince George Right Face/Right Flank	—	—	—	—	—	—	—	—	/2	—	—

Prince George Left Face/Left Flank	—	—	—	—	—	—	—	—	/2	—	—
Cavaller	—	3	—	3	4	—	—	—	—	—	—
Curtain to Prince Christian Bastion	—	—	—	—	—	—	—	—	—	—	2
Prince Christian Bastion, Blunted Salient	—	2	—	2	—	—	—	—	—	—	—
Prince Christian Right Face/Right Flank	—	—	—	—	—	—	—	—	/2	—	—
Prince Christian Left Face/Left Flank	—	—	—	—	—	—	—	—	/2	—	—
Curtain to Queen Bastion	—	—	—	—	—	—	—	—	—	—	2
Queen Bastion, Blunted Salient	—	1	—	2	—	—	—	—	—	—	—
Queen Bastion, Right Face/Right Flank	—	—	—	—	2/	—	—	—	/2	—	—
Queen Bastion, Left Face/Left Flank	—	—	—	—	—	—	—	—	/2	—	—
Curtain	—	—	—	—	—	—	—	8	—	—	2
King Bastion	—	—	—	1	—	—	—	—	—	—	—
King Right Face/Right Flank	—	1/	—	—	—	—	2/	—	/2	—	—
King Left Face/Left Flank	—	1/	—	—	—	—	—	—	/2	—	—
King Cavaller	—	—	—	—	2	—	—	—	—	—	—
Denmark Bastion	—	1/	—	6/	—	—	—	—	/2	4/	—
Norway Bastion Left Flank	—	1	—	1	—	—	2	—	—	—	—
Norway Fausse Braie	—	—	—	—	—	—	4	—	—	—	—
Redoubt I	—	3	—	2	—	—	5	—	—	2	—
Redoubt II	—	4	—	4	1	5	5	—	—	2	—
Redoubt III	—	8	1	6	2	—	2	—	—	—	—
Redoubt IV	—	7	1	7	1	—	5	4	—	—	—
Redoubt V	—	—	8	—	—	1	—	—	—	—	—
Totals	4	36	10	39*	14	16	43	12	34	12	10

Generalstaben, Volume III, Appendix 3

Figures shown on the left of an oblique indicate ordnance on the 'Face', and on the right of the oblique that on the 'Flank'

During pre-war works to the fortress, the salients of three bastions, Prince George, Prince Christian, and Queen, had been flattened and widened. Hence the use of this term.

Four of these guns were rifled

In addition to the above, nine Espignol guns were present, three in the Oldenborg Outwork, four at the Kolding Outwork, and two in Redoubt I

XVII

Order of Battle, Prussian Combined III Corps

26th April 1864

Commander	Lieutenant-General von der Mülbe
General Staff Officer	Major von Alvensleben
Commander, Artillery	Lieutenant-Colonel Scherdening, Brandenburg Artillery Brigade Nr. 3
Engineer Officer	Premier-Lieutenant Scheibert
Adjutants	Captain von Notz, 2nd Foot Guards Regiment
	Premier-Lieutenant von Henniges, 1st Guard Grenadier Regiment

Combined Foot Guard Brigade

Commander	Major-General Count von der Goltz
Adjutant	Premier-Lieutenant Freiherr von Ende, 1st Guard Grenadier Regiment

3rd Foot Guards Regiment – Colonel von der Groeben
    I Battalion
    II Battalion
4th Foot Guards Regiment – Major von Conta (Colonel von Korth, wounded)
    I Battalion
    II Battalion

Combined Guard Grenadier Brigade

Commander	Colonel von Bentheim
Adjutant	Premier-Lieutenant von Wrochem, 2nd Foot Guards Regiment

3rd Guard Grenadier Regiment – Colonel von Winterfeld
    I Battalion
    II Battalion
4th Guard Grenadier Regiment – Colonel von Oppell
    I Battalion
    II Battalion
    Fusilier Battalion

10th Infantry Brigade

Commander	Colonel von Kamienski, 8th Brandenburg Infantry Regiment Nr. 64

Adjutant   Premier-Lieutenant Luft, 1st Silesian
                                      Grenadier Regiment Nr. 10
1st Posen Infantry Regiment Nr. 18 – Colonel von Kettler
    I Battalion
    II Battalion
    Fusilier Battalion
6th Brandenburg Infantry Regiment Nr. 52 – Lieutenant-Colonel von
Blumenthal
    I Battalion
    II Battalion
    Fusilier Battalion
    Westphalian Jäger Battalion Nr. 7 – Major von Beckedorff
Westphalian Dragoon Regiment Nr. 7 – Lieutenant-Colonel von Ribbeck
(4 Squadrons)
3rd Guard 6 Pounder Battery – six smoothbore cannon
Guard 4 Pounder Battery – eight rifled 4 pounder field guns
1st 6 Pounder Battery, Brandenburg Artillery Brigade Nr. 3 – six
smoothbore cannon
Westphalian Pioneer Battalion Nr, 7 (minus 1st Company) - Captain von
Rohrscheidt

Ancillary Units

    Ammunition Trains Nrs. 1, 2, and 3, Brandenburg Artillery Brigade Nr. 3
    Provisions Trains Nr. 1 and 2 (detached from Train Battalion of I Corps)
    1st Heavy Field Hospital (from VII Corps)
    Combined Guards Division Light Field Hospital
    Combined Guards Division Sick Transport Company
    Field Telegraph Detachment Nr. 2 (attached to III Corps from Headquarters)

XVIII

Order of Battle, Combined Division Münster

20th April, 1864

Commander	Major-General Count Münster-Meinhövel
General Staff Officers	Major von Stedink, Magdeburg Dragoon Regiment Nr. 6
	Major Count von Wartensleben
Adjutants	Second-Lieutenant von Noville, Westphalian Uhlan Regiment Nr. 5
	Second-Lieutenant von Grimm, Ziethen Hussar Regiment Nr. 3
Orderly Officer	Second-Lieutenant von der Horst, Westphalian Hussar regiment Nr. 8
On Active Service	Major Prince Heinrich von Hesse

Combined Guard Infantry Regiment – Lieutenant-Colonel von Esebeck, 4th Foot Guards
Fusilier Battalion, 3rd Foot Guards
Fusilier Battalion, 4th Foot Guards
Fusilier Battalion, 3rd Guard Grenadiers
3rd 6 Pounder Battery, Artillery Brigade Nr. 6 – six rifled 6 pounder cannon

21st Infantry Brigade

Commander	Major-General von Bornstedt
Adjutant	Premier-Lieutenant von Lieres und Wilkau, 2nd Upper Silesian Infantry Regiment Nr.23

1st Silesian Grenadier Regiment Nr. 10 – Colonel Freherr von Falkenstein
I Battalion
II Battalion
Fusilier Battalion
3rd Lower Silesian Infantry Regiment Nr. 50 – Colonel von Hackewitz
I Battalion
II Battalion
Fusilier Battalion
4th 12 Pounder Battery, Brandenburg Artillery Brigade Nr. 3 – six smoothbore 12 pounder cannon

Combined Cavalry Brigade

Commander	Colonel Flies

Adjutant	Premier-Lieutenant von Rudolphi, 1st Brandenburg Uhlan Regiment, Nr. 3

Guard Hussar Regiment – Lieutenant-Colonel Kerssenbroigt
  – four squadrons
Brandenburg Cuirassier Regiment Nr. 6 – Colonel, His Royal Highness, The Duke of Mecklenburg
  Schwerin – four squadrons
Westphalian Hussar Regiment Nr. 8 – Lieutenant-Colonel von Rantzau (minus 1st Squadron) – four squadrons
5th Horse Artillery Battery, Westphalian Artillery Brigade Nr. 7 – four smoothbore 6 pounder cannon

XIX

Order of Battle, Royal Danish Army

26th June 1864

A. On Funen Island

Headquarters

Commander	Lieutenant-General G.D. Gerlach
Chief of Staff	Lieutenant-Colonel F.C. Stiernholm
Deputy Chief of Staff	Ritmester J.Z. Schroll
Adjutants	Captain F.E. Bille
	Premierlieutenant E.G. Gotschalk
	Premierlieutenant F.F. Jacobi
	Premierlieutenant A.L. le Maire
	Premierlieutenant C.A.S. Dahlberg
Personal Adjutant	Second-Lieutenant L.H. Westphal
Also attached to Headquarters	Ritmester V.F.G. Bülow
	Second-Lieutenant Count C. Moltke-Bregentved
Senior Officer, Artillery	Colonel J. Vahl
Senior Officer, Engineers	Lieutenant-Colonel J.C.F. Dreyer
Naval Liaison Officer	(Naval) Captain A.C. Schulz
Commander, Train	Ritmester H.C.W.F. Deichmann
Orderly Officers	Ritmester C.E. Hansen
Staff Quartermaster	Captain A.J.C.E. Madsen
Staff Auditor	Auditor V.C. Ussing
Staff Surgeon	Senior Surgeon J. Rørby
Staff Veterinarian	Staff Veterinarian C.L. Friis
Army Telegraph & Topography	Lieutenant R.W.F. Abrahamson
Head of Administration	Principal of the War Ministry, Premierlieutenant C. J. Westergaard

Army Artillery

Commander	Colonel J. Vahl
Chief of Staff	Lieutenant-Colonel J.T. Wegener
Attached from Staff	Captain S.W. Pfaff
	Premiellieutenant C.T. Müllertz
	Premierlieutenant A.M. Gjern
	Premierlieutenant Count C. Moltke-Hvitfeldt

4th Field Artillery Battery – Captain C.P.F.J. de Conick (mustering)
Fortress Artilley Command – Captain J.J. Bahnson

2nd Fortress Company – Captain C.G.J. Schmidt
Artillery Depot

Engineer Command - Field Army

Commander	Lieutenant-Colonel C.E.F. Dreyer
Chief of Staff	Captain F.C. Good
Adjutant	Premierlieutenant F.L.J. Keyper
Attached from Staff	Premierlieutenant C. Bayer
	Second-Lieutenant S.B.W. Dyhr

2nd Engineer Company – Captain P.F.H. Bruun
6th Engineer Company – Captain J.C.G. Hedemann (as bridging company)
7th Engineer Company – Captain H.F.F. Jastrau (serving as Engineer Park)

Third Division

Commander	Major-General F.C.W. Caroc
Chief of Staff	Captain L.E. Fog
Adjutants	Premierlieutenant F. Grüner
	Second-Lieutenant T. Westergaard
Orderly Officer	Premierlieutenant C.M. Wildenradt, personal adjutant
Senior Engineer Officer	Captain W.O.W. Lehmann

3rd Brigade

Commander	Colonel J.A.P.F. Wørishøffer
Adjutants	Premierlieutenant J.P.F. Colding
	Second-Lieutenant E.O. Mygind

16th Infantry Regiment – Lieutenant-Colonel C. Wolle
    I Battalion (1st, 2nd, 5th, 6th Companies)
    II Battalion (3rd, 4th, 7th, 8th Companies)
17th Infantry regiment – Major E.G.E. du Plat
    I Battalion (1st, 2nd, 5th, 7th Companies)
    II Battalion (3rd, 4th, 6th, 8th Companies)

7th Brigade

Commander	Colonel F.L.A. Hein
Adjutant	Premierlieutenant F.J. Buchwaldt
Orderly Officer	Second-Lieutenant (of the War Reserve) O.W. Fischer

11th Infantry Regiment – Lieutenant-Colonel J.M.F.F. Rist
    I Battalion (1st, 3rd, 5th, 7th Companies)
    II Battalion (2nd, 4th, 6th, 8th Companies)
12th Infantry Regiment – Major M. Arntz
    I Battalion (1st, 2nd, 3rd, 4th Companies)
    II Battalion (5th, 6th, 7th, 8th Companies)

8th Brigade

Commander	Colonel P.U. Scharffenberg

Adjutant   Second-Lieutenant H. Holbøll
Orderly Officer   Second-Lieutenant (of the War Reserve)
                            F.W. Kraft
2nd Infantry Regiment – Major C.F.A.. Olufsen
    One Battalion only (1st, 2nd, 3rd, 4th Companies)
9th Infantry Regiment – Major J. Nørager
    One Battalion only (1st, 2nd, 3rd, 4th Companies)
20th Infantry Regiment – Major A.D.B.X. de Plane
    One Battalion only (1st, 2nd, 3rd, 4th Companies)
22nd Infantry Regiment – Major C.F. Schøning
    One Battalion only (1st, 2nd, 3rd, 4th Companies)
13th Infantry Regiment – Major P.E. Klingsey
    I Battalion (1st, 2nd, 3rd, 4th Companies)
    II Battalion (5th, 6th, 7th, 8th Companies)
    Funen Work Battalion – Captain C.F. Bülow
Divisional Cavalry   Lieutenant-Colonel Baron F.W. Rosenkrantz
                            Guard Hussar Regiment
1st Half Regiment – Major D.W. Hegermann-Lindencrone
(2nd, 4th, 6th Squadrons)
4th Dragoon Regiment
2nd Half-Regiment – Major C.A.F. Lillienskjold
(4th, 5th, 6th Squadrons)

Divisional Troops

Divisional Artillery   Lieutenant-Colonel R.O. Holm
    6th Field Artillery Battery – Captain E.E.S. Thestrup
        Eight smoothbore 12 pounder cannon
    10th Field artillery Battery – Captain H.P.W. Mønster
        Eight smoothbore 12 pounder cannon
    11th Field Artillery Battery – Captain M.E. Fallesen
        Eight rifled 4 pounder field guns
    12th Field Artillery Battery – Major J.D.Z. von der Recke
        Eight smoothbore 12 pounder cannon
    13th Field Artillery Battery – Captain J.W. Salto
        Eight rifled 4 pounder field guns

5th Brigade (Former Infantry Reserve – unassigned to a higher formation)

Commander   Colonel C.F.M. Müller
Adjutant   Second-Lieutenant A. Hartung
Orderly Officer   Premierlieutenant P.H.W. Lange
8th Infantry Regiment – Major C.F. Bauditz
    I Battalion (1st, 2nd, 5th, 8th Companies)
    II Battalion (3rd, 4th, 6th, 7th Companies)
15th Infantry regiment – Lieutenant-Colonel A..F. Zepelin
    I Battalion (1st, 2nd, 5th, 6th, Companies)
    II Battalion (3rd, 4th, 7th, 8th Companies)
Attached

1st Squadron, 4th Dragoon Regiment
8th Field Artillery Battery – Captain F.W.F. Messerschmidt
    Eight rifled 4 pounder field guns
5th Engineer Company – Premierlieutenant M.O. Asmussen
Streifkorps – Captain B.C.M. Aarøe
In transit from Frederikshavn (northern Jutland) to Nyborg (on Funen Island):

2nd Division

Commander Major-General E.H.C. Wilster
Chief of Staff Captain C.M.W. Tvaermoes
Adjutants   Premierlieutenant H.E.E. Nysted
    Premierlieutenant M.S.F. Hedemann
Orderly Officer   Second-Lieutenant Harboe

1st Brigade

Commander	Lieutenant-Colonel G.J.W. Nielsen
Adjutant	Second-Lieutenant E.A.A. Marcussen
Orderly officer	Premierlieutenant (of the War Reserve) J.F.S. Øst

7th Infantry Regiment – Lieutenant-Colonel L.H.L. Muus
    I Battalion (1st, 2nd, 5th, 8th Companies)
    II Battalion (3rd, 4th, 6th, 7th Companies)
14th Infantry Regiment – Major H. Junghaus
    I Battalion (1st, 2nd, 3rd, 4th Companies)
    II Battalion (5th, 6th, 7th, 8th Companies)

B. In North Jutland

The North Jutland Army Corps

Commander	Lieutenant-General C.D. Hegermann-Lindencrone
Chief of Staff	Major S. Anckjær
Deputy Chief of Staff	Ritmester T. Freiesleben
Adjutants	Premierlieutenant J.E.C. Rosen
	Premierlieutenant H.H. Lüttichau
	Premierlieutenant T.G. Rohde
	Second-Lieutenant F.E.W. Paulsen
Attached	Ritmester A.W.R. Oppen-Schilden
On Service with the Staff	His Royal Highness, Crown Prince Frederik
Adjutant	Captain L. Lund
Senior Officer, Artillery	Lieutenant-Colonel J.C. Just
Senior Officer, Engineers	Major C.T. Jørgensen
Orderly Officer Detachment	Premier-Lieutenant V. Saurbrey

4th Division

Commander	Major-General J.J. Honnens
Chief of Staff	Major F.J. Heramb

Deputy Chief of Staff	Captain J.B. Scholten
Adjutants	Captain C.C. Zahlmann
	Premierlieutenant C.C. Engelbrecht

9th Brigade

Commander	Lieutenant-Colonel L. N. Færch
Adjutants	Second-Lieutenant M.A, Karmark
	Second-Lieutenant (of the War Reserve) T.E. Frisch
Attached from the Staff	Second-Lieutenant (of the War Reserve) J.Petersen

19th Infantry Regiment – Lieutenant-Colonel L.N. Færch
    I Battalion (5th, 6th, 7th, 8th Companies)
    II Battalion (1st, 2nd, 3rd, 4th Companies)
21st Infantry Regiment – Major O.C.F. Saabye
    I Battalion (1st, 2nd, 3rd, 4th Companies)
    II Battalion (5th, 6th, 7th, 8th Companies)

1st Cavalry Brigade

Commander	(Divisional Commander)
Adjutant	Premierlieutenant H.B. Dahl
Orderly Officer	Second-Lieutenant A.L. Baadsgaard

3rd Dragoon Regiment – Major F.L. Brock
    (1st, 2nd, 3rd, 4th, 5th, 6th Squadrons)
5th Dragoon Regiment – Lieutenant-Colonel N.S. Brock
    (1st, 2nd, 3rd, 4th, 5th, 6th Squadrons)
      3rd Field Artillery Battery – Captain A.L. Klein
        Eight rifled 4 pounder field guns
      5th Field Artillery Battery – Captain C.J.F. Lønborg
        Eight rifled 4 pounder field guns
Divisional Engineers
3rd Engineer Company – Captain E.M. Dalgas

Under Corps Command

2nd Cavalry Brigade

Commander	Colonel H.L. Scharffenberg
Adjutant	Second-Lieutenant H.F. Hegermann-Lindencrone
Orderly Officer	Second-Lieutenant (of the War Reserve) Baron C.F.S.W. Juel-Brockdorff

2nd Dragoon Regiment – Major E.P. Bruhn
    (1st, 2nd, 3rd, 4th, 5th, 6th Squadrons)
6th Dragoon Regiment – Lieutenant Colonel F.C.A. Bauditz
    (1st, 2nd , 3rd, 4th, 5th, 6th Squadrons)
1st Infantry Regiment – Lieutenant-Colonel H.G.J. Beck
    I Battalion (1st, 2nd, 6th, 7th Companies)

II Battalion (3rd, 4th, 5th, 8th Companies)
7th Field Artillery Battery – Captain W.P.J. Johansen
Eight rifled 4 pounder field guns

C. On the Island of Als

1st Division

Commander	Major-General P.F. Steinmann
Chief of Staff	Captain J.C. Blom
Deputy Chief of Staff	Captain C.E. Meldahl
Adjutants	Premierlieutenant C.G.F. Rønnov
	Second-Lieutenant C. Søltov
	Second-Lieutenant (of the War Reserve) P.E.M. Ramsing
Orderly Officer	Premierlieutenant W.F. Bendz
Attached from the Staff	Captain F..A. Moltke
	Premierlieutenant (of the War Reserve) A.C.N.W. Holstein

2nd Brigade

Commander	Colonel H.A.T. Kauffmann
Adjutant	Second-Lieutenant C.F.F.E Tuxen
Orderly Officer	Second-Lieutenant J.W.B. Benedictsen

3rd Infantry Regiment - Lieutenant-Colonel H.W. Mathiesen
    I Battalion (1st, 2nd, 5th, 6th Companies)
    II Battalion (3rd, 4th, 7th, 8th Companies)
18th Infantry Regiment – Major E.A. Lundbye
    I Battalion (1st, 2nd, 5th, 7th Companies)
    II Battalion (3rd, 4th, 6th, 8th Companies)

4th Brigade

Commander	Colonel E.A. Faaborg
Adjutant	Premierlieutenant G.C.C. Zachariae
Orderly Officer	Second-Lieutenant (of the War Reserve) P.O.R. Olrik

4th Infantry Regiment – Major M.A.F. Rauch
    I Battalion (1st, 2nd, 5th, 7th Companies)
    II Battalion (3rd, 4th, 6th, 8th Companies)
6th Infantry Regiment – Lieutenant-Colonel G.W. Caroc
    I Battalion (1st, 2nd, 5th, 6th Companies)
    II Battalion (3rd, 4th, 7th, 8th Companies)

6th Brigade

Commander	Colonel O.C.S.A. Bülow
Adjutant	Second-Lieutenant C.J.C.F Kranold
Orderly Officer	Second-Lieutenant (of the War Reserve) W.L. Dinesen

5th Infantry Regiment – Major A.C.J. Myhre
  I Battalion (1st, 2nd, 5th, 6th Companies)
  II Battalion (3rd, 4th, 7th, 8th Companies)
10th Infantry Regiment – Major W.E.S. Gedde
  I Battalion (1st, 2nd, 5th, 7th Companies)
  II Battalion (3rd, 4th, 6th, 8th Companies)
Divisional Cavalry
4th Dragoon Regiment
1st Half Regiment – Major A.W. Gerlach
(2nd and 3rd Squadrons)

Als Artillery Command

Commander   Major E.V. Schreiber
Attached from Headquarters   Premierlieutenant H.A. Elben
                                 N.A. Wolff
  1st Field Artillery Battery – Captain N.P.C.T. Bruus
    Eight rifled 4 pounder field guns
  2nd Field Artillery Battery – Captain O. Lunn
    Eight rifled 4 pounder field guns
  9th Field Artillery Battery – Premierlieutenant M.F.L. Bentzon
    Eight smoothbore 12 pounder cannon
3rd Fortress Company – Captain A. Grove
4th Fortress Company – Captain F. Bartholin
6th Fortress Company – Captain H.C. Hertel
Als Artillery Depot – Captain G. Hagerup

Als Engineer Command

Commander   Major C.F.N. Schrøder
Attached from Headquarters   Major C. Ovesen
                                 Captain N.A. Brummer
                                 Captain W.A. Thulstrup
                                 Premierlieutenant J.H.K. Bangert
                                 Premierlieutenant A.K. Larsen
1st Engineer Company – Premierlieutenant W. Kolderup-Rozenvinge
Detachment of 6th Engineer Company
Work Company – Premierlieutenant J.W.F. Arnoldi

XX

Danish Army Combatants with Designated Units

Fit for duty - August 1st 1864

	Officers				NCO's				Musicians			Undercorporals	Men	Total
	Line	Reserve & Temprary	Foreign	Total	Line	Reserve	Temporary	Total	Line	Reserve	Total			
1st Infantry Brigade Staff	2	1	—	3	—	—	1	1	—	—	—	—	3	7
2nd Infantry Brigade Staff	3	—	—	3	—	—	—	—	—	—	—	—	5	8
3rd Infantry Brigade Staff	3	1	—	4	—	—	—	—	—	—	—	—	9	13
4th Infantry Brigade Staff	2	1	—	3	—	—	—	—	—	—	—	—	3	6
5th Infantry Brigade Staff	3	—	—	3	—	—	—	—	—	—	—	—	5	8
6th Infantry Brigade Staff	3	—	—	3	—	—	—	—	—	—	—	—	6	9
7th Infantry Brigade Staff	2	1	—	3	1	—	—	1	—	—	—	—	4	8
8th Infantry Brigade Staff	3	—	—	3	—	—	—	—	—	—	—	—	11	14
9th Infantry Brigade Staff	2	2	—	4	—	—	—	—	—	—	—	—	5	9
Life Guards Infantry	13	1	—	14	37	—	1	38	45	—	45	72	660	829
1st Infantry Regiment	14	20	—	34	23	9	43	75	13	5	18	143	1313	1583
2nd Infantry Regiment	8	11	—	19	16	3	22	41	6	5	11	59	900	1030
3rd Infantry Regiment	11	16	3	30	21	5	38	64	12	7	19	87	1146	1346
4th Infantry Regiment	8	8	2	18	15	7	25	47	10	7	17	80	885	1047
5th Infantry Regiment	10	13	4	27	17	5	54	76	12	7	19	100	925	1147
6th Infantry Regiment	14	16	2	32	30	3	46	79	15	7	22	123	1462	1718
7th Infantry Regiment	15	16	1	32	28	16	37	81	13	13	26	127	1471	1737
8th Infantry Regiment	14	17	5	36	25	13	45	83	9	8	17	138	1555	1829
9th Infantry Regiment	10	9	—	19	19	7	33	59	10	5	15	89	823	1005
10th Infantry Regiment	6	8	4	18	18	5	29	52	5	6	11	58	705	844
11th Infantry Regiment	20	16	1	37	24	6	55	85	11	9	20	141	1369	1652
12th Infantry Regiment	15	20	2	37	29	7	39	75	17	4	21	127	1261	1521
13th Infantry Regiment	15	17	—	32	33	6	39	78	15	2	17	147	1173	1447
14th Infantry Regiment	15	15	1	31	24	1	26	51	15	7	22	108	1152	1364
15th Infantry Regiment	15	22	1	38	25	1	51	77	14	11	25	102	1324	1566
16th Infantry Regiment	14	14	4	32	27	*	60	87	10	13	23	134	1323	1599

17th Infantry Regiment	12	17	3	32	16	*	72	88	8	2	10	136	1256	1522
18th Infantry Regiment	11	15	3	29	16	4	41	61	11	14	25	109	1265	1489
19th Infantry Regiment	16	18	—	34	27	15	29	71	15	10	25	132	1330	1592
20th Infantry Regiment	11	7	2	20	19	4	30	53	8	6	14	76	833	996
21st Infantry Regiment	16	20	—	36	26	7	43	76	13	10	23	136	1367	1638
22nd Infantry Regiment	7	12	3	22	16	*	28	44	9	2	11	73	660	810
Aaroes Corps	6	5	6	17	3	*	31	34	8	—	8	—	628	687
Garrison Battalions	6	17	—	23	26	*	23	49	14	—	14	74	1298	.458
1st Cavalry Brigade Staff	4	—	—	4	—	—	—	—	1	—	1	1	9	15
2nd Cavalry Brigade Staff	2	1	—	3	—	—	—	—	—	—	—	—	6	9
Life Guards Cavalry	6	—	—	6	13	—	—	13	7	—	7	8	109	143
Guard Hussar Regiment	22	2	1	25	44	—	16	60	12	—	12	46	592	735
2nd Dragoon Regiment	13	8	—	21	30	—	32	62	12	—	12	37	524	656
3rd Dragoon Regiment	16	5	—	21	36	—	31	67	11	—	11	47	657	803
4th Dragoon Regiment	13	6	2	21	33	1	22	56	8	3	11	46	627	761
5th Dragoon Regiment	17	4	—	21	39	—	30	69	11	—	11	48	716	865
6th Dragoon Regiment	18	2	—	20	49	3	14	57	13	—	13	46	614	750
1st Division Artillery Command	2	—	—	2	—	—	—	—	—	—	—	2	4	8
2nd Division Artillery Command	2	—	—	2	—	—	—	—	—	—	—	2	—	4
3rd Division Artillery Command	2	—	—	2	2	—	—	2	—	—	—	—	2	6
4th Division Artillery Command	2	—	—	2	—	—	—	—	—	—	—	—	3	5
Artillery Command/Little Belt	3	1	—	4	—	—	—	—	—	—	—	—	5	9
1st Battery	2	2	—	4	8	1	3	12	2	—	2	14	135	167
2nd Battery	2	1	—	3	6	2	3	11	2	—	2	16	136	168
3rd Battery	2	1	—	3	6	2	3	11	2	—	2	13	142	171
4th Battery	—	—	—	4	—	—	—	—	—	—	—	—	—	4
5th Battery	3	—	—	3	6	3	3	12	2	—	2	15	132	164
6th Battery	2	2	—	4	7	3	—	10	2	—	2	14	178	208
7th Battery	3	1	—	3	7	2	1	10	3	—	3	14	141	171
8th Battery	2	—	—	2	10	1	2	13	3	—	3	11	140	169
9th Battery	2	1	—	3	5	3	4	12	1	—	1	10	116	141
10th Battery	2	1	—	3	7	1	4	12	3	—	3	13	164	195
11th Battery	2	2	—	4	9	1	2	12	2	—	2	12	145	175

2th Battery	2	2	—	4	10	—	4	14	2	—	2	14	181	215
13th Battery	2	2	—	4	8	—	4	12	2	—	2	17	155	190
Copenhagen Fortress Company*	4	17	1	22	3	29	13	45	—	—	6	24	810	907
2nd Fortress Company	1	5	1	7	7	3	5	15	—	—	—	13	383	418
4th Fortress Company	—	—	—	4	4	6	—	10	—	—	—	7	170	191
6th Fortress Company	1	6	2	9	10	6	3	19	—	—	—	13	332	373
Engineer Troops	12	3	—	15	27	34	—	61	2	—	2	51	481	610
Headquarters and Ordnance	14	2	—	16	6	—	4	10	25	—	25	5	45	101
Telegraph & Topography	1	1	—	2	9	—	—	9	—	—	—	2	42	55
Engineer Command Field Army	12	—	—	12	5	—	3	8	—	—	—	—	6	26
Army Artillery	4	—	1	5	4	—	—	4	—	—	—	1	11	21
1st Division Staff	6	—	—	6	3	—	2	5	—	—	—	2	23	36
2nd Division Staff	6	—	—	6	3	—	2	5	—	—	—	1	13	24
3rd Division Staff	7	—	—	7	3	—	1	4	25	—	25	2	21	59
4th Division Staff	8	3	—	11	2	—	1	3	1	—	1	1	20	36
Nyborg Command	2	1	—	3	1	—	—	1	—	—	—	2	23	29

Source, Generalstaben, *Statistiske Meddelelser angaaende den danske Krigsmagt*, Volume I, Copenhagen 1867, pp. 70-71

*For these units, Reserve NCO's are included in the Line total

A Note on Sources

Writing this book has necessitated the consultation of a wide range of sources. The sheer amount of literature on the war is astonishing. For such a small conflict, there are vast quantities of published and unpublished material. I have consulted many of these for the purposes of comparison, clarification, corroboration, or simply to gain the "flavour" of something.

The starting point for information on the 1864 War are two bibliographies, published in 1915 and 1970 respectively. The first was compiled by Lieutenant-Colonel Albert Buddecke, the head of the Imperial German General Staff Library for many years, and published as the first of his intended series on (then) recent German wars. Appearing in the midst of the First World War, it was in fact the only one completed. In 1970, the State Library of Schleswig-Holstein and the Royal Library in Copenhagen collaborated in the publication of the second, an excellent work covering both printed and pictorial sources. Both have been invaluable to me.

Of published sources, I would specifically highlight the following. Further details may be found in the bibliography:

Fischer, Friedrich von – The Austrian official history (1870), this is a good work, which pulls few punches in its criticisms. It is used as a standard textbook on the campaign at the Danish Defence Academy.

Fontane, Theodor – One of the earlier major works on the subject (1866), this is a highly detailed account of the war, written in a journalistic style. There are many personal accounts. Fontane had a clear political agenda in all his writing, based upon simple Prussian directed German nationalism. One must be clear about this in interpreting his material.

Generalstaben – The Danish official history (1890-92). It is a massively detailed description of the campaign, which has been described as "dry as dust". It relates facts, but makes no criticisms and few observations.

Grosser Generalstab – The German General Staff history (1886-87), very probably written by Count Moltke himself. An analytical study of the war, primarily from German language sources – much technical detail.

Jensen, N.P. – A very good turn of the 20th Century history (1900), by a Danish officer who served in the war. Written primarily from Danish sources, but with a generally even-handed approach.

Johansen, Jens – The author penned three books (1936, 1938, 1942) on different aspects of the war, two of them in conjunction with J. Nordentoft. All three are packed with detailed information and comment. The Danish Army archive librarian, Johansen had complete access to vast amounts of information for almost 30 years, but, infuriatingly, he rarely gives any sources for his assertions.

Lecomte, Ferdinand – A contemporary work by a Swiss officer (1864), this is an extremely good source. Written with a pro-Danish viewpoint, it is nevertheless objective in its analysis.

Liljefalck & Lütken, O. – A detailed, good and generally accurate book, (1904) though with an element, perhaps inevitably, of "good Danes" and "beastly Germans". It was written in a sense to bring the country together 40 years after the event. There are several editions.

Rüstow, Wilhelm – Another contemporary book (1864), also by a resident of Switzerland. An exile from the 1848 revolutions, Rüstow takes a pro-German stance, but like Lecomte, his analysis is objective, and he is critical of both sides.

Sørensen, Carl Th. – A very detailed study of the war (1883), by a former company commander, using material from both sides. This work was originally envisaged as the official Danish history of the war, Sørensen being at the time an officer on the General Staff. However, he was forced to publish it privately, because of his political views.

Skinner, J.E.H. – A first-hand description of the first part of the campaign, by the British correspondent of the *Daily News*. This is probably the best contemporary account in English, although the author's sympathies are completely biased in favour of the Danes. A reprint of this book was issued in 2002.

Vaupell, Otto – Another very detailed work, by a decorated former Danish officer who served in the war (1889). A very useful source, but it suffers from the author's great hostility to Lieutenant-General de Meza, the Danish Commander-in-Chief in the initial phase of the war, to whom the author rather insultingly refers as "General Meza".

Waldersee, Count – Waldersee wrote his account immediately after the campaign (1865), in which he served as a major on the staff of Prince Friedrich Carl. This is a very detailed and informative book, inevitably viewed from one side.

A number of official and semi-official periodicals are also a rich source of information on the subject, particularly (as relevant) in the year of and those immediately following the war. Again, I would highlight the following:

Danebrog – Danish (published 1880-1884)

Militært Tidsskrift – Danish (published 1871-to date)

Militärische Blätter – Prussian/German (published 1863-1873), and subsequently, *Neue Militärische Blätter* (1873-1901)

Militär-Wochenblatt – Prussian/German (published 1816-1942)

Österreichische Militärische Zeitschrift – Austrian (published 1860-1914)

Tidsskrift før Krigsvæsen – Danish (published 1855-1874)

Vort Forsvar – Danish (published 1881-1908)

In addition, four popular periodicals covered the war in some detail in their contemporary issues. These are:

Harper's Weekly – A Journal of Civilization, New York

The Illustrated London News, London

Illustreret Tidende, Copenhagen

Über Land und Meer – Allgemeine Illustrierte Zeitung, Leipzig & Stuttgart

A large amount of unpublished information resides in the Danish and Austrian Archives, and in the Royal Garrison Library in Copenhagen.

Bibliography

Unpublished Sources

Kriegsarchiv, Vienna
KA – AFA – Dänemark 1864. Reports shown by month, document number, and title in relevant footnote.

Hæren's Arkiv, Copenhagen
Reports shown by unit and date in relevant footnote.

Private Correspondence listed in relevant footnote.

Dechange, Marcus, "Die dänische Marine und ihre Operationen im Deutsch-Dänische Krieg 1864" (Dissertation, Hamburg Universität der Bundeswehr 1998)

Johansen, Jens, "Hovedbegivenhederne I Krigen 1864" (Typed manuscript in Royal Danish Military Library, Copenhagen 1952)

Kiær, L.H. "Dagbog fra Krigen 1864 11 Reg./1 Kmp." (Typed manuscript in Royal Danish Military Library, Copenhagen, from original diary in the Military Archives) 1987

Norrie, J.W.G. "Begivenhederne 1. – 6. Februar 1864" (Typed manuscript in Royal Danish Military Library, Copenhagen 1963)

Norrie, J.W.G. "Overgangen over Alssund den 29/6/1864" (Typed manuscript in Royal Danish Military Library, Copenhagen 1963)

German Books

(Anon.), Auszug a.d. *Geschichte d. k.u.k. FeldJägerBataillons Nr. 9*, (Graz 1890)

(Anon.), *Die hervorragenden Waffenthäten der Unteroffiziere und Mannschaft des k.k. 6. Armeekorps aus dem feldzüge 1864 gegen Dänemark,* (From 'Der Kamerad', Vienna 1865)

(Anon.), *Der Feldzug in Schleswig im Jahre 1864,* (Josef Stockhauser v. Hirschfeld, Vienna 1864)

(Anon.), *Der schleswig-holstein'sche Krieg für's deutsche Volk in treuer Schilderung,* (Beck, Vienna 1864)

(Anon.), *Exercier-Reglement fur kaiserlich-königlichen Fusstruppen 1862,* (Vienna 1862)

(Anon.), *Exerzier-Reglement für die Infanterie der Königlich Preussischen von 25 febr. 1847,* (Berlin 1847)

(Anon.), *Geschichte des K.u.K, Husaren-Regimentes Graf Nadasdy Nr.9,* (Sopron 1903)

(Anon.), *Illustrierte Kriegs-Berichte aus Schleswig-Holstein. Gedenkblätter an den Deutsch-Dänischen Krieg von 1864,* (Weber, Leipzig 1864)

(Anon.), *Der Befreiung Schleswig-Holsteins im Jahre 1864. Nach den Berichten des Königl. Staats-Anzeigers zusammengestellt,* (Schultze, Berlin 1864)

(Anon.), *Manövrir-Reglement fur die kaiserl. Königl. Infanterie 1863*, (Vienna 1863)

Altrock, Constantin v., *Geschichte des Königin Elisabeth-Garde-Grenadier-Regiments Nr. 3., von seiner Stiftung bis zum Jahre 1896*, (E.H. Mittler & Son, Berlin 1909)

Bader, Werner, *Pionier Klinke: Tat und Legende*, (Westkreuz Verlag, Berlin/Bonn 1992)

Bartsch, Rudolf, et al, *Kriegsbilder der österr.- ungar. Armee aus der 19.Jahrhunderte*, (E. Beyer, Vienna & Leipzig 1913)

Behn, Alfred, *Die Volkstimmung in Schleswig-Holstein im letzten Jahre vor ausbruch des Krieges von 1864,* (Stefanstifts, Hanover 1920 – dissertation)

Blasendorff, K., *Der Deutsch-Dänische Krieg von 1864*, (Weidmann, Berlin 1889)

Bleibtreu, Carl, *Düppel Alsen*, (Carl Krabbe, Stuttgart c.1905)

Bloch, Eduard, *Preussen und Oesterreicher in Schleswig*, (Lustige Soldatenbilder 7, Lassar, Berlin 1864)

Braumüller, Maximilian, *Geschichte des Königen Augusta Garde-Grenadier Regiments Nr.4*, (E.S. Mittler & Son, Berlin 1901)

Bremen, W.von, *Düppel und Alsen. Schleswig-Holsteins Befreiung 1864*, (Wohlfahrtsgessellschaft, Berlin c 1914)

Buddecke, Albert, *Die Literatur über den Feldzug 1864*, (Georg Bath, Berlin 1915)

Bunge, C., *Aus meinem Kriegstagebuche. Erinnerungen an Schleswig-Holstein 1864*, (Max Babezien, Rathenow nd,1865)

Camphausen, Walter, *Ein Maler auf dem Kriegsfelde. Düppel und Alsen 1864. Illustriertes Tagebuch*, (Velhagen & Klasing, Bielefeld & Leipzig 1916)

Cramer, Alfred, *Geschichte des Infanterie-Regiments Prinz Friedrich der Niederlande (Westfälischer) Nr. 15*, (Eisenschmidt, Berlin 1910)

Crousaz, A. von, *Die Organisation des Brandenburgischen und Preussischen Heeres seit 1640*, (Riemenschneider, Berlin 1873)

Dedenroth, V., *Der Winterfeldzug in Schleswig-Holstein*, (Friedrich Schulze, Berlin 1864)

Fischer, Friedrich von , *Der Krieg in Schleswig und Jütland im Jahre 1864*, (*Österreichische Militärische Zeitschrift*, Vienna 1870)

Friedjung, Heinrich ,*Der Kampf um die Vorherrschaft in Deutschland 1859 bis 1866*, (Cotta, Stuttgart & Berlin 1912)

Friedrich, R., Ritter von Wiser, *Die Besetzung der nordfriesischen Inseln im Juli 1864*, (Danzer's Armee Zeitung, Seidel, Vienna 1914)

Foerster, Wolfgang, *Prinz Friedrich Karl von Preussen. Denkwürdigkeiten aus seinem Leben*, (Deutsche Verlags Anstalt, Stuttgart and Leipzig 1910)

Fontane, Theodor, *Der Schleswig-Holsteinsche Krieg im Jahre 1864*, (Decker, Berlin 1866)

Gentz, Hauptmann, *Geschichte des 8. Brandenburgischen Infanterie-Regiments Nr. 64*, (E.H. Mittler and Son, Berlin 1878)

Granier, Herman, *Der Feldzug von 1864*, (M. Felix, Berlin 1897)

Grois, Victor, *Geschichte des k.k. Infanterie-Regimentes Nr. 14*, (Verlage des Regiments, Linz 1876)

Grosser Generalstab, *Der Deutsch-Dänische Krieg 1864*, (E.H. Mittler und Son, Berlin 1886/87)

Gründorf von Zebegény, Wilhelm Ritter, *Memoiren eines österreichischen Generalstäblers 1832-1866*, (Robert Lutz, Stuttgart 1913)

Günther, Peter P. E., *Namentliches Verzeichnis der Todten der Preussischen Armee und Marine des Deutsch-dänischen Krieges 1864, (Berlin 1978)*

Haeseler, Graf. V, *Zehn Jahre im Stabe des Prinzen Friedrich Karl*, (E.H. Mittler & Son, Berlin 1910/12)

Hake, M. (Volume 1), Horn, A., & Lichtenstein, Major, *Geschichte des Leib-Grenadier Regiments König Friedrich Wilhelm III (1 Brandenburgischen) Nr. 8 1898-1908*, (E.H. Mittler & Son, Berlin 1908)

Hegenbarth, Hans, *Furchtlos und treu. 300 Jahre Infanterie-Regiment Nr. 27*, (Ulrich Moser, Graz 1982)

Hellighausen, Otto, *Denkwürdigkeiten aus dem deutsch-dänischen Kriege 1864*, (Freiburg im Breisgau 1914)

Helmert, Heinz, & Usczeck, Hansjürgen, *Preussischdeutsche Kriege. Von 1864 bis 1871*, (Militärverlag, Berlin 1984)

Herrmann, E., *Översee*, (Kleinmayer & Bamberg, Laibach 1904)

Herzog, R., *Dueppel 1864-1914*, (E. Marcks, Potsdam 1914)

Hohenlohe-Ingelfingen, Prinz, *Aus meinem Leben*, (E.S. Mittler & Son, Berlin 1897-1907)

Honthumb, Kaspar Alexander, *Mein Tagebuch. Erinnerungen aus Schleswig-Holstein von Casper, Musketier des 53. Regiments*, (Theissing, Münster 1865)

Isenburg, Franz, *Das Brandenburgische Füsilier Regiment Nr. 35 1815-1870*, (E.S. Mittler & Son, Berlin 1879)

Jena, Carl, *Erinnerungen an einen Heimgegangenen*, (G. A. König, Berlin 1864. Major Jena's letters to his family)

Junck, C., *Aus dem Leben des K.K. Generals der Cavallerie Ludwig Freiherrn von Gablenz*, (Faesy & Frick, Vienna 1874)

Kessel, V., *Die Ausbildung des Preussischen Infanterie-Battalions im praktischen Dienst*, (E.S. Mittler & Son, Berlin 1863)

Knorr, E., *Von der Eider bis Düppel*, (Perthes-Besser & Mauke, Hamburg 1864)

Knorr, E., *Von Düppel bis zur Waffenruhe*, (Perthes-Besser & Mauke, Hamburg 1864)

Knorr, E., *Von Alsen bis zur Frieden*, (Perthes-Besser & Mauke, Hamburg 1865)

Kohl, Horst, *Der Deutsch-dänische Krieg 1864*, ((Deutschlands Einigungskriege 1864-1871,Volume I, Voigtlander, Leipzig 1917)

Koht, Halvdan, *Die Stellung Norwegens und Schwedens im Deutschen-Dänischen Konflikt, zumal während der Jahre 1863 und 1864*, (Jacob Dybwad, Kristiania 1908)

Kreipner, Julius, *Geschichte des k. und k. Infanterie-Regimentes Nr. 34 für immer während Zeiten Wilhelm I deutscher Kaiser und König von Preussen 1733-1900*, (Kaschau 1900)

Kufittich, Hans, *Unsere Offiziere vor dem Feinde*, (Militär-Verlagsanstalt, Berlin 1900)

Kusserow, Ludwig von, *Geschichte des Brandenburgischen Jäger-Battalions Nr. 3 und des Magdeburgischen Jäger Battalions Nr. 4 von 1815 bis 1865*, (Bath, Berlin 1865)

Lehman, Gustav, *Die Trophäen des Preussischen Heeres in der königlichen hof und Garnisonskirche zu Potsdam*, (E. S. Mittler und Son, Berlin 1899)

Lüdinghausen, General, & Wolf, Hauptmann, *Organisation und Dienst der Königlich Preussisches Kriegsmacht*, (War School and Cadet Academy, Berlin 1863)

Magirus, Adolf, *Herzog Wilhelm von Württemberg, K.u.K. Feldzeugmeister*, (W. Kohlhammer, Stuttgart 1897)

Mahler, Heinrich, *Über die Eider an den Alsensund*, (Ulrich Frank, Berlin 1864)

Mahler, Heinrich, *Wieder in der Krieg*, (Ulrich Frank, Berlin 1864)

Mellenthin, X von, *Jungens holt fast. Der Überfall auf Fehmarn*, (Schmitz & Bukofzer, Berlin 1914)

Moltke, Helmuth, Count v., *Moltkes Militärische Werke 1. Militärische Korrespondenz. Krieg 1864*, (E.S. Mittler & Son, Berlin 1892)

Moltke, Helmuth, Count v., *Moltkes Militärische Werke 3*, (E.S. Mittler & Son, Berlin 1899)

Müller, Hermann v., *Kriegerisches und Friedliches aus den Feldzügen von 1864, 1866, und 1870/71*, (Ernst Mittler & Son, Berlin 1909)

Müller, K., *Tegetthoffs Marsch in die Nordsee, Oeversee – Düppler Schanzen -Helgoland im deutsche-dänischen Krieg 1864*, (Styria, Graz 1991)

Neumann, R., *Über den Angriff auf die Düppler Schanzen in der Zeit vom 15. März bis zum 18. April 1864*, (E. H. Mittler & Son, Berlin 1865)

Pfaundler, Leopold, *Heldenzüge der Mannschaft des k k 27 Infanterie Regimentes König der Belgier aus dem Feldzüge 1864*, (Dimbock, Vienna 1864

Pflug, Ferdinand, *Der Deutsch-Dänische Krieg*, (F.F. Weber, Leipzig 1865)

Prettenthaler, T., *90 Jahre Översee*, (Stiasny, Graz, 1954)

Prybila, Karl v., *Geschichte der Kriege der k und k Wehrmacht von 1848-1898*, (Rudolf Brzezowsky & Son, Graz 1899)

Prybila, Karl v., *Geshichte des k.k. Infanterie-Regiments Leopold II, König der Belgier Nr. 27 von dessen Errichtung 1682 bis 1882*, (Vienna 1882)

Pulkowski, Erich, *Kurzgefasste Geschichte des Fussartillerie-Regiments General Feldzeugmeister (Brandenburgischen) Nr. 3*, (E.H. Mittler & Son, Berlin 1914)

Rehtwisch, ,Theodor, *Schleswig-Holstein Stammverwandt. Bilder aus dem Kriege von 1864*, (Turm, Leipzig, c. 1907)

Rothpletz, Emil, *Bericht eines schweizerischen Offiziers uber seine Mission nach Dänemark (1864)*, (Ernst Bircher, Bern/Leipzig 1924)

Rüstow, W, *Der deutsch dänische Krieg 1864*, (Friedrich Schulthek, Zurich 1864)

Scheel, Otto, *Das Gefecht von Oeversee*, (Heimat und Erbe, Flensburg 1939)

Schmiterlöw, Bernhard von, *1864 Düppel und Alsen*, (c 1895)

Schnayder, Ladislaus, *Oesterreichisch-Preussischer Krieg gegen Dänemark*, (F. B. Geitler, Vienna 1865)

Smagalski, Ladislaus, *K.K. 'Fürst Liechtenstein' 9. Husaren-Regiments Geschichtliche Skizze aus dem Feldzuge 1864 Gegen Dänemark*, (Chrudim 1866)

Stolz, Gerd, *Anekdoten vom Militär*, (Husum Druck-und Verlagsgessellschaft, Husum 1983)

Stolz, Gerd, *Das deutsche-dänische Shicksaljahr 1864 in seinen Ereignissen*, (Heimatkundlichen Arbeitsgemeinschaft fur Nordschleswig, Aabenraa 1988)

Stolz, Gerd. *Die 'Eroberung' der nordfriesischen Inseln im Jahre 1864: eine 'Affaire' aus dem deutsch-dänischen Krieg*, (Husum Druck – und Verlagsgessellschaft, Husum 1988)

Stolz, Gerd, *Kriegsgräber aus den deutsch-dänischen Kriegen von 1848/51 und 1864*, (Eckenförde 1982)

Vinke, C. v., *Die Reorganisation des Preussischen Heerwesens nach dem Schleswig-Holsteinschen Kriege*, (Reimer, Berlin 1864)

Voights-König, Captain & Becker, P., *Geschichte des Infanterie-Regiments Großherzog Friedrich Franz II von Mecklenburg-Schwerin (4 Brandenburgischen) Nr. 24*, (Mittler & Sons, Berlin 1908)

Vogel, Winfried, *Entscheidung 1864: das Gefecht bei Düppel im Deutschen-Danischen Krieg und eine Bedeutung für die Lösung der Deutsche Frage*, (Bernard & Grafe, Koblenz 1987)

Voss, Wilhelm, *Illustrierte Geschichte der deutschen Einigungskriege 1864-1866*, (Union Deutsche Verlagsgesellschaft, Stuttgart 1914)

Wagner, Walter, *Von Austerlitz bis Königgratz. Österreichisches Kampftaktik im Spiegel der Reglements 1805-1864*, (Studien zur Militärgeschichte, Militarwissenschaft und Konliktforschung, Number 17, Biblio, Osnabruck 1978)

Waldersee, G. Gr. W., *Der Krieg gegen Dänemark im Jahre 1864*, (Duncker, Berlin 1865)

Went von Römo, Karl, *Ein Soldatenleben*, (Braumüller, Vienna 1904)

Widdern, Georg v., *Küstenschütz und Unternehmungen gegen denselben an der Schleswig-holsteinisch-jütisch Nord- und Ostseeküste in Feldzuge 1864*, (Eisenschmidt, Berlin 1906)

Winterfeld, C. von, *Der Schleswig-Holstein'sche Krieg von 1864*, (Doring, Potsdam 1865)

Wirtgen, Rolf, *Das Zündnadelgewehr*, (Wehrtechnik und wissenschaftliche Waffenkunde, Volume 7,E.S. Mittler & Sohn, Herford and Bonn 1991)

Wiser, Friedrich Ritter von, *Der Besetzung der nordfriesischen Inseln im Juli 1864*, (Danzer's Armee Zeitung, Vienna 1914)

Zimmer-Vorhaus, Otto, *Offizier Stammliste des Infanterie-Regiments Lützow (1 Rhenischen) Nr. 25 1813-1913*, (Otto Beckmann, Berlin 1913)

German Articles

(Anon.), „Antheil des 2. Bat. 1 Posenschen Inf. R. am gefecht vor Düppel am 28 März", (*Militärische Blätter*, Volume 12, Number 15, Berlin 1864)

(Anon.), „Beleuchtung der Vorwurfe, welche von der Untersüchungs-Kommission des Folkedhing's gegen die dänischen Armee und die Kriegführung im Jahre 1864 erhoben sind", (Supplement to *Militair-Wochenblatt*, Berlin January 1865)

(Anon.), „Das Gefecht vom 28. März 1864", (*Militärische Blätter*, Volume 14. Number 6, Berlin 1865. See follow on article below, 'Zum Gefecht vom 28 März 1864)

(Anon.), „Das Zündnadelgewehr", (*Allgemeine Militär-Zeitung*, Number 13 Darmstadt 1864)

(Anon.), „Der 18 April, der Tag von Düppel", (*Allgemeine Militär-Zeitung*, Number 31, Darmstadt 1882)

(Anon.), „Der Feldzug in Schleswig", (*Militärische Blätter*, Volume 12, Numbers 6, 11, 12, 13, 14, and 20, and Volume 13, numbers 29, 34, 37, 39, and 40, Berlin 1864)

(Anon.), „Der Krieg 1864, (*Militär-Wochenblatt*, Numbers 17 and 18, Berlin 1914)

(Anon.), „Der Krieg gegen Dänemark im Jahre 1864", (*Unsere Zeit*, Leipzig 1865)

(Anon.), „Die Aufgaben und das verhalten des Rolf Krake im Feldzuge von 1864, besonders bei dem Übergange auf Alsen", *(Militärische Blätter*, Volume 21, Berlin 1869)

(Anon.), „Die Befestigungen im schleswig-holstein'schen Krieg 1864", (*Österreichische Militärische Zeitschrift*, Volume 1, Vienna 1865)

(Anon.), „Der Österreichische Feldtelegraph in Schleswig-Holstein", *(Allgemeine Militär-Zeitung*, Number 7, Darmstadt 1864)

(Anon.), „Die Belagerung und Erstürmung von Düppel", (*Militärische Blätter*, Volume 12, Number 18, Berlin 1864)

(Anon.), „Die Düppler Schanzen und ihre Vertheidigung", (*Allgemeine Militär-Zeitung*, Number 23, Darmstadt 1864)

Anon.) , „Die Ereignisse von und in der Festung Fredericia während des Feldzugs gegen Dänemark 1864", (*Allgemeine Militär-Zeitung* 1866, Numbers 21-26)

(Anon.), „Die Eroberung bei der Insel Alsen unter besonderer Berücksichtigung der Theilnahmeder Westphälischen Truppen", (*Militärische Blätter*, Volume 13, Number 43, Berlin 1864)

(Anon.), „Die Eroberung von Alsen", (*Allgemeine Militär-Zeitung*, Number. 28, Darmstadt 1864)

(Anon.), „Die Erstürmung von Jagel am 3. Februar 1864", (*Österreichische Militärische Zeitung*, Volume 1, Vienna 1864)

(Anon.), „Die Gefechte bei Sönder-Tranders und Lundby am 3. Juli 1864", (Supplement to *Militair-Wochenblatt*, Berlin October/November 1864)

(Anon.), „Die Gefechte bei Veile am 8. Mai 1849 und am 8 März 1864, unter Anwendung der älteren und neuartigen Feuerwaffen", (*Österreichische Militärische Zeitschrift,*, Volume 2, Vienna 1864)

(Anon.), „Die gegenwartige Stand des Krieges in Schleswig-Holstein", (*Allgemeine Militär-Zeitung*, Number 11, Darmstadt 1864)

(Anon.), „Die Kriegsereignisse in Schleswig, (*Allgemeine Miltär-Zeitung*, Numbers 7 and 12, Darmstadt 1864)

(Anon.) , „Die Kriegsoperationen in Schleswig vom 1.-6.Februar 1864",
(*Allgemeine Militär-Zeitung*, Numbers 8 and 9, Darmstadt 1864)

(Anon.), „Die Landwehr im Felde", (Militärische Blätter, Volume 14, Number
8, Berlin 1865)

(Anon.) , „Die militärische Bedeutung des Feldzuges 1864", (*Unter Gablenz und
Tegetthoff 1864, Danzer's Armee Zeitung*, Vienna 1904)

(Anon.), „Die Seegefechte bei Rügen und Helgoland", (*Allgemeine
Militär-Zeitung*, Number 21, Darmstadt 1864)

(Anon.), „Die Theilnahme des 1. Posenschen Inf. R. Number 18 an der
Erstürmung der Düppler Schanzen am 18. April 1864", (*Militärische
Blätter*, Volume 13, Number 46, Berlin 1864)

(Anon.), „Die Verluste bei der Erstürmung von Düppel", (*Militärische Blätter*,
Volume 12, Number 19, Berlin 1864)

(Anon.), „Die Verluste der Alliirten und der Danen im Jahre 1864", (*Allgemeine
Militär-Zeitung*, Number 48, Darmstadt 1865)

(Anon.), „Die Verluste der K. preussischen Armee im dänischen Kriege",
(*Allgemeine Militär-Zeitung*, Number 1, Darmstadt 1865)

(Anon.), „Die Waffenwirkung in den preussischen gefechten im Feldzüge 1864,
bis nach derErstürmung der Düppler Schanzen", (*Militärische Blätter*,
Volume 13, Number 49, Berlin 1864)

(Anon.), „Ephemeriden des Feldzüges in Schleswig und Jütland", (*Militärische
Blätter*, Volume 12, Numbers 21, and 22; Volume 13, Number 28, Berlin
1864)

(Anon.), „Erfährungen und Reflexionen über den Dänischen Feldzug von
1864", (*Allgemeine Militär-Zeitung* 1866, Numbers. 2, 3 and 5)

(Anon.), „Fechtweise der preussischen und österreichischen Infanterie",
(*Militärische Blätter*, Volume 12, Number 8, Berlin 1864)

(Anon.), „Ist es in dem Gefechte bei Översee wirklich zum Handgemenge
gekommen?", (*Österreichische Militärische Zeitschrift*, Volume 2, Vienna
1865)

(Anon.), „Kritische Betrachtungen über die Operationen im Feldzüge 1864 bis
zur Einnahme der Dannewerke", (*Neue Militärische Blätter*, Numbers 45
and 46, Berlin, 1894, 1895)

(Anon.), „Missunde. Der Übergang über die Schlei. Von der Avant Garde.",
(*Militärische Blätter*, Volume 12, Number 8, Berlin 1864)

(Anon.), „Munitionsverbrauch der Preuss. Truppen in dem Feldzüge gegen
Dänemark", (*Militärische Blätter,* Volume 14, Numbers 3 and 4, Berlin
1865)

(Anon.), „Officieller preussischer Bericht uber die Kriegereignisse bei der Armee
in Schleswig-Holstein in dem Zeitraum vom 1. bis einschliesslich 10.
Februar", (*Österreichische Militärische Zeitschrift*, Volume 1, Vienna 1864)

(Anon.), „ Ordre de Bataille und Dislokation der Königl. Dänischen Armee und
Bemerkungen dazu", (*Militärische Blätter*, Volume 12, Number 5, Berlin
1865)

(Anon.), Ordre de Bataille der Königlich Preussischen Truppen in Schleswig
und Jütland", (*Militärische Blätter*, Volume 13, Number 29, Berlin 1864)

(Anon.) „Über die Verwendung der technischen Truppen und der Infanterie-Pionnere im Felde. Mit Berücksichtigung der im schleswig-holstein'schen Feldzüge 1864 diesfalls gemachten Erfahrungen", (*Österreichische Militärische Zeitung*, Volume 4, Vienna 1864)

(Anon.), „Über die ersten Nachrichten und Urtheile in Betreff der Kriegführung in Schleswig im Jahre. 1864", (*Österreichische Militärische Zeitschrift*, Volume 1, Vienna 1864)

(Anon.), „Vom Schauplatz der 13 Division", (*Militärische Blätter*, Volume 12, Numbers 4, 5, 7, and 9, Berlin 1864)

(Anon.), „Wahrnemungen über die Leistungen der k.k. Artillerie und der Neuartigen österreichischen Geschütze im Kriege gegen Dänemark im Jahre 1864", (*Österreichische Militärische Zeitschrift*, Volume 1, Vienna 1864)

(Anon.), „Welchem Nutzen hatte die Anwendung von recognoscierungsballons auf dem Kriegstheater in Schleswig dem Verbündeten und dänischen Heere bringen konnen?", (*Allgemeine Militär Zeitung*, Number 9, Darmstadt 1864)

(Anon.), „Wie bewahrt die Ausrüstung und Bewaffnung der königlich preussischen Armee im Kriege?", (*Allgemeine Militär-Zeitung*, Number 11, Darmstadt 1864)

(Anon.) „Zum Gefecht vom 28. Marz 1864", (*Militärische Blätter*, Volume 14, Number 12, Berlin 1865)

(Anon.), „Zur Erstürmung der Düppler Linien", (*Allgemeine Militär-Zeitung*, Number 17, Darmstadt 1864)

(Anon.), „ Zur Schilderung der Kriegsoperationen im Herzogthume Schleswig im Jahre 1864", (*Österreichische Militärische Zeitschrift*, Volume I, 1 to 7 February and II, 8 to 21 February, Vienna 1864)Adami, Geza Dell', „Die k. u. k. Kriegsmarine im Jahre 1864" (*Unter Gablenz und Tegetthoff 1864*, *Danzer's Armee Zeitung*, Vienna 1904)

Adler, F., „Ballegaard und Alsen", (*Archiv. für die Offiziere der preuss. Artillerie u. Ing. Korps*, Number 57, Berlin 1864)

Attems, Count, „Nachtrag zu dem Artikel: "Ist es in dem Gefechte bei Översee wirklich zum handgemenge gekommen?", (*Österreichische Militärische Zeitschrift*, Volume 2, Vienna 1865. See entry under Anon, below)

Berger, Oberst v., „Bericht des Leib-Grenadier-Regiments über seine Theilnahme an der Erstürmung der Düppler Schanzen am 18. April 1864", (*Supplement to Militair-Wochenblatt*, Berlin October/November 1864)

Buddecke, Albert, „Preussens Kriegsrüstung 1864", (*Jahrbücher für die deutsche Armee und Marine*, July-December, Berlin 1914)

Buddenbrock, Oberst v., „Das 5. Westphälische-Infanterieregiment Nr. 55, das 1. Battalion 6. Westphälischen Infanterieregiments Nr. 53, und die 2. Kompagnie des Westphälischen Pionier-Battalions Nr. 7 am 18. April 1864", (*Militair-Wochenblatt*, supplement to Number 37, Berlin 1865)

Bugge, Gen. Baurat, „Kriegserinnerung aus dem Jahre 1864 (Missunde, Düppel, Alsen)" (*Preussische Jahrbücher*, Number 140, Berlin 1910)

Canstein, Freiherr v., „Bericht über die Betheiligung der 11. Infanterie-Brigade an der Erstürmung der Düppler Schanzen Am 18. April 1864", (Supplement to *Militair-Wochenblatt*, Berlin June 1864)

Christl, Oskar, „Das österreichische 6. Armeekorps im Kriege gegen Dänemark 1864", (*Unter Gablenz und Tegetthoff 1864, Danzer's Armee Zeitung*, Vienna 1904)

Estorff, Obltnt v., „Taktische Aufgaben auf kriegsgeschichtlicher Unterlage von 1864", (*Militär Wochenblatt*, Numbers 61, 67, 68, Berlin 1910)

Gablenz, Freiherr von, „Officieller österreichischer Bericht über die Operationen des k.k. Österreichischen 6. (II. Armeekorps der verbündeten Armee) in Schleswig-Holstein, in der zeit vom 1 bis 7 Februar 1864", (*Österreichische Militärische Zeitschrift*, Volume1, Vienna 1864

Goeben, Generalmajor von, „ Das Gefecht bei Rackebüll am. 17. März 1864", (*Militair-Wochenblatt*, Number 13, 1865)

Guggenberger, Josef, „Erinnerungen eines alten Belgier Offiziers aus den Erlebnissen des Jahres 1864", (*Unter Gablenz und Tegetthoff 1864, Danzer's Armee Zeitung*, Vienna 1904)

Hake, v., Gen.-Lt., „Actenstücke über die Besitznahme Rendsburgs durch die Preussen am 21. Juli 1864", (*Österreichische Militärische Zeitung*, Volume 3, Vienna 1864)

Heinrich, Prince, „Kriegstagebücher vom Prinzen Heinrich von Hessen", (*Allgemeine Militär-Zeitung*, Numbers 1 – 6, Darmstadt 1902)

Herwarth (von Bittenfeld), „Officieller Bericht über den am 29. Juni 1864 ausgeführten Stürm auf Alsen", (*Österreichische Militärische Zeitung*, Volume 3, Vienna 1864)

Heymann, Gefreiter, „Unsere Compagnie bei Lundby", (*Der Soldatenfreund*, Number 32, Berlin 1864/65)

Holzing, Max von, „General v. Moltkes Einwirkung auf den strategischen Gang des Krieges gegen Dänemark 1864", (Supplement to *Militär-Wochenblatt* 1898)

H. v. O, „Die dänische Artillerie und ihre Theilnahme von 1864", (*Allgemeine Militär Zeitung*, Numbers 1-3, Darmstadt 1866)

Kade, von, „Aus meinem Feldzugs-Erinnerungen von 1864", (*Allgemeine-Militär-Zeitung*, Numbers 83, 84,and 85, Darmstadt 1899)

Kammeier, Heinz-Ulrich, „Der Krieg gegen Dänemark 1864 in Briefen von Soldaten aus dem Kreis Lubbecke", (*Zeitschrift der Gesellschaft für Schleswig-Holsteinsche Geschichte,* Volume 114, 1989)

Kettler, Oberst, „Bericht des 1. Posenschen Infanterie-Regiments Nr. 18 über seine Theilnahme an der Erstürmung der Düppler Schanzen am 18. April 1864", (*Militair-Wochenblatt*, Supplement to Number 18, Berlin 1865)

Klose, Olaf, „Briefe des preussischen Gefreiten Wilhelm Gahter aus dem Jahre 1864 vom Kriegsschauplatz", (*Zeitschrift der Gesellschaft für Schleswig-Holsteinische Geschichte*, Volume 100 1975)

Meyernink, D., „Ereignisse im Kriege gegen Dänemark beim (kombinirtes) Armee-Korps, vom 20. Januar bis 7. Februar", (*Jahrbücher für die deutsche Armee und Marine*, Number 90, Berlin 1894)

Minarelli-Fitzgerald, Alexander Chevalier, „Moltke und seine Einflussnahme auf die Operationen des Feldzuges 1864", (*Organ der Militär-wissenschaftliches Vereine*, Number 46, Vienna 1893)

M., v., 'Frieden im Kriege!' Einiges aus meinem erlebnissen wahrend des Feldzuges 1864 in Jutland", (*Jahrbücher für die deutsche Armee und Marine* Number 109, Berlin 1898)

Moltke, Helmuth, Freiherr v., „Bemerkungen uber den Einfluss der verbesserten Schusswaffen auf das Gefecht", (*Militair-Wochenblatt*, Supplement to Number 27, Berlin 1865)

Moranow, Karl Morawetz von, „Die Belgier, Zur Erinnerung an der Jahrestag des Gefechtes bei Översee 6. Februar 1864", (*Militärische Rundschau*, Number 7, Vienna 1913)

Müller, Oberlieut., „Übersicht der von königlich preussischen und den kaiserlich österreichischen Pionnieren im Feldzuge gegen Dänemark i. Jahre 1864 ausgeführten Brückenbauten und Überschiffungen", (*Österreichische Militärische Zeitschrift*, Volume 3, Vienna 1868)

Oberlindober, Major, „Die Erstürmung der Düppler Schanzen (18. April 1864)", (*Jahrbücher für die deutsche Armee und Marine*, January-June, Berlin 1914)

Oberlindober, Major, „Die Übergang auf Alsen (29. Juni 1864)", *Jahrbücher für die deutsche Armee und Marine, January-June*, Berlin 1914)

"Officier", „Der Sieg in Schleswig,(Von einem deutschen Officier)", (*Preussische Jahrbücher*, Number 13, Berlin 1864

"Officier", „Die militärische Action in Schleswig und Jutland (Von einem deutschen Officier)", (*Preussische Jahrbücher*, Number 13, Berlin 1864)

"Officier", „Schleswig-Holstein und die Preussischer Waffen (Von einem deutscher Officier)", (*Preussische Jahrbücher*, Number 13, Berlin 1864)

Österreicher, Tobias, „Die Artillerie im Seegefecht vor Helgoland", (*Österreichische Militärische Zeitschrift*, Volume 2, Vienna 1864)

Schmid, Generalmajor von, „Ein Tagebuch von1864 des Generalmajors v.Schmid, Kommandeurs der 25. Infanteriebrigade", (Supplement to *Militär-Wochenblatt*, Berlin 1914, Numbers 2 and 3)

Saenger, D. von, „Über die theilname der reitenden Artillerie (der 1., 3., 4., und 6. Batterie) der Westphälischen Artillerie-Brigade Nr 7 an dem Gefecht von Missunde am 2. Februar 1864, als Ergänzung und Berichtigung zu den Angaben in dem Werke: 'Der Krieg gegen Dänemark im Jahre 1864 von G. Gr. W (aldersee)...", (*Militärische Blätter*, Volume 21, Berlin 1869)

Schwarz, Anton, „Die Beschiessung von Fredericia", (*Militärische Rundschau*, Number 73, Vienna 1914)

Sommerfeldt, E.J. & Wagner, Reinhold, „Düppel 1864", (*Jahrbücher für die deutsche Armee und Marine*, January-June, Berlin 1902)

Stolz, Gerd, „Missunde: 1848, 1850, und 1864 –Zwei Kriege und drei Gefechte", (*Jahrbüche Heimatsgemeinschaft* Number 57, Eckernförde 1999)

Stolz, Gerd, „Översee – 6. Februar 1864 Und Seine Tradtion", (*HeimatvereinsSchleswigsche*, Geest 1983)

Strombeck, Freiherrn von, *„Der Stürm auf Alsen am 29. Juni 1864"*, (Allgemeine Militär-Zeitung, Numbers 6 and 7, Darmstadt 1869)

Tegetthoff, Wilhelm v., „Das Seetreffen bei Helgoland am 9. Mai 1864", (*Österreichische Militärische Zeitschrift*, Volume 2, Vienna 1864)

W., General St., „Der Übergang nach Alsen am 29. Juni 1864", (*Militär-Wochenblatt*, Numbers 86 and 87, Berlin 1914)

Went von Römö, Karl, „Errinerungen eines österreichischen Kriegsmannes",(*Österreichische Militärische Zeitschrift*, Volume 39, Number 1, Vienna 1898)

Werner, Bartolomaus v., „Das Seegefecht bei Helgoland am 9. Mai 1864", (*Unsere Zeit*, Leipzig 1889, Volume 1)

Wolff, Gustav, „Der Übergang der Preussen über der Alsensund am 29. Juni 1864", (*Österreichische Militärische Zeitschrift*, Volume 36, Number 1, Vienna 1895)

Woinovits, Paul, „Österreichische Pioniere bei Düppel", (*Militärische Rundschau*, Number 100, Vienna 1914)

Zernin, Hauptmann, „Vor 20 Jahren", (*Allgemeine Militär-Zeitung*, Number 50 Darmstadt, 1884)

Danish Books

(Anon.), *Armeens Overcommando's Dagesbefalinger Felttoget 1864*

(Anon), *Bidrag Til 17. Battalions Historie 1657-1907*, Centraltrykkeriet, Copenhagen 1907)

(Anon.), *De Slesvigske Krige 1848-50 og 1864*, (Military Academy, Copenhagen, 1955)

(Anon.), *Dronningens Livregiment 1657-1957*, (Ael Scholins, Aalborg 1957)

(Anon.), *Exerceer-Reglement for det Kongelige danske Infanterie 1863*, (Copenhagen 1863)

(Anon.), *Fra Februar til August*, (Michælsen & Tillge, Copenhagen 1864)

(Anon.), *Mine Krigserfaringer paa Dybbøl 1864*, (Mohr & Co., Copenhagen 1909)

(Anon.), *Officerernes Fordeling wed den active Armee og paa Flaaden*, (Lose & Delbanco, Copenhagen 1864)

(Anon.), *3 Bataillon 1842-1942*, (Carl Nielsen, Haderslev 1942)

Andersen, Bo Benthin, *En dansk husars dagbog 1863-1864*, (H.C. Lorenzen, Nordborg 1988)

Andersen, Jens, *Oplevelser fra krigen 1864*, (Hobro Bogtrykkeri, Hobro 1989)

Andersen, Ole, *Bøffelkobbel*, (Dybbøl Centre, 1996)

Askgaard, Finn (et. al), *Tøjhusmuseets bog om 1864*, (Copenhagen 1964)

Bauditz, F., *Den danske hærs Reorganisation*, (C.C. Lose, Copenhagen 1865)

Birkeland, Palle, & Klose, Olaf, *Bibliografi og Ikonografi 1864/Bibliographie und Ikonographie 1864*, (Joint edition, Schleswig-Holstein Library, Kiel, and Royal Library, Copenhagen, Karl Wachholtz, Neumünster 1970; bilingual, Danish – German)

Bjerager,Oberstløjtnant, *Kaptajn Aarøes Strejfkorps i Marts og April 1864*.

Beretning til Krigsministeriet 1893, (R. Levin & Co. 1978)

438 BISMARCK'S FIRST WAR

Bjørke, Svend, Kjaer, Henning F., & Norrie, J.W.G, *Krigen 1864,* (Strube, Copenhagen 1968)

Boeck, Hector, *12 Bataillons Historie 1679 –1925,* (Gyldendahl, Copenhagen 1929)

Bokkenheuser, V., *Fra Ejderen til Als,* (Bergmann, Copenhagen 1889)

Borberg, Lauritz, *I Krig og Kantonnement 1864,* (H. Hagerup, Copenhagen 1936)

Bredsdorff, Chr., *Paa Feltfod,* ("Danmark", Copenhagen 1911)

Bruun, Daniel, *Fra Krigens Tid,* (G.E.C. Gad, Copenhagen 1913)

Bruun, Helge , *Dannebrog og danske Faner gennem Tiderne,* (Jespersen & Pios, Copenhagen 1949)

Castenschiold, C., *Indtryk og Minder fra Dybbøl,* (Gad, Copenhagen, 1908)

Christensen, C., *Kriegsminder fra Dannevirke og Dybbøl,* (K. Jørgensen, Kolding 1886)

Christensen, Rolf, & Henriksen, Anders, *På forpost ved Dybbøl i Krigen 1864,* (Devantier, Næstved 2000)

Dinesen, W., *Fra Ottende Brigade,* (Gyldendal, Copenhagen 1945)

Dockum, C. van, *Østersoes-Eskadren i 1864,* (C.C. Lose, Copenhagen 1864)

Edsberg, V., *Minder fra 10. Batteri i 1864,* (J. Jørgensen & Co., Copenhagen 1889)

Essmann, N. C., *Det Aarøe'ske Strejfkorps i 1864,* (Bianco Lunos, Copenhagen 1884)

Falkenskjold, Oberst, *22de Infanteri-Regiments Deeltagelse I Krigen 1864,* (Chr. Hanson, Frederiksborg 1866)

Friis, Aage, *D.G. Monrads Deltagelse i Begivenhederne 1864,* (Copenhagen 1914)

Friis Moller, M. & Mentze, Ernst, *1864 – et hundredårsminde/ Med bidrag af Egon Eriksen,* (Martin, Copenhagen 1963)

Generalstaben, *Den dansk-tydske krig 1864,* (Copenhagen 1890/92)

Generalstaben, *Statistiske Meddelelser angaaende den dansk Krigsmagt,* (Copenhagen, 1867 & 1871)

Graae,G. Fr.A., *Mellem Krigene 1851-1864. Efterladte Optegnelser og Breve,* (Schutbothe, Copenhagen 1887)

Hammer, Otto Chr., *Vesterhavsøernes Forsvar i Aaret 1864,* (Gyldendal, Copenhagen 1865)

Hansen, Christen, *Dagbog, holdt af en Menig i 17. Reg. 6 Komp. i Vinterfelttoget 1864,* (Andr. Hals, Copenhagen 1865)

Hansen, F.F., *En Compagniecommandeurs Erindringer fra Krigen 1864,* (J. Frimodt, Copenhagen 1911)

Hansen, Frederik, *Dagbog fra 1864. Optegnelser af menig Frederik Hansen, Nybøl,* (Claus Nielsen & J. Slettebo, Copenhagen 1964)

Hansen, H.G., *Kampen ved Mysunde 2.februar 1864,* (H.G, Hansen, Holbaek 1981)

Hedemann, Marius, *Fra front og Kantonnement i 1864,* (Royal Garrison Library, Copenhagen 1995)

Hegermann-Lindencrone, Cai, *Betragtninger i Anledning af D.G. Monrads politiske Breve,* (C.A. Reitzel, Copenhagen 1875)

Hegermann-Lindencrone, Cai, *Om Krigsaaret 1864*, (C.A. Reitzel, Copenhagen 1874)

Helms, Ludvig, *Tilbagetoget i Jylland 1864*, (Compiled by Helge Søgaard Th. Thrues, Aarhus 1971)

Hoffmann, Chr. A., *Erindringer Fra Krigen 1864*. (Gyldendahl, Copenhagen 1892)

Holbøll, H., *En Brigadeadjutants erindringer fra Krigen 1864*, (Vilhelm Trydes, Copenhagen 1912)

Jensen, N.P., *Den anden slesvigske krig 1864*, (Det Nordiske forlag, Copenhagen 1900)

Johansen, J., & Nordentoft, J., *4de Division i Nørrejylland 1864*, (General Staff, Copenhagen 1936)

Johansen, J., & Nordentoft, J., *Hæren ved Danevirke 1864*, (General Staff, Copenhagen 1938)

Johansen, Jens, *Dybbøl 1864*, (General Staff, Copenhagen 1942)

Jonquieres, H. de, *Bemærkninger Om Det Danske Artilleri samt om dets Deeltagelse i Krigen 1864*, (H. de Reitzel, Copenhagen 1865)

Kauffmann, W., *Tilbagetoget fra Dannevirke og dets hemmelige historie*, (J. Schulz Copenhagen, 1865)

Kjerrsgaard, Erik & Wemund, Bendtsen, *Fra Dannevirke til Dybbøl*, (P. Haase & Sons, Copenhagen 1963)

Lauring, Palle, *1848-1864*, (Gyldendal, Copenhagen, 1963)

Leschly, E., *Historisk Beretning om 5' Dragonregiment*, (J.M. Elmenhoff & Sons, Randers 1929)

Liljefalk, Axel and Lütken, Otto, *Vor sidste Kamp for Sønderjylland*, (H. Hagerup, Copenhagen 1904)

Lindeberg, Lars, *De så det ske*, (Forlaget Union, Copenhagen 1964)

Lütken, O., *Nordsø-Eskadren og Kampen Ved Helgoland*, (Gyldendal, Copenhagen, 1884)

Lütken, Otto, *Søkrigsbegivenhederne i 1864*, (Gyldendal, Copenhagen 1896)

Michelsen, Poul, *21 Bataillons Historie 1788-1918*, (Hasselbalch, Copenhagen 1918)

Mogensen, Aage, *Soldaten og den tabte krig*, (Forlaget Fremad 1963)

Møller, H.L., *Krigen 1864 I Samtidens Digtning*, (G.E.C. Gads Forlag, Copenhagen 1913)

Mørch, F.C.E.,*En Dansk Militærafdeling Gennem 325 Aar*, (H. Hagerup, Copenhagen 1939)

Nellemann, S., *Nogle Bemærkninger til Forsvar for ,Rolf Krakes' Chef*, (Th. Lind, Copenhagen 1867)

Nielsen, Søren, *Danske Livregiments Historie 1763-1963*, (Copenhagen, 1963)

Niergaard, E., *18de Bataillons Historie 1785-1885*, (Pontoppidan, Copenhagen 1885)

Norrie, J.W.G., *Løjtnant Voldbyes breve fra 1864*, (Reprint from Sønderjyske Årbøge1961)

Rasmussen, Knud, *General de Meza og den dansk-tyske Krig 1864*, (Odense Univesitetsforlag 1997)

Rasmussen, L., *Minder fra Krigen 1864*, (Th. Vennervald, Odense 1907)

Ravn, J.T., *Fremstilling af Krigsbegivenhederne paa Als, fra den 18de April til den 1ste Juli 1864*, (Gyldendahl, Copenhagen 1870)

Rist, P.F., *En Rekrut fra Fire og Treds*, (Gyldendahl, Copenhagen & Christiania 1920)

Rockstroh, C.A., *General de Meza og Dannevirkes Rømning*, (C.A Reitzel, Copenhagen 1930)

Rockstroh, K.C., *Fortællinger Af 2. Battalions Historie 1657-1907*, (Centraltrykkeriet, Copenhagen 1907

Schau, Major E., *En Generalstabsofficer i 1864. Breve fra Major E. Schau*, (August Bang, Copenhagen 1974)

Schiøtt, F.C.. *1864 i Billeder og Text*, (Nordstjern, Copenhagen, 1889)

Schøller, F., *Forsvaret af Dybbølstillingen i 1864*, (C.C. Lose, Copenhagen 1867)

Skov, Sigvard, *1864*, (Konrad Jorgensen, Kolding 1963)

Sørensen, Carl Th., *Den anden slesvigske krig*, (Gyldendahl, Copenhagen 1883)

Sørensen, Carl Th., *Erindringer fra Første Regiment 1864*, (Copenhagen 1891)

Spur, Erik, *Vi oplevede det – Tidsbillede fra 1864*, (Konrad Jørgensen, Kolding 1963)

Stavenstrup, P., *D.G. Monrad – Politiker og Gejstlig*, (Berlingske, Copenhagen 1948)

Stilling, Valdemar, *Danske Livregiment til Fods. 1' Bataillon 1763-1913*, (Gyldendahl, Copenhagen 1913)

Stub-Jørgensen, Christian, *1864 Bornholm og Krigen om Sønderjylland*, (Colberg, Rønne 1963)

Theide, C.E., *1. Bataillons Historie*, (Copenhagen, 1947)

Thornit, P., *1864 – Den danske soldat i samtidige billeder*, (Bent Carlsen, Copenhagen 1978)

Thorson, Th., *Skildringer fra den slesvigske Krig 1864*, (F. Woldike, Copenhagen 1865)

Treschow, O.G., *Danmarks mørkeste Nat*, (Copenhagen 1864)

Tusch, E. Jensen, *11 Bataillon I Krigsaarene 1848-50 og 64*, (Magnus A. Schultz, Aalborg 1897)

Vaupell, Otto, *Krigene 1848-50 og 1864. Kampen ved Sønderjylland 1864*, (Reitzel, Copenhagen 1889)

Vogel-Jørgensen, T., *Krigen 1864 i samtidens billeder*, (Berlingske, Copenhagen 1963)

Waagepetersen, J.T. & Norrie, J.W.G, *Fortællinger af 18' Battalions Historie*, (Jørgen Otsen, Sønderborg 1935)

Weitemeyer, Waldemar, *Breve mellem front og hjem 1864: breve til og fra Waldemar Weitemeyer under felttoget 1864*, (Compiled by Mogens Weitemeyer, Museum Tusculanum, Copenhagen University 1995)

Zimmerman, Axel, *Erindringer fra felttoget 1864*, (F. Woldike, Copenhagen 1867)

Danish Articles

(Anon.), „*Beretning fra Krigsministeriet om Fægtningerne foran Dannevirke (Selk, Kongshøj, Bustrup og Jagel) den 3die Februar 1864*"

(Anon.), „*Beretning fra Krigsministeriet om Tilbagetoget fra Dannevirke, for Arrieregardens Vedkommende, og om Kampen ved Sankelmark Sø den 6te Februar 1864*"

(Anon.), „*Beretning fra Krigsministeriet om Fægtningen foran Fredericia den 8de Marts 1864*"

(Anon.), „*Beretning fra Krigsministeriet om Fægtningen ved Vejle den 8de Marts 1864*"

(Anon.), „*Beretning fra Krigsministeriet over Fægtningen den 17. Marts 1864*"

(Anon.), „*Beretning fra Krigsministeriet om Fægtningen den 28de Marts 1864*"

(Anon.), „*Foreløbig Beretning fra Krigsministeriet om Kampen i Dybbølstillingen d. 18de April 1864*"

(Anon.), „*Beretning fra Krigsministeriet om Kampen den 18de April 1864*"

(Anon.), „*Beretning fra Krigsministeriet angaaende Kampen paa Als den 29de Juni 1864*"

(Anon.), „*Beretning fra Marineministeriet........Overgang til Als Natten mellem den 28de og 29de...*"

(Anon.), „*Beretning fra Marineministeriet om Vesterhavsøernes Overgivelse*"

(Anon.)"En Officer" „Det sidste Geværskud den 6te April 1864" (*Daneborg*, Volume 2, Copenhagen, 716-717)

(Anon.), „Fra Affæren ved Helgoland den 9de Mai 1864. Den officielle danske Rapport." (*Danebrog*, Volume 2, Copenhagen 1881-82)

(Anon.), „General de Meza i 1864" (*Vort Forsvar*, Numbers 280 and 282, Copenhagen, 1891)

(Anon.), „Kampen ved Sankelmark den 6te Februar 1864" (*Vort Forsvar*, Number 447, Copenhagen 1898)

Andersen, C., „En Episode fra Dybbøl kampen" (*Vort Forsvar*, Number 99, Copenhagen 1884)

Andersen, C., „Fra Sundeved til Als 1864" (*Krigshistorisk Tidsskrift*, Number 1, Copenhagen 1974)

Andersen, O., „Preussernes overgang til Als 1864" (*Aarsskrift for Sottrup Sogn*, 1985)

Andersen, O., „Smol Vold som Preussisk skanse i 1864" (*Krigshistorisk Tidsskrift*, Number 2, Copenhagen 1995)

Andresen, H., „En Oplysing", (*Danebrog*, Volume 1, Copenhagen 1880-81)

Bajer, Frederik, „Paa Tilbagetoget over Limfjorden 1864" (*Danebrog*, Volume 2, Copenhagen 1881-82)

Berg, Captain, „Oplysning om den 18de April 1864" (*Vort Forsvar*, Number 101, Copenhagen 1884)

Bernth, J.C.E., „Fra Rendsborg til Sankelmark" (*Vort Forsvar*, Numbers, 87 & 88, Copenhagen 1884)

Bjerregard, Niels, „Hærens overgeneral i 1864. Christian Julius De Meza, de Siger,'De Siger, At De – Er Gaet Fra Danevirke' (*Krigshistorisk Tidsskrift*, Number 1,Copenhagen 1996)

Bluhm, E., „Tabet af Als" (*Tidsskrift før Søvæsen*, Copenhagen 1865 - A criticism: see below, Ravn, 'Tabet af Als')

Bokkenheuser, Chr., „De Nordiske frivillige i vore slesvigske krige" (*Militært Tidsskrift*, Number 65, Copenhagen 1936)

Bokkenheuser, V., „Erindringer fra 1864" (*Danebrog*, Volume 3, Copenhagen 1882-83)

Bokkenheuser, V. „Nogle Minder fra Als i 1864" (*Danebrog*, Volume 1, Copenhagen 1880-81)

Bokkenheuser, V. „ Premier Løjtenant P R Bruuns Død den 22de Februar 1864" (*Vort Forsvar)*, Number 141, Copenhagen 1886)

Bork, F.F., „Dannevirke" (*Krigshistorisk Tidsskrift*, Number 2, Copenhagen 1987)

Bork, F.F., „Kampene om Vesterhavsøerne 1864 –Eller guerilla i Danmark (*Krigshistorisk Tidsskrift*, Number 3, Copenhagen, 1985)

Bronnum, Villiam, „Et Indlæg" (*Danebrog*, Volume 1, Copenhagen 1880-81)

Bruun, B., „Kampene på Als 1864" (*Krigshistorisk Tidsskrift*, Numbers 2 & 3, Copenhagen 1978)

Cajus, „Fra Groften. Erindringer fra Als 1864." (*Danebrog*, Volume 1, Copenhagen 1880-81)

Cajus, „Fra Sankelmark 1864" (*Danebrog*, Volume 4, Copenhagen 1883-84)

Castenschiold, C., „Minder fra Dybbøl 1864" (*Vort Forsvar*, Number 448, Copenhagen 1898)

Christensen, J. Kaare, „Helgoland i maj 1864" (*Krigshistorisk Tidsskrift*, Number 3, Copenhagen 1988)

Christensen. J. Kaare„ Krigen 1864. Beretninger fra krigsskuepladsen" (*Krigshistorisk Tidsskrift*, Number 2, Copenhagen 1988)

Dinesen, W., „Fra Dannevirke" (*Vort Forsvar,* Number 111b, Copenhagen 1885)

Dinesen, W., „Kampen om Dybbøl Mølle 18. April 1864" (*Vort Forsvar,* Number 97, Copenhagen 1884)

Daue, Captain H. v, „Det 20de Infanteri-Regiments 1ste Compagni under Fægtningen den 8de Marts 1864" (*Tisskrift for Krigsvæsen*, Copenhagen 1866)

Dockum, C. van, „Den Officielle danske Rapport om Fægtningen ved Rügen den 17de Marts. 1864" (*Danebrog*, Volume 2, Copenhagen 1881-82)

Duch, Theodor Sophus, „Fra 1864. Et Minde fra den 17. Marts" *Vort Forsvar,* Number 609, Copenhagen 1904)

Eg Bæk, C.P., „'64' fortæller" (*Vort Forsvar*, Number 634, Copenhagen 1905)

Feddersen, Oscar, „Fra Vejle den 8de Marts 1864" (*Danebrog*, Volume 3, Copenhagen 1882-83)

Feddersen, Oscar, „Paa Hirsholmen" (*Danebrog*, Volume 3, Copenhagen 1882-83)

Feddersen, Oscar, „Ved 3. Dragonregiment i 1864" (*Danebrog*, Volume 3, Copenhagen 1882-83

Filskov, Anders Nielsen, „En Taksigelse" (*Danebrog*, Volume 2, Copenhagen 1881-82)

Gerlach, General, „*Rapport fra 1ste Armeedivision* (General Gerlach) *over kampen ved Mysunde den 2den Februar 1864*

Hagen, Major C.F., „Krigen 1864   Dansk Strategi og Foring belyst I Relation til Krigsførelsens Principper" (*Militært Tidsskrift*, Copenhagen 1964)

Hansen, H.C., „Min Tilfangetagelse og fangenskab i 1864" (*Danebrog*, Volume 1, Copenhagen 1880-81)

Hansen, P.W., „Bevæbning og Stodttaktik i Danmark og Østrig 1864" (*Militært Tidsskrift*, Volume 75, Copenhagen 1946)

Hansen, P.W., „Var en offensiv mulig?" (*Militært Tidsskrift*, Volume 93, Copenhagen 1964)

Hansen, Wilhelm, „Minder fra Skanse 5" (*Vort Forsvar*, Number 104, Copenhagen 1884)

Hedegaard, E.O.A., „Generalstabs værket. Om 1864 – En Konfliktfyldt Udgivelse" (*Militært Tidsskrift*, Copenhagen, Number 11995)

Hedegaard, Major O. A., „Hærens faner i krigen 1864" (*Militært Tidsskrift*, Number. 1, Copenhagen 1993)

Hedemann, Holger, „Danevirke 1864" (*Militært Tidsskrift*, Number 36, Copenhagen 1907)

Helms, H. St., „Erindringer fra min Soldatertid" (*Danebrog*, Volume 3, Copenhagen 1882-83)

Hertel, Capitain, „*Rapport fra det Fæstningscompagni (Capitain Hertel) over Træfningen ved Mysunde den 2den Februar 1864*"

Holbøll, H., „Kampen om Kongshøj. Mine oplevelser den3die Februar 1864" (*Militært Tidsskrift*, Number 39, Copenhagen 1910)

Honnes de Lichtenburg, G., „Fæstningen Rømmes" (*Krigshistorisk Tidsskrift*, Number 1, Copenhagen 1985)

Honnes de Lichtenburg, G., „Troppettransportbåndene" (*Militært Tidsskrift*, Number 93, Copenhagen 1964)

Jensen, N.P., „Forsvaret af Slien" (*Militært Tidsskrift*, Number 36, Copenhagen 1907)

Jensen, N.P., „Mysunde 2. Febr. 1864-2. Febr. 1904" (*Militært Tidsskrift.*, Number 33, Copenhagen 1904)

Johansen, Jens, „3' Division ved Dannevirke den 3' Februar 1864. Taktiske Studie" (*Militært Tidsskrift*, Numbers 50 and 51,Copenhagen 1921 and 1922)

Jørgensen, A., „Sankelmark d. 6te Februar 1864" (*Vort Forsvar*, Numbers 580, 582, and 586, Copenhagen 1903)

Jørgensen, Anders, „Eskadronen Posselt syd fra Sankelmark den 6te Februar 1864" (*Vort Forsvar*, Number 583, Copenhagen 1903)

Kielberg, A., „En Soldats Erindringer fra 1864" (*Danebrog*, Volume 1, Copenhagen, 1880-81)

Kielberg, A., „Fra Dannevirke til Sønderborg. Erindringer fra 1864" (*Danebrog*, Volume 2, Copenhagen 1881-82)

Kirkegaard, Jens, „Østrigerne paa Mors 1864" (*Danebrog*, Volume 4, Copenhagen 1883-84)

Klint, Helge, „Kommentar til Halding: Krisen og Krigen" (*Krigshistorisk Tidsskrift*, Number 1,Copenhagen 1969 - see entry above, under Halding, Ole)

Kofoed-Jensen, C., „Nogle Bemærkninger angaaende ‚Kampene den 3' Februar 1864‘, taktisk studie af Oberstl. Jens Johansen." (*Militært Tidsskrift*,

Number 50, Copenhagen1921 - see above, Johansen, Jens-"3' Division ved Dannevirke")

Knub, H., „Kaptejn Redsted" (*Vort Forsvar,* Number 573, Copenhagen 1902)

Koren, G., Martens, D.G. & Reimert, T.D., „Beretning fra Korpslægerne T.D. Reimert og D.G. Martens samt frem Compagnikirurg G.Koren efter deres Besøg ved den danske Armee I 1864." (*Tidsskrift for Krigsvæsen,* Copenhagen 1866)

Krag, F.V., „I Brohovedet paa Dybbøl (8.4. 1864)." (*Danebrog,* Volume 1, Copenhagen 1880-81)

Krieger Thomsen, P.B, „I krigsfangenskab i 1864" (*Krigshistorisk Tidsskrift,* Number 3, Copenhagen 1992)

Larsen, „Erindringer om Slaget ved Sankelmark d. 6. Febr. 1864" (*Militært Tidsskrift,* Number 39, Copenhagen 1910)

Larsen, A., „Overfaldet ved Assendrup" (*Danebrog,* Volume 2, Copenhagen 1881-82)

Larsen, Axel, „Lidt fra Aarøeske Strejfkorps" (*Danebrog,* Volume 1, Copenhagen 1880-81)

Larsen, Kay, „Vore Priseskibe 1864" (*Tidsskrift for Søvæsen,* Number 136, Copenhagen 1936)

Lesser, J.A.L., „En Episode af Slaget den 18de April 1864" (*Danebrog,* Volume 3, Copenhagen 1864)

Lesser, Captain, „Om 9de Infanterieregiment" (*Vort Forsvar,* Nr. 355, 1894)

Liljefalk, Axcl, „ Preusserne i Bjerge Herred i Marts ogApril 1864" (*Vejle Amts Arbøger,* Vejle 1906)

Liljefalk, J.A., „Fra Skanse II i 1864" (*Krigshistorisk Tidsskrift,* Nr. 1, Copenhagen 1994)

Lunding, General, „ Breve fra General Lunding i 1864" (*Danebrog,* Volume 3, Copenhagen 1882-83)

Lutken, O., „ Kampen ved Helgoland den 9de Maj 1864" (*Danebrog,* Volume 4, Copenhagen 1883-84)

Moe, Ritmester, „Et enkelt Afsnit af en detacheret dansk Escadrons Virksomhed under fjendtlige Armeens Fremrykning Over Kongeaan i Februar 1864" (*Tidsskrift for Krigsvæsen,* Copenhagen 1865)

Moltke, A., „Krigen 1864" (*Vort Forsvar,* Number 702, 1907)

Müller, Oberst M., „Mere i Anledning af " Bajonnettens Anvendelse Under Fægtninger" (*Tidsskrift for Krigsvæsen,* Copenhagen, 1865)

Muxoll, Orlogscapitain, „I Anledning af Major Ravns Artikel ‚Tabet af Als' (*Tidsskrift for Krigsvæsen,* Copenhagen 1865 - See below, Ravn, "Tabet af Als)

Muxoll, Orlogscapitain, „Modbemærkninger til Major Ravn's Afhandling ‚Tabet af Als' og Efterskridt til samme" (*Tidsskrift for Krigsvæsen,* Copenhagen 1867. See entry below, Ravn, "Svar paa en Kritik…")

Muxoll, Orlogscapitain, „Berigtigelser, Pantserbatteriet ‚Rolf Krake' vedkommende, til Afhandlingen" Forsvaret af Dybbølstillingen i 1864" (*Tidsskrift for Krigsvæsen,* Copenhagen 1867. See entry in books, Schøller, F.)

Muxoll, Orlogscapitain & Rothe, „Gjensvar til Forfatteren af 'nogle
    Bemærkninger etc.' (*Tidsskrift for Krigsvæsen*, Copenhagen 1868. See entry
    below, Schøller)
Nielsen, H.A., „Fra Affæren ved Helgoland den 9de Mai 1864. Erindringer."
    (*Danebrog*, Volume 2, Copenhagen, 1881-82)
Nielsen, Johs., „De preussisk-østrigske krigsplaner og krigsførelse" (*Militært
    Tidsskrift*, Vol. 116, Number. 6) Copenhagen 1987
Nielsen, Johs., „Den uundgåelige krig" (*Krigshistorisk Tidsskrift*, Number 1,
    Copenhagen 1989)
Nielsen, Tonne, „Nyaarsaften 1863", (*Danebrog*, Volume 1, Copenhagen
    1880-81)
Norretranders, H.F.F.. „Erindringer fra felttoget i 1864" (*Danebrog*, Volume 2,
    Copenhagen 1881-82)
Norrie, J.W.G., „Løjtnant Voldbyes breve fra 1864" (*Sønderjydske Arboger*,
    1961)
Norrie, J.W.G.. „Ministeren og Generalen" (*Militært Tidsskrift*, Volume 93,
    Copenhagen 1964)
Ornstedt,E., „Hugo v. Siemsen – en underlæge fra 1864" (*Krigshistorisk
    Tidsskrift*, Number 3, Copenhagen 1976)
Petersen, Bernhard, „Den første Uge 1864" (*Danebrog*, Volume 3, Copenhagen
    1882-83)
Petersen, H., „Af min Dagbog fra Dannevirke til Dybbøl" (*Vort Forsvar*,
    Number 149, Copenhagen1886)
Petersen, H., „Krigskammeraterne af 7de Regiments 6te Kompagni (1864)"
    (*Danebrog*, Volume 4, Copenhagen 1883-84)
Pontopiddan, L., „Et Par Bemærkninger I Anledning af Oberstløjtnant
    Johansens Artikel: 3'Division ved Dannevirke 3' Februar 1864. (*Militært
    Tidsskrift*, Number 50, Copenhagen 1921 - see item above, Johansen, Jens
    –3' Division ved Dannevirke...)
Ravn, Major, „Tabet af Als" (*Tidsskrift for Krigsvæsen*, Copenhagen 1865)
Ravn, Major, „Svar paa en Kritik i Tidsskrift for Søvæsen i Anledning af Artiklen
    ,Tabet af Als' „ (*Tidsskrift for Krigsvæsen*, Copenhagen 1866. See above,
    Bluhm)
Ravn, Major, „Et Forsvar for Artiklen 'Tabet af Als', I Anledning af Hr
    Orlogscapitain Muxolls Modbemærkninger" (*Tidsskrift for Krigsvæsen*,
    Copenhagen 1867)
Ravn, Oberst, „Bemærkninger og Oplysninger I Anledning af Oberst Vaupells;
    Rettelse" (*Tidsskrift for Krigsvæsen*, Copenhagen 1870. See entry below,
    Vaupell, "En Rettelse......")
Rordam, C.H., „Uddrag af en tysk Officers Dagbog fra Krigen 1864"
    (*Danebrog*, Volume 2, Copenhagen 1881-82)
Rothe, H.P., „Fornøden Berigtigelse, ,Rolf Krake' ved Kommende, til
    Afhandlingen: ,Forsvaret af Dybbølstillingen i 1864" (*Tidsskrift for
    Krigsvæsen*, Copenhagen 1867 - See entry in books, Schøller, F., and above,
    Muxoll, "Berigtigelser, Panserbatteriet 'Rolf Krake' etc.")
Rothe, H.P., „Rolf Krake den 18de April 1864" (*Vort Forsvar*, Number 98,
    Copenhagen 1884)

Schøller, G.F., „Nogle Bemærkninger, fremkaldte ved Orlogs-Capitain Muxolls ,Berigtigelser, Pandserbatteriet Rolf Krake vedkommende, til afhandlingen 'Forsvaret af Dybbølstillingen i 1864' og Orlogscapitain Rothes" Fornøden Berigtigelse,'Forsvaret af Dybbølstillingen i 1864" (*Tidsskrift for Krigsvæsen*, Copenhagen 1867 - See entries mentioned above, Rothe and Muxoll))

Skytte, Jens, „Smaatræk fra Krigene" (*Danebrog*, Volume 1, Copenhagen 1880-81)

Sørensen, Augustinus, „Minder fra Krigen 1864" (*Danebrog*, Volume 1, Copenhagen 1880-81)

Sørensen, Augustinus, „Minder fra Krigen i 1864" (*Danebrog*, Volume 3, Copenhagen 1882-83)

Stockholm, Lars, „Minder fra den første Uge i februar 1864" (*Vort Forsvar*, Numbers 694, 695, and 703, Copenhagen 1907)

Svane, F., „De i 1864 faldne svenske frivillige" (*Danebrog*, Volume 1, Copenhagen 1880-81)

Svane, F., „Gjensvar" (*Danebrog*, Volume 1, Copenhagen 1880-81)

Teisen, J., „Reserve løjtnanter 1861-1864" (*Tidsskrift for Søvæsen*, Number 135, Copenhagen 1964)

Thalbitzer, C.W., „Erindringer fra 1864" (*Danebrog*, Volume 1, Copenhagen 1880-81. ,En Tilføjelse' – correction, also in this volume)

Thalbitzer, C.W., „Uddrag af Breve fra krigen 1864" (*Danebrog*, Volume 4, Copenhagen 1883-84)

Tranberg G., „2den Paaskedag den 28de Marts 1864" (*Danebrog*, Volume 2, Copenhagen 1881-82)

Tranberg G., „Minder fra 1864" (*Danebrog*, Volume 2, Copenhagen 1881-82)

Vaupell, O., „Danevirke" (Vort Forsvar, Numbers 134 and 135, Copenhagen 1886)

Vaupell, O., „Johan Anker og Skansen Nr. II's Forsvar" (*Danebrog*, Volume 2, Copenhagen, 1881-82)

Vaupell, O., „Kampen ved Mysunde den 2den Februar 1864" (*Danebrog*, Volume 1, Copenhagen 1880-81)

Vaupell, Oberst, „En rettelse til den af Oberst Ravn givne ,Fremstilling af Krigsbegivenhederne paa Als' (*Tidsskrift for Krigsvæsen*, Copenhagen 1870. See entry in books, Ravn, and also above, "Bemærkninger og Oplysninger")

Vaupell, Otto, „Kampen for Sønderjylland" (*Vort Forsvar*, Numbers 137, 142, and 143,Copenhagen 1886)

Vaupell, Otto, „Paa Forpost (14. Marts 1864)" (*Vort Forsvar*, Number 43, Copenhagen 1882)

Vaupell, Otto, „Smaatraek fra Krigen 1864" (*Vort Forsvar*, Numbers 110 and 114, Copenhagen 1885)

,V.B'., „Et Minde fra den 18de April 1864" (*Danebrog*, Volume 1, Copenhagen 1880-81)

Wandler, G., „Smaatræk fra Indtagelsen af Als i 1864" (*Danebrog*, Volume 3, Copenhagen 1882-83)

Wenck, Kaptajn i Flaaden, „Krigsledelsen I 1864. Et Studie over dansk og

Preussisk Strategi I 1864 med særligt Henblik Paa Erobringen af Als." (*Tidsskrift for Søvæsen, 1914*)

Westrup, Premierlieutenant, „En Bemærkning om Bygning af dækkede Opholdssteder I Felten" (*Tidsskrift for Krigsvæsen*, Copenhagen 1865)

Wørishoffer, Carl Jul. Fr., „3. Brigade 15.4.1864" (*Vort Forsvar*, Number 64, Copenhagen 1883)

Worm, F.C., „2 Regiment under Kampen ved Dybbølstillingen" (*Danebrog*, Volume 3, Copenhagen 1882-83)

English Books

(Anon.), *The Empress Frederick - A Memoir*, (James Nisbet & Co., London 1913)

Anderson, Eugene N., *The Social and Political Conflict in Prussia, 1858-1864*, (University of Nebraska Press, Lincoln 1954)

Brackenbury, C.B. et al, *Report of a Professional Tour by Officers of the Royal Artillery in 1865*, (George E. Eyre & William Spottiswoode, London 1866)

Buchholz, Arden, *Moltke and the German Wars, 1864-1871*, (Palgrave, New York 2001)

Carr, William, *The Origins of the Wars of German Unification"*, (Longman, London 1991)

Craig, Gordon A., *Theodor Fontane Literature and History in the Bismarck Reich*, (Oxford University Press, Oxford 1999)

Dicey, Edward, *The Schleswig-Holstein War*, (Tinsley Brothers, London 1864)

Gallenga, Antonio, *The Invasion of Denmark in 1864*, (Richard Bentley, London 1864)

Halicz, Emanuel, *Russia and Denmark 1856-1864. A Chapter of Russian Policy towards the Scandinavian Countries*, (Reitzel, Copenhagen 1990)

Herbert, Auberon, *The Danes in Camp. Letters from Sonderborg"*, (Saunders, Otley & Co., London 1864)

Hohenlohe-Ingelfingen,Prince Kraft zu, *Letters on Artillery*, Translated by Major N.L. Walford, (Royal Artillery Institution, Woolwich 1887)

Horsetzky, A. von, *The Chief Campaigns in Europe since 1792*, (Translated by K.B. Ferguson: John Murray, London 1909)

Maurice, Sir J. F., *The Balance of Military Power in Europe"*, (W. Blackwood & Sons, Edinburgh & London 1888)

Nielsen, Johs., *The Danish-German War 1864*, (Tøjhusmuseet, Copenhagen 1991)

Oliphant, Laurence, *Episodes in A Life of Adventure"*, (William Blackwood & Sons, London and Edinburgh 1888)

Peel, Peter H., *British Public Opinion and the Wars of German Unification*, (International Research Institute For PoliticalScience, College Park, Maryland 1981)

Rothenburg, Gunther E., *The Army of Francis Joseph*, (Purdue University Press, W. Lafayette 1976)

Sandiford, Keith A.P., *Great Britain and the Schleswig-Holstein question 1848-1864: a study in diplomacy, politics, and public opinion,* (University of Toronto Press, Toronto & Buffalo 1975)

Schioldann-Nielsen, Johann, *The Life of D.G. Monrad 1811-1887. Manic-Depressive Disorder and Political Leadership",* (Odense University Press, 1998)

Showalter, Dennis E., *Railroads and Rifles",* (The Shoe String Press, New Haven 1988)

Skinner, J.E.H., *The Tale of Danish Heroism",* (Bickers and Son, London 1865)

Sokol, Anthony, *The Imperial and Royal Austro-Hungarian Navy",* (United States Naval Institute, Annapolis 1968)

Sondhaus, Lawrence, *Preparing for Weltpolitik. German Sea Power before the Tirpitz Era",* (Naval Institute Press, Annapolis 1997)

Steefel, Lawrence D., *The Schleswig-Holstein Question",* (Harvard University Press, Cambridge 1932)

Ward, A. W., &Wilkinson, S., *Germany 1815-1890",* (Cambridge University Press, Cambridge 1916-1918)

Westergaard, Waldemar, *Denmark and Slesvig 1848-1864",* (Arnold Busck & Oxford University Press, Copenhagen/London 1946)

English Articles

(Anon.), „The Naval Action in the North Sea", (*The Times,* London May 13th 1864)

(Anon.), „The War in Schleswig-Holstein", (*Army and Navy Journal,* New York 1864, Number 27)

(Anon.), „The War in Denmark", (*Army and Navy Journal,* New York 1864 Numbers 28, 29 and 32)

(Anon.), „Capture of Duppel", (*Army and Navy Journal,* New York 1864 Numbers 37 and 42 1864)

(Anon.), „Narrative of the campaign in Schleswig-Holstein", (*Colburn's United Service Magazine andNaval and Military Journal,* London 1864, Parts 2 and 3)

(Anon.), „The Invasion of Denmark and the political crisis", (*Colburn's United Service Magazine and Naval and Military Journal,* London 1864, Parts 1 and 2)

Cecil, Robert Arthur Talbot Gascoyne, Marquis of Salisbury, „The Danish Duchies", (*The Quarterly Review,* London January 1864)

Hall, W.E., „A personal narrative of recent military events in Denmark", (Reprinted from *The Spectator,* London & Oxford 1864)

Harvie, Ian, „HMS Aurora and the Battle of Helgoland", (*Marinehistorisk Tidsskrift,* Number 3, August 2001)

Laughton, J.K., „Vice-Admiral Baron von Tegetthoff", (*Fraser's Magazine,* London 1878)

Putnam, Arnold A., „Rolf Krake: Europe's first turreted Ironclad", (*The Mariner's Mirror,* Volume 84, number 1, Southampton 1998)

Showalter, Dennis E., „Infantry Weapons, infantry tactics, and the Armies of Germany 1849-1864", (*European Studies Review*, Number 4, London, April 1974)

Smith, Percy (Translator), „Notes upon the attack of the Duppel Entrenchments in March and April, 1864", (*Papers on subjects connected with the Duties of the Corps of Royal Engineers*, Vol. 14, Woolwich 1865. This is a much truncated version. See, Fritsch-Lang, Captain, "L'artillerie rayée prussienne…", for complete article)

Wylly, H.C., „A lesson in invasion", (*The United Service Magazine*, Nr. 41, London 1910)

French Books

Anvers, R., & Brialmont, Major, *Reflexions a propos de la brochure institulée: La Guerre du Schleswig, envisagée au point de vue Belge*, (General Staff, Brussels 1865 – see entry below)

(Brialmont) par officier, d'etat-major *La guerre du Schleswig, envisagée au point de vue Belge*, (General Staff, Brussels 1864)

Burdin d'Entremont, F. M., *L'Armée Danoise et la Defense du Sundevit en 1864*, (L. Baudoin, Paris 1885)

Crousse, Franz, *Invasion du Danemark en 1864*, (Dumaine, Paris 1865-66 - Parts 1 and 2)

'Dannebrog', Captain, *Invasion du Danemark en 1864*, (C. Mucquart, Brussels 1864)

De Bas, F., *L'Armée Danoise en 1864. Le Dannevirke et Dybböl*, (J. van Egmond, Arnhem 1867)

Lecomte, F., *Guerre du Danemark en 1864*, (Tanera, Paris 1864)

Leurs, J., *L'artillerie de campagne Prussienne de 1864 à 1870, son rôle dans les grand batailles autour de Metz*, (*Brussels and Leipzig*, 1874)

Mermor, Andreas, *L'allemagne nouvelle 1863-1867*, (E. Dentu, Paris 1879)

Saint-Nexant, Charles de, *La Spoliation du Danemark*, (J. Rozez, Brussels 1865)

French Articles

(Anon.), „De la manière don't les Allemands font la guerre contre le Danemark et traitent surtout le Slesvig"('*les principaux libraires*', Paris 1864

(Anon.), „Guerre de Schleswig", (*Journal de l'armée belge*, Brussels 1864, Nr. 27)

(Anon.), „Notes sur le nouveau materiel de campagne autrichien pendant la guerre de Danemark 1864", (*Revue de technologie militaire*, Paris 1864)

(Anon.), „Sur la Guerre de Danemark", (*Journal de l'armée belge*, Brussels 1863, Nr. 25)

A.D.B., Colonel, „Notice sur la position de Duppel-Alsen", (*Journal de l'armée belge*, Brussels 1864, Nr. 26)

A.D.B., Colonel, „Sur le siège de Duppel", (*Journal de l'armée belge*, Brussels 1864, Nr. 26)

Desfeuilles, P., „Le défense de l'ile Als par l'armée danoise en 1864", (*Revue internationale d'histoire*, Paris 1966, Nr. 25)

Fritsch-Lang, A., „L'artillerie rayée prussienne a l'attaque de Düppel d'apres les auteurs allemands", (*Le Spectateur Militaire*, Paris 1865, Nr. 50)

Martin, Ch., „Forces militaires et navales du Danemark", (*Le Spectateur Militaire*, Paris 1864, Nr. 45)

Martin, Ch., „Précis des événements militaire du Danemark", (*Le Spectateur Militaire*, Paris 1864, Nrs. 45 and 46)

Seinguerlet, Eugene, „Douze anées de la domination danoise dans les duchés de Schleswig-Holstein 1852-1864", (*Salomon*, Strasbourg 1864)

Index

Index of Places/Features

Index of People

Schütze, Engineer Capt, 190
Secher, P Lt C., 195
Seegenberg, Capt von, 253
Sehested, Ritmstr H., 138, 164
Sellin, Capt von, 182, 259, 263
Senkel, P Lt, 257
Seydlitz, 2nd Lt von, 228
Seydlitz, Capt von, 255-256
Seyffarth, P Lt G., 51
Skibsted, Reserve Lt, 298
Skinner, J.E.H., 198, 243
Smidth, Officer Aspirant, 256
Snertinge, P Lt N.O., 310-311
Sommer, Ritmstr, 125
Sonnerup, Dragoon A.L., 262
Sørensen, Reserve Lt, 298
Sørensen, P Lt C., 179
Sørensen, P Lt Carl Th., 92, 100-102, 151, 154
Sperling, Capt, (later Maj), A., 148, 262
Sperling, P Lt W., 164
Spiess, Captain von, 253
Spinn, Lt, 258
St. Julien, Ober Lt Count A., 101
Staggemeier, Capt A. W., 67-68, 103, 151
Stammer, 2nd Lt, 314, 319
Stampfer, Maj, 68, 71
Steinmann, P Lt C., 69, 146, 148, 299
Steinmann, Maj Gen P.F, 79, 87, 89, 95-96, 102, 110, 217, 226, 266, 289, 298, 302, 318-320, 323, 340
Stiernholm, Maj (later Lt Col), 113, 168, 229
Stickmann, 2nd Lt, 220
Stockfleth, Capt F., 163, 262, 264
Stockhausen, Capt von, 196
Stoephasius, P Lt, 257
Stolzenberg, Rtmstr W., 92,
Stonor, P Lt W.B., 183, 310
Stransky, Maj, 68, 71
Stricker, Capt E.A.S., 302, 310, 317
Stricker, Capt W., 96, 102-103, 105, 151
Strohmeyer, Warrant Offr., 92
Strombeck, P Lt Baron von, 144
Strubberg, Lt Col von, 223
Struensee, Capt, 253
Stuart, The Honorable W., 291
Studnitz, Capt von, 132
Stülpnagel, Capt von, 253
Stwolinski, Capt, 260
Suenson, Commodore E, 281-283, 285-286, 339

Svane, Capt L. 318
Szwykowski, Capt, 314
Taulow, Maj H. Ritter von, 91, 104, 152
Tegetthoff, Capt W., 281, 283-286
Tersling, Lt Col H., 262
Thaden, P Lt von, 138
Thalbitzer, Capt J., 65, 95, 100
Thesen, Capt C.A., 312
Thestrup, Capt E.E.S., 86
Thestrup, Lt Gen J.T., 31-32
Thiele, P Lt, 110
Thomsen, Capt C.A.F., 164-165
Thorkelin, Capt B., 116-117
Thorson, P Lt, T., 228
Thrane, P Lt J., 302, 307
Thurn und Taxis, Ritmstr E., 92
Tiedemann, Col von, 140
Tippelskirch, Lt Col von, 203
Tomas, Maj Gen, 39, 57, 78,
Tranberg, P Lt G.C.F., 193
Trepka, 2nd Lt C., 319
Treskow, P Lt von, 265
Treumann, Capt, 222
Troiel, P Lt E., 121
Tümpling, Lt Gen von, 140, 192
Uexküll, Captain Count, 150
Uldall, 2nd Lt J., 333
Unruh, Capt (GR8), 195
Unruh, Maj von, 306, 316
Unruhe, Captain von, 178, 306
Urschitz, Capt, 73, 334-335
Vetter, Lt. Col G Count, 91
Vahl, Col J., 168
Varberg, P Lt C. F., 102
Vaupell, Capt O., 32, 302, 310, 312
Vaupell, P Lt V., 72,
Vetter, Lt Col Count G., 154
Victoria, Queen, 24, 136
Vilstrup, P Lt J., 312
Voght, Maj Gen C.A., 47-50, 84, 168, 194, 289
Voldby, 2nd Lt, 170-171, 173
Volkersen, 2nd Lt F.C., 102
Volkvartz, Capt A.C., 44, 125, 170, 313
Voss, P Lt E., 73
Wachtmeister, Count, 291
Wandler, 2nd Lt G.G., 311
Wartensleben, 2nd Lt Count, 138
Wedefeldt, Capt H., 72,
Wedege, Capt S.J., 181-183
Wegener, Maj J.T., 79, 86
Weien, P Lt, 147

Index of Military/Naval Units

Related titles published by Helion & Company

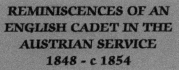

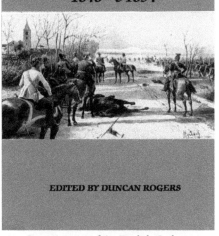

Reminiscences of An English Cadet in
the Austrian Service 1848–c1854
edited by Duncan Rogers
44pp   Pamphlet
ISBN 978 1 874622 04 8

The Prussian Campaign of 1866
A Tactical Retrospect
Captain Theodor May
68pp   Paperback
ISBN 978 1 874622 14 7

A selection of forthcoming titles

The First Schleswig-Holstein War 1848–50
Nick Svendsen   ISBN 978 1 906033 08 8

The Prussian Artillery in the Campaign of 1866
Lieutenant S. Gore-Brown   ISBN 978 1 906033 05 7

The Seven Weeks' War of 1866: Its Antecedents & Incidents,
based upon letters reprinted from 'The Times'
H.M. Hozier   ISBN 978 1 906033 06 4

The Invasion of Denmark 1864
Antonio Gallenga   ISBN 978 1 906033 07 1

HELION & COMPANY
26 Willow Road, Solihull, West Midlands, B91 1UE, England
Tel 0121 705 3393   Fax 0121 711 4075
Website: http://www.helion.co.uk

Lightning Source UK Ltd.
Milton Keynes UK
UKHW022037240519
343285UK00006B/593/P

9 781906 033033